HITLER'S WAR

Volume One

HITLER'S WAR

VOLUME ONE

David Irving

The Viking Press • New York

Copyright © David Irving, 1977

First published in 1977 by The Viking Press
625 Madison Avenue, New York, N.Y. 10022

Published simultaneously in Canada by
The Macmillan Company of Canada Limited

Printed in the United States of America

Contents

VOLUME TWO

4 TOTAL WAR

5 THE WORMS TURN

6 ENDKAMPF

Acknowledgments

I like to think that I chose precisely the right ten years to work on Hitler. Any earlier, and the archives would not have begun to disgorge their captured papers; any later, and those who came closest to enjoying Hitler's confidence would have died. Hitler's secretaries and adjutants were without exception of the utmost help. Traudl Junge and Christa Schroeder provided unpublished manuscripts and letters of the period; his adjutants Admiral Karl-Jesco von Puttkamer (navy), General Gerhard Engel (army), and Colonel Nicolaus von Below (Luftwaffe) did the same, and labored through much of the resulting manuscript. Without the memories of Colonel Erik von Amsberg, Max Wünsche, Fritz Darges, and Otto Günsche, many a gap in our knowledge would have remained unfilled. But many other adjutants attending Hitler's conferences also assisted—of whom I must single out for mention Major General Ottomar Hansen, Lieutenant Colonel Ernst John von Freyend, Admiral Kurt Freiwald, and Captain Herbert Friedrichs, and particularly Johannes Göhler and Wolf Eberhard for the important diaries and letters they made available to me for the first time.

The most important documents were provided by Professor Hugh Trevor-Roper and by Lev Besymenski. Dr. Cortez F. Enloe, Washington, D.C., furnished medical records on Hitler. François Genoud, Lausanne, Switzerland, supplied key extracts from Bormann's personal files; Frau Asta Greiner, Wiesbaden, Germany, her husband's unpublished diaries and private correspondence; the stenographer Karl Thöt, Bonn, his war diary; the late Colonel Karl-Heinz Keitel, papers from his father's collection; Albert Speer, Heidelberg, Germany, his office Chronik and other papers; Reinhard Spitzy, Austria, certain letters; Günter Peis, Munich, selected items from his unique collection; and Dr. Heinrich Heim, Munich, papers originating from his period as Martin Bormann's adjutant; furthermore Hitler's doctors Professor Hanskarl von Hasselbach, Dr. Erwin Giesing, and Dr. Richard Weber provided papers or other aid.

Many of the collections deposited in the archives would have remained closed to me without the kindness of the following: Isabella Adam, Ursula Backe, Anni Brandt, Ilse Dittmar, Friedl Koller, Paula Kubizek, Baroness Jutta von Richthofen, the late Lucie Rommel, Anneliese Schmundt, Gertrud Seyss-Inquart, Ruth von Vormann, Elisabeth Wagner, Elisabeth Todt, Margarete von Waldau, Baroness Marga von Weichs, Baroness Marianne von Weizsäcker—all of whom either permitted me to see or provided me with direct access to their husbands' papers, letters, and diaries. (The Weizsäcker diaries have been expertly transcribed by my colleague Professor Leonidas E. Hill.) Frau Blanda Benteler allowed me the diaries of her husband Walther Hewel; Liselotte von Salmuth those of her husband, the Colonel General; Else Renate Nagy the manuscripts and papers of her late husband Dr. Wilhelm Scheidt—adjutant of Hitler's court historian General Walter Scherff; Frau Gerta von Radinger the private letters of her late husband, Alwin-Broder Albrecht (whom she had married in 1940). Frau Anneliese Schmundt gave me her private war diary. I am also grateful to Dr. Peter von Blomberg, Manfred Brückner, General Heinz-Günther Guderian, Joachim Hoepner, Hermann Leeb, Fritz von Lossberg, Rüdiger von Manstein, and Roland Schaub for permission to use the private papers of their fathers. The late Karl-Otto Saur, Field Marshal Erhard Milch, Major General Ivo-Thilo von Trotha, General Walter von Seydlitz-Kurzbach, Ambassador Dr. Hasso von Etzdorf, and the late Ludwig Krieger, stenographer, all made diaries and papers available to me.

Of those who gave up their time for long conversations or to write letters I must mention these: Ludwig Bahls, Werner Best, Karl Bodenschatz, Herta Berger—widow of the stenographer killed on July 20, 1944 —Herbert Büchs, Eugen Dollmann, Peterpaul von Donat, Xaver Dorsch, Baron Sigismund von Falkenstein, Ambassador André François Poncet, Reinhard Gehlen, Otto-Heinz Grosskreutz, Werner Grothmann, Hedwig Haase, Ernst "Putzi" Hanfstaengl, Heider Heydrich, Ralph Hewins, Ambassador Hans von Herwarth, Professor Andreas Hillgruber, Professor Raul Hilberg, Gebhard Himmler, Walter Huppenkothen, Professor Hans-Adolf Jacobsen, Elisabeth Kaltenbrunner, Hans Kehrl, Werner Koeppen, Marlene Kunde (née Exner), Dr. O. H. Schmitz-Lammers, Helmut Laux, Heinz Linge, Field Marshal Friedrich List, Heinz Lorenz, Colonel J. L. McCowen, Johanna Morell, Josef Müller, Pastor Martin Niemöller, Max Pemsel, Leo Raubal, the late Anneliese von Ribbentrop, Walter Rohland, Jürgen Runzheimer, Professor Ernst-Günther Schenck, Henriette von Schirach, Richard Schulze-Kossens, Dietrich Schwencke, former Federal Chancellor Dr. Kurt von Schuschnigg, General Curt Siewert, Otto Skorzeny, Gertrud and Friedrich Stumpfegger, the late Helmut Sündermann, Admiral Gerhard Wagner, Winifred Wagner, Karl Wahl, Walter Warlimont, and Karin Weigl. Walter Frentz placed his photographic collection at my disposal; Peter Hoffmann his expertise; Frau Luise Jodl her husband's papers.

For most of the ten years I also plagued archives and institutes with my inquiries. I am most indebted to the exemplary Institut für Zeitgeschichte in Munich, and to its then director Professor Helmuth Krausnick and above all its head of archives Dr. Anton Hoch, who guided me as friend and mentor with great objectivity and ability from October 1966 onward; Frau Karla Götz, Hermann Weiss, and Anton Zirngibl fulfilled my often immodest demands, and Dr. Wolfgang Jacobmeyer permitted me to use his prepared edition of the Hans Frank diaries. In transferring to the Institut my entire Hitler document collection, including the interview and interrogation records, Hitler's armament decrees, the Canaris/Lahousen fragments, a correct transcription of Greiner's war diary notes, the Scheidt papers, and much else, I hope to have recompensed in part for the assistance given me. Much of the material was microfilmed by the Imperial War Museum, London S.E. 1, before I transferred it to Munich; these films are available from the museum's Foreign Documents Centre. I also transferred my collection of records on Hitler's medical history to the Bundesarchiv in Koblenz, Germany (where it is filed as item *Kl. Erw. 525*). I placed a copy of the Fritzsch Papers, 1938–39, in the Bundesarchiv-Militärarchiv in Freiburg, Germany, where Dr. Friedrich-Christian Stahl, Alfred Bottler, and Colonel Helmuth Vorwieg aided me. At the neighboring Militärgeschichtliches Forschungsamt (of the German Defense Ministry) I was guided by Colonels Karl Gundeslach, Manfred Kehrig, Rolf Elbe, and Dr. Georg Meyer through the intricacies of their own archives. At Nuremberg's State Archives Dr. Puchner and Dr. Schuhmann aided me; and at the Führungsakademie der Bundeswehr in Hamburg Colonel Helmuth Technau was kind enough to allow me to carry volumes of original records—including the important Koller diaries—to London with me to put on microfilm. In the Operational Archives Branch at Washington Navy Yard I met with the fullest cooperation of Dr. Dean C. Allard and Mrs. Mildred D. Mayeux; and Robert Wolfe, John E. Taylor, Thomas E. Hohmann, and their colleagues provided assistance at the National Archives. I must also mention Mrs. Agnes F. Peterson of the Hoover

Library, Stanford, California; Detmar Finke of the Office of the Chief of Military History (OCMH), Washington, D.C.; and Mr. George E. Blau, chief historian of USAEUR headquarters, Heidelberg, Germany. The U.S. Mission's Berlin Document Center provided speedy and efficient assistance while under its director Richard Bauer, as did the heads of archives of the German, French, Finnish, and British foreign offices. In London I encountered particularly useful help from Dr. Leo Kahn of the Imperial War Museum; Squadron Leader L. A. Jackets of the Air Historical Branch; Mr. Brian Melland, Mr. Clifton Child, and Mrs. Nan Taylor of the Cabinet Office Historical Section; and Mr. K. Hiscock at the Foreign Office Library. World War II researchers will find many of the special microfilms of materials prepared by me while researching this book available now from E. P. Microform Ltd., East Ardsley, Wakefield, Yorkshire, England.

This book would have been impossible without the patience and generosity of the many publishers who waited long years for the scaffolding to be removed from this *monumentum aeris* which I have erected. My editors, Alan Williams of the Viking Press and Stanley Hochman, provided me with many a stimulus and useful reproof. Without the indulgence of my wife, Pilar, in putting up with the years of turmoil and inconvenience the book might not have appeared. Nor shall I forget the nameless legions who typed, translated, or trudged the archives with me: Mrs. Jutta Thomas, the only one of my secretaries to survive the full marathon, and my colleague Elke Fröhlich, who encouraged me to persist and helped me to scale the mountains of records in Berlin, Munich, London, Freiburg, and Bonn that had daunted and dissuaded other writers and would otherwise have discouraged me.

Introduction

"To historians is granted a talent that even the gods are denied—to alter what has already happened!"

I bore this scornful adage in mind when I embarked on this study of Hitler's war years late in 1964. I saw myself as a stone-cleaner—less concerned with a wordy and subjective architectural appraisal than with scrubbing years of grime and discoloration from the facade of a silent and forbidding monument, uncertain whether the revealed monument would prove too hideous to be worthy of the effort.

In earlier books, I relied on the primary records of the period rather than published literature; I naïvely supposed that the same technique could within five years be applied to a study of Adolf Hitler, little realizing that it would be eleven years before I would lay bare the factual bedrock on which the legend of Hitler had been built. But I believe that hard rubbing has disclosed a picture of the man that nobody until now had suspected.

My conclusion on completing the research startled even me: while Adolf Hitler was a powerful and relentless military commander, the war years saw him as a lax and indecisive political leader who allowed affairs of state to rot. In fact he was probably the weakest *leader* Germany has known in this century. Though often brutal and insensitive, Hitler lacked the ability to be ruthless where it mattered most, *e.g.,* he refused to bomb London itself until the decision was forced on him in the late summer of 1940. He was reluctant to impose the test of total mobilization on the German "master race" until it was too late to matter, so that with munitions factories crying out for manpower, idle German housewives were still employing half a million domestic servants to dust their homes and polish their furniture. His military irresolution also showed through, for example, in his panicky vacillation at times of crisis like the Battle for Narvik in 1940. He took ineffectual measures against his enemies inside Germany for too long, and seems to have been unable to take effective action against strong opposition at the very heart of his High Command. He suffered incompetent ministers and generals far longer than the Allied leaders did. He failed too to unite the feuding Party and Wehrmacht factions in fighting for the common cause, and he proved incapable of stifling the OKH (War Department's) corrosive hatred of the OKW (the Wehrmacht High Command). I believe I show in this book that the more hermetically Hitler locked himself away behind the barbed wire and minefields of his remote military headquarters, the more his Germany became a Führer-Staat without a Führer. Domestic policy was controlled by whoever was most powerful in each sector—by Hermann Göring as head of the powerful economics office, the Four-Year Plan; by Hans Lammers as chief of the Reich Chancellery or by Martin Bormann, the Nazi party boss; or by Heinrich Himmler, minister of the interior and "Reichsführer" of the black-uniformed SS.

The problem is that Hitler was a puzzle even to his most intimate advisers. Joachim Ribbentrop, his foreign minister, wrote in his Nuremberg prison cell in 1945:

> I got to know Adolf Hitler more closely in 1933. But if I am asked today whether I knew him well—how he thought as a politician and statesman, what kind of man he was—then I'm bound to confess that I know only very little about him; in fact nothing at all. The fact is that although I went through so much together with him, in all the years of working with him I never came closer to him than on the first day we met, either personally or otherwise.

As a historian I have resorted to the widest possible spectrum of source materials. I have not only used the military records and archives; I have burrowed deep into the contemporary writings of his closest friends and personal staff, seeking clues to the real truth in their diaries or in the private letters they wrote to their wives and friends. In this way I have tried to understand the intricacies and contradictions in Hitler's last years.

The sheer complexity of that character is evident from a comparison of his extreme brutality in some respects and his almost maudlin sentimentality and stubborn adherence to long-abandoned military conventions in others. In the chapters that follow, we shall find Hitler cold-bloodedly ordering the execution of fifty or a hundred hostages for every German occupation-soldier killed; dictating the massacre of Italian soldiers who turned their weapons against the German troops in 1943; ordering the systematic liquidation of Red Army commissars, Allied Commando troops, and—in 1945—even captured Allied aircrews; in 1942 he announces to the General Staff that the entire male populations of Stalingrad and Leningrad will eventually be exterminated, and he justifies these orders to himself and to his staff by political doctrines and the expediencies of war. Yet the same Adolf Hitler indignantly exclaimed, in one of the last war conferences of his life, that Soviet tanks were flying the Nazi swastika as a ruse during street fighting in Berlin, and he flatly forbade his Wehrmacht to violate flag rules! In an age in which the governments of the democracies, both during World War II and in later years, unhesitatingly attempted, engineered, or condoned the assassination of the inconvenient—from General Sikorski, Admiral Darlan, Field Marshal Rommel, and King Boris to Fidel Castro, Patrice Lumumba, and Salvador Allende—we learn that Hitler, the unscrupulous dictator, not only never resorted to the assassination of foreign opponents, but flatly forbade the Abwehr (Intelligence Agency) to attempt it (in particular he rejected Admiral Canaris's plans to assassinate the Red Army General Staff).

The negative is traditionally always difficult to prove; but it seemed well worth attempting to discredit accepted dogmas if only to expose the "unseaworthiness" of many current legends about Hitler. The most durable of these concerns the Führer's involvement in the extermination of the Jews. My analysis of this controversial issue serves to highlight two broad conclusions: that in wartime, dictatorships are fundamentally weak—the dictator himself, however alert, is unable to oversee all the functions of his executives acting within the confines of his far-flung empire; and that in this particular case, the burden of guilt for the bloody and mindless massacre of the Jews rests on a large number of Germans, many of them alive today, and not just on one "mad dictator," whose order had to be obeyed without question.

I had approached the massacre of the Jews from the traditional viewpoint prevailing in the mid-1960s. "Supposing Hitler was a capable statesman and a gifted commander," the argument ran, "how does one explain his murder of six million Jews?" If this book were simply a history of the rise and fall of Hitler's Reich, it would be legitimate to conclude: "Hitler killed the Jews." He after all created the atmosphere of hatred with his anti-Semitic speeches in the 1930s; he and Himmler created the SS; he built the concentration camps; his speeches, though never explicit, left the clear impression that "liquidate" was what he meant. For a full-length war biography of Hitler, I felt that a more analytical approach to the key questions of initiative, complicity, and execution would be necessary. Remarkably, I found that Hitler's *own* role in the "Final Solution of the Jewish Problem" has never been examined. German historians, usually the epitome of painstaking essaying on every other subject, to whom no hypothesis is acceptable unless scrutinized from a thousand angles, suddenly developed monumental blind spots when Hitler himself cropped up: bald statements were made, legends were created, blame was laid, without a shadow of historical evidence in support. British and American historians followed suit. Other writers quoted them. For thirty years, our knowledge of Hitler's part in the atrocity has rested on inter-historian incest.

Many people, particularly in Germany and Austria, had an interest in propagating the accepted version that the order of one madman originated the entire massacre. Precisely when the order was given and in what form has, admittedly, never been established. In 1939?—but the secret extermination camps did not begin operating until December 1941. At the January 1942 "Wannsee Conference"?—but the incontrovertible evidence is that Hitler ordered on November 30, 1941, that there was to be "no liquidation" of the Jews (without much difficulty, I found in Himmler's private files his own handwritten note on this). On several subsequent dates in 1942 Hitler made—in private—statements which are totally incompatible with the notion that he knew that the liquidation program had in fact begun. In 1943, and again in early 1944, I find that documents being submitted to Hitler by the SS were tampered with so as to camouflage the truth about the pogrom: sometimes the files contain both the original texts and the "doctored" version submitted to Hitler. Small wonder that when his closest crony of all those years, SS General Josef ("Sepp") Dietrich, was asked by the American Seventh Army for an opinion on Hitler on June 1, 1945, he replied, "He knew even less than the rest. He allowed himself to be taken for a sucker by everyone."

My own hypothesis, to which I point in the various chapters in which I deal in chronological sequence with the unfolding persecution and liquidation of the European Jews, is this: the killing was partly of an *ad hoc* nature, what the Germans call a *Verlegenheitslösung*—the way out of an awkward dilemma, chosen by the middle-level authorities in the eastern territories overrun by the Nazis—and partly a cynical extrapolation by the central SS authorities of Hitler's anti-Semitic decrees. Hitler had unquestionably decreed that Europe's Jews were to be "swept back" to the east; I describe the various phase-lines established by this doctrine. But the SS authorities, Gauleiters, and regional commissars and governors in "the east" proved wholly unequal to the problems caused by this mass uprooting in midwar. The Jews were brought by the trainload to ghettos already overcrowded and underprovisioned. Partly in collusion with each other, partly independently, the Nazi agencies there simply liquidated the deportees as their trains arrived, on a scale increasingly more methodical and more regimented as the months passed.

A subsidiary motive in the atrocity was the animal desire of the murderers to loot and plunder the Jewish victims and conceal their traces. (This hypothesis does not include the methodical liquidation of Russian Jews during the "Barbarossa" invasion of 1941, which came under a different Nazi heading—preemptive guerrilla warfare; and there is no indication that Hitler expressed any compunctions about it.) We shall see how in October 1943, even as Himmler was disclosing to audiences of SS generals and Gauleiters that Europe's Jews had virtually been exterminated, Hitler was still forbidding liquidations—*e.g.*, of the Italian Jews in Rome—and ordering their internment instead. (This order his SS also disobeyed.) Wholly in keeping with his character, when Hitler was confronted with the facts—either then or, as Kaltenbrunner later claimed, in October 1944—he took no action to rebuke the guilty. His failure or inability to act in effect kept the extermination machinery going until the end of the war.

It is plausible to impute to Hitler that not uncommon characteristic of Heads of State who are overreliant on powerful advisers: a conscious desire "not to know." But the proof of this is beyond the powers of any historian. What we *can* prove is that Himmler several times explicitly accepted responsibility for the liquidation decision.

Given the brutality of Hitler's orders to "dispose of" the entire male populations of two major Soviet cities, his insistence on the execution of hostages on a one hundred to one basis, his demands for the liquidation of Italian soldiers, Polish intellectuals, clergy and nobility, and captured Allied airmen and Red Army commissars, his apparent reluctance to acquiesce in the extermination of Europe's Jews remains a mystery. His order in July 1944, despite Himmler's objections, that Jews be "sold" for foreign currency and supplies suggests to some that like contemporary terrorists he saw these captives as a potential "asset," a means by which he could blackmail the civilized world. In any case, by April 1945 whatever inhibitions he may have felt were overcome, and we find him ordering Himmler to liquidate any unevacuated prisoners from concentration camps that were in danger of being overrun by American troops.

My central conclusion, however, is that Hitler was a less than omnipotent Führer and that his grip on his immediate subordinates weakened
as the war progressed. Hitler certainly realized this, but too late—in the
final days, in his Berlin air raid shelter. In the last two chapters we see
him struggling vainly to turn the clock back, to reassert his lost authority by securing one last tactical victory over his enemies. But there are
few generals—either Wehrmacht or SS—who now heed him.

I also found it necessary to set very different historical accents on the
doctrinaire foreign policies Hitler enforced—from his apparent unwillingness to humiliate Britain when she lay prostrate in 1940 (as I believe I establish on pages 165–67, for example), to his damaging and
emotional hatred of the Serbs, his illogical and over-loyal admiration of
Benito Mussolini, and his irrational mixtures of emotions toward Josef
Stalin. For a modern English historian there is a certain morbid fascina-
tion in inquiring how far Adolf Hitler really was bent on the destruction
of Britain and her Empire—a major raison d'être for her ruinous fight,
which in 1940 imperceptibly supplanted the more implausible one
proffered in August 1939: the rescue of Poland from outside oppres-
sion. Since in the chapters that follow evidence extracted again and
again from the most intimate sources—like Hitler's private conversations
with his women secretaries in June 1940—indicates that he originally
had neither the intention nor the desire to harm Britain or destroy the
Empire, surely British readers at least must ask themselves: What, then,
were we fighting for?

Given that the British people exhausted their assets and lost their
Empire in defeating Hitler, was he after all right when he noted that
Britain's essential attitude was "Après moi le déluge—if only we can get
rid of the hated National Socialist Germany?"

Unburdened by ideological idealism, the Duke of Windsor suspected
in July 1940 that the war continued solely in order to allow certain British statesmen to save face, even if it meant dragging their country and
the Empire into financial ruin. Others pragmatically argued that there
could be no compromise with Adolf Hitler and the Nazis. But did Britain's leaders in fact believe this?

Dr. Bernd Martin of Freiburg University has revealed that secret negotiations on peace continued between Britain and Germany in October
1939—negotiations on which, curiously, Sir Winston Churchill's files
have officially been sealed until the twenty-first century! Similar negotiations were carried on in June 1940, when even Churchill showed him-

self in Cabinet meetings to be willing to make a deal with Hitler if the price was right.

Of course, in assessing the real value of such negotiations and of Hitler's publicly stated intentions it is salutary to know that in 1941 he confidentially admitted to Walther Hewel (as the latter recorded in his diary): "For myself personally I would never tell a lie; but there is no falsehood I would not perpetrate for Germany's sake!" It is also necessary to take into account a string of broken promises that kept Europe in paralyzed inactivity for the better part of a decade.

Nevertheless, one wonders how much suffering the (Western) world might have been spared if both sides had pursued this line. But modern historiography has chosen to ignore this possibility as heresy.

The facts revealed here concerning Hitler's recorded actions, motivations, and opinions should provide a basis for fresh debate. Americans will find much that is new about the months leading up to Pearl Harbor. The French will find additional evidence that Hitler's treatment of their defeated nation was more influenced by memories of France's treatment of Germany after World War I than by his respect for Mussolini's desires. Russians can try to visualize the prospect that could conceivably have unfolded if Stalin had accepted Hitler's offer in November 1940 of inclusion in the Axis Pact; or if, having been defeated in the summer of 1941, Stalin had accepted Hitler's offer to rebuild Soviet power beyond the Urals; or if Hitler had taken seriously Stalin's alleged peace offer of September 1944.

In each case, this book views the situation as far as possible through Hitler's eyes, from behind his desk. This technique was bound to yield different perspectives, while answering many questions that arose in the past as to the motives for his actions and decisions. For example, I have devoted great effort to accumulating the same Intelligence material that was presented to Hitler—like the rare intercepts of Göring's *Forschungsamt* (literally, "Research Office"), which monitored telephone lines and decoded international radio signals; these explain, for instance, Hitler's alarm in July 1940 over Stalin's intentions.

Because this tragic moment in history is told from Hitler's point of view, we inevitably *see* the sufferings of the Germans, whereas the destruction and death inflicted on other nations remains somewhat more abstract. However, it is well to keep in mind that conservative estimates are that Hitler's War resulted in 40,000,000 military and civilian deaths. Of this number approximately 2,500,000 were Germans.

In modern Germany, some of my conclusions proved unpalatable to many. A wave of weak, repetitive, and unrevealing Hitler biographies had washed through the bookstores two or three years before my manuscript (running to over three thousand pages in the first draft) was published. The most widely publicized was that written by a German television personality, Joachim Fest; but he later told a questioner that he had not even visited the magnificent National Archives in Washington, which houses by far the largest collection of records relating to recent European history. Stylistically, Fest's German was good; but the old legends were trotted out afresh, polished to an impressive gleam of authority. The same Berlin company also published my book shortly after, under the title *Hitler und seine Feldherren;* their chief editor found many of my arguments distasteful, even dangerous, and without informing me, suppressed or even reversed them: in *their* printed text Hitler had not told Himmler there was to be "no liquidation" of the Jews (on November 30, 1941); he had told him not to use the word "liquidate" publicly in connection with their extermination program. Thus history is falsified! (My suggestion that they publish Himmler's note as a facsimile had been ignored.) I prohibited further printing of the book, two days after its appearance in Germany. To explain their actions, the Berlin publishers argued that my manuscript expressed some views that were "an affront to established historical opinion" in their country.

The biggest problem in dealing analytically with Hitler is the aversion to him as a person created by years of intense wartime propaganda and emotive postwar historiography. My own impression of the war is limited to snapshot memories of its side effects: early summer picnics around the wreckage of a Heinkel bomber on the fringe of the local Bluebell Woods; the infernal organ note of the V-1 flying bombs awakening the whole countryside as they passed overhead; convoys of drab army trucks rumbling past our country gate; counting the gaps in the American bomber squadrons straggling back from Germany in formation after the day's operations; the troopships sailing in June 1944 from Southsea beach, heading for Normandy; and of course VE-Day itself, with the bonfires and beating of the family gong. Our knowledge of the Germans responsible for all this was scarcely more profound. In *Everybody's* magazine, long defunct, I recall "Ferrier's World Searchlight" with its weekly caricatures of a club-footed dwarf called Goebbels and the other comic Nazi heroes.

The caricatures of the Nazi leaders have bedeviled the writing of history ever since. Writers have found it impossible to de-demonize them. Confronted by the phenomenon of Hitler himself, they cannot grasp that he was an ordinary, walking, talking human weighing some 155 pounds, with graying hair, largely false teeth, and chronic digestive ailments. He is to them the Devil incarnate. The process flourished even more after his death: at the Nuremberg Trials, the blame was shifted from general to minister, from minister to Party official, and from all of them invariably to Hitler. Under the system of "licensed" publishers and newspapers enforced by the Allies in postwar Germany, the legends prospered. No story was too absurd to gain credence; the authority of the writers who created them passed unchallenged.

Among these creative writers the German General Staff must take pride of place. Without Hitler, few of them would have risen higher than to the rank of colonel; they owed him their jobs, their medals, their estates, their endowments. Often they owed him their military victories too—the defeat of France in 1940 (see pages 47–48, 87–88, 124, 127–29), the Battle of Kharkov in 1942 (page 423), to mention just two. After the war those who survived—which was not infrequently because they had been dismissed, and thus removed from the hazards of the battlefield—contrived to divert the blame away from themselves to the erstwhile Führer and Supreme Commander. I have exposed the frauds and deceptions in their biographies. Thus in the secret files of the Nuremberg prosecutor Justice Robert H. Jackson, I found a note addressed to his investigator warning about the proposed tactics of General Franz Halder, the former German Army Chief of Staff: "I just wanted to call your attention to the CSDIC intercepts of Halder's conversations with other generals. He is extremely frank on what he thinks should be suppressed or distorted, and in particular is very sensitive to the suggestion that the German General Staff was involved in anything, especially planning for war." Usually, these tactics involved labeling Hitler a "madman"—although the medical experts who treated him are unanimous that clinically speaking he remained quite sane to the very end.

Fortunately, this embarrassed adjusting of consciences and memories was more than once, as above, recorded for posterity by the hidden microphones of the Combined Services Detailed Interrogation Centers. When General Heinz Guderian—one of Halder's successors as Chief of Staff—and the arrogant, supercilious General Leo Geyr von Schweppenburg were asked by their American captors to write their history of the war, they felt obliged to obtain the permission of Field Marshal Wilhelm von Leeb as senior officer at the Seventh Army CSDIC. Leeb replied:

> Well, I can only give you my personal opinion: . . . You will have to weigh your answers carefully when they pertain to objectives, causes,

and the progress of operations in order to see where they may affect the interests of our Fatherland. On the one hand we have to admit that the Americans know the course of operations quite accurately; they even know which units were employed on our side. However, they are not quite as familiar with our motives. And there is one point where it would be advisable to proceed with caution, so that we do not become the laughingstock of the world. I do not know what your relations were with Hitler, but I do know his military capacity. . . . You will have to consider your answers a bit carefully when approached on this subject, so that you say nothing that might embarrass our Fatherland. . . .

Geyr von Schweppenburg: The types of madness known to psychologists cannot be compared with the one the Führer suffered from. He was a madman surrounded by serfs. I do not think we should express ourselves quite as strongly as that in our statements. Mention of this fact will have to be made, however, in order to exonerate a few persons. The question is whether now is the right time to mention all this.

After an agonized debate on whether and which German generals advocated war in 1939, Leeb suggested: "The question is now, whether we should not just admit openly everything we know." The following discussion ensued:

Geyr von Schweppenburg: Any objective observer will admit that National Socialism raised the social status of the worker, and in some respects even his standard of living as long as that was possible.
Leeb: This is one of the great achievements of National Socialism. The excesses of National Socialism were in the first and final analysis due to the Führer's personality.
Guderian: The fundamental principles were fine.
Leeb: That is true.

I was startled and, as a historian, depressed by the number of "diaries" which close scrutiny proved to have been faked or tampered with—invariably to Hitler's disadvantage. Two different men claimed to possess the entire diaries of Admiral Wilhelm Canaris—the legendary Abwehr chief hanged by Hitler as a traitor in April 1945. The first produced "documents of the postwar German Intelligence Service (BND)" and original papers "signed by Canaris" in his support; the second, a German High Court judge, announced that his set of the diaries had recently been returned by Generalissimo Francisco Franco to the West German government. Forensic tests on the paper and ink of a "Canaris" document supplied by the first man, conducted for me by a London laboratory, proved them to be forgeries. An interview with Franco's chef de bureau—his brother-in-law Don Felipe Polo Valdes—in Madrid disposed of the German judge's equally improbable claim. Neither ever provided the actual diaries for inspection. The Eva Braun diaries published by the film actor Luis Trenker were largely forged from the "memoirs" written decades earlier by Countess Irma Larisch-Wallersee; the forgery was established by the Munich lawcourts in October 1948. (Eva Braun's genuine diaries, and her entire correspondence with Hitler, were acquired by a CIC team based on Stuttgart-Backnang in the summer of 1945; they have not been seen since. I identified the team's commander and visited him in New Mexico; he admitted the facts, but I failed to persuade him to make the papers available for historical research—perhaps he has long since sold them to a private dealer.) The oft-quoted "diaries" of Himmler's masseur Felix Kersten are equally fictitious, as for example the "twenty-six-page medical dossier on Hitler" described in them shows. Oddly enough Kersten's real diaries—containing political dynamite on Sweden's elite—do exist and have not been published. Similarly, the "diaries" published by Rudolf Semmler in *Goebbels—the Man Next to Hitler* (London, 1947) are phony too, as the entry for January 12, 1945, proves: it has Hitler as Goebbels's guest in Berlin, when the Führer was in fact still fighting the Battle of the Bulge from his HQ in West Germany. And there are no prizes for spotting the anachronisms in Count Galeazzo Ciano's extensively quoted "diaries": for example Marshal Rodolfo Graziani's "complaints about Rommel" on December 12, 1940—two full months *before* Rommel was appointed to Italy's North African theater! In fact Ciano spent the months after his dismissal in February 1943 rewriting and "improving" the diaries himself, which makes them very readable but virtually useless for the purposes of history. Ribbentrop warned about the forgery in his prison memoirs—he claimed to have seen Ciano's real diaries in September 1943—and the Nazi interpreter Eugen Dollmann described in his memoirs how the fraud was actually admitted to him by a British officer at a prison camp. Even the most superficial examination of the handwritten original volumes reveals the extent to which Ciano doctored them and interpolated material—yet historians of the highest repute have quoted them without question as they have Ciano's so-called "Lisbon Papers," although the latter too bear all the hallmarks of subsequent editing. They have all at some time been retyped on the same typewriter, although ostensibly originating over six years (1936–42).

Other diaries have been amended in more harmless ways: the Luftwaffe Chief of Staff Karl Koller's real shorthand diary often bears no resemblance to the version he published as *Der letzte Monat* (Mann-

heim, 1949). And Helmuth Greiner, keeper of the official OKW operations staff war diary until 1943, seized the opportunity in 1945, when
asked by the Americans to retranscribe his original notes for the lost
volumes from August 1942 to March 1943, to excise passages which
reflected unfavorably on fellow prisoners like General Adolf Heusinger
—or too favorably on Hitler; and no doubt to curry favor with the
Americans, he added lengthy paragraphs charged with pungent criticism of Hitler's conduct of the war which I found to be missing from
his original handwritten notes when I compared them with the published
version. This tendency—to pillory Hitler after the war—was also strongly
evident in the "diaries" of General Gerhard Engel, who served as
Hitler's army adjutant from March 1938 to October 1943. His-
toriographical evidence alone—*e.g.,* comparison with the 1940 private
diaries of Reichsminister Fritz Todt or the wife of General Rudolf
Schmundt, or with the records of Field Marshal von Manstein's Army
Group Don at the time of Stalingrad—indicates that whatever they are,
they are *not* contemporaneous diaries (regrettably, the well-known Institut für Zeitgeschichte in Munich has nonetheless published them in a
volume, *Heeresadjutant bei Hitler 1938–1943* [Stuttgart, 1974], rather
feebly drawing attention to the diaries' inconsistencies in a short Introduction).

My exploration of sources throwing light on Hitler's inner mind was
sometimes successful, sometimes not. Weeks of searching with a proton-
magnetometer—a kind of supersensitive mine-detector—in a forest in
East Germany failed to unearth a glass jar containing stenograms of
Goebbels's very last diaries, although at times, according to the map in
my possession, we must have stood right over it. But I did obtain the
private diaries written by Walther Hewel, Ribbentrop's liaison officer on
Hitler's staff, and by Baron Ernst von Weizsäcker, Ribbentrop's state
secretary. Field Marshal Wolfram von Richthofen's widow made available to me the two thousand-page original text of his unpublished diaries
too; in fact every officer or member of Hitler's staff whom I interviewed
seemed to have carefully hoarded diaries or papers, which were eventually produced for my exploitation here—mostly in German, but the research papers on the fringe also came in a Babel of other languages:
Italian, Russian, French, Spanish, Hungarian, Romanian, and Czech;
some cryptic references to Hitler and Ribbentrop in the Hewel diaries
defied all my puny codebreaking efforts, and then proved to have been
written in Indonesian! For the sake of completeness, I would add that
Field Marshal Fedor von Bock's diary was pruned by him, but he does
not seem to have interpolated fresh material; and that General Halder's

diary is completely trustworthy (having been originally transcribed from the shorthand by the British) but is best employed *without* reference to Halder's postwar footnotes.

Many sources of prime importance are still missing, although enterprising West German publishers have now obtained the full text of Goebbels's diaries. That those of Hewel and Weizsäcker remained hitherto unexplored by historians is a baffling mystery to me. They only had to ask the widows, as I did. The diaries of Hans Lammers, Wilhelm Brückner, Karl Bodenschatz, Karl Wolff, and Professor Theo Morell are missing, although known to have fallen into Allied hands in 1945. Nicolaus von Below's are probably in Moscow. Himmler's missing pocket notebooks certainly are. Alfred Rosenberg's remaining diaries are illicitly held by an American lawyer in Frankfurt. The rest of Field Marshal Erhard Milch's diaries—of which I obtained some five thousand pages in 1967—have vanished, as have General Alfred Jodl's diaries covering the years 1940 to 1943; they were looted with his private property by the British 11th Armored Division at Flensburg in May 1945. Only a brief fragment of Benito Mussolini's diary survives (see pages 591–92): the SS copied the originals and returned them to him in January 1945, but both the originals and the copy placed in Ribbentrop's files are missing now; a forgery perpetrated by two Italian nuns temporarily and expensively deceived the London *Sunday Times* some years ago, before it was exposed by the same laboratory that tested the "Canaris" document for me. The important diaries of Schmundt were unhappily burnt at his request by his fellow adjutant Admiral Karl-Jesco von Puttkamer in April 1945, along with Puttkamer's own diaries. The diary of Dr. Stephan Tiso, the last Slovak premier (from August 1944), is unaccountably held in the closed files of the Hoover Institution.

As for autobiographical works, I preferred to rely on the original manuscripts rather than the published texts, as in the early postwar years apprehensive publishers (especially the "licensed" ones in Germany) made changes in them—for example in the memoirs of Karl-Wilhelm Krause, Hitler's manservant. Thus I relied on the original handwritten memoirs of Himmler's Intelligence chief, Walter Schellenberg, rather than on the mutilated and ghostwritten version subsequently published. I would go so far as to warn against the authoritativeness of numerous works hitherto accepted as "standard" sources on Hitler—particularly those by Konrad Heiden, Dr. Hermann Rauschning, Dr. Hans Bernd Gisevius, Erich Kordt, and by Hitler's dismissed adjutant Fritz Wiedemann. (The latter unashamedly explained in a private 1940 letter to a friend: "It makes no difference if exaggerations and even falsehoods do creep in.")

With the brilliant exception of Professor Hugh Trevor-Roper, whose book *The Last Days of Hitler* was based on the records of the era and is therefore virtually unassailable even today, each successive biographer has repeated or engrossed the legends created by his predecessors, or at best consulted only the most readily available works of reference themselves. Since it proved impracticable to study in detail such a dictator's whole life within this one volume, I limited myself to his war years; I eschewed as far as possible all *published* literature, since by 1964 when I began the research it was possible to speculate that "books on Hitler" outnumbered page for page the total original documentation available. This proved a sad underestimate.

Idle predecessors had gratefully lamented that most of the documents had been destroyed. They had not—they survived in embarrassing superabundance. The official papers of the Luftwaffe Field Marshal Milch, Göring's deputy, were captured by the British and total over 60,000 pages (not that Göring's most recent biographer consulted even one page of them). The entire war diary of the German naval staff, of immense value far beyond purely naval matters, survived; it took many months to read the 69 volumes of main text, some over 900 pages long, in Washington, and to examine the most promising of the 3,900 microfilm rolls of German naval records held there too.

And what is the result? Hitler will long remain an enigma, however hard the historians burrow and toil. Even his intimates realized they hardly knew him. I have already quoted Ribbentrop's puzzlement; but General Alfred Jodl, his closest strategic adviser, also wrote in his Nuremberg cell on March 10, 1946:

. . . But then I ask myself, did you ever really know this man at whose side you led such a thorny and ascetic existence? Did he perhaps just trifle with your idealism too, abusing it for dark purposes which he kept hidden deep within himself? Dare you claim to know a man, if he has not opened up the deepest recesses of his heart to you —in sorrow as well as in ecstasy? To this very day I do not know what he thought or knew or really wanted. I only knew my own thoughts and suspicions. And if, now that the shrouds fall away from a sculpture we fondly hoped would be a work of art, only to reveal nothing but a degenerate gargoyle—then let future historians argue among themselves whether it was like that from the start, or changed with circumstances.

I keep making the same mistake: I blame his humble origins. But then I remember how many peasants' sons have been blessed by History with the name, The Great.

"Hitler the Great"? No, contemporary History is unlikely to swallow such an epithet.

From the first day that he "seized power," January 30, 1933, Hitler knew that only sudden death awaited him if he failed to restore pride and empire to post-Versailles Germany. His close friend and adjutant, Julius Schaub, recorded Hitler's jubilant boast to his staff on that evening, as the last celebrating guests left the Berlin Chancellery building: "No power on earth will get me out of this building alive!"

History saw this prophecy fulfilled, as the handful of remaining Nazi faithfuls trooped uneasily into his underground study on April 30, 1945, surveyed his still warm remains—slumped on a couch, with blood trickling from the sagging lower jaw, and a gunshot wound in the right temple—and sniffed the bitter-almonds smell hanging in the air. Wrapped in a gray army blanket, he was carried up to the shell-blasted Chancellery garden. Gasoline was slopped over him in a reeking crater and ignited while his staff hurriedly saluted and backed down into the shelter. Thus ended the six years of Hitler's War. We shall now see how they began.

—David Irving,
London, January 1976

Hitler's People

As an aid to following the narrative, brief biographical details follow of the principal German personalities referred to in the text.

ALBRECHT, Alwin-Broder: Until June 1939 Hitler's naval adjutant, his replacement was demanded by Raeder after an unfortunate marriage; Hitler demurred and made him a personal adjutant instead. He is presumed to have died in the last days in Berlin.

AMSBERG, Colonel Erik von: A former adjutant of Keitel's, he stepped in as Hitler's Wehrmacht adjutant after Below, Puttkamer, and Schmundt were injured in the July 20, 1944, bomb explosion.

ASSMANN, Admiral Heinz: Jodl's naval staff officer, who frequently attended Hitler's war conferences from 1943 to 1944.

BACKE, Dr. Herbert: The very capable state secretary in the food ministry, who virtually supplanted the minister, Richard Walter Darré, in 1942.

BECK, General Ludwig: Was Army Chief of Staff until August 1938, when he was replaced by Halder and began to intrigue against Hitler; after the July 20, 1944, bomb plot failed, he committed suicide.

BELOW, Colonel Nicolaus von: Genteel and educated, Below served as Hitler's Luftwaffe adjutant from 1937 until the Führer's suicide.

BERGER, SS General Gottlob: Chief of Himmler's SS Main Office (*Hauptamt*).

BEST, Dr. Werner: A department head in the Gestapo, he was appointed Hitler's Plenipotentiary in Denmark in 1942.

BLASCHKE, Professor Johannes: Hitler's principal dentist—his postwar interrogation by the Americans provides the main evidence that Hitler's was the corpse found by the Red Army in Berlin.

BLOMBERG, Field Marshal Werner von: The first field marshal created by Hitler—in 1937—Blomberg was fired as war minister in early 1938 after marrying way, way below his station; but Hitler had a soft spot for him until the very end.

BOCK, Field Marshal Fedor von: One of Hitler's toughest and most successful soldiers in France (1940) and Russia (1941–42), he died in an air raid in 1945.

BODENSCHATZ, General Karl: Officially Göring's chef de bureau, Bodenschatz became his permanent representative at Hitler's HQ.

BONIN, Colonel Bogislaw von: Latterly the chief of operations in the German General Staff.

BORGMANN, Colonel Heinrich: Succeeded Engel as Hitler's army adjutant in 1943; killed by air attack on his car in April 1945.

BORMANN, Albert: Younger brother of Martin Bormann, but not on speaking terms with him; Albert was an adjutant in Hitler's Private Chancellery.

BORMANN, Martin: Rose from relative obscurity as Hess's right-hand man to position of vast personal power upon Hess's defection in May 1941. Head of the Nazi Party Chancellery, and from 1943 the "Führer's secretary" as well. He was the dynamo inside the Nazi machine, converting Hitler's half-spoken thoughts into harsh reality. Hard working, hard living—condemned to death at Nuremberg in absentia, his lawyer's appeal for clemency is still on the case file, undecided.

BOUHLER, Reichsleiter Philipp: As Chief of the Chancellery of the Führer of the Nazi party, Bouhler handled the incoming mail of German citizens; as such his office dealt with applications for clemency and thus became involved in the murderous euthanasia projects and the technicalities of the liquidation of Jews and other "undesirables." He took his own life in May 1945.

BRANDT, Dr. Karl: Hitler's accompanying surgeon from the mid-Thirties onward, he was dismissed in October 1944 by Martin Bormann; the Americans hanged him in 1947 for his part in the euthanasia planning.

BRAUCHITSCH, Field Marshal Walther von: Appointed Commander in Chief, Army, by Hitler in 1938 for want of a better general; Hitler tolerated him only reluctantly until his ill-health provided sufficient cover for his retirement in December 1941. He died in British captivity in 1948.

BRAUN, Eva: Hitler's only known mistress from 1931 onward; she provided conversation and company, and according to Hitler's secretaries, developed from the humble laboratory assistant she had been before then into a woman of great poise and charm. He formally married her thirty-six hours before their joint suicide in April 1945.

BRÜCKNER, SA Gruppenführer Wilhelm: A chief adjutant of Hitler's, dismissed in October 1940—having, like Albrecht and Blomberg, contracted a much-criticized marriage.

BURGDORF, General Wilhelm: Succeeded Schmundt as Hitler's chief Wehrmacht adjutant and chief of the army personnel branch after Schmundt was wounded in the July 20, 1944, bomb explosion; previously Schmundt's deputy. A rough diamond and heavy drinker, he committed suicide soon after Hitler.

CANARIS, Vice Admiral Wilhelm: Chief of the Abwehr—the OKW Intelligence Branch—until its absorption by the SS in 1944, Canaris weathered many storms. A man of few friends, with Indian manservants, Greek blood, and a liking for warm champagne for breakfast, he slipped off his tightrope between the traitors and the SS in 1944 and was hanged in the last month of the war.

CHRISTIAN, General Eckhard: He had been Jodl's chief staff officer until he married Hitler's personal secretary Gerda Daranowski in November 1942; then he rose rapidly until he was the chief of the Luftwaffe operations staff.

CHRISTIAN, Frau Gerda: One of Hitler's four private secretaries, and certainly the most attractive—as the Führer is known to have appreciated. She joined his staff before the war, retired on her marriage in November 1942, but returned a year later and stayed with Hitler until the end.

DARGES, Fritz: Martin Bormann's adjutant until 1939, he became Hitler's personal adjutant from March 1943—until Hitler sacked him in July 1944, ostensibly because of an incident with an insect during a war conference, more probably because Darges had jilted Eva's sister Gretl Braun. He was sent to the Russian front.

DIETRICH, Dr. Otto: Hitler's press spokesman.

DIETRICH, SS General Josef "Sepp": One of the Party Old Guard, he commanded the SS Leibstandarte (Life Guards) and then the SS Sixth Panzer Army.

DÖNITZ, Grand Admiral Karl: Commander in Chief of the German U-boat service until 1943, he stepped into Raeder's shoes when the latter resigned as Commander in Chief, Navy, that January. Dönitz supported Hitler's bolder strategic decisions—*i.e.*, to hold on to the Crimea and the eastern Baltic provinces—and satisfied Hitler that he was the best successor as Führer in April 1945.

DORSCH, Dr. Xaver: After Fritz Todt, one of the Reich's most outstanding civil engineers; became head of the Todt Organization building military sites in Reich-occupied countries.

EICHMANN, SS Colonel Adolf: A minor official in Kaltenbrunner's Reich Main Security Office, Eichmann was responsible for the smooth running of the Jewish deportation programs; he was one of the driving forces behind the extermination of the Jews.

EICKEN, Professor Carl von: The ear, nose, and throat specialist who operated on Hitler's throat in 1935 and again in November 1944.

ENGEL, Colonel Gerhard: Hitler's army adjutant from 1938 to 1943, he then distinguished himself as a division commander.

ETZDORF, Major Hasso von: Liaison officer between the General Staff and Ribbentrop's foreign ministry, his often cryptic penciled notes were deciphered by the Americans postwar and present vital information on Hitler's foreign strategy.

FALKENHAUSEN, General Alexander von: The aristocratic Nazi Military Governor of Belgium, he entered into a liaison with an equally aristocratic Belgian lady which resulted in his dismissal in July 1944; this probably spared him from the hangman's noose some weeks later, as his implication in the bomb plot escaped the attention of the Gestapo.

FEGELEIN, SS General Hermann: Himmler's representative at Hitler's HQ from 1944 to the end; married Gretl Braun (*see also* Darges) but left her a widow, as he was shot for attempted desertion in the last days.

FELLGIEBEL, General Erich: Chief of the Wehrmacht's and Army's Signals Branches, he was executed after the failure of the 1944 bomb plot in which he was implicated.

FRANK, Dr. Hans: One of Hitler's oldest friends and his personal legal adviser in the Thirties. Hitler appointed him Governor General of rump Poland after that country's defeat in 1939.

FRANK, Karl-Hermann: Deputy Protector of Bohemia-Moravia.

FRICK, Dr. Wilhelm: Minister of the Interior, until Himmler supplanted him in August 1943.

FROMM, General Friedrich: A deadly enemy of Keitel, Fromm commanded the Replacement Army—divisions being raised and trained in Germany; he was implicated in the July 20, 1944, conspiracy, but only vaguely—the People's Court found no evidence, for example, that he had known of the plot, but condemned him to death for cowardice in not having acted more energetically against his Chief of Staff, Stauffenberg, that afternoon.

GIESING, Dr. Erwin: Army ENT-specialist summoned from Rastenburg hospital after July 20, 1944, bomb explosion to treat Hitler's head injuries.

GLOBOCNIK, SS Brigadier Odilo: Formerly police commander in occupied Polish district of Lublin, he ranked with Eichmann as one of the Nazis behind the massacre of the Jews.

GOEBBELS, Dr. Joseph: One of the Party's Old Guard; Gauleiter of Berlin, and after 1933 Reich propaganda minister—an outstanding speaker and master of dialectics, but undoubtedly one of the evil geniuses behind the Führer. Took his own and his family's lives after Hitler's suicide.

GOERDELER, Dr. Carl: Former mayor of Leipzig, Goerdeler was political leader of the anti-Hitler conspiracy culminating in the July 20, 1944, bomb explosion.

GÖRING, Reichsmarschall Hermann: A man of many titles, but principally important as Commander in Chief of the Luftwaffe and head of the Four-Year Plan office. Alternating between bouts of laziness and spasms of intense activity, he was most closely identified by the German public with their eventual misery and defeat—but somehow his popularity remained virtually unimpaired until his October 1946 suicide.

GUDERIAN, General Heinz: Ranks as one of World War II's leading tank commanders; was dismissed by Hitler in December 1941 to satisfy Kluge and remained in a command limbo until Hitler appointed him his personal Inspector of the Panzer Service in February 1943. Even then Guderian wavered in his loyalty; he certainly had advance warning of the July 20, 1944, bomb explosion and prudently absented himself from the Führer's HQ that day—to return only hours later, to his own surprise, as the army's new Chief of General Staff until March 1945.

GÜNSCHE, SS Colonel Otto: Formerly a private in Hitler's escort squad, Günsche—a big, blond bulldog of an officer—became his personal adjutant and bodyguard, and was entrusted by the Führer with burning his corpse after his suicide in April 1945—and with giving him a coup de grâce with his pistol if necessary.

HAASE, Professor Werner: Had treated Hitler before the war, became his doctor again briefly in the last days in Berlin.

HALDER, General Franz: Succeeded Beck as the army's Chief of General Staff in 1938; generally acknowledged to have been a good tactician, Halder retained this post until Hitler could stand him no longer—in September 1942.

HASSELBACH, Dr. Hanskarl von: Dr. Karl Brandt's deputy as Hitler's accompanying surgeon until October 1944.

HESS, Rudolf: Hitler's official "deputy" until his flight to Scotland in May 1941.

HEWEL, Ambassador Walther: He had joined the Nazi party as a student in the early Twenties, shared Hitler's Landsberg imprisonment briefly in 1923, then emigrated as a planter to Java; he returned to become a member of Ribbentrop's staff—serving through the period of this book as liaison officer at Hitler's HQ.

HEYDRICH, SS General Reinhard: Kaltenbrunner's predecessor as chief of the Reich Main Security Office of the SS; as such he was more interested in the "executive" side—the building of a formidable police organization throughout Germany. Appointed "Reich Protector" of occupied Czechoslovakia in October 1941, embarked on reforms there, assassinated by British-trained agents in May 1942. As he was the brain behind the extermination camps, he merits no sympathy.

HIMMLER, Heinrich: SS Reichsführer, chief of police, and—after August 1943—Minister of the Interior. "Himmler," said the Nazi party newspaper chief Max Amann, "considered it his duty to eliminate all enemies of the Nazi ideology and he did so calmly and impersonally, without hate and without sympathy." A rare mixture of crackpot and organizational genius.

JESCHONNEK, General Hans: A lieutenant at sixteen in World War I, he seemed marked out for a brilliant career; by 1939 he was Luftwaffe Chief of Staff—by August 1943 he was dead, a suicide.

JODL, General Alfred: A pure soldier, of unquestionable loyalty to his Führer, Jodl served as chief of the OKW operations staff (*Wehrmachtführungsstab*) from August 1939 to the very end. His strategic insight was profound. He was hanged at Nuremberg in 1946.

JUNGE, Frau Traudl: Youngest of Hitler's secretaries, she joined his staff when Gerda Daranowski married in 1942; she herself married Hitler's manservant Hans Junge, was widowed by 1944, and stayed with Hitler to the end. (Née Traudl Humps.)

JUNGE, Captain Wolf: Jodl's naval staff officer until August 28, 1943, then again from summer 1944 onward while Assmann recovered from injuries sustained on July 20, 1944.

KALTENBRUNNER, SS General Dr. Ernst: Heydrich's successor as chief of the Reich Main Security Office—but personally more interested in the Intelligence side and less in the police and executive aspects, in which "Gestapo" Müller grew in influence.

KEITEL, Field Marshal Wilhelm: Chief of OKW (German High Command) in title only; he exercised his ministerial functions well; the military and strategic side he—wisely—left to Jodl. Loyal and hardworking, Keitel shared Jodl's fate at Nuremberg.

KESSELRING, Field Marshal Albert: He held important air commands during the invasions of Poland, France, and Russia. Supreme commander of German forces in Italy (1943–45), in March 1945 he took over from Rundstedt as Commander in Chief West. In 1947 he was condemned to death for war crimes against Italian civilians, but this sentence was later commuted to life imprisonment. He was pardoned in 1952.

KLUGE, Field Marshal Günther Hans von: A good commander of men, like Rommel—always in the battle line with his troops, but politically ambitious too. Lent an ear to various groups of plotters, but would not commit himself. Fearing implication in the failed July 20, 1944, plot, Kluge took cyanide and closed his "big blue, patrician eyes" for the last time on August 18, 1944, his personal admiration for Adolf Hitler undiminished.

KOCH, Erich: Gauleiter of East Prussia, he was appointed Reich Commissioner in the Ukraine in 1941, pursuing policies of such brutality as to achieve the impossible—a pro-Soviet Ukraine.

KOEPPEN, Dr. Werner: Rosenberg's representative at Hitler's HQ, he recorded the Führer's political Table Talk for some months in 1941.

KOLLER, General Karl: Luftwaffe Chief of Staff from November 1944 to the end; Bavarian, dour but capable, having risen from the enlisted ranks.

KORTEN, General Günther: Luftwaffe Chief of Staff following Jeschonnek's 1943 suicide, he died an agonizing death when a fragment of table pierced him after Stauffenberg's bomb exploded beneath it in July 1944. Korten was the first to campaign for a strategic bomber force in the Luftwaffe.

KRANCKE, Vice Admiral Theodor: Permanent representative of the Commander in Chief, Navy, at Hitler's HQ after September 1942.

KREBS, General Hans: Last Army Chief of Staff, he negotiated with the Russians in Berlin following Hitler's death, then committed suicide.

KREIPE, General Werner: Luftwaffe Chief of Staff from August 1 to September 21, 1944, when Hitler banished him from war conferences at his HQ.

LAMMERS, Dr. Hans Heinrich: A legacy of the Hindenburg regime, Lammers was an expert on constitutional law and, as chief of the

Reich Chancellery, the most important civil servant of the Third Reich.

LEY, Dr. Robert: Party Organization chief, he took over the trade unions in 1933 and molded them into the monolithic German Labor Front (DAF).

LINGE, Heinz: Hitler's manservant until the very end in Berlin.

LOSSBERG, Colonel Bernhard von: Jodl's army staff officer.

LUTZE, Victor: Succeeded the murdered Ernst Röhm as chief of the SA brown-shirt army in 1934. A heavy drinker and loose talker, he engaged Himmler's displeasure by remarks about the SS, and died in a car crash in 1943.

MAISEL, General Ernst: Burgdorf's deputy in the Army Personnel Branch—a quiet, intelligent officer manhandled by postwar writers for his unfortunate part in Rommel's death.

MANSTEIN, Field Marshal Erich von: Universally acclaimed as Germany's most outstanding General Staff product, as he displayed in offensive operations in Poland (1939), the west (1940), and the Russian campaign.

MEISSNER, Dr. Otto: Like Lammers, a leftover of the Hindenburg era; head of the Presidential Chancellery (*Präsidialkanzlei*).

MILCH, Field Marshal Erhard: Founder of Lufthansa airline, Milch was called upon by Hitler and Göring to build the secret Luftwaffe in 1933. After years of intense rivalry with Göring, Milch—who had labored to conceal a serious defect in his family tree (he was pure Aryan, but accepted popular legend to the contrary to conceal the fact that he was the product of the illicit relationship between his mother and her mother's brother)—was sacked in 1944.

MODEL, Field Marshal Walter: Monocled, highly schooled, modern in outlook, he was the antithesis of Manstein; when a front line needed holding or restoring, Hitler sent for Model.

MORELL, Professor Theo: Morell alone had been able to cure Hitler of a gastric disorder in 1936; he appointed him personal physician and turned a deaf ear on all his critics until the very end.

MÜLLER, SS General Heinrich: Chief of *Amt IV* (the Gestapo) under Kaltenbrunner, he vanished in the last days of the war and has not been positively seen since.

PAULUS, Field Marshal Friedrich: Led his Sixth Army into Soviet captivity after the Battle of Stalingrad, 1943.

PUTTKAMER, Admiral Karl-Jesco von: Hitler's naval adjutant from March 1935 to June 1938, then again from August 1939 to the end—

one of the most important witnesses still surviving from Hitler's circle.

RAEDER, Grand Admiral Erich: Was already Commander in Chief, Navy, when Hitler came to power in 1933, and forcefully resigned exactly ten years later.

RATTENHUBER, SS Brigadier Hans: Chief of Hitler's police bodyguard at HQ, responsible for his security, he sought to conceal his brutal and intriguing nature beneath a veneer of Bavarian charm.

RIBBENTROP, Joachim von: Reich foreign minister after 1938, he realized that many of Hitler's foreign policies were doomed to failure but allowed the Führer to overrule him every time; hanged at Nuremberg in 1946.

RICHTHOFEN, Field Marshal Wolfram von: Perhaps the toughest Luftwaffe strike commander, Richthofen commanded first an air corps, then an air force (Luftflotte); Hitler always committed Richthofen where the battle was fiercest, and listened readily to the field marshal's extravagant complaints about his army counterparts.

ROMMEL, Field Marshal Erwin: Commandant of Hitler's HQ 1939–40, he secured command of a panzer division in time for the attack on France, fought a brilliant if reckless campaign there, and repeated his triumphs on a larger scale in North Africa, until the lack of supplies and the Allied superiority in tanks and aircraft beat him back; his loyalty to Hitler remained unchanged, but his hatred of the OKW and Jodl reached pathological proportions in 1944. Implicated by others in the July 20, 1944, conspiracy, he took the consequences —poison—in October that year.

ROSENBERG, Alfred: Verbose Party philosopher; bitter opponent of Koch, particularly after Rosenberg as Minister for the Occupied Eastern Territories had to deal with him; notorious anti-Semite.

RUNDSTEDT, Field Marshal Gerd von: Blunt, chivalrous, loyal, but elderly and easygoing in later years, Rundstedt was the senior serving German soldier; Hitler was fond of him and rightly trusted him— thrice appointing him to high commands, and thrice relieving him when expediency demanded. From 1942 to 1945 Rundstedt was— with a brief interval in the summer of 1944—Commander in Chief West.

SAUCKEL, Fritz: Gauleiter of Thuringia, Sauckel was appointed by Hitler in 1942 to take charge of the manpower procurement program of the Reich; this Sauckel achieved by contracts, inducements, or slave labor. Hanged at Nuremberg.

SAUR, Karl-Otto: Outwardly the typical Nazi—stocky, forceful, crude—

Saur was first Todt's, then Speer's right-hand man in the munitions ministry; his phenomenal memory for dates and statistics made him one of Hitler's favorites.

SCHAUB, Julius: Joined the Nazi party in 1925, served as Hitler's personal adjutant and factotum until the end; of too limited an intellect to intrigue—hence valued highly by the Führer in his entourage.

SCHEIDT, Dr. Wilhelm: Adjutant to Hitler's court historian Scherff. After Scherff's injury on July 20, 1944, Scheidt took his place for many months at Hitler's war conferences. But through his friendship with Beck, Goerdeler, and Kurt von Hammerstein, Scheidt was the source (unwittingly perhaps?) of much secret Intelligence that reached the enemy, direct from Hitler's HQ.

SCHERFF, General Walter: Chief OKW historian, appointed by Hitler in 1942 to write the Reich war history; but he never got around to it —and on his orders the shorthand records of most of Hitler's war conferences were burned in May 1945.

SCHMUNDT, General Rudolf: Hitler's chief Wehrmacht adjutant after 1938, and chief of the army personnel branch after October 1942 as well; his role as private adviser to Hitler needs intensive research. He died a lingering death, blind and burnt, after the July 20, 1944, bomb blast.

SCHÖRNER, Field Marshal Ferdinand: Like Model, Schörner was usually assigned to sectors where other generals had failed, and he usually succeeded.

SCHROEDER, Christa: Hitler's private secretary after 1933, she stayed with him until ordered to leave Berlin on April 20, 1945. Hitler warmed toward her, despite her sharp tongue and feline comments on the war's progress.

SEYSS-INQUART, Dr. Arthur: A quiet-spoken Austrian lawyer, propelled by the 1938 union between Germany and Austria into high office in Vienna as a Nazi sympathizer, Seyss-Inquart was Hans Frank's deputy in Poland until May 18, 1940, when he was appointed Hitler's viceroy in the Netherlands. Hanged at Nuremberg.

SONNLEITNER, Dr. Franz von: Diplomat, stood in for Hewel during his recovery from air crash injuries in 1944.

SPEER, Albert: Nominated by Hitler as architect for Berlin, despite his youth; ambitious, vain, publicity-conscious, but possessing—like Göring—undoubted *presence* and organizing ability. Hitler shrewdly appointed him Todt's successor as munitions minister in February 1942, but became disillusioned with him in the last weeks of his life.

STUMPFEGGER, Dr. Ludwig: A well-known surgeon on Himmler's staff, who began treating Hitler in October 1944.

TODT, Dr. Fritz: Hitler's main civil engineer, who had built the autobahn network on his orders, and then the West Wall in 1938–39; in March 1940 Hitler nominated him to head a new munitions ministry. When Todt was killed in a plane crash in February 1942, Speer succeeded him.

VORMANN, General Nikolaus von: Appointed by Brauchitsch to act as army representative at Hitler's HQ in August and September 1939.

VOSS, Vice Admiral Hans-Erich: Succeeded Krancke as naval representative at Hitler's HQ on March 1, 1943.

WAGNER, General Eduard: Quartermaster General of the German army—until his suicide after the July 20, 1944, bomb plot failed.

WARLIMONT, General Walter: *De facto* deputy to Jodl in the OKW operations staff, Warlimont deeply felt that he should have held Jodl's position (which by rights was his).

WEIZSÄCKER, Baron Ernst von: Ribbentrop's state secretary at the foreign ministry after 1938; from early 1943 onward he was German ambassador to the Vatican.

WOLF, Johanna: Oldest of Hitler's private secretaries.

WOLFF, SS General Karl: Chief of Himmler's personal staff, SS representative at Hitler's HQ until early 1943—when he was involved in a marriage scandal—and from September 1943 chief of police in Nazi-occupied Italy.

ZEITZLER, General Kurt: Dubbed "Thunderball" (*Kugelblitz*) because of his intensive energy as Chief of Staff to a panzer corps in Russia, 1941–42; Hitler fetched him from his position as Rundstedt's Chief of Staff in France (1942) to succeed Halder as Army Chief of Staff. Zeitzler put up with Hitler's tantrums until June 30, 1944, when he simply vanished and reported sick.

PART 1

HITLER'S WAR BEGINS

"White"

Late on the evening of September 3, 1939, Hitler exchanged the elegant marbled halls of the Chancellery for the special train, *Amerika,* parked in a dusty Pomeranian railroad station surrounded by parched and scented pine trees and wooden barrack huts baked dry by the central European sun.

Never before had Germany's railroads conveyed a train like this—a cumbersome assemblage of twelve or fifteen coaches hauled by two locomotives immediately followed by armored wagons bristling with 20-millimeter antiaircraft guns; a similar flak wagon brought up the rear. Hitler's personal coach came first: a drawing room about the size of three regular compartments, a sleeping berth, and a bathroom. In the drawing room, there was an oblong table with eight chairs grouped around it. The four remaining compartments in Hitler's coach were occupied by his adjutants and manservants. Other coaches housed dining accommodations and quarters for his military escort, private detectives, medical staff, press section, and visiting guests. Joachim von Ribbentrop, Hans Lammers, and Heinrich Himmler followed in a second train code-named *Heinrich.* Göring's private—and considerably more comfortably furnished—train, *Asia,* remained with him at Luftwaffe headquarters near Potsdam.

The nerve center of Hitler's train was the "command coach" attached to his own quarters. One half was taken up by a long conference room dominated by a map table, and the other half by Hitler's communications center, which was in constant touch by teleprinter and radio-telephone with the OKW and other ministries in Berlin, as well as with military headquarters on the front. Hitler was to spend most of his waking hours in this hot, confined space for the next two weeks, while Colonel Rudolf Schmundt, Hitler's chief adjutant, valiantly kept the stream of importunate visitors to a minimum. Here General Wilhelm

Keitel introduced to the Führer for the first time his chief of operations, Major General Alfred Jodl, a placid, bald-headed Bavarian mountain-warfare officer a year younger than Hitler, whose principal strategic adviser he was to be until the last days of the war. (Jodl was to be called upon by the Americans in the postwar period for his advice on the defense of western Europe, then hanged as a war criminal at Nuremberg.) Jodl took one of the chairs in the middle of the long map table, while Keitel regularly sat at one end and Colonel Nikolaus von Vormann, the army's liaison officer, sat next to the three telephones at the other.

In the train, as at the Chancellery, the brown Nazi party uniform dominated the scene. Generally speaking, Hitler's adjutants were the only others who found room there. Even Rommel, the new commandant of the Führer's headquarters, could not live in this train. Hitler hardly intervened in the conduct of the Polish campaign anyway. He would appear in the command coach at 9 A.M. to hear Jodl's personal report on the morning situation and to inspect the maps that had been flown in from Berlin. His first inquiry of Colonel von Vormann was always about the dangerous western front situation, for of 30 German divisions left to hold the three-hundred-mile line, only 12 were up to scratch; and against them France might at any time unleash her army of 110 divisions. But contrary to every prediction voiced by Hitler's critics, the western front was curiously quiet. On September 4, an awed Colonel von Vormann wrote: "Meanwhile, a propaganda war has broken out in the west. Will the Führer prove right after all? They say that the French have hung out a banner at Saarbrücken reading *We won't fire the first shot*. As we've strictly forbidden our troops to open hostilities, I can't wait to see what happens now."

It was indeed a mystery. While Poland reeled toward defeat, her allies made ominous noises but remained inactive as their precious opportunities dwindled with each passing day.

Poland was overrun in three weeks. Neither the bravery of her soldiers nor the promises of her allies prevented this overwhelming defeat; it startled Stalin, astonished the democracies, and confirmed Hitler's belief in the invincibility of his armies. They had fallen upon Poland from Pomerania and East Prussia, from Silesia and from the protected territories of Slovakia as well; at no stage were the Poles able to establish a stable front. The gasoline engine, the tank, and the dive-bomber should not have taken the Poles by surprise, but they did. Hitler's armored and mechanized units swept through the brittle Polish defenses in the west and encircled the enemy armies while they were still massed to the west of the Vistula, where they were deployed partly in defense of their country and partly in preparation for the drive to Berlin—the thrust which would bring about an anti-Nazi revolution in Germany, as the Polish government had so naïvely been led to believe. German expectations came off somewhat better. What had been planned on the maps of the German General Staff throughout the summer now took precise shape in the marshlands and fields of Poland in September 1939.

Hitler left General Walther von Brauchitsch in unfettered control of the army's operations. He listened unobtrusively to all that went on about him in the command coach, soaking up the debates and discussions and no doubt comparing the course of the campaign with the events his self-taught knowledge had led him to expect. His being there did not distract his staff, as one member wrote, except that they were forbidden to smoke in his presence—a prohibition that fell heavily on his chain cigar-smoking naval adjutant, Captain Karl-Jesko von Puttkamer. Hitler's only strategic influence had been on the "grand pincer" plan, with its powerful southward thrust with mechanized forces from East Prussia behind the Vistula. He had attempted to veto the appointments of Generals Johannes Blaskowitz to command the Eighth Army and Günther von Kluge the Fourth Army—the latter because of Göring's personal antipathy, and the former because he recalled that in maneuvers three years before, the general had not committed his tanks as he himself would have considered best; but on these appointments Hitler allowed himself to be overruled, although he did later find fault with the conduct of the Eighth Army's operations. This produced the only real crisis of the campaign; but the crisis occurred precisely where Hitler had expected, and he had ordered countermeasures in anticipation. The few days in which Kluge commanded his Fourth Army before an aircraft accident put him temporarily *hors de combat* convinced Hitler that here was a general to whom he should always entrust the most demanding operational commands; the resulting affection probably spared Kluge from the gallows, though not from death, five years later.

The Poles had committed the basic strategic error of concentrating their forces forward in the Posen (Poznan) salient, instead of establishing a main line of defense that could be more readily held, for example on the Vistula River. As it was, these forces were encircled and destroyed in the first phases of the campaign. The western border fortifications were weak and obsolete—those near Warsaw dated back to the Great War; the capital's fortifications were incorporated into its suburbs, and this inevitably resulted in heavy fighting there. But by that time the outcome was a foregone conclusion.

———

At eight o'clock on the morning of September 4, after his train's arrival at the front, General Fedor von Bock, the commander of Army Group North, joined Rommel in reporting to Hitler, and the three men set out on an extended tour of the battle areas. Accompanied by his adjutants and a manservant, Hitler rode in a heavy six-wheeled Mercedes, and the rest of his staff and escort followed in six identical vehicles. The little convoy, headed by two armored scout cars, with two more bringing up the rear, drove off to visit Fourth Army headquarters; seventy or more cars packed with Party and ministerial personages jostled for position behind the Führer's convoy, completely ignoring the vehicle-sequence orders the frantic Schmundt had drawn up. A choking cloud of Pomeranian dust was flung up from the unpaved country roads. At each brief halt the same undignified scenes were repeated as Hitler's generals and Party leaders elbowed their way into the foreground of the photographs being taken and then galloped back to their cars to urge their chauffeurs into even closer proximity to the Führer's Mercedes. Once when Martin Bormann angrily rebuked Rommel for these scenes of disorder the general coolly snapped back: "I'm not a kindergarten teacher. You sort them out, if you want!" Hitler affected not to notice all this—no doubt seeing it as further proof of his own popularity. During the first days of the campaign, no way could be found to shake off this horde of idle camp followers, but eventually Schmundt did manage to elude most of them by beginning each visit to the front with a short flight in the three available Junkers 52's to an airfield where a little motor convoy was waiting.

The Wehrmacht was already steamrolling northward toward Thorn, and General Heinz Guderian's armor was entering his birthplace, Chelmno (Culm). These were fields long steeped in German blood; ancient German land was coming under German rule again. Everywhere Hitler was surrounded by jubilant soldiers who sensed that this was an historic hour and that the injustices of Versailles were at last being wiped out. On the sixth he toured the battlefield of Tucheler Heide, where a powerful Polish Corps had been encircled and now desperately struggled to break out. (Apparently convinced that the German tanks were only tinplate dummies, the Polish cavalry attacked with lances couched.) Here the roads were hideous with the carnage of unequal battle. A radio message told Hitler that Cracow was now in German hands. As he had hoped, the greater part of the Polish army had been trapped west of the Vistula, while the strong force assembled at Posen for the attack on Berlin was now aimless and isolated—far from the main scene of events.

At 10 P.M. that evening, September 6, Hitler returned to his command coach. Colonel von Vormann briefed him on the western front. "The phony war continues," he wrote later that day. "So far not a shot has been fired on the western front. On both sides there are just huge loudspeakers barking at each other, with each side trying to make it clear to the other how impossible their behavior is and how stupid their governments are. Tomorrow Brauchitsch and Raeder are due here. . . . Poland's situation is worse than desperate." Vormann already talked of the dissolution of the Polish army: "All that remains now is a rabbit hunt. Militarily, the war is over." Hitler stared at him incredulously; then, beaming with pleasure, he took the colonel's hand in both of his and pumped it up and down before leaving the command coach without a further word.

The situation in the west had a comic-opera quality. From both sides of the Rhine, loudspeakers assured the enemy they would not open fire first. At some places the troops were bathing in the river. There were secret exchanges of food and drink between the French and German lines. French deserters disclosed that their frontline sentries were not permitted to load live ammunition in their rifles. German commanders had the strictest possible instructions not to fire into French territory or permit flights over the frontier. In addition, Hitler went out of his way to avoid provoking British public opinion: when Göring begged for permission to bomb the British fleet riding peacefully at anchor at Scapa Flow, Hitler rejected the Luftwaffe commander's request as overeager. He was furious when Britain announced on September 4 that one of her transatlantic liners, the *Athenia,* had that morning been torpedoed off the Hebrides by a German submarine, with some loss of life among the eleven hundred British and American passengers. Admiral Erich Raeder checked with his submarine commander, Karl Dönitz, and assured Hitler that none of their handful of U-boats could have been near the alleged incident and that in any case they were under orders not to attack British passenger vessels. Hitler suspected that Winston Churchill, as First Lord of the Admiralty, had himself ordered the liner sunk to provoke American public opinion, and he instructed the propaganda ministry to expose this "lord of the liars" forthwith. Shortly afterward, however, Raeder advised him confidentially that a U-boat commander had now admitted the sinking. The liner, he contended, had been blacked-out and zigzagging, and he had mistaken it for a cruiser and sunk it. The damage had been done. Raeder and Hitler agreed to keep the truth to themselves, and it is doubtful that even Goebbels learned it.

Submarines were henceforth forbidden to attack passenger vessels even if in convoy with naval forces.

Hitler's territorial plans for Poland were still indeterminate. He had expected to be forced to accept Italian mediation and an eventual armistice, and to improve his position at the bargaining table he had seized as much Polish territory as possible in the first days. But the armistice offer never came. As his armies surged on, his appetite grew. In a secret speech to his generals on August 22 he had set as his goal "the annihilation of the Polish forces"—an orthodox Clausewitzian objective—rather than any particular line on the map. A week later he still talked only of fighting his "first Silesian war" and wrote off eastern Poland to the Russian claim. But on September 7, when Stalin had not yet moved his armies, Hitler also mentioned to his army Commander in Chief, General von Brauchitsch, the possibility of founding an independent Ukraine.

Hitler's hazy notion was to mark the ultimate frontier between Asia and the West by gathering together the racial German remnants scattered about the Balkans, Russia, and the Baltic states to populate an eastern frontier strip along either the Bug or the Vistula River. The troops in their garrisons would be like the Teutonic knights in their castles or like the northwest frontier of India in more modern times. To the west of the 1914 Polish-German frontier, the Poles and Jews would be uprooted and displaced eastward; the land would be resettled by the skill and industry of the Germans—those whom Himmler was already extracting from the South Tyrol would populate the northern slopes of the Beskid Mountains, for example. Warsaw would become a center of German culture; or alternatively it would be razed and replaced by green fields on either side of the Vistula. Between the Reich and the "Asian" frontier, some form of Polish national state would exist, to house the ethnic Pole—a lesser species of some ten million in all. To stifle the growth of new chauvinistic centers, the Polish intelligentsia would be "extracted and accommodated elsewhere."

With this independent rump Poland, Hitler planned to negotiate a peace settlement that had some semblance of legality and thereby spike the guns of Britain and France. If, however, this rump Poland fell apart, the Vilna area could be offered to Lithuania, and the Galician and Polish Ukraine could be granted independence—in which case, as Abwehr Chief Wilhelm Canaris noted, Keitel's instructions were that his Abwehr-controlled Ukrainians "are to provoke an uprising in the Galician Ukraine with the destruction of the Polish and Jewish element as its aim." On no account was this Ukrainian nationalist ferment to spill over into the Soviet Ukraine, Keitel warned. Moscow's attitude toward Poland was still uncertain, however; the Russians were eager to amputate a slice of territory but reluctant to wield the knife in public.

Hitler's army fell upon the hated Poles with well-documented relish. Colonel Eduard Wagner, as Quartermaster General initially responsible for occupation policy, wrote privately on September 4: "Brutal guerrilla war has broken out everywhere, and we are ruthlessly stamping it out. We won't be reasoned with. We have already sent out emergency courts, and they are in continual session. The harder we strike, the quicker there will be peace again." And a week later: "We are now issuing fierce orders which I have drafted today myself. Nothing like the death sentence! There's no other way in occupied territories."[1]

Hitler's own anti-Polish feelings were comparatively new; born of his frustrated plan in the fall of 1938 for an alliance with Poland against Stalin, they were now reinforced by events in this campaign. There is no trace of his crueler plans for Poland among the documents predating the outbreak of the war. In Poland, however, Hitler and his generals were confronted by what they saw as still warm evidence that Asia did indeed begin just beyond the old Reich frontier in the east. In the western Polish town of Bydgoszcz (Bromberg) the local Polish commander had ordered the massacre of several thousand German residents on the charge that some of them had taken part in the hostilities. Göring's paratroopers were being shot on the spot when captured by the Poles. It was also charged that the Poles had used poisonous blister-gases in manufacturing booby traps. Hitler was particularly angered by a report that a Polish prisoner who had jabbed out the eyes of a wounded German soldier had been routinely sent to the rear through regular army channels. (Hitler said he should have been tried and executed on the spot by a drumhead court-martial.)

On the evening of the eighth, moreover, Warsaw radio imprudently appealed to civilians to join in the fight to defend their invaded homeland, and this was deplored as an open incitement to franc-tireur warfare. The population was instructed, for example, to pour gasoline over disabled German tanks and set them on fire. "Against Germany the Polish people fight side by side with the Polish soldiers, building barricades

---

[1] From unpublished letters of Wagner, in my possession. When the tide turned against Hitler, Wagner joined the opposition; he committed suicide in July 1944. By the whims of modern historiography, he was transformed into a hero of the anti-Nazi resistance.

and combating the German operations and positions by every means they can."

There was no acceptable explanation for Stalin's inactivity. While Hitler could easily finish off Poland alone, he was particularly eager for Russia's strategic involvement because then Britain and France would have to think twice about implementing their guarantee. As Reinhard Heydrich explained to his department heads: "Then Britain would be obliged to declare war on Russia too."[2] Above all Hitler wanted to get the Polish campaign over before the U.S. Congress reassembled on the twenty-first.

His heavy special train, *Amerika,* had left for Upper Silesia on the ninth. It finally halted in a railway siding at Illnau. The pleasing draft in the corridors ceased, and the temperature within the camouflage-gray walls and roofs rose. The air outside was thick with the hot dust-particles of mid-September. His secretary Christa Schroeder wrote plaintively:

> We have been living in this train for ten days now. Its location is constantly being changed, but since we never get out the monotony is dreadful. The heat here is unbearable, quite terrible. All day long the sun beats down on the compartments, and we just wilt in the tropical heat. I am soaked to the skin, absolutely awful. To top it all, there is hardly anything worthwhile to do. The Chief drives off in the morning leaving us condemned to wait for his return. We never stay long enough in one place. Recently we were parked one night near a field hospital through which a big shipment of casualties was just passing. . . . Those who tour Poland with the Chief see a lot, but it's not easy for them because the enemy are such cowards—shooting in the back and ambushing—and because it is difficult to protect the Chief, who has taken to driving around as though he were in Germany, standing up in his open car even in the most hazardous areas. I think he is being reckless, but nobody can persuade him not to do it. On the very first day he drove through a copse still swarming with Polacks—just half an hour earlier they had wiped out an unarmed German medical unit. One of the medics escaped and gave him an eyewitness account. . . . Once again, the Führer was standing in full

[2] Britain was not in fact obliged to declare war on Russia when she invaded Poland on September 17, 1939, as by a secret clause in her August treaty with Poland she had providently specified that the only "European Power" to which the treaty referred was Germany.

view of everybody on a hummock, with soldiers streaming toward him from all sides. In a hollow there was this Polish artillery; obviously they saw the sudden flurry of activity and—since it's no secret that the F. is touring the front—they guessed who it was. Half an hour later the bombs came raining down. Obviously it gives the soldiers' morale a colossal boost to see the F. in the thick of the danger with them, but I still think it's too risky. We can only trust in God to protect him.

"The Führer is in the best of moods; I often get into conversation with him," wrote General Rommel. "He says that in eight or ten days it'll all be over in the east and then our entire battle-hardened Wehrmacht will move west. But I think the French are giving up the struggle. Their soldiers are bathing in the Rhine, unmolested by us. This time," he concluded, "we are definitely going to win through!"

That day, September 12, Hitler summoned Göring, Brauchitsch, and Keitel to his train at the Illnau railway siding and flatly forbade them to provoke the French in any way. Late that afternoon he received Admiral Wilhelm Canaris, Keitel's chief of Intelligence, for a rare audience. Canaris was white-haired, weary, and elderly, a frail stooping figure with a soft lisping voice, a studied sloppiness of dress, and an apparent naïveté of manner that were designed to disarm his critics. The admiral was known widely as "that slimy Greek"—a soubriquet he sought to disprove by circulating a family tree which supported his claim to Italian ancestry.

Hitler walked into the command coach just as Canaris was outlining to Keitel the unfavorable effect a German bombardment of Warsaw would have on foreign opinion. When asked for news from the western front, Canaris craftily replied that the French were systematically marshaling troops and artillery opposite Saarbrücken for a major offensive.[3] Hitler remained politely incredulous. "I can hardly believe that the French will attack at Saarbrücken, the very point at which our fortifications are strongest." They would also then run into second and third lines of even stronger defenses. They might, Hitler conceded, invade across the Rhine or even—though less probably—through Belgium and Holland in violation of their neutrality. Keitel agreed, and Jodl added that the artillery preparation for a major offensive would take at least

[3] Canaris, a confirmed anti-Nazi, had deliberately exaggerated reports of a planned minor French attack—in regimental strength—in the hope of disrupting Hitler's Polish campaign strategy, according to Colonel Lahousen, who accompanied him.

three weeks, so the French offensive could not begin before October. "Yes," responded Hitler, "and in October it is already quite chilly, and our men will be sitting in their protective bunkers while the French have to wait in the open air to attack. And even if the French should manage to penetrate one of the weaker points of the West Wall, we will in the meantime have brought our divisions across from the east and given them a thrashing they'll never forget."

Before Canaris left, Keitel forbade him to brief Mussolini on the German military situation. Hitler no longer trusted the Italians, as he had found out that they were in contact with the French.

Hitler's tours of these battlefields were his first real contact with "the East." They reinforced his unhealthy fantasies about the "subhumans" and the Jews.

On September 10 he had visited the Tenth Army, busy finishing off the Polish forces encircled at Radom. The Polish countryside struck him as tangled and unkempt, as though from prehistoric times. Was this still Europe? Indiscriminately scattered about the untended acres were wretched wooden hutlike dwellings with thatched roofs; between them were miles of endless swamps with occasional farmsteads and rare, magnificent castles gleaming on the horizon. The laborers' buildings were caked with filth, the barns and sheds were dilapidated, the roads were treeless and rutted by centuries of wheels. At the roadsides, knots of submissive Polish civilians stood in the swirling dust of Hitler's motorcade. Among them he glimpsed Jews in high-crowned hats and caftans; their hair in ritual ringlets; they looked for all the world like figures out of medieval anti-Semitic drawings. Time had stood still here for centuries.

The Jews were the enemy. He had given them clear warning in a bellicose speech to the Reichstag eight months before. How often in his life had his prophecies been laughed at by them! How the Jews had mocked his earnest prediction that one day he, a humble street agitator, would lead the German people to true greatness! Their peals of laughter had died to a croak in their Jewish throats, Hitler had jeered in January 1939. "Today I am going to be a prophet again. If the international finance-Jewry inside and outside Europe manages just once more to precipitate the world into war, the outcome will be, not the bolshevization of the earth and the consequent triumph of Jewry, but the annihilation of the Jewish race in Europe." The Berlin newspapers had headlined the

Reichstag speech as one of Adolf Hitler's greatest: PROPHETIC WARNING TO THE JEWS.

Now, in September 1939, Hitler was upon the verge of world war. And Dr. Chaim Weizmann, the president of the Jewish Agency, had written to Neville Chamberlain promising explicitly that all Jews everywhere stood by him and would fight on the side of the democracies against Nazi Germany. *The Times* published Weizmann's letter on September 6, and Hitler no doubt considered it an unorthodox Jewish declaration of war. He often referred to it in later years—by which time his grim prophecy was being cruelly fulfilled. "For the first time we are now implementing genuine ancient Jewish law," he boasted on January 30, 1942. "An eye for an eye and a tooth for a tooth." And on November 8 he reminded his Party faithfuls of that unique 1939 "prophecy," adding with ominous ambiguity: "As a prophet they always laughed at me. But of those who laughed loudest then, countless laugh no longer today. Nor are those who are still laughing even now likely to laugh when the time comes . . ."

While Hitler's overall anti-Jewish policy was clearly and repeatedly enunciated, it is harder to establish a documentary link between him and the murderous activities of the SS "task forces" (*Einsatzgruppen*) and their extermination camps in the east.

For the pogroms that now began, Himmler and Heydrich provided the initiative and drive themselves, using arguments of Reich security. Hitler's only order to the Reichsführer SS, Himmler, in this context was one for the general consolidation of the German racial position; there is no evidence that Hitler gave him any more specific instruction than this, nor did Himmler ever claim so. When army generals became restless about deeds being enacted by the SS in Poland, Himmler reassured them in a secret speech at Koblenz in March 1940, of which his handwritten notes survive—though they are infuriatingly cryptic in parts. He explained that now for the first time, under Adolf Hitler, the solution of the thousand-year-old historical problem of Poland was possible: only the infusion into Poland of Germanic blood during the years of Germany's weakness had made some Poles great and dangerous; now that Germany was strong she must see to the "final annexation of the area, its purification and Germanization"; a simple merging of the peoples was impossible for racial reasons. But a "Bolshevik method"— which Himmler defined in a memorandum two months later as downright extermination of the minority races—was "equally impossible." He conceded that the "leading brains of the resistance" were being executed but this was not, stressed Himmler in this *pièce justificative,* "a wild excess by subordinate commanders—still less by me." Here Himmler's jottings show a German phrase (*Weiss sehr genau, was vorgeht*) which might be translated either as "(I) know precisely what is happening" or "(He) knows precisely what is happening."[4] Two weeks later Himmler spoke in a Ruhr city. Here his notes read: "The Führer's mission to the Reichsführer SS: the quality of the German species. Blood our most supreme value. New territories not a political, but an ethnological problem."

This ethnological mission had been assigned to Heydrich. As in Austria and Czechoslovakia, the advancing tide of German army units had been followed by his police net. In the present Polish campaign his task forces were subordinated directly to the generals. Each army had its *Einsatzgruppe,* and each corps an *Einsatzkommando* of a hundred officials in Waffen SS uniform with SD (*Sicherheitsdienst,* security service) emblems on their sleeves. Their primary role was Intelligence—seizing enemy documents—and counterinsurgency operations, or what the army orders more formally described as "combating any anti-Reich or anti-German elements in rear areas." According to Heydrich, writing ten months later, the special order directing the task forces to conduct "security operations of a political and ideological nature in these new territories" was issued by Hitler himself. But the order's practical interpretation—embodying what Heydrich calmly referred to as the liquidation of Polish leaders "running into several thousands"—evidently sprang from him. On September 7 he briefed his staff (without any mention of a Führer Order) as follows: "The Polish ruling class is to be put out of harm's way as far as possible. The lower classes that will remain will not get special schools, but be kept down in one way or another." To Heydrich, the prophylactic mission of his task forces was the essential one—hunting down the thousands of leading Poles already listed in black books and liquidating them before they could unite in opposition.

Parallel to the SS task forces attached to the armies, there was an independent "special duties" task force which rampaged through Poland under the command of the arrogant and brutal SS General Udo von Woyrsch. Most of the early savagery against the Poles and Jews was

---

[4] General Ulex, who was present, recalled this after the war as "I am doing nothing of which the Führer does not know." (*Cf.* Professor Helmut Krausnick, "Hitler and the Murders in Poland," *VfZ,* 1963, 196ff.) However, nobody else recalled this. And General von Leeb, whose diary has been available to me, would certainly have mentioned such a candid statement in it, given his pronounced Christian convictions. Ulex had been humiliated by Hitler late in 1938. No other authors have bothered to transcribe Himmler's speech notes. Colonel Eduard Wagner wrote his wife on the following day: "It was highly interesting yesterday. In the evening Himmler spoke to the Commander in Chiefs at Koblenz. More about that verbally . . ."

Woyrsch's work. When he was eventually kicked out of Poland on German army orders, he loudly protested that he had received direct instructions from the Führer via Himmler to spread "fear and terror" in what would seem an illogical attempt to dissuade the Poles from committing acts of violence. (Himmler's orders to Woyrsch survive, dated September 3: he was charged with the "radical suppression of the incipient Polish insurrection in the newly occupied parts of Upper Silesia"; Hitler is not mentioned.) Heydrich was nettled by Woyrsch's ouster and later ascribed the army's interference to its ignorance of the "political mission" entrusted to the task forces by Himmler, who was acting, Heydrich claimed, on the directives of the Führer and Göring; it was wrong for the army to see the task force operations as "arbitrary acts of brutality," he complained.

There is no surviving record of when—or if—Heydrich conferred with Hitler during the Polish campaign. But the German army's records of briefings by Hitler are voluminous, and they offer a curious and distasteful picture. In short, many of Hitler's generals learned from him that he planned to eliminate the Polish intelligentsia one way or another; either they welcomed it, or they joined a conspiracy of silence.

Not until October 1939 did the major "mopping up" of "potential dissidents" begin in Poland. It was evidently delayed at the request of the army, even though Heydrich was eager to get on with the job. Hitler's blood was already boiling at the ponderous court-martial procedures being implemented against Polish guerrillas—he wanted their swift and summary execution; but Heydrich had his eye on bigger game. He was quoted as saying, "We will let the small fry off; but the nobility, the papists, and the Jews must all be killed." He proposed discussing with the army ways and means of eliminating these enemies after the Germans entered Warsaw. On September 7 Hitler met with Brauchitsch in his private coach and for two hours discussed the political future of Poland. He instructed the army to abstain from interfering in the SS operations.

The next day Hitler issued a set of guidelines in which the emphasis was on the appointment of Party functionaries as civil commissars—to do the dirty work—whose task it was to parallel the army's military government in Poland. Little is known in detail of what Hitler told Brauchitsch. After talking to General Franz Halder on the ninth, Eduard Wagner noted in his diary: "It is the Führer's and Göring's intention to destroy and exterminate the Polish nation. More than that," Colonel

Wagner noted in his diary, "cannot even be hinted at in writing." The same day a member of Hitler's staff—Colonel von Vormann—wrote: "The war in Poland is over. . . . The Führer keeps discussing plans for the future of Poland—interesting but scarcely suited for committing to the written word." Yet another colonel on Halder's staff joined this dumb chorus a few days later. "A lot is happening and the questions looming ahead give rise to much food for thought, above all the proposals over Poland's fate. . . . Too hush-hush to write even one word about them." Only General Walther Heitz, the new military governor of West Prussia, lifted a corner of this veil of secrecy in writing up a conference with Brauchitsch on September 10: "Other business: I am to rule the area with the mailed fist. Combat troops are overinclined toward a false sense of chivalry."

That the nature of the SS task force operations had been explained to Brauchitsch was established two days later when Admiral Canaris reminded Keitel of the damage the planned "widespread executions" of Polish clergy and nobility would inflict on the Wehrmacht's reputation. Keitel retorted that this had long been decided on by the Führer, who had made it plain to Brauchitsch—who had visited Hitler with Göring that morning—"that if the Wehrmacht wants nothing to do with it, they will merely have to put up with the SS and Gestapo appearing side by side with them." Hence the creation of parallel civil authorities in Poland. On them would fall the job of "demographic extermination," as Canaris recorded Keitel's phrase. In fact Heydrich, recognizing that time was on his side, readily heeded the army's urgent appeal to postpone the really bloody business until it was out of Poland. Thus, when Heydrich informed a member of Halder's staff—Colonel Wagner—that the planned "mopping up" of Poland would embrace "the Jewry, intelligentsia, clergy, and nobility," the army officer asked only that the army not be compromised—in other words, that the murderous orders flow directly from Heydrich to his task forces in the field. Preferably, even this would not happen until full control of the occupied areas had been transferred to the Party and its civil commissars.

But Heydrich had not in fact secured Hitler's approval for liquidating the Jews. On September 14 he reported to his staff on his tour of the task forces. The discreet conference record states: "The Chief [Heydrich] enlarged on the Jewish problem in Poland and set out his views on this. The Reichsführer [Himmler] will put certain suggestions to the Führer, on which only the Führer can decide, as they will also have considerable repercussions abroad." Hitler, however, favored only a deportation of the Jews, as became clear to both Brauchitsch and Himmler when they conferred separately with Hitler at Zoppot on September 20. To Brauchitsch he talked only of a ghetto plan for the Jews (causing Halder to warn that nothing must happen to give foreign countries a peg for "atrocity propaganda"). Hitler's somewhat more moderate instructions to Himmler were presumably those echoed by Heydrich to his task force commanders in Berlin next day: the formerly German provinces of Poland would be reannexed to the Reich; an adjacent *Gau,* or district, made up of a Polish-speaking population, would have Cracow as its capital and probably be governed by the Austrian Dr. Arthur Seyss-Inquart. This Gau—the later *Generalgouvernement*—would be a "kind of no-man's-land" outside the planned East Wall: it would accommodate the Polish Jews. Hitler also authorized Heydrich to unload as many Jews as possible into the Russian zone. To facilitate this expulsion the Jews were to be concentrated in the big Polish cities. They would be joined by the Jews and the remaining thirty thousand gypsies from Germany. About 3 percent of the former Polish ruling class remained, said Heydrich; they would be put in concentration camps. The educated class of teachers, clergymen, aristocrats, and demobilized officers would be rounded up and dumped in the rump Polish Gau. The working class would provide a reservoir of migratory labor for the Reich. Hitler asked Himmler to act as overlord of this resettlement operation.

For his part, General von Brauchitsch circularized his field commanders thus: "The police task-forces have been commanded and directed by the Führer to perform certain ethnographical (*volkspolitische*) tasks in the occupied territory." The commanders were not to interfere, nor would they be held responsible. The only stipulation Brauchitsch made when he met Heydrich on September 22 was that the expulsion operations must not interfere with the army's movements or Germany's economic needs. Heydrich readily agreed.

Hitler's positive enjoyment of the battle scenes was undeniable. He visited the front whenever he could, heedless of the risk to himself and his escort. It irritated him when his convoy took a wide detour around the city of Lodz en route to Eighth Army headquarters, and he ordered that on the way back the convoy was to drive right through the heart of the city (an order the unhappy army authorities fulfilled by cordoning off the entire route, clearing away the Polish population in neighboring streets and conducting Hitler's convoy at an uninterrupted fifty miles an hour, two vehicles abreast, from one end of the city to the other). He enjoyed meeting his troops and, for all we know, was exhilarated by the smell of cordite and sight of blood. At a divisional headquarters set up in a school within range of the Polish artillery, he made the acquaintance of General von Briesen, who towered head and shoulders above him. Briesen had just lost an arm leading his division into an action which warded off a desperate Polish counterattack by four divisions and cavalry on the flank of Blaskowitz's Eighth Army; he had lost eighty officers and fifteen hundred men in the fight, and now he was reporting to his Führer not far from the spot where his father, a Prussian infantry general, had been killed in the Great War. Hitler could only stare entranced as this monumental officer reported the battle situation to him. Afterward he exclaimed to his staff, "That is just what I always imagined Prussian generals looked like when I was a child!" He repeated these words a dozen times to different listeners that evening and insisted that Briesen immediately be awarded a Knight's Cross. "That is the commander I have been looking for for years for my SS"—a less than realistic appraisal of so blue-blooded an officer. On the fifteenth we find Hitler at Jaroslav, watching his soldiers bridging the river San.

By September 16, 1939, the greatest strategic triumph of the campaign was complete: the Polish army optimistically assembled at Posen for the attack on Berlin had been encircled, and Kutno had been captured by the Fourth and Eighth armies. In a model operation that the legendary Field Marshal von Schlieffen himself could not have improved on, a former corporal had destroyed the last vestiges of Polish military strength west of the Vistula. The bold pincer operation starting from bases nearly two hundred miles apart could have been blunted by a successful Polish stand, but now it was only a matter of days before Warsaw itself fell.

Hitler had begun to debate the fate of that city with Jodl on the fifteenth. As has been noted he was particularly eager to have the capital in his hands by the time the U.S. Congress reconvened. Since he wanted to avoid the high casualties inherent in house-to-house fighting, he hoped that the mere threat of concerted ground and air attack would bluff the city's commandant into capitulating. On the thirteenth he had repeatedly plagued General Blaskowitz for estimates on how long it would take to starve the city into submission, and a few days later he worried at his own liaison officer with the same question. The General Staff, erroneously believing that the armies parked outside Warsaw would not be immediately needed for other purposes, favored a bloodless siege of the Polish capital; but this would take weeks and Hitler could not spare the time.

Early on the sixteenth a German officer carried to the Polish lines a written ultimatum giving the commandant six hours in which to surrender unconditionally. If he failed to do so, the Germans would regard the city as a defended fortress, with all that that implied.

Hitler's bid for an easy and bloodless victory was rejected. The Polish commandant refused even to receive the ultimatum. He had spent every waking hour since September 9 preparing the capital for the German assault. The civilian population had been urged to join with the military in defending the city against the invaders; all fortifications and defenses had been strengthened; every suburban building had been reinforced by sandbags, concrete, and barbed wire, its basement linked by a honeycomb of tunnels to a network of resistance strongpoints; deep antitank trenches cut across Warsaw's main thoroughfares, and there were barricades formed of heaped-up streetcars, cobblestones, and rubble; the parks and squares bristled with heavy artillery. Surrender was unthinkable.

As Blaskowitz was later to report: "What shocked even the most hardened soldier was how at the instigation of their military leaders a misguided population, completely ignorant of the effect of modern weapons, could contribute to the destruction of their own capital."

Until then, Hitler had limited the bombardment of the capital to dive-bomber and artillery attacks on strategic targets. But whatever inhibitions he may have felt about the presence of a million civilians and nearly two hundred foreign diplomats were apparently about to break down under the demands of his timetable. At three o'clock on the afternoon of the sixteenth, Luftwaffe aircraft released over Warsaw several tons of leaflets giving the civilian population twelve hours to leave by two specified roads, and Hitler ordered a saturation bombardment for the next day.

The people of Warsaw were never able to take advantage of the leaflet offer because by some incredible oversight nobody had informed the local German army commanders of it. As a result, they of course had kept the two egress roads under heavy artillery fire. Shortly before midnight, Hitler called off the scheduled bombardment.

At midday on the seventeenth, the Germans monitored a Warsaw Radio message asking them to accept a Polish officer who would come toward their lines under a flag of truce. His mission would be to negotiate the release of the civilian population and the foreign diplomatic corps.

Hitler immediately began to suspect that the Polish commandant was playing for time—that he planned to wage a bitter house-to-house resistance and that under those circumstances civilians were likely to be encumbrances and useless mouths to feed. Better, therefore, that Warsaw's civilians should remain bottled up in the city.

At 6 P.M. the Deutschland Sender broadcast an invitation to the Polish forces to send officers to the German lines for negotiations to begin at 10 P.M. Meanwhile, Keitel telegraphed Brauchitsch that since the civilian population had failed to leave the city by the earlier deadline, that offer was now void.

Any Polish officers who turned up for negotiations were to be instructed to hand to their commandant an ultimatum calling for the unconditional surrender of the capital by 8 A.M. the next day. Arrangements for the evacuation of the diplomatic corps would be made on request, but the civilian population had to stay put. Leaflets to this effect were dropped.

When by 11:45 A.M. on the eighteenth no Polish officer had appeared at the German lines, Hitler ordered Brauchitsch and Göring to prepare at once to attack Warsaw from the eastern suburb of Praga. His attempts to obtain the city's bloodless capitulation were apparently sufficient to give him a clear conscience in ordering death to rain down on its one million inhabitants.

The Polish government and military command had already escaped to neutral Romania, thus the Russians could now claim that the Poland with whom they had concluded their nonaggression pact no longer existed. "To protect the interests of the Ukrainian and White Russian minorities," two Soviet army groups invaded eastern Poland in the small hours of September 17. The news reached Hitler's train soon after. He canceled his planned flight to Cracow and at about 4 A.M. entered the command coach of his train, where he found Schmundt waiting with Keitel and Jodl. All of them were grouped around the maps of Poland, guessing at the Soviet army's movements until the arrival of Ribbentrop, who on Hitler's instructions now revealed to the astonished generals the details of secret arrangements made with Moscow for Poland. "We decided with Stalin on a demarcation line between the two spheres of interest running along the four rivers—Pissa, Narev, Vistula, and San," the foreign minister explained as he somewhat crudely drew the line on the map. The generals frostily pointed out that Russian aircraft were evidently even now taking off without any notion of where the leading

German units were, and that the Wehrmacht had suffered considerable casualties in capturing territory which was apparently a hundred miles and more beyond the demarcation line secretly agreed upon. Now joint staff talks with the Russians had to begin at once—Ribbentrop somewhat tactlessly suggested Brest-Litovsk, the scene of Russia's World War I humiliation, as a venue—and the most advanced German units had to disengage from the fighting immediately and withdraw to the proposed line.

By September 19, when Hitler and his staff drove into Danzig, the Polish campaign was all but over; it had lasted only eighteen days, a breathtaking victory that confounded all his opponents. How he now privately mocked the foreign ministry Cassandras who had predicted military disaster![5] Only the garrisons of Warsaw, Modlin, and Hela were still holding out. It was a soldier's world. He had spent two hours last evening talking with Rommel about the problems of war. "He is exceptionally friendly to me," wrote Rommel.

As the victorious Führer drove through the streets of Danzig for the first time, flowers rained down from the windows, swastika flags draped the streets, and the crowds of German Danzigers were wild with emotion. When the convoy of cars stopped outside the ancient Artus Hof, Schmundt was heard to comment to a newer staff member who was overwhelmed by this reception, "It was like this everywhere—in the Rhineland, in Vienna, in the Sudeten territories, and in Memel. Do you still doubt the mission of the Führer?" Here, in a long, columned fourteenth-century hall built in the heyday of the Germanic knightly orders, Hitler delivered a lengthy speech on which he had been working for many days. He pathetically compared the humanity with which he was fighting this war and the treatment the Poles had meted out to the German minorities after Pilsudski's death. "Tens of thousands were deported, maltreated, killed in the most bestial fashion. These sadistic beasts let their perverse instincts run riot and—this pious democratic world looks on without batting one eyelash." In his peroration he spoke not of the blessing of Providence, but of "Almighty God, who has now given our arms his blessing."

Afterward his staff cleared a path for him through the heaving Danzig population packed into the Long Market outside. A bath was provided

[5] *Cf.* Hewel's unpublished diary, October 10, 1941: "Triumphant conversation [with the Führer] about the foreign ministry. Who in 1939 believed in victory? The state secretary at the foreign ministry [Weizsäcker]?"

for the sweat-soaked Führer in one of the patrician houses, and he worked over the text of his speech for release to the press. Then he took up quarters for the next week in the roomy seafront Kasino Hotel at Zoppot, near Danzig, where Ribbentrop, Lammers, and Himmler also found rooms for themselves and their staffs. Hitler received most of his official visitors in his suite of rooms—numbers 251, 252, and 253 on the second floor—while the war conferences were conducted in Jodl's suite, rooms 202 and 203. His mood was irrepressible. At midnight two days after his arrival, followed by one of his manservants with a silver tray of champagne glasses, he burst into Jodl's room, where a number of generals were celebrating Keitel's birthday. Despite the thick fog of cigar smoke, he stayed there an hour or more drinking and talking. His Polish victory had convinced him that the Wehrmacht he had created was equal to any task he set before it.

Here at Zoppot Hitler began weighing a course of action as hideous as any that Reinhard Heydrich was tackling in Poland: "mercy killing," or euthanasia. The ostensible occasion for this formal decision was related to war needs. About a quarter of a million hospital beds were required for Germany's mental institutions; of Germany's disproportionately large insane population (a result of centuries of lax and indiscriminate marriage laws) of some seven or eight hundred thousand people all told, about 10 percent were permanently institutionalized. Others were in and out of hospitals. They occupied bed space and the attention of skilled medical personnel which Hitler now urgently needed for the treatment of the casualties of his coming campaigns. Above all they were a glaring genetic impurity marring the blood of the German race. According to Dr. Karl Brandt, his personal surgeon, Hitler wanted between 40 and 60 percent of the permanently hospitalized insane to be quietly put away.

To his suite at the Kasino Hotel the Führer now summoned his constitutional and medical advisers, and in particular Hans Lammers, chief of the Reich Chancellery, and Dr. Leonardo Conti, chief medical officer of the Reich, together with the ubiquitous Martin Bormann; Reichsleiter Philipp Bouhler, chief of the "Führer's Chancellery" (an essentially Party authority) was also present for a reason that will shortly become plain. Hitler instructed Dr. Conti that in view of the war, a program for the painless killing of the incurably insane should be initiated; this would release badly needed hospital beds and nursing facilities for patients with a greater national priority. Dr. Conti appears to have suggested restricting this program to only the most hopeless cases, and he questioned whether there was any scientific basis for assuming it would produce eugenic advantages. He believed the authorities would be justified only in aiding, for example, a terminal case of paralysis through the most painful stages to a rapid end. During the conference the word "euthanasia" was actually used, but Hitler made it plain that under no circumstances was the real cause of death to be divulged to the next of kin. There was some discussion of the actual mechanics of the program. Dr. Conti proposed the use of narcotics to induce in the patients a sleep from which they would not awaken; but in separate discussions with Dr. Brandt Hitler learned that barbiturates would be too slow to be "humane" and that most physicians considered carbon monoxide gas the fastest and most peaceful lethal dose, if somewhat unmedical in character. Hitler asked Brandt shortly to investigate which was the fastest way consequent with the least amount of pain.

After this Zoppot discussion, some time passed without any results. In fact Dr. Conti had become involved in lengthy discussions with Lammers, with the ministry of justice, and with psychiatric and legal experts, in which the legal and ethical bases of Hitler's proposals were explored. Lammers favored the enactment of a secret law which would protect the doctors and nurses involved in the program against potential criminal charges. The consequence of this delay was that Hitler bypassed both Lammers and Conti, and peremptorily dictated onto a sheet of his private stationery, which bore a gold-embossed eagle and "Adolf Hitler," an order that was both simple and unorthodox, and that considerably enlarged the scope of the euthanasia project:

> Reichsleiter Bouhler and Dr. Brandt, M.D., are herewith given full responsibility to enlarge the powers of certain specified doctors so that they can grant those who are by all human standards incurably ill a merciful death, after the most critical assessment possible of their medical condition.
>
> (*signed*) Adolf Hitler.

It was a curious confirmation of the fact that Hitler regarded the war as Germany's struggle to the end that this Führer Order was symbolically backdated to September 1, the start of what he had envisaged as his "first Silesian war." Now it was no longer a local campaign but a bloody crusade in the course of which the German people were to become ennobled by conflict and purged of the impure elements in their blood and seed.

An extensive camouflage organization was set up by Bouhler's Chancellery; census forms, ostensibly for statistical survey purposes, were circulated to doctors and hospitals as from October 9, 1939; on these forms there were separate listings of the senile debilitated, the criminally insane, and patients of non-German blood. Panels of three assessors then decided the life or death of each patient on the basis of these forms alone. As Hitler had told Bouhler, he wanted a process untrammeled by red tape. He resisted every effort Lammers made to codify the procedure in a Reich law, for this would have led to too many ministries and officials learning what was afoot.

Hitler had been an enthusiastic advocate of the racial rejuvenation of the German people ever since the Twenties, supporting his beliefs with an inadequate grasp of the Mendelian laws of genetics. (In fact, the processes of "negative eugenics" are extraordinarily slow: if all living epileptics were sterilized, for example, it would still take three centuries for the incidence of epilepsy in a population to be reduced by one quarter!) In 1929, however, Hitler had brutally summed up his views as follows: "If Germany were to have a birthrate of a million children a year, and to put away seven or eight hundred thousand of the weakest, then the end result might even be a net increment in strength." On the pretext that—according to some authorities—20 percent of the German population had hereditary biological defects, the National Socialists had instituted a program of racial hygiene immediately after they came to power; Minister of the Interior Wilhelm Frick was a fervent advocate. In July 1933 the Cabinet had passed the first related law; it was henceforth obligatory for doctors to report on patients with hereditary diseases so that they could be sterilized. From sterilization and abortion it was an easy step to the "destruction of human beings unworthy of life," the program initiated by Hitler in 1939. An elderly Darwinian (Alfred Ploetz) whom the Reich had made a professor after 1933 was to point out in 1935 that "the contraselective effects of war must be offset by an increase in the extermination quotas." In other words, so much fine blood is lost in battle that equal quantities of impure blood must be let if the race is not to be polluted—a pseudoscientific justification which emerged openly and unmistakably in arguments adduced by Hitler in private in 1943.[6]

Frick had drafted the necessary laws concerting the operations of the local health offices in 1934, parallel to which functioned the racial-politics agencies of the Party in each Party district. In that same year, the Bavarian provincial commissioner of health affairs urged that sterilization alone was not enough. Psychopaths, imbeciles, and other subnor-

[6] See page 577 below.

mals must be sorted out and exterminated. "This is a policy," he added, "which has in part already begun in our concentration camps." Over the next ten years tens of thousands of senior medical officials were to pass through special courses in racial hygiene, and perhaps significantly these were attended after 1938 by senior officers and staff of all the Wehrmacht services as well. Subtle appeals were made to their latent racial psychoses, the economic burden represented by these unworthy specimens was explained, and particularly repulsive samples were fed and housed at the institutions as walking laboratory exhibits. In June 1935 a Reich law allowed abortions for genetic reasons. In the same year Hitler openly told Dr. Conti's predecessor that should war come he would "tackle the euthanasia problem," since a wartime psychology would reduce the risk of opposition from the church.

But it was not until the end of 1938 that Hitler was directly involved in any euthanasia decisions, and then it was in "mercy killing," rather than the infinitely more controversial blanket program to eliminate the insane. Bouhler's Chancellery had repeatedly submitted to him appeals from patients in intolerable pain, or from their doctors, asking Hitler to exercise the Head of State's prerogative of mercy and permit the doctor to terminate the patient's life without fear of criminal proceedings. When Hitler received such an appeal from the parents of a malformed, blind, and imbecile boy born in Leipzig, he sent Dr. Brandt early in 1939 to examine the child, and on hearing the doctor's horrifying description of the pathetic case, he authorized the doctors to put him to sleep; at the same time he orally authorized Bouhler and Brandt to act accordingly in any similar cases in the future. A ministerial decree was eventually passed in August 1939 requiring all midwives and nurses to report to the local health office the details of such deformed newborn babies; a panel of three assessors judged each case, and if all three agreed, the infant was procured from the parents either by deception or by compulsion and quietly put away with as little pain to the child and sorrowing parents as possible. From a theological expert[7] Hitler had in 1939 secured formal assurances that the church need not be expected to raise basic objections to euthanasia. Perhaps as many as five thousand children were eventually disposed of in this way.

The "mercy killing" of the few was followed by the programmed elimination of the burdensome tens of thousands of insane; and all this was but a platform for far wider campaigns of extermination on which the Reich was to embark now that it was at war.

[7] The rector of the theological high school at Paderborn, a Professor Maier.

Overtures

Hitler's train idled on a siding in outer Pomerania until 9:30 A.M. on September 26 and then began the eight-hour haul back to Berlin. The journey passed in heavy silence. Hitler went into the command coach, but Keitel was in Berlin and Jodl must have been in his private compartment, for only Colonel von Vormann was there, seated at his customary place next to the telephones, writing and sorting the heaps of papers that had accumulated. For the next few hours Hitler spoke no word but restlessly paced the length of the swaying carriage while the train drew closer to Berlin. There were no messages, no calls, no visitors. Just after 5 P.M. the train reached Berlin's Stettin station, unheralded by any crowds or scenes of jubilation. The motor pool had sent cars to pick them up; Hitler and his entourage drove almost stealthily to the Reich Chancellery, where dinner was served at the large round table in his residence. The atmosphere was funereal. After a while Hitler abruptly rose, bid the others good night, and retired to his rooms.

Without doubt his thoughts now revolved around the next step he must take: could the western powers be made to see reason, or must he defeat them as he had defeated Poland? In January 1944 he was secretly to address his skeptical generals with words that he might well have been thinking now. "If I am now taken to task about what concrete prospects there are of ending the war, then I should just like to ask you to look at the history of wars and tell me when in the major campaigns any concrete idea emerged as to how each would end. For the most part there was not even a concrete idea as to how the campaign should be conducted. Moltke himself wrote that it is erroneous to expect that any plan of war can be drawn up that will hold good after the first battles." In the same speech he was to explain: "In my position one can have no other master than one's own judgment, one's conscience, and one's sense of duty. Those are the only masters to whose commands I bow."

The army had already taken matters into its own hands, issuing in mid-September 1939 an order for the withdrawal of most of the combat divisions from Poland and their partial demobilization. Keitel warned General Halder that such an order was unthinkable without Hitler's consent; and when Hitler heard of it he sat sharply upright and ejaculated, "We are going to attack the west, and we are going to do it this October!"

There are small indications that Hitler had known all along that he was on the threshold of a long and bitter war with Britain—that Britain would not withdraw even now that Poland no longer existed. As early as September 5 the Führer instructed Walther Hewel—Ribbentrop's liaison officer on Hitler's staff, who as a student had spent several months with him in Landsberg prison in 1923—to use every possible diplomatic channel to rescue his disconsolate friend "Putzi" Hanfstaengl from the consequences of his own stubbornness in London and arrange his escape to Germany.[1] A few days later, the British Cabinet announced that Britain was preparing for a war that was expected to last at least three years; this blunt statement evidently jolted Hitler, for he was still referring to it three weeks later. Britain was clearly going to play for time until her rearmament was complete—and this was the one development Hitler feared most. On the evening of September 12 he confidentially disclosed to Colonel Schmundt that as soon as Poland had been defeated he would swing around and *attack* in the west; he must exploit the western weakness while he could. But he deliberately kept General von Brauchitsch uninformed of his thinking.

A few days later, on the fourteenth, he discussed with his chief engineer, Fritz Todt, architect of the West Wall fortifications, the need for a proper permanent headquarters site in the west, as his special train would be too vulnerable to air attack. One site was debated and discarded, and another near Munstereifel was eventually selected. To his adjutants, Hitler explained that his Great War experience in Flanders had taught him that until January the weather would hold good for an offensive, after which it would be imprudent to launch a large-scale campaign before May. He admitted that he did not expect the victorious campaign in Poland to influence the western powers; he proposed to

---

[1] After a ham-handed joke by Hitler and Göring in February 1937 had misfired, Hanfstaengl had fled to England, believing his life to be in danger.

make one more peace offer to Britain, but he had small hopes for it. He did not seriously expect Britain to come to terms until the Wehrmacht was arrayed on the English Channel, he said. On the twentieth, General Keitel, chief of the OKW (Wehrmacht High Command), warned a member of his staff that Hitler was planning to launch an offensive in the west as soon as it became clear there was no chance of reaching an understanding with the western powers.

In a long speech, Hitler revealed this intention to his startled supreme commanders on September 27, the day after his return to the Chancellery: what disturbed the army was Hitler's insistence that since German superiority of arms and men was only temporary, the offensive against France must therefore begin before the end of 1939, and, as in 1914, it would have to be carried through Belgium and at least the southern tip of a Holland he hoped would bow before the inevitability of such action. Hitler explained that he was unconvinced of Belgium's honest neutrality, for she was clearly fortified only along her frontier with Germany, and there were indications that she would permit a rapid invasion by the French and British forces massing on her western frontier—perhaps a secret military convention already existed between Belgium and the western powers to that end. (In this belief he was mistaken.) Thus the Ruhr, seat of Germany's armaments industries, would be lost and so would the war. He ordered General von Brauchitsch to establish the earliest date by which the German buildup could be complete. Aware that Brauchitsch inwardly rebelled against this new campaign, Hitler tolerated no discussion of his decision or of the prospects. He terminated the conference by shredding his brief notes and tossing them into the fire burning in the study grate.

As he privately informed Reichsleiter Alfred Rosenberg on September 29, he intended to propose a grand peace conference to arrange an armistice, demobilization, and the general settlement of outstanding problems, but if need be he would launch an offensive in the west. He was not afraid of the Maginot line. If the British would not accept the peace he offered, then he would destroy them. And Baron Ernst von Weizsäcker recorded Hitler as saying in his presence that day that the new offensive might cost Germany a million men—but it would cost the enemy the same number, and the enemy could ill afford the loss. Hitler repeated his arguments to his army and army group commanders when he assembled them in the Chancellery the next day to receive his thanks for the Polish triumph.

Warsaw had just fallen. It had been at the mercy of German ground and
air bombardment since September 10. Elsewhere in Poland the towns
had largely escaped damage. In Cracow, only the railroad station and
the airfield had been bombed. But this was not to be the fate of Warsaw, whose commandant Hitler suspected of stalling for time in which
to fortify the city against the encircling German armies. By the twenty-
first it was clear that Warsaw would have to be taken by storm. The two
hundred foreign diplomats were allowed to escape through the German
lines, and the artillery bombardment of the city's vital gas, power, and
water installations was stepped up. On the twenty-fifth Hitler had visited
the Tenth and Eighth armies; the latter had a hundred and fifty batteries
of artillery drawn up for the final bombardment due to begin next day.
From the roof of a sports stadium Hitler and a handful of his followers
watched with binoculars as the artillery pounded Warsaw. Blaskowitz's
final report states:

> On September 25 the Führer and Commander in Chief of the Wehr-
> macht visited the Warsaw front with the Commander in Chief of the
> army and his Chief of Staff. He was briefed on the Eighth Army's
> plan of attack: according to this the main artillery assault on the for-
> tress will commence early on September 26. Until then only identified
> military objectives, enemy batteries, and vital installations such as
> gas, water, and power stations are being bombarded by ground and
> air forces. Thirteenth Army Corps' attack is to begin at 0800 hrs on
> September 26, followed by Ninth Army Corps one day later; oppor-
> tunities of improving on the opening positions before then will be
> exploited. . . .
> After the plan of attack has been outlined broadly to him and been
> given the detailed approval of the Commander in Chief of the army,
> the Führer, who is deeply troubled by the suffering that lies in store
> for the population of the fortress [Warsaw], suggests that one more
> last attempt should be made to persuade the military command of
> Warsaw to abandon its lunatic course. He guarantees that the officers
> of the fortress will be granted honorable captivity and may retain
> their daggers if they surrender forthwith, and orders that the NCOs
> and troops are to be assured of their early release after the necessary
> formalities.

Millions of new leaflets publishing these terms were dropped over
Warsaw that evening. The Polish commandant made no response. Early
on the twenty-sixth, therefore, the target of the artillery bombardment
was changed to the city itself, and the infantry assault began. The next
day it was all over; the Poles had capitulated with virtually no further
military resistance. For a week there had been no water in the city; the

railroads were in ruins; there was no food or electric power. Unburied in
the ruins lay some twenty-six thousand civilian dead, over twice the
total German military casualties of the entire Polish campaign. On October 2, General Rommel and Colonel Schmundt visited Warsaw and
afterward reported to Hitler on the terrible scenes of destruction. Rommel wrote to his wife the next day: "All went according to plan yesterday. Flight to Berlin, flight to Warsaw, talks and inspection there, flight
back to Berlin, report in the Reich Chancellery, and dinner at the
Führer's table. Warsaw is in bad shape. There is hardly a building not in
some way damaged or with its windows intact. . . . The people must
have suffered terribly. For seven days there has been no water, no
power, no gas, and no food. . . . The mayor estimates there are forty
thousand dead and injured. . . . Apart from that everything is quiet.
The people are probably relieved that we have come, and that their ordeal is over. The NSV[2] and the 'Bavaria' rescue convoy and the field
kitchens are besieged by starving, exhausted people. It's raining here in
Berlin, and there are low-lying clouds. In Warsaw the weather was fine
but cloudy."

A pall of death still hung over Warsaw as Hitler flew in for his big
victory parade there on October 5. The stench of rotting bodies soured
the Polish air. Handpicked regiments of the finest infantry divisions
stomped past in a parade-march that could not have been improved
upon, but according to his closest staff the Führer was unnerved by the
spectacle of the death and destruction all about. Outwardly he remained
hard and callous. To the foreign journalists swarming around him as he
returned to the airfield he said menacingly, "Take a good look around
Warsaw. That is how I can deal with any European city. I've got enough
ammunition." But when he saw the banquet that the army had prepared
at the airfield, either his stomach rebelled or his instinct for bad publicity warned him not to sit at a vast, horseshoe-shaped table with spotless
white linen and sumptuous food at a time when hundreds of thousands
of Warsaw's inhabitants were starving. He turned on his heel and instructed Keitel and his staff to follow him immediately to the aircraft.
He had wanted to eat at a field kitchen with his troops, he said.

The frontiers of eastern Europe had now been agreed upon between
Germany and the Soviet Union. Hitler had insisted that his foreign
minister personally fly to Moscow to settle the details. Since Ribbentrop
was unenthusiastic about the mission, Hitler told him with some feeling:
"Laying down the definitive frontiers between Asia and Europe for the

---

[2] *National-Sozialistische Volkswohlfahrt*, the Party's civilian welfare organization.

next thousand years is after all a task worthy of the foreign minister of the *Grossdeutsches Reich!*" The partition of Poland had caused some anguish in Germany. Göring, a fanatical huntsman—a member of what Hitler called "that green freemasonry of men"—turned greedy eyes on the forests of Bialystok, rich with game, and he persuaded General Hans Jeschonnek to telephone Hitler's train to point up the importance of the Bialystok wood supply to the German economy; Hitler had bellowed with laughter. "He talks of wood and he means stags!" and he instructed that Bialystok should nevertheless be assigned to the Russian side of the demarcation line.

Ribbentrop settled the line on a small-scale map of Europe in Stalin's Kremlin office on September 28. Whereas the line provisionally agreed upon in mid-September had run along the Vistula River, it now followed the Bug River far to the east, since Stalin had also assigned to Germany the districts of Warsaw and Lublin in exchange for the Baltic state of Lithuania, which the August pact had placed within Germany's sphere of influence. So now the German troops who had advanced to the Bug, only to be ordered to withdraw to the Vistula, had to march eastward once again, spanning the difficult terrain for the third time in as many weeks. Stalin offset the only other dissatisfaction with the partition—the fact that the oil-producing region at Lvov (Lemberg) was on his side of the line—by a promise to supply Germany with three hundred thousand tons of the oil annually. All in all, as Ribbentrop remarked to Hitler on his return to Berlin, talking with Stalin and the other Kremlin potentates he had felt he was among comrades barely distinguishable from his National Socialist acquaintances.

Rosenberg almost choked when he heard of Ribbentrop's flattery of Stalin. He saw the strategic weakness in the new eastern frontiers almost at once. The new demarcation line would give Germany no common frontier with Romania, thus Germany's sole railway link with the Romanian oil fields and the Black Sea would run through Soviet-controlled territory. As another minister commented to Rosenberg, "If the Russians now march into the Baltic states, we shall have lost the Baltic as well, strategically speaking; Moscow will be more powerful than ever and they will be able to act against us in concert with the West any time they choose." Rosenberg probably put this view to Hitler with some emphasis when he saw him on the twenty-ninth. In fact the indecent haste with which Stalin moved to take up the options extended to him gravely embarrassed Ribbentrop's ministry; it can only be explained by the Soviet leader's alarm at the speed with which Hitler's Wehrmacht had polished off Poland and by his fear that peace might break out. Under

pressure from him Estonia conceded air and naval bases to Russia on
September 29, and Latvia and Lithuania followed suit a few days later.
Finland, however, made it clear from the outset she would offer the
most determined resistance to similar Russian demands.

For the first two weeks of October 1939, Hitler unquestionably wavered
between continuing the fight—which meant launching an almost immediate offensive in the west—and making peace with the remaining bellig-
erents on the best terms he could get. The fact that he had ordered the
Wehrmacht to get ready for "Operation Yellow" (*Fall Gelb,* the attack
on France and the Low Countries) in no way detracts from the reality
of his peace offensive. Whatever his final decision, there was no time to
be lost.

Hitler saw powerful arguments against stopping the fighting while the
Reich's military advantage was at its height. Nevertheless, he would
probably have settled for what he had already conquered—if only to be
able to return to his grandiose architectural dreams. Besides, Germany
would have needed at least fifty years to digest the new territories and
carry out the enforced settlement programs planned by Heinrich
Himmler to fortify the German blood in the east. Thus Hitler's peace
feelers toward London were sincere—not just a ploy to drive a wedge
between Britain and France. Weizsäcker wrote early in October: "The
attempt to wind up the war now is for real. I myself put the chances at
20 percent, [Hitler] at 50 percent; his desire is 100 percent. If he obtained peace, the thesis that Britain would sacrifice Poland would be
proven quasi right. And besides, it would eliminate the awkward decision as to how to reduce Britain by military means." Early in September
Göring had hinted to the British through Birger Dahlerus, the Swedish
businessman whom Hitler had already accepted as an unofficial intermediary to London during August, that Germany would be willing to restore sovereignty to a Poland shorn of the old German provinces excised
from the Fatherland at the end of the Great War; there would also be
an end to the persecution of the Jews and a reduction in German armaments. The British response had been a cautious readiness to listen to
the detailed German proposals.

But since these proposals had been made, the Russians, as per their
agreement with the Nazis, had seized eastern Poland. Hitler told
Göring and Dahlerus in Berlin late on September 26 that if the British still wanted to salvage anything of Poland, they would have to make
haste. They would have to send a negotiator who would take him
seriously, and now he could do nothing without consulting his Russian

friends. As for the Jewish question, the Germans proposed that it be solved by using the new Poland as a sink into which Europe's Jews should be emptied. Hitler approved the proposal that a secret meeting take place between German and British emissaries—perhaps Göring himself and General Sir Edmund Ironside—in Holland. Dahlerus left for London at once.[3]

The German army had good reason to keep anxious track of Hitler's peace offensive. Late in September, Halder's deputy had gloomily—and wholly inaccurately—warned that the German army could not launch a frontal assault on the French before 1942. Hitler was aware of the army's reluctance to apply its mind to "Yellow"; this was one reason for his speech of September 27. But even in that speech he had referred to a western assault only as a necessary evil if the French and British failed to see reason. If that happened, then "we must resolve to batter the enemy until he gives in."

The army marshaled what arguments it could against executing "Yellow" now: the tactics which had proved so successful in Poland would not suffice against the well-organized French army; the foggy weather and short hours of autumn daylight would set the Luftwaffe at a disadvantage; the army lacked ammunition, stores, and equipment. Brauchitsch enumerated these arguments to Hitler on October 7, and Hitler—already angered by the reluctance of his soldiers to follow him—asked the Commander in Chief to leave his notes behind, an ominous sign that he was not satisfied. Over the next two days he dictated a fifty-eight-page memorandum for the eyes of Keitel and the three commanders in chief alone; in it he explained just why they must launch "Yellow" at the very earliest opportunity and just why time was working against Germany.

The Führer read this formidable document to his uncomfortable generals on the tenth. We shall return to it at greater length shortly. In it, he insisted that Britain's long-range goal remained unchanged: the disintegration of the powerful German bloc, and the annihilation and dissolution of this new Reich with its eighty million people. The long-range German war aim must therefore be the absolute military defeat of the West (in which the destruction of the enemy's forces was more important than the gaining of enemy territory). This was the struggle which

[3] From the papers released to the Public Record Office in London it is clear that neither Chamberlain nor Halifax rejected Hitler's terms out of hand when Dahlerus described them. Even Churchill talked approvingly of an armistice. However, the file that evidently contains notes of Chamberlain's talk with Dahlerus on September 29, 1939, is closed until 1990, and forty-five pages of the foreign office file on Germany and future policy (F.O.371/22,985) covering the crucial period of October 3–4, 1939, are unavailable until the year 2015. A two-volume history of Anglo-German peace negotiations by Dr. Bernd Martin, of the University of Freiburg, is to appear shortly.

the German people must now assume. Despite all this, he added, a rapidly achieved peace agreement would still serve German interests—provided that Germany was required to relinquish nothing of her gains.

Hitler ignored none of the various unofficial channels for negotiation with the West now that Poland had been laid low. Over the next few days, however, it became clear that while some circles in Britain—notably in the air ministry—wanted an armistice, there was in the British Cabinet a hard core of opposition to whom all talk of making a deal with Hitler was anathema. Hitler was probably right in identifying the main source of this stubborn anti-German line as Churchill, now First Lord of the Admiralty, and the clique around him. On September 29, Alfred Rosenberg secured Hitler's permission to take up feelers put out through an intermediary in Switzerland by officials of the British air ministry; but this glimmer of hope was shortly extinguished when the intermediary reported that the forces for peace in that ministry had been pushed to the wall by the more militant forces at Churchill's beck and call. Little more was heard of these diffident approaches from London.

At this stage in Hitler's thought processes there came an ostensible intervention by President Roosevelt that was as abrupt in its approach as it was enigmatic in denouement. At the beginning of October an influential American oil tycoon arrived in Berlin on a peace mission for which he had apparently received a ninety-minute personal briefing from Roosevelt. He was William Rhodes Davis, whose own personal interest lay in preventing any disruption of his oil business with Germany. He had been brought into contact with Roosevelt by John L. Lewis, leader of the CIO, the United States labor federation whose fourteen million members represented a political force no president could afford to ignore. Lewis was originally both anti-Fascist and anti-Communist, but he had, said Davis, been impressed by the significant rise in the living standards of the German worker under National Socialism. Anxious about the effects of a long war on American export markets, Lewis had obliged Roosevelt to entrust this unofficial peace mission to Davis.

In Berlin the oilman met Göring, and a seven-page summary of the discussion of the alleged Roosevelt proposals survives.[4] It was evidently given wide confidential circulation in Berlin, for sardonic references to Roosevelt's sudden emergence as an "angel of peace" bent on securing a third term figure in several diaries of the day.

---

[4] Signed by Ministerialdirektor Wohlthat, this remarkable docment was not published in the postwar volumes of captured German documents; nor were the German reports on the Dahlerus missions that followed.

President Roosevelt is prepared to put pressure on the western powers to start peace talks if Germany will provide the stimulus. President Roosevelt asks to be advised of the various points Germany wants to settle, for example, Poland and the colonies. In this connection President Roosevelt also mentioned the question of the purely Czech areas, on which however a settlement need not come into effect until later. This point was touched on by President Roosevelt with regard to public opinion in the United States, as he must placate the Czech voters and the circles sympathizing with them if he is to exercise pressure on Britain to end the war.

Davis assured Göring that Roosevelt's main strategic concern was to exploit the present situation to destroy Britain's monopoly of the world markets. "In his conversation with Davis, Roosevelt explained that he was flatly opposed to the British declaration of war. He was not consulted by Britain in advance." Roosevelt suspected that Britain's motives were far more dangerous and that they had nothing to do with Poland; he himself recognized that the real reason for the war lay in the one-sided *Diktat* of Versailles which made it impossible for the German people to acquire a living standard comparable with that of their neighbors in Europe. Roosevelt's proposal, according to the unpublished summary, was that Hitler be allowed to keep Danzig and all the now Polish provinces taken from Germany by the treaty of Versailles, that all Germany's former African colonies be restored to her forthwith, and that the rest of the world give Germany financial assistance in establishing a high standard of living.

This was not all. If Daladier and Chamberlain refused to comply, then President Roosevelt would support Germany—Davis reported—in her search for a just, tolerable, and lasting peace: he would supply Germany with goods and war supplies "convoyed to Germany under the protection of the American armed forces" if need be. John L. Lewis had privately promised Davis that if some such agreement could be reached between Germany and the United States his unions would prevent the manufacture of war supplies for Britain and France.

Göring outlined Davis's message in detail to the Führer immediately after the meeting, and on October 3 the field marshal announced to the American that in his important speech to the Reichstag on the sixth Hitler would make a number of peace proposals closely embodying the points Davis had brought from Washington. (Hitler's more detailed proposals as described by Göring indeed went so far that their sincerity is open to question.) Göring told Davis: "If in his [Roosevelt's] opinion the suggestions afford a reasonable basis for a peace conference, he will then have the opportunity to bring about this settlement. . . . You may assure Mr. Roosevelt that if he will undertake this mediation, Germany will agree to an adjustment whereby a new Polish state and an independent Czechoslovak government would come into being. However this information is for him [Roosevelt] alone and to be used only if necessary to bring about a peace conference." Göring was willing to attend such a conference in Washington.

When Davis went back to the United States with the five detailed points Hitler proposed, he was accompanied by a German official, a "special ambassador" appointed to settle any details. Hitler hoped for an interim reply from Roosevelt by the fifth. (As Rosenberg wrote: "It would be a cruel blow for London to be urgently 'advised' by Washington to sue for peace!") But something had gone wrong with the mission: when Davis reached Washington he was not readmitted to the President, and they did not meet again.

A different aspect of Roosevelt's policy was revealed by the Polish documents ransacked by the Nazis from the archives of the ruined foreign ministry building in Warsaw. The dispatches of the Polish ambassadors in Washington and Paris laid bare Roosevelt's efforts to goad France and Britain into war with Germany while he rearmed the United States and psychologically prepared the American public for war. In November 1938, William C. Bullitt, his personal friend and ambassador in Paris, had indicated to the Poles that the President's desire was that "Germany and Russia should come to blows," whereupon the democratic nations would attack Germany and force her into submission; in the spring of 1939, Bullitt quoted Roosevelt as being determined "not to participate in the war from the start, but to be in at the finish"—the United States without doubt would fight, but "only if France and Britain kick off first." Bullitt was said by the Poles to have carried with him to Paris a "suitcase full of instructions" outlining the pressure he was to put on the Quai d'Orsay not to compromise with the totalitarian powers; at the same time Washington was applying "various exceptionally significant screws" to the British. Washington, Bullitt had told the Polish diplomats, was being guided not by ideological considerations but solely by the material interests of the United States. The Warsaw documents left little doubt as to what had stiffened Polish resistance to German demands during the August 1939 crisis.

On Friday October 6, Hitler spoke to the Reichstag. His "appeal for peace" was addressed to the British in more truculent and recriminatory language than many of his more moderate followers would have wished.

He singled out Churchill—who was then First Lord of the Admiralty—as a representative of the Jewish capitalist and journalistic circles whose sole interest in life lay in the furtherance of arson on an international scale.

On the ninth, he issued to his commanders in chief a formal directive to prepare for "Yellow" with all haste, in the event that "Britain and, under her command, France as well" were not disposed to end the war. His soldiers were, however, full of optimism. General Rommel wrote from Berlin on the seventh: "The reaction of the neutrals [to the Führer's speech] seems very good. The others will be able to think it over during the weekend. There is not much going on here otherwise. If the war ends soon, I hope I will soon be able to go home. . . ."

Hitler had sent Dahlerus to London for talks with Chamberlain. Late on October 9 the Swede reported to him the conditions Britain was attaching to peace negotiations: in addition to insisting on a new Polish state, Britain wanted all weapons of aggression destroyed forthwith; and there must be a plebiscite in Germany on certain aspects of her foreign policy. These were hard terms to swallow, for in public Hitler was still claiming that the future of Poland was a matter for Germany and Russia alone to decide, and Britain was blithely ignoring the growing armed strength of the Soviet Union and her expansionist policies. Nevertheless, on the tenth, Dahlerus was instructed to advise London that Hitler would *accept* these terms on principle. The Swedish negotiator saw Hitler twice that day before he departed for a promised rendezvous with a British emissary at The Hague. He took with him a formal letter from Göring and a list of Hitler's proposals—which included a new Polish state; the right for Germany to fortify her new frontier with Russia; guarantees backed by national plebiscite; nonaggression pacts between Germany, France, Britain, Italy, and the Soviet Union; disarmament; and the return of Germany's former colonies or suitable substitute territories.[5] Dahlerus noted to one German officer after meeting Hitler that "Germany for her part was able to swallow even tough conditions, provided they were put in a palatable form." He said he was taking with him to Holland more than enough to dispel Britain's smoldering mistrust of Hitler.

In Holland, however, Dahlerus waited in vain for the promised British emissary. The British foreign office asked him to describe Hitler's proposals to their local envoy and to remain at The Hague until he

[5] The brief treatment of this episode in Sir Llewellyn Woodward's *British Foreign Policy in the Second World War,* Vol. II (H.M.S.O., 1971), page 186, includes an inadequate summary of the proposals.

heard from London. Berlin optimistically viewed this request as a positive token of British interest and agreed that he should wait there. But
Chamberlain's eagerly awaited speech to the House of Commons the
next day, October 12, exploded Hitler's confident expectation that peace
was about to descend on Europe after five weeks of war. Chamberlain
dismissed Hitler's public offer (of the sixth) as "vague and uncertain"—
he had made no suggestion for righting the wrongs done to Czechoslovakia and Poland. If Hitler wanted peace, said Chamberlain, "acts—not
words alone—must be forthcoming." That same evening Hitler sent for
Göring, Milch, and Udet of the Luftwaffe and instructed them to resume
bomb production at the earliest possible moment. "The war will go on!"
Dahlerus was asked to return from The Hague to Berlin forthwith.
Édouard Daladier's reply to Hitler was no less abrupt. "Before these
answers came," Weizsäcker wrote two days later, "the Führer himself
had indulged in great hopes of seeing his dream of working with Britain
fulfilled. He had set his heart on peace. Herr von Ribbentrop seemed
less predisposed toward it. He sent the Führer his own word picture of a
future Europe like the empire of Charlemagne."

To the Swedish explorer Sven Hedin a few days later Hitler voiced
his puzzlement at Britain's intransigence. He felt he had repeatedly extended the hand of peace and friendship to the British, and each time
they had blacked his eye in reply. "The survival of the British Empire is
in Germany's interests too," Hitler noted, "because if Britain loses
India, we gain nothing thereby." *Of course* he was going to restore a
Polish state—he did not want to gorge himself with Poles; as for the rest
of Chamberlain's outbursts, he, Hitler, might as well demand that Britain "right the wrongs" done to India, Egypt, and Palestine. Britain
could have peace any time she wanted, but they—and that included that
"brilliantined moron" Eden and the equally incompetent Churchill—
must learn to keep their noses out of Europe.

And in a fit of anger Hitler complained to Dahlerus about "the unbe-
lievable behavior of Mr. Chamberlain"; from now on Germany would
fight Britain tooth and nail—he did not propose to bargain with her any
longer. Dahlerus left the Chancellery in a huff at the failure of his peace
effort, but was later soothed by Göring, who sent an important German
decoration around to him that same evening.

To Hitler it was clear there was no alternative but to proceed with the
war. The *urgency* of resuming the offensive was what he had most
impressed on his supreme commanders in his memorandum of October

9. While German military advantage was now at its very zenith, every month that passed in idleness would see a relative weakening vis-à-vis the enemy; in Italy, moreover, Mussolini was not getting any younger; the West might succeed in blackmailing Holland or Belgium into abandoning their neutrality, or in bribing the venal Balkan countries to the same effect; Russia's attitude could easily change. And there were other reasons why Germany must strike swiftly and avoid a protracted war: as Britain patched up her military resources and injected fresh units into France, the psychological boost this gave to the French could not be ignored; conversely it would become progressively more difficult to sustain the German public's enthusiasm for war or to feed the German war effort with foodstuffs and raw materials as each month passed. Germany's air superiority was only temporary—the moment the enemy believed *he* had achieved air superiority he would exploit it regardless of any reprisals Hitler might announce. Above all the British and French knew of the vulnerability of the Ruhr industries, and the moment the enemy could base aircraft or even long-range artillery on Belgian and Dutch territory, Germany would have to write off the Ruhr from the war effort; enemy bombers would have to fly barely a sixth of the distance that German bombers would have to cover to reach important British targets from the small strip of Germany's North Sea coast. This was why Hitler was convinced that the occupation of Belgium and Holland *must* be on the western powers' agenda already, and this was how he justified ordering his army to prepare to attack France through Belgium.

If the coast of western Europe were in Hitler's hands, the advantages to Germany would be decisive if the war against Britain was to continue: for sound strategic reasons the German navy needed submarine bases west of the English Channel. (On the tenth, Raeder also proposed that Germany obtain naval bases in Norway for the same reasons.) Similarly the Luftwaffe would have a disproportionate advantage in striking power if its flying distance to British targets involved only the short shuttle route from Holland, Belgium, or even the Pas de Calais in France.

The battle performance of the arms, men, and leadership of the German Wehrmacht had been strikingly demonstrated in Poland. In the fighting in the west, Germany could field a modern army of proud and battle-hardened soldiers. Their weapons were up-to-date and plentiful, particularly in the panzer and air forces; the artillery had at least two to three times as much ammunition per gun as at the onset of the war in 1914. Hitler proclaimed himself unimpressed by France's superiority in heavy howitzers and long-range artillery. But he warned emphatically against underestimating the value of the British divisions; as each month brought more to the shores of France, it would become increasingly awkward for the French government to extricate itself from the war.

These were the reasons Hitler gave for asking the Wehrmacht to put the offensive first, attacking in the west "this very autumn," and en masse; after all this might well be the push that ended all the fighting in Europe. The German army would attack the French along a front from south of Luxemburg to north of Nijmegen, in Holland. Splitting into two assault groups on either side of the Belgian fortress of Liège, it would destroy the French and British armies which would have come to meet it. The German armored formations would be used with such speed and dexterity that no cohesive front could be stabilized by the enemy; on no account were the tanks to become entangled in the endless maze of Belgian streets. The cities were to be bypassed, invested by lesser troops, and starved into submission. The Luftwaffe was to concentrate on shattering enemy railroad and road networks, rather than squander effort on hunting down individual aircraft. "Extreme restrictions are to be imposed on air attacks on cities themselves"; they were to be bombed only if necessary as reprisals for raids on the Reich cities. The war aim of the Wehrmacht, he drilled into his supreme commanders in this carefully-thought-out memorandum, was the destruction of the Anglo-French armies, not the destruction of public property and installations.

The German navy and air force accepted Hitler's arguments without demur, but the army leadership began a kicking and struggling that was to last until the spring of 1940. Perhaps this was because for the first time the generals clearly saw that Hitler took his position as Supreme Commander of the Wehrmacht seriously—that he now proposed to "interfere" more radically with the overall strategic direction of the war. Admiral Raeder not only shared the views expressed in the memorandum, but added an urgency of his own when he saw Hitler on the evening of the tenth of October: if Britain was to be defeated, she must be beleaguered and besieged regardless of army objections and the risk of American involvement. "The earlier we begin, and the more brutally, the earlier we shall see results; the shorter will be the war." Hitler thought the same way and stressed the importance of maintaining the submarine construction program right through 1940. Rudolf Hess meantime furnished him with several studies urging the use of magnetic mines to blockade Britain's sea lanes. In short, everybody accepted the need to defeat the western powers except the German army: the OKH (War Department) considered the army unready for a new campaign;

army group commanders Bock and Leeb echoed this skepticism with different degrees of vehemence, and army commanders like Reichenau and Kluge were equally unenthusiastic about the campaign—they would not even favor such an attack if the western powers were to invade Belgium forthwith. General von Brauchitsch found in mid-October that Hitler turned a deaf ear on his hesitations. Only a sound thrashing would make the British see reason, the Führer said. "Yellow" was provisionally to begin the third week of November; this early date would be dependent only on the weather forecast for Luftwaffe operations and not on the recalcitrant army's whims.

An indirect but readily traceable result of the British snub of his peace overture was a further hardening in Hitler's attitude to the future of Poland. After his Reichstag speech of October 6, he did not renew his offer to set up a rump Polish state. The Poland of 1939 would be subdivided, dismembered, and repopulated in such a way that it would never again rise to embarrass Germany or the Soviet Union. The eastern half, of course, had gone to Stalin; in the west, part would be absorbed by the Reich, while central Poland, *i.e.,* the districts of Warsaw, Radom, Lublin, and Cracow, would become a Polish reservation under exclusively German rule—a reservoir of cheap labor for the Reich's industries. By the end of September, Hitler had already drafted the first decrees for radical surgery of Poland's population under the overall direction of Heinrich Himmler as "Reich Commissioner for the Consolidation of the German Population." The Polish and Jewish populations in western Poland were to be displaced to a reservation in central Poland, and refugees of German descent from the Baltic states and eastern Poland would take their place.

A series of radical decrees signed by Hitler heralded this new order in Poland. On October 4 he amnestied all deeds committed by Germans "enraged by the atrocities perpetrated by the Poles." The Hitler decree appointing Himmler gave him the job of "eliminating the injurious influence of such non-German segments of the population there as are a danger to the Reich"; it was signed on the seventh. On the eighth Hitler signed a decree setting up new Reich Gaue (districts)—"West Prussia" and "Posen"—while former Polish frontier regions around Kattowitz and Zichenau were annexed to Silesia and East Prussia, respectively. As for the remaining German-occupied area, the Polish reservation, on the twelfth Hitler drafted a decree "for the restoration . . . of public order" there, subjugating these remaining regions to a German Governor General, a viceroy responsible only to himself; the new setup was to go into effect the moment the military government was withdrawn.

The Generalgouvernement was about one quarter the area of prewar Poland. As Governor General, Hitler selected Dr. Hans Frank, the Party's legal adviser; Frank, a former member of the Faculty of Law at Munich University, had specialized in industrial law. He rapidly gained a reputation for slipperiness with the army generals assigned to the eastern command, and since he shortly fell out with Himmler—who did not even attend Frank's installation ceremony at Lodz—his reign from Cracow castle was to be a lonely one.

These were the twilight days of the German army's rule in Poland. At a conference at the Chancellery on October 17, Hitler announced to Keitel, Frank, and Himmler that the army was to hand over control to the civilian administrations set up under Hans Frank and Gauleiters Albert Forster and Artur Greiser. The army ought to be glad to be rid of this unwholesome task, Hitler noted, and warming to his theme he ordered that in the Generalgouvernement it was no part of the administrators' duty to establish a model province along German lines or to put the country economically back on its feet. On the contrary, this was to become a "Polish economy"[6] par excellence! Significantly Frank's task in Poland would be to "lay the foundations for a military buildup in the future" and to prevent the Polish intelligentsia from creating a hard-core opposition leadership. The fight would be cruel, but this alone, Keitel noted in his record of Hitler's remarks, would spare Germany the need to go onto the battlefield once again because of Poland. Poland must become so poor that the people would *want* to work in Germany; the Jews and other vermin must be given speedy passage eastward. To an army colonel who arrived at the Chancellery that evening Keitel frankly admitted: "The methods to be employed will be irreconcilable with all our existing principles." According to yet another version, Hitler ended by announcing that he wanted Gauleiters Greiser[7] and Forster to be able to report to him ten years from now that Posen and West Prussia were pure and Germanic provinces in full bloom, and Hans Frank to be able to report that in the Generalgouvernement—the Polish reservation—the "devil's deed" had been done.

[6] Literal translation of *polnische Wirtschaft,* a phrase of which the sense would better be given, however, by a "Polish pigsty."
[7] On March 7, 1944, Gauleiter Artur Greiser cabled the Führer that 1,000,000 Germans had been officially transplanted to his Reich Gau "Wartheland" from the old Reich, from the rest of Europe, and most recently from the Black Sea regions; the Jews had all but vanished from the area, and the number of Poles had been reduced from 4,200,000 to 3,500,000 by forced migration. This indicates the kind of population movements that Hitler set in train in October 1939. In May 1945, with the approval of the western governments, the tides were reversed, but even more dramatically. About 40,000,000 Germans, Poles, and Czechs were forcibly resettled by 1948.

The population surgery prescribed by the redrawn map of eastern Europe inflicted hardship on Germans too, and German refugees crowded the roads of the territories of southeastern Poland beyond the San River, an area which had been assigned to Russia. Here there were scores of villages and hamlets where the language and the culture was German, where Germans had tended land given to their ancestors by Maria Theresa and Joseph II—villages with names like Burgthal and Wiesenberg, or Neudorf and Steinfels, where the farms were laid out and worked in an orderly and scientific manner that set them apart from the farms of Polish and Ukrainian neighbors.

In the last days of October 1939, Captain Engel, Hitler's army adjutant, handed him a Fourteenth Army report on the evacuation of these thousands of ethnic Germans before the advancing Red Army troops occupied their villages. In the five days after September 22, about five thousand bewildered villagers and their livestock had been marched westward, helped by army transport of the withdrawing Wehrmacht units and looked after by NSV welfare teams. No orders had been given; none were necessary. "In the majority of cases the villagers had experienced enough during the Great War (when the Germans were transported to Siberia) and during the years of Bolshevik rule, 1919 and 1920, for them to abandon their property without further ado and take to their heels." These were pious and deeply patriotic Germans, untainted by Polish ways, the report concluded; they would be excellent stock for the resettlement of Germany's newly won eastern provinces. As this westward movement was in progress, a more ominous eastward flow began: from their half of Poland, the Russians began deporting dangerous intellectuals and officer classes; and in the German half the Jews were being rounded up, confined, and spilled over the demarcation line into the Russian zone where possible.

Hitler's attitude toward the Kremlin at this time revealed a fascinating conflict between his short-term desire for a stable eastern front and an assured supply of raw materials, and his long-term, immutable hatred and mistrust of Stalin and communism; his imperial eastern ambitions had only temporarily been anesthetized by the rapid conquest of Poland. In private conferences with such loquacious personalities as Count Galeazzo Ciano, both the Führer and Ribbentrop spoke reverently of the treaties signed with Moscow. But secretly Hitler acted as though the Russians were infected by some contagion which must at all costs be prevented from spreading to the Reich. Contacts between the German and Soviet armies along the demarcation line were prohibited by Berlin. The repatriation of the ethnic Germans was actively encouraged, and at one time there was even a suggestion that the navy protect the interests of the German communities trapped by the Russian encroachment on the Baltic states. How long could he rely on the Kremlin to respect the demarcation line? In his long October memorandum to his supreme commanders Hitler had warned: "Through no treaty and no agreement can the lasting neutrality of Russia be guaranteed with certainty. For the present all the indications are that Russia will not abandon this neutrality. But that may change in eight months, in a year, or even in several years' time." Only the clear demonstration of Germany's superiority in arms would dissuade Stalin from tearing up his pact with Berlin the moment it suited him. This latent mistrust was voiced even more emphatically by Hitler to Keitel on the seventeenth: Poland was to be left in decay except insofar as was needed to work up the roads, the rail systems, and the signals networks to turn the area into an important military springboard; without doubt he was thinking in terms of an attack on Russia.

In a long speech behind closed doors to senior Party officials and Gauleiters on October 21, he promised that once he had forced Britain and France to their knees he would revert his attention to the east and show who was the master there. It had become clear that the Russian army was not much use, he was quoted as explaining, and that their soldiers were badly trained and poorly equipped. "Once he had [dealt with the East] as well he would set about restoring Germany to how she used to be. . . ." He wanted Belgium; and as for France, Hitler was now thinking in terms of the ancient frontier of 1540—when the Habsburg empire of Charles V had embraced Switzerland and a multitude of duchies like Burgundy and Lorraine as far to the west as the Meuse.

In summary, Hitler proposed to exploit his alliance with Stalin as long as possible and then to attack Russia before Stalin attempted to destroy him. It was plain that Russia was prepared to pay a high price in raw materials for German industrial expertise, machine tools, modern artillery, aircraft, and ship designs. Russia even signed a trade agreement with Britain to procure the rubber and tin needed by Berlin. Nevertheless, to his closest associates Hitler betrayed his true feelings about the alliance. A week after his speech to the Gauleiters, he assembled two dozen generals and admirals for an investiture at the Chancellery, and during the banquet that followed, he suddenly asked the panzer general, Guderian, what the army reaction to his Moscow Pact had been. Guderian replied the army had breathed a sigh of relief, but this was evidently anything but the answer Hitler wanted. The Führer lapsed into a brooding silence and then changed the subject.

Incidents

By November 1939 Adolf Hitler had faced up to the fact that the war would go on. In mid-October his propaganda ministry had already instructed editors to mute reporting of peace proposals from abroad so that no false hopes would be raised in the German public. When Alfred Rosenberg came to him on November 1 with nebulous reports of fresh peace moves within the British air ministry, the Führer belittled the prospects: while he himself would still favor a German-British rapprochement, London was in the grip of a Jewish-controlled, lunatic minority against whom Chamberlain was a characterless and impotent old man. Hitler said he failed to see what the British really wanted. "Even if the British won, the real victors would be the United States, Japan, and Russia." England, even if victorious, would emerge from a war in ruins, and her fate if she were militarily defeated would be worse.

Early in November, the Belgian and Dutch monarchs appealed to the warring parties to seek ways of restoring a lasting peace, but their well-intentioned appeal was immediately rejected by Lord Halifax in a public speech using language described by Ribbentrop as of such brazenness that he actively discouraged all further unofficial feelers, and the appeal was left unanswered by Berlin. German propaganda now portrayed the British whom Hitler had unsuccessfully wooed as murderers, liars, hypocrites, and it used a veritable thesaurus of other uncomplimentary terms. Hitler gathered that the peace party in Britain had lost. British Fascist leader Oswald Mosley had put up a good fight, but he had been silenced. The only good Briton, in Hitler's view, was Lloyd George. That Britain was continuing the fight was an unpalatable truth he now had to face.

Upon his return from Poland, Hitler had equipped the big Congress Room in his official Berlin residence as a war conference room. In its center was a large map table.

Here the Führer conducted all his war conferences in Berlin until the chamber was ruined by a bomb five years later. The OKW generals Keitel and Jodl moved into neighboring rooms vacated by Hitler's adjutants. Jodl's status was still relatively weak. When he ventured an appreciation of the overall strategic situation, Hitler cut him short after the first few sentences and delivered a lecture on what *he* thought. But Hitler's regard for Jodl grew as his contempt for the army's representatives became more explicit. He told Jodl in the middle of October, when they were discussing the new "Yellow" offensive in the west: "We are going to win this war even if it contradicts a hundred General Staff doctrines—because we've got the better troops, the better equipment, the stronger nerves, and a united, resolute leadership!" Throughout that month and the next, the army's Commander in Chief and Chief of Staff showed equal determination in waging a rearguard action against "Yellow," and it is not impossible that Hitler got wind of military and political conspiracies constantly being hatched by the army generals and civilian dissidents. At any rate, that autumn he pithily commented to Luftwaffe officers waiting for one conference to begin, "Here comes my Coward Number One!" as Brauchitsch, the army Commander in Chief, came through the door, and added, ". . . and Number Two!" when Halder, the Chief of Staff, joined him.

On October 19, 1939, the reluctant war department had at Hitler's behest issued its first hasty directive on "Yellow." It envisaged a massive main attack being carried through Belgium by seventy-five divisions whose object it was to meet and destroy the British and French armies on French and Belgian soil. As a token of their distaste for the whole affair, Brauchitsch and Halder deliberately left it to General Keitel to read out the details to Hitler. While General von Bock's Army Group B and the powerful *Armeeabteilung* Niederrhein (Army Sector Lower Rhine) would deliver the main thrust through Liège and Namur, General von Rundstedt's Army Group A would follow up with a subsidiary attack on the southern wing; Army Group C, commanded by General von Leeb, would remain on the defensive with sixteen divisions behind the West Wall.

The big push into Belgium would involve crossing a fifteen-mile-wide sliver of Dutch territory at Maastricht, but at this stage Hitler hoped it might be possible to avoid hostilities with Holland over this "temporary" claim on Dutch hospitality. (If the British landed in Holland, of course, the German army must have plans ready to occupy the whole country immediately.) Meanwhile, to justify invading neutral Belgium the military and Intelligence agencies were instructed to compile detailed summaries of instances of Franco-Belgian collusion and to allow their imaginations free rein in doing so.

The military prospects of this OKH plan did not encourage Bock and Rundstedt, who expressed their pessimism in memoranda to the war department in October. Leeb added a similar study, questioning the propriety of violating Belgian and Dutch neutrality. General von Reichenau, commanding the Sixth Army, put his objections to Hitler in person more than once, and when Hitler voiced his own fear that if "Yellow" was not executed forthwith, "one fine winter's night Britain and France may arrive at the Meuse without a shot being fired," the general stubbornly retorted, "That would be preferable in my view." When Keitel returned from a brief visit to General Staff headquarters at Zossen, impressed by the arguments Brauchitsch and Halder were deploying against "Yellow," Hitler bitterly accused his OKW chief of "conspiring with the generals" against him. He insisted that in the future Keitel loyally transmit the Führer's will to the war department—an order whose implications provoked the upright, traditionalist general into offering Hitler his resignation both orally and in writing; Hitler told him not to be so touchy. Hitler's staff believed Göring was behind the Führer's growing animosity toward the army, but even Göring was uneasy about launching "Yellow" so soon; however, he failed to win Ribbentrop's support, and after Hitler turned a deaf ear on him, the field marshal privately vowed to be a good soldier and obey orders in the future.

A basic difference of opinion lay in the Intelligence estimate of the enemy, inadequate because of the Abwehr's almost total failure to establish a network in the west. The army put the strength of the French army far too high, in Hitler's view; what perturbed Hitler was the growing British force in France, for he considered each British division was worth three or four French. But the expert tactical opinions could not be ignored. Bock warned that the British would land in Antwerp and before the Wehrmacht could prevent it there would again be a long and bloody war of attrition in Belgium. Other generals pointed out that the winter nights were long and that the combination of long nights and rainy, foggy days would make a war of movement difficult. But Hitler wanted a war of movement in which his armored and mechanized formations could sweep forward, exploiting the "inflexibility" of the French and the "inertia" of the British armies, and the more he pored over the maps the less he liked the war department's proposed operational plan. In the third week of October he commented acidly to Keitel and Jodl that Halder's plan, with its strong right wing along the coast, was no different from the Schlieffen Plan drafted before World War I: "You cannot get away with an operation like that twice. I have something very different in mind. I will tell you two about it in the next few days and then discuss it with the army."

This was the alternative possibility—a vast encirclement of the enemy, spearheaded by the armored units thrusting eventually up to the coast between the Meuse River and Arras and Amiens; this was terrain he had fought on as a young man, and he knew it would be ideal for the tanks. Farther to the north, in Flanders, the tanks would get into terrain difficulties. The idea obsessed him, and at the end of a discussion with the senior "Yellow" generals at the Reich Chancellery on October 25 he tentatively put it to the Commander in Chief. Bock, who was also present, wrote in his diary that the Führer

> said in reply to a question from Brauchitsch that from the very outset he has had the following wish and idea: to deliver the main offensive *only south* of the Meuse, perhaps coupled with a subsidiary attack on Liège, so that by our advancing in a roughly westerly and then northwesterly direction the enemy forces already in or pouring into Belgium will be cut off and destroyed.
>
> Brauchitsch and Halder are obviously taken completely by surprise, and a "lively" debate rages to and fro over this idea.

This was the germ of the campaign plan that was to bring about France's defeat. But it seemed so bold, staking everything on one card—namely whether the German armies would succeed in breaking through to the Channel coast or not—that Hitler hesitated to order such a radical change of emphasis, the more so since three days before he had provisionally ordered that "Yellow" was to begin on Sunday, November 12. But he asked the army to look into his idea, and from a side remark it was clear that he was not averse to postponing the offensive until spring if need be.

Hitler was aware that the army's opposition was not limited to objective debate of the merits of "Yellow."

There was a clique of as yet unidentifiable officers bent on his forcible removal from power, and their contacts with the western governments made them potentially very dangerous men indeed. During October he accordingly authorized Heydrich's secret service to develop its contacts with the British Intelligence network in Holland. Heydrich's men were to pretend to represent dissident German army generals willing to risk all in a plot to overthrow the Führer. If they could secure the British agents' confidence, the names of the real German conspirators might be revealed, or gleaned from the subsequent radio traffic between the agents and their Intelligence masters in London. This was the SS plan, and it worked up to a point. After a convincing series of false starts and unkept rendezvous, the first clandestine meeting between the British agents and Heydrich's "army generals" took place on Dutch soil in the second half of October; certain questions were submitted for the British Cabinet to answer, on the assumption that the generals captured Hitler and ended the war; and an additional rendezvous was arranged for early November. Hitler was intrigued by the possibility of embarrassing the Dutch government by exploiting the evidence of Anglo-Dutch staff collaboration revealed by these SS ploys, and he discussed this with Ribbentrop and Heydrich's lieutenant, Dr. Werner Best; a plan to kidnap the British agents was first considered, then shelved for the time being.

The Abwehr was not consulted by Heydrich. The Abwehr had its hands full with a very different kind of operation, again at Hitler's command. If he invaded Belgium on November 12, the Albert Canal and the nearby fortress of Eben Emael would present serious obstacles to the advance of Reichenau's Sixth Army. The canal linked Antwerp to the Meuse; at Eben Emael it had been designed from the outset as a moat, an integral part of the Belgian eastern defenses, and it was fortified with bunkers, blockhouses, and walls ramped to steep slopes. Only three bridges crossed the canal, and these had been built with pillboxes and demolition chambers controlled by detonating squads housed in impregnable blockhouses some distance away. The Eben Emael fortress had eighteen heavy guns emplaced in casemates and armored turrets and manned by a thousand Belgian troops living underground in the tunnels and bunkers; it commanded the Meuse and the southern reaches of the canal. Since the whole system was some twenty miles from the Reich frontier, the bridges could be demolished long before German army advance parties could reach them; the Germans would then have to cross the wide Meuse by the two available bridges on the Dutch side at Maastricht, and these had also been prepared for demolition.

This complex problem occupied Hitler as much as the rest of "Yellow's" problems put together. In the last week of October he proposed setting up a camouflaged Abwehr battalion under Reichenau's control— some four or five hundred Germans under a Captain Fleck and a Lieutenant Hokke, who were skilled in clandestine operations. This battalion would be rigged out in uniforms used by the Dutch frontier police in the Maastricht enclave. As Hitler was to say, "In wartime, a uniform is always the best camouflage. But one thing is vital—that the leaders of Hokke's shock troops be the spitting image of Dutch police officers as far as language, dress, and behavior go." Their job would be to put the detonating cables and charges out of action.

Hitler lamented his army generals' inability to come up with ideas like these. "These generals are too prim and proper," he scoffed after one such conference. "They haven't got a *ruse de guerre* among the lot of them. They ought to have read more Karl May!"[1] He had a solution for the fortress of Eben Emael as well: at the same time as the "Trojan horse" policemen were silencing the Dutch guards on the bridges, some three hundred airborne troops would *silently* cross the Maastricht enclave in squadrons of gliders and land within the fortress walls in the darkness before dawn; they were to be equipped with deadly fifty-kilo "hollow-charge" explosives capable of knocking out the big guns there. At the beginning of November, the Seventh Air Division commanded the immediate activation of an airborne assault unit for the glider operation; its orders were to seize the bridges, knock out the fortress, and hold these positions until the army's advance guards had fought their way up from the Reich frontier. The unit was to be ready for action by the twelfth.

There was much that could, and did, go wrong. Canaris's Abwehr bungled the preparatory work: an official of the Munster Abwehr office was detected purchasing large quantities of Dutch police uniforms in the province of Groningen; he was arrested trying to smuggle them across the frontier, and by November 5 there was a public uproar in Holland. For several days Dutch newspapers featured cartoons speculating on the manner in which the Nazi invaders would be dressed when they came. One cartoon that reached the Chancellery in Berlin showed Göring skulking in the uniform of a Dutch streetcar conductor; another had him preening himself in a mirror as a Dutch policeman.

With the attack on France and Belgium ostensibly just one week away, the German army command was in a high state of nervousness. Generals who attempted to remonstrate with Hitler had been sent away unheeded or unheard. At noon on November 5, General von Brauchitsch himself secured an audience with the Führer, and the next hour

[1] German author of popular and ingenious American Indian stories.

saw one of the strangest encounters in the history of their uncomfortable partnership. The General Staff was now on a different tack: with facts and figures supplied by the quartermaster general, they were trying to point up the army's unreadiness and unwillingness for a new campaign. Brauchitsch himself wrote out in longhand his answer to Hitler's memorandum of October 9.

His main concern was the state of the army in the west. In the Polish campaign the infantry had shown little verve in attack, the general contended, and at times the NCOs and officers had lost control. Brauchitsch even spoke of "mutinies" in some units, and he recounted acts of drunken indiscipline at the front and on the railways during the transfer west that invited comparison with the uglier scenes of 1917 and 1918. Reports from railway officials and of resulting courts-martial had reached Brauchitsch. On hearing this, Hitler, who had listened in silence, lost his temper and, interrupting the Commander in Chief, demanded the identities of the units involved. His hoarse, angry voice could be heard by the secretaries outside. Snatching Brauchitsch's memorandum from his hands, he tossed it into his safe and thundered at the general that it was quite incomprehensible to him how an army commander could blacken and condemn his entire army because of a handful of excesses. "Not one frontline commander mentioned any lack of attacking spirit in the infantry to me. But *now* I have to listen to this, after the army has achieved a magnificent victory in Poland!" He insisted that Brauchitsch furnish him with the reports he had mentioned, and with details of the death sentences passed in the east and west in consequence. He would fly to the units concerned immediately. Sweeping out of the room, Hitler slammed the door behind him and left Brauchitsch trembling.

Keitel afterward suggested to Hitler that it was the older recruits—the oft-mentioned "white years" of young men who because of Versailles Treaty prohibitions had not undergone early conscription and intensive training—who were to blame for these acts of indiscipline. Hitler agreed; he had fought in vain against the refusal of Brauchitsch's predecessor to train these men in good time. Later that evening he angrily discussed with his adjutants Schmundt and Engel this "army sabotage" of his plans. He dismissed General von Brauchitsch's written memorandum as a pack of lies, and Captain Gerhard Engel, Hitler's army adjutant, was ordered to visit the front and report to him on the "mutinying army units." To Fräulein Schroeder he dictated an aide-mémoire on the ugly scene with Brauchitsch; this too was locked away in the safe for future use. He also dictated a document dismissing Brauchitsch, but Keitel

talked him out of this. There was no suitable successor for the courtly
and pliable Commander in Chief of the German army. The Brauchitschs
had served their country as officers and servants of the state for many
centuries, and Nietzsche's aphorism could have been their family motto:
"Rebellion is the distinguishing mark of the slave; let *your* mark be obe-
dience." A Herr von Brauchitsch would not rebel.

Two days later Hitler provisionally postponed "Yellow" by three
days, giving the weather as the reason.

That evening, November 7, his special train left for Munich—his first return to Bavaria since he had departed from the Berghof to confront an
uncertain future in August. He was loath to leave Berlin, but the annual
Party anniversary of the 1923 beer-hall putsch was the next day, and he
must speak to the "Old Guard" at the Bürgerbräukeller. He was uneasy
about the security risks involved in annual public appearances—the best
safeguard against assassination was always an irregular routine. This
Bürgerbräu assembly and the long march through Munich's narrow
streets were annual opportunities no less inviting to an assassin than the
Nuremberg rally or that approach road to the Kroll opera house in
Berlin. On November 9, 1938, a Swiss waiter named Maurice Bavaud
had trained a gun on him on this very march through Munich, but
Bavaud's aim had been spoiled by the sudden forest of hands raised in
salute. Hitler learned of the attempt only when Bavaud was stopped by
railway police at Augsburg—as he was attempting to leave Germany—for
not having a valid ticket. He was found to be carrying an envelope
addressed to the Führer, and under interrogation he also confessed to
having stalked Hitler with a gun during his daily walks on the Obersalzberg mountain in October. Bavaud was to come up for secret trial by
the People's Court in December 1939.[2]

Hitler was supposed to remain in Munich until the ninth and then,
after further ceremonies, fly back to Berlin; however, on the morning of
the eighth his residence was telephoned from Berlin that the army was
demanding a fresh decision on the next day's deadline for "Yellow,"
and since his chief pilot warned him that the weather forecast was
against flying, he sent an adjutant to arrange for his private coaches to
be attached to the regular express leaving Munich that same evening.
His adjutant returned with word that this train would get him to Berlin
by 10:30 the next morning, but it would be cutting things fine if he was
to catch it after his speech. Hitler irritably asked if there were no later

[2] He was beheaded.

trains, but the next express to Berlin would not arrive there until too late for the army's purposes. He therefore brought forward the beginning of his speech by five minutes, to 8:10 P.M., and ordered Hess to stand in for him during ceremonies scheduled for the next day.

At seven-thirty the Munich police chief arrived to escort him to the beer hall, and an adjutant telephoned the Bürgerbräu with instructions that the speeches must begin punctually, as they now had a very tight schedule. At eight o'clock sharp, the Führer entered the cavernous beer hall, the local Party band stopped playing in mid-march, and Christian Weber (a former horse-dealer who was now one of the Party's leading figures in Bavaria) spoke a few brief words of welcome.

Normally Hitler spoke for about ninety minutes, but this time he spoke for just under an hour, standing at a lectern in front of one of the big, wood-paneled pillars. Many of the Old Guard were away at the front, so the hall was filled with other senior Party members and local dignitaries as well as the next of kin of the sixteen Nazis killed in the 1923 putsch. Hitler's speech was undistinguished, a pure tirade of abuse against Britain, whose "true motives" for this new crusade Hitler identified as jealousy and hatred of the new Germany, which had achieved in six years more than Britain had in centuries. Julius Schaub, who was responsible for seeing to it that his chief reached the railroad station on time, nervously passed him cards on which he had scrawled increasingly urgent admonitions: "Ten minutes!" then "Five!" and finally a peremptory "Stop!"—a method he had previously had to use to remind his Führer, who never used a watch, of the passage of mortal time. "Party members, comrades of our National Socialist movement, our German people, and above all our victorious Wehrmacht: *Siegheil!*" Hitler concluded, and stepped into the midst of the Party officials who thronged forward. A harassed Julius Schaub managed to shepherd the Führer out of the hall at twelve minutes past nine. The express was due to leave from the main railway station in nineteen minutes.

At the Augsburg station, the first stop after Munich, confused word was passed to Hitler's coach that something unusual, though as yet undefined, had occurred at the Bürgerbräu. At the Nuremberg station, the local police chief, a Dr. Martin, was waiting with more detailed news: just eight minutes after Hitler had left the beer hall a powerful bomb had exploded in the paneled pillar right behind where he had been speaking. There were many dead and injured. Hitler's Luftwaffe aide, Colonel Nicolaus von Below, later wrote: "For a moment Hitler refused to believe it. He had been there himself and nothing had happened then. . . . The news made a vivid impression on Hitler. He fell very silent, and then described it as a miracle that the bomb had missed him."[3] He spoke by telephone with SS General von Eberstein, the Munich police chief (who had been flatly forbidden to encroach on this strictly Party preserve with regular police security measures), and consoled the anguished SS general: "Don't worry—it was not your fault. The casualties are regrettable, but all's well that ends well." By 7 A.M. the news was that six people had been killed (the death toll later rose to eight) and over sixty injured.

At the Anhalt station in Berlin, Hitler's chauffeur persuaded him at last to inspect the bulletproof Mercedes limousine he had ordered for the motor pool. The vehicle was driven into the Chancellery's entrance hall for Hitler's approval; its windshield was of quarter-inch laminated glass, its body of toughened steel armorplate, and its floor was extra thick in order to protect the occupants against mines. Turning to Martin Bormann, Hitler said, "In the future I will only ride in this car. You can never tell when some idiot may lob a bomb in front of you."

At first the SS security agencies ran around in circles. Himmler reported that the manager of the Bürgerbräu was known to the Heydrich office as a high-ranking freemason who "dealt only with Jews, freemasons, and other sinister elements." The Abwehr indulged in even wilder flights of fancy and suspected that the perpetrators would be found among old Party luminaries whose noses had been put out of joint. Perhaps they had even been in league with Göring! Hitler evidently hoped it would prove to be the work of agents of a foreign power. The people who feared Hitler's renewed disfavor hurried to dissociate themselves from the outrage at Munich, and for several days afterward his adjutants Brückner and Wünsche brought to the ruffled Führer telegrams of congratulation from people like Admiral von Horthy, the king and queen of Italy, Benito Mussolini, the still-exiled Kaiser Wilhelm, and Field Marshal von Blomberg. Queen Wilhelmina of the Netherlands cabled Adolf Hitler:

> Herr Reich Chancellor, may I send to you my most heartfelt congratulations on your escape from the abominable attempt on your life.

Even as Hitler had been speaking at the Bürgerbräu, however, a man had been apprehended at Konstanz, attempting to cross illegally into Switzerland. On the night of November 13 this man, Georg Elser, a

---

[3] Below's account goes on to say that Hitler often excitedly repeated the circumstances that had led to his leaving the Bürgerbräu early (see also Rosenberg's diary, November 11). "He joked that this time the weather expert had saved his life. Otherwise, commented the Führer, the expert was pushing him into an early grave with his weather forecasts, for the weather outlook was black and likely to continue so."

thirty-six-year-old Swabian watchmaker, confessed that he had single-handedly designed, built, and installed a time bomb in the pillar. In his pockets were found a pair of pliers, sketches of grenade and fuse designs, pieces of a fuse, a picture postcard of the Bürgerbräu hall's interior; a badge of the former "Red Front" Communist movement was found concealed under his lapel. Under Gestapo interrogation a week later the whole story came out—how he had joined the Red Front ten years before but had long lost interest in politics, and how he had been angered by the regimentation of labor and religion as well as by the relative pauperization of craftsmen such as himself in the early years of Nazi rule. The year before he had resolved to dispose of Adolf Hitler and had begun work on an ingenious time-bomb controlled by two clock-mechanisms for added reliability. After thirty nights of arduous chiseling at the pillar behind the paneling, he installed the preset clocks in one last session on the night of November 5, the evening after Hitler's furious altercation with Brauchitsch in Berlin. The mechanism was soundproofed in cork to prevent the ticking from being heard, and Elser's simple pride in his craftsmanship was evident from the records of his interrogations. He refused to agree he had been acting on higher orders, even though the customs officials who had arrested him both described how they saw a man in a light-colored overcoat apparently waiting for him just inside the Swiss frontier. He probably was telling the truth, and there is no doubt that one watchmaker acting alone had nearly accomplished what after years of debate, planning, and self-indulgent conspiracy a platoon of officers and intellectuals were to fail to do five years later.

To Hitler it seemed an impossible coincidence that his archenemy, the Nazi renegade Otto Strasser, was at that time in Switzerland, and he later claimed that the Dutch prime minister and Anthony Eden had known of the plot. In private he assured his staff that one day he would publish the whole story but not yet, as he also wanted to round up those who had pulled the strings. Security measures were tightened. General Rommel, commandant of Hitler's headquarters, wrote on November 9: "Six feet of rubble cover the spot where the Führer spoke yesterday evening. That was how strong the explosion was. One dare not think what would have happened if the assassination had succeeded. My only hope is that now in the Führer's headquarters too the security precautions will be better organized with everything in one person's hands (mine). Because if anybody is going to take *this* responsibility, he cannot share it with anybody else." And on the fifteenth, referring to "Operation Yellow," Rommel wrote: "The Führer's mind is absolutely made up. The assassination attempt in Munich has only made his resolution stronger. It is a marvel to witness all this."

On the day after the Munich explosion Hitler again postponed "Yellow," and on November 13 he further instructed that the offensive would not begin before the twenty-second.

There is some reason to believe that Hitler himself did not intend these deadlines to be serious—that they were designed to keep the army at maximum readiness in case the western powers should themselves suddenly invade the Low Countries. Nor would the western powers have to violate Belgian and Dutch sentiment in so doing, for with the exception of Flemish minority elements, popular sympathies in the Low Countries lay with the West; the Belgian armed forces were concentrated almost wholly against the German frontier, where British and French forces could join them virtually overnight, leaving Germany's "Achilles' heel," her Ruhr industrial zone, in a precarious situation indeed. Hitler did not doubt that the West had economic means enough to pressure the Low Countries into "appealing for help" at a propitious moment. "Let us not credit the enemy with a lack of logic," Hitler said later in November. "If we respect their [the Low Countries'] neutrality, the western powers will just march in during the spring."

Hitler was also under pressure from Göring and the Luftwaffe's Chief of Staff to occupy the whole of Holland rather than just temporarily violate the Maastricht enclave: possession of Holland would be vital for the future air war between Britain and Germany. After the Munich bomb attempt, Hitler came around to this view.

The time had come to compromise the Dutch. He instructed Heydrich to wind up the cat-and-mouse game being played with the British agents in Holland. Heydrich's "army officers"—who had not shown up at the agreed rendezvous on November 8—now appeared on the ninth at Venlo, just inside the Dutch frontier. The British agents drove up, there was a rapid exchange of gunfire, and they were dragged across the border into Germany together with the driver and another officer, mortally wounded; this latter turned out to be a Dutch Intelligence officer accompanying them. The Dutch government formally requested the return of the body; that was "Holland's biggest blunder," Hitler afterward ominously said. This was proof that the ostensibly neutral Dutch were working hand in glove with the British. "When the time comes I will use all this to justify my attack," he told his generals. "The violation of Belgian and Dutch neutrality is unimportant," he explained. "Nobody will ask about such things after we have won."[4] On November 12, Hitler personally presented the Iron Cross to the SS major who had directed the kidnapping.

One unexpected bonus from the Venlo incident was that the British agents turned out to be Britain's top agents in Holland; from them Heydrich's officers learned that the British secret service was evidently in touch with genuine Wehrmacht officers who were planning a revolt against Hitler. But Heydrich's ambition to establish a direct link between the Bürgerbräu explosion in Munich and the British secret service remained unfulfilled (which did not prevent Himmler from claiming later in November that proof to that effect had been obtained).

On November 13, General Jodl instructed the war department that a new Führer Directive was on its way: the army must be prepared to occupy as much of Holland as possible to improve Germany's air defense position. This was on the assumption that the British, who had already eroded Holland's neutrality by repeated overflying of RAF planes, would attempt to set foot in Holland as soon as Hitler's troops marched across the Maastricht enclave. Hitler would justify his violation of Dutch neutrality by claiming the involvement of the Dutch General Staff in the Venlo incident. Three days later he again postponed "Yellow," this time to November 26 at the earliest; on the twentieth the operation was postponed to December 3. On November 20, meanwhile, Hitler issued a further directive to the services which finally ranked the attack on Holland equal to those on Belgium and France:

> In variation of the earlier directive, all measures planned against *Holland* are authorized to commence simultaneously with the beginning of the general offensive, without special orders to that effect. The reaction of the Dutch forces cannot be estimated in advance. Where no opposition is encountered, the invasion is to be given the character of a peaceful occupation.

According to the diary of a member of Jodl's staff, during a conference in the OKW's map room Hitler expressed the opinion that "the planned attack in the west would lead to the biggest victory in the history of the world."

In the east, meanwhile, the "devil's work" was well in hand. Gruesome reports of massacre and persecution began to filter up through army channels. Not all of them reached Hitler, since Brauchitsch had in September tacitly agreed that Heydrich should have free rein for his spe-

---

[4] This was an argument of some force. Who later questioned the various Allied encroachments on neutral nations: the planned invasions of Norway and Eire in 1940 (see below) and the actual occupation of Iceland that same year?

cial tasks; for Brauchitsch to have protested now would have been hypocritical, and besides, his row with Hitler on November 5 had made him
reluctant to set foot in the Chancellery again. But consciences had to be
salved, and the reports were dutifully shuttled about between the adjutants. Thus, soon after the Munich plot, Captain Engel received from
Brauchitsch's adjutant a grisly set of eyewitness accounts of executions
by the SS at Schwetz. An outspoken medical officer addressed to Hitler
in person a report summarizing the eyewitness evidence of three of his
men:

> Together with about 150 fellow soldiers they witnessed the summary
> execution of about 20 or 30 Poles at the Jewish cemetery at Schwetz
> at about 9:30 A.M. on Sunday, October 8. The execution was carried
> out by a detachment consisting of an SS man, two men in old blue
> police uniforms, and a man in plain clothes. An SS major was in com-
> mand. Among those executed were also 5 or 6 *children aged from
> two to eight years old.*

Whether Engel showed this document and its attached eyewitness accounts to Hitler is uncertain. He returned it to Brauchitsch's adjutant almost immediately with a note: "The appropriate action to be taken at
this end will be discussed orally." Apparently he asked Himmler to investigate the executions. A few days later, however, Brauchitsch's adjutant submitted a further report, this time by General Blaskowitz, the
military commander in the east, protesting at the wave of illegal executions. Engel later recorded: "I showed this report, which is absolutely
objective in tone, to the Führer that same afternoon. He took note of it
calmly enough at first but then began another long tirade of abuse at the
'childish ideas' prevalent in the army's leadership; you cannot fight wars
with the methods of the Salvation Army."

If Hitler still regretted having kindled this holocaust, it was not because of the horrors that were beginning to spread like a medieval
plague across eastern Europe: they were inevitable byproducts of his
program, and he was more concerned to justify them inwardly than to
prevent them. What unsettled him was the unscheduled delay the war
would inflict on his grand plans for the reconstruction of Germany. On
nocturnal drives through the deserted, blacked-out streets of Berlin he
would mentally survey and supervise the architectural reshaping of the
city. One night he ordered his driver to stop outside the half-completed
"House of Tourism" near Potsdam Bridge and sadly commented that it
was a pity the war had to put a stop to so many of these fine building
projects throughout the Reich.

In the Reich Chancellery, the large table in the old Cabinet Room, where Bismarck's Berlin Congress had assembled, was now dominated by a huge relief map of the Ardennes—the mountainous, difficult region of Belgium and Luxemburg that was twice to be the scene of Hitler's unorthodox military strategy. The Chancellery cleaning women must have dusted around the contoured models of Belgium and Luxemburg without realizing the map's significance. Many an hour Hitler stood alone in the evenings, tracing the narrow mountain roads and asking himself again and again whether his tanks and mechanized divisions would be able to get through.

By now he had been provided with the original construction plans of the bridges across the Albert Canal; previously he had only aerial photographs and picture postcards of these important targets. The blueprints showed where each demolition chamber had been built into the bridges and pinpointed each detonation fuse and bunker. From other sources he had similar details on the toughness of the concrete and armorplate of the fortress at Eben Emael. Belgian deserters proved particularly useful. A scale model of the fortress had been built, and intensive training of the glider crews had begun under top security conditions.

The bridges, and particularly those in the Dutch town of Maastricht, presented the most intractable problem, the more so since the Dutch had evidently been warned by anti-Nazi agents in Berlin and even alerted to the date originally set for the attack, for on November 12 extensive security precautions had suddenly been introduced at the Maastricht bridges.[5] Had the Abwehr's four hundred special duties agents infiltrated the border in Dutch uniforms, they would have been slaughtered. Hitler discussed the operations with Canaris and his chief of sabotage operations, Colonel Erwin Lahousen, on November 16; but he did not believe they would capture the bridges over the Albert Canal by surprise alone, and he began casting around for other means of preventing the bridges' destruction. Though he asked to meet the two Abwehr officers who would lead the clandestine operation, he also reflected that should the bridges be blown the most urgent need would be to displace the army's mechanized units from the northern to the southern wing, for it was in this thrust through the Ardennes that the main chance lay. The British and French were expecting Hitler to attack through Holland, so

[5] Colonel Hans Oster, Canaris's Chief of Staff in the Abwehr, had himself warned the Belgian and Dutch legations that Hitler planned to attack on November 12. The uniform scheme was not mentioned.

Oster had been cashiered from the Reichswehr over a morals scandal in 1934 and immediately conscripted into the Abwehr by Canaris. Both men were hanged in April 1945.

all their best units were in the north. He ordered a full-scale secret conference on the bridges plan, starting at 3 P.M. on November 20, and directed that Brauchitsch should come too.

General von Reichenau made it clear from the outset that since the invasion of Holland had already been compromised once, he had no faith in the Abwehr's "Trojan horse" plan. The "Dutch policemen" must not cross the frontier before the glider operations had begun. Since the Dutch authorities were now expecting the police uniforms to be used, as was shown by the fact that they had issued special armbands to their police, there was little prospect of the Abwehr getting away with it. Hitler replied, "Then the entire operation as at present planned is pointless!" Canaris did what he could to salvage the plan (according to Lahousen, he lied) by suggesting that the Dutch were still in the dark, as the Munster agent who had been arrested had not himself known the purpose of the uniform purchases. Hitler was unconvinced. "None of the plans is *bound* to succeed." But after they had surveyed the large relief map and all the other possibilities had been scrutinized—including attacking the bridges with light bombs to destroy the demolition cables, and rushing them with tanks and 88-millimeter guns[6]—he had to fall back on the Trojan horse. "There must be some means of getting these bridges into our hands," he complained. "We have managed to solve even bigger problems before."

When the conference ended four hours later, Hitler had provisionally adopted the sequence proposed by Göring: at X-hour proper, fifteen minutes before dawn, the gliders would land silently on the fortress at Eben Emael and the bridge at Canne; five minutes later dive-bombers would attack the other Albert Canal bridges to disrupt the demolition charges; the bombers would be followed five minutes later by the arrival of more glider-borne troops just east of the bridges themselves. At the same time the Abwehr's disguised advanced party would seize the Maastricht bridges; for this they would have to cross the frontier in Dutch uniform forty-five minutes before X-hour. Within the first hour after X, it was hoped, the tanks and artillery of the Sixth Army would be close enough to relieve them. A special liaison officer with the army would at once radio back to Hitler's staff a report on the fate of the bridges, for on this would depend the course of the rest of the campaign.

The weather was still against "Yellow." Each day the Luftwaffe's chief meteorologist was consulted on the long-term forecast. Göring, indeed, expended large sums on a charlatan who claimed to have developed an electronic machine capable of influencing the weather. (It

[6] "If it can't be accomplished by trickery," Hitler said, "then brute force must do."

proved on investigation to be a broken radio.) General Halder, ignoring the fact that the Führer had never consulted horoscopes, unrealistically proposed bribing Hitler's soothsayer, since he no longer heeded his generals' prophecies of doom. (When Hitler later learned the role astrology had played in persuading his own deputy, Rudolf Hess, to fly to the enemy he clamped down on astrologers in general.)

Every morning, Berlin was in the grip of icy frost and fog, which lifted in the afternoons to let a weak sun filter through. On November 21 the Führer issued surprise orders for his leading generals and admirals to hear an exposure of his views two days later. Had not Frederick the Great summoned his defeatist generals to just such a talk before the battle of Leuthen? To the large audience that packed the Great Hall of the Chancellery at noon on the twenty-third Hitler depicted the coming battle as the operation that would finally ring down the curtain on the world war that Germany had been fighting ever since 1914. He repeated the compelling arguments for early action that he had first marshaled in his October memorandum. He recited the many occasions since having first decided on the arduous life of a politician in 1919, when aided only by Providence he had ignored the grim prophecies of others to exploit the brief opportunities that opened to him. How many opportunities the politicians and generals had lost in the years since Moltke's death in 1891! At that time, too, the generals had claimed that they were unready.

He, Adolf Hitler, had now provided the generals with a strategic situation unparalleled since 1871. "For the first time in history we have only to fight on one front. The other is at present open. But nobody can be certain how long it will remain so." His own indispensability had been forcefully impressed on him by the recent assassination attempt; that there would be other attempts was probable, for what the enemy called a fight against "Hitlerism" was, he warned, nothing less than a war against the presence of any powerful, determined government in Germany. In the same degree the immediate future depended on the lifespans of Mussolini and Stalin, for if the Duce died, the basically hostile monarchy would convert Italy's imperialist strategy into a fundamentally anti-German one; and if the Russian dictator died, the treaty with Russia might become worthless. Thus there was no time to be lost. This was why the defensive strategy his cowardly army generals were calling for was shortsighted; had Moltke in his studies of 1871 and after proposed defensive strategies? On the contrary, Moltke had clearly shown that only through offensives could wars be decided. Germany's present enemies were weak and unready: here, he illustrated his point

by listing in turn the number of French tanks and guns, and British
ships. The United States might on the other hand prove dangerous in
one or two years' time. He was convinced that Italy would join in as
soon as Germany made the first move against France, just as Russia had
waited before joining in against Poland.

His speech bristled with concealed barbs against the army generals.[7]
While he praised the "aggressive spirit" of the navy and Luftwaffe, in an
evident reference to Brauchitsch, he sneered: "If our commanders in
chief are going to have nervous breakdowns as in 1914, what can we
ask of our simple riflemen?" He had been "deeply wounded" by suggestions that the German army was inferior insofar as infantry was concerned, and that the officers had had to precede their men into battle,
with consequently disproportionately high officer losses. He dismissed
this curtly. "That is what the officers are there for." He recalled how in
1914 after months of training the infantry attack on Liège had broken
up in panic and disaster; nothing like that had happened in the Polish
campaign. "I will not hear of complaints that the army is not in shape.
It is all a matter of military leadership. Give the German soldier proper
leadership and I can do anything with him."

It was not as though Germany had a real choice between armistice
and war. The West wanted war, Hitler said, therefore Germany must
fight on until victory. A more tortuous argument he deployed was that
since the German people had already sacrificed so much to rebuild the
Wehrmacht, it would be irresponsible not to make the fullest use of it
now. "People will accuse me: war and yet more war! But I regard
fighting as the fate of all the species. Nobody can opt out of the struggle,
unless he wants to succumb." He had spent his whole life preparing for
this fight. A few minutes later he said, "Victory or defeat! And it is not
a matter of the future of National Socialist Germany, but of who will
dominate Europe in years to come. For this it is *worth* making a supreme effort." In a dark reference to conspirators, Hitler warned that
wars could not be ended except by destroying the enemy. "Anybody
who thinks differently is irresponsible." He believed the present favorable strategic situation would last perhaps six more months, but then the
British troops, "a tenacious enemy," would vastly strengthen their foothold in France, and "Yellow" would be a different proposition altogether.

"My own life is of no importance," he concluded. "I have led the

---

[7] Rommel wrote the next day: "The Führer spoke very bluntly. But that seems quite necessary,
too, because the more I speak with my comrades the fewer I find with their heart and conviction
in what they are doing. It is all very depressing."

German people to great achievements even if we are now an object of hatred in the outside world." His was the choice between victory or annihilation. "I have chosen victory." If he had to die, he would do so honorably, because he did not propose to survive the defeat of his country. Germany would neither capitulate to the enemy nor dissolve in internal revolution.

The speech lasted two hours. Afterward, Hitler instructed his principal generals and admirals to join him in his study. According to one of them, Hitler explained that he realized it was unusual for the supreme commander to explain his decisions and orders to his subordinates. He had made this exception because he had detected the negative mood prevailing among the generals. He ended this little speech with the words: "This will be the last war Germany fights against France, because I am going to smash France to smithereens. I can clearly see that coming, with my prophetic eye." Then he shook each of them by the hand and released them from the Chancellery.

General von Brauchitsch reappeared in the evening and stiffly informed the Führer that if he had no confidence in him he ought to replace him. Hitler retorted that the general must do his duty like every other soldier; he was not oblivious to "the spirit of Zossen" prevailing in the army, and he would stamp it out. Zossen was the headquarters of the General Staff and seat of the conservative and conspiratorial elements of the German army.

Clearing the Decks

Whether or not Hitler's often expressed fears that time was working against Germany were a purely tactical device to spur his wary generals is uncertain. Until the spring of 1940, although delay after delay postponed the launching date of "Yellow"—his campaign in the west—time certainly worked in his favor: lifeblood was being pumped into his armies massing in the west far faster than the enemy could strengthen their own forces. Indeed, Hitler not only had time to remold the strategy of his campaign—he now prepared and sent an expedition to Scandinavia. This was something he had not even been contemplating in the autumn of 1939. True, the Wehrmacht had not yet reached that peak of perfection he had hoped to attain by 1944, but he was sure that this was to be only a short war; the armies that had defeated Poland would carve up France with equal facility. It was also true that there was no popular, jingoistic support for this war: on the very first day of the Polish campaign Dr. Goebbels had come to the Chancellery with a fast public-opinion poll his agencies had just conducted in Berlin; sitting on a table, dangling his legs, the propaganda minister had complacently revealed a complete lack of enthusiasm or patriotic exuberance among the Berliners—they were resigned to the coming of fresh tribulations, but it would not be a popular war, he told the Führer.

Hitler knew that his pact with Stalin was misunderstood. In his November 1939 speech to the generals he had laid bare his own suspicions about Stalin. "Russia is *at present* harmless," he assured them—and more than one of them noted the emphasis he laid on "*at present.*" Pacts were respected only until they no longer served a purpose. "Russia will abide by the pact only as long as she considers it to her advantage." Stalin had far-reaching goals, and among them were the strengthening of Russia's position in the Baltic—which Germany could only oppose once she was unencumbered in the west—the expansion of Russian influence in the Balkans, and a drive toward the Persian Gulf. It was the aim of German foreign policy that Russia should be deflected toward the Persian Gulf, as this would bring her into conflict with Britain; but she must be kept out of the Balkans. Hitler hoped the present situation between Germany and Russia would prevail for two or three more years, but if Stalin were to die, there might be a rapid and ugly *volte face* in the Kremlin. There was clear evidence of a Russian military buildup that could be unleashed against Germany. Blaskowitz reported from Poland that four military airfields were being built, and two to three hundred Russian bombers had been counted, around Bialystok. In addition, wrote Blaskowitz, Russian propaganda was making plain that this was nothing less than a war against fascism: "Germany is said [in the USSR] to be planning an attack on Russia as soon as she is victorious in the west. Therefore Russia must be on guard and exploit Germany's weakness at the right moment." Blaskowitz described Russian infantry as poor, but the armored troops were considered good (if badly equipped), and the general's command had clearly identified Russian espionage and Communist subversive activity behind German lines in Poland. Moreover, he reported, the Russians were doing all they could to help the Poles establish a Polish Legion in France. In short, Hitler must conclude that war with Russia was inevitable—and that victory would go to the side which was ready first.

To strengthen her position in the Baltic, Russia now made of Finland demands similar to those she had successfully pressed against the three other Baltic states two months before. When Finland snubbed the Russians, the Red Army attacked on the last day of November 1939; Hitler was extremely embarrassed vis-à-vis his Italian ally, who was unaware that Finland had been abandoned to Soviet influence in a secret codicil to the August pact with Stalin. Russia had justified her demands on Finland as necessary to safeguard her communications to the far north and the Baltic approaches to Leningrad; but who could menace those communications if not Germany? Berlin regarded the invasion of Finland as a further token of Stalin's mistrust of Hitler. But even though German sympathy was solidly for Finland, Hitler instructed his foreign missions to adhere to an anti-Finnish line, for the integrity of his brittle pact with Stalin was to be his most powerful weapon in the attack on France. This loyalty to Stalin further tarnished Hitler's image with his allies, for Mussolini openly supplied Finland with arms and recalled his ambassador from Moscow. The Kremlin's gratitude to Hitler was expressed in a November revolutionary Comintern proclamation which lumped Germany with the other capitalist plunderers and not inaccurately predicted that once victory in the west had become clear for one side or the other, Italy would join in like a battlefield hyena.

But the Finnish war thrust the Russians further into Hitler's arms. They needed military supplies and aid. The Führer even agreed to a Russian request for the transfer of fuel and provisions from German steamships to Soviet submarines blockading Finland. (This did not prevent the Russians from torpedoing a German vessel steaming out of a Finnish port a few days later; the survivors were abandoned to their fate.)

Soviet compliance was the economic key to Hitler's continued warmaking capacity. Under the economic treaty signed between the two powers on August 19, Russia was to supply Germany with such raw materials as grain, oil cake, phosphates, platinum, and petroleum; it was also to act as a safe channel to Germany for goods exported by Japan, Manchuria, Afghanistan, Iran, and Romania but subject to British naval blockade. The Soviet Union imported rubber and zinc from Britain and cotton from the United States and immediately re-exported them to Germany. Hitler also needed the oil produced in Russia and Soviet-occupied Poland (where two-thirds of Poland's oil resources were located), and he knew that Stalin could exert pressure to control the supply of Romanian oil to Germany. It thus behooved him to behave like a proverbial friend in need; and throughout the winter he was a Soviet friend indeed as he instructed his military and economic authorities to do their utmost to meet the Russian demands. An additional trade treaty with the USSR was signed in December, and this was supplemented by a far-reaching commercial agreement in Moscow on February 11, 1940.

Russia's list of requirements was not easy to fulfill. The Russians wanted the half-built cruiser *Lützow* and the aircraft carrier *Graf Zeppelin;* they also wanted the blueprints of these and even more up-to-date German warships including the *Bismarck* and the *Tirpitz.* They asked for sets of the heaviest ship's armament, and for the 57,000 blueprints prepared for the new Krupp 406-millimeter triple-turret guns, the fire-control sets, and the ammunition that went with them. The Soviet navy wanted samples of accumulators and periscopes for submarines, they wanted a supply of top-grade German armorplate for a cruiser to be built in Russia, and they wanted hydroacoustical gear, torpedoes, and mines as well. The German air force was to supply the Soviet Union with prototypes of its most modern equipment—fighters and bombers, high-performance aircraft engines, antiaircraft artillery, control gear, and bombs. The army was to hand over field artillery, samples of modern explosives, tanks, engineer corps equipment, radio gear, and chemicals. Hitler sided with Ribbentrop and urged on his service commanders complete acceptance of almost all these demands. Such delays in delivery as he did propose were clearly the result of his country's own pressing arms requirements and shortages of raw materials, rather than of any ulterior plotting for the future. During negotiation for the commercial agreement, he told Keitel he wanted it signed as rapidly as possible. He told Raeder that his only anxiety in handing over the blueprints of the battleship *Bismarck* to the Russians was that these revealed that the vessel had been planned on a far larger scale than was permitted by the international agreements binding on Germany at the time. Raeder assured him it would take the Russians six years to copy the *Bismarck;* however, he conceded that it would be unfortunate if the blueprints fell into British hands.

Hitler attentively followed the course of the Russian invasion of Finland. He had been alerted by the navy to the danger that the Soviet attack might bring the western powers to Finland's aid. Such a course of action would give the Allies a foothold in Scandinavia, and this would have immense consequences for Germany. For the first time, the strategic importance of Norway was forcibly brought home to Hitler.

So far, he had assigned his navy a largely passive role in the war. Raeder's small force had supported the land operations against Poland in a modest way, while the pocket battleships *Admiral Graf Spee* and *Deutschland* dispatched in August into the south and north Atlantics, respectively, had for many weeks lain low in remote waters to avoid incidents. Hitler initially forbade his submarines to attack even Anglo-French naval forces, but as the enemy's attitude hardened toward Germany he gradually stripped away these irksome restrictions until eventually all-out and unrestricted submarine warfare was the order of the day. Raeder's navy was vastly inferior to the combined Anglo-French force. Its major expansion plan had been due for completion in 1944; Raeder had canceled that and made his production capacity available for submarine and surface vessel construction. During the first year of the war, the German navy had on average only a dozen submarines with which to blockade the British Isles. Since the Luftwaffe was given priority in raw materials, the navy's steadily reduced steel allocation further limited its expansion.

In one respect, however, Raeder had an advantage over Brauchitsch and Göring: he had discouraged Hitler from interfering with naval strategy and operations, and within the broad directives which the Führer now began to issue, the navy had a free hand to dispose of its fleet as it thought best. To Hitler the sea was an unwholesome element, an area of uncertainty he did not understand, and he was relieved to trust Grand Admiral Raeder to act as he saw fit. Raeder in turn committed his crews wholeheartedly to the war effort, with none of the carping that characterized the army generals. His destroyers executed bold sorties into the very jaws of the enemy, laying magnetic minefields in the estuaries of the principal British rivers. A U-boat sank the aircraft carrier *Courageous;* another U-boat penetrated Scapa Flow and torpedoed the battleship *Royal Oak.* Toward the end of November, the German fleet attacked the British northern patrol and sank the ill-armed merchant cruiser *Rawalpindi.* Hitler had a faulty understanding of the strategy of cruiser warfare and of the long-term benefits to be drawn from such costly fleet operations, but the sinking of the *Royal Oak* by Lieutenant Guenther Prien brought scenes of wild enthusiasm to the streets of Berlin for the first time. The Führer saw the huge crowds that packed the Wilhelmstrasse when he invited Prien's crew to the Chancellery, and this was a language he understood.

In the South Atlantic the *Graf Spee* had now begun raiding enemy convoys, but the Luftwaffe—and Göring particularly—wanted to bring the war closer to Britain's shores: when on November 28, in reprisal for the German mining of the coastal waters, Britain issued an Order-in-Council blockading Germany's export shipments, Raeder advised Hitler the British order was a triple violation of the Paris Declaration of 1856. Göring and his deputy, General Erhard Milch, hurried to Hitler that same afternoon with proposals for a crushing Luftwaffe offensive against British shipyards, docks, and ports. It was suggested that the Luftwaffe attack shipping west of Britain, while the German navy dealt with the shipping off the east coast. Hitler turned down the Luftwaffe's idea, but he did issue a new directive specifying that the best way to defeat Britain would be to paralyze her trade. The German navy and the Luftwaffe were to turn to this task, in conjunction with the more tenebrous forces of German sabotage and fifth-column organizations, as soon as "Yellow" had been successfully completed. Since Hitler would then control the Channel coast, the Luftwaffe really could attack on the lines Göring had proposed.

Afraid lest Britain secure a foothold in northern Norway, in December 1939 Hitler issued the first secret instructions for a German operation against Norway to be studied. In October,[1] Raeder had left him in no doubt as to Germany's grim strategic position should the British occupy Norway: in winter all Germany's Swedish iron-ore requirements passed through the ice-free port at Narvik; German merchant ships and warships would no longer be able to traverse the neutral Norwegian waters; the British air force could dominate northern Germany from Norwegian bases; and the Royal Navy would command the Baltic. Though he had realistically advised Hitler that a Norwegian campaign might end in a massacre of the German fleet, Raeder saw no alternative to such a campaign if the strategic dangers inherent in a British occupation of Norway were to be obviated.

Raeder's view took Hitler by surprise. His own strategy had always envisaged respecting and preserving Norway's neutrality, but neither his political nor his naval advisers gave him respite once the Russo-Finnish war broke out. At noon on December 11, Alfred Rosenberg, head of the Party's foreign policy department, briefed Hitler on an idea that had originated with one of his Norwegian contacts: the Norwegian would use his organization to create disturbances in Norway, and he would then appeal to the German forces to occupy key Norwegian bases.

In the event, a different plan was adopted, but room was still found in it for Rosenberg's contact man—Major Vidkun Quisling. Quisling had been Norway's defense minister until 1933, after which he had founded his own party, the anti-Jewish Nasjonal Samling. He was a convinced anti-Communist. After World War I he had for many years been a military attaché in Moscow, and had afterward come to regard bolshevism as the greatest danger confronting Europe and, more immediately, Scandinavia. He now dreamt of a common alliance of the Germanic peoples, and he was concerned about anti-German sentiments provoked in Norway by Germany's acquiescence in the Russian assault on Finland. Rosenberg told Hitler that Quisling's idea was that Germany should invade Norway at the request of a government he would himself set up. For once Ribbentrop and his state secretary, Weizsäcker, were unanimous in warning Hitler against even agreeing to see this Norwegian. But Quisling had hard evidence that Britain had designs on Norway. Hitler thought the matter over and the next day told Rosenberg he was willing to meet Quisling and form a personal impression of him. Quisling

[1] See page 39 above.

brought the Norwegian businessman Viljam Hagelin with him. "In this conversation," Rosenberg's office recorded, "the Führer repeatedly emphasized that what he most preferred politically would be for Norway and, for that matter, all Scandinavia to remain absolutely neutral. He had no intention of enlarging the theaters of war by dragging still more countries into the conflict. But if the other side was planning such an enlargement of the war with the object of forcing a further constriction and threat upon the German Reich, then he must obviously feel compelled to take steps against the move. In an effort to offset the increasing enemy propaganda activity, the Führer then promised Quisling financial aid for his Pan-Germanic movement." Quisling had claimed that the Norwegian press was under British control and that Carl Hambro—the Jewish president of the Norwegian Storting, or parliament—had allowed the British secret service to infiltrate Norway's Intelligence service (of which he was also head) from stem to stern. Quisling said he had two hundred thousand followers, many in key positions in Norway. Since constitutionally the Hambro government—which had prolonged its tenure—would be in office illegally as of January 10, Quisling suggested that his movement overthrow it after that date and then appeal to Hitler to move troops into Oslo.

Hitler was not convinced that Quisling's following was so large, and he privately asked the OKW to draft two alternative operations, one following Quisling's suggestions, but the other projecting an occupation of Norway by force. Through foreign ministry channels, Hitler initiated inquiries into Quisling's background. The replies were not wholly satisfactory, and Hitler shortly decided *not* to rely on him for any assistance beyond the kind of subversive operations that Konrad Henlein, the Sudeten German leader, had undertaken within Czechoslovakia in 1938. Before they returned to Oslo, Quisling and Hagelin met Hewel and Schmundt, who instructed them to commence operations designed to cause economic unrest in Norway by ruining the country's shipping, foreign trade, and fisheries industries. A number of handpicked Norwegians would undergo secret guerrilla-warfare training in Germany; when Norway was invaded, they were to seize key buildings in Oslo and elsewhere, and thus present the king with a *fait accompli*. The military details of the invasion would be drawn up by a special OKW study group. No date for the operation was set.

Though Admiral Raeder had not raised the related problem of Denmark, which lay across the access route to Norway, Hitler was without compunction in ordering this little country to be occupied at the same time as Norway. He had signed a nonaggression treaty with Denmark as recently as August.

The General Staff continued their open hostility to Hitler. After his unequivocal speech to the generals in the Chancellery on November 23, General Guderian privately taxed Hitler with his astonishing attitude toward the leaders of an army that had just won such a victory for him in Poland. Hitler retorted that it was the army's Commander in Chief himself who displeased him, adding with an expression of extreme distaste that there was unfortunately no suitable replacement for the general. Brauchitsch's chief of Intelligence noted: "There is as little contact between Br. and the Führer as ever. A changeover is planned."

When Jodl toured the western front and returned to Berlin on December 12, he confirmed that the military airfields in the west were largely waterlogged. Hitler postponed a decision on "Yellow" until after Christmas so that his troops could get some leave. He suspected the hand of the General Staff against him everywhere. When the *Deutsche Allgemeine Zeitung* published a sensational and sloppy article on the "Great Headquarters," Hitler was furious at an implicit suggestion that history was being made by the General Staff and not himself; Keitel was obliged to admonish Halder on that score. But the Führer was hard to please, for when at Christmas the *Essener National-Zeitung* ventured a seasonal comparison between Adolf Hitler and the Messiah, Goebbels confidentially informed the entire German press that the Führer would prefer them to abstain from such comparisons in the future. Through Colonel Schmundt Hitler also arranged for the suppression of General von Rabenau's biography of General Hans von Seeckt—Brauchitsch's great predecessor. It was in Seeckt's own interest, as Hitler put it. He exercised this personal censorship with increasing arbitrariness: when—evidently from telephone-tapping reports—he learned that the editor of the General Staff's *Military Weekly* had privately questioned the veracity of the OKW war communiqués, he demanded the general's immediate resignation. As a military commander, however, Hitler was still only flexing his muscles.

Indeed, in moments of military crisis, Hitler was to display an indecisiveness and lack of precision that was otherwise wholly out of character. This contributed to the loss of the *Graf Spee*.

On December 13 the pocket battleship fell foul of three British cruisers off the coast of neutral Uruguay. During the following night a series of disjointed radio messages reached Berlin. The first read: "Action with *Exeter, Ajax,* and *Achilles.* Damaged *Exeter* and light cruiser." Five hours later, the battleship signaled her attendant supply ship *Altmark:* "On your own." Obviously, things were not going well, but it was not until the small hours of the fourteenth that the first details reached the Berlin admiralty. "I have taken fifteen hits, food stores and galleys destroyed, I am making for Montevideo." To those familiar with the political stance of Uruguay it was clear the battleship's fighting days were probably over: the country had a pro-British president, a pro-French foreign minister, and a rich and powerful British embassy; it was also a hotbed of British secret service activity. *Graf Spee* could hardly have run for a more hostile haven. It would take many days for the damage to be repaired. The government at Montevideo granted only three days. Meanwhile British naval forces began to mass in uncertain strength at the mouth of the Plate River, waiting for the lame warship to leave the neutral waters.

At 1 P.M. on the sixteenth, Raeder arrived at the Chancellery with the latest cable from the battleship. Captain Hans Langsdorff had signaled:

1. Military situation off Montevideo: apart from cruisers and destroyers [there are also] *Ark Royal* and *Renown.* Tightly blocked at night. No prospect of breakout into open sea or reaching home.
2. Propose emerging as far as neutral waters limit. Should it be possible to fight through to Buenos Aires using remaining ammunition, this will be attempted.
3. In event that breakout would result in certain destruction of *Spee* with no chance of damaging enemy, I request decision whether to scuttle despite inadequate depth of water? Estuary of the Plate? Or internment?
4. Please radio decision.

The German admiralty was puzzled: its Intelligence had—accurately, as we now know—ascertained from the radio emissions of the aircraft carrier *Ark Royal* and the battle cruiser *Renown* that both ships were still many days to the north of Montevideo; they could not arrive before the nineteenth. But Langsdorff's signal breathed despair.

Even before he read it, Hitler met Admiral Raeder at the door of his study with a demand that *Graf Spee* must attempt to break through to the open sea; if she must go down, at least she could take some of the enemy with her. He put a hand on the admiral's shoulder. "Herr Grossadmiral, I can well understand how you feel. Believe me, the fate of this ship and her crew is as painful to me as to you. But this is war, and when the need is there, one must know how to be harsh." But he followed this firm speech with an inexplicable act. Raeder showed him the admiralty's draft reply to Captain Langsdorff: *Graf Spee* was to stay at Montevideo as long as the authorities would allow; a "breakout" to Buenos Aires would be "approved," internment in Uruguay would not. "If scuttling, thoroughly destroy everything first." Although this reply was wholly out of keeping with Hitler's heroic demand, he nonetheless allowed Raeder to transmit it around the world to Montevideo at once. Hitler's naval adjutant was perplexed.

Hitler eagerly awaited the news of *Graf Spee*'s last battle. During the seventeenth, however, the stunning news arrived that the battleship had sailed out of Montevideo, discharged her crew onto a waiting steamer which had borne them safely to a friendly Buenos Aires, and then gently settled down onto the shallow bed of the river's estuary.[2] In a savage mood, that evening Hitler pondered the damage Langsdorff had done to Germany's fighting image. At three in the morning he ordered the official announcement of the battleship's loss altered to read: "Under these circumstances the Führer ordered Captain Langsdorff to destroy the ship by blowing her up." The neutral press appraised the episode with reserve and even respect; but Germany's enemies responded with shrieks of spiteful glee, and this exposed a further weakness in the Führer—his inability to accept misfortune with equanimity. He developed an aversion to cruiser warfare, with its doctrine of hit-and-run; out of this aversion grew a hostility toward the maturer officers of the German navy, which contrasted with his admiration of the dashing destroyer and submarine commanders. Langsdorff himself had been an officer on Jodl's staff; he had been given the *Graf Spee*, it transpired, almost as a cure for his chairbound attitudes. But the cure had apparently not worked—perhaps the injuries he had suffered when a shell hit the bridge earlier had affected the captain's judgment. He shot himself on reaching Buenos Aires.

When the *Deutschland*, sister ship of the ill-fated *Graf Spee*, returned to Germany, Hitler—fearful of the loss of prestige Germany would suffer should a "Deutschland" ever go under—ordered her renamed. *Spee*'s supply ship *Altmark*, laden with prisoners plucked from the decks of the battleship's victims, was ordered to return home to Germany.

---

[2] Her vital equipment was undestroyed, and some time later British Intelligence officers were able to examine her radar gear. Shortage of explosives was the probable reason for this.

Hermann Göring did what he could to use this incident to impugn the honor of the navy's big ships. His Luftwaffe's prestige was running high. With insignificant loss to the German fighter defenses, a marauding squadron of RAF bombers attacking Wilhelmshaven in broad daylight on the eighteenth was virtually wiped out. The British realized their attempts at visual daylight bombing raids were fraught with perils and decided to convert to a night-bomber force.

Hitler left Berlin for a brief respite at the Berghof. Passing through Munich, he paid his annual Christmas visit to his friends and patrons, the Bruckmanns; without Else Bruckmann's salon twenty years before, he might never have got this far. He stayed two hours, chatting about his plans to conquer Britain, to force her to her knees over the next eight months by using magnetic mines and other fabulous weaponry. In private circles such as these, Hitler had no sense of security precautions but would happily ramble on about his future strategy, revealing all. Warsaw, he said, was a desolate heap of rubble thanks to the intransigence of its defenders. Only a small area was worth rebuilding. But when peace came, he would turn to the magnificent reconstruction of the new Reich—whose Nordic dimensions he hinted at in his entry in the Bruckmanns' guest book: "In the year of the fight for the creation of the great German-Teutonic Reich!"

For three days Hitler toured the western front, joining the Christmas celebrations of Luftwaffe squadrons, antiaircraft batteries, infantry, and SS regiments. It was clear that the French were not making any move to attack. In the autumn the army's cryptographers had broken the main French codes, and the ability to decode the flood of signals transmitted by the French war ministry more than compensated for the shortcomings of Canaris's Abwehr organization. The signals revealed that the French were having problems in manufacturing antitank weapons and in activating new units in the interior; the weakness of the French Ninth Army between Sedan and Mauberge was also evident. At Spichern, near Saarbrücken, the French had fallen back under local German pressure and Hitler was able to cross the French frontier for the first time since 1918. Here the famous frontier battles of 1870 had been fought.

On his return to Berlin, Hitler again postponed "Yellow," this time to mid-January. The long-range weather forecast predicted a period of cold, clear wintry weather for then; failing that, the Führer resolved, he would call off "Yellow" until the spring.

As in years past, he retreated to the Berghof to await the New Year. Here Eva Braun and her friends brought a relatively civilized touch to his surroundings, but the photographs in her albums show that even when the Führer sat faintly smiling at the delight of the offspring of Speer, Goebbels, and Martin Bormann at a Berghof children's party, he still wore the field-gray army tunic, with its solitary Iron Cross, that he had emotionally donned on the day his troops attacked Poland. In one photograph, however, Hitler is shown in somber evening dress, spooning molten lead into a bowl of water—a New Year's Eve tradition. Some believe that a man's future can be predicted from the contorted shapes the solidifying metal assumes. Hitler's face betrays a certain lack of confidence in this procedure.

At the Berghof he received a long, angry, and frightened letter from Benito Mussolini. It broke the months of silence which followed a mid-December speech in which Foreign Minister Ciano had revealed that Rome had not been consulted at the time of Hitler's pact with Stalin and that the Führer had broken promises given to the Italians about the imminence of war. Mussolini's letter marked the lowest point in Axis relations, which had been soured by Hitler's continued flirting with Moscow. As recently as December 22, Hitler had on Stalin's sixtieth birthday cabled him greetings coupled with his best wishes for the Soviet peoples; Stalin had cordially replied. In Mussolini's eyes Hitler was a traitor to the Fascist revolution; he had sacrificed the principles of that revolution to the tactical requirements of one given moment.

> You cannot abandon the anti-Semitic and anti-Bolshevist banners which you have flown for twenty years and for which so many of your comrades died; you cannot abjure your gospel, which the German people have blindly believed. . . . The solution for your *Lebensraum* is in Russia and nowhere else. Russia has twenty-one million square kilometers and nine inhabitants per square kilometer. It is outside Europe, in Asia—and this is not just some theory of Spengler's.

> Not until they, the Axis leaders, had jointly demolished bolshevism would they have kept faith with their revolutions. "It will then be the turn of the great democracies. . . ." wrote Mussolini.

In this letter—which Hitler deliberately left unanswered for two months —Mussolini also voiced concern about rumors reaching him on German treatment of the Poles. He proposed that Hitler should take steps to restore some kind of Polish state.

Hitler's policy in Poland had undergone a radical change in the autumn of 1939. Initially he had regarded a future "Polish state" as a bargaining counter against the western powers. But as the prospects of an armistice receded, his attitude hardened—although he lagged perceptibly behind the SS and Party in degree. Early in October he had indicated to Governor General Frank that the Generalgouvernement was to be a kind of Polish reservation, but in November he bluntly told Frank: "We are going to keep the Generalgouvernement. We will never give it back." Although Hitler's long-standing personal friend, Frank was only a verbose and pettifogging lawyer. He did not have the Führer's confidence to the inexplicable extent that SS Reichsführer Himmler had —and it was Himmler's SS and police agencies that wielded the *executive* power in German-occupied Poland.

Himmler's rule in the east derived its authority from an official commission granted to him by Hitler in September. Though the Reichsführer made much of it in his public and private speeches, this commission did not exist in writing, and its limits became increasingly ill-defined. Basically, Himmler's job was the Germanization of the new provinces of West Prussia and Posen. On this Hitler and Himmler agreed, but thereafter their opinions differed. Hitler saw no great urgency about the matter and had himself told Himmler: "I don't want these eastern Gauleiters in a frantic race to be the first to report to me after two or three years, 'Mein Führer, my Gau is fully Germanized.' I want the population to be racially flawless, and I'll be quite satisfied if a Gauleiter can report that in ten years." (In March, Hitler even told Mussolini that he expected it would take forty or fifty years to develop these regained provinces.) Himmler, however, wanted greater urgency. Acting on a cruel directive he had issued at the end of October, the two Gauleiters concerned—Forster and Greiser—and SS Generals Krüger and Odilo Globocnik, police commanders based in Cracow and Lublin, respectively, began the ruthless midwinter expulsion from their domains of the 550,000 Jews, the post-1919 Polish settlers, and the principal anti-German and intellectual elements; they used Frank's Generalgouvernement as a dumping ground.

Himmler gave them until February 1940 to complete the job. Long forced marches took a heavy toll of these unwanted human beings. Early in January, both Göring and Lammers took protests about this impossible state of affairs to Himmler and evidently to Hitler as well— but to no avail. Yet in some respects Hitler did act as a brake. From Himmler's scrawled notes on his private confrontations with the Führer we know that he was obliged to report in person on the "shooting of 380 Jews at Ostro" on November 19; and that when at the end of November the archbishop and suffragan bishop of Lublin were condemned to death along with 13 priests for the possession of arms and subversive literature, Hitler ordered their reprieve and deportation to Germany instead.

What Himmler did not include in his notes was the fact that Heydrich —blithely disregarding Frank's authority in the Generalgouvernement— had found his own ways of simplifying the midwinter population movements. In January 1940 he converted a remote camp at Soldau, near the East Prussian border, to a liquidation center for Poles who survived the day-to-day brutalities. A ripple of protest disturbed the German armies poised in the west to unleash "Yellow." Hitler learned that on January 22, Major General Friedrich Mieth, Chief of Staff of the First Army, had told his assembled officers about atrocities in Poland: "The SS has carried out mass executions without proper trials. There have been disturbances. There have been certain incidents between the SS and regular forces. . . . The SS has besmirched the Wehrmacht's honor." Mieth was dismissed. Soon after, the army's Commander in Chief East, General Johannes Blaskowitz, sent to Berlin a formal list of specific SS and police atrocities in Poland—including murder, looting, and general bestiality. He challenged the very basis of the occupation policies: "The view that the Polish people can be intimidated and kept down by terrorism will definitely be proven wrong. They are far too resilient a people for that." Blaskowitz added that the atrocities would provide the enemy with powerful ammunition throughout the world.

When Frank next came to the Reich Chancellery, he criticized Blaskowitz's unhelpful attitude. One of Hitler's adjutants wrote: "Reichsminister Frank . . . described the programs for the rounding-up and resettlement of the Jews. He bitterly attacked the army's Supreme Commander [Blaskowitz] and the field-administration officers. They are interfering with the work of 'pacification'; the officers 'have no instinct' and are getting in the way of his agencies. He asked the Führer to tell the army not to interfere, particularly in political matters, as it is flatly opposed to the Party line. The Führer had a fit of anger, which lasted until the war conference began."

The wording of this note, which talks of "resettlement," may mean that at this point the real fate of the Jews was being withheld from Hitler; he does, however, appear to have issued orders to Hans Frank for regular prophylactic massacres of the Polish intelligentsia, cruelly and cynically justifying this step as a security measure. The first two thousand Poles were to die as soon as "Yellow" began to cause sufficient diversion in the west. How else can Frank's confidential remarks at the end of May 1940 to his police authorities in Poland be interpreted? "The Führer has said to me, 'The problem of dealing with and safeguarding German interests in the Generalgouvernement is a matter for the men in charge of the Generalgouvernement and for them alone.' And he used these words: 'The ruling class that we have already unearthed in Poland is to be exterminated. We must keep close watch on whatever grows up in its place, and dispose of that too after a suitable time has elapsed.'" And Frank hastened to recommend to his minions: "There's no need for us to burden the Reich or its police bodies with all this. There's no need for us to cart off all these elements to concentration camps in the Reich first. That'll just result in a lot of bother and unnecessary correspondence with next-of-kin. No—we'll liquidate this business here, on the spot."

It was General von Brauchitsch who quelled the rumors along the western front. He of course had long ceased to cavil at the SS operations. Indeed, he arranged for Himmler to explain and justify them to the troubled army generals in the west, in a speech at Koblenz on March 13. When Blaskowitz submitted two further thick dossiers on SS atrocities in April, Berlin handled them as gingerly as nitroglycerine: Keitel refused to sign for their receipt; the Luftwaffe's General Milch locked his copy in a safe and threatened Blaskowitz's courier with arrest. Blaskowitz was relieved of his command in May, and when his successor wrote still more reports on the atrocities in Poland in July, Keitel abruptly instructed him to stop meddling in matters which did not concern him.

The directive issued by the Eighteenth Army on its transfer to Poland in August 1940 is an eloquent statement of the army's surrender to the Party. It forbids any criticism of the struggle being waged there against minorities, Jews, and the clergy. "For centuries an ethnological struggle has raged along our eastern frontier. To put an end to it once and for all has called for a short, sharp solution. Specific Party and government agencies have been put in charge of waging this ethnological war in the east. This is why our soldiers must keep their noses out of what these units are doing. We are not to make their job more difficult by criticizing them."

Under Party sponsorship, lawlessness flourished in the east. Hitler turned a blind eye on the excesses. An army major procured the arrest of eight Polish whores and did four of them clumsily to death in prison that evening; a fifth survived a bullet in the brain and escaped. Gauleiter

Forster made representations to Hitler against executing this major for one drunken offense and—contrary to the recommendations of Brauchitsch, Keitel, and Schmundt—Hitler commuted the sentence to a prison term. In another case, one of the innumerable young SA officers appointed magistrate in Poland ordered fifty-five Polish prisoners out of their cells and shot them all in a drunken orgy. Here too the local Gauleiter, Greiser, begged the ministry of justice not to blight the young officer's promising career, and Hitler—learning that the man had a clean Party record—granted him a reprieve. In later years, it fell to Hitler's naval adjutant, Karl-Jesko von Puttkamer, to brief him on the court-martial sentences requiring confirmation by him as Supreme Commander. A level-headed and incorruptible ex-destroyer commander, Puttkamer succeeded in influencing Hitler to the necessary degree so that what were considered the most deserving cases did not escape the firing squad or, sometimes, the hangman's rope.

Within Germany itself, Himmler's police agencies were now acting as a law unto themselves. When the first German citizen was summarily shot for refusing to work on a defense project, the Gestapo quieted all criticism by informing the ministry of justice that before leaving for the Polish front on September 3 the Führer had instructed Himmler to maintain order in the interior "as he saw fit." More executions followed, although Göring warned Heydrich that no Germans were to be executed without formal sentencing. At the end of September, the minister of justice submitted to Hitler a file on summary executions of Germans; Hitler replied that he had not given Himmler any *general* instruction but that he had ordered certain executions himself, as the regular military and civil courts were not adjusting themselves to the special war conditions. "This is why he has now ordered the Teltow bank robbers to be put before a firing squad," his staff explained. But the files also show that Hitler drew much of his information on civilian crime from casual references in the newspapers. A thoughtless editor had only to headline a story MAN SWINDLED SOLDIERS' WIVES for the Führer to send Schaub scurrying to a telephone with instructions that the modest prison sentence passed on the defendant was incomprehensible and that the Führer wanted the man to be shot.

Hitler's attitude to the Party's own courts was even more ambivalent, as his reaction to the trial of Julius Streicher showed. Streicher, the stocky, balding Gauleiter of Franconia, was an insensitive and rigid member of Hitler's "Old Guard" with an obsession against the Jews and accepted morality. His enemies were legion—the armed forces as a whole, Nuremberg's mayor and police president, and above all Rudolf

Hess and his bustling deputy Martin Bormann. Hitler saw in Streicher an idealist and a true revolutionary, but when the clamor against the Gauleiter reached its climax at the end of 1939 he yielded and permitted Streicher—one of the very few men allowed to address the Führer by the familiar *du*—to be put on trial by the Party's Supreme Court. The actual charges against him seem uncertain. Treason may have been among them; four days after Hitler's speech to the Gauleiters in October,[3] Streicher had revealed Hitler's military plans to local Party members in a speech, and he had repeated this imprudent step in a larger assembly a few days later. Speaking of Hitler's decision to invade neutral Belgium, Streicher had explained, "We need the coast for our attack on Britain." His recent speeches—of which the police president privately showed a dossier to the local military authorities—included blasphemous attacks on the clergy, libelous references to the generals of the Great War, and an address to a young female audience in November in which he exhorted them to find nothing improper in the desire to seduce married men. "Any woman or lady who gets worked up about this is in my eyes just a pig." According to Major Walther Buch, the Party's chief judge, Streicher was indicted for dishonest monetary dealings in the confiscation of Jewish property; for libeling Göring over the true paternity of his daughter Edda; for brutality and improper relations with a very young girl. Streicher himself said he was accused of having called war widows "silly geese," but was acquitted of this charge.

Whatever the charges, the Supreme Court—six Gauleiters and three Party judges—met in February and on the sixteenth decided on a verdict against Streicher. Hitler suspended Streicher from office and forbade him to make further public speeches; but he was not ejected from the Party, as Hess had demanded, and he was allowed to continue publishing his newspapers—including the despicable *Stürmer*. To Hitler the trial smacked of a kangaroo court, and he told other Party leaders like Ley that he felt an injustice had been done to Streicher: the legalists had paid too little attention to Streicher's Party record in the past. After all, Streicher had won Nuremberg, the stronghold of the Marxists, for the Nazi party just as Goebbels had won Berlin.

On January 6, 1940 the Führer had returned from Munich to Berlin.

Over the following days he submitted to a series of medical examinations by his corpulent physician, Dr. Theodor Morell—blood-serum and

[3] See page 44 above.

sedimentation-rate tests, urinalyses, and fecal examinations. The records of these have survived, and are unremarkable except that the urine was alkaline, as was to be expected of a vegetarian, and that a routine series of tests for syphilis all proved negative. Morell's heart examination on January 9 revealed a normal pulse and blood pressure for a man of Hitler's age, and there is as yet no reference to the rapidly progressive coronary sclerosis that seems to have first been detected in mid-1941.

"We Must Destroy Them, Too!"

An icy winter descended on Germany. The canals froze, the railways were clogged with military movements, population and industry alike were starved for coal and the most elementary daily requisites. These domestic worries Hitler transferred to the willing shoulders of Field Marshal Göring. He himself was concerned only with the coming offensive against France and the Low Countries. Day and night he talked and dreamed of "Yellow"—of how the armored divisions could best be employed, of how the bridges could be seized intact, of how the Dutch government could be persuaded not to fight back, and of how each operation should be devised to shed as little German blood as possible—a consideration that weighed less on him with each successive year. By Christmas 1939 he had already decided where the big hole was to be punched through the French defenses: at Sedan; and it was indeed at Sedan that the foundations of the Nazi triumph over France were laid.

It was now January 1940, and the Führer was back at his Chancellery in Berlin. He had heeded neither the entreaties of his generals, the admonitions of his diplomats, nor the anxious counsels of his vacillating Italian ally. The frightened letter Mussolini had written early in January proved how little Hitler could rely on Italy. Why else should the Italians offer to mediate with the West unless they intended to use Hitler's inevitable refusal as an alibi? A few days later Mussolini repeated the familiar complaint that Ribbentrop had in August 1939 promised Ciano that the West would stay out of the war; what was the point of such carping observations if Italy were not planning to welsh on her obligations when the time came?

It was indeed a curious alliance, for the *Forschungsamt,* Göring's remarkable telephone-tapping and codebreaking agency, now intercepted a coded telegram in which the Belgian ambassador in Rome reported to his foreign ministry in Brussels that Count Ciano had betrayed to him Germany's firm intention of attacking Belgium and had revealed the date currently set for that adventure. Since the records show that the Forschungsamt was reading the coded dispatches from the Italian embassy in Berlin to Ciano, Hitler must have known that the military attaché General Marras had supplied this information to Rome; at any rate, when Hitler later in the month proposed spreading *false* rumors about his new plans, Marras figured significantly among those with whom the rumors were to be planted!

Hitler assured Ambassador Bernardo Attolico, "1940 will bring us victory," but at the beginning of March, though Mussolini now made loyal noises, the Italians were still sitting uncomfortably on the fence. "The Italians are strange people," wrote Weizsäcker at that time. "Loyal glances toward us, so as to share in any success we may achieve. And gifts and minor acts of treachery for the West, so as to keep in their good books too."

Hitler was satisfied in his own mind that neither Belgium nor Holland would long maintain its strict neutrality. He was (wrongly) convinced that Brussels had long since reached secret agreement with London and Paris. Not surprisingly, Belgium had shifted her main defensive effort to her frontier with Germany, and the anti-German trend of all Belgian military preparations was highlighted by a secret report submitted by German army Intelligence in January 1940: Belgium had been fortified solely against Germany; fraternization was actively encouraged between Belgians and the French and British forces in the west; since mid-October, over two-thirds of all Belgium's forces were massed in the east, apparently oblivious of the growing Anglo-French concentration in the west; the Belgian gendarmerie had received instructions to speed any French invasion of the country, and while signposts in western Belgium had been replenished and improved to that end, those in the east had been wholly removed to hamper a German invasion. In the west, throughout November the Belgians had allegedly accumulated railway stock and convoys of trucks to aid the French. Mayors of Ardennes villages were ordered to prepare billets for French troops. Mufti-dressed French soldiers "on leave" were observed on the Belgian transport systems with uniforms in their suitcases. The fortifications at Liège and on the Albert Canal were far beyond the Belgian military capacity to defend—they had clearly been designed to accommodate French and British troops as well. One glance at an Intelligence map was enough to show that the Allies were preparing the left wing of their offensive through Belgian territory. "With the exception of one division, every single mechanized infantry, armored, and cavalry division is standing on the Belgian frontier." In short, Hitler saw no reason to have compunctions about attacking this "little neutral."

Hitler still frowned on the notion that he had unleashed a second World War. Later in January he was to authorize the navy to refer to the campaign from time to time as the "English war." For more general consumption, he decided that the best overall title was the "Great German War of Liberation." Neither term caught the public imagination—perhaps the public still hoped peace was just around the corner.

On the afternoon of January 10, the Führer discussed "Operation Yellow" with his commanders in chief. The weather report was excellent—for the next ten to fourteen days they could count on clear wintry weather in the west. He decided "Yellow" would begin fifteen minutes before dawn on the seventeenth, preceded perhaps by four or five days of saturation bombing attacks on French airfields and flying schools. As January 10 ended, Germany was closer to launching "Yellow" than ever before. Two million men waited with their tanks and guns confronting the armies of France, Belgium, and Holland.

Shortly before noon the next day, however, infuriating news reached the Chancellery. A Luftwaffe major carrying a suitcase of the most secret documents had strayed in a light aircraft across the Belgian frontier and crash-landed near Mechelen-sur-Meuse. Hitler stormed into Jodl's room and demanded a complete list of all the documents the major had been carrying. "It is things like this that can lose us the war!" he exclaimed—an outburst of startling frankness when spoken by the Führer. The major had contravened a direct embargo on flying with secret papers. Even now Hitler did not waver on his decision to launch "Yellow" on the seventeenth, and at 3:15 P.M. he confirmed this.

He also issued a drastic "Basic Order No. 1" on security—a regulation that was from now on to be displayed in every military headquarters as a wallposter—stipulating that nobody was to hear of any secret matter unless absolutely necessary and that then he was to be told no more, and no earlier, than necessary. "I forbid the thoughtless dissemination, just on the basis of some distribution list or other, of orders whose secrecy is of prime importance!" As a concrete restatement of general security principles the order was sound and admirable, but in later years Hitler came to wield it as a capital weapon in his tactic of *divide et impera:* soldiers should not interfere with diplomacy, nor diplomacy with the affairs of government; one army group commander was not to learn the orders and intentions of his neighboring army group. Only Adolf Hitler, as Führer and absolute commander, had the right to know it all.

Most of the Belgian newspapers reassuringly reported that the Luftwaffe major had managed to destroy all the papers he was carrying, but one journal (correctly as we now know) stated that same evening that this was not so: the German major had hurled the documents into a stove in the room where he was being interrogated; but a Belgian officer had thrust his hand into the stove and retrieved the smoldering fragments. On January 12, Jodl set out to Hitler the maximum the Belgians could deduce from the secret documents. If they had all fallen intact into enemy hands, then the situation was indeed serious. Later that day the attaché in Brussels cabled that the major and his pilot had assured him they had burned all the papers apart from an unimportant residue, and he repeated this in person to Hitler at the Chancellery at 11 A.M. on the thirteenth.

The Mechelen incident was not enough to deter Hitler from launching "Yellow." But shortly afterward a bad weather report—of warmer air coming from the northeast and resulting in periods of fog in the west— unsettled him, and at about one o'clock that afternoon he ordered all movements stopped. "Yellow" was provisionally postponed by three days to the twentieth. But the weather picture worsened. Hitler told his staff: "If we cannot count on at least eight days of fine and clear weather, then we will call it off until the spring." And on the afternoon of the sixteenth he directed that the whole offensive was to be dismantled until then, and that its reassembling was to be made on a new basis: that of security and surprise. He left Göring in no uncertainty about his anger at the Luftwaffe's loose security regulations, for two more incidents had occurred: in one, an officer had dropped a dispatch case out of a train, in the other a Luftflotte adjutant had lost a file of secret documents. Göring reacted characteristically: he dismissed both General Helmuth Felmy, the major's superior, and Felmy's Chief of Staff, and he then calmly informed Hitler that he had consulted a clairvoyant, who had also reassured him that the most important papers had been destroyed.

The Intelligence reports from Belgium gave this Delphic utterance the lie. Extensive mobilization was carried out in both Holland and Belgium late on the thirteenth. The Belgian General Staff ordered military units stationed in southern Belgium to offer no resistance whatever to French and British troops that might march in—indeed, the frontier barriers were to be taken down to speed their entry. Since the Forschungsamt was reading the Belgian codes, it is reasonable to assume that Hitler had by now also read the telegram sent by the Belgian military attaché in Berlin, Colonel Goethals, on the evening of January 13, warning that the German invasion was due next day, according to what an *"informateur sincère, de valeur discutable"* had told him.[1] By the morning of the seventeenth, it was clear from the official *démarches* of the Belgian government that the Mechelen documents had betrayed most of "Yellow" in its original form. Belgium and Holland now knew that Germany planned to disregard their neutrality and mount an airborne landing operation at Namur; fortunately for Hitler, the documents could not have compromised the delicate plan to seize the bridges across the Meuse and the Albert Canal.

In a sense Hitler must have been relieved that this Luftwaffe *bêtise* had forced a major decision on him. Besides, the enemy would now surely concentrate his best forces in the north to meet the new German "Schlieffen-style" attack; so the prospects of an encirclement operation beginning at Sedan and ending at the Channel coast were much enhanced. Everything depended on keeping this, his real intent, concealed from the enemy, and in a series of conferences at the end of January 1940 Hitler impressed this on his army commanders. As he said on the twentieth, he was convinced Germany would win the war, "but we are bound to lose it if we cannot learn how to keep our mouths shut." He ordered the preinvasion timetable to be overhauled in such a way that he need no longer decide on the date of the attack seven days in advance. He directed that paratroop units also be employed in the north, for he now wanted the whole of Holland occupied. When "Yellow" began, a foreign ministry official would be sent secretly to The Hague to invite the Dutch monarchy to accept the Wehrmacht's "armed defense of Dutch neutrality."[2] A constant state of alert was to be maintained in the west on the assumption that "Yellow" might start at any moment.

---

[1] Goethals sent further telegrams to Brussels on January 14, 15, and 17, 1940, indicating that his source was passing on to him Hitler's decisions with a time lag of about twenty-four hours; the source may have confused the beginning of "Yellow" with the preceding Luftwaffe strike, which was to take place on January 14 (later canceled). Goethals's source was his Dutch colleague, Major G. J. Sas, who saw him at about 5 P.M. on the thirteenth and told him that when Hitler had learned of the Mechelen incident he was furious. "He stormed about and ordered the immediate beginning of the offensive in the west, before the Allies could take countermeasures." Sas's source was a Colonel Hans Oster.

[2] Major Werner Kiewitz, who had carried Hitler's first surrender ultimatum to Warsaw on September 16 (see page 19), was selected for this mission. He was to persuade Queen Wilhelmina of the futility of opposing the German invasion. In the event, the Dutch were forewarned, and they refused to issue an entry visa to him; a desperate plan to parachute him into The Hague was abandoned, as by then the queen had escaped to England.

This placed an almost intolerable burden on the goodwill of the towns and villages on which the armies had been billeted since October. The army commanders reminded Hitler of the undesirable consequences for the local female residents, but he reflected that at present there was far more at stake.

At the end of January 1940, the Führer had sent his chief military adjutant on a flying tour of the western front. On his return to Berlin on February 1, Colonel Rudolf Schmundt was bursting to report what he had found at General von Rundstedt's army group headquarters at Koblenz. Rundstedt's former Chief of Staff, General Erich von Manstein, was as adamantly opposed to the current war department (OKH) offensive plan in the west as was Hitler; moreover, he was advocating a radical alternative almost identical to what Hitler had been debating with his closest staff ever since October—breaching the French lines at Sedan after crossing the awkward Ardennes region of southern Belgium and then pushing a strong armored force straight up to the Channel to cut off the British and French elite forces as they advanced into Belgium. When Hitler had toured the western front over Christmas, he had talked of little else to his adjutants. But while he had contemptuously referred to the war ministry plan as "the same old Schlieffen medicine as before," Hitler had not convinced himself to the extent of issuing a concrete order redisposing the armored divisions for the attack through the Ardennes.

Hitler's respect for General von Manstein's ability bordered on fear. That Manstein had independently had the same idea as he, convinced him of its soundness; and that the OKH bureaucrats had removed Manstein from his post with Rundstedt and given him command of a corps in the rear, impressed him even more. On February 13, Hitler told Jodl of his decision to commit the mass of his armor to the breakthrough at Sedan, where the enemy would now least expect it. Jodl urged caution. It was an "underhand approach"; the Gods of War might yet catch them napping there, for the French might launch a powerful flank attack. But now Hitler was deaf to criticism. On the seventeenth he buttonholed Manstein in person when the general attended a Chancellery dinner party for the new corps commanders. Manstein assured him that the new plan was the only means by which to obtain a total victory on land; everything else was just a half-measure. The next day Hitler sent for General von Brauchitsch and his Chief of Staff and after explaining the underlying strategy dictated the new operational plan to them. On February 24, the war department issued the new directive for "Yellow."

The eventual outstanding success of the new strategy—which has gone down in history not wholly unjustly as the Manstein Plan, for it was he who elaborated it in all the staff detail of which Hitler was incapable—convinced Hitler of his own military genius. Henceforth he readily mistook his astounding intuitive grasp for the sound, logical planning ability of a real warlord. His reluctance to heed his professional advisers was ever after magnified. He told one of his elder civil servants, experts should be on tap—not on top.

To undermine the French soldier's morale Hitler ordered German propaganda to hint that the real quarrel was with the British. Millions of rust-brown "autumn leaves" were released over the French lines, imprinted with Goebbels's famous message: *"Automne. Les feuilles tombent. Nous tomberons comme elles. Les feuilles meurent parce que Dieu le veut. Mais nous, nous tombons parce que les Anglais le veulent. Au printemps prochain personne ne se souviendra plus ni des feuilles mortes ni des poilus tués. La vie passera sur nos tombes."*[3]

But Hitler's true attitude toward Britain and France was the reverse of what this melancholy warning would seem to suggest. It was for the British that he had a maudlin, unrequited affection that caused him to pull his punches throughout 1940 to the exasperation of his strategic advisers. As Halder explained Hitler's program to the chief of army Intelligence late in January: "The Führer wants to win the war *militarily:* defeating France, then a grand gesture to Britain. He recognizes the need for the empire." During lunch at the Chancellery in these weeks of early 1940, Rudolf Hess once inquired, "Mein Führer, are your views about the British still the same?" Hitler gloomily sighed, "If only the British knew how *little* I ask of them!" How he liked to leaf through the glossy pages of *The Tatler,* studying the British aristocracy in their natural habitat! Once he was overheard to say, "Those are valuable specimens—those are the ones I am going to make peace with." And how he envied the ease with which the British got away with their "trickery and double-dealing!" The Chancellery dinner attended by Manstein and the other corps commanders fell on the day after the *Altmark* incident, in which the Royal Navy had coolly violated Norwegian neutral waters

---

[3] "Autumn. The leaves are dropping. We too will drop like them. The leaves die because God wills it. But we die because the British want it. Next spring nobody will remember either the dead leaves or the fallen French soldiers. Life will go on above our graves."

under circumstances to be explained below. Hitler could talk of little else and expounded loudly on the inherent *properness* of such actions—whatever the international lawyers might subsequently proclaim. History, he explained, judged only between success and failure; that was all that really counted—nobody asked the victor whether he was in the right or wrong.

Characteristically, nobody interrupted or contradicted Hitler. A general who was present later wrote: "Among his listeners sat Manstein, his face absolutely motionless. Some time before I had heard him make comments on the Nazi creed that were of an acerbity rare in army circles. Another general sat nodding sagely at each and every remark that Hitler made, like a mandarin toy with its head on a spring. The very astute General Schmidt listened with his head cocked attentively to one side." Rommel—who had been given an armored division a few days before—left the Chancellery clutching the copy of *Mein Kampf* Hitler had just given him. It was inscribed: "To General Rommel with fond memories, Adolf Hitler, February 3, 1940." Rommel wrote that afternoon: "I am enormously pleased with it."

The *Altmark* incident had revealed the frailty of the neutrality of a small country which falls foul of the interests of two great powers. The *Altmark* was the 15,000-ton German supply ship which had ministered to the needs of *Graf Spee* in the South Atlantic; since the action off the Uruguayan coast, she had lain low, her holds packed with three hundred British seamen captured from *Graf Spee*'s victims. Until mid-February 1940, the worried German admiralty had heard no sound from her, but on the fourteenth she signaled that she was about to enter northern Norwegian waters. In those waters she should be immune to enemy attack; under The Hague Rules she was entitled to passage through them, for she was not a man-of-war but a naval auxiliary flying the flag of the German merchant marine. Such defensive armament as she had boasted in the Atlantic was properly stowed away below. The Norwegian picket boats interrogated her; her captain denied the presence of any prisoners —the position in law would not have altered if he had admitted them—and the *Altmark* was allowed to proceed.

The Norwegians undertook to escort her, but in Berlin late on the sixteenth the admiralty began intercepting British naval signals which left no doubt but that an attempt was afoot to capture the *Altmark* even if it meant violating Norwegian neutral waters. By 6 A.M. next morning these fears were confirmed. A radio signal of the British commander to the admiralty in London had been decoded in Berlin: the British destroyer *Cossack* had been alongside the *Altmark,* and he and his group were returning to Rosyth. By midday a full report of this incident was in Hitler's hands, telephoned through by the legation in Oslo. Seeing the British force—a cruiser and six destroyers—closing in, the *Altmark*'s captain had sought refuge in Jøssing Fjord. Two Norwegian vessels had held the British ships at bay until dusk, when the *Cossack,* her searchlights blazing, had forced her way past them into the fjord and ordered the German ship to heave to. The *Altmark*'s report described how a boarding party had seized the ship's bridge "and began firing like blind maniacs into the German crew, who of course did not have a gun among them." Six men died, many more were injured. A handful of the crew fled across the ice which hemmed the vessel in, or they sprang into the water; the British boarders opened fire on these as well—an outrage to which the Norwegians also later testified. The three hundred prisoners were liberated, the ship and its crew were looted, and the *Cossack* withdrew. The Germans had not fired one shot.

Hitler did not have to await the official decoration of the *Cossack*'s captain with the Victoria Cross to know that this violation of Norwegian neutrality had the highest sanction in London. London had even signaled the captain the previous afternoon that the destroyers were to open fire on the Norwegian patrol boats if the latter resisted the British approach. These and other British signals were decoded by Berlin. The German naval staff war diary concluded: "From the orders of the admiralty and the steps taken by the British naval forces it is clear beyond a doubt that the operation against the supply vessel *Altmark* was premeditated and planned with the deliberate object of capturing the *Altmark* by whatever means available, or of releasing the prisoners, if necessary by violating Norway's territorial waters." Now if never before Hitler realized how real was the possibility that the Allies would use the Russo-Finnish war as a pretext for a full-scale invasion of Norway. He ordered that in the ensuing operation to recover the damaged *Altmark* Norway's neutrality was to be respected to the utmost; but his own resolve to violate it once and for all dated from this naval episode.

More than the wish to repair his prestige, injured by the *Altmark* affair —more even than the strategic need to occupy the Norwegian coast before the Allies could do so—there began to weigh with Hitler the belated consideration that since the Scandinavian peoples were also of Germanic stock they naturally belonged within the Nazi fold. There is no other explanation for his later persisting in his plan to occupy Norway, even after the initial pretext had gone.

It is important to recall that in none of his Wehrmacht directives or secret speeches to his generals had Hitler adumbrated the occupation of Scandinavia. Only after Quisling's visits in December 1939 had the Führer ordered Jodl's staff to study such a possibility, but he had sat on the resulting document for some weeks before forwarding it to the service commands on January 10. The OKW study recommended that a special working staff under a Luftwaffe general, with navy and army assistants, should devise a suitable operational plan. Assuming the code name "Oyster," this staff began work under General Erhard Milch a week later, but almost immediately Hitler ordered the unit dissolved and the OKW study withdrawn; he was not convinced that the Luftwaffe knew how to safeguard the secrecy of such planning. Instead, a top-secret unit was established within the OKW itself under Hitler's personal supervision; its senior officer was a navy captain, Theodor Krancke, and it was from the very scanty Intelligence material available that Krancke and his handful of army and Luftwaffe aides drafted the first blueprint for the campaign. He proposed simultaneous amphibious landings at seven Norwegian ports—Oslo, Kristiansand, Arendal, Stavanger, Bergen, Trondheim, and Narvik—the troops being carried northward by a fleet of fast warships; paratroops of the Seventh Air Division and waves of bombers and fighters would support the invasion. Diplomatic pressure on the Oslo government would do the rest.

Characteristically, Hitler consulted neither Brauchitsch nor Göring at this stage. The Luftwaffe's reluctance to coordinate its operations with the other services was notorious—indeed, its truculent and disastrous spirit of independence was borne out by the bombing and sinking of two German destroyers late in February with heavy loss of life. Göring refused to attach a Luftwaffe officer to Krancke's staff and remained in haughty ignorance of the Norwegian plan until early March. Hitler meanwhile accepted General Jodl's recommendation that the campaign preparations be put in the hands of an infantry general, Nikolaus von Falkenhorst, a fifty-five-year-old veteran of the 1918 German campaign in Finland; summoned to the Chancellery on February 21, Falkenhorst accepted the mission with alacrity and returned to the Chancellery on the twenty-ninth with a complete operational plan which now embraced not only Norway but Denmark as well, for the lines of communication between Germany and Norway had to be secured. Hitler had still not firmly decided whether the invasion was to be launched before, after, or even simultaneously with the attack on France and the Low Countries;

but since Jodl had recommended making the two theaters entirely independent of each other, that decision could be postponed.

On March 1, Hitler signed the directive for the occupation of Norway and Denmark. Daring and surprise were the essence of the campaign. The army at once protested the introduction of a new theater. Göring stormed into the Chancellery and refused to subordinate his squadrons to Falkenhorst's command (eventually General Milch commanded Luftwaffe operations "in consultation with" Falkenhorst). Only the navy committed itself body and soul to the campaign, which was just as well, since Raeder's fleet was to suffer dearly.

Hitler wanted the campaign launched *soon,* before the British and French could beat him to it. Hewel brought him telegram after telegram from Helsinki, Trondheim, and Oslo hinting at the Allied preparations to land in Scandinavia on the pretext of helping Finland. On March 4, Hitler orally ordered the service commands to speed up their planning; it was to be completed within six days so that the simultaneous landing operations, including northern Norway, could begin on the seventeenth. "Yellow" could then follow about three days later. Göring was still discontented, and when Falkenhorst reported progress on March 5, he expressed loud contempt for all the army's joint planning work so far; but to Hitler this was a strategic crisis transcending interservice rivalries.

The risk of an Allied intervention in Scandinavia was too great. Through Rosenberg, Hitler received from Quisling's men in Oslo urgent proof that the British and French invasion plans were far advanced: communications within Scotland, just twenty-four hours from the Norwegian coast, had been blacked out. Something was clearly afoot. At lunch on the sixth, Hitler leaned over to Rosenberg and said, "I read your note. Things are looking bad."

The crisis reached its blackest point on March 12, as a torrent of dispatches from Moscow and Helsinki revealed that armistice talks had begun. If the western powers wished to act, it had to be now; if there was no war in Finland, Britain and France would have no legitimate reason to land in Scandinavia. London began desperate attempts to keep the war alive a few more days. Winston Churchill had evidently flown to Paris on the eleventh to inform the French government that on March 15 his expeditionary force was to sail for Narvik, for at 3:30 P.M. on March 12 the Forschungsamt intercepted an urgent telephone call from the Finnish envoy in Paris to his foreign ministry in Helsinki. The envoy reported that Churchill and Daladier had promised him that if the Finns appealed for help immediately, British and French troops would be landed in Norway; the Norwegian government would merely be "notified" of this; Britain and France would then break off diplomatic relations with the Soviet Union at once. (Whether the Forschungsamt intercepted the actual date of the invasion is uncertain.) Thus the fat really was in the fire. Hitler ordered all German invasion plans accelerated, and the forces to stand by for the so-called *Immediate Op.* emergency. By next morning, however, the Russians had signed the armistice with Finland, and the immediate crisis was over.

The German admiralty's intercepts of coded British radio messages clearly indicated that the British and French had been on the very brink of a major landing in Norway. Destroyers had been attached to the British Commander in Chief Home Fleet, submarines stationed as a flank defense across the Skaggerak, and troop embarkation for an unspecified "Plan Three" completed. The fact that the troop transports had now been placed on extended sailing alert indicated that the Allies had only postponed their invasion and not canceled it altogether. German invasion preparations returned to a more leisurely pace; for the time being, Hitler withheld the executive order for the operation. "He is still searching for a sufficient reason," Jodl wrote in his diary. The true root of the Norwegian campaign was laid bare by Hitler in a remark to Rosenberg three weeks later, the day the amphibious operation began: "Just as Bismarck's Reich dates from the year 1866, so today has seen the birth of the Greater Germanic Reich."

We have seen how as Führer Hitler concerned himself not only with grand strategy—with all the chains of Intelligence combining only in his hands—but with the minutest interlocking elements of each operation: the position of the demolition charges on canal bridges, the thickness of the concrete in his fortifications, the strength of the guns commanding the Norwegian fjords. In this he was aided by a phenomenal memory and technical insight into weapons design, although his knowledge was limited to ships, tanks, and guns rather than to the weapons of air war. It was he who first demanded that 75-millimeter long-barrel guns be installed in German tanks. And it was he who pinpointed the common error in German warship design—building the forecastle so low that in heavy seas it tended to cut beneath the waves: on his birthday in 1937, the proud navy had presented him with a model of the *Scharnhorst,* and late that evening he had sent for his adjutant Puttkamer and invited him to crouch and squint along the model's decks with him; he was right, of course, and even at that late stage the forecastle had to be redesigned. On his bedside table his manservants always laid out the latest edition of

Weyer's naval handbook—the German Janes'—for the Führer to commit to memory as though he were preparing for some astounding music-hall act. His own staff had already witnessed the scene at headquarters during the Polish campaign when Admiral Raeder telephoned news of the sinking of some British warships; Hitler had beamed with pleasure, put down the telephone, and told Puttkamer the news, adding without the slightest hesitation the displacement, armament and armor thickness of each vessel. "Am I right, Puttkamer?" he had inquired, and the naval adjutant had reassured him, "Without doubt, mein Führer!" (Nonetheless he had privately checked in Weyer's immediately afterward and exclaimed to the other adjutants that Hitler's figures had been right "down to the last Pfennig!")

Did Hitler have some secret method, or was it that rarity—a photographic memory? We cannot tell. When the Red Book of arms production reached him each month, he would take a scrap of paper and, using a colored pencil selected from the tray on his desk, scribble down a few random figures as he ran his eyes over the columns. Then he would throw away the paper—but the figures remained indelibly in his memory —column by column, year after year—to confound his bureaucratic but more fallible aides with the proof of their own shortcomings. One month he pounced on a printing error in the current Red Book: an "8" instead of a "3." He had remembered the right figure from the previous month's edition. Late in 1940 Keitel took his new adjutant for an arms production conference with Hitler at the Berghof. Keitel started with figures on the total ammunition expended in the recent French campaign, and added more to allow for an extended war now; but Hitler responded that in 1916 the German armies had consumed far more 210-millimeter and 150-millimeter ammunition each *month,* and he stated the precise quantities from memory. Afterward Keitel instructed his adjutant to forward those new figures to General Georg Thomas of the OKW's munitions procurement office. "That is the new program." When the adjutant suggested they should at least check Hitler's figures Keitel wearily replied, "This is something you still have to learn. If the Führer says it, you can take it that it's right."

Hitler's seeming omniscience, and the eloquence of the arguments by which he gradually wore everybody down while apparently refreshing himself, had one disadvantage. While the less frequent visitors on technical affairs like the minister of posts, the elderly Wilhelm Ohnesorge, or the chief of naval construction, Admiral Karl Witzell, were flattered by the genuine interest the Führer displayed in their reports, Hitler's regular staff were discouraged by the feeling that since the Führer had already thought of everything himself there was little they could contribute by way of suggestion or initiative.

Although the OKW maintained its own munitions procurement office under General Thomas, Keitel readily echoed Hitler's mounting criticism of the arms production effort during the winter. He made no discernible effort to point out to Hitler that it was his own insistence on German armament in breadth for Blitzkrieg warfare—or war by bluff—rather than in depth for an extended war on many fronts, that was to blame for the present low ammunition production capacity. Again and again Hitler dinned into Keitel's head the disparity between current production programs and the achievements of the German munitions industry in World War I. In vain Keitel warned that such huge production figures could not be attained if the high quality of modern ammunition was not to be jeopardized. Hitler himself drew up a new production program in which priority was given to mine production for the naval and Luftwaffe blockade of Britain and to huge monthly outputs of artillery ammunition. He virtually doubled previous figures in a new program he issued on December 12, 1939.

Keitel issued the program to the army ordnance office—at that time headed by a sixty-year-old professor, General Karl Becker. By mid-January 1940, the latter had objected that Hitler's program could not be met "to the remotest extent": there was no point squandering scarce steel and nonferrous metal stocks manufacturing millions of shells if the chemical and explosives industry was not big enough to fill them. Keitel refused to tell this to the Führer. The Führer's munitions program must be fulfilled. If the ordnance office could not do it, the Führer would give the job to somebody else. Hitler was already toying with the idea—first put to him by Göring, who lost no opportunity to criticize the army's feeble ordnance office—of appointing a civilian munitions minister to take arms and munitions production out of the hands of the bureaucratic army staff officers. When Keitel himself asked for the power to control the arms industry, Hitler turned him down. In view of the increasing Allied strength in the West he was planning to establish ten more army divisions as well as new Luftwaffe squadrons which would concentrate on minelaying operations; he must at all costs have the increased mine and munitions production now.

When in February the army ordnance office reported the previous month's production figures, Hitler found this the last straw. Production of the most important weapons had actually declined. In the two main calibers of shell the Führer's program figures would not be reached even by April. Throughout January and February Hitler cursed General

Becker's lethargic and inadequate ordnance office. Nor did he have any confidence in the ability of Keitel's staff to prod the arms industry into activity.

At the end of February, Göring appointed Dr. Fritz Todt as a special troubleshooter to locate the bottlenecks in the munitions industry and recommend ways of stepping up production. Hitler trusted Todt implicitly, and Todt had also won the respect of the Party. He shortly convinced Hitler that if the industry was given a voice in how it was to fulfill its orders—the system of self-responsibility that had functioned so well in the construction of the autobahns and of the West Wall—Hitler's "impossible" production figures could be achieved. In March, Hitler appointed Todt his munitions minister. It was as much a rebuff to Keitel as to General Becker. But when the pained General Thomas, whose gloomy analyses of Germany's economic position had continually irritated Hitler, voiced objections, he was silenced by Keitel with the blunt comment that the less he reminded the Führer of his existence the better. Fritz Todt effectively wielded the powers Hitler had earlier denied to Keitel and Becker, for by the summer of 1940 the munitions crisis had virtually been surmounted. General Becker sensed his failure keenly, despite Hitler's endeavors to preserve his self-esteem, and he committed suicide not long after—the first of a sad band of Germans whose only common denominator was a failure to come up to Hitler's expectations.

At the end of February 1940, Hitler had secretly convened the Party leaders in the Chancellery and assured them the war would be over in six months—his new weapons would force the enemy to their knees; without doubt he was alluding to the mass minelaying operations the Luftwaffe was shortly to begin, using the deadly magnetic mine against which he believed the Allies had no defense.

Italy's uncertain stance continued to trouble him. Roosevelt had sent his undersecretary of state, Sumner Welles, to tour the engaged European capitals and sound their leaders on the prospects of peace. Hitler observed this uninvited diplomat's first port of call, at Rome, with as much disquiet as the British, though for different reasons. He was concerned that Welles's vague peace proposals might strengthen the neutralist elements in Rome, or even drive Italy into the arms of the Allies. Hitler studied the official Italian communiqués on the Rome talks and compared them closely with the Forschungsamt intercepts of the secret Italian dispatches relating to them. The Duce, however, appeared to have loyally defended Germany's claims. In his own talks with Sumner Welles, Hitler adhered rigidly to his argument that since this was Britain's war, it was up to Britain to end it. No amount of flattery by the American diplomat could cajole the Führer from this attitude. On March 4, Hitler repeated it to a General Motors vice president, James D. Mooney, to whom he granted an audience. "The current war can only be brought to an end by the other countries giving up their war aims," meaning the annihilation of Germany; Germany, he said, had no war aims.[4]

Britain's heavy-handed dealings with Mussolini reinforced his Axis position. To force him to take his trade negotiations with Britain seriously, the British imposed a naval blockade on Italy's coal supplies at the beginning of March. Hitler stepped in with an immediate offer of a million tons of coal a month, to be supplied over land to his harassed Axis partner. On March 8 he sent Ribbentrop to Rome with an overlong and profuse letter replying at long last to the Duce's missive of two months before. When Ribbentrop reported back that Mussolini had at last agreed on principle to take up arms against Britain and France, Hitler asked for an immediate meeting to be arranged with the Fascist leader. He instructed Jodl's staff to provide him with a folder of charts, including one grossly faking Germany's actual military strength (crediting her with 207 divisions instead of her actual 157), and met Mussolini at the Brenner Pass on March 18.

It was their first meeting since Munich. How much of his far-reaching program Hitler had achieved since then! Mussolini, on the other hand, arrived with the air of a schoolboy who had not done his homework, as Hitler later put it. The Führer impressed upon Mussolini that the Duce could decide the best moment to declare war, but that he, Hitler, would recommend doing so only after the first big German offensive. The Duce promised to lose no time, but he would prefer "Yellow" to be delayed for three or four months until Italy was properly prepared. Hitler hugely exaggerated Germany's prospects: her armies were more powerful than in 1914, she had more ammunition than she could use, production of Junkers 88 aircraft and submarines was surging forward. As for the British, once France had been subdued, Britain would come to terms with Hitler. "The British are extraordinarily determined in defense but

---

[4] The only American who made a good impression on Hitler at this stage was the traveling journalist Colin Ross, sent to him by Youth Leader Baldur von Schirach. Ross described to him the "fantastic slyness" and organizing talent of the American Jews, who had achieved so much that nobody in the United States now dared to support fascism openly, although there was much that was Fascist about the American government and way of life. Roosevelt's pathological envy of Hitler, said Ross, was caused by seeing how Hitler had put all his ambitious plans into practice, while he, who had come to power in the same year, had not.

quite hopeless at attacking, and their leadership is poor." More than once he assured Mussolini that for Germany there could now be only one partner; however, despite all these protestations he evidently still mistrusted the Italians, for he imparted to Mussolini neither the impressive operational plan he and Manstein had evolved for victory in the west, nor the slightest mention of his intentions in Scandinavia. And in the directive he soon after issued to Keitel, a directive in which the Wehrmacht was instructed to resume staff talks with Italy, he stated explicitly that any Italian forces must be assigned a task as independent from the main German operations as possible, to minimize "the problems inevitable in a coalition war."

Italy was still angry with Germany about the pact with Russia, which had been supplemented in February by an important economic agreement. Hitler attempted in both his letter and his private talk with Mussolini to convince him that Russia was changed—though how far these words were intended for Soviet consumption is a matter of speculation. "Without doubt," Hitler had written the Duce, "since Stalin's final triumph Russia has been undergoing a change from the Bolshevik principle to a more nationalist Russian way of life." At the Brenner meeting he reminded Mussolini that he had always wanted to march side by side with the British, provided that the British respected Germany's claims to expand eastward and returned to her the colonies lost after the Great War. "But Britain preferred war. This was why I was forced into partnership with Russia."

Yet there were surely less abstract reasons for his insistence that German industry deliver the goods to Stalin in abundance and on time—an insistence he voiced urgently throughout the spring of 1940. The British were known to be wooing the Russians even now. So long as the pact with Stalin was in force, it effectively released sixty high-grade divisions for Hitler to employ in the attack on France. Hitler's innermost intentions lay just below the surface. Perhaps the Russians should have guessed at them, for in 1940 millions of copies of the latest reprint of *Mein Kampf* went on sale, in which Chapter Fourteen, with its clear statement of his plan to invade the east, remain unexpunged. And when Hitler touched in conversation with Mussolini on the enforced evacuation of the German-speaking population from the South Tyrol—a mountainous province claimed by both Italy and Austria—he cryptically explained that he planned to resettle these people in a beautiful region "that I do not yet have but will certainly be procuring"; he must have already been looking ahead to the day when his armies would have turned eastward and be standing astride the Crimea, the region he formally assigned to the South Tyroleans in mid-1941.

On March 22, 1940, four days after his pregnant aside to Mussolini, Adolf Hitler again headed south, flying this time from Berlin to the Berghof for the Easter weekend. Captain Engel took the opportunity of this long flight to hand the Führer a lengthy report General Guderian had compiled on the wretched equipment and training standards of the Soviet troops in Finland. According to Engel, Hitler returned it with the laconic commentary: *"Auch die müssen wir vernichten!"*—"We must destroy them, too!"

Hors d'oeuvre

On Easter Monday, March 25, 1940, Hitler drove with his staff down the winding road from the Berghof and returned to the Chancellery in Berlin. The next time he was to see the Obersalzberg mountain it would be high summer, and he would be master of all northern Europe from North Cape to the Pyrenees.

The risks involved in the Norwegian operation were daunting, but he felt he must eliminate this constant source of worry implanted in his mind by Admiral Raeder—the fear that the Allies might obtain a foothold in Norway and cut Germany off from her iron-ore supplies. For the present his plans were delayed because the Baltic ports were still icebound and the transport ships he needed could not yet be assembled there. The world press slowly filled with speculation about the Allied designs on Scandinavia, but so far no word of Hitler's own daring intentions had leaked out. This was the first success of his stringent new security regulations. He had not even breathed a word of his military plan to Ribbentrop.

At noon on the day after Hitler's return to Berlin, Admiral Raeder put it to him that although a British invasion of Norway now seemed less acutely imminent than it had two weeks earlier, the Germans would do well to seize the initiative there now. It would be best to occupy Norway in a surprise operation timed to coincide with the new moon on April 7; by the fifteenth the dark nights would already be too short. Hitler agreed, but opted for a date between the eighth and tenth so that "Yellow" could begin four or five days after, if conditions were right. Raeder also asked Hitler to authorize an immediate resumption of Luftwaffe minelaying operations, as it seemed that the secret of the magnetic mine was now out; although both Keitel and Göring wanted the minelaying campaign delayed until "Yellow" began, the Führer directed that it must begin immediately. Against Göring's advice, Hitler also allowed himself to be persuaded by Raeder on another issue: the Führer had originally wanted the dozen destroyers that were to carry troops to Narvik and Trondheim to remain as a source of artillery support and to boost the morale of the troops they had landed; as he put it to Jodl one evening in his map room, he could not tolerate "the navy promptly scuttling out of the Norwegian ports." What would the landing troops make of that? But Raeder dug his heels in. The most perilous phase of the whole invasion campaign, he insisted, would be the withdrawal of the warships from northern Norway to the safety of German waters under the nose of the most powerful navy in the world. If the destroyers were detained one moment too long, they would be bottled in by the British and wiped out when they emerged. Raeder was prepared to risk his fleet for Norway, but he would not stand by and see it frittered away, and in a private clash with Hitler on March 29 he told him so. Hitler yielded to the force of argument.

Intelligence on Britain's intentions in Scandinavia hardened, although on March 22, Raeder's codebreakers found to their dismay that the British had just changed one of their most important codes; this might hamper cryptanalysis for two weeks. The Scandinavian press began to speculate on an imminent Allied operation in Norwegian waters. Raeder warned Hitler of a perceptible stiffening in Norway's attitude toward Germany. Far more important was that Hitler now learned of an Allied Supreme War Council decision in London on March 28 to develop a two-stage Scandinavian operation early in April: the cynical Allied master plan was to provoke Hitler into an overhasty occupation of *southern* Norway by laying mines in Norway's neutral waters; Hitler's move would then "justify" a full-scale Allied landing at Narvik in the north to seize the railroad to the Swedish ore fields. This first stage would later be coupled with several operations farther south. On March 30 German Intelligence intercepted a Paris diplomat's report on a conversation with Paul Reynaud, France's new premier. According to a summary in the naval staff's war diary, Reynaud had assured this unidentified diplomat that the dangers in western and southern Europe would shortly pass, as in the next few days the Allies would be launching all-important operations in northern Europe. On the same day, Churchill broadcast on the BBC a warning to Norway that Britain would no longer tolerate a pro-German interpretation of neutrality; the Allies would continue the fight "wherever it might lead them." (Churchill's designs on Norway were known to German Intelligence from a series of incautious hints he dropped in a secret press conference with neutral press attachés in London on February 2.) Small wonder that Hitler later referred more than once to the indiscretions committed by Reynaud and Churchill as providing the final urgent stimulus for his own adventure.[1]

On March 30, German cryptographers also intercepted a cable from the Romanian legation in Oslo conveying the impression being created by the British envoy there: conspicuous protestations that no far-reaching decisions had yet been taken in London or Paris about violating Norwegian waters were coupled with British denials that they intended to land troops in Norway. The combination finally convinced the German naval staff that "in reality a British operation against Scandinavia is imminent," and that a race between Britain and Germany was developing. An intercepted Swiss legation report from Stockholm claimed that British *and* German invasions of the Norwegian coast were imminent. Major Quisling said the situation was so urgent that the Germans should not wait for him to build up his organization first; British and French officers were being installed in key points in Norway, disguised as consular officials. Admiral Raeder nervously pressed Hitler to launch the invasion on April 7, the earliest possible date; but after spending two days investigating every detail of the operation with all the commanders involved, Hitler decided on April 2 that the first assault on Norway's coastline was to take place at 5:15 A.M. on the ninth.

The nervous strain on Hitler would have overwhelmed most men. Perhaps the very idea was too audacious to succeed? How could train-loads of South German mountain troops heading for the Baltic coast be plausibly explained? How could ponderous transport ships laden with hundreds of troops, guns, and ammunition be safely dispatched toward the Arctic without alerting the British fleet in time to wipe out the German navy? When on April 1, Hitler personally addressed the hand-picked commanders, one report noted: "The Führer describes the operation . . . as one of the 'cheekiest operations' in recent military history. But in this he sees the basis for its success." He offered the familiar preventive reasons for occupying Norway but added that the time had come for Germany to win safe channels to the outside world. "It is intolerable that each generation is subjected to renewed pressure from Britain.

---

[1] Ambassador Hewel recorded Hitler's dinner-table reminiscences on July 5, 1941, thus in his diary: "For instance, if we had formally declared war against Norway, we would have lost it; yet Norway is absolutely vital to the future of Germany. And vice versa, if Churchill and Reynaud had kept a still tongue in their heads, I might well not have tackled Norway. A week earlier Churchill sent his nephew [Giles Romilly] to Narvik, just typical of his American-Jewish journalistic character. Treason."

Sooner or later the fight with Britain would have been inevitable. It has to be fought. It is a matter of life and death for the German nation."

At 2 A.M. on April 3, Hitler's operation passed the point of no return. The first three transports camouflaged as coal vessels sailed from Germany, bound with the tanker *Kattegat* for Narvik, a thousand miles to the north. Four more "coal ships"—three for Trondheim and one for Stavanger—were ready in German ports. All carried heavy equipment, artillery, ammunition, and provisions concealed beneath the coal. The initial assault troops would be carried on fast warships, some entering the Norwegian ports under cover of the British flag: ten destroyers would carry two thousand troops to Narvik, escorted by the battleships *Scharnhorst* and *Gneisenau;* another seventeen hundred troops would be landed at Trondheim by the cruiser *Hipper* and four destroyers. Thousands of assault troops would be landed at five other ports by virtually the rest of the German navy—a fleet of cruisers, torpedo boats, whalers, minesweepers, submarine chasers, tugs, and picket boats. Troop reinforcements would arrive during the day in fifteen merchant ships bound for Oslo, Kristiansand, Bergen, and Stavanger. If anything prematurely befell even one of these ships laden with troops in field-gray, the whole operation would be betrayed.

Hitler ordered the OKW to disclose the impending operation to Ribbentrop. By April 5, the admiralty in Berlin could recognize that a fresh British operation had begun. An imperfectly broken British radio message of very unusual length appeared to be an operational order to fifteen or twenty submarines; since the operation seemed to be one of particular importance, it was decided that either the British were deploying against Hitler's operation or that "the enemy has his *own* plans to invade Norway." The German naval staff correctly deduced the two-stage character of the Allied plan—first the British would lay a mine barrage, then, as soon as the Germans retaliated, the Allies would use this as justification for an invasion. Since there was no other evidence at all that the Allies might have detected Germany's strategic plan, let alone the audacious scale on which Hitler had prepared the invasion, the naval staff concluded on April 6 that "the enemy is on the threshold of conducting operations in Norwegian waters or on Norwegian soil." In Berlin, the foreign ministry learned that the Allied governments had sent to the Scandinavian governments crisply worded notes indicating that since the latter were no longer "entirely free agents" in handling their foreign affairs, the Allies reserved all rights.

In his Chancellery, Hitler feared that at any moment word would arrive that the Allied invasion had begun. On the afternoon of the sixth

the war department notified him that the railroad movement of invasion
troops from their assembly areas in the heart of Germany to the Baltic
dockyards had begun on schedule. From Helsinki came fresh word of an
imminent British operation against Narvik; Swedish and Norwegian
officers tried to assure Berlin that the Allies were just trying to provoke
Germany into an ill-considered preventive campaign, but Hitler remained unconvinced. He already felt that the Swedes knew more than
was good for them. He had arranged for all the foreign military attachés in Berlin to tour the West Wall over the next few days—but the
Swedish legation had declined the invitation, explaining that the attaché
would be urgently needed at the time scheduled. Equally ominous were
the telephone conversations the Forschungsamt now intercepted between the Danish military attaché and the Danish and Norwegian ministers in Berlin, in which the attaché urgently asked for immediate in-
terviews with them as he had something of "the utmost political
significance" to tell them.[2]

During the night of April 6-7, the German fleet operation began. The
battleships, cruisers, and destroyers sailed from their North Sea ports. A
further stiffening in the Norwegian attitude to Germany was detected.
Norwegian coastal defenses were on the alert, troop movements were reported, lighthouses and radio beacons were extinguished. Norwegian
pilots for the "coalships" waiting to pass northward through the Leads
to Narvik and Trondheim were only slowly forthcoming—was this deliberate Norwegian obstructionism, or had the German admiralty simply
failed to impress on these ships' captains the importance of the timetable? It was too late to speculate now, for the entire German invasion
fleet was at sea. Hitler was committed to either a catastrophic defeat,
with the certain annihilation of his navy, or to a spectacular victory.

Early on April 8, the German legation in Oslo telephoned Berlin with
the not altogether unexpected news that British warships had just begun
laying minefields in Norwegian waters. This violation of Norway's neutrality could hardly have been more flagrant, nor more opportune for
Hitler's cause. Now he could present his seizure of the Norwegian coast
as a dramatic, and highly effective, answer to the Allied action; and a
gullible world would believe it. In Oslo, there was uproar and anger at

---

[2] The Abwehr office of the OKW had been involved in some of the dealings with Major Quisling's
men and was thus apprised of the coming Norwegian invasion. Admiral Canaris's Chief of Staff,
Colonel Hans Oster, warned the Dutch military attaché Major Sas of this—presumably to restore
his own credibility after the many false alarms he had given in the winter. Sas passed the information on to the Danish and Norwegian legations, though neither was greatly impressed by it.

the Allied presumption; the redoubled Norwegian determination to defend their neutrality caused Raeder to order his warships to abandon their original intention of entering the Norwegian ports under the British flag, as he could now see little profit in the deception.

The elation in Berlin at the Allied action was shattered by a second telephone call from the Oslo legation in the early evening. The *Rio de Janeiro,* a slow-moving merchant ship headed for Bergen with horses and a hundred troops, had been torpedoed a few hours earlier off the Norwegian coast. Troops in field-gray uniforms had been rescued from the sea and were presumably even now being interrogated by the Norwegians. But Hitler's luck still held. The hours passed, and although word came that the Norwegian Cabinet had been urgently called into session, it seemed to have resolved upon no clear course of action. From intercepted radio messages the British admiralty was known to have identified the fast warship groups heading for Narvik and Trondheim during the eighth. But in Berlin the naval staff was confident that the British would wrongly conclude that this was an attempted breakout into the Atlantic. Raeder had insisted on attaching battleships to the first group, and this was now vindicated, for the British were indeed deceived, and deployed their forces far to the north of the true seat of operations.

In the small hours of April 9, Berlin picked up a Norwegian radio signal reporting strange warships entering the Oslo Fjord. Now Hitler knew that the toughest part of the operation—running the gauntlet of the Norwegian coastal batteries—had begun. But shortly before 6 A.M. German signals from the forces landed at Narvik, Trondheim, and Bergen were monitored; they called for U-boats to stand guard over the port entrances. Access to Norway had now been forced. Hitler and Jodl read the signals with evident relief, though not until later did the full measure of this German victory dawn on them.

By the evening of April 9, 1940, Norway and Denmark appeared securely in German hands. General von Falkenhorst reported at five-thirty: "Norway and Denmark occupied . . . as instructed."

Hitler himself drafted the German news-agency report announcing that the Danish government had submitted, grumbling, and almost without a shot having been fired, to German *force majeure.* Grinning from ear to ear, Hitler congratulated Rosenberg: "Now Quisling can set up his government in Oslo." The unbelievably sluggish British naval command had fumbled every countermove. In southern Norway the strategically well-placed airfield at Stavanger had been captured by German paratroops, assuring Hitler of immediate air superiority—the key to the later campaign; at Oslo itself—where the seaborne forces arrived three hours late—five companies of paratroops and airborne infantry landed on Fornebü airfield. A small party of infantry marched with band playing into the Norwegian capital and Oslo fell.

At the Reich Chancellery in Berlin there was the heady scent of victory and relief. When the gold-embossed supper menu was laid before Hitler that evening, the main course of macaroni, ham, and green salad was appropriately prefaced by *smörrebröd*. Scandinavia was indeed just the hors d'oeuvre; as soon as the Luftwaffe could disengage itself from Norway, "Yellow" would begin—a feast of military conquest which Hitler was already savoring in advance.

As Admiral Raeder had predicted, the German navy had suffered grievous losses and was to suffer yet more; but Hitler confided to his adjutants that if his navy was to do naught else in this war, it had justified its existence by winning Norway for Germany. In the final approach to Oslo along the fifty-mile-long Oslo Fjord, Germany's newest heavy cruiser, the *Blücher,* had been disabled by the ancient Krupp guns of a coastal battery and finished off by torpedoes with heavy loss of life. Off Bergen the cruiser *Königsberg* was also hit by a coastal battery; it limped into port and was sunk the next day by British aircraft. South of Kristiansand, the cruiser *Karlsruhe* was sunk by a British submarine. Three more cruisers were damaged and many of the supply vessels sunk, for during their own invasion preparations the British had stationed sixteen submarines in the area; this was the operational signal the German admiralty had been unable to decipher completely.

In one incident, the cruiser *Hipper* and four destroyers bearing seventeen hundred troops to Trondheim were challenged by the coastal batteries guarding the fjord; the *Hipper*'s commander, Captain Heye, steered directly toward the batteries, signaling ambiguously in English: "I come on government instructions." By the time the puzzled gunners opened fire, the ships were already past.

It was at Narvik that the real crisis began. Ten destroyers landed General Eduard Dietl's two thousand German and Austrian mountain troops virtually unopposed, for the local Norwegian commander was a Quisling sympathizer. But the three camouflaged supply ships and the tanker *Kattegat* never arrived from Germany. Only the tanker *Jan Wellem* arrived punctually from the naval base provided by Stalin at Murmansk; as the ten destroyers could refuel only slowly from this one tanker, they could not be ready to return before late on the tenth. But earlier that day five British destroyers penetrated the fjord in a blinding snowstorm; in the ensuing gunplay and the battle fought there three days later, the aging British battleship *Warspite* and a whole flotilla of destroyers sank all ten German destroyers—though not before they had taken a toll from the British. Thus half of Raeder's total destroyer force had been wiped out.[3] Hitler had that morning already radioed Dietl to hold on to Narvik at all costs. He was to prepare frozen Lake Hartvig as an airfield ready to receive Luftwaffe supply planes. After word came of the sinking of the destroyers, Rosenberg found the Führer slumped deep in thought following a conference with Göring. When over the next two days news arrived of British troops landing at Harstad, not far north of Narvik, and at Namsos, to the north of Trondheim, the military crisis brought Hitler to the verge of a complete nervous breakdown.

Had the diplomatic offensive in Oslo been prepared with the same thoroughness as the military invasion, the Norwegian government could have been won over or effectively neutralized. Thus armed Norwegian resistance would have been avoided and the interior lines of communication secured from one end of Norway to the other. But bad luck had dogged events in Oslo: when the *Blücher* had sunk in Oslo Fjord, the assault party detailed to arrest the Norwegian government had foundered with her; in addition, the airborne troops due to land at Fornebü airport were delayed by fog. As a result, the king and government had had time to escape the capital, and the local German envoy, Kurt Bräuer, was not equal to the situation.

On April 10, both king and government in refuge outside Oslo—had been amenable to negotiation, but Bräuer wanted them to recognize Major Quisling's new government and left the talks without awaiting the outcome of his proposals. Back in Oslo, Bräuer learned that the proposals were rejected: the king refused to violate the constitution by appointing Quisling, whom the Norwegian public regarded as a traitor. The fugitive government issued a call to arms and sabotage, and a confused but still undeclared war between Norway and Germany began. Had Bräuer not insisted on Quisling but dealt with the existing government instead, this situation would not have arisen.

Hitler's support for Quisling was short-lived. On April 14, the foreign

---

[3] The German destroyer commodore at Narvik was killed in the action on the tenth. His successor notified the German admiralty that during the second raid, on April 13, the British destroyers caused additional casualties by machine-gunning the German sailors thrown into the sea. Whatever the substance of such wholly uninvestigated allegations, they will have contributed to the atmosphere at the Reich Chancellery.

ministry flew Theo Habicht, a Nazi revolutionary and ministry official, to Oslo to straighten matters out. His instructions were to make a last attempt to secure agreement with the king. Quisling was forced to climb down next day; but with the British operations in Narvik stiffening the Norwegian resolve, Germany's position was weaker politically than it had been four days earlier. Ribbentrop's representatives scraped together an "Administrative Council" of leading Oslo citizens including the chief justice of the Norwegian Supreme Court, Paul Berg, but progress was slow and quite the opposite of what Hitler had wanted. He was apoplectic with rage at Bräuer and Habicht for allowing these "Norwegian lawyers" to dupe them; he had wanted to see Quisling at the head of an ostensibly legal Norwegian government—not some lawyers' junta. Habicht and Bräuer were fetched back to Berlin and dismissed from the foreign service—it was all Ribbentrop could do to save them from incarceration in a concentration camp. Hitler fumed that all he desired in these northern lands was law and order; since the foreign ministry had failed, the army and Party must now try.

Next to the old Reich Cabinet Room Hitler used for his war conferences were the rooms his military advisers Jodl and Keitel occupied; additional offices were supplied for their adjutants and clerical staff. It was on this small stage that in mid-April 1940 the command crisis over Narvik was played. It shed such unfavorable light on Hitler's qualities of leadership that Colonel Schmundt, his faithful Parsifal, ordered all reference to it excised from the official records of the High Command; it showed Hitler in an all too mortal posture—when the strain upon him grew too great, his nerves cracked and he lost his powers of reason.

Neither Luftwaffe nor submarines could carry munitions, reinforcements, or artillery to General Dietl in any quantity. Eleven Junkers 52 transport planes had landed on Lake Hartvig with the components of a mountain battery, but no sooner were the aircraft unloaded than the ice thawed and all eleven aircraft sank. With his own two thousand troops now augmented by the two thousand shipless sailors of the destroyer force, Dietl could not hold Narvik—the whole point of the Norwegian campaign—once the main British assault on the port began. Together with Göring, Hitler studied one plan after another for the relief of the Narvik force. It worried him that they were mostly Austrians, for he had not yet wanted to place such a burden on the Anschluss. By April 14, he was already talking to Brauchitsch of abandoning Narvik and concentrating all effort on the defense of Trondheim, threatened by the British beachhead at Namsos and now by the onset of a fresh invasion at Aandalsnes to the south. He planned to expand Trondheim into a strategic naval base that would make Britain's Singapore seem "child's play." Over the next few days, after repeated conferences with Göring, Milch, and Jeschonnek, he ordered the total destruction of Namsos and Aandalsnes, and of any other town or village in which British troops set foot, without regard for the civilian population. He frowned at his adjutants and said, "I know the British. I came up against them in the Great War. Where they once get a toehold there is no throwing them out again."

On the fourteenth, he had somehow gained the impression that the British had already landed at Narvik. He knew of no other solution than that Dietl should fight his way southward to Trondheim. Jodl scorned the idea. "Mein Führer, I have been there. An expedition there is like a Polar expedition!" Jodl knew and trusted Dietl; he also knew Narvik, and he considered it quite possible to defend it for a long time with meager resources. But Hitler had no intention of wasting more aircraft in supplying Dietl. He announced Dietl's promotion to lieutenant general and at the same time dictated to Keitel a message ordering Dietl to evacuate Narvik forthwith. The British would now take Narvik unopposed; that Sweden would defend her iron-ore fields, as Göring believed, seemed to Hitler unlikely. Jodl wrote in his diary: "The hysteria is frightful." His deputy later recalled that when Hitler was not loudly giving vent to irrelevant suggestions, he sat glowering in one corner of Jodl's room. Hitler had acted like this once before, during a minor crisis over the capture of Warsaw. If he was plagued by nervous fits in a subsidiary campaign like this, it augured ill for "Yellow," which was to begin as soon as the Luftwaffe's paratroops and transport squadrons were released from their commitment in Norway. Jodl's staff was scandalized by the Führer's lack of comportment in these days.

In fact Hitler's radio message to Dietl was never sent. It reached the OKW offices at Bendlerstrasse, and at 10:40 A.M. on the morning of April 15 it was back in Jodl's room, in the quivering hands of his army staff officer, Colonel Bernhard von Lossberg. Lossberg angrily refused to send out such a message—it was the product of a nervous crisis "unparalleled since the darkest days of the Battle of the Marne in 1914." The whole point of the Norwegian campaign had been to safeguard Germany's iron-ore supplies. Was Narvik now to be relinquished to the British without a fight? Jodl quietly advised him that this was the personal desire of the Führer. Keitel turned his back on Lossberg and left the room. With Jodl's permission, Lossberg visited the Commander in

Chief of the army and urgently begged him to talk Hitler around, but Brauchitsch curtly refused. "I have nothing whatever to do with the Norwegian campaign. Falkenhorst and Dietl are answerable to Hitler alone, and I have not the least intention of going of my own free will to that clip joint," meaning the Reich Chancellery. However, the colonel craftily persuaded Brauchitsch to sign another message to Dietl, one congratulating him on his promotion and ending: "I am sure you will defend your position, which is so vital to Germany, to the last man." Lossberg handed this text to Jodl and tore up Keitel's handwritten Führer Order before their eyes. Thus ended one day of the Narvik crisis.

It is clear Hitler feared the blow that the loss of Narvik would inflict on his prestige. Now Jodl began to assert his authority as strategic adviser. He openly rejected Hitler's muttered reproaches against the army and navy operations. When Hitler drew ugly comparisons between the scuttling of the disabled destroyers at Narvik and the ignominious end of the *Graf Spee,* Jodl pointed out that when a warship has no fuel and has expended her last ammunition she has no choice if she is to avoid capture. As each day of this Narvik crisis passed, Jodl's voice was raised with more assurance. Eventually the Allies had landed some twelve thousand British, French, and Polish troops to confront Dietl's lesser force. Jodl remained unimpressed; and when Hitler again began talking of abandoning Narvik, he lost his temper and stalked out of the Cabinet Room, slamming the door behind him with a noise that echoed around the Chancellery building.

Upon reflection, however, Jodl decided that his faith in Hitler had not been misplaced. Had not precisely the same despondency smitten Frederick the Great at the battle of Mollwitz two hundred years before? When that battle had turned against the great Prussian monarch, he had taken flight with his cavalry. And hadn't it been Schwerin and his infantry who had saved the day without him?

Jodl expressed his opposition to Hitler's policy of despair with the advice: "You should not give up anything until it is really *lost*." Throughout the seventeenth the argument raged back and forth between them. Hitler had already drafted a radio message ordering Dietl to withdraw. "There must be some way out!" he exclaimed, leaning over the chart of Norway. "We cannot just abandon those troops." Jodl retorted in his earthy Bavarian accent, "Mein Führer, in every war there are times when the Supreme Commander must keep his nerve!" Between each word, he rapped his knuckles on the chart table so loudly that they were white afterward.

The psychological effect of this drama on Hitler was interesting. He composed himself and with deliberate controlled evenness replied, "What would you advise?" Thereupon Jodl showed him an appreciation by his staff, appended to which was a draft directive to Dietl to hold out and contain enemy forces there as long as possible. That evening Hitler signed the order; but he made it abundantly clear in a preamble that he thought the whole northern position was bound to be overwhelmed by the Allies eventually, since all the odds were against Dietl and his four thousand ill-armed men. It was not one of his more felicitously worded messages.

His fifty-first birthday passed without noticeable public enthusiasm. When Alfred Rosenberg presented him with a large porcelain bust of Frcdcrick the Great, tears welled up in the Führer's eyes. "When you see him," he said, "you realize how puny are the decisions we have to make compared with those confronting him. He had nothing like the military strength we command today!"

But military strength, if mindlessly applied, often proves counterproductive. In Norway, Falkenhorst had begun draconian reprisals to quell the incidence of sabotage. Hostages were taken. Göring mentioned during an audience with Hitler that a mass resistance movement in Norway was growing. By late on April 18 it was clear that earlier attempts at kid-glove tactics had failed. On that day, the fugitive Norwegian government declared itself at war with Germany. All diplomatic talks ceased, and Hitler told his staff that from now on brute force was the only answer. At the war conference he announced his intention of transferring executive authority to Falkenhorst; the tough young Gauleiter of Essen, Josef Terboven, would be appointed Reich Commissioner for Norway, answerable only to the Führer himself. Keitel—rightly fearing that Norway was now to suffer as Poland was already suffering—raised immediate objections. When Hitler's only reply was to snub the OKW chief, Keitel took a leaf from Jodl's book and stormed out of the conference chamber. Afterward he privately cornered Hitler and warned that friction was bound to arise between Terboven and the military commander. Nevertheless, by that evening Terboven was already at the Chancellery; the next day saw him ensconced in private with Hitler, Himmler, and Martin Bormann; and on April 21, Terboven and his staff were en route for Oslo and ready to introduce a reign of terror to the Norwegian people.

Again Hitler was plagued by sleepless nights. What was the true situation in Norway? If the Luftwaffe generals were to be believed, Falkenhorst was in despair and already giving up Trondheim as lost. During the day, the trickle of information reaching the Chancellery along the one scrambler-telephone link between Oslo and Berlin was never enough to quench Hitler's thirst for detail. He sent one officer after another by special plane to Norway to report to him on the progress of his two divisions of infantry struggling to bridge the three hundred miles between Oslo and Trondheim.

On April 22, he sent his own adjutant, Schmundt, by plane to Oslo with Jodl's army staff officer, Colonel von Lossberg. Lossberg—a towering figure with a game leg and a fearless nature—reported back to Hitler the next evening after a hazardous flight. So struck was he by the contrast between the confident resolution he had found at Falkenhorst's Oslo headquarters and the air of dejection in the Chancellery, that he apparently forgot himself; when the downcast Führer asked in what strength the British had now landed at Namsos and Aandalsnes, he exclaimed, "Five thousand men at most, mein Führer!" This, to Hitler, was a disaster, but the colonel briskly interrupted him: "*Jawohl*, mein Führer, *only* five thousand men. Falkenhorst controls all the key points, so he could finish off the enemy even if they were far stronger. We must rejoice over every Englishman sent to Norway rather than to meet us in the west on the Meuse." When Hitler emphasized that the army must move reinforcements to Falkenhorst, Lossberg recommended that he leave matters in Falkenhorst's hands. Germany needed every division it could retain in the west for "Yellow." Hitler allowed Lossberg to lecture him no longer on elementary tactics. Perhaps the ill-concealed sarcasm the colonel had voiced over Hitler's panicky and pernickety command methods from the Chancellery had found their mark. Lossberg was curtly dismissed from the conference chamber, and for weeks afterward he was not allowed into the Führer's presence.

On the chart table, Lossberg had left behind him a small sheaf of recently captured British military documents which he had brought with him from Oslo. On the following day this little dossier was greatly augmented by additional British documents, which arrived from Oslo with one of Jodl's officers. A British infantry brigade fighting south of Aandalsnes had been put to flight by the advancing Germans, and important files captured. The immense political importance of the find sank in overnight: the brigade commander, in private life a London soap manufacturer, had previously been briefed on the plan to capture Stavanger—long before the German invasion of Norway. The British orders were dated April 2, 6, and 7! Other British landing operations had been planned at Bergen, Trondheim, and Narvik. The German operation had cut right across the British scheme, and the troop transports, which had actually been sighted by the Luftwaffe on April 9, had been recalled to port to enable the navy to engage the German fleet. These documents, in conjunction with files seized from French and British consulates in Norway, showed the whole history, dating back to January, of the Allied plan to invade Norway. It was equally clear that certain Norwegian leaders were determined the Allied operation should not be resisted.

Hitler was overjoyed. He had taken much booty since his invasion began, including a million tons of shipping in Norwegian ports, but this haul of secret Allied documents was the stroke of real luck he had been waiting for. He personally mapped out the propaganda campaign to exploit them; until the small hours of the morning, he, Schmundt, and Jodl checked over the White Book the foreign ministry was preparing. The hasty publication contained document facsimiles, translations, and statements of British officers as to the documents' authenticity. Hitler himself met and talked to the British prisoners brought to Berlin from Norway.[4] At midday on the twenty-seventh, Ribbentrop distributed the damning publication to the assembled foreign diplomats in the main Chancellery building. That afternoon, he broadcast a lengthy tirade that was heard worldwide, from North America to the Russias; in it he emphasized the cant and humbug of British assurances to the little neutrals.

The speech was due to begin at 2:30 P.M., and Hitler made it one of the rare occasions when he himself listened to the radio. Ribbentrop as usual kept his huge audience waiting several minutes before he began, and Rosenberg, the minister's archenemy, slyly observed to Hitler: "Not a very punctual start!" Hitler waved his hand in a characteristic gesture and laughed. "The foreign minister is always too late." (Once Ribbentrop had kept him waiting for several minutes before deigning to come

---

[4] One of Halder's staff wrote at this time about the British army's problems: "And what military dilettantes they are is clear from the volumes of written material found on a British brigade commander in Norway. It is very valuable to us. . . . The first British prisoners were flown to Berlin, shown to the Führer, wined and dined, and driven around Berlin for four hours. They just could not understand how things can look so normal here and that the public is not being fed from soup kitchens. They are staggered to see the shops open and people in the streets. Above all they were in perpetual fear of being shot: that's what they had been tricked into believing." Hearing a few days later that Polish prisoners had attacked the new British arrivals, Hitler asked that next time photographers should be present to capture the scene of supposed allies at one another's throats.

to the telephone; Hitler had recommended that he not repeat this threadbare tactic with him again.)

There was no denying the effect Ribbentrop's White Book on the Norwegian documents had on world opinion. Well might Hitler ask, Who now dares condemn me for assailing Belgium and Holland if the Allies care so little for small states' neutrality themselves? At all events, on the very day the captured documents were released to the world, April 27, 1940, Hitler secretly announced to his staff the decision over which he had wavered these many months. He would launch "Yellow" in the first week of May.

To open the assault in the west, Hitler had marshaled 137 divisions, with over 2,400 tanks and 3,800 aircraft at their command; yet even so he was facing a numerically superior enemy. His Intelligence agencies had pinpointed the position of 100 French divisions and 11 more divisions from the British Expeditionary Force; the Belgians had raised 23 divisions, and the Dutch 13. Added to this total of 147 divisions were 20 more holding the fortifications. The French had committed only 7 divisions, plus 3 fortification divisions—immobile units capable only of defense—to their frontier with Italy. In short, instead of launching his offensive with the traditional superiority of numbers, Hitler's army had the odds against it. Superior morale, tactics, and weaponry would have to make up for this deficiency. The weather for the Luftwaffe must be perfect from the first moment.

Hitler did not doubt the outcome of the forthcoming passage of arms. He would command this campaign himself, and by rapid initiative and superior strategy he would annihilate the enemy, whose "bureaucracy and hidebound tactics" had already proven their undoing in Norway. Jodl was years later to write: "Only the Führer could sweep aside the hackneyed military notions of the General Staff and conceive a grand plan in all its elements—a people's inner willingness to fight, the uses of propaganda, and the like. It was this that revealed not the analytic mind of the staff officer or military expert in Hitler, but the grand strategist." On the eve of the assault on France and the Low Countries, Hitler was to proclaim to his assembled staff, "Gentlemen: you are about to witness the most famous victory in history!" Few viewed the immediate future as sanguinely as he.

Now the real pressure was on. On April 29, Hitler ordered the Luftwaffe to stand by to open "Yellow" on May 5; on April 30, he ordered the entire Wehrmacht to be ready to launch "Yellow" at twenty-four hours' notice from the fifth. That day, General Jodl had confirmed to him that in Norway the German forces that had set out weeks before from Trondheim and Oslo had now linked; the Führer was delirious with joy. "That is more than a battle won, it is an entire campaign!" he exclaimed. Before his eyes he could already see the autobahn he would build to Trondheim. The Norwegian people deserved it. How utterly they differed from the Poles! Norwegian doctors and nurses had tended the injured until they dropped with exhaustion; the Polish "subhumans" had jabbed their eyes out. Moved by this comparison, on May 9, Hitler was to give his military commander in Norway an order which began as follows:

> . . . In the course of the campaign in the east German soldiers who had the misfortune to fall injured or uninjured into Polish hands were usually brutally ill-treated or massacred. By way of contrast, it must be said of the Norwegian army that not one single such incident of the debasement of warfare has occurred.
> The Norwegian soldier spurned all the cowardly and deceitful methods common to the Poles. He fought with open visor and honorably, and he tended our prisoners and injured properly and to the best of his ability. The civilian population acted similarly. Nowhere did they join in the fighting, and they did all they could for the welfare of our casualties.
> I have therefore decided in appreciation for this to authorize the liberation of the Norwegian soldiers we took prisoner. Only the professional soldiers will have to remain in captivity until such time as the former Norwegian government withdraws its call to arms against Germany, or individual officers and men give their formal word not to take part under any circumstances in further hostilities against Germany.

The Allies had evacuated their forces from Namsos and Aandalsnes at the beginning of May, leaving only the twelve thousand troops landed at Narvik to continue the fight. The British press admitted frankly that the defeat in Norway was having a disastrous effect on public opinion. When the British submarine *Seal* showed the white flag and surrendered to a German naval aircraft on May 5, the naval staff saw it as a "sad sign of Britain's lack of resolution and readiness."

Hitler assembled his staff for a last run of secret conferences on the details of "Yellow": everybody was now standing by—the glider and parachute troops who were to seize bridges, forts, and key points in Holland and Belgium; the disguised "Dutch policemen"; the emissary who was to present to the queen of Holland a demand that the Dutch proffer no resistance; the little scout force of radio vehicles detailed by Jodl to report directly to him on the operation against the bridges and Fort Eben Emael; and two million men. The weather forecasts were of crucial importance; the Luftwaffe's chief meteorologist sweated blood over the burden of responsibility he alone now carried. On May 3, Hitler postponed "Yellow" on his advice by one day, to Monday. On the fourth he again postponed it, to Tuesday. On Sunday the fifth the forecast was still uncertain, so "Yellow" was set down for Wednesday the eighth. On this deadline Hitler was determined: he ordered a special timetable printed for his headquarters staff as part of the elaborate camouflage of his real intentions. The timetable showed his train departing from a little station near Berlin late on May 7 and arriving next day in Hamburg en route for "an official visit to Oslo."

Hitler would not brook weather delays any longer. At the end of April the SS obtained the transcript of a telephone conversation between the prime ministers of Britain and France, indicating that they were planning an operation themselves. Hitler later mentioned this as his reason for fearing that "at any moment the Allies might march into Holland and Belgium" (in fact the two prime ministers were discussing a French air attack on Russia's oil fields). But the Luftwaffe's meteorologist was adamant, in conference with Hitler on May 7, that there was still a strong risk of morning fog; so Hitler again postponed "Yellow" by one day.

Hitler was even more alarmed by what the Allies might now learn of *his* plans. On May 7, the Forschungsamt showed him two coded telegrams the Belgian ambassador to the Vatican had just sent to his government: a German citizen who had arrived in Rome on April 29 had warned that Hitler was about to attack Belgium and Holland. The Abwehr was ordered to search out the informant—a supreme irony as the SS was to realize four years later, for the culprit was a minor member of Canaris's Abwehr network.[5] In any case, the fat was in the fire. At 5 P.M. Dutch radio announced that all leave was canceled, and by early on the eighth Holland was in a state of siege. Telephone links with foreign countries were cut, members of Anton Mussert's pro-Nazi movement in the Dutch forces were arrested, cities began evacuation meas-

[5] This was Dr. Joseph Müller, a Catholic lawyer, who later became the postwar Bavarian minister of justice. Colonel Oster also repeated his earlier acts of subversion by giving the Dutch military attaché a running commentary on each postponement of "Yellow" and the final definitive warning at 9 P.M. on the very eve of the offensive. His complicated motives can be summarized thus: recognizing Hitler's immense popular support by 1940, Oster desired to inflict on him such a military defeat that a coup against him would stand a better chance; he also desired the Allies to take him seriously as a negotiating partner. The Dutch military commander considered him "a pitiful specimen."

ures, the government district of The Hague was cordoned off, and—most irritating of all for Hitler—the guard on important bridges was increased. Hitler wanted to wait no longer, but Göring kept his nerve and promised that although there was still fog in the morning, the weather was improving daily: May 10 would be ideal. Hitler was torn between the counsels of his experts and the whispering voice of his intuition. Against all his instincts he reluctantly agreed to postpone "Yellow" to May 10, "but not one day after that."

Early on the ninth Puttkamer, the duty adjutant, telephoned one of the westernmost corps headquarters, at Aachen; the Chief of Staff there told him there was some mist, but the sun was already breaking through and tomorrow would probably be as fine. When the naval adjutant repeated this to Hitler, he announced, "Good. Then we can begin." The service commands were informed that the final orders to attack or postpone (code words "Danzig" and "Augsburg," respectively) would be issued by 9:30 P.M. at the latest.

Extraordinary security precautions were taken, even within Hitler's own staff. Martin Bormann was left in the belief that they were to visit Oslo, and the Party authorities there made great plans to welcome the Führer. Hitler instructed his female secretaries to pack their bags for a long journey, and when these innocents asked Julius Schaub "How long?" he replied with an air of mystery, "It might be a week, it might be two. It could be a month or even years!" In fact, even Schaub, Hitler's long-time intimate, did not know. During the afternoon Hitler and his staff drove out of Berlin, heading north toward Staaken airfield. But the column of cars bypassed Staaken and went to the small railroad station at Finkenkrug, a popular excursion spot. Here Hitler's special train was waiting for them. It left at 4:38 P.M., heading north toward Hamburg; but after dusk fell, it pulled into the little country station of Hagenow. When it set off again, even the uninitiated could tell it was no longer heading north. At about nine o'clock it halted outside Hanover; the telephones were linked up, and the latest weather forecast was obtained from Luftwaffe headquarters near Potsdam. It was still good. Hitler ordered the code word "Danzig" issued to the commands.

Still the secret was closely kept. Over dinner Schmundt asked the secretaries nonchalantly, "Have you got your Sick-Sick tablets?" After a while Hitler joked, "If you behave yourselves, you can all take home sealskins as souvenirs." He retired early to his sleeping quarters, but the movement of the train and his apprehensions kept him from sleeping. Hour after hour he gazed out of the carriage window, watching for the first telltale signs of fog shrouds forming. The initial success of "Yellow" depended on the Luftwaffe's striking force, and fog was Göring's worst enemy.

An hour before dawn, at 4:25 A.M., the train glided into a small station from which all the name indications had been removed—it was Euskirchen, thirty miles from the Allied lines. A column of the three-axled field limousines that had served Hitler so well in Poland was awaiting him in the semidarkness. For half an hour he and his entourage drove through the little Eifel villages, in which the signposts had been replaced by stark yellow plates with various military symbols on them. Hitler broke the silence only once. Turning to Major von Below, the Luftwaffe adjutant sitting with Schaub on the jump seats of his car, he asked, "Has the Luftwaffe taken into account that here in the west the sun rises several minutes later than in Berlin?" Below set his mind at rest.

After a while the country lanes began to climb a hill through scattered woods. When his limousine stopped, Hitler clambered stiffly out. A former antiaircraft position on the side of a hill had been converted and strengthened to serve as his field headquarters. The nearest village had been completely evacuated, and would serve for his lesser staff. It was already daylight. The air was filled with the sound of birds heralding the arrival of another dawn. Hitler stood outside his bunker, watching the sun slowly bring color to the countryside. This was to be the first real day of spring weather. From the two main roads in the valleys on each side of this hill they could hear the heavy rumble of convoys of trucks heading westward. An adjutant pointed wordlessly to his watch: it was 5:35 A.M. Far away they could hear the growing clamor of heavy artillery begin, and from behind them swelled a thunder of aircraft engines as the Luftwaffe fighter and bomber squadrons approached.

PART 2

"WAR OF LIBERATION"

The Warlord at the Western Front

On May 10, 1940, the *Völkischer Beobachter*—chief organ of the Nazi party—rolled off the presses in Berlin, Munich, and Vienna with red banner headlines: GERMANY'S DECISIVE STRUGGLE HAS BEGUN! and THE FÜHRER AT THE WESTERN FRONT. After half an hour's tough arguing, Keitel had persuaded Hitler to allow the OKW communiqué to end with the announcement that he himself had gone to the western front to take command. Hitler was loath to steal his generals' thunder, but the OKW generals, fresh from their command triumph in Norway, wanted to keep the army's General Staff firmly in its secondary place. Hitler's prestige was high. General Erwin Rommel—now commanding a panzer division in the west—had in a letter on April 21 written a private eulogy of the Führer's victory over Denmark and Norway. *"Ja,* if we didn't have the Führer! Who knows whether any other German exists with such a genius for military leadership and such a matching mastery of political leadership too!"

Hitler had patiently gone over every aspect of "Yellow" with the leading generals—with Walther Reichenau, Günther von Kluge, and the panzer general Ewald von Kleist, whose tanks would spearhead the thrust to the English Channel, and with General Ernst Busch, whose Sixteenth Army would string out a powerful flank defense south of the armored thrust. Hitler found high praise for the meticulous logistics work of Kleist's Chief of Staff, General Kurt Zeitzler.

Just as he was godfather to the strategy underlying "Yellow," so Hitler was the progenitor of the special raids which opened the campaign—the "Trojan horse" trick used to seize the Dutch bridges, the paratroop raids against Rotterdam and the Moordijk bridge in "Fortress

Holland," and above all the glider landings on the key bridges in Belgium and on the daunting fortress-site at Eben Emael. "Suffice to say this," was the appraisal of one of Jodl's staff in September, "this operation against the bridges was *the* factor that would determine whether the Sixth Army could advance or not. That it came off was thanks to the Führer alone, as regards both the decision itself and the preparation."

As a military commander, Adolf Hitler remained an enigma even to his closest associates. They admired him for his past achievements for Germany but still feared for the future. In victory his generals worshipped him; but those whom he rejected turned sour, abominated him, and eventually conspired against him. The depth of hatred he stirred in the souls of these intelligent outcasts can be read in the countless essays they composed in vain endeavors to synthesize and express their memories. Alfred Jodl, perhaps his most able strategic adviser, was to write from a prison cell that he still kept asking himself whether he had really known the man at whose side he had led such a thorny and self-denying existence. "I keep making the same mistake: I blame his humble origins. But then I remember how many peasants' sons were blessed by History with the name The Great." And General Zeitzler—one of Hitler's last chiefs of the General Staff—also grappled in vain with this phenomenon, though more analytically. "I witnessed Hitler in every conceivable circumstance—in times of fortune and misfortune, of victory and defeat, in good cheer and in angry outburst, during speeches and conferences, surrounded by thousands, by a mere handful, or quite alone, speaking on the telephone, sitting in his bunker, in his car, in his plane; in brief on every conceivable occasion. Even so, I can't claim to have seen into his soul or perceived what he was after."

Zeitzler saw him as an actor, with every word, gesture, and grimace under control, his penetrating stare practiced for hours before some private mirror. He won over newcomers from the first handshake and piercing look, and paradoxically appeared the very embodiment of the strong and fearless leader, of honesty and open heart. He cultivated the impression that he cared deeply for his subordinates' well-being. He would telephone a departing general at midnight: "Please don't fly. It's such foul weather and I'm worried about your safety." Or he would look a minor official in the eye and explain, "Now I'm telling you this privately, and you must keep it strictly under your hat."

The surviving records are full of examples of the congenial impression Hitler made on others. Rommel proudly wrote on June 3: "The

Führer's visit was fabulous. He greeted me with the words, 'Rommel! We were all so worried about you during the attack!' He was beaming from one ear to the other, and asked me to walk with him afterward—I was the only division commander there." Milch wrote down Hitler's words to him on April 21, 1941, after a particularly hazardous return flight from North Africa: "Thank goodness you got back!" In June 1941 Albert Speer's office chronicle noted: "The Führer sent a telephone message from the Obersalzberg begging Herr Speer to drop the proposed visit to Norway, as things are too uncertain up there and Herr Speer is indispensable to him." In February 1943 Field Marshal Wolfram von Richthofen wrote in his diary: "Finally the Führer inquired very anxiously about my health." In midwar Hitler would halt urgent conferences with hungry generals for half an hour to allow his stenographers to eat. One wrote in his diary on February 20, 1943: "The midday conference was short—57 minutes—but cold. The Führer must have noticed that we were freezing, because he mentioned it to us. I said that if you sit still a long time you do get cold. The Führer . . . then promised a heater for us. I replied, 'That would be very nice, mein Führer!' " And next day: "At the noon conference the heater promised by the Führer is indeed there—a small china stove. . . . In the afternoon, before a brief reception of seven officers handpicked for special missions for which the Führer briefs them in a short speech, he inquired in General Schmundt's presence whether the stove was warm enough for us. When we said it was, he was hugely pleased and laughed out loud."

His assessment of character was instant and deadly. A member of Jodl's staff, Captain Ivo-Thilo von Trotha, who was often present at Hitler's supper table during the French campaign, wrote in 1946: "My impression was that the Führer clearly recognized the human weaknesses of his colleagues and stood aloof from them." Hitler knew precisely how far he could go with each general. Once he snatched a document from Keitel's hands and threw it on the floor. Keitel meekly gathered it up. Hitler judged newcomers after only a glance. Of one army commander he sourly commented, "He looks like a schoolteacher!"—and since for him every teacher was a *"Steisstrommler,"* or buttock-thrasher, that general's career was clearly at an end. But his staff abounded with misfits—like his personal adjutant, the crippled nonentity Julius Schaub—whose value was in their undivided loyalty to him.

Of his gifts as a leader, even a military leader, there is no doubt. Halder was to refer to his unusual intellect and grasp, his imaginativeness, his tenacity and willpower. Jodl wrote that in the French campaign Hitler's leadership was clear, consistent, and capable; here Hitler was to prove himself a "classical commander." Jodl considered that in drafting the terms of the armistice with fallen France, Hitler ostensibly showed a generosity that gave cause to hope that of the two warring impulses within him it was the better that was gaining ground.

By decades of planned reading, Hitler had soaked up a huge amount of technical and military learning. His memory was proverbial. He had not only read the works of Frederick the Great, Moltke, Schlieffen, and Clausewitz, he could confound his generals with quotations from memory. What he lacked was the ability to assess and analyze a military situation logically, unhurriedly, and calmly—as a staff officer would have; in that respect he was still the World War I corporal who had no mastery of the time and space problems involved in the deployment of great armies. In the French campaign he was to prove as timid and cautious in the conduct of operations as he had been bold, almost brash, in designing them; in later campaigns he asserted himself to the other extreme. The classical Führer Directive, in which his commanders were given a broad mission and left to their own discretion in carrying it out, was increasingly supplemented and supplanted by Führer Orders, in which Hitler intervened in the tactical operations at every level. His victory in France confirmed him in his belief that he was a predestined military commander.

Hitler's headquarters for "Yellow" were at Münstereifel. The underground command post was very cramped. Alone in his room, with its folding bed, table, and chair, he could hear every sound made by Keitel and Jodl next door. Jodl's operations staff was billeted down in the village and worked in a wooden encampment hidden three miles away in the woods. Hitler toured it briefly one day—the only time he ever set foot inside Security Zone II. He preferred to hold his war conferences in the open air, for the spring landscape enchanted him. He privately suggested to his staff that when the war was over they should all return each year—just this little select group around him now—to Münstereifel, "my bird paradise." The site remained unchanged until 1944, with even the names of the occupants left painted on the doors; it had been intended as a permanent memorial to Hitler's "war of liberation."

As the Luftwaffe predicted, May 10, 1940, dawned fine. He rewarded the meteorologist responsible for the brilliant forecasting with a gold watch. During the night, his Luftwaffe had already begun mining the Belgian and Dutch ports. Now Göring struck simultaneously at seventy airfields, destroying between three and four hundred planes, and thus seizing for Hitler an air superiority that was to remain unchallenged for the next two weeks. Soon messengers brought him the exhilarating news that the British and French armies had begun pouring into Belgium. In October 1941, his armies now before Moscow, Hitler still remembered the thrill of that moment. "When the news came that the enemy was advancing along the whole front I could have wept for joy! They'd fallen right into my trap! It was a crafty move on our part to strike toward Liège—we had to make them believe we were remaining faithful to the old Schlieffen Plan. . . . How exciting it will be later to go over all those operations once again. Several times during the night I used to go to the operations room to pore over those relief maps."

The Belgians and Dutch were not unprepared. The Forschungsamt had intercepted a last frantic telephone warning from the Dutch military attaché to his government the previous evening, but the delicate "Trojan horse" operations went ahead—a calculated risk, in view of the enemy's foreknowledge. As one of Jodl's staff noted: "Our troops were storming an enemy who was ready and waiting for our attack to begin early on May 10." The Dutch government had cannily refused an entry visa to Major Kiewitz, Hitler's special emissary to Queen Wilhelmina. Ironically it was Canaris's Abwehr that was appointed to find out how the Dutch suspicions had been aroused; the Abwehr adroitly diverted suspicion to a senior foreign ministry official.

Extreme anxiety reigned at Hitler's headquarters as word of the vital commando-operations was awaited. One of Jodl's officers was accompanying the first wave of tanks invading Holland and Belgium with a radio truck, to report direct to Hitler on the state of the bridges over the Meuse and the Albert Canal. Between 9 and 10 A.M. the first three coded signals arrived from this officer, Captain von Trotha: the Dutch had evidently managed to blow up both bridges across the Meuse north and south of Maastricht; the railway bridge farther north had also been blown up, but was now in German hands; the Abwehr's Special Battalion 100, the "Trojan horse," had suffered fearful casualties.

But in the afternoon Trotha had better news: the Belgian bridges across the Albert Canal—where a hundred troops had silently landed in gliders as dawn broke—were intact, except for one at Canne. A Belgian infantry division close by had as yet done nothing to mop up this diminutive German holding force. By 4:30 P.M., Hitler learned that the 4th Panzer Division had actually forded the Meuse, leaving its armor temporarily behind, and was pouring into the two bridgeheads seized across the Albert Canal. At Eben Emael a band of intrepid German engineer troops armed with hollow-charge explosives had landed by glider and immobilized the entire fortress: the underground gun-crews were sealed in, their artillery was knocked out. By early next morning, May 11, a temporary bridge had been thrown across the Meuse at Maastricht, and an armored brigade had crossed. The 4th Panzer Division now spearheaded the advance of Reichenau's Sixth Army. Eben Emael capitulated at midday, and with this, Belgium's fate was effectively sealed.

In the evening, Captain von Trotha brought to Hitler the first impressions of the front line. On the approaches to Maastricht the German armor had encountered little resistance; the frontier forces had thrown their weapons away and fled by bicycle. The Dutch population had stood curiously watching the tanks and infantry pass. The people were friendly, Trotha reported; some of them gave the Hitler salute, others willingly helped the invaders on their way with directions stuttered in Dutch or broken German. As Trotha had entered Maastricht in his armored radio vehicle, two colossal detonations, shattering millions of windows, had heralded the demolition of the bridges. A stolid Dutch citizen had espied his red-striped General Staff trousers and besought advice: he had left home and crossed the bridge, hatless, just to fetch milk —how was he to get back? Trotha had replied the Germans also regretted that the bridge was down, but that all complaints were to be addressed to the Dutch military authorities. "I was opposed to it from the start," said the Dutchman. Trotha replied, "Well you must just wait until our troops have finished crossing." The Dutchman asked how long that would be. "We will try and get everybody across by the time the war ends," joked the army officer. "But what will my wife think?" "I expect the people over there will also learn in time that the war has come," responded Trotha. In fact, by afternoon the Germans were already ferrying Dutch citizens from one side of the river to the other.

In southern Holland the German troops had found the Dutch garrisons of towns and villages standing idly around without their guns or gear and passively awaiting the invaders. But in the north a four-day battle raged as the Dutch tried to wipe out the paratroops and gliderborne infantry landed at Rotterdam and The Hague; bomber squadrons had already taken off to relieve the pressure on General Kurt Student's paratroops at Rotterdam when word arrived that the Dutch were capitulating. Only half the bombers could be recalled—the rest dropped nearly a hundred tons of bombs on the town; nine hundred people died in the subsequent fires. The next day Holland formally surrendered.

It was now time for Hitler's masterstroke.

Every indication until now had persuaded the enemy that the offensive through Belgium and Holland was the somewhat unoriginal linchpin of Hitler's strategy. For months Canaris's organization had been feeding clues to that effect to the enemy, using every conceivable method from elegant women agents to "indiscreet" telephone conversations on lines known to be tapped by the enemy.

But Hitler's main offensive was to start far to the south, at Sedan, on the other side of the Ardennes, where General von Kleist's armor had just crossed the Meuse and established a bridgehead. On May 14, Hitler directed that all available panzer and mechanized divisions were to assemble for a rapid push from this bridgehead westward and then northwestward to the English Channel; that he should have issued a Führer Directive which merely repeated what had long been ordered was an augury of the extent to which he proposed to take command himself.

> The course of the operations so far shows that the enemy has not perceived the basic idea of our own operation, the eventual breakthrough by Army Group A [Rundstedt]. They are still moving up powerful forces to a line extending from Antwerp to Namur and apparently neglecting the sector confronting Army Group A.

Bock's Army Group B was given the task of luring as much of the enemy into Belgium as possible before Rundstedt's armor cut them off in the rear by driving to the Channel. Leeb's Army Group C had meanwhile so successfully simulated preparations for a frontal assault on the Maginot line that the French had hesitated to withdraw troops from the south until it was too late, for the Luftwaffe had destroyed the railway lines. Their path now flattened before them by the bombers of Richthofen's Eighth Air Corps, Kleist's armored units rolled out of the Sedan bridgehead toward the Channel coast.

From this moment on, only a resolute commander supported by outstanding military Intelligence could have saved France. General von Rundstedt, Germany's oldest active soldier, is said to have remarked that he would have found it much more interesting to fight the rest of the campaign in the shoes of France's Army Chief of Staff, General Maurice Gamelin. It was now clear that the cream of the Allied forces had mustered north of Kleist's advance and was penetrating Belgium. German army Intelligence had located a new French Seventh Army referred to explicitly as an *"armée d'intervention dans la Belgique."* Since the end of March, Halder's Intelligence branch, "Foreign Armies

West," had consistently estimated that half the Anglo-French forces were in the north, waiting to be cut off.[1]

Again, as in the Norwegian campaign, Hitler's nerve briefly left him. He was wary of his own good fortune. When Brauchitsch made his regular twice-daily telephone call, Hitler nervously bombarded him with minutiae of which the army's thorough preparations had long taken care. As Kleist's armor swept onward toward the Channel coast, on May 17 Hitler intervened to order that they halt to allow the slower infantry divisions time to catch up and consolidate the flank before the French could penetrate it. Army Intelligence argued in vain that the French were presently concerned only with stabilizing their own defensive line along the Aisne and the Somme: radio Intelligence had found a new French army headquarters west of Verdun, and aerial reconnaissance showed that the French transport movements were purely defensive. Hitler would not be convinced. He drove to Rundstedt's headquarters, nervously studied the maps, and on his return to his own headquarters spread a wholly unnecessary gloom about the danger from the south. When Halder and Brauchitsch saw him the next day, he was raging that the army was about to ruin the whole campaign and that it was needlessly running the risk of defeat. On the nineteenth Hitler had fresh occasion for alarm when army Intelligence lost all sight of the three-quarters of a million Allied soldiers believed trapped in the north; for hours on end it seemed that the bulk of the British and French forces had succeeded in escaping southward after all. Not until May 20 was this first personal crisis over. The army reported that there were at least twenty enemy divisions trapped north of the Somme; in the evening, when Brauchitsch telephoned Hitler with the news that the tanks had reached Abbeville—and hence the Channel coast—Hitler was ecstatic with praise for the army and its commanders.

He spoke with such emotion that General Keitel made a written record of his words, which is, however, lost. According to Jodl, the Führer spoke of the peace treaty he would now make with France—he would demand the return of all the territories and properties robbed from the German people these last four hundred years, and he would repay the French for the ignominious terms inflicted on Germany in 1918 by now conducting the first peace negotiations at the same spot in the forest of

[1] The Allied superiority in tanks was vast. The French and British had 3,432 tanks, not including either the obsolete Renault F.T. or the light British tanks. The Germans had started the campaign with 2,574 tanks, of which, however, 523 were the light Mark I, and 955, the hardly better Mark II. (Among the rest were 345 Mark IIIs, 278 Mark IVs, 106 Czech Mark 35, and 228 Czech Mark 38s.)

Compiègne. As for the British: "The British can have their peace as soon as they return our colonies to us."

According to an officer who read Keitel's missing account, Hitler jubilantly predicted that this victory would at last right the wrongs done by the Peace of Westphalia which had concluded the Thirty Years' War and established France as the dominant power in Europe. To Keitel he exclaimed, "I must not forget how much I owe to Field Marshal von Blomberg at this moment! Without his help the Wehrmacht would never have become the magnificent instrument that has reaped us this unique victory!"

But it was this victory psychosis, prematurely sprung upon his military staff, this belief that total victory had been achieved by May 20, 1940, that was to prove his undoing at Dunkirk.

Hitler now turned his attention to long-range planning.

On May 20 he had already conferred with Brauchitsch and Halder on the outline of the second phase of the campaign, code-named "Red," in which German forces would sweep southward from the Somme and Aisne toward the lower Seine and the Swiss frontier. His earlier eagerness for Italian divisions to join in a mid-June offensive ("Brown") on the Upper Rhine front had evaporated. He wrote frequently to Mussolini with word of his latest victories, but Mussolini's replies were an uninspiring amalgam of polite applause and qualified promises of later belligerency. Indeed, an awkward disparity of aims was now emerging: for Italy the main enemy was now Britain, while Hitler believed that with France laid low he could oblige Britain to come to terms with him. There were disquieting rumors that Italy was preparing to invade Yugoslavia, which might set the whole of the Balkans on fire. An urgent question of priorities would have to be faced.

When Admiral Raeder privately disclosed to Hitler on the twenty-first that the admiralty had been studying the problems of a seaborne invasion of the British Isles since November, Hitler did not noticeably welcome this diligence; and when Jodl a few days later suggested that an immediate invasion be prepared, the Führer roundly rejected the idea without explaining why. We must conclude that he believed that submarine and bomber attacks would force Britain to submit, for he indicated that after France's defeat he would concentrate on the production of submarines and Junkers 88 bombers. He left Raeder at least in no doubt that he thought the war still far from over.

In one respect Russia's posture gave immediate cause for alarm, for it could instantly shut off Germany's Romanian oil supplies. Russia's main threat to Germany was still a distant one: from the slow rate at which airfield construction was progressing in the Russian-occupied border regions, it seemed clear that Germany still had a breathing space during which the Kremlin would continue to appease Hitler. Molotov had expressed Russia's genuine relief that Germany had managed to invade Norway before the Allies had, and he had received word of "Yellow" with equal sympathy; but this honeymoon would not last any longer than served the Russian purpose. Hitler probably believed that if he could attack the Soviet Union in the spring of 1941 he would thwart Stalin's intentions. How else is one to interpret the Führer's cryptic remark to Halder on April 24, 1940: "We have an interest in seeing to it that the [Romanian] oil fields keep supplying us until next spring at the least; after that we will be freer." Romania was now exporting over 130,000 tons of oil a month to Germany—nothing must endanger these oil fields or the countries through which the Danube and the railroad links brought that oil to Germany.

At the end of May 1940 the risk did become acute as rumors multiplied of Italian plans to attack Yugoslavia; this would free Hungary to attack Romania—from Forschungsamt intercepts of the Hungarian legation's cables from Berlin, the Germans knew how hollow were Hungary's declarations of solidarity with the Axis—and Russia would use this as a pretext to invade Romania as well. On May 20 the German military attaché in Moscow quoted to Berlin reliable details of Soviet troop concentrations on the Romanian frontier. Molotov denied them, but the facts spoke for themselves. Brauchitsch (unaware that Bessarabia, or Moldávia, had already been assigned to Stalin by the secret August 1939 pact) urged Hitler on the twenty-second to do something to curb these Russian ambitions; Hitler responded that he "hoped" to limit the Russian expansion to Bessarabia. Weizsäcker wrote a curious passage in his private diary on May 23: "Assuming there *is* a crushing victory in the west, the obvious next move would be to create order in the east as well, that will give breathing space and river frontiers—an order that will endure. Whether Britain submits at once or has to be bombed into her senses, the fact is there will probably have to be one more squaring of accounts in the east. . . ." In the event, Italy undertook not to attack Yugoslavia, and after a few days this eastern crisis subsided. But all this was symptomatic of the raw nerves constantly exposed in the Balkans, where Hitler's sole interest was the economic necessity of keeping the peace at all costs. Even at the height of battle, the absolute political leader must keep more than immediate military problems on his mind.

Many intricate and interrelated factors explain how the British Expeditionary Force (BEF) escaped from Dunkirk in the last days of May 1940, while German armor was pulled back on orders first from Rundstedt and then from Hitler himself.

The first factor, often overlooked in retrospective works of history, was that the realization that the British were deserting the field of battle en masse did not dawn on the German High Command until about May 26—a full week after the decision had been taken in London. The jealousy with which the war department (OKH) guarded its own affairs from OKW interference contributed to this. Halder's Foreign Armies West branch had certainly reported as early as May 21 that the unusual number of troop transports in Dunkirk and Boulogne might indicate that British troops were about to be evacuated; and the permanent radio link between the war office in London and the BEF in France, first monitored the next day, also suggested events were being removed from French control. But to Hitler all this was unthinkable. Had he not always warned that once the British got a toehold anywhere it was almost impossible to dislodge them? He was convinced that the British would fight to the last man in France and that he must deploy his forces accordingly. Not until May 26 was this fundamental error realized. German army Intelligence intercepted a radio message from the war office in London to the British commandant in Calais just after noon. "Every hour you continue to exist is of the greatest help to the BEF." Aerial reconnaissance had sighted thirteen warships and nine troop transports in Dunkirk harbor that morning. Foreign Armies West concluded: "It is probable that the embarkation of the British Expeditionary Force has begun." Only now did Hitler permit the armored advance on—though not into—Dunkirk to begin again. His artillery would finish the job.

The sequence of events which had resulted in the halting of the armor two days before had begun with a brief local crisis on May 21, when British and French tanks launched an unexpected attack on the inner flank of the German Fourth Army at Arras. Hitler and Rundstedt both regarded this as proof that the armored spearhead of Army Group A had advanced too fast for an effective flank defense to be established, and Rundstedt ordered the Fourth Army and Kleist's armored group to delay its advance on the Channel ports until the Arras crisis had been resolved. Brauchitsch and Halder regretted Rundstedt's overcautious conduct of Army Group A operations—bearing up on the Channel ports from the southwest—and without informing Hitler they ordered control of the Fourth Army transferred to General von Bock's Army Group B, which was advancing on the ports from the east. Bock was to command the last act of the encirclement. Hitler learned of this when he visited Rundstedt's headquarters at Charleville with Jodl and Schmundt the next morning, May 24. Thus an element of contrariness, a subconscious desire to spite Brauchitsch and the General Staff, must have contributed to Hitler's peremptory cancellation of their order: the Fourth Army was not to be transferred to Bock's command—for the time being it was to stay where it was. It was tactically foolhardy, claimed Hitler, to commit their tanks, which were vital to the success of "Red," in the swampy Flanders lowlands to which the war department would have sent them.

At Charleville, Hitler found every support for his views. Indeed, the previous day the Fourth Army's General von Kluge had himself persuaded Rundstedt it would be better not to attack on the twenty-fourth but to allow Kleist's armor time to regroup for a more methodical assault on the twenty-fifth. (With gross exaggeration, Kleist was claiming that half his tanks were out of action, and this figure must have worried Hitler.) Rundstedt's proposal to Hitler on May 24 went one stage further: his armor should remain where it was, commanding the high ridge along a line of canals west of Dunkirk, and give an appropriate welcome to the enemy forces swept westward by Bock's Army Group B; this would give the tanks a valuable respite. The possibility that the British might escape to England was not discussed. Hitler was obsessed by two visions: his precious armor floundering in the swampy Flanders fields that he, Keitel, and Jodl had all seen with their own eyes in World War I; or alternatively, his tanks being pointlessly shot to pieces in the streets of Dunkirk, as they had in fact been in the suburbs of Warsaw eight months before.

There was a political factor too. Hitler desired to spare Belgium's relatively friendly Flemish population the destruction of property this closing act of "Yellow" would entail.

At all events, Hitler did not hesitate to lend his authority to Rundstedt's decision to halt the tanks. How far he was also motivated by Göring's boast that the Luftwaffe alone would annihilate the encircled enemy is open to dispute. Göring certainly telephoned Hitler to this effect. Afterward, Hitler told his army adjutant that Göring would do the job, and he contrasted the Luftwaffe's ideological reliability with that of the army leaders. At twelve-thirty the Führer's headquarters telephoned the "halt order" to the army group and army commanders:

they were to stand fast west of the canal line; that same day, in a directive giving guidelines for "Red" and the campaign against Britain, Hitler merely indicated in passing that the Luftwaffe's present job in the north was to break all resistance of the "encircled enemy" and prevent any British forces from escaping across the Channel. To a protesting staff member, Jodl soothingly said, "The war is won; it just has to be ended. There is no point in sacrificing a single tank if we can do it much more cheaply with the Luftwaffe."

Thus the tanks remained "rooted to the spot," as Halder bitterly commented in his diary on May 26. Hitler had still not set the tanks in motion. One more factor had arisen. On the evening of the twenty-fifth he explained to his adjutants that he particularly wanted the SS elite brigade under Sepp Dietrich to join in this crucial action at Dunkirk. His intention was to show the world that he had troops equal to the best even such a racially advanced nation as Britain could field against him. Heinrich Himmler—who conferred with Hitler that day on his radical plans for the eastern territories[2]—may well have asked this favor of Hitler, although his own agenda makes no explicit reference to the military operations. By May 26, Sepp Dietrich's Leibstandarte Adolf Hitler —Life Guards Brigade—was in position. On that morning, too, Rundstedt's staff changed their attitude, since radio monitoring suggested that their appreciation of the enemy's intentions was wrong. Colonel Henning von Tresckow, one of Rundstedt's staff, telephoned his friend Schmundt at Hitler's headquarters about this, with the result that at 1:30 P.M. Hitler informed Brauchitsch that the tanks might resume their eastward drive at once. They were to come within artillery range of Dunkirk, and the army's heavy artillery and the Luftwaffe would do the rest. But Kleist's tank drivers were now resting, or their tanks were being overhauled, and many hours would pass before the attack began.

Meanwhile the Luftwaffe could see that the British were apparently embarking only their troops, abandoning all their weapons and equipment as they fled. The beaches were thick with waiting Englishmen, the roads were choked with truck columns fifteen miles long. Göring landed at Hitler's headquarters in a light aircraft and boasted of the carnage his bombers were wreaking in Dunkirk harbor. "Only fishing boats are getting through. Let's hope the Tommies can swim!" The reality, however, was soon different: the Luftwaffe bombers were based largely on airfields back in Germany, and either their bombs were ineffective

[2] See pages 134–35 below.

against small ships or they exploded harmlessly in the sand dunes; more ominously, the German bombers proved no match for the short-range British fighters based just across the Channel. The Germans found that for the first time the enemy had local air superiority, and their troubles were added to by the fact that at the end of May the Luftwaffe's Eighth Air Corps was grounded by fog for three days. In Dunkirk the British rearguard fought on with undiminished tenacity as the last British and French troops were embarked.

Göring failed to see the warning signs for his Luftwaffe, which Hitler had now ordered to open direct air attacks on the British Isles as soon as possible, beginning "with an annihilating attack in reprisal for the British raids on the Ruhr." The Luftwaffe commander confidently leaned his vast bulk across the map table in Hitler's headquarters, stabbed a finger at the map, and promised that when his planes began their attacks on London no stone would be left atop another.

While these momentous events were transpiring in the west, in Germany's new eastern domains a ruthless program of subjugation and pacification had begun. "Yellow" distracted the world's press from what was going on.

On Sunday May 25, the Reichsführer SS outlined to Hitler and the head of his Chancellery, Lammers, proposals for dealing with the various racial strains in Poland, whether Poles, Jews, Ukrainians, White Russians, Gorals, Lemkes, or Kashubs. Himmler showed the Führer his six-page plan for screening the 23 million people in these new dominions for adults and children of sufficiently pure blood to allow their assimilation into Germany. He proposed that all other children should be taught only what he saw as the necessary rudiments: "Simple counting up to five hundred, how to write their names, and lessons on the divine commandant to obey the Germans and be honest, industrious, and well-behaved." It was unnecessary for them to learn to read. Racially acceptable children could be evacuated to the Reich to receive a proper education after separation from their parents. As Himmler pointed out, in what now seems a significant explanation when the plan's recipient is considered: "Each individual case may seem cruel and tragic, but this method is the mildest and best if we are to reject as ungermanic, impossible, and incompatible with our convictions the Bolshevik method of physically exterminating a race."

After a few years of this racial sifting, a low-grade potpourri of races would remain in the east. "This population will be available to Germany as a leaderless labor force, providing us with seasonal migratory labor for special projects like roadbuilding, quarrying, and construction work. They themselves will eat and live better than under Polish rule. And, given their own lack of culture, they will be well appointed to work under the strict, forthright, and just leadership of the German nation on its eternal cultural mission." As for the Jews, Himmler's six-page plan disclosed, "I hope to effect the complete disappearance of the Jew [from Europe] by means of a mass emigration of all Jews to Africa or some other such colony."[3]

Afterward, Himmler scribbled in his notebook: "Memorandum on Poland. Führer warmly approves." Hitler commanded Lammers to provide an oral briefing for Hans Frank, the Gauleiters, top SS officials, and police officials of the eastern provinces. Himmler stipulated that the document's contents must never be quoted in any orders that these men issued (an interesting embargo).

A month later, Himmler took the opportunity of a train journey with Hitler to show him an eight-page plan for settling these eastern provinces with strong German stock. It provided for one-eighth of the indigenous population to be transplanted as racially acceptable stock to Germany; the other seven-eighths would be displaced eastward, into Hans Frank's Generalgouvernement. To provide healthy German stock, Himmler proposed that after two years of military service or four years in the SS young unmarried German soldiers be induced to settle.and work the land in the eastern provinces for up to eight years before marrying and taking over a farmstead or estate. The Generalgouvernement was to serve them as a reservoir of cheap labor. The foreign laborers were to be kept in serfdom; attempts at sexual relations with their German overlords would be punishable by death or heavy prison sentences. It was the lack of racial purity, Himmler argued, that had led to the downfall of the Greek and Roman empires. He afterward noted on the document: "Shown to the Führer in the train from Freiburg i.Br. to Ottersweiser on June 30, 1940. The Führer said that every point I made was right."

By that time, as we shall see, Hitler was already considering provinces far to the east of Poland.

There is much less to be learned from an examination of the military events of the rest of the French campaign. On May 28, the king of Bel-

---

[3] After France's defeat, Hitler decided in July 1940 that Madagascar would make a suitable destination for Europe's Jews. See pages 148–49.

gium capitulated, and by June 2 the British evacuation of Dunkirk was over. German army Intelligence estimated that half the enemy forces had been swept from the battlefield; Brauchitsch telephoned this information to Hitler that evening. The German army, with 136 divisions, was virtually intact. It would embark on "Red," the final defeat of France, with a 2 to 1 superiority.

Events were fast pushing Europe's frontiers back to those of the sixteenth century. German bomber squadrons based in the Artois region and Flanders could keep the British Isles in check. But nothing was further from Hitler's mind than an invasion of Britain now. The great strategic option, between striking north or south after Dunkirk, was not recognized at the time. His blueprint for "Red" was largely determined by short-term psychological or political factors: Verdun must be captured as rapidly as possible. Overland contact must be made with Spain—a decoded cable had just revealed that Franco had assured Britain of his neutrality and lack of aggressive intentions against Gibraltar. Paris itself would be bypassed to the east and west, for Hitler feared nothing more than that an 1871-style Communist uprising in the capital might bring his forces into armed conflict with Soviet-backed Communists. The Maginot line would be taken from the rear. "Red" would begin at 5 A.M. on June 5.

Meanwhile, surrounded by Party officials and personal bodyguards, Hitler toured the battlefields in Belgium and Flanders. At the end of May the new Italian ambassador, Dino Alfieri,[4] had brought him Mussolini's offer to attack France's Alpine frontier on June 5. Since this might well lead world opinion to believe that it was this Italian "second front" and not "Red" that brought France down, Hitler asked the Duce to wait a few days. Even so, Italy's belated belligerency and her transparent self-interest aroused the anger of the generals to whom Hitler now revealed Mussolini's intentions in conferences at Brussels and Charleville on the first two days of June. At Brussels, where Bock had assembled his senior generals, Hitler explained his Dunkirk decisions: "Gentlemen, you will have wondered why I stopped the armored divisions outside Dunkirk. The fact was I could not afford to waste military effort. I was anxious lest the enemy launch an offensive from the Somme and wipe out the Fourth Army's weak armored force, perhaps even going so far as Dunkirk. Such a military rebuff," as he put it, "might have had intolerable effects in foreign policy. . . ." Afterward he drove

---

[4] The Forschungsamt had detected the anti-German utterances of his sixty-year-old predecessor, Bernardo Attolico, and Hitler had requested his recall.

with Army Group Commander von Bock in an open car through Brussels—which he had last seen as a Bavarian infantryman.

At Charleville the next day, June 2, he addressed Rundstedt and his generals, by chance in the villa which had once housed Kaiser Wilhelm II during World War I. He outlined "Operation Red" to them and informed them that Italy would shortly join in. He spoke of the reparations he proposed to exact from France; then his voice softened, and he once again extolled Britain and her mission for the white race. It was not, he said, a matter of inconsequence to him which power ruled India. One general wrote in his diary: "He points out that without a navy the equal of Britain's we could not hold on to her colonies for long. Thus we can easily find a basis for peace agreement with Britain. France on the other hand must be stamped into the ground; she must pay the bill." Another general wrote: "Hitler never drew the proper consequences from his admiration of the British; his threats against France revealed his boundless greed for conquest."

As he left the villa, crowds of cheering soldiers thronged his car. Hitler, every inch the victorious warlord, acknowledged their acclaim.

To Hitler the war seemed already won. He said as much to Admiral Canaris on June 3 when the Intelligence chief came to report on the Abwehr agents who had been killed in the campaign so far. And he repeated it to Admiral Raeder the next day. Within a few weeks France would be knocked out, and German industry could resume work on equipping the navy and Luftwaffe; he would demobilize large sections of the army to provide the industrial manpower. In the far north, the Allies suddenly abandoned their last foothold in Narvik, losing an aircraft carrier, two destroyers, and a troop transport in skirmishes with the diminished German battle fleet that chanced upon the scene; Hitler generously credited General Jodl alone with the decision to retain Narvik in mid-April, despite his own dark hours of despair for Dietl's survival. Jodl's position on Hitler's staff was henceforth unassailable.

Hitler's occupation policy in Holland and Belgium was to establish these Germanic states as border dependencies around a mighty German core. As early as November he had drafted a decree on the administration of the countries to be occupied in "Yellow." In the version he had signed on May 9 he had deleted the words "There is to be no exploitation of the occupied regions in a selfish German interest." In Holland as in Norway he established a Reich Commissar to fill the vacuum left by the fleeing monarchy; he chose an Austrian, Arthur Seyss-

Inquart, evidently on Himmler's recommendation. Seyss-Inquart had felt ill at ease with his job in the Generalgouvernement and had pleaded for an army commission so he could serve Germany as he had in the previous war; but Hitler knew the lawyer had a crippled leg and gave him Holland to administer instead, ignoring the angry outcry this civilian appointment provoked in the army. On May 22 he explained that by appointing Reich commissars in Norway and Holland he hoped to remold these countries along National Socialist lines.

In Holland, as in Belgium, there had been embryonic Nazi organizations, but Hitler had little time for them. He regarded his own rise to power as unique and inimitable. He scorned Holland's Anton Mussert and Britain's Sir Oswald Mosley as plagiarists of his own ideas, and he discarded Quisling in all but form. Only for Belgium's Léon Degrelle did he have some respect, and he betrayed real anger when at one stage of the French campaign he was told—quite falsely—that Degrelle was among a large number of foreign Nazis shot by the French in May.

Since Belgium had fought honorably and capitulated unconditionally, Hitler was inclined to leniency. He agreed to Göring's heartfelt request— the Luftwaffe chief had telephoned Hitler the moment the Belgian capitulation was announced—that King Leopold be chivalrously treated. A senior statesman, Otto Meissner, was sent to tell the king that if Belgium now acted sensibly his kingdom might yet survive—otherwise Hitler would create a new Gau: "Flanders." A telegram in German army files indicates that King Leopold was furious at the looting and willful destruction of his country by the withdrawing French and British troops, so Hitler's political wisdom in ordering his armies to spare the cities of Flanders from unnecessary visitations undoubtedly paid dividends. But here Hitler too appointed a German military governor: General Alexander von Falkenhausen was a liberal commander and maintained liaison with the king. There was in consequence little resistance to the Nazi presence in Belgium until Falkenhausen incurred Hitler's displeasure in 1944 and was replaced by a civilian, the Gauleiter of Cologne. Hitler retrieved for Germany the former German areas of Eupen, Malmedy, and Moresnet which had been annexed by Belgium in 1918; he ordered Brauchitsch to separate the Belgian prisoners of war into Flemings and Walloons—the former, 200,000 men of trusty Germanic stock, were to be released forthwith, while the latter, 150,000 less friendly prisoners, were to be held in continued pawn.

For "Red," the second half of the French campaign, Hitler's staff had found a new headquarters site in southern Belgium—in the deserted village of Brûly-de-Pêche in a forest clearing. Fritz Todt had rapidly erected three barrack buildings to house Hitler, a dining hall, and Jodl's staff; he had converted a church to house the rest. The whole headquarters, code-named "Forest Meadow," was ready with its antiaircraft batteries and barbed-wire entanglements by the time Hitler arrived on June 6.

He never felt as secure here as at Münstereifel. Perhaps it was the swarms of mosquitoes that rose from the dense undergrowth all around to plague him. Perhaps it was a general impatience to end the war. There was less for him to do during "Red"; Brauchitsch, who had phoned him regularly during "Yellow," now came in person. Hitler had mellowed toward him, and seems to have taken him more into his confidence about his future military plans. For a while Hitler abandoned his idea of discarding Brauchitsch—he could hardly do this to the Commander in Chief of a victorious army, as he mentioned to one adjutant. Ribbentrop was also a frequent visitor. After Dunkirk he asked Hitler whether he might draft some sort of peace plan for the British, but Hitler replied, "No, I shall do that myself. It will be only a very few points. The first point is that nothing must be done which would in any way injure Great Britain's prestige; secondly Britain must give us back one or two of our old colonies; and thirdly, we must reach a stable *modus vivendi* with Britain."

A member of the headquarters staff wrote of these weeks of waiting for the French collapse: "I have the happiest memories of those weeks, partly because of the fine military victories, partly because of the magnificent landscape in the Eifel and in Belgium. Of course we had a lot to do, usually far into the night, but the work was a pleasure in contrast to the often barely tolerable weeks of tension that had gone before. Every evening the Führer ate privately with ten or twelve others, regularly joined by one or two officers of the Wehrmacht operations staff; my turn came every eight or ten days. He was on top of the world and in splendid humor, and we talked about anything but shop. I remember we all debated the reason why the cuckoo makes a point of laying its eggs in other birds' nests." And one of Hitler's secretaries wrote on June 13: "For a week now we have been out front again, in a deserted village. For the first few nights I had to sleep with the other girl in a former pigsty, which had been boarded up and was frightfully damp. Yesterday the barracks were ready for us, *Gottseidank,* so we are on dry land again. . . . Every night we get the same performance: at precisely twenty past twelve, enemy aircraft come and circle over the village. We don't know if they are looking for us or the approach road to the front. We can't get them down because they fly too high. If they don't come then, the Chief"—meaning Hitler—"inquires, 'Where's our office airman today then!' At any rate every night finds us standing until half past three or four in the morning with the Chief and other members of his staff in the open air watching the nocturnal aerial maneuvers until the reconnaissance planes vanish with the onset of dawn. The landscape at that hour of the morning reminds me of a painting by Caspar David Friedrich. . . ."

On June 10, 1940, Italy formally declared war on Britain and France. Hitler had known of the date for a week in advance and had again tried to persuade Italy to wait, as he could not spare the Luftwaffe to help Mussolini's divisions penetrate France's Alpine fortifications. He made no attempt to disguise his contempt and forbade Keitel to permit staff talks with the Italian forces. A member of Keitel's staff noted: "The Führer's view is that since Italy left us in the lurch last autumn we are under no obligation to her now." In the foreign ministry sardonic comparisons were drawn between Mussolini and the traditional circus clown who rolled up the mats after the acrobats completed their performance and demanded that the audience applaud *him;* or again, the Italians were dubbed the "harvest hands." Over dinner on the eleventh, hearing that the Italians had only now bombed Malta, Hitler commented sourly, "I would have done everything the other way around." That Mussolini had formally declared war on France instead of first launching a lightning invasion of Malta left him almost speechless with vexation. "That must be the last Declaration of War in history," he exclaimed. "I never thought the Duce was so primitive." And, waving at his adjutants Mussolini's letter announcing his intention, he added, "I always knew he was naïve, but this whole letter is a warning to me to be much more careful with my dealings with the Italians in the future."

There survives among the papers of Walther Hewel the government communiqué announcing Italy's inauspicious action, with eloquent amendments written in Hitler's own hand. Where the original text proclaimed: "German and Italian soldiers will now march shoulder to shoulder and not rest until Britain and France have been beaten," Hitler irritably crossed out "Britain" and then redrafted the latter part to read ". . . *and will fight on until those in power in Britain and France are prepared to respect the rights of our two peoples to exist.*" He commented scornfully that Mussolini evidently expected this "looting expedition" to be some kind of excursion on which he could proceed at a *passo romano* goose-step. "He is in for the surprise of his life. The

French respect the Italians far less than us." He cursed, "First they were too cowardly to join in with us, and now they fall over themselves to be in on the spoils." After a while he reflected: "Declarations of war always were the mark of a hypocritical political attitude—an attempt to keep up an appearance of chivalry. They only became fashionable with the rise of civilization. In olden times they didn't Declare War—there were just sudden raids and invasions, and by and large that is the proper, healthy way. Never in my life will I sign a declaration of war. I will always strike first."

Paris was abandoned by the French government and declared an open city to prevent its destruction. At the last meeting of the Supreme War Council held in France that day, Winston Churchill, the new British prime minister, begged the French to tie the German forces down by defending Paris, or to resist until the Americans came in.[5] His appeal for yet more French blood to be spilled in Britain's cause may have rung cynically in his allies' ears; the French commanders left him in no doubt the war was lost. Hitler's Intelligence services must have worked brilliantly now, for the next day, June 13, one of Hitler's secretaries wrote: "I personally cannot believe the war will go on after June. Yesterday there was a War Council in Paris: Weygand declared the battle for Paris lost and suggested a separate peace, in which Pétain supported him; but Reynaud and some other members thundered their protests against him. . . . To know precisely what the situation is and still order your men to fight on until they die, shows complete lack of principle."

The French Cabinet resigned in the face of this defeat, and the aged Marshal Henri Philippe Pétain, veteran and hero of World War I, took over. On June 17 word reached Hitler through Spain that Pétain desired an armistice and wanted to know the German terms. One of Jodl's staff later wrote: "When he heard this news Hitler was so delighted that he made a little hop. I had never seen him unbend like that before." He decided to meet Mussolini to discuss the terms at once. Meanwhile, the Wehrmacht was ordered to keep up its pressure on the defeated enemy—

[5] Hitler devoted some thought to keeping the United States at bay. He granted an exclusive interview to the Hearst Press correspondent Karl von Wiegand on June 13 to stress his total lack of predatory interest in either North or South America, or for that matter in the British Empire; of Britain he demanded only the return of the former German colonies. "But as Britain lost battle after battle, her men in power besought America with tear-swollen eyes to help them. They declared that Germany was threatening the British Empire and intended to destroy it. One thing will, admittedly, be destroyed in this war—a capitalist clique which is and always has been willing to destroy millions of people for its own despicable ends."

to take Cherbourg and Brest as a matter of honor, and to occupy the Alsace and particularly Strasbourg as a matter of geography.

For many days Hitler had deliberated on the armistice itself: he would invite the French to undergo the same indignities as they had visited on the defeated German generals in 1918 at Compiègne; he ordered his staff to find out precisely how the French had behaved then. It had been raining in 1918, and the Germans had been kept waiting in the downpour to humiliate them still further. Hitler at first prayed that this time as well it would rain at Compiègne. Eventually, his mood changed somewhat: it must be the purpose of *this* armistice to give France no cause to fight on from North Africa; above all, Hitler wanted to show the British how magnanimous he could be in victory.

The terms of the armistice betrayed a master hand. Weizsäcker noted approvingly: "They are so elastic that Pétain can hardly reject them. . . . On the other hand the terms leave room for an *annihilating* peace." At Munich, Hitler privately persuaded Mussolini to shelve the Italian territorial claims on France until a final peace treaty. Only northwestern France would be occupied by the Germans as far as the Spanish frontier. The rest would remain under Pétain's control. The delicate problem of the French fleet called for brilliant handling, for Hitler did not want it to escape to the British. When Admiral Raeder asked him on the twentieth if Germany could claim the fleet, Hitler replied that the German navy had no title to the ships as the French fleet was unbeaten. Besides, the French ships were beyond their reach. The armistice therefore formally renounced all claim to the French fleet: the French might retain part to preserve their colonial interests; the rest was to be taken out of commission. Otherwise the ships would be left unmolested—in fact Hitler wished for nothing better than that they might be scuttled by their crews. In short, for reasons of strategy the German armistice terms bore no comparison with the humiliating terms inflicted on Germany in 1918 or indeed with the terms of armistice recently drafted by France in anticipation of defeating Hitler.[6]

At noon on June 21, Hitler drove through the fog-shrouded roads of northern France to the forest of Compiègne. Ever since Pétain's armistice request had reached him four days before, Hitler's headquarters staff had toiled to set the scene for the world's press and cameramen. The old wooden dining car in which Marshal Foch had dictated his terms to the Germans on November 11, 1918, had been retrieved from its permanent display in Paris and set up on a short length of railway

---

[6] The captured French document, dated November 9, 1939, analyzed in particular means of ensuring that the reparations could be extracted from Germany without the errors made in 1919.

track in the same spot in the forest, near the French armistice memorial. A guard of honor awaited Hitler's arrival. Forty minutes later the French officers arrived. Hitler sat on one side of the long table set up in the dining car, while General Keitel began reading out the preamble to the three stony-faced Frenchmen.

Hitler himself had composed these words: "After a heroic resistance, France has been vanquished. Therefore Germany does not intend to give the armistice terms or negotiations the character of an abuse of such a gallant enemy. The sole object of the German demands is to prevent any resumption of the fighting, to provide Germany with the necessary safeguards for her continued struggle against Britain, and to make possible the dawn of a new peace whose primary element will be the rectification of all the brutal injustices inflicted on the German Reich. . . ." After this twelve-minute introduction Hitler rose and left with his party, while Keitel continued to dictate the terms to the Frenchmen. Schmundt had dictated the order in which the German officers were to leave at this stage, and it spoke volumes for Hitler's mentality: Hitler was to be followed by Göring, and then by Ribbentrop, Hess, and Raeder; Brauchitsch was to leave last of all. The railway coach was now shipped to Berlin as an exhibit; the French memorial at Compiègne was demolished with explosives—only the statue of Marshal Foch himself remained untouched, on Hitler's personal instructions.

The French signed the armistice document with Keitel the next afternoon and then left for Italy to bargain with the Italians. Hitler could now fulfill a lifelong dream to visit Paris and see its architecture. He sent for his three favorite intellectuals—the architects Albert Speer and Hermann Giesler and the sculptor Arno Breker—and they arrived at Brûly-de-Pêche that evening, June 22. Over dinner Hitler could talk of nothing but the next day's visit. At 4 A.M. the next morning he flew secretly to Le Bourget airport with Keitel, a handful of his staff, and the court architects clad in incongruous field-gray. Here at last, towering above him in stone and iron and stained glass, were the monuments so familiar to him from the pages of his architectural encyclopedias. He was actually *inside* the modern baroque Opéra, asking the gray-haired usher to show him long-forgotten chambers of whose existence he was aware from the architectural plans. For these three brief hours shortly after dawn he wandered around the Tour Eiffel, the Arc de Triomphe, and Les Invalides, where he stood in bareheaded awe of Napoleon's sarcophagus. When it was light enough he gazed out across the undamaged city from the forecourt of Sacré-Coeur and Montmartre. At ten that morning he flew back to Belgium. That evening he commanded Speer to draft a decree for the complete reconstruction of Berlin—it must outshine everything he had seen in Paris. He signed the document three days later, ordering the Reich capital's facelift to be completed by 1950.

The Italians and French came to terms as well. Hitler told Brauchitsch he believed the British would soon give way. An hour after midnight on June 25, 1940, a bugler of the 1st Guards Company took up station at each corner of the Führer's village headquarters. Seated at the bare wooden table in his requisitioned cottage, Hitler waited with Speer, his adjutants, secretaries, and personal staff; he had also invited two of his fellow infantrymen from World War I to join him—one Ernst Schmidt, a master painter, and his old sergeant Max Amann, now chief of the Party's printing presses. Throughout Europe millions of radios were tuned in to this quiet forest acre. Hitler ordered the lights in the dining room switched off, and the window opened. A radio turned low whispered a commentary. At 1:35 A.M., the moment prescribed for the armistice to take effect, the buglers sounded the cease-fire.

It was the most moving moment of his life. Nobody would ever understand what this victory meant for him; for four years he had once fought as an anonymous infantryman, and now as Supreme Commander it had been granted to him to lead his people to a unique victory. After a while he broke the silence. "The burden of responsibility . . ." But he did not go on.

The Führer asked for the lights to be turned on again.

The Big Decision

While Schmundt packed up the headquarters, and a never-ending stream of telegrams and congratulations reached the Chancellery in Berlin—from the exiled kaiser in Holland, from the crown prince, from Hindenburg's daughter, and even one from Hitler's old schoolmaster in Austria—the Führer contentedly toured the Flanders battlefield of World War I with his old comrades Amann and Schmidt. He even found the house where he had been billeted as an infantryman and delightedly showed it to Schaub and the select handful who accompanied him on this nostalgic pilgrimage around those corners of his memory. At one point he darted off and clambered up an overgrown slope, looking for a concrete slab behind which he had once taken cover. His memory had not deceived him, for the same nondescript slab was still there and for all we know lies there to this day.

Schmundt had prepared for him an interim headquarters, "Tannenberg," high up in the Black Forest near Freudenstadt. Hitler did not want to return to Berlin until he had some unofficial response to the peace feelers he had extended to the British through Sweden. He would then stage a triumphal return to the capital on July 6 and make his formal offer in a Reichstag speech two days later. After that he would be free to attend to Russia in 1941.

The anti-Bolshevik urge, like some Wagnerian motif, continued to inspire his private deliberations, occasionally breaking to the surface in moments of triumph or repose—much to the consternation of his unready associates. Every time the Russians made some move, he reminded himself that this motif was his real raison d'être: he had analyzed the inexplicable Russian armistice with Finland with this in mind, and he had concluded that Stalin must have been bluffing about his military weakness; but to what end? Unlike "the alcoholic dilettante" into whose hands British power had now been thrust, Stalin was a national leader of whose strategic capability Hitler was in no doubt; he knew how to think in terms of centuries—he set himself distant goals which he then pursued with a single-mindedness and ruthlessness that the Führer could only admire.

As early as June 2, Hitler had mentioned to Rundstedt when discussing "Red" at Charleville, "Now that Britain will presumably be willing to make peace, I will begin the final settlement of scores with bolshevism." He obviously regarded the August 1939 pact with Stalin with increasing cynicism. It was a life insurance policy to which he had steadfastly contributed but which he now felt had served its purpose; his victory in France had given him a feeling of immortality.

The Russian and British problems were inseparably entangled with the British: if Russia were neutralized as a military power, Britain would be obliged to accept just the kind of *bloodless* defeat Hitler was reserving for this troublesome brother-country. Her last "Continental dagger" would be smitten from her grasp.

There is an abundance of contemporary evidence that in June 1940 Hitler was still well disposed toward the British Empire. The archives of the High Command and the navy provide examples. This was why Keitel rejected a proposal that Britain's food supplies be sabotaged, and on June 3 Hitler explicitly forbade Canaris to introduce bacterial warfare against Britain. On June 17, Jodl's principal assistant confirmed to the naval staff that

> . . . the Führer has anything but the intention of completely destroying the British Empire, as England's downfall would be to the detriment of the white race. Hence the possibility of making peace with Britain after France's defeat and at the latter's expense, on condition that our colonies are returned and Britain renounces her influence in Europe. With regard to an invasion . . . the Führer has *not* so far uttered any such intention, as he is fully aware of the extreme difficulties inherent in such an operation. That is also why the High Command has as yet undertaken *no* studies or preparations. (The Commander in Chief, Luftwaffe, has put certain things in hand, *e.g.*, the activation of a parachute division.)

Hitler also lengthily discussed his friendly attitude toward Britain with Rudolf Hess, and together with Göring he hatched a plan to offer Britain twelve divisions for "overseas purposes"—the defense of her Empire against aggression. Göring criticized the plan as meaningless, since Britain could now in increasing measure rely on the United States for military support.

Hitler persisted in believing that with the fall of France the British government would see reason. Admiral Raeder urged him to launch immediate air raids on the main British naval bases and to prepare a seaborne invasion; for the latter, of course, aerial supremacy was essential. Hitler, however, believed an invasion quite superfluous. "One way or another the British will give in." On June 25 one of his private secretaries wrote: "The Chief plans to speak to the Reichstag shortly. It will probably be his last appeal to Britain. If they don't come around even then, he will proceed without pity. I believe it still hurts him even now to have to tackle the British. It would obviously be far easier for him if they would see reason themselves. If only they knew that the Chief wants nothing more from them than the return of our own former colonies, perhaps they might be more approachable. . . ." On the same day General Jeschonnek, the Chief of Air Staff, refused to assist the OKW's invasion planning since "in his [Jeschonnek's] view the Führer has no intention of mounting an invasion." When the air member of Jodl's staff nonetheless pressed Jeschonnek to help, the general bitingly replied, "That's the OKW's affair. There won't *be* any invasion, and I have no time to waste on planning one."

Hitler felt that the British public was being deliberately misled as to his war aims. In a democracy, public opinion—and that meant *published* opinion—made it difficult to reverse one's course of action; perhaps, he reasoned, there was nobody in Britain with the courage to admit the error in declaring war on Germany. "Naturally, it matters a lot what the Britons expect the Führer's purpose to be in fighting their country," wrote Hewel to a contact in Switzerland on June 30 (the letter is important, since it appears to have been submitted to Hitler for approval.) "They were cajoled into this catastrophe by emigrés and liberal-thinking people . . . now it is up to them to find some way out of this mess. The point is, Can the British grasp the genius and greatness of the Führer, not only as a benefit to Germany but to the whole of Europe too? Can they swallow their envy and pride enough to see in him not the conqueror but the creator of the new Europe? If they can they will automatically come to the conclusion that the Führer does not want to destroy the Empire, as the emigrés duping them claim." Hitler was minded to give the British one last chance shortly, added Hewel. "If they continue to wallow in their present pigheadedness, then God help them." A few days later Weizsäcker summed up the situation in his diary: "We'd like to call it a day, put out a Germanic hand to Britain and thus win added pressure for our threat against the Russians, who are currently reaping all the advantages—which are, indirectly, against us. In addition, perhaps we automatically shy from taking over the immense task of inheriting both Europe and the British Empire. 'Conquer Britain—but what then, and what for?'—This question of the Führer's is countered by others, like Herr von Ribbentrop, with a comparison to two great trees that cannot prosper if they grow up close together." In Weizsäcker's view Britain would not give in unless clubbed to the ground—and only after Churchill had been disposed of.

Deep in the Black Forest, the Führer waited for word from Britain and planned the Reich's new frontiers. Now that victory was his, he saw no reason not to gather the spoils of war. He would throw France back to the frontiers of 1540. He personally instructed the two western Gauleiters, Josef Bürckel and Robert Wagner, to reannex Alsace and Lorraine by stealth; any formal German announcement would have prompted Mussolini to enforce Italy's territorial claims against France, or even provoked Marshal Pétain to transfer his fleet and African colonies to the enemy. Meanwhile German troops stopped the thousands of French refugees from returning to these provinces; German civilian governments were set up, and all French official protests were ignored. Many of Hitler's own staff, like Otto Meissner and Rudolf Schmundt, had been born in Alsace.

Small wonder that Hitler warned his legal experts to "put as little down on paper as possible," for the new Germany would have a western frontier not enjoyed since the late Middle Ages; it would embrace all of Holland, Belgium, and Luxemburg, and much of modern France besides. The line he envisaged ran from the Somme estuary southward; it gave Germany the Channel ports of Boulogne, Calais, and Dunkirk, much of Flanders, all of Lorraine, the Franche Comté and part of Burgundy, as far as Lake Geneva. (Hitler also asked Jodl's operations staff to draft a contingency plan for the invasion of Switzerland.) France herself was to be reduced to an impotent collection of self-governing provinces.

Under the peace settlement Hitler also intended to oblige his former enemies, as well as the pro-Axis countries, to agree on a uniform solution of the Jewish problem. France would be required to make available an overseas territory to accommodate Europe's Jews—he considered Madagascar best suited. Hitler revealed this decision to Admiral Raeder on June 20 and evidently to Ribbentrop and Himmler soon after, for experts in the foreign ministry worked eagerly on the Madagascar plan throughout the summer, and the Reichsführer SS definitely issued corresponding instructions to the police generals in the east. He told a relieved Governor General Hans Frank that the Führer had ordered an end to the dumping of Jews in the Generalgouvernement of Poland after all, as they were to be deported overseas, including those now in Poland. Gauleiter Greiser, governor of the newly annexed Warthegau, was not pleased, however, for he had herded 250,000 Jews into the Litzmannstadt (Lodz) ghetto to await their transfer to the Generalgouvernement; further delay would place a huge medical and foodstuffs burden on his administration that winter. But "of course he would bow to these instructions," he promised. At a Cracow conference, SS General Streckenbach quoted Himmler: "When and how the deportation begins, depends on the peace settlement."

It is difficult to relate the political and military developments of the summer of 1940 to the industrial—and hence longer-range—decisions Hitler took. His political posture from early June onward was one of conviction that Britain could be persuaded by diplomatic means to yield to his will. Nevertheless, in the second week of June he ordered Keitel, Göring, and the arms industry to convert to the special needs of the war against Britain: all effort must be applied to the mass production of Junkers 88 bombers and of submarines. But though the ammunition dumps were to be replenished, the peacetime consumer-goods industry was restarted. The field army was to be reduced in strength immediately by thirty-five divisions, which would provide industry with the manpower it now lacked.

The key to the uncertainty this reflected was Russia. Jodl felt that Hitler's "huntsman's instinct" told him that Stalin meant him no good, and twice during June Russian actions fed these suspicions. On the twelfth, Moscow issued an ultimatum to the Baltic state of Lithuania, followed four days later by similar ultimata to Estonia and Latvia. Soviet troops invaded these countries, and from the concentrations of troops on Romania's frontier it was clear that further moves were intended.

Now Germany's oil supplies were in real danger. Army Intelligence recorded a flood of reports that the Russians were going to invade Germany, that heavy tanks had been heard massing across the frontier, and that Germany was to receive an ultimatum to hand over Memel. The rapidity with which Hitler finally defeated France must have taken Stalin by surprise, for on the twenty-third Molotov informed Germany that despite an earlier promise to avoid war with Romania over the Bessarabian region, the Soviet Union would brook no further delay and was resolved to "use force if the Romanian government refuses a peaceful settlement." To Hitler's evident consternation, the Russians also laid claim to Bukovina, a region formerly owned by the Austrian crown and never by Imperial Russia; Bukovina was densely populated by ethnic Germans. Hitler asked Ribbentrop to refresh his memory as to the content of the 1939 pact with Stalin, but the secret protocol was alarmingly vague: "With respect to the southeast, the Soviet party stresses its interest in Bessarabia. The German party declares its total political *désintéressement* in these regions." The plurality of "regions" was an embarrassment, but the protocol bore Ribbentrop's signature, and war in the Balkans had to be avoided at all costs. Molotov agreed to limit the Russian claim to northern Bukovina, and under German pressure the Romanian government bowed to *force majeure* on the twenty-eighth.

To his adjutants Hitler expressed all the private anger about these two Russian moves—into the Baltic states and eastern Romania—that he was unable to vent in public. He termed them the first Russian attacks on western Europe and as such to be taken very seriously indeed. "This is Russia trying to safeguard her flanks." Since the autumn of 1939 Stalin had now annexed over 286,000 square miles, with a population of over twenty million people.

During the last days of June, Hitler had a number of private talks with Brauchitsch, the army's Commander in Chief, some of which General Halder also attended. Halder was concerned about Russia's growing militancy, her steadily increasing strength along the September 1939 demarcation line in Poland, and her colossal armaments program; he pointed out that the few divisions left in the east were not even sufficient for customs purposes and asked for an increase in German strength there. On June 23, Hitler discussed this at length with Brauchitsch—a long note of their decisions was taken by Colonel von Lossberg. Basically Hitler ruled that the army was to be reduced from 155 to 120 divisions (although 20 of the 35 divisions to be disbanded could be reactivated on short notice if necessary); he directed that the armored and mechanized divisions were to be doubled—itself an interesting provision; and that no fewer than 17 divisions were to be stationed in the east, together with the headquarters of General Georg von Küchler's Eighteenth Army. The Russians were to be reassured that this redeployment was merely a "transfer home."

Hitler's political appreciation of the situation was that if Britain continued to fight, it could only be because she hoped to enlist the United States and Russia on her side. Two days later, Halder is to be found briefing his staff on the new element in all this: "Germany's striking power in the east." In an order to the three army group commanders on June 25, General von Brauchitsch mentioned innocuously that the various organizational changes would be effected "partly in occupied areas, partly in Germany, and partly in the east." Discussing the reasons underlying the transfer of the Eighteenth Army to the east, in a letter to Brauchitsch on the twenty-eighth,[1] Halder wrote: "The purpose here for the time being is to demonstrate the physical presence of the German army; but it is important not to show an attitude of open hostility." Two days later he apparently told Weizsäcker that Germany must keep a weather eye on the east. "Britain will probably need a display of military force before she gives in and allows us a free hand for the east."[2] And on July 3 Halder was even more explicit in his discussion of the eastern problem. "It has to be examined from the angle of how best to deliver a military blow to Russia, to extort from her a recognition of Germany's dominant role in Europe."

Tannenberg was not one of Hitler's most attractively sited headquarters. It consisted of a number of wooden barracks and concrete block houses partly below ground level, deep in the Black Forest. The tall pine-trees sighed in the wind, and it rained heavily. There were only a few days of sunshine in the week he stayed there, beginning June 28. While Jodl's staff applied itself to the theoretical problems of defeating Britain, Hitler began to draft the speech he would deliver to the Reichstag upon his return to Berlin.

The Italian ambassador called on him here; Hitler hinted that Germany was on the threshold of "big new tasks," without being more specific. In truth, he had not yet made up his own mind which way to turn. He mentioned to Schmundt that he was turning over in his mind whether or not to fight Russia. The Wehrmacht adjutant afterward told Below about it as they walked gloomily through the dripping forest. (The scene of this exchange remained indelibly in the Luftwaffe adjutant's memory and helped to fix the time of Hitler's portentous remark in the rush of history that summer.) Hitler also seems to have discussed

---

[1] The letter is quoted in a restricted British monograph but is not among the files restituted to Germany; it is presumably still in British hands.

[2] In the published version of his diaries, Halder annotates the quotation to suggest that Weizsäcker was quoting Hitler *to him*, but taken in conjunction with the entry of July 3, 1940, it is difficult to defend that interpretation.

this possibility with his foreign minister, and one of Jodl's staff—whether on Hitler's direct command cannot now be discerned—privately began drafting an OKW plan for an attack on Russia.[3]

By late June 1940, Hitler suspected that the British had no intention of submitting; by the end of the first week in July, this suspicion had hardened to a certainty.

Not only had Germany's own unofficial soundings through Sweden met with a rebuff, but Hitler's agencies had intercepted the formal British reply to an offer of mediation by the Pope. The extent of Britain's determination was displayed vividly on July 3, when Churchill's navy opened fire on the remnants of the French fleet at Mers-el-Kebir, killing 1,150 French sailors; this was Hitler's own language and the message reached him loud and clear. Moreover, Allied documents captured in France demonstrated unmistakably the kind of war that Britain was preparing: among the records of the Supreme War Council was one of a November 1939 meeting at which Chamberlain had disclosed that the British air staff had developed a plan to use its new long-range bombers for the destruction of the Ruhr, site of an estimated 60 percent of German industry. Aerial photographs had been taken; plaster models had been built of the entire region. The RAF bombing offensive as planned would continue for several months and would inevitably, Chamberlain admitted, take a heavy toll of civilian life in Germany, which was a drawback from a world-opinion point of view. French War Minister Daladier had begged the British to think again, fearing that the German reprisals would fall most heavily on France.

Hitler's agents had also discovered notes written by Daladier during a visit to Paris by Churchill and British air marshals on May 16, while the archives of the Quai d'Orsay were being burned outside the windows. ". . . Churchill thinks the [German] salient can be cordoned off just as in 1918. I explain to him there can be no comparison between the two wars. A long technical argument with his generals, who declare to me that the German advance into France can be slowed down by bombing the Ruhr. I retort it is absurd to believe that. The Germans are interested only in pressing on into France and finishing off Britain afterward. The damage to the Ruhr won't matter two hoots to them; they won't let their spoils slip through their fingers now. . . . London must be defended *here*. Air Marshal Joubert de la Ferté and Churchill contradict, they point out the importance of defending the British arms facto-

[3] This was Colonel Bernhard von Lossberg; for his plan ("Operation Fritz") see page 177 below.

ries. . . ." A last desperate telegram from Reynaud to Churchill appealed for the RAF to stop its futile attacks on the Ruhr and send aircraft instead in direct support of the French infantry, now standing alone in battle with the Germans. This document was also in Hitler's hands by the end of June.

So the British planned to fight on—relying on their air force for the defense of their isles and a strategic attack on Germany's rear. It was an unwelcome revelation for Hitler and the OKW operations staff. As one of Jodl's officers was later to write: "We had in truth not the slightest desire for such a passage of arms. Our worries centered solely on the gathering Bolshevik menace far in the east, against which no natural frontier protected us. This was why we had built up our costly arms industry." On June 30, Jodl drafted a first appreciation of the continued war with Britain. It was dominated by the specter of a Britain resurgent and able to strike at Germany's arms industry—in essence it was concerned with defensive and preventive strategy, with ways of breaking Britain's will, and of defeating her bomber force either in the air or in the factories themselves. Jodl regarded the invasion of Britain as an extreme to be adopted only if all else failed to bring Britain to her senses; meanwhile, the country could be blockaded or bombed into abandoning her war against Germany. Hitler ordered his service commanders to start invasion preparations since "under certain circumstances" the need might arise, but the mere thought of committing upward of thirty good divisions to an *opposed* operation "overseas" must have smitten the Führer with grave apprehension. He willingly allowed the invasion preparations to go on, but apparently only for the diversionary[4] and political effect they had on Britain and Russia.

On July 6, 1940, Hitler returned to Berlin, two months after he had sallied forth to fight the French. A public holiday had been declared in the capital, the shops had shut at noon, a million swastika flags had been distributed free to the packed mass of humanity lining the streets to the Chancellery, and roses were scattered in the roads for Hitler's

[4] An unpublished OKW directive signed on June 28 by Lossberg—who certainly knew that a Russian campaign was now in the cards—ordered the Intelligence services to use all available channels to dupe the British into believing "Germany is preparing war against the British mainland and overseas possessions with all dispatch in the event that Britain desires to continue the fight." The British were to be led to believe that their blockade and bombing offensive were ineffective, that a German air offensive would start once the Luftwaffe had recovered its breath, and that there would be new secret weapons (super-artillery, tanks) by September; moreover Germany, Italy, and Russia would soon open a campaign against the British position in the Middle East —this was the "real" explanation for the five panzer divisions and the infantry divisions being withdrawn from France to the Reich. (These were the divisions being moved up against Russia.)

cars to crush. As a military band struck up the Badenweiler march and Dr. Goebbels himself broadcast the running commentary over the radio network, at 3 P.M. Hitler's special train pulled into Anhalt station.

The strategic alternatives facing Hitler were of nightmarish magnitude. Every other decision he had taken on impulse, with an instinctive lunge after a night of deep contemplation. But the choice between attacking Britain or Russia was one that occupied him continuously until the end of July and to a lesser degree until autumn. Unexpectedly he was now confronted by two enemies, but he had only one bullet left in the breech, as he himself later graphically put it. Britain was the less urgent of the dangers; Churchill might conceal from his own people the magnitude of the defeat suffered at Dunkirk, but the debris of an army in flight, left on the beaches of northern France, was concrete evidence of Britain's inability to intervene directly on land for several years to come. That the RAF might bomb German industry concerned Hitler less than the mischief Britain might create in the Balkans—the source of Hitler's oil—where Churchill could set one jealous country at its neighbor's throat with little risk to British life and limb.

The Allied planning documents recently captured in France had been an eye-opener, betraying, as they did, the sympathetic attitude shown by Turkey, Greece, and particularly Yugoslavia toward the various moves contemplated by the Allies: the Greek war minister had secretly announced his country's readiness to allow the Allies to land troops in Salonika, and Turkey had agreed to allow French aircraft overflights from Syria to bomb the Russian oil fields in the Caucasus. In short, the Balkans could prove Hitler's undoing, and he told Italy's foreign minister as much on the day after his return to Berlin. The Italians wished to invade Yugoslavia now, but Hitler urged them not to since then Hungary could invade Romania, the Balkans would go up in flames, and Russia might cross the Danube into Bulgaria, where Communist and Pan-Slav influence was rife and the royal house dangerously insecure. "The Russians would therefore certainly advance toward their ancient Byzantine goal, the Dardanelles and Constantinople," said Hitler. He added explicitly, "So long as the conflict with Britain has not been brought to a victorious conclusion, a Balkan conflict would present great difficulties for us. Things might go so far that Britain and Russia, under the pressure of events, could discover a community of interest."

By July 1, 1940, both General von Brauchitsch and Colonel von Lossberg, a member of Jodl's staff, had realized that Hitler proposed a Russian campaign. Brauchitsch asked the OKH to "do some operational thinking" about this, and Halder accordingly asked General Hans von Greiffenberg to start planning in the operations branch of the General Staff. In addition, "Foreign Armies East" was directed to investigate the distribution of Soviet forces confronting them. Lossberg's OKW study of a Russian campaign[5] was some thirty pages long, with a number of appendices and maps; early in July, during the subsequent sojourn of the OKW command train *Atlas* on a siding at Grunewald station in Berlin, Lossberg directed Captain von Trotha—his assistant—to obtain maps of Russia. The Lossberg study in its final form—the plan was code-named "Fritz," after his son—bore a striking resemblance to the campaign that was actually begun in the summer of 1941.

Lossberg was undoubtedly right when he later suggested that there was a psychological factor in Hitler's decision to deal with Russia first. It was not just that the Führer realized that risking a seaborne invasion of Britain despite her crushing naval supremacy might on the first day cost him a hundred thousand men—men he would one day need to achieve his distant goal, the black nugget of National Socialist ambition, the subjugation of the Soviet Union. It was the realization that victory in France had produced both in his command staffs and in the German people a smugness and a self-satisfaction and a savoring of the peace to come that threatened to undermine all hope of launching a superhuman crusade against the Bolsheviks. It was now or never: never again would Germany have a leader of such authority and following. In April 1941 he was to say:

Of course the people will never see the point of this new campaign. But the people never does grasp what must be done for its own advantage. The people must always be led by the nose to paradise. Today we are more powerfully armed than ever before. We cannot keep up this level of armament much longer. I would never be able to tackle my real peacetime ambitions otherwise. That is why we have to use the arms we have now for the real battle—the one that counts, because one day the Russians, the countless millions of Slavs, are going to come. Perhaps not even in ten years' time, perhaps only after a hundred; but they will come.

In spite of all this, throughout the summer of 1940 Hitler allowed the invasion preparations against Britain to continue in the hope that this threat coupled with propaganda, blockade, and if need be air bombard-

---

[5] *I.e.,* before July 5. Sources differ as to Lossberg's inspiration. After the war, he himself privately claimed to have drafted the plan on a contingency basis on his own initiative and not, for example, on Jodl's instructions. But his cousin was to state under interrogation that "in about August" Lossberg had told him the Führer had commissioned the rough study from him.

ment would bring the British people to their senses. Admiral Raeder felt that the British would not make peace without, figuratively speaking, a taste of the whip first: he urged Hitler first to order heavy air raids on some big city like Liverpool, and then to deliver his "peace offer" in the Reichstag; an invasion must be regarded only as a last resort. Hitler agreed in principle, but refused to unleash the Luftwaffe against Britain as this might stir up irreparable hatred.

The signs were in fact conflicting. It was rumored that the new British ambassador in Moscow, Sir Stafford Cripps, had predicted that an invasion was bound to succeed, forcing the government to emigrate to Canada; and the expatriate Duke of Windsor—who had served with the French military mission near Paris but had now escaped through Spain to Portugal—bitterly attacked Churchill's unnecessary prolongation of the war and categorically foresaw that "protracted heavy bombardment would make Britain ready for peace." He considered that his return to Britain would result in a powerful boost for the peace party there, and that was why Churchill was sending him away to govern the Bahamas.[6] But by July 11 it was clear that Churchill's hard line was prevailing.

Hitler was perplexed by this continued intransigence. He assumed that Churchill had deliberately misinformed his colleagues, for Cripps was heard to explain in Moscow that Britain could not make peace "because Germany would without doubt demand the entire British fleet to be handed over to her"—a charge devoid of even the smallest shred of support in the German documents. Yet, could not the British people realize, Hitler reasoned, that Churchill's opportunist war would mean the end of their empire? Halder wrote on the thirteenth: "The Führer . . . accepts that he may have to force Britain to make peace; but he is reluctant to do so, because if we do defeat the British in the field, the British Empire will fall apart. Germany will not profit therefrom. We should be paying with German blood for something from which only Japan, America, and others would draw benefit." Hitler now shared the army's suspicion that the only explanation for Churchill's stand was that through Cripps he was working out a deal with Moscow. Could Stalin be making common cause with Britain, despite all he had just learned

---

[6] The American ambassador in Madrid reported to Washington that on July 1 the Duke of Windsor had told him: "The most important thing now to be done [is] to end the war before thousands more [are] killed or maimed just to save the faces of a few politicians." The duke is quoted as saying that French and other societies were so diseased that they ought never to have declared war on a healthy organism like Germany. These views, stated the ambassador, reflected a possibly growing element in Britain of people "who find in Windsor and his circle a group who are realists in world politics and who hope to come into their own in event of peace." His dispatch is in U.S. government files.

from copies supplied to him of captured French documents about the Franco-British plans of April 1940 to bomb the Caucasus oil fields?

Hitler had postponed the Reichstag session and left Berlin on July 8. For the next ten days he drifted purposelessly about Bavaria and Austria—attending a reception for Munich artists at Bormann's house, persuading the Hungarian leaders to moderate their territorial demands on Romania, and then retiring to the Obersalzberg for a week of quiet reflection on the future. The Hungarian premier, Count Paul Teleki, had brought him a letter from his regent, Admiral Nicholas Horthy, on July 10; only Horthy's handwritten draft survives in the Budapest archives, but it shows that he strongly hinted—as in an earlier letter in November —that Germany was the only power that could prevent Stalin and the Red Army from "devouring the whole world like an artichoke, leaf by leaf." Between the lines was Horthy's undertaking to lend his forces to an anti-Soviet campaign.

With Hitler's acquiescence, Joachim von Ribbentrop had begun an extended maneuver to win the support of the Duke of Windsor, who was now staying with the duchess at the Lisbon mansion of one of Portugal's leading bankers, Ricardo de Espirito Santo Silva, prior to taking up his new post at Bermuda. Hitler's respect for the duke (whom he had met in 1937) was increased by the reports that now reached him of the latter's unconcealed loathing of Churchill and the war, as well as his conditional willingness to accept high office in a Britain humbled by armistice. The duke had assured the Spanish foreign minister he would return to Britain if the duchess were recognized as a member of the Royal Family. For the moment, German policy was limited to arranging the duke's safe arrival in an area within Germany's sphere of influence, for example southern Spain. Ribbentrop genuinely feared the British secret service had evil designs on the duke, for he sent Walter Schellenberg, chief of Heydrich's security service, to Lisbon with instructions to ensure that no harm came to him. Schellenberg was also to enable the duke and duchess, whose passports had been impounded by the British embassy in Lisbon, to cross back into Spain if they wished.

There was an air of high intrigue about the German diplomatic cables that now arrived from Lisbon and Madrid. On July 9 the news was that the duke had asked the Spanish foreign minister to send somebody he could trust to Lisbon to pick up a message. Two days later Ribbentrop confidentially cabled his ambassador in Madrid that only the Churchill clique stood in the way of peace and that if the duke so desired Ger-

many was willing to smooth the path for "the duke and duchess to occupy the British throne." The duke told the Spanish emissary that he
had been offended by the tone of Churchill's letter appointing him governor of the Bahamas and that its delivery had been accompanied by an
oral threat of court-martial if he disobeyed. By the last week of July it
seemed Ribbentrop might succeed: the Spanish emissary quoted the
duke as saying that he was not afraid of his brother the king, who was
"of copious stupidity," so much as of the queen, who was shrewd and
forever intriguing against the duke—and particularly the duchess. For
two pins, he would break with his brother and Britain's present policies
and retire to a life of peace in southern Spain—but the Lisbon embassy
had impounded his passports. To Ribbentrop this cannot have seemed a
serious obstacle. On the twenty-fourth, the Spanish emissary com-
municated to Ribbentrop that the duke and duchess had said they were
willing to return to Spain. When the duke had been told the time might
come when he would again play an important part in English public life,
and perhaps even return to the throne, he had replied in astonishment
that the British Constitution made this impossible for a king who had
once abdicated. Ribbentrop's ambassador reported, "When the emissary
then suggested that the course of the war might bring about changes
even in the British Constitution, the duchess in particular became very
thoughtful."

Hitler's suspicion of collusion between Russia and Britain was powerfully reinforced by reports of conversations of Russian diplomats in
Moscow; these reports were partly intercepted by the German Intelligence service and partly furnished by the Italian government in the innocent belief that proof of the antagonism of Yugoslavia and Greece toward Germany would soften Hitler's stern opposition to any Italian
adventure against Yugoslavia. Hitler was far more concerned with them
as concrete proof of Soviet duplicity, however. Thus on July 5 the
Turkish ambassador reported to Ankara on a conversation with Sir
Stafford Cripps: Mikhail Ivanovich Kalinin, the President of the Presidium of the Supreme Soviet, had assured the Briton that Britain and
Russia had many interests in common; but while it was necessary for
them to arrive at an understanding he recommended that nothing be
done hastily.

In Hitler's eyes, this cautious utterance exposed Stalin's hypocrisy.
According to Molotov's version of Stalin's meeting with Cripps, the Soviet dictator had refused to convert his policies into anti-German ones.

Yet in mid-July the Italians supplied Ribbentrop with a decoded Greek telegram sent to Athens by the Greek legation in Moscow. It reported on a two-hour interview with Cripps on July 6, the contents of which demonstrably alarmed Hitler when he read them on his return to Berlin. Cripps had emphasized that the Russians were feverishly making war preparations ("*which is quite correct,*" noted the Greek telegram) and that if the war lasted, then within one year the Soviet Union would join in on Britain's side. Significantly the Greek envoy had retorted that "it appears questionable to me that if Germany believes the Kremlin definitely intends to attack she will give the Russians a year to get ready and not take action immediately." Cripps had claimed in reply that because Germany could not be ready to attack Russia before autumn, and even then could not endure a winter campaign, "she will be forced to postpone the war against Russia until next spring—by which time the Russians will be ready too." Until then both parties would avoid any disruption of their mutual relations. Speaking to the Turkish ambassador on July 16—it was the Hungarian foreign ministry that supplied Ribbentrop with an account of this conversation—Cripps had indicated Stalin's evident inclination to accept the collaboration proposed to him by Churchill in a personal letter; as Cripps had admitted to the Turkish ambassador, "I fully understand how delicate this matter is, but faced by imminent German attack . . . we are forced to come to some arrangement with the Russians whatever the cost."

Russia for its part seemed to be trying to set the Balkans at Germany's throat. In an "unusually cordial" interview with the new Yugoslav minister in Moscow, Kalinin had insidiously cast aspersions on sharp business practices adopted by Germany in exporting to Yugoslavia. "This is no way for the Germans to safeguard the peace," the Russian had hinted. "Indeed, they always demand more and more. No, you must struggle against it; you must be vigilant—you must stand together." The Yugoslav diplomat's dispatch on this pregnant interview was also in Hitler's hands on his return to Berlin.

On July 16, Hitler had without noticeable enthusiasm accepted Jodl's draft order to the Wehrmacht to prepare an invasion of Britain "and if need be carry it out," since Britain still failed to draw the proper consequences from her hopeless position. The army generals, exhilarated by their recent victories, were eager to go and jostling for the most favored positions on the Channel coast. But the navy was more circumspect. The withdrawal of a thousand heavy barges from the German waterways would paralyze large sections of industry; in addition, adequate local air superiority was a *sine qua non* for any invasion operation. On the fifteenth the OKW had orally asked the commanders in chief whether everything could theoretically be ready by August 15; on his arrival now in Berlin Hitler learned from Raeder that this would be quite impossible. Nonetheless the Führer ordered the stage to be set—the transport ships and crews were to be marshaled along the Channel coast in full view of the British. His aim was transparent, for the Luftwaffe meanwhile operated with a decorum and restraint hardly compatible with the strategic objective of fighting for air supremacy.

Hitler now delivered his long-delayed speech to the Reichstag. The flower-bedecked Kroll opera house was packed to overflowing—the generals and admirals in the dress circle and the "deputies" in the orchestra. There is no need here to analyze his speech—effective as ever, now narrating, now mocking, now ranting, now appealing. Its burden was an "appeal to Britain's common sense," an appeal Hitler had long known would fall on deaf ears, but nonetheless a necessary tactic if he was to justify himself to history and the German people. What was unorthodox was that he unexpectedly announced an avalanche of promotions for all his principal commanders on the western front. He had kept them secret even from his staff, but Hermann Göring must have learned that he was to be created a *Reichsmarschall*—one rung higher even than field marshal—for he had already ordered a gaudy new uniform which he paraded before Hitler immediately after his return to the Chancellery; the Luftwaffe generals were disappointed that Göring no longer saw fit to wear Luftwaffe uniform. Among the dozen field marshals Hitler had just created, he reluctantly included Brauchitsch, although against his better judgment, as he told his adjutants. Before the day was over he privately assured the sixty-five-year-old Field Marshal von Rundstedt, who was about to return to France, that he had not the slightest real intention of launching a cross-Channel invasion; that would be quite superfluous.

Hitler evidently repeated to Brauchitsch his demand that a Russian campaign now be explored. He had established—perhaps from the Lossberg study—that the Wehrmacht could regroup for an attack on Russia within four to six weeks. Lossberg's "Fritz" draft certainly indicated that the regrouping could be very rapid, and the strategic objective Hitler outlined to Brauchitsch echoed Lossberg: "To defeat the Russian army or at least to take over as much Russian territory as is necessary to protect Berlin and the Silesian industrial region from enemy air raids.

It would be desirable to advance so far into Russia that we could devastate the most important areas there with our own Luftwaffe."

The Führer was now convinced that Britain was playing for time and reposing her hopes in American and Russian intervention. By all accounts she had already lost the war, if things did not improve; the British ambassador in Washington was openly conceding that Britain had been defeated and must expect to pay. Before leaving Berlin on July 21, Hitler collected Raeder, Brauchitsch, and Göring's Chief of Staff, Jeschonnek, in the Chancellery and explained to them the need to take the necessary political and military steps to safeguard the crucial oil imports should—as was "highly unlikely"—the Romanian and Russian supplies threaten to dry up. The ideal strategy now would be to invade Britain and end the war, but this would not be just an enlarged river-crossing operation; he asked Raeder to report to him within a week on the prospects for an invasion that must be completed by September 15 at the latest. Brauchitsch was optimistic, but Raeder was not. "If the preparations cannot definitely be completed by the beginning of September, it will prove necessary to ponder other plans," Hitler concluded. By this he meant that he would postpone the decision on England until next May and attack Russia this very autumn.

While awaiting Raeder's report on the prospects for an invasion of Britain, Hitler toured Weimar and Bayreuth. What thoughts must have inspired him now, listening to *Götterdämmerung*? But now there were air raid wardens in the theater, air raid shelters everywhere, and the program in his hands included a full-page announcement on what to do if the sirens sounded. Since May the British air offensive, now conducted almost entirely under cover of darkness, had begun causing perceptible discomfiture in Germany.

On the twenty-fifth Hitler was back in the capital and Raeder again tried to dissuade him from an invasion of Britain; the admiral used economic arguments and the unreadiness of the Luftwaffe to mask his basic opposition from a naval point of view. Hitler asked him to report again on the position in a few days' time. But his final decision may have been spurred by an intercepted telegram that was shown him before he left Berlin for the Berghof late that evening. In it, the Yugoslav ambassador in Moscow, Gavrilovic, a pro-Russian member of the Serbian Agrarian party, reported to his government and quoted Sir Stafford Cripps's view that France's collapse had put the Soviet government in great fear of Germany. "The Soviet government is afraid that the Germans will launch a sudden and unexpected attack. They are trying to gain time. The Soviet government thinks Germany will not be ready for a war against them this winter."

Gavrilovic had also discussed the growing Russian military strength with his Turkish colleague. "The army's mechanization is much more advanced than people believe. The Red Army has 180 divisions according to his information, and is more powerfully organized than any other at this moment. Apparently this is all aimed at Germany, while Japan is only of subsidiary interest." The Turkish ambassador also considered war between Germany and Russia a foregone conclusion.

Hitler arrived at the Berghof in time for lunch on July 26. Over the next few days a series of meetings followed with Balkan potentates. Hitler urged the Romanians to concede the territorial claims now raised by Hungary and Bulgaria, painful though they were, coming so shortly after Russia's invasion of Bessarabia and Bukovina. The Russians were now known by the German army to have stationed in the former Romanian provinces powerful forces—including the bulk of their cavalry and mechanized units. Small wonder that the king of Romania had begged Hitler to guarantee the rest of his country, if only because of Germany's concern over the oil wells there. But it was the proximity of the Russian air force that also nagged at Hitler. In one of these Berghof conferences, on the twenty-eighth, he explained, "The long-term political lineup in Europe must be straightened out. Only if one no longer has to fear being exposed to enemy bombing attack can one embark on far-reaching economic plans."

One morning after the regular war conference in the Berghof's Great Hall, Hitler asked General Jodl to stay behind and questioned him on the possibility of launching a lightning attack on Russia *before* winter set in.[7] He explained that he was perfectly aware that Stalin had only signed his 1939 pact with Germany to open the floodgates of war in Europe; what Stalin had not bargained for was that Hitler would finish off France so soon—this explained Russia's headlong occupation of the Baltic states and the Romanian provinces in the latter part of June. It was now clear from the increasing Soviet military strength along a frontier on which Germany still had only five divisions stationed that Russia had further acquisitions in mind. Hitler feared Stalin planned to bomb

---

[7] Hitler's sudden insistence on an autumn campaign against Russia was unquestionably an echo of the mocking tone adopted by Soviet leaders in their (intercepted) conversations with Balkan diplomats. Hitler himself referred to "intercepted conversations" in this connection on July 31.

or invade the Romanian oil fields that autumn; in such an event, Germany would be open to all manner of Soviet blackmail. Hitler would then be unable to launch a winter counteroffensive, and by spring—from all that he had heard—Russia's entire military potential would be marshaled against him. Russia's aims had not changed since Peter the Great: she wanted the whole of Poland and the political absorption of Bulgaria, then Finland, and finally the Dardanelles. War with Russia was inevitable, argued Hitler; such being the case, it was better to attack now—this autumn; postponement was only to Russia's advantage. Jodl doubted whether they could be ready by autumn, but he undertook to find out at once. Hitler's decision was to start *preparations* nonetheless; meanwhile he would make one last political attempt to explore Stalin's intentions before making up his mind to attack.

A few days later Jodl returned to the Berghof with his operations staff's analysis of the prospects for an attack against the USSR. Spreading out railway maps on the large red marble table at the Berghof, he had to advise Hitler that for transport reasons alone it would be impossible to attack Russia that autumn. Hitler ordered the OKW to attach top priority to expanding the handling capacity of the railways in the east.

When the Führer called his OKW, army, and navy chiefs to the Berghof on July 31, 1940, his reluctance to reach a firm decision on an invasion of Britain contrasted strongly with his powerful arguments in favor of attacking Russia.

Admiral Raeder had flown down from Berlin. He sedulously gave the impression that the navy would be ready for the invasion by mid-September 1940; but he advanced formidable technical reasons why they should wait until May 1941. May and June were the ideal months, while from a moon and tide point of view in the coming autumn only two periods were attractive—from August 20 to 26, and from September 19 to 26; the first was too early for the navy, the second fell in what records showed to be a traditional foul-weather period. Hitler took the weather risk very seriously. Meanwhile, warned Raeder, the commandeering of barges and fishing ships required for the invasion was having catastrophic effects on the German economy. In passing he raised basic tactical objections to the army's plan to invade southern England on such a broad front. If Hitler waited until May, on the other hand, the navy's fleet of battleships would be brought up to four by the new *Tirpitz* and *Bismarck,* and there would also be many more smaller warships. Hitler thanked the navy for its splendid achievement so far, and the admiral returned to Berlin.

After he had gone, Hitler commented to Brauchitsch and Halder—who had flown up from General Staff headquarters at Fontainebleau—that he doubted the technical practicability of an invasion. He was impressed by Britain's naval supremacy and saw no real reason to take "such a risk for so little." The war was already all but won. With more marked enthusiasm—Halder underlined in his diary several of Hitler's following statements—the Führer turned to the other, less risky, means of dashing Britain's hopes. Submarine and air war would take up to two years to defeat Britain. Britain still had high hopes of the United States, and she was clutching at Russia like a drowning man: if Russia were to drop out of the picture, then the United States must, too, because with the USSR eliminated Japan would be released as a threatening force in the Far East. That was the beauty of attacking Russia. "If Russia is laid low, then Britain's last hope is wiped out, and Germany will be master of Europe and the Balkans."

This then was Hitler's strategy. The Wehrmacht must prepare to finish off Russia as a military power by capturing Moscow, launching a huge encirclement operation from the north and south and following this up with a subsidiary offensive against the Caucasian oil fields.

The main campaign had to be completed in one stage. There was, alas, no time to commence it that autumn, as winter would have set in before the operation could be concluded; but if it were started in the spring—May 1941—the army would have five clear months in which to defeat the Soviet Union. The army he had so recently ordered cut back to 120 divisions would now be expanded to a record 180 divisions; whereas on June 23 he and Brauchitsch had agreed to allocate 17 infantry divisions to the east, he now proposed that by spring his strength there be built up to 120 divisions, including most of his armored units. He would explain this imbalance to the Russians by stressing the need to have an area well away from the danger of British air attack in which to set up new divisions for "campaigns in Spain, North Africa, and Britain."

Neither Brauchitsch nor Halder offered any objections.

The Dilemma

Winston Churchill's resistance in the summer of 1940 overthrew the very basis of Hitler's calculations. For twenty years he had dreamed of an alliance with Britain. Until far into the war he clung to the dream with all the vain, slightly ridiculous tenacity of a lover unwilling to admit that his feelings are unrequited. When Japan joined the war in December 1941, the dream still lingered dimly on, although Britain and Germany had by then dealt each other blows of unexampled savagery. In his unpublished diary, Walther Hewel recorded Hitler's melancholy lament: "How strange that with Japan's aid we are destroying the positions of the white race in the Far East—and that Britain is fighting against Europe with those swine the Bolsheviks!" But Britain's persistent war aims were clear beyond a doubt from a secret 1939 document captured by Hitler's troops in France: Germany was to be defeated and dismembered, regardless of whether Hitler was overthrown by internal revolution or not; but these true war aims were not to be published, as they would only implacably unite the Germans behind their Führer.

As Hitler told Major Quisling on August 18, 1940: "After making one proposal after another to the British on the reorganization of Europe, I now find myself forced against my will to fight this war against Britain. I find myself in the same position as Martin Luther, who had just as little desire to fight Rome but was left with no alternative. In this fight now I will destroy the England of old, and go alone about establishing a New Order in Europe. My interests are only in northern Europe, not the south. The Mediterranean countries have always been death to the Germans."

This was the dilemma confronting Hitler that summer. He hesitated to crush the British. Accordingly, he could not put his heart into the invasion planning—Göring at least noticed this and drew the appropriate conclusions. More fatefully, Hitler initially stayed the hand of the Luftwaffe and forbade any attack on London under pain of court-martial; the all-out saturation bombing of London, which his strategic advisers Raeder, Jodl, and Jeschonnek all urged upon him, was vetoed for one implausible reason after another. Though his staffs were instructed to examine every peripheral British position—Gibraltar, Egypt, the Suez Canal—for its vulnerability to attack, the heart of the British Empire was allowed to beat on, unmolested until it was too late and its armor of fighter squadrons and antiaircraft batteries rendered it impregnable. In these months an adjutant overheard Hitler heatedly shouting into a Chancellery telephone, "We have no business to be destroying Britain. We are quite incapable of taking up her legacy," meaning the empire; and he spoke of the "devastating consequences" of the collapse of that empire.

Perhaps he felt his peace feelers had not "got through" or had been expressed in the wrong language. Rudolf Hess believed so, for early in September he told a confidant: "The Führer never wanted to batter the empire to pieces, nor does he want to now. Is there nobody in Britain willing to make peace?" If the war continued, the white race would be committing suicide, since even if Germany secured an absolute victory in Europe she was incapable of taking over the imperial legacy overseas, Hess noted. This was unquestionably Hitler's language, which makes it likely that when Hess urgently asked his friend about ways and means of communicating Hitler's serious wish for peace to leading Britons he was acting as the Führer wanted. The views of the Duke of Windsor may have influenced Hitler's assessment of the British mentality: it was reported from Lisbon that he had described the war as a crime, Halifax's speech repudiating Hitler's "peace offer" as shocking, and the British hope for a revolution in Germany as childish. The duke delayed his departure for the Bahamas as long as he could, but he explained through intermediaries he would intervene actively only if he was convinced he had the support of the majority in Britain, as his return to England might lead to civil war. He assured his Portuguese host that he could return by air from Bermuda within twenty-four hours if need be. "Undiminished though his support for the Führer's policies are," reported the Lisbon ambassador, "he thinks it would be premature for him to come right out into the open at present."

Ribbentrop—clearly with Hitler's knowledge—cabled his Madrid ambassador to send confidential word to the Portuguese banker host that Germany was determined to use as much force as was necessary to bring Britain to the peace table. "It would be good if the duke could stand by to await further developments." If the duke could not be dissuaded from leaving (a loyal friend of King George's and a handful of Scotland Yard detectives had just arrived in Lisbon to persuade him), then the banker was to arrange a private channel of communication with him. The Duke of Windsor left Lisbon for the Bahamas on August 1. In his last conversation with his host he replied to Ribbentrop's message: he praised Hitler's desire for peace and reiterated that had he still been king there would have been no war, but he explained that given an official instruction by his government he had no choice but to obey. To disobey would be to show his hand too soon—it would cause a scandal and rob him of his prestige in Britain. A code word had been prearranged with the banker for his immediate return to Lisbon.

From the reports of friendly neutrals like Spain, Hitler had a detailed picture of the situation in Britain. From an agent in the State Department in Washington he also obtained copies of the reports of the American ambassador in London, Joseph P. Kennedy, who at the beginning of August predicted that the Germans would get their way without invading Britain. They had only to continue the blockade: the east coast harbors were already paralyzed, the rest were badly damaged.

This was Hitler's view too. To Göring it was one more reason not to sacrifice his Luftwaffe in preparations for an invasion he believed would never take place—despite the fact that the primary task assigned to him in Hitler's directive of August 1 was the defeat of the British air force. Göring's proposal was to feint with a great bomber force toward London, forcing the bulk of the enemy's fighter force into the air, and then to wipe this out with the combined fighter strength of Field Marshal Albert Kesselring's and Field Marshal Hugo Sperrle's commands; he could have everything ready by August 5. The attacks would continue until the enemy air force was defeated or the weather worsened. Hitler was back in Berlin on the fourth, but Göring repeatedly postponed the attack, giving the weather as his excuse. On the sixth the army's Chief of Staff complained in his diary: "We now have a peculiar situation in which the navy is tongue-tied with inhibitions, the Luftwaffe is unwilling to tackle the task which they first have to accomplish, and the OKW—which really does have some Wehrmacht commanding to do here—lies lifeless. We are the only people pressing ahead."

On the eighth Hitler returned to the Berghof, where he awarded Frau Bormann the Mother's Cross in gold for her considerable procreative accomplishments, and he inspected the new beehives Bormann had laid out—as though there were no more pressing problems.

At the Berghof, the tapestry at one end of the Great Hall was drawn aside to reveal the projection room, and a cinema screen was set up at the other end. Every available Russian and Finnish newsreel film of their recent war was run and rerun, while Hitler and his staff studied the Russians' weapons and the tactics the film revealed. When the lights went up, little knots of officers excitedly discussed the eastern enemy. The Intelligence reports reaching Hitler were unmistakable and disconcerting: a gigantic rearmament effort had begun in Russia; in addition, according to Heydrich's organization, the Soviet trade missions were spreading Communist propaganda and organizing cells in German factories. At the Brown House, the Nazi party headquarters in Munich, one day Hitler told Ribbentrop that he did not intend to stand by idly and allow the Soviet Union to steamroller Germany; Ribbentrop begged him not to contemplate war with Russia, and he quoted Bismarck's dictum about the unwillingness of the gods to allow mere mortals to scan the cards of Fate.

The real face of Stalinism had been unmasked in the Baltic states, where less than two months after the Red Army had taken over, the entire intelligentsia had been liquidated with a ruthless efficiency not even Himmler was achieving in Poland. When Keitel submitted a handwritten memorandum against waging war with Russia if it could possibly be avoided, Hitler summoned him to a private interview and scathingly reduced the field marshal's arguments one by one: Stalin had as little intention of adhering to their treaty as he did; moreover, Stalin was alarmed by Hitler's military successes. Keitel was hurt and suggested that the Führer find an OKW chief whose strategic judgment meant more to him. Rising to his feet, Hitler angrily denied him the right to resign—Brauchitsch too had tried that last autumn. Keitel was on his feet as well. Without a word he turned on his heel and left the room. Hitler retained the memorandum. Presumably it vanished into his safe along with his collection of other incriminating documents.

Keitel had already, on August 2, instructed his armaments staff that an upheaval in all their planning might prove necessary, as the Führer now recognized that Britain might not collapse that year. In 1941 the United States might intervene and "our relationship to Russia might undergo a change." Admiral Canaris, Keitel's Intelligence chief, was also briefed in August on Hitler's intention of attacking Russia in the spring.

Ways and means must be found of camouflaging the buildup of German strength in the east. The OKW had already issued an order to that end and transparently code-named it "Eastern Buildup." According to this plan, because of the vulnerability of the western provinces to British air attack, Germany's eastern provinces were to accommodate more divisions and their transport systems were to be modernized. Eastern mapping sections were also to be enlarged for the same reason. Even Admiral Raeder was informed by Hitler during August that these growing troop movements to the eastern front were just an outsize camouflage to distract from the imminent invasion of Britain. In fact, the truth was the reverse. The OKW's war diary stated explicitly on the eighth: "'Eastern Buildup' is our camouflage order for preparations against Russia."

Hitler's mind was on the shape of the Greater German Reich to come —and above all on how Germany was to police the more turbulent and dissident peoples that would come within the Reich's frontiers. This, he declared to Colonel Schmundt on August 6, must be the peacetime task of his Waffen SS. An elite force of "state police troopers" was to maintain the authority of the central government so that there would never be any need to call on the regular forces to take up arms against their fellow countrymen.[1] These police troopers, noted Schmundt, must be of the best German blood and unconditional champions of the Nazi ideology—a body of men of a purity and pride that would never make common cause with the seditious proletariat; to increase their authority in the eyes of the people, the Waffen SS must prove their value on the coming battlefields; they must be an elite, and Hitler laid down that the Waffen SS must therefore not exceed 5 to 10 percent of his army's peacetime size. The Wehrmacht objected bitterly to this further entrenchment of Himmler's private army, but Keitel agreed with Hitler's arguments and ordered them given the widest circulation within the army.

Among close friends at the Berghof, Hitler often thought out loud about his plans for all Europe when it was finally in his hands. He would build great autobahns far into the east, he would build new cities; on Victory Day the people of Berlin must dance in Wilhelmsplatz, and then the rebuilding of Berlin was to begin. He would be gracious and magnanimous to the vanquished enemy heads of state—even to Churchill, whom he would "give leave to paint and write his memoirs."

---

[1] At his very first Cabinet meeting on January 30, 1933, Hitler had asked that in the event of a general strike the Reichswehr not be used to put it down; Blomberg, as defense minister, expressed his gratitude for this view and emphasized that the soldier was accustomed to treating only foreigners as potential enemies.

Göring told Hitler he needed three days of good weather to begin the air attack on the British fighter defenses. On August 12, he announced that the attack would begin the next day. At 11:20 A.M. Hitler therefore left the Berghof for Berlin. When Raeder warned on the thirteenth that the invasion of Britain was a last resort, not to be undertaken lightly, Hitler reassured him that he would first see what results the Luftwaffe obtained. Thus he postponed his decision. But those who knew him realized the invasion would never take place. "Whatever his final decision, the Führer wants the *threat* of invasion of Britain to persist," the naval staff's war diary noted on August 14. "That is why the *preparations,* whatever the final decision, must continue." In fact, Hitler's attention was already very much on Russia. It is evident that he was unsettled by signs that the USSR was preparing to swallow Finland once and for all, for he told Göring to supply the Finns secretly with war goods and particularly with antitank mines, forthwith; he asked Raeder to fortify northern Norway against any Russian designs on that area as well.

When the newly created field marshals assembled in the Chancellery on August 14 to receive their magnificently bejeweled batons from Hitler's hands, he was explicit about his strategic thinking. His remarks about Britain would have bemused the British people, who even now believed that Hitler was hell-bent on destroying and devouring the British Empire. In addition to the naval staff's account of his speech, there are two surviving records by field marshals. Hitler referred to Germany's greatest strength as her national unity. Since Britain had rejected Hitler's hand of peace, a conflict was inevitable but was initially to be restricted to Luftwaffe operations. "Whether the army will have to be employed can't be predicted. In any case it would only be used if we were absolutely forced to. . . ." Hitler expressed doubts that the Luftwaffe would succeed in altering British determination before bad weather set in: should it fail, he would postpone a decision about an invasion until May 1941.

Leeb's account[2] of Hitler's revealing *political* speech toward the end of the luncheon is important enough to quote at length:

Probably two reasons why Britain won't make peace.

    Firstly, she hopes for U.S. aid; but the U.S. can't start major arms deliveries until 1941.

    Secondly, she hopes to play Russia off against Germany. But Germany is militarily far superior to Russia. The film of Russian warfare

[2] Field Marshal Leeb's diaries are being published by the West German government; I am indebted to Leeb's heirs and to Dr. George Meyer for access to the manuscript.

in Finland contains quite ludicrous scenes. The loss of gasoline [from Russia] can easily be made up by Romania.

There are two danger-areas which could set off a clash with Russia: number one, Russia pockets Finland; this would cost Germany her dominance of the Baltic and impede a German attack on Russia. Number two, further encroachment by Russia on Romania. We cannot permit this, because of Romania's gasoline supplies to Germany.

Therefore Germany must keep fully armed. By the spring there will be 180 divisions.

As for Europe: there is no justification for the existence of small nations, and they particularly have no right to big colonial possessions. In the age of air forces and armored divisions small nations are lost. What matters today is a unified Europe against America. Japan will have to seek contact with Germany, because Germany's victory will tilt the situation in the Far East against Britain, in Japan's favor. But Germany is not striving to smash Britain because the beneficiaries will not be Germany, but Japan in the east, Russia in India, Italy in the Mediterranean, and America in world trade. This is why peace is possible with Britain—but not so long as Churchill is prime minister. Thus we must see what the Luftwaffe can do, and await a possible general election.

The first two days of the Luftwaffe attack were a disappointment—not that the defenses were proving insuperable, but the unpredictable English summer foiled every effort to coordinate the operations of Göring's three air forces. Hitler ruled nonetheless that the air war must go on and that invasion preparations should take September 15 as their target date. But in the latter part of August haze and even fog made the air war progressively less profitable. A "total blockade" of the British Isles was declared, but even this was a half-measure, for it was followed up a week later by an OKW compendium of practices forbidden to the German forces—the use of poison gases, unrestricted attack on certain types of shipping in specific areas, and of course Hitler's on-going embargo on air raids on London town; he forbade any kind of "terror attack" without his permission.

On August 15, Germany's Lisbon embassy learned that the Duke of Windsor had cabled his former host to let him know when he should "act"; but that time was still far off. The next evening, Hitler again left Berlin for the Obersalzberg; such hopes as he may have reposed in the Luftwaffe's campaign were temporarily disappointed.

At the Berghof Hitler busied himself less with plans for invading Britain than with other ways of crushing her people's will.

He studied an earlier Brauchitsch proposal that if the invasion were abandoned, a German expeditionary force should be sent to Libya to support an Italian attack on the British position in Egypt: Germany could spare an armored corps until the following spring. Hitler also asked Ribbentrop to explore ways of bringing Spain into the war, and Jodl's staff attracted Hitler to the idea of capturing Gibraltar with Spanish complicity. But General Francisco Franco was reluctant to declare war, for his country's economy had not yet recovered from three years of civil war; he informed Ribbentrop's Madrid embassy that Spain would need an annual supply of four hundred thousand tons of gasoline and large quantities of wheat and other imported commodities as well. Hitler instructed Keitel to examine Germany's ability to meet these requirements.

Hitler had renewed cause for anxiety about the situation in the Balkans. The Italians were pressing him to enable them to invade Yugoslavia; in addition, after a week of talks between Hungary and Romania on the disputed Transylvania region, war between those two countries became imminent on August 23. Hitler needed complete peace on Germany's southeastern border, and he urgently warned Italy against giving Britain the least excuse to station air force squadrons in Yugoslavia.[3] The Romania situation led to more far-reaching decisions: Romania appealed to Germany to arbitrate the dispute and—without consulting Moscow, as he was bound to under the pact with Stalin—Hitler agreed. Meanwhile he ordered the German army to stand by to occupy the vital Romanian oil region to prevent "third parties"—meaning Russia—from getting there first should the arbitration talks break down. Canaris already had several hundred counter-sabotage troops in the region. Hitler's decision was not determined by sheer opportunism, for there were firm reports of Russian troop movements on the new frontier with Romania. When Field Marshal von Brauchitsch visited the Berghof on the twenty-sixth, Hitler explained to him the need to safeguard Romania without "as yet" provoking the Russians too much; he now wanted ten good divisions moved eastward to the Generalgouvernement and East Prussia.

The Vienna Award of August 30, in which Germany and Italy obliged Romania to cede the disputed territories to Hungary and guaranteed these new frontiers, removed the immediate risk of conflagration in the Balkans. However, the forces Hitler had now set rolling continued in motion, and on September 2 he decided to send a German military mis-

---

[3] Marshal Pietro Badoglio assured Germany a few days later that Italy had no intention of attacking Yugoslavia or Greece.

sion to Romania at the king's request. The Russians would, of course, regard this as yet another provocative act, but Hitler had already figured out the consequences. On August 27 Colonel Schmundt flew to East Prussia with Dr. Fritz Todt to search for a suitable site for the Führer's headquarters during the coming Russian campaign.

One night late in August 1940, British aircraft appeared over Berlin for the first time and dropped a few scattered incendiary bombs. Hitler refused to believe that Churchill could have authorized such a folly, given the Luftwaffe's intimidating superiority in bombers; but in the early hours of the twenty-ninth word was telephoned to the Berghof that the bombers had again struck Berlin and that this time ten civilians had been killed. Evidently the Reich capital now faced an ordeal of fire by night. That same afternoon Hitler flew back to Berlin. He announced to Jodl that as soon as the weather was right he would permit the Luftwaffe to raid London itself in strength—as punishment for Churchill's "downright stupidity," as he told his adjutants. That night the bombers came again. On the fourth of September, Hitler authorized the Luftwaffe to attack Britain by night, too.

That afternoon he delivered one of his most forceful public orations, taunting Churchill for his recent failures and officially inaugurating the new air war. Germany was all-powerful. One year's war had brought her Norway and all Europe from the Bug River in the east to the Spanish frontier in the west; only Britain's "skill in scurrying" had saved her skin so far. He mocked the thesaurus of reassuring predictions used by British officialdom to hint at Hitler's ever-imminent downfall. "For example they say, 'We learn that,' or 'As we understand from well-informed circles,' or 'As we hear from well-placed authorities,' or 'In the view of the experts'—in fact they once went as far as announcing, 'It is believed that there may be reason to believe . . .'" It was this kind of jargon, the Führer told his delighted audience in the Sportpalast, that had made of Dunkirk a glorious feat of British arms. "I saw the vestiges of that feat of arms with my own eyes, and it looked quite a mess to me." He mocked that after Germany had thrown the Allies out of Norway they had chanted: "We only wanted to lure the Germans up there. What a unique triumph that was for us!" After France's defeat Britain had rejoiced that now she need only defend herself. "And if Britain is now consumed with curiosity and asks, Well, why doesn't he invade? I answer, Calm down, he's coming!" Britain and her pathetic collection of exiled monarchs did not frighten him. "We German National Socialists

have come up through the toughest school imaginable. First we fought
as soldiers in the Great War, and then we fought the fight of the German revolution." As for the night bombardment of Germany's Ruhr
cities that Churchill had begun three months before, Hitler now announced he would reply measure for measure and more. "If they proclaim they will attack our cities on a grand scale, we will *wipe their
cities out!*"

Whether Göring had formally been advised that Hitler proposed to
fulfill his cherished ambition of attacking Russia is uncertain, but Jodl's
staff certainly noticed on the fifth that the Reichsmarschall showed no
interest in preparing for the invasion "as he does not believe it will be
carried out." Perhaps Göring saw the bombing of London and the
blockade of Britain as convenient and antiseptic alternatives. He established headquarters on the Channel coast and personally directed the
new offensive, which opened that night with a bombardment of the
docks and oil refineries east of London.

Admiral Raeder certainly saw the handwriting on the wall, for
Hitler's naval adjutant had privately informed him that a Führer headquarters was already being built for the Russian campaign. On September 6 the naval chief arrived at the Chancellery with a series of powerful
arguments as to why—if the invasion of England fell through—Germany
ought to concentrate her attack on Britain's Mediterranean positions
and on a sea and air blockade of the British Isles (which a captured Allied document showed to be most feared of all). Raeder did not as yet
attempt to dissuade Hitler from an attack on the Soviet Union, a move
which the admiral discreetly referred to in his notes as "the *S*-problem";
however, he warned Hitler that it would be impossible to launch both
the attack on Russia and the invasion of Britain simultaneously; the
navy preferred the attack to be undertaken when the ice in the Baltic
was melting, as this would tilt the balance against the Russian navy.
Hitler agreed to tell the OKW this and assured the admiral that if he did
drop the invasion, he would eject the British from the Mediterranean
that coming winter; and for the first time he mentioned that Germany
and Italy must secure footholds in the Azores, the Canaries, and the
Cape Verde Islands before the British—and later the Americans—could
do so. As Raeder summarized it to the naval staff: "The Führer's decision to invade Britain is by no means definite, as he is convinced Britain
can be subdued even without an invasion."

Hitler's hesitation became even more marked when Raeder briskly
announced on September 10 that the navy would complete its accumulation of troop transports in the Channel ports within the set time; in-

deed, Hitler was visibly taken aback and consequently welcomed the various doubts voiced about the seaworthiness of the barges and the probable onset of autumn gales. Hitler again postponed the fateful decision for three more days, blaming the weather and the strength of British air defenses; the weather forecast for September had indeed proven wrong—while the navy tactfully termed the current weather "wholly abnormal," Hitler went further and described it (gratefully, we suspect) as "exasperating," as the kind of conditions from which only a defender could draw profit.

When Hitler assembled his commanders in the Chancellery once more at 3 P.M. on the fourteenth—with Field Marshal Milch deputized to represent Göring, who was still on the Channel coast—he explained why he would not formally cancel the invasion even though the primary requirement, the defeat of the British air force, had not been met. He began with a political survey. "Moscow is dissatisfied with the way things have gone; they were hoping we would bleed to death." He was giving military aid to Romania because Germany needed the oil, and to Finland because of the balance of power in the Baltic. While it was difficult to see into the future, anything might happen. "New conflicts are quite possible"; but he contemplated them calmly. He did not expect America's modest rearmament, which was mostly naval, to take effect before 1944, and he certainly did not want the war to last that long. "We have attained our objectives, so we have no interest in prolonging it." He reminded them that the Reichsmarschall had asked for five or six consecutive days of perfect weather and had never gotten them; this had enabled the enemy fighter defenses to take breath between each hammering. While the exact number of British fighter planes was uncertain, the RAF had surely suffered grievously. From now on it would be a war of nerves, with the bomber attacks and the *threat* of invasion gradually wearing the British people down. "If eight million inhabitants [of London] go crazy, that can lead to catastrophe. If we get good weather and can neutralize the enemy air force, then even a small-scale invasion can work wonders." He proposed, therefore, to wait a few more days before finally canceling the operation. If it were dismantled altogether, it would come to the ears of the enemy and the nervous strain would be that much less. He would still not permit the Luftwaffe to carry out saturation bombing raids on London's residential districts, as Göring's Chief of Staff Jeschonnek had requested. "That is our ultimate reprisal!" He wanted key targets like railroad stations and water and gas works attacked first! *"Not* the population, for the time being." Three days later Hitler postponed the invasion "until further notice."

His commanders knew what that meant; from now on only the *threat* of invasion was to be maintained. In reality, Hitler's mind was elsewhere.

During September and October 1940, foreign diplomats in Moscow reported mounting Soviet bitterness toward Hitler over the controversial Vienna Award and his guarantee to Romania—a guarantee which could only be directed against Russia. A secret analysis by Foreign Armies East in mid-September provided chapter and verse for Russia's hostility; anti-German propaganda in the Red Army was continuing undiminished, and there were caricatures of Hitler, Göring, the "Nazi hydra," and the omnivorous "Fascist shark" in Red Army barracks even in the newly occupied areas. In addition, as recently as August the Red Army had appealed to Finnish war veterans to fight with it "against German and Italian fascism and create a Soviet Europe in which there will be no more exploitation." German Intelligence had also learned of a meeting of the Supreme Soviet on August 2 in which while Molotov and Marshal Kliment Voroshilov, Commissar for Defense, had tried to lull their listeners with details of Russia's western frontier fortifications, others warned against trusting Germany because "certain information indicated that after her victory in the west she would start a war against Russia." "Indeed," these others had continued, "we must get in our attack before our thieving neighbor in the west can get in hers."

The heavily camouflaged German buildup in the east was due to reach its interim conclusion at the end of October. Under the now familiar rubric of "dispersing the forces tightly concentrated in the west," Brauchitsch personally signed an order for additional divisions to move east immediately on September 6. Significantly enough, Field Marshal von Bock's army group headquarters was to take over command, from Posen, and two more armies were to join the Eighteenth—the Fourth and the Second. This would bring up to thirty-five the number of divisions on the eastern frontier, among them six armored divisions. On that same day, General Jodl ordered the Abwehr to dupe Russian agents known to be taking an increasing interest in these movements by feeding to them false information indicating that the bulk of Germany's strength was at the southern end of the front; the Russians were "to draw the conclusion that we are able to protect our interests in the Balkans from Russian clutches at any time with powerful forces."

In fact for strategic reasons Jodl's staff recommended that the main military effort at the start of the attack on Russia should be in the north, even though concentrating strength in the south would have taken better account of the Russian threat to the Romanian oil. In the north, explained Colonel Lossberg in his draft campaign plan ("Fritz") submitted to Jodl later in September, there were better road and rail facilities, the Russian influence in the Baltic region could be quickly extinguished, and it would be possible to cooperate with Group XXI operating from northern Norway through Finland into Russia; above all, an attack in the north would rapidly bring Leningrad and Moscow under the German guns. Lossberg proposed occupying all of Russia up to a line easy to defend against "Asiatic Russia." Tactically, they must prevent the Russians from withdrawing in strength into their vast hinterland, as they had before Napoleon's Grand Army in 1812.

Lossberg's plan undoubtedly formed the basis of Hitler's later grand strategy against Russia.[4] The main thrust north of the Pripyet Marshes was proposed by the colonel as follows: "An attack by two army groups from the general line east of Warsaw to Königsberg, with the southern group the more powerful (the group assembling around Warsaw and southern East Prussia) and being allocated the bulk of the armored and mechanized units." The latter army group would wheel north at an appropriate moment and cut off the Russian armies to the north from the rear. Lossberg predicted that Russian military resistance south of the Pripyet Marshes would be feebler—plagued by internal unrest in the Ukraine fomented by the Abwehr's advance subversive operations. The further strategy of the campaign, and its terminal objectives, must depend on whether and when Russia caved in under the force of the initial German onslaught. Had not Hitler himself exclaimed, according to his army adjutant, "If we can just tackle this colossus the right way, it will crumple up quicker than was ever dreamed possible!"

Only one possibility remained open to Moscow—to take the offensive first in order to disrupt the half completed German invasion preparations; or even more pertinently to invade the Romanian oil fields, perhaps using airborne troops alone. It would be the job of a future German military mission in Romania to forestall such a Soviet move. In Lossberg's view, however, the Russians would be forced for political reasons to try to thwart the German attack close to the frontier; otherwise they would be abandoning the flanking positions they had so recently secured on the Baltic and Black Sea coasts.

In Romania the king had abdicated in the crisis evoked by the Vienna Award, and the ruthless but incorruptible General Ion Antonescu had been appointed the national leader. Antonescu secretly asked Hitler to

---

[4] The only surviving copy is now in Russian archives, which explains why it escaped the attention of other postwar historians.

modernize the Romanian army with German tanks and artillery and to lend German instructors and staff officers. In return, he would deploy his forces exclusively on the Russian frontier. When Keitel put these requests to Hitler on the afternoon of September 19, Hitler decided instead to send about one division of German troops into Romania as a "military mission," as Lossberg had suggested; in addition, Romania was to be supplied with captured Polish equipment rather than the superior German models, for Hitler still suspected the Romanians might use them on their neighbors. A Luftwaffe mission would also be housed in Romania. On the same day the OKW issued a document stating that while these missions' ostensible purpose was to help the Romanians reorganize and train their forces, the "real jobs"—which were not to be made apparent to either the Romanian or the German missions' members—were:

1. to protect the oil fields from the clutches of a third power, and from destruction;
2. to enable the Romanian forces to fulfill specific tasks to a rigid plan aligned with German interests; and
3. to prepare the operations of German and Romanian forces from Romanian soil in the event we are forced into war with Soviet Russia.

The reader should be reminded that even at this stage no irrevocable order for an attack on Russia had been given; Hitler was still only preparing the military machine. But as E. M. Robertson has commented: "The consequences of having set in motion the planning machinery for the eastern campaign cannot be overlooked. With forces gathering on either side of the frontier and the political situation continuing to deteriorate, only some unfortunate and prodigious event would cause a final cancellation of the most cherished venture of his career."

Molotov

The six weeks preceding the doom-charged visit of Vyacheslav Molotov to Berlin in November 1940 are a period when Hitler's foreign policy becomes almost impossible to disentangle. With the direct assault on the British Isles all but abandoned and the Luftwaffe's murderous bombardment producing no visible collapse, he took counsel with the Spanish and Italians on ways of striking the British Empire at the periphery; he brought Japan into the Axis in a Tripartite Pact ostensibly designed to warn the United States against intervention, and he even pawed over the possibility of an alliance with France. This much is clear. But what are we to make of his more determined attempts to lure the Soviet Union into joining the Tripartite Pact as well? Was it a realistic alternative to inflicting military defeat on her, or was it a cynical attempt to force Britain to give way and enable Hitler to concentrate his undivided effort in the east?

The impulse toward a *peripheral* solution was provided by Admiral Raeder—and perhaps by Göring too, although the date of his often-mentioned "three-hour argument" with Hitler, urging against a Russian campaign is still obscure. Early in September Raeder had examined with Hitler the strategic options open to Germany; by the twenty-sixth, when he came for a long private talk on the same subject, he was convinced there were ways of pacifying Russia more elegant than brute force. Germany should throw the British out of the Mediterranean that winter, before the United States was roused; it should provide assistance to Italy for the capture of the Suez Canal and then advance through Palestine to Syria. Turkey would then be at Germany's mercy. "Then the Russian problem would assume a very different aspect. Russia is basically frightened of Germany"—a point on which Hitler agreed. "It is unlikely that any attack on Russia in the north would then be necessary." Hitler appeared to like this plan: they could then invite Russia to turn toward Persia and India—again on the British periphery—which were far more important to her than the Baltic. After the admiral left, the Führer mentioned to his naval adjutant, Puttkamer, that the interview had been enlightening, as it had checked with his own views and he could see how far he was right.

The key to any peripheral strategy was, however, Italy, and Italy was ruled by a vain Mussolini whose reach far exceeded his grasp. The Italians had haughtily declined Hitler's offer of an armored corps for the attack on Egypt: the attack had opened on September 13 and petered out four days later. Hitler's plan for France to join in a coalition war against Britain by fighting in the defense of North Africa—a plan inspired by Vichy's determined repulse later that month of the powerful British naval force that attempted to land General Charles de Gaulle's Free French troops at Dakar—would also depend on the extent to which Italy's distrustfulness could be overcome. North Africa was in her sphere of interest, and the Italians were reluctant to moderate their demands for the disarmament of French forces there or to allow the French fleet units stationed at Toulon to put to sea.

The most intractable barrier to Franco-German cooperation was the interest both Italy and Spain were declaring in substantial portions of France's African territories: Spain expected to be given the whole of French Morocco in return for declaring war on Britain. In other respects as well, the talks conducted in Berlin and Rome by Franco's future foreign minister, Ramón Serrano Suñer, remained unproductive. Hitler postponed reaching a final decision on problems affecting Spain and France until he could meet their leaders and Mussolini. Small wonder that the High Command's exasperated war diarist lamented: "Our command policy of late seems to be dictated only by regard for the feelings of the Reichsmarschall and the Italians."

One thing Hitler was certain of by late September 1940: it would be impossible to gratify the territorial dreams of Italy, France, and Spain simultaneously. If Spain were to join the war and seize Gibraltar, and if France were also to be encouraged to join the grand coalition, he must resort to "fraud on a grand scale," as he disarmingly put it to Ribbentrop: *each* aspirant would have to be left in the happy belief that his wishes would be largely fulfilled. The first claimant to be deceived was Hitler's senior partner, Benito Mussolini, whom he met on the Brenner frontier between Italy and Germany at midday on October 4. Hitler cunningly suggested that they lure Spain into the war by promising to deal with her colonial demands in the final peace treaty with France; in return for the loss of part of Morocco to Spain, France could have a slice of British Nigeria and the honor of defending her remaining colonies and reconquering those she had forfeited—to say nothing of the privilege of permitting Germany to establish bases in West Africa. Mussolini was promised Nice, Corsica, and Tunis. There would be something for everybody in the coalition.

On leaving the Brenner frontier, Hitler's train immediately headed for Berchtesgaden. By 9 P.M. he was back at the Berghof. For three days he idled in the autumn sunshine, reflecting on the implications of his new political strategy. His timetable was clearly mapped out: he would first like to see the former French ambassador, André François-Poncet (whom he liked) in Berlin; then he would embark on a grand tour, seeing Marshal Pétain in France and next General Franco in Spain, before returning to France to settle with Pétain the terms of their future collaboration. First, however, he would write to Stalin to tempt him with a share of Britain's legacy in return for Russia's participation in the coalition. "If we manage that," Brauchitsch was told, "we can go all out for Britain." The alternative of course—war with Russia—was already being quietly prepared, and with increasing reason, for there was a steady trickle of reliable Intelligence that behind her well-disposed if occasionally frosty facade the Soviet Union was contemplating carrying the world revolution further to the west. Hitler instructed Göring to ensure that all the Russian contracts with German industry were punctiliously fulfilled so that Stalin would have no cause for complaint on that score; but he also authorized the Luftwaffe to start extensive high-altitude photographic reconnaissance missions far into Russia.

On October 9, Hitler was back in the Chancellery in Berlin. Hungary, Romania, and Bulgaria were all showing a willingness to join the Tripartite Pact; Spain, he decided upon reflection, seemed so torn by internal malaise as to be valueless—Germany might have to take Gibraltar without Spain's aid; Italy's value as an ally was mitigated by her generals' sloth and Count Ciano's latent hostility. This was how Hitler apparently summarized the position to Field Marshal von Brauchitsch.

In conversation with Ribbentrop, Hitler debated the best approach to Moscow. Ribbentrop suggested a summit meeting between Stalin and the Führer, but Hitler pointed out that Stalin would not leave his country. Hitler himself dictated a lengthy letter to Stalin on the thirteenth inviting Molotov to visit them very shortly in Berlin. The letter bore all Hitler's familiar trademarks—the inveighing against Britain's duplicity, the portrayal of her leaders as conscienceless political dilettantes who dragged one reluctant country after another into battle on Britain's behalf and then abandoned them in their hour of need; he reminded Stalin of the captured Allied documents which revealed plans to bomb the Soviet oil fields, and he sought—though unconvincingly—to explain Germany's guarantee to Romania and her military mission there as a necessary safeguard in case of *British* sabotage or invasion. If Molotov came to Berlin, the letter concluded, Hitler would be able to put to him his concrete ideas on the joint aims they could pursue.

On October 12, Hitler had issued a secret message to the services formally canceling all invasion preparations against Britain. The army units would be needed for other purposes; the tugs and fishing boats were to be returned to the civilian economy. Göring's bombers alone would continue the war against the British people. As Hitler gloated to a visiting Italian minister on the fourteenth: "Let the British announce what they will—the situation in London must be horrific. Recently an American newspaper triumphantly claimed the Luftwaffe cannot have inflicted all that much damage, because of eighty-two American firms only eight have been completely destroyed and another seventeen damaged; but I am completely satisfied with such figures, even if the American newspaper isn't. It is far more than I expected. Let's wait and see what London looks like two or three months from now. If I cannot invade them, at least I can destroy the whole of their industry!" The aerial photographs his bomber crews brought back proved the extent of the damage done to Britain night after night. Churchill announced that over eight thousand Britons had been killed by the Luftwaffe.

What perplexed Hitler was the total lack of plan and purpose behind the British bombing offensive. Germany had feared an attempt to paralyze her transport system or, even worse, a ceaseless onslaught on her oil refineries—oil was Germany's Achilles' heel—yet Churchill was making the fundamental error of attacking Germany's civilians and inflicting only negligible damage on her war effort in the process. Nevertheless, Hitler had ordered Reichsleiter von Schirach to organize the evacuation of children from the biggest cities, and he had increased the antiaircraft batteries around Berlin from nineteen to thirty. He had also sent for Fritz Todt and commanded that air raid shelters be built. The blackout was perfected, blue lights were installed in streetcars, trains, and hospitals, and the whole civil defense organization was handed over to Field Marshal Milch.

The uncomfortable realization that as yet there was no defense against the enemy night-bomber confronted Hitler with a host of new problems. If only one aircraft approached Berlin, should the entire city be sent scurrying for the air raid shelters by sirens? How long before the all clear could be sounded? On the night of October 14 a typical episode angered Hitler: first an enemy bomber arrived without any advance warning; then there was an all clear followed by a fresh alert as more enemy bombers were spotted approaching over Magdeburg. The injured and sick in Berlin's hospitals were twice forced to trek down into their shelters—this was not a burden he had planned to inflict on the *German* population at all. He sent for Milch the next day and ordered him to sort the matter out. Hitler was glad he was leaving Berlin for the tranquility of the Berghof that night.

In Berchtesgaden, his only engagement of consequence was a private visit from the Italian Crown Princess Maria-José, the elegant spouse of Crown Prince Umberto and sister of King Leopold of Belgium. Hitler entertained her at afternoon tea on the seventeenth in the mountaintop "Eagle's Nest." The tea party started well—Hitler's majordomo Artur Kannenberg had as usual prepared it exquisitely. (Hitler would never hear a word said against the obese and sycophantic Kannenberg; whether softly playing an accordion in the background while the Führer and Eva Braun warmed themselves on a sofa before a crackling log fire, or organizing the great state banquets that passed flawlessly and without incident, Kannenberg had become indispensable.) A number of Hitler's most presentable womenfolk were also invited to meet the princess— among them Henriette von Schirach and the dazzlingly attractive wife of Robert Ley. While white-jacketed servants ministered to their needs, the princess haltingly begged Hitler to allow her brother to come and meet with him secretly. She assured Hitler of Leopold's loyalty, despite the domestic troubles caused by the food shortage in Belgium and Hitler's unwillingness to release the rest of the Belgian prisoners. When Hitler refused, she steadfastly repeated her request and then pleaded for the release of at least the more ailing prisoners. Hitler was impressed by her plucky manner with what was after all now the most powerful man in Europe. After the princess left his mountain, he joked feebly with his staff: "She is the only real man in the House of Savoy!"

In the special train *Amerika,* Hitler left Bavaria toward midnight on October 20, 1940, on the first leg of a rail journey that was to cover over four thousand miles within the next week. Every hundred yards or so sentries patrolled to the right and left of the railroad track; the Luftwaffe had provided exceptional air cover, too. The French leaders were still unaware that Hitler was coming to them.

Hitler had eventually abandoned his desire to meet François-Poncet, the former French ambassador, again. He had always warmed toward this Frenchman and believed he had won him over, but Ribbentrop had recently reeducated him by brandishing quantities of captured French diplomatic papers in which the former ambassador's confidential pronouncements were more pithy and colorful than either the Forschungsamt had succeeded in decoding or the French had published after war broke out. François-Poncet had no real sympathy for the spirit of National Socialism, for all his recognition of the injustices of Versailles and the wayward genius of the Führer; Hitler, warned the ambassador, was bent only on securing for Germany a hegemony in Central Europe. But "the remarks he [François-Poncet] occasionally drops about the Führer and other leading Reich figures are often so pointed and spiteful as to be incompatible with an even moderately loyal attitude." "As far as I am concerned," the ambassador had written in July 1937, "this mistrust has never left me. I am too well aware of the Third Reich leaders' powers of hypocrisy, mendacity, and cynicism to discard this mistrust one instant whatever the smiles and the amiability I outwardly adopt."

Hitler's train pulled into the little railroad station at Montoire, "somewhere in occupied France," at 6:30 P.M. on October 22. Ribbentrop's train, *Heinrich,* was already there. The station area had been freshly graveled and a thick red carpet had been rolled out. Antiaircraft batteries had been stationed on the surrounding hills. At seven, the short, stocky Pierre Laval, French deputy premier, sporting the familiar Gallic moustache and white tie, arrived by car. He had learned only a few minutes earlier that he was about to meet the Führer himself. In the dining car Hitler briefly indicated his wish to speak with Pétain in person on the lines France's future collaboration with Germany might take. The defeat of Britain was inevitable, he prophesied, and Laval earnestly assured him that he too desired this defeat, as must every redblooded Frenchman. Britain, said Laval, had dragged France into an unwanted war, abandoned her, and then besmirched her honor at Mersel-Kebir and more recently at Dakar. That the French had not wanted the war was shown by the two million troops who had allowed themselves to be taken prisoner.[1] Hitler emphasized that he was determined to mobilize every conceivable force necessary to defeat Britain. "Per-

[1] In fact the maximum number of French prisoners in German hands was 1,538,000.

haps the immediate future would prove this was no empty phrase"—a hint at his intention of drawing Russia into the Tripartite Pact. Laval, who had scribbled notes throughout the interview, promised to return with Pétain in two days' time.

At 4 A.M. Hitler's train left for the Spanish frontier. Upon General Franco's willingness to enter the war, and the consequent claims Hitler would have to support against France's colonial possessions, would depend the tenor of the main approach to Pétain. By 4 P.M. his train had reached the frontier town of Hendaye. A guard of honor was drawn up on the platform. Franco's train was half an hour late, but at four-thirty it drew alongside on another platform, where the Spanish-gauge railway ended. Hitler invited the Caudillo to inspect the guard of honor. Then the hard business of the day began in the drawing room of Hitler's train.

The argument that followed was to haunt Hitler to the end of his life. He later told Mussolini, "I would rather have three or four teeth extracted than go through that again." In vain he tried to persuade the plump, swarthy Spanish dictator to enter into an immediate alliance and allow German troops to capture Gibraltar. Twice during the summer Admiral Canaris had visited Spain in this connection, and mountain troops were already conducting experiments on the cliffs and caves of the Côte d'Azur in France—trying out various projectiles, explosives, and drilling techniques. Franco refused to rise to Hitler's bait. It was clear he doubted the likelihood of an Axis victory. Hours of argument brought Hitler no closer to his goal. He barely controlled his fury when Franco's foreign minister several times interrupted in a tactless way that Ribbentrop would certainly never have dared with *his* chief—usually at the precise moment when Hitler believed Franco was on the point of accepting the German terms.

Once he stood up abruptly and said there was little point in talking any longer, but talk on he did until dinner was served in his dining car. The Spanish leaders were scheduled to leave immediately afterward, but Hitler tackled Franco again, arguing with him about Spain's requirements of guns, gasoline, and foodstuffs until far into the night. When at 2:15 A.M. the Spanish leader's train left the little frontier station to the strains of the Spanish national anthem, General Franco was no nearer to joining the Axis. It was clear to all who crossed Hitler's path in these hours of his jolting journey back to Montoire that he was furious. He mouthed phrases about "Jesuit swine"—referring to Spain's Foreign Minister Serrano Suñer—and the Spaniards' "misplaced sense of pride." Over the next weeks, his anger at having been cold-shouldered turned to contempt. "With me, Franco would not even have become a minor

Party official," he scoffed to Jodl's staff, and he sneered at the quirk of fortune that had made a man like Franco head of state. (Another general had started the Spanish uprising in 1936, only to meet his death in an air accident.) But history was to prove that General Franco was wise enough to outlive by twenty years the Axis that now was wooing him.

At three-thirty the next afternoon, October 24, Hitler arrived back at Montoire. Ribbentrop and his staff had stayed behind for one more round of talks with the Spanish and so returned by plane—the foreign minister seething with anger at the fresh snub he had that morning been dealt by Serrano Suñer, who had failed to appear at the meeting they had arranged, and had sent only a junior official in his place. A secret protocol drawn up between the three governments—of which only Hitler, Mussolini, and the foreign ministers were to learn—was the only tangible product of the journey to Hendaye. But Franco was rightly suspicious of the vagueness of the territorial offers it contained, and his suspicions grew stronger as Hitler's demands grew shriller in the months to come.

Hitler now set much greater store in persuading Marshal Pétain to bring France into the "continental bloc" he was organizing against Britain. Spain's territorial claims could now safely be ignored. Hitler nervously left his train after lunch to make sure that a proper guard of honor was awaiting the French leaders, and he placed Field Marshal Keitel in front of the guard of honor to greet the "victor of Verdun" as his car drew up shortly before 6 P.M. Pétain stepped out wearing a long French military greatcoat and a general's red cap, beneath which gleamed his silver hair. Laval followed. Pétain was evidently gratified at the dignity of the German welcome, but he avoided inspecting the guard of honor. Hitler conducted him to his drawing room and repeated the impressive catalog of German arms, stressing the certainty of the Axis victory.

But when he asked Pétain for his response, the latter answered evasively that he must consult his government. The marshal would go no further than to confirm in principle his country's readiness to collaborate with Germany. Nonetheless, Hitler was pleased with the outcome. Pétain's military bearing, and even his reserve, had enhanced his admiration for him. He afterward said in Schaub's hearing, "France should be proud to have such a leader, a man who wants only the best for his own country." Although he suspected Pétain would meet with opposition from his government, he believed the Montoire conferences had accomplished all he had set out to achieve, and this was echoed in the first paragraph of the next directive he issued to the forces:

> It is the aim of my policy toward France to collaborate with that country in the most effective possible way to fight Britain in the future. For the time being there will fall to France the role of a "non-belligerent" obliged to tolerate military steps taken by the German war command in her territories, and particularly in the African colonies, and to support those steps where necessary by operations of her own defensive forces. The most urgent duty of the French is the defense—both by defensive and offensive means—of their possessions in West and Equatorial Africa against Britain and de Gaulle's movement. From this duty there can flow France's wholehearted participation in the war against Britain.

Pétain's meeting with Hitler had ended at 7:45 P.M. on October 24, a Thursday. Hitler accompanied the marshal back to his car while a guard of honor presented arms; then the marshal was driven away, never to be seen by him again.

Hitler's special train remained overnight at the Montoire station. He had planned to return to Berlin to prepare for Molotov's visit—the Russians had secretly accepted the invitation two days before—but now something unexpected occurred. Hewel brought him a long, jealous letter from Mussolini which had just arrived via the OKW's coded-teleprinter service. The letter, dated five days before, contained an impassioned appeal by the Duce to the Führer to set aside his dangerous flirtation with the French. Mussolini warned that he had information that the Vichy government was in secret touch with London via Lisbon; the French would always hate the Axis, and certainly no less now that they were in defeat. As for his own plans, Mussolini again mentioned that the British menace looming over Greece was comparable with that which Hitler had so successfully forestalled in Norway. "As far as Greece is concerned," Mussolini noted, "I am determined to act without hesitation—in fact to act very rapidly indeed."

After reading this, Hitler took fright and instructed Ribbentrop to arrange a meeting with Mussolini in a few days' time in Upper Italy. The lack of greater urgency suggests that the Duce's reference to attacking Greece was only of secondary importance to Hitler's concern to assuage Mussolini's fears about the approaches to France. Surely the Italians would not attack Greece *now,* with the autumn rains and winter snows almost upon them? That would be "downright madness"—it would be an open invitation to the British to occupy Crete and other Greek islands well within bomber range of the Romanian oil fields. Ribbentrop telephoned his Italian counterpart from the first railroad station inside the German frontier, and in the small hours of Friday morning Hewel brought the Führer a teletyped note from Ribbentrop's train, *Heinrich:* "I just spoke with Count Ciano on the phone and told him the Führer would very much like to speak with the Duce early next week. Count Ciano put this to the Duce and replied latter would be happy to welcome the Führer and Reich Chancellor on Monday in Florence.—*Ribbentrop.*"

During his Brenner meeting with Mussolini, on October 4, Hitler had probably given theoretical support for an Italian occupation of Greece if—and only if—necessary to forestall a British invasion. Admittedly the Abwehr had reported rumors of an Italian attack on Greece some days earlier; during Friday October 25 the German military attaché in Rome cabled that Marshal Badoglio himself had informed him that they now had information that the British intended to occupy Greek territory and that the Italians had for their part taken all necessary precautions to intervene the moment the first Briton sets foot on Greek soil. But he had reassured him: "I will inform you if it comes to that."

Hitler heard no more until Monday morning. His train reached Munich eventually late on Saturday, and he spent the next day killing time there. Ribbentrop's foreign ministry remained placidly unperturbed by the multiplying reports of Italian preparations in Albania, which Italy had occupied in April 1939. The two key dispatches from Rome that Sunday evening—the military attaché's discovery that Italy *was* going to attack Greece next morning, and the ambassador's report on Ciano's communication to the same effect at 9 P.M.—were not deciphered by their Berlin recipients until Monday morning and had certainly not reached Hitler, whose train left Munich punctually at 6 A.M. for Florence; so punctually indeed that Field Marshal Keitel, who had flown down from Berlin, had to leap onto the train as it was pulling away from the platform.

Mussolini's troops had invaded Greece at five-thirty that morning. The stunning news reached Hitler's train at Bologna, fifty miles north of Florence. Mussolini had obviously withheld his plan from him, to pay him in his own coin for Norway—and more pertinently for sending German troops into Romania, of which Mussolini was joint guarantor. Hitler's purpose until now had been at least to persuade the Duce not to attack Greece until after the American presidential elections, which were one week away. Hitler also wanted to be in a position to give his friend his expert advice on the best thrust direction for the offensive, and to mount a German airborne assault on Crete by divisions first moved to North African soil. Possession of Crete was after all the key to the command of the eastern Mediterranean. By the time Hitler's train steamed into Florence an hour later, 11 A.M., however, he had pocketed his intense disappointment at his ally's rash and thoughtless move, though he was hard put to control his anger when Mussolini strutted up to him and announced in German: "Führer—*wir marschieren!*" "We are on the march!"

Seven hours of discussions followed. At one stage Mussolini hinted incoherently at his real motive for attacking Greece. "You see, I trust my soldiers; but not my generals. They can't be trusted." But Hitler's mistrust extended to *all* Italians from now on. Why had they not given expression to their military aspirations by completing their assault on Egypt? The capture of the British naval base at Alexandria would have had immense consequences for their Mediterranean position. The Italians were comparing their Greek campaign with the German campaign in Norway, but they had left Crete and the Peleponnesian Islands unmolested; had Hitler shown no interest in Trondheim or Narvik in April? There was nobody on Hitler's staff who did not see this Greek adventure as a strategic error of the first magnitude, although Mussolini was optimistic that it would soon all be over. One of Hitler's adjutants noted that Hitler "swore at all German liaison staffs and attachés who knew their way around the best restaurants but were the world's worst spies," and hinted that "this was going to spoil many a scheme he was hatching himself."

All his fears proved only too well founded. Italy had not committed enough strength to the campaign. On the day after the Florence meeting, British ground and air forces landed on Crete. On November 3 the first British army units landed on the Greek mainland near Athens. Mussolini's invading divisions were thrown back. A member of Jodl's staff noted on October 29: "At present no participation in Greece is planned; nor is anything being undertaken with regard to Crete for the time being." But within a week Hitler had been forced to order the Wehrmacht to prepare an offensive against Greece to take the pressure off his harassed and headstrong ally. Out of this plan emerged perforce the need to invade Yugoslavia as well, and the schedule for spring 1941—already crowded with possible major operations in east and west —was finally thrown out of joint. On this day in October 1940 was sown the first seed of later defeat. "There is no doubt about it," the Führer was to lament as the shadows of that defeat began to fall across him, "we have had no luck with the Latin races! While I was occupied, first in Montoire, buttoning up a futile policy of collaboration with France, and then in Hendaye, where I had to submit to receiving gaudy honors at the hands of a false friend, a third Latin—and this time one who really was a friend—took advantage of my preoccupation to set in motion his disastrous campaign against Greece."

Nevertheless, the signs had been there to see, had Hitler not been so afflicted with blind trust in Mussolini; nor can Ribbentrop escape his share of the blame. Hitler's naval adjutant, Puttkamer, has stated that his chief refused to take the warning signals seriously. On October 18 Jodl's staff had first heard rumors that Italy was planning to hurl up to ten divisions at Greece at the end of the month. On the seventeenth a colonel on the Italian General Staff had confidentially told a German liaison officer in Rome that the Italian attack would begin eight or nine days later. A senior official of the foreign ministry had then drafted a telegram to the German ambassador in Rome directing him to deliver a stern demarche to the Italian government, but Ribbentrop had prevented the dispatch of this telegram, saying that its tone was too strong and that the ambassador should merely direct a "friendly inquiry" to Count Ciano. Almost simultaneously Hitler was shown a telegram in which his ambassador in Rome referred to the Italian plans against Greece, and not long afterward he saw a full report by the ambassador on a conversation with Ciano. In this exchange, the Italian foreign minister pointed out: "Italy has complete freedom of action over Greece. The Führer has conceded this to the Duce"—words which caused Ribbentrop to telephone his ministry and stop even the telegram about the "friendly inquiry." The whole matter must be decided by the Führer, said Ribbentrop; and Hitler's decision was that Italy must be trusted, and that no inquiry was to be sent to Rome.

Hitler returned to Berlin. For the next two weeks—ending with Molotov's arrival from Moscow—he lost the initiative, thanks to Mussolini's untimely attack on Greece. He unenthusiastically examined one peripheral project after another: the capture of Gibraltar, support for the Italians in Egypt, the mining of the Suez Canal, and even the occupation of various Atlantic islands as bases for a possible future war with the United States. Now he began to regret that he had not invaded Britain, and the diaries of his staff show him repeating years later that the navy had smart-talked him out of it. Julius Schaub recalled, "The Führer told me afterward, 'So long as I acted on instinct I acted rightly; the moment I allowed myself to be persuaded, things went wrong—as with the invasion of Britain.'"

During this period of indecision, only the Luftwaffe bombing—which had now killed fourteen thousand people in Britain—and the U-boat blockade continued. Meanwhile, Mussolini's humiliation by the Greeks restored British morale. For a time Hitler considered the possibility of seeking an armistice with Britain at the expense of Italy or France; but his instinct was against that, and he told Göring—as chief of the Four-Year Plan—to prepare the war economy for a long fight. Some time before, on returning through France from his meeting with Franco, he had cabled Admiral Karl Dönitz, the wiry commander of the German U-boat fleet, to join his train; he had ordered him to build huge concrete shelters to protect the U-boats from enemy air attacks on new submarine bases in western France. The navy had not thought them really necessary, but on his return to Berlin now Hitler sent for Fritz Todt and showed him precisely what he wanted. By Easter 1941 the first "U-boat pens" were ready—a good example of Hitler's foresight.

The Axis alliance as such had again reached low ebb. Throughout the summer the German army had encouraged Hitler to offer Italy armored units to ensure victory in Egypt, but the Italians had proudly snubbed this offer. At the Brenner meeting early in October, however, the Duce had hinted that he could use German tanks after all, and throughout that month Hitler had prepared to send his 3rd Panzer Division to help the Italians capture Marsa Matrûh; the army had sent a panzer general to carry out an on-the-spot investigation in North Africa. By the time the general reported to Hitler at the beginning of November, the Führer had determined to let the Italians stew in their own juice all winter. He would, instead, use the spare troops to invade Greece from Bulgaria and thus secure an outlet to the Aegean Sea; and he also planned a simultaneous attack on Gibraltar together with Spain but without Italy, since he could meet Spain's territorial demands at Italy's expense. He told his army adjutant he was so angry with Italy that he was minded to send no troops to North Africa and none either to Albania—into which Italian attack divisions had retreated after a Greek counterattack.

The panzer general's report from North Africa was the last straw: the Italians were highly unready to resume their offensive; their army commanders were inadequate, the water supplies for the attacking troops were insecure, and German mechanized units would be adversely affected by engine breakdowns under desert conditions. Hitler forthwith "wrote off" all idea of sending troops to North Africa; he ordered the planning to continue on a purely caretaker basis only. Ironically, it was to General Rommel that the Führer now bluntly proclaimed, "Not one man and not one pfennig will I send to North Africa." A few days later the disgrace of the Italians was complete. They had kept their battle fleet in harbor rather than risk it in an assault on Crete; now a handful of British torpedo planes attacked the warships in Taranto harbor and crippled three battleships, including Mussolini's most modern battleship. *Schadenfreude* in Berlin was tempered by the realization that the strategic balance in the Mediterranean had been ominously tilted.

Hitler's lack of strategic purpose was most clearly expressed in his rambling discussion with his supreme commanders on November 4 and in the resulting Wehrmacht directive issued a week later. General Franco had just personally written to Hitler that he took his oral promises very seriously—which meant that he intended to declare war on Britain. Hitler now told his commanders that he wanted to speed up Spain's entry into the war and tackle Gibraltar—the key to the western Mediterranean—as soon as the political negotiations were out of the way. A wing of Junkers 88 dive-bombers would fly from French airfields, wipe out the British warships sheltering in Gibraltar, and land in Spain; at the same time powerful German ground forces would cross into Spain and invest the British fortress. Since the British would probably covet the Canaries or Portugal's Cape Verde Islands once Gibraltar had fallen, the Germans must occupy those Atlantic islands, too. The political talks were to start at once.

In the Balkans, an operation for the occupation of northern Greece (Macedonia and Thrace) was to be planned should need arise. That Hitler desired the Dardanelles to come under German control is also evident, though this would eventually mean war with Turkey. However, on November 4 he commented to General Halder: "We cannot go on down to the Dardanelles until we have defeated Russia." Russia remained the one great area where Hitler could take a bold initiative, and it came higher in his list of priorities than invading Britain. At the end of October, a member of Jodl's staff had noted that even though the Soviet Union had just occupied still more Romanian territory—three islands in the Danube estuary, on the pretext that they were part of Bessarabia—this encroachment was for the present being played down. "No orders of any kind have been issued for Case East, nor are any as yet to be expected." And in the admiralty it was optimistically believed that "Case East is no longer considered likely as things are going at present." But, on November 4, Hitler said to Halder that Russia remained the nub of Europe's problems: "Everything must be done so that we are ready for the final showdown."

What triggered Hitler's remark? From the Forschungsamt reports Hitler now knew that in Moscow Molotov had recently discussed Russia's interest in the Dardanelles with Sir Stafford Cripps and had even demanded a naval base there. The ultimate clash between Germany and the USSR seemed inevitable if Hitler could not deflect Moscow's interests toward the Persian Gulf and India. But the Nazi party also seems to have reminded Hitler where his real mission lay. On the last day of October, the ruthless Gauleiter of Posen, Arthur Greiser, lunched with Hitler and Bormann at the Chancellery and complained at the way the eyes of the German people were currently turned west instead of east. The conquests in the west had brought Germany a bigger population to feed, and this was the very opposite of the Lebensraum policies Hitler had preached to the Party: Lebensraum could only be assured by conquests in the east. "The Führer agreed that this opinion was a correct one," noted Bormann, "and emphasized that when peace is concluded absolutely every young and capable civil servant aspiring to promotion will have to serve a number of years in the eastern territories."

On the eve of Molotov's arrival in Berlin, Hitler visited Field Marshal von Bock, his formidable new Commander in Chief in the east. Bock wrote:

The Führer called, sat half an hour at my bedside, and was very friendly and concerned. The overall situation was covered in detail. He is furious at Italy's escapade in Greece; not only did Italy keep it secret from us, she actually denied it when we taxed her with it. The Führer described how he tried to prevent the mischief by going down to Florence, or at least to keep things on ice long enough for us to lend a helping hand; but in vain—Mussolini had announced he could no longer call off the operation that had begun. The ultimate—and highly undesirable—outcome is that the Romanian oil fields will be threatened by the British air force units from Salonika. This danger is so great that it may oblige us to take countermeasures. . . . What will transpire in the east is still an open question; circumstances may force us to step in to forestall any more dangerous developments.

The outcome of Molotov's visit would determine whether or not Hitler would attack the Soviet Union. In the secret directive he circulated to his service commanders on November 12 after a week of drafting and redrafting, Hitler approved this wording: "*Russia*. Political discussions have been initiated with the aim of establishing what Russia's posture will be over the coming period. Irrespective of the outcome of these discussions, all the preparations orally ordered for the east are to continue. Directives thereon will follow as soon as the army's basic operational plan has been submitted to and approved by me."

Molotov had his first encounter with Hitler at three o'clock that day.

The Soviet foreign minister arrived at Anhalt station with a big bodyguard. Ribbentrop's state secretary, Weizsäcker, described them as "good gangster types for a film"—he found it depressing that 130 million Russians were being represented by such a shabby bunch. The station building was brilliant with fresh greenery and flowers, Russian flags waved, and a military band greeted the delegation. Every member seemed to be under his neighbor's surveillance. Molotov had even had to radio Moscow for permission to eat in the German dining car. He was accompanied by a young official, ostensibly an interpreter, though he spoke not one word to the Germans. Weizsäcker wrote in his diary: "Molotov seems to be a thorough worker. His men are timid. All are obviously afraid of us. Many of them quote Bismarck and his concept of a German-Russian collaboration. . . . From our viewpoint too a cooling off in the east is worthwhile. This summer it has become à la mode to wish for war with Russia or regard it as necessary." And in an entry he added some days later: "Why not let them stew in their own stupid bolshevism? So long as the country is ruled by officials like those we have seen here, it's less to be feared than when the czars were in power!"

Not since his talks with the British before Munich, in 1938, had Adolf Hitler heard such tough language as Molotov used on November 12 and 13. Hitler had always contended that the Soviet Union and the Reich were two different worlds, but might try to live together. As Ribbentrop had done before him, he harangued the Russian minister as though he were at a Party rally. He put it to Molotov candidly that it was in their interests to stand back to back, rather than try to outstare one another. If Russia wanted to share in the booty as the British Empire fell apart, then now was the time to declare Soviet solidarity with the Tripartite Pact powers. He was not asking for an outright military alliance from Russia; he sympathized, he said, with Russia's desire for an outlet to the high seas and suggested she should expand southward from Batum and Baku toward the Persian Gulf and India; Germany would expand into Africa. As for Russia's interest in the Dardanelles, Hitler restated his willingness to call for the renegotiation of the 1936 Montreux Convention, which governed the straits, to bring it into line with Moscow's defensive interests.

Molotov—one year younger than Hitler, a stocky, nondescript figure who reminded Weizsäcker of "a schoolmaster type"—itemized with an occasional frosty smile the price demanded by the Soviet Union for any explicit alignment with the Axis. Stalin himself had dictated these points to him before he left, he said. Russia wanted another stab at Finland—she intended to occupy and annex the whole country, which had, after all, been assigned her by the 1939 pact Molotov had signed with Ribbentrop in Moscow. But Hitler was adamant that there must be no fresh war in the Baltic; he was at war, and he needed Finland's nickel and timber supplies. When Molotov complained—"crudely," as he himself apologetically noted—that Hitler's recent guarantee to Romania and the troops he had just sent there could only be directed against Russia, Hitler acidly reminded him that Romania had herself asked for them. And when Molotov announced Russia's intention of inviting Bulgaria to sign a nonaggression pact which would permit the establishment of a Soviet base near the Dardanelles and would guarantee the safety of King Boris, Hitler ironically inquired whether Bulgaria too had *asked* for such assistance; pressed later by Molotov for a reply to Soviet terms, Hitler evasively answered that he must consult Mussolini!

Molotov was unconvinced: he was unconvinced that Hitler was serious in his offer of partnership; since Italy's crippling reverses in Greece and at Taranto, he was unconvinced of Axis supremacy; above all he was unconvinced that Britain's days were numbered. Each of his conferences with Hitler was terminated by the warning of approaching British aircraft, and his dinner at the Soviet embassy on the thirteenth ended abruptly for the same reason. Ribbentrop invited him to the concrete shelter at his home and here—who will ever know what prompted Molotov's untimely candor?—the Soviet foreign minister revealed that Moscow's long-range interests extended far beyond the Balkans—as though that was not ominous enough! Molotov asked Ribbentrop whether Germany really was interested in preserving Sweden's neutrality, and he declared that Russia could never entirely forego an interest in the western approaches to the *Baltic* either—the Kattegat and Skagerrak.

When Ribbentrop told the Führer of Molotov's revelations in the shelter, Hitler was stunned. Like Italy, the Soviet Union had suffered only military disgraces—most recently in Finland—while Hitler's Wehrmacht had crushed the resistance of one country after another. Yet Molotov had made immense demands. "He demanded that we give him military bases on Danish soil on the outlets to the North Sea," Hitler was to recall in the last week of his life. "He had already staked a claim to them. He demanded Constantinople, Romania, Bulgaria, and Finland

—and *we* were supposed to be the victors!" While the public was deliberately fed the impression that the formal discussions had been harmonious and successful, within the OKW and Hitler's Chancellery there was no doubt that the parting of the ways had come. Keitel's adjutant recalled that when he entered the Führer's daily war conference the next day it was like entering the house of a dying man: a funereal aura clouded the proceedings. One of Hitler's own adjutants wrote: "[The Führer] says he never had expected much from it all. The discussions have shown, he says, which way the Russians' plans are lying: M[olotov] has let the cat out of the bag. He (the Führer) is vastly relieved, this won't even have to remain a *mariage de convenance*."

Irrevocable and terrible in its finality, the decision Adolf Hitler now took was one he never regretted, even in the jaws of ultimate defeat.

The "Barbarossa" Directive

After Molotov's trainload of advisers and secret police officials had crossed the demarcation line back into Russia's share of Europe, an air of uncertainty and gloom shrouded Hitler's Chancellery. One of his adjutants recorded his conviction that the Führer himself was at a loss which way to turn next: his confidence in his own military commanders —and particularly in Göring's Luftwaffe—was waning. Perturbed at Britain's unexpected tenacity, uncertain about Russia's true military strength, again and again he repeated that he alone would decide the next move. The talks with Molotov had betrayed Russia's designs on Europe. He could not afford to surrender the Balkans; it would be awkward enough to have Finland in Russia's sway. As for Ribbentrop's deal with Stalin in August 1939, Hitler now admitted: "That pact never was an honest one, because the gulf between the ideologies was just too wide."

Opinion among Hitler's principal advisers was divided about the Russian campaign. Ribbentrop had been convinced there was no alternative. Brauchitsch certainly did not oppose it. Halder gave no clear lead one way or the other: his papers show him to have regarded now Britain, now Russia, as Germany's most important opponent; his mind was in confusion. Keitel's opposition had been stilled. Jodl unquestionably regarded the Russian campaign as inevitable and was optimistic about the outcome. The Party leaders gloated in anticipation of the new empire awaiting them. Only Göring and Raeder voiced pertinent objections.

The Reichsmarschall confronted Hitler with them on November 13: it would be foolish to court a war with Russia. His Luftwaffe had only just got its teeth into Britain's industrial flesh; in addition, Germany could never police such a huge area in the east. Far better to let Russia attack Finland and advance toward the Dardanelles, since this must surely bring Britain into open conflict with Russia (such was also Papen's advice). Hitler replied that the danger from Russia was so singular that it must be met squarely before the Soviet industrial buildup was complete. He evidently also explained to Göring that in a long war Germany could beat Britain's food blockade only by expanding to the east; similarly, the oil requirements of large-scale air war against Britain—and no doubt the United States—could only be covered by capturing the Caucasian oil fields. Göring was told to assume that the attack on Russia would start on May 1, 1941, and last only a few months; he thereupon ceased objecting, and instructed Keitel's chief economic officer to supply him with a dossier on Russia's arms economy. On the fourteenth, it was Raeder's turn to voice the admiralty's emphatic opposition to attacking Russia before Britain had been defeated, and the admiral maintained this vigorous criticism of the plan until the end of the year.

Heinrich Himmler probably echoed Hitler's views most closely in a November speech to Party officials in which he pinpointed the frontier between Europe and Asia. People suggested it was the Ural Mountains, but the Mongol strains permeated the people both sides of that barrier too strongly to escape Himmler's racialistic scrutiny:

That is why this Russian people will never make a purely European or even a pure Asiatic race. It must be treated as a potpourri of races and kept within its frontiers. By brute force if by no other means. At present there is no need for that; we have our friendship pact with Russia. But this friendship pact is not a love affair; it's a pact designed to meet the most elementary requirements of our two nations. Up to now, by means of this pact Russia has subjugated entire countries and nations, apart from Finland, without drawing her sword from its scabbard; she has annexed large territories on her western and southern frontiers. Her appetite threatened to grow gigantically, so it became necessary for us to map out our mutual interests to each other afresh. In his long overdue visit to Berlin, Molotov has been given the necessary instructions. If what I have heard is true, then Stalin is not permitted to start any wars for the moment, or any fighting, as otherwise he will be dealt a sharp rebuke by our own guns. This order holds good both for her [Russia's] evil designs on Finland and for any she may have in the south or southeast. She is permitted to launch military operations only with the Führer's express permission. To put muscle into our orders, we have based enough troops along our eastern frontier for the Red czar in Moscow to take them seriously. Anyway, as I said in my last speech, Russia is militarily quite harmless. Her officer corps is so poor that they do not even bear comparison with our NCOs; her army is as badly equipped as trained. They cannot possibly be any danger to us.

Before ten days had passed, it was clear the Russians' aims were irreconcilable with Hitler's. Ribbentrop had submitted to Moscow a draft treaty embodying in secret protocols the substance of Hitler's oral offer to Molotov: Germany's territorial expansion would take place in Central Africa; Italy's in north and northeast Africa; Japan's in the Far East; and the Soviet Union's toward the Indian Ocean. On November 25, Molotov submitted the four conditions on which Russia would sign. The first two—a demand that Hitler evacuate from Finland the troops sent in August 1940, and that Bulgaria conclude a pact with Russia granting her military bases within range of the Bosphorus—were wholly unacceptable to Hitler. He instructed Ribbentrop to make no reply at all.

The Führer had retreated from these traumatic events in Berlin on November 16 and spent the next few days at the Berghof. He had, of course, privately notified King Boris of Bulgaria of the proposals Molotov had outlined for Soviet "protection" of his country, and on the seventeenth Hitler conferred with the king at the Berghof. He had a certain mistrust of all kings, but the short, swarthy Bulgarian monarch spoke fluent German and had an easygoing manner which tended to win over the Führer. (During this private visit to Germany he stayed at the Hotel Vier Jahreszeiten in Munich, where he caused consternation to his personal detectives by slipping out of the hotel's back door and strolling through Munich's bohemian quarter and the English Gardens.) Boris was a shrewd businessman, and provided that Hitler did not compromise him too early—after all, Bulgaria was exposed to attack from Turkey and the Soviet Union—he was willing to let German divisions cross Bulgarian territory when the time came to attack northern Greece. Hitler offered him western Thrace as an outlet to the Aegean if Bulgarian troops would participate, but in the king's view this was going too far. Boris also warned Hitler that road conditions were so poor in winter that it would be advisable to postpone the assault on Greece until early March. Bulgaria was also reluctant to join the Tripartite Pact at present.[1]

By the end of the following week, Hungary, Romania, and Slovakia had all joined the Tripartite Pact. The Greeks had now started a coun-

[1] She joined on March 1, 1941, simultaneously with the entry of the first German divisions. See page 226 below.

teroffensive into Albania. Italy begged Hitler to supply German trucks to replace the inferior Italian transport, but Hitler refused. He saw no realistic way of helping Italy until the spring. In Vienna, the Hungarian prime minister agreed to allow German troops to cross into Romania. Yugoslavia would have to be cajoled into refraining from molesting the German movements toward the Greek frontier: to the chagrin of the Italians—who had designs of their own on Yugoslavia—Hitler insisted on luring Yugoslavia toward the Axis by offering her part of northern Greece (Salonika) and guaranteeing her possessions. The greatest impression on Hitler was made by the new Romanian leader, General Antonescu, who paid a first visit to Berlin on the twentieth. His contempt for the Slavs, his admiration for the National Socialist movement, and his soldierly bearing won the Führer immediately; Antonescu announced that in signing the Tripartite Pact, Romania was not just acting out a formality but was ready "to fight sword in hand beside the Axis powers for the victory of civilization." Hitler adroitly hinted that the anti-Romanian Vienna Award might yet be rescinded in Romania's favor when peace came.

Italy's disgrace made it easier to reshuffle Spanish and Italian claims on African territory—all the more necessary now that the Gibraltar operation's importance had been enhanced by the British foothold in Greece. When General Franco's foreign minister, Serrano Suñet, had visited the Berghof on the eighteenth, Hitler had given him "the friendly advice" to declare war on Britain as soon as possible: "Any hesitation by politicians can easily cost thousands of brave soldiers their lives!" He bluffed the Spaniard with fictitious figures of Germany's armed might and glibly promised to supply all the wheat and oil Spain would need; but he had no real answer to the minister's argument that the Spanish people were not psychologically ready for a new war, and he could make no concrete moves to replace the vague assurances he had offered both at Hendaye and in a secret agreement Spain had since signed with Italy and Germany concerning the African territories it was to receive. Hitler knew that if he made public the inroads that were to be made in Morocco, the French there would immediately declare for de Gaulle.

There were already signs that Pétain was treating with the enemy. The Spanish foreign minister advised Hitler that Pierre Laval was one of the most hated men in France for collaborating with Germany, and that this fact indicated the true sentiments of the French people. Hitler instinctively agreed—he feared that every weapon he provided to Vichy would one day be turned against him. When Washington announced the appointment of an admiral as ambassador to Vichy in place of its present lowly chargé d'affaires, Hitler's suspicions of the "old fogy"—Pétain —intensified. The Forschungsamt had reported on November 11 that secret talks were going on in New York between emissaries of Pétain and Churchill.

Hitler for his part did nothing to strengthen the French people's affection for Laval. He authorized Gauleiter Josef Bürckel, the civil administrator of Lorraine, to expel a hundred thousand hostile French citizens from the province, and later in November nearly seven thousand German Jews from Baden and the Palatinate were on Hitler's orders transported into Vichy France. Both actions aroused Pétain's indignation. Meanwhile the Franco-German talks on military collaboration were conducted desultorily at the German embassy in Paris. The fact that Hitler appointed only Major General Walter Warlimont, Jodl's deputy, as Germany's representative showed how little importance he attached to them.

Hitler's timetable began to take shape, dominated by the need to program the commitment of his scarcest resources most efficiently—in this case the Junkers 88 dive-bomber squadrons, which were only gradually coming off the production lines. Their commitment in Spain must be over by February if they were to be available for the attack on Greece (an operation now code-named "Marita," after the daughter of one of Jodl's junior staff). On May 1 the attack on Russia would begin. (This had not prevented Hitler from "confidentially" informing the talkative Ciano that he would be invading Britain in May.)

A number of untidy residual problems remained. King Leopold of Belgium, now a prisoner, had been brought to the Berghof on November 19, where he had hinted that if Hitler would broadcast an explicit guarantee of Belgium's future independence—as the British were doing— the Belgians might be open to military and political agreements. Hitler did not rise to the bait: he saw no need. Nor would he release the Belgian prisoners, as they supplied him with a useful labor force, whereas Belgium already had widespread unemployment.

The second area that briefly attracted Hitler's attention was southern Ireland, which had remained neutral though with pronounced pro-German sympathies. In mid-November, the OKW had examined the possibility of an appeal from Dublin for German aid; but it was not until the twenty-second that Hitler directly considered the matter.

Early that morning German army Intelligence picked up a British radio message reading: "Fifty wireless operators (no Jews) are to be

202 "WAR OF LIBERATION"

provided for transferring GHQ. Depart Carlisle November 22 1940
1300 hrs for operation Ireland. Starting point for operation Ireland is
Rosslea in Ulster." Taking the political situation into account, the German High Command deduced that a British invasion of southern Ireland was imminent. This would provide Britain with airfields and submarine and escort bases which would gravely set back the German
U-boat operations west of Ireland. To deprive London of her apparent
motive, the German foreign ministry denied any German intention of
occupying Ireland, and this was welcomed by Eire's President Eamon
De Valera; Berlin believed that Dublin's determination to beat back any
British invasion had given London second thoughts. Hitler's attention,
once attracted to the Emerald Isle, characteristically lingered on, however. On the twenty-seventh he asked his High Command to analyze the
pros and cons of invading Ireland, whose fall into German hands would
spell the end of Britain. Perhaps no episode illustrates so vividly the
whims which inspired Hitler's *ad hoc* military strategy as the winter of
1940 approached. It was not difficult for Admiral Raeder to demonstrate that a prolonged German occupation of Ireland in the face of
Britain's huge naval superiority was quite out of the question.

Despite the remarkable resilience of the British people under heavy
air attacks, all Hitler's advisers—and particularly Admiral Raeder—saw
the continued bombing of British industry and dockyards—coupled with
the submarine campaign—as the most likely way to bring Britain to her
knees. Nothing was to be allowed to distract effort from this remorseless
campaign. Coventry, and now Birmingham, had been devastated by
night attacks before once again worsening weather forced a halt to German raids. (Indeed, bombers were one reason why Hitler wanted the
Azores, which provided his only chance of striking at the United States
with long-range Messerschmitts—still on the drawing board, but he had
seen a mock-up at Augsburg in 1937—and forcing the Americans to
set up their own system of air defense at the expense of helping the British.) But Hitler still lacked the determination needed to use the strategic
bomber force to maximum effect. On the morning after Birmingham's
first raid he told a Hungarian visitor that he was sorry about the fine
cities and the people being destroyed in Britain; it was all the fault of incompetent British politicians. Perhaps he admired the ability of the
"Germanic" British to stand up to the bombers. Himmler explained to
Party officials: "The Führer had no desire to destroy the British people
or their empire. The British are a race related to our own and in their
bones they are as uncowed as ever. This is displayed by the unheard-of
toughness with which the British people has taken its beating from the

Luftwaffe, month after month. The bombardment of London and the wiping out of entire cities has not sufficed . . ."

Bored by the failure of his squadrons in the Battle of Britain, Reichsmarschall Göring had gone on an extended hunting leave on his estate at Rominten. On November 25, Hitler explored with Field Marshal Milch and Chief of Air Staff Jeschonnek ways of attacking the British position in the eastern Mediterranean from Italian-controlled airfields. The most important target would be the British fleet at Alexandria, but this could not be tackled until the Italians had taken Marsa Matrûh; the Luftwaffe was to prepare to mine the Suez Canal, though the Italians were still unwilling to agree. Meanwhile, until the German attack on Greece started in the spring, the Luftwaffe was to help the Italians out of their predicament by attacking military targets in Greece. The Italian squadrons which had briefly assisted in the attack on Britain were to be transferred to Albania. Hitler complained to the air force generals that the Italians failed to realize how grave the situation was: they were "frittering" their forces away, and had brought the British bomber squadrons so close that Germany must now supply sorely needed antiaircraft batteries to Romania (to protect her oil interests) and to southern Germany.

On December 4, Milch brought Hitler details of Göring's proposals: by basing the Tenth Air Corps, with two squadrons of Junkers 87 dive-bombers, on Sicily, and two more squadrons of Junkers 88 dive-bombers (the heavier, longer-range aircraft) in southern Italy, Germany could effectively block the narrows between Sicily and North Africa. Jeschonnek's deputy wrote after this conference: "Discussion between Führer and Milch on possibilities of battering British position in Mediterranean. This is necessary as the Italian disaster in Greece is having psychological effects quite apart from any military disadvantages: Africa and Spain are beginning to waver in their attitude toward us." Hitler handed Milch a letter to carry immediately to Mussolini. In it he warned the Duce that he must have these squadrons back by early February for use elsewhere. By the seventh, Milch and the Deputy Chief of Air Staff were back from Rome, reporting to Hitler on Mussolini's optimism about the situation in Albania. "Midday, back in Berlin," wrote Jeschonnek's deputy. "Conference with Führer, who is considerably upset by the unpleasant consequences of the situation in the Mediterranean. He fears this may have an effect on Spain's attitude."

That this was no idle fear was shown a few days later. On November 28, Ribbentrop's ambassador in Madrid had reported that General Franco was willing for the proposed preparations for Spain's entry into the war to proceed; Hitler assumed that this meant "proceed immediately," and on December 4 he sent Admiral Canaris to Franco with a personal letter proposing that German troops formally cross the Spanish frontier on January 10, which would mean starting the assault on Gibraltar, six hundred miles from the frontier, in the first week of February.

Field Marshal von Reichenau would command the assault; it would start on February 4 or 5 and last four weeks. By mid-May 1941, Hitler could have the troops back for other purposes. The Führer demanded that the assault open with a saturation bombing attack on Gibraltar—particularly on the fleet units and dockyard there. Then the gun batteries were to be silenced, and the Rock itself battered with thousands of rounds of artillery fire; the level ground between the Rock and the Spanish frontier was to be plowed through and through to neutralize enemy minefields. The heaviest available tanks would tackle the British troops sheltering in the galleries, and the remnants would be driven out by colossal demolition charges. "The principle must be to use as much equipment as possible to avoid [German] bloodshed."

Like so many other projects, the capture of Gibraltar was an operation Hitler had vividly pictured in his imagination night after night.

The directive for the Gibraltar operation, code-named "Felix," had already been prepared, and General Jodl was already packing his bags for Madrid, where he was to explain the plan to Franco, when a telegram arrived from the Spanish capital bringing everything to an abrupt halt. In a long audience on the evening of the seventh, Franco had stated that for economic reasons Spain could not be ready by January 10: what good would Germany's deliveries do Spain if her transport network could not distribute the foodstuffs to the starving populace? Besides, Britain would seize the Canary Islands and Spain's other overseas possessions. It was in both their countries' interests, Franco suggested, that he decline Hitler's proposal; he did not want Spain to become a burden on the Axis.

Hitler ordered Keitel to ask by what date Spain *could* be ready; Canaris replied from Madrid that Spain could only join in the war if Britain was on the brink of collapse. The alacrity with which Hitler now abandoned "Felix"—though in later years he again toyed more than once with this idea—suggests that his instinct was screaming warnings against accepting obligations toward a second Latin nation. In the immediate aftermath of Franco's rebuff he lamented this further proof that Mussolini's misadventures in the Balkans had undermined the awe in which the world held the Axis. He also greatly regretted forfeiting the psychological bonus the capture of Gibraltar would have bestowed.

Molotov's negative reply to Hitler's proposals at the end of November 1940 dispelled whatever hesitations Hitler still had about attacking Russia. Visiting the sick General von Bock again briefly on December 3, the field marshal's sixtieth birthday, Hitler warned that the "eastern problem" was now coming to a head; there seemed to be links running between Russia and the United States, and this in turn made a joint Anglo-Russian enterprise more likely. "It would be dangerous to sit back and wait for the end of a development like that. But if the Russians are eliminated, Britain will have no hope whatever of defeating us on the Continent, particularly now that America is prevented from interceding effectively by Japan, whose rear is free of danger now." To Brauchitsch, two days later, Hitler announced, "The hegemony of Europe will be decided in the fight with Russia."

Hitler's strategic timetable took shape. He would execute "Marita" early in March. Of course, if the Greeks saw the light and showed their British "guests" the door, he would call off "Marita" altogether—he had no interest whatever in occupying Greece. Then he would attack Russia during May. "In three weeks we will be in Leningrad!" Schmundt heard him say.

This confident prediction was symptomatic of the German army's crass underestimate of their Russian opponent's strength. Virtually nothing was known about the Red Army: a complete search of archives in France—Russia's own ally!—had yielded nothing. Hitler was confident that the German Mark III tank with its 50-millimeter gun provided clear superiority over the obsolete Red Army equipment; they would have one thousand five hundred by spring. "The Russian himself is inferior. His army has no leaders," he assured his generals. "Once the Russian army has been beaten, the disaster will take its inevitable course."

At 3 P.M. on December 5, Hitler's military advisers—Brauchitsch and Halder of the army, and Keitel and Jodl of the OKW—came to the Chancellery to argue out each phase of the coming operations and their tactical details. Now for the first time the two varying concepts of the Russian campaign—the meticulous studies drawn up and exercised by Halder's staff and the draft operational plan submitted by Jodl's Colonel Lossberg—were brought into informal synthesis. Halder's proposal was distinguished by a particularly powerful main drive toward Moscow, the hub of the Soviet political and transport system; Lossberg's "Fritz" attached more weight to the northernmost army group and the occupation of the Baltic coast.[2] Lossberg's plan was evidently not actually discussed at this conference, but its influence on Hitler is clear, for in his reply to Halder the Führer now drew heavily on Lossberg's arguments. Both Halder's plan (which had been originated by General Erich Marcks and completed by General Friedrich Paulus) and Lossberg's assumed that the Russians must of necessity defend the western areas of the Soviet Union and the Ukraine; and both stated that the Russians must be prevented from staging an ordered retreat as in 1812—the Russian front must be pierced by armored spearheads, encircled from the rear, and liquidated. The army and OKW were also agreed that they must occupy as much Soviet territory as necessary. This would prevent the Russian air force from reaching Reich territory; it would also enable Göring's bomber squadrons to attack Russian industries and thus prevent a resurgence of armed Soviet might. Halder proposed that the offensive end along a line from the Volga River to Archangel.

Where Hitler took exception, though at first with noticeable mildness, was to Halder's insistence that nothing detract from the main assault on Moscow. Hitler wanted the Russian forces in the Baltic countries to be encircled first; a similar huge encirclement action by Army Group South, south of the Pripyet Marshes, would liquidate the Russian armies in the Ukraine. Only after that should it be decided whether to advance on Moscow or to bypass the Soviet capital in the rear. "Moscow is not all that important," he explained. This was the first hint of a strategic controversy that was eventually to rage between Hitler and the General Staff in the summer of 1941, though neither Halder nor Brauchitsch took it seriously as yet. Indeed, when the first draft directive for the Russian campaign was brought to Hitler by Jodl, it still conformed with Halder's recommendation of a main thrust toward Moscow ("in conformity with the plans submitted to me"). But Hitler ordered the document redrafted in the form *he* had emphasized: the principal task of the two army groups operating north of the Pripyet Marshes was to drive the Russians out of the Baltic countries. "Only after this, the most urgent task, has been accomplished, followed by the capture of Leningrad and Kronstadt, are the offensive operations to be continued with the object of seizing the vital transport and armaments center, Moscow."

Hitler's motives for seizing the Baltic coast first were clear. The admiralty attached particular importance to restoring peace in the Baltic

---

[2] Details of the Lossberg plan, dated September 15, 1940, are summarized on pages 176–77 above.

as soon as possible. The Baltic was the navy's training ground and the route Germany's ore supplies from Scandinavia must take; besides, when the Russians had been destroyed in the Baltic countries, great forces would be released for other operations. The Russian campaign would be a short one; indeed, it must be settled together with all other continental problems before 1941 was over—for from 1942 onward the United States would be capable of intervening.

Toward the United States, where Roosevelt had just been elected for a third term, Hitler was to display unwonted patience despite what he regarded as extreme provocations for one long year. Technically neutral, the United States under the Roosevelt administration had violated neutrality time and again; both Roosevelt and Churchill yearned for the incident that would swing American public opinion around toward open intervention. Until then American aid was limited to the trade of over-age destroyers for British bases in the Western hemisphere, the exporting of aircraft and munitions, and a fringe of illegal military activities: American citizens fought in the Royal Air Force; a blind eye was turned on British violations of the Pan-American security zone; and United States warships chased, harried, and shadowed Axis merchant ships plying their trade in transatlantic waters. These warships were ostensibly escorting the German steamships for their own safety, but the admiralty in Berlin knew from its radio reconnaissance and decoding sections that in reality the Americans were passing on to the British all the information they could about these blockade-runners.

In vain Admiral Raeder protested to Hitler about this "glaring proof of the United States' nonneutrality." He asked whether this active hostility was to be allowed to go unchallenged, and whether this was "compatible with the honor of the German Reich." But to Hitler the United States was still a *quantité négligible* and he wanted it to stay that way in 1941. Nothing must happen to increase the tension between Germany and the United States. Throughout the year that followed, the dossier of American violations thickened; and now that the foreign ministry and Forschungsamt were also reading the American diplomatic ciphers, the evidence against Roosevelt hardened. But nothing would alter Hitler's determined refusal to take up the gauntlet flung down to Germany.

His eyes were now fixed on Russia. On December 18, Jodl brought him the final version of the campaign directive, retyped on the large "Führer typewriter." "Fritz," Lossberg's code name for the coming campaign, was replaced by the more majestic-sounding "Barbarossa," the name by which the first Emperor Friedrich had gone into history eight hundred years before as the founder of a mighty empire. Partly the handiwork of Jodl, a master stylist whose spoken German was very clear and simple, and partly the product of Hitler's pen, the eleven-page document instructed the Wehrmacht to be prepared to "overthrow Soviet Russia in a rapid campaign even before the war with Britain is over." The Luftwaffe would have a purely support role, rather than one of strategic bombardment. All preparations were to be complete by mid-May 1941; he, Hitler, would give the word for the necessary troop concentrations to begin eight weeks before the chosen date "if Russia should fail to change in her attitude toward us." Nine copies of the directive were signed for the commanders in chief and the OKW; those let into the dreadful secret were to be kept to an absolute minimum, and every single phase was to be camouflaged against Russian scrutiny.

From now on his intention of disposing of the Soviet menace was the one constant in Hitler's grand strategy. His goals in Africa and his policies toward Spain and France had been reduced to a shambles by Italy's military ignominy. He expected General Maxime Weygand, the French Resident in North Africa, to declare for de Gaulle at any moment. Franco's rebuff robbed Hitler of direct access to Morocco. At short notice the army and OKW drafted a campaign plan, "Attila," in case Germany had to occupy Vichy France as well and stop the French home fleet from crossing to North Africa.

Mussolini blamed his political and military advisers for the Greek calamity: they had promised him it would take little more than a "military two-step" to invade Greece, but now the Greek army was deep inside Albania, outnumbering the Italian divisions more than 2 to 1. Badoglio, chief of the Italian armed forces, resigned; Mussolini replaced him with General Ugo Cavallero and sent the Italian ambassador with a pathetic appeal to Hitler to speed Yugoslavia's entry into the Tripartite Pact as a warning to Greece. Hitler responded that the only methods that would halt the Italian army's headlong flight were barbaric ones "like putting the guilty generals and colonels before the firing squad and decimating the other ranks." Yugoslavia had little love for Italy and refused even to allow German trucks to pass through to the Italian forces in Albania. Hitler supplied a squadron of transport planes to help Mussolini fly divisions from Italy, and he suggested that the Duce come and see him personally on December 10. But on the ninth a further disaster began for Italy as the British army in Egypt opened a counteroffensive which was to throw back the Italian forces into Libya and result within a matter of days in the capture of thirty-eight thousand Italian troops and four of Mussolini's generals. British casualties were a little over a hundred men.

Not that Italy's disgrace was wholly a disadvantage, for now, as Hitler explained on the ninth to General Halder, "There is no need to pay any significant attention to the Italians." In addition, Franco's rebuff had absolved Hitler from keeping the pledges he had given since Hendaye. In short, he could promise France everything—and in particular that it would keep its territories intact if it would collaborate with the Axis. This honeymoon was to last less than a week, however.

In the early hours of December 14 the text of a personal letter from Marshal Pétain reached Hitler. He thanked the Führer for his honorable intentions in transferring to Les Invalides in Paris the mortal remains of Napoleon's beloved son, the Duke of Reichstadt, which had since 1832 reposed in Vienna; but he also advised Hitler that he had dismissed Pierre Laval, the deputy premier with whom the German leaders had so recently conferred at Montoire, and replaced him by Admiral Jean François Darlan who would continue the policy of cooperation and in whom Vichy had greater confidence. In vain Ribbentrop tried to secure Laval's restoration; the luckless minister was held incommunicado on Pétain's orders. Even greater was the further affront to Hitler of Pétain's refusal to attend the ceremony at Les Invalides. The marshal initiated the rumor that this was just a German trick to lure him to Paris and kidnap him—a canard which enraged Hitler. He again withdrew the hand he had extended toward France. Who needed France anyway? A vision still haunted him—the possibility of signing a peace with Britain, but this time at France's expense.

Something distantly resembling the spirit of Christmas overcame Hitler. He instructed the Luftwaffe to suspend bombing missions against Britain until Christmas was over.[3] A fortnight of aimless meandering ensued. He spoke at noon on December 18 to the new batch of officer cadets—2,375 from the Luftwaffe alone—and submitted to various medical tests in a checkup by Dr. Morell. With the "Barbarossa" decision made, a forced levity entered his conversation. On the nineteenth, when Ribbentrop's lanky SS adjutant Richard Schulze came to announce the birth of the foreign minister's son, Hitler was sitting on a bench in the Chancellery entrance hall, his hands characteristically clasped around

[3] Much to the annoyance of the British foreign office, who had prepared to reap propaganda capital. See Sir Alexander Cadogan's *Diary*.

one knee. He asked Schulze to stand beside his brother, Hansgeorg, who was one of the Führer's own SS aides, and quizzically inquired, "How big do you have to be to get into the Leibstandarte regiment?" "Six feet tall, mein Führer." Hitler sighed. "Then that rules me out. It will be back to the infantry for me!"

Keitel, Halder, and much of Jodl's staff had gone on leave. Protected by extra antiaircraft trains, Hitler set out with his personal staff on a Christmas tour of the western front. He wanted to inspect the big gun batteries which Todt's organization had installed to command the Channel coast—the sites had names like "Great Elector," "Siegfried," and "Gneisenau"—and he wanted to celebrate the holiday with the aircrews of Göring's fighter and bomber squadrons. (Göring himself was spending a comfortable Christmas and New Year at his Rominten estate, some twenty miles from the Russian frontier in East Prussia.) Only one frosty interview with Admiral Darlan, Pétain's "crown prince," chilled the atmosphere of Hitler's special train; Darlan recounted how his family had always hated the British and had been fighting them now for three hundred years—a perhaps inappropriate confidence, given Hitler's present mood. One of Hitler's secretaries wrote to a friend: "We have not stopped moving since December 21. Christmas on the French coast —Calais and Dunkirk. As we were eating dinner in the dining car of our special train on the twenty-third at Boulogne, the British came and started bombing, and our antiaircraft roared back at them. Even though we were shunted into a safe tunnel"—guarded by antiaircraft trains at each end—"I couldn't help feeling 'a bit queer'. . . . On New Year's Eve the mood was more than painful. . . ."

Hitler had returned to the Berghof to spend New Year with Eva Braun and his "family" of adjutants and staff. Goebbels would be making the traditional speech to the Reich. Hitler had already seen and approved the script, and marked it with spidery ink amendments of a trivial, grammatical nature, except for one: where Goebbels had wanted to proclaim "Never will we capitulate, never will we tire, and never will we be despondent," Hitler had expunged the first four words.[4]

---

[4] In June 1943 he again censored a Goebbels speech in the same sense; see below, page 570.

Let Europe Hold Its Breath

Hitler entered the new year, 1941, with two distantly related ambitions: to knock out Soviet Russia and thus force Britain to submit with no injury to her empire, and to rescue fascism in Italy from threatened oblivion. All else was subsidiary to these aims. He had no designs on Greece and fervently hoped that now the Greeks had thrown the Italian invaders out they would rid themselves of their British guests as well; then he could cancel the "Marita" operation against Greece. Through Admiral Canaris he had offered, using obscure Spanish and Hungarian diplomatic channels, to mediate between Greece and Italy, but in vain. As for the Italian defeats in Africa, he would not have been alarmed by them were it not for the danger that Mussolini's regime might collapse in consequence. "The fact is, for better or for worse Germany is tied to the Duce," explained Hitler on January 4. "In the long run you can only make history by loyalty," he mused virtuously. Hitler's loyalty to Mussolini is indeed worthy of an odd niche in history.

In North Africa, Hitler saw no problems that a small force of German tanks and aircraft could not put right. In the Balkans, however, a dangerous situation had developed since Italy's ill-timed attack on Greece in October. Over Hitler's broad desks at the Chancellery, and now at the Berghof, flowed the dispatches from Ribbentrop's experts. Familiar and unfamiliar Balkan potentates and diplomats were ushered past—the queen mother of Romania, prattling endlessly about the problems of Europe's other monarchs, about cousin Christian of Denmark, and about her brother King George II and Crown Prince Paul of Greece; then in January the prime minister of Bulgaria, followed a week later by King Boris again, still promising to join the Tripartite Pact but genuinely fearing that the Russians, and possibly Turkey too, would invade the moment the Germans set foot in Bulgaria, which the Russians were loudly proclaiming was in *their* sphere of interest. Here too was Antonescu, reaffirming the Romanian willingness to fight for Hitler but asking now for mines and for big guns to defend his Black Sea port of Constanta (where seven hundred thousand tons of German oil was stockpiled) against Russian attack. Walther Hewel brought Hitler file after file of top-secret Forschungsamt intercepts and surveys. From these sources Hitler gained confidence that Turkey would not as yet intervene. Nonetheless he had ordered that the divisions assigned to "Marita" be split into three groups—one to protect Romania against Russian invasion, one in southeastern Bulgaria to dissuade Turkey from interfering, and one for the actual operation against Greece.

No terrain could be less promising for a modern army than the Balkans. Before his armies could even get into Bulgaria, they would have to throw pontoon bridges across the swirling Danube River, nearly a mile wide; the one existing railway bridge could handle only six trains a day. The roads were virtually impassable in winter and became morasses when the snow thawed. The crumbling bridges crossing the countless Balkan streams and dikes would never support the loads an army would impose on them.

Nevertheless, the Wehrmacht overcame all these obstacles: in the remaining weeks before "Marita" German staff officers in plain clothes and Volkswagens were sent throughout Bulgaria to supervise the strengthening of the bridges and the resurfacing of the roads. And when the campaign was over, Hitler was to relate to the Reichstag: "In barely three weeks this triumphant campaign has extinguished the fighting in two countries, following rutted tracks, demolished roads, across jagged slopes and boulders, along the narrowest rocky paths, through raging torrents, over towering mountain passes, across demolished bridges and bare mountainsides!"

To Hitler, early in 1941, the Balkans meant two things: the Ploesti oil field in Romania, now well within the reach of the RAF bombers even if the Athens government still refused them the necessary overflight permission; and Salonika, in northern Greece, from which the Allies had launched their deadly assault on Austria-Hungary in World War I. That must not happen this time. In 1918 there was no great power waiting on the sidelines to benefit. This time there was the Soviet Union, her eyes firmly fixed on the Dardanelles.

Hitler called together his leading military advisers and Ribbentrop for a council of war at the Berghof. It began on January 7 and ended on the ninth with a major secret speech in which he outlined the reasoning underlying his grand strategy at a length and level of frankness unfamiliar since his harangues of 1939. Keitel and Jodl were already at the Berghof; they were joined on the eighth by Raeder's chief of operations, the studious and intellectual Rear Admiral Kurt Fricke, and Halder's deputy, Paulus; and by the ninth, the afternoon of the speech itself, Brauchitsch and the army's chief of operations, Adolf Heusinger, had also been driven up the snow-covered lanes to the Berghof with General Jeschonnek, the Luftwaffe's Chief of Staff.[1] Jeschonnek was a slim, cool-headed, ruthless staff officer of an ability outstanding for his youth: at sixteen he had been an infantry lieutenant in World War I, then a fighter pilot; still only forty-one, he had a typically Silesian mentality—an abrupt, single-minded attitude with neither the ability nor the inclination to argue with those who disagreed with him. It was Jeschonnek who had confidently predicted that Britain would cave in under the pressure of the Luftwaffe bombing offensive. Now, not even Hitler accepted that: the British people's "toughness" was a wholly unexpected factor, he admitted.

As for Britain, Hitler had long since decided that an invasion would be a "crime" unless the country was so paralyzed that his army would have the kind of walkover the French had had in the Ruhr in 1923 when Germany failed to keep up reparations payments. "Terror raids by the Luftwaffe have little point or prospect of success," he explained. The Luftwaffe must concentrate on reinforcing the naval blockade of Britain's imports and on attacking bottlenecks in the arms industry. This combined offensive could produce results by July or August 1941; Britain was already admitting a 10 percent loss in arms output, and as her aluminum imports were being stifled, Hitler was skeptical about the British air force's prospects of expansion without direct American aid. Rumors of Britain's growing military strength could easily be discounted by the simplest analysis of the raw materials position: Germany had produced as much pig iron as Britain and France put together; at present she was producing twenty-four million tons a year compared with less than eight million in Britain. Germany produced far more aluminum, and as a dictatorship she could marshal far greater reserves of manpower; in Britain the number of jobless was actually increasing—a sure measure of the enemy's industrial problems. The German naval blockade was only just beginning: fifty submarines were in training, three would be in service by January, five in February, eight in March;

---

[1] Jeschonnek is presumably the author of the hitherto unpublished note on Hitler's speech of January 9, 1941, which I found among the papers of his deputy, Hoffmann Waldau.

from June onward, there would be fifteen new submarines a month. "The destruction of the English mother country is inevitable in time," Hitler concluded.

Britain, of course, realized this and the fact that Germany could be defeated only here, on the continent. "Britain," asserted Hitler, as he had consistently since the fall of France, "is propped up by her faith in the United States and Russia." Her wooing of Stalin was betrayed by many clues: Churchill had two weeks before appointed Anthony Eden, whom Hitler suspected of having pronounced pro-Bolshevik sympathies, to the foreign office; from intercepts and other sources, Hitler was aware of the diplomatic overtures Britain was preparing in Moscow; Britain had announced her lack of interest in the Dardanelles; and Russia's chorus of increased demands since the summer of 1940 was unlikely to be coincidence. Stalin was infinitely the cleverest and most cautious of Hitler's opponents—he must be seen as an ice-cold blackmailer who would not hesitate to tear up every written treaty if it served his purposes. Russia's *Drang nach dem Westen* would lead Stalin to exploit every temporary indisposition of Germany or her allies, and the British would do everything to egg him on.

Apart from Russia, Germany's position was now impregnable, at least for the coming year, Hitler noted. Norway was safe from invasion—at most the British might launch minor prestige raids for their nuisance value. Occupied France wanted an end to the war; the unoccupied half still dreamed of a reverse in its fortunes, but he had prepared "Operation Attila" to occupy this sector and seize or immobilize the French fleet at Toulon should General Weygand, that "German hater," declare North Africa for the Allies. He was still undecided about Spain: Franco had more than once broken his promise concerning Gibraltar, and he would still go no further than agree to enter the war once Britain was down and almost out—a promise that had come to Britain's ears. In the Balkans, only Romania was deliberately and unreservedly friendly; Antonescu had made "the best impression imaginable" on Hitler. Bulgaria was loyal, had feared Russian intervention until recently, but would join the Tripartite Pact in good time. Turkey would take no action at this time. Hungary was "usable" at present. Yugoslavia was cool. Poland was no longer any problem.

Therefore Russia must be Britain's last hope. "They will only give up when we have smashed this last hope on the continent to smithereens." The British were no fools, said Hitler; they must realize that if they lost this war they would no longer have the moral authority to hold their empire together. "On the other hand, if they can pull through and raise forty or fifty divisions, and if the United States and Russia help them, then Germany will be in a precarious situation. That must not be allowed to happen." He had always believed in destroying the enemy's most powerful positions first. "That is why Russia must now be defeated." If Britain did not give in even then, Germany need leave only some fifty divisions in the east; her army could be cut back to provide manpower for the Luftwaffe and naval construction programs, for the antiaircraft defenses, and for the dispersal of industry out of reach of the British bombers. Meanwhile Russia's defeat would enable Japan to put pressure on the United States, and Roosevelt would have second thoughts about attacking Germany.

Since Russia must be defeated, it must be defeated now. "True, the Russian forces are a clay colossus with no head, but who knows how they will develop in the future?" He believed the Russian arms industry was still hamstrung by development problems.[2] The defeat of the Soviet Union must be swift and final; under no circumstances must the Russians be allowed to regroup after the first, brutal breakthrough. Again he called for the rapid occupation of the Baltic coast first of all. The generals' strategic targets were the annihilation of the Russian army, the capture of the most important industrial regions and the destruction of the rest, and the occupation of the oil fields at Baku—on the Caspian Sea. Though immense and new, this latter demand should not, however, daunt them; their armies had also covered immense distances in the few weeks of the French campaign, Hitler reminded them. He concluded, "Germany will then be unassailable. The vast spaces of Russia will yield hoards of incalculable wealth. Germany must dominate them economically and politically, without annexing them bodily. Thus we will have all we need to be able to fight whole continents in the future, if need be; we will be invincible. When we fight this campaign, let Europe hold its breath!" From now until June 1941, Hitler made no mention whatsoever of Russia in his public speeches.

Mussolini was still loath to meet with Hitler. Small wonder, for on January 5 a small British force had captured the Italian fortress of Bardia in Libya, taking forty-five thousand Italians prisoner. There were now only five Italian divisions left in Cyrenaica and five more in Tripolitania. Meanwhile the Luftwaffe corps Hitler had transferred to the Mediterranean had opened its attack on January 6, sinking a British cruiser and

---

[2] In April 1941, Hitler learned for the first time how advanced the huge Soviet arms industry was. See page 258.

damaging an aircraft carrier. Mussolini finally agreed to come to a meeting later in January but stipulated that there must be no fuss and no photographers—he even suggested their two trains should meet somewhere in the open countryside.

Hitler sought for ways of helping the Italians out of their self-created mess without hurting Mussolini's prestige at home. He considered sending a mountain division to Albania and a small "blocking force" of German tanks and engineers to help the Italians hold on to Tripoli; his ambassador in Rome accompanied Ribbentrop to the Berghof on the ninth and urged that Germany exert a greater influence on Italian strategy in the Mediterranean, but Hitler characteristically refused to do anything that would damage the Duce and thus impair the "most valuable link in the Axis," the mutual trust between Mussolini and himself. Two days later he signed the directive ordering the army and Luftwaffe to prepare to support the Italian defense of Albania and Tripolitania.

Hitler collected Mussolini from a small railroad station near Salzburg at 10 A.M. on January 19. Two days of conferences and strolls about the snow-clad Obersalzberg followed. Hitler had one 90-minute talk privately with the Duce, but from the record of the other conferences it is clear he revealed nothing he had not already stated to his own generals on the ninth, except that he made no mention of his plan to attack Russia soon. Indeed, he again averred that so long as the wise and prudent Stalin was alive Russia would adhere to her treaties. (On January 9, according to a note taken by Admiral Fricke, Hitler had explained he had no intention of revealing his own plans to the Italians because of the very real danger that the Italian monarchy would forward this Intelligence to Britain.) He did, however, reveal that "in the British Cabinet's secret meetings Churchill referred to the helping hand Russia would perhaps one day lend, in addition to America." Britain, however, would lose the war before then. "The British may get used to living a troglodyte existence, or to having no windows in their houses and the like," states the record of Hitler's comments, "but when their food imports are no longer safe they will have no option but surrender. This is why Germany is trying to sink as much shipping as possible—particularly refrigerated vessels, as they take a long time to build. In the three such ships sunk in recent weeks Britain has lost two whole weeks' meat supplies."

This meeting brought to an end Mussolini's dream of fighting an independent war, parallel to Hitler's, in the Mediterranean. He accepted the offer of a "blocking force" for Tripoli but could not accept the mountain division for Albania, as he needed the Albanian port space for his own reinforcements. On January 22, Tobruk with twenty-five thousand

Italians fell into British hands. The whole of Tripolitania was now in peril. The panzer specialist General Hans von Funck, sent to North Africa in mid-January, reported to Hitler on February 1 in the most pessimistic terms at the Chancellery in Berlin: the Italians had no will to resist the British onslaught in North Africa. What was needed was not a defensive "blocking force," but a force capable of launching a determined counterattack on the extended British mechanized units. "The crazy feature is," said Hitler afterward to his staff, "that on the one hand the Italians are shrieking for help and cannot find drastic enough language to describe their poor guns and equipment, but on the other hand they are so jealous and childish that they won't stand for being helped by German soldiers. Mussolini would probably like it best if our troops could fight in Italian uniforms there, and our aircraft flew with the Italian fasces on their wings!"

In conference with his army and Luftwaffe chiefs two days later, Hitler again declared that militarily the loss of Italian North Africa would mean little; however, its political and psychological effects could be devastating, for Britain could then deal with Mussolini at pistol point and force him to make peace. Conversely, if Hitler could win quick successes for the Axis in Libya, this might speed a peaceful settlement in the Balkans. He decided to send more than just a "blocking force" to North Africa; he would send a light infantry and a panzer division to Libya, with a German corps staff. Who should command this Afrika Korps? Erich von Manstein and Erwin Rommel were suggested to him. He chose Rommel. (In August 1942 he explained to Italy's Ambassador Alfieri: "I chose Rommel because he's like Dietl—he knows how to carry his troops forward with him; and this is absolutely vital for the commander of an army fighting under extremes of climate, be it in North Africa or in the Far North.") Son of a Württemberg schoolmaster, Rommel had won the *Pour le Mérite* medal fighting the Italians in World War I. Between the wars he had written a brilliant manual, *Infantry Attack*. In the French campaign of 1940 he had fought his 7th Panzer Division through to the Channel coast heedless of personal risk and exhaustion; as recently as December, Schmundt had shown Hitler an illustrated divisional history Rommel had devised of the French campaign—for the future "desert fox" was nothing if not a capable public relations man, too.

On February 6, 1941, Rommel and General Enno von Rintelen, the military attaché in Rome, were briefed by Hitler in Berlin. Rintelen was instructed to ask Mussolini to put all the Italian mechanized units in Libya under Rommel's new command. That evening Hitler leafed through the British and American illustrated weeklies to show Rommel what his enemies in Cyrenaica looked like. These magazines and boys' adventure books were Hitler's main source of information. ("Your experts should read more Karl May and attend fewer courses," he said in rebuke to the Luftwaffe's Field Marshal Milch in October 1942. "Then they'd be of more use in this war!") Rommel was instructed to hold Tripolitania for the Axis powers, tying down the British and preventing them from breaking through to the French in Tunisia. "Saw army's Commander in Chief [Brauchitsch] first," wrote Rommel in his hotel afterward. "Then the Führer. There's no time to be lost. My luggage is being sent on afterward. . . . My head reels to think of all that can still go wrong. It will be months before things take effect!" On February 9, Mussolini's agreement to hand over tactical command to Rommel arrived, and after some delay Rommel's first troops and equipment began disembarking at Tripoli on the twelfth. It was a beginning, but it would be April or May before the last of his corps was finally assembled there.

Spurred on by Admiral Raeder, by the ambiguous attitude of Vichy, and by the deteriorating situation in the Mediterranean, during January 1941 Hitler put renewed pressure on General Franco to revise his views on Gibraltar. He could not understand why the Spanish dictator had rejected his offers of material aid, for the British were certain—he argued—to let Spain down in the end. When Mussolini came to the Berghof, Hitler also persuaded him to pressure Franco at a forthcoming personal meeting: Gibraltar in the hands of the Axis would put a new complexion on the whole North African dilemma. Air bases and two German divisions in Spanish Morocco would soon keep General Weygand in his place.

At Salzburg on January 18, Ribbentrop briefed his ambassador to Madrid on the tough line to adopt with the Caudillo, but this new approach did not bring possession of Gibraltar any nearer. Franco, of course, had no inkling of the strict timetable Hitler had already drawn up for the attacks on Greece and Russia, a timetable into which "Felix," the attack on Gibraltar, must be slotted, if it was to take place at all; this explains the increasing irritability of Ribbentrop's telegrams to Madrid over the next two weeks. On the twentieth the ambassador cabled from Madrid that Franco had cleverly skirted around the central issue— "As to *whether* Spain would enter the war there is no question, that was settled at Hendaye; it is only a question of *when*." If Germany would not send food supplies until Spain entered the war, they would arrive too late. The ambassador had replied that if Germany was expected to send food shipments in advance—for example, the one hundred thousand tons of grain tantalizingly held up in ships in Lisbon—then Germany must be permitted to stipulate the date of Spain's entry into the war, and Franco must agree to it in advance.

Ribbentrop's ploy was not likely to flatter Franco's self-esteem. The ambassador was instructed to read out to Franco six points, of which the first was: "Without the help of the Führer and the Duce there would not be any Nationalist Spain today. Nor any Caudillo." If Franco did not abandon his "vacillating attitude," then the end of Nationalist Spain was only a matter of time. Franco angrily denounced this as unjust: he had never vacillated, and he still intended to enter the war; but the ambassador cabled Ribbentrop that the Caudillo seemed more hesitant than before. Ribbentrop cabled him to see Franco yet again and read out a message beginning: "Only the immediate entry by Spain into the war is of any strategic value to the Axis." (This was the harsh truth.) Given the necessary promise Germany would at once release one hundred thousand tons of grain from Lisbon. In a lengthy reply to Ribbentrop's earlier demarche the Spanish government amiably reminded Berlin of the German foot-dragging the previous summer—Germany had still not sent the economic experts Spain had asked for in September; the Spaniards also suggested the German High Command had taken little account of the extremes of weather encountered in southern Spain in the winter. Ribbentrop now concentrated his venom on his ambassador, for having allowed Franco to slither away from a clear Yes or No answer to the question of whether or not he was willing to enter the war at once.

On January 28, Jodl pointed out to Hitler that even if they could resume preparations for "Felix" on February 1, it would be impossible to launch the actual assault on Gibraltar before mid-April, which meant that the hundreds of artillery pieces and troops involved could not be released for "Barbarossa" in mid-May. Hitler told Jodl they must dispense with "Felix," but evidently he still pinned some hopes on Mussolini's talks with the Caudillo on February 12. A few days beforehand he wrote the Caudillo a personal letter suggesting that in times of crisis nations could be saved "less by prudent foresight than by a bold heart." This poetic appeal made no impression on Spain's realistic leader. On the fourteenth Ribbentrop telephoned to the Berghof a message from the Duce, which the Italian chargé in Berlin had just delivered to the foreign ministry. Hitler's senior secretary, Fräulein Wolf, took the telephone message down in shorthand. By raising demands which it was clear Hitler would not accept, Franco had made it abundantly clear that Spain would not join the war. Spain was to be given military and economic aid; the Hendaye secret protocol was to be reworded more precisely, so as to grant Spain the whole of French Morocco; and the assault on Gibraltar was to be executed by *Spanish* forces, perhaps with German support. Mussolini's general impression was that Spain was in no position to declare war. To Hitler, however, Franco was failing to honor a promise. Walther Hewel, Ribbentrop's liaison with Hitler, wrote in his diary that day: "Telegram from Rome on Mussolini's meeting with Franco. Negative, as we expected. The Führer is going to drop Spain. They will just go under."

"In the evening, we sat for a long time with the Führer around the fireside," continued Hewel's diary. "The Führer talked about his pension—that of a middle-grade civil servant! He is going to write books—a third volume of *Mein Kampf* . . . entitled *Collected Broken Promises,* and books on Frederick the Great, Luther, and Napoleon." Earlier that afternoon he had spent two-and-a-half hours nervously trying to persuade the Yugoslav prime minister to join the Tripartite Pact. By now Field Marshal Sigmund Wilhelm List's Twelfth Army preparations in Romania were so far advanced that bridge-building across the Danube—the frontier with Bulgaria—could begin the next day if need be. But so many uncertainties were involved in occupying Bulgaria, let alone attacking Greece, that Hitler was still looking for alternatives; not until the end of the month would he finally allow the bridge-building to begin.

The Yugoslav prime minister indicated that his country was no keener to join the Axis than it had been in November. The most he would offer was to mediate between Italy and Greece. Hitler suggested that it was illusory to expect the British to evacuate their foothold in Greece now. "Only when our dive-bombers and armored corps appear will they get out of Greece as hastily as they have on every other occasion we employed these means. Germany has no demands whatever against Greece. Here as elsewhere Britain is the root cause of all the difficulties."[3] Of course, added Hitler, he was aware from the Allied documents captured in France (which were duly published) of the extent to which the Greeks had offered their country as a front for Britain. What he did not say was that a recently intercepted French diplomat's

[3] Had Italy not attacked Greece, the difficulties would not have arisen. But Hewel was echoing his master's views when he wrote to a friend on January 23, 1941: "It is actually regrettable that we are forced to smash and destroy so much that we do not want to smash and destroy and that should not have been destroyed for European culture and the mastery of the Germanic races."

report from Belgrade recounted a conversation with the state secretary in the Yugoslav foreign ministry: "Yugoslavia is trying to gain time until May. Britain has assured her that from May onward Britain's military strength and the entry of the United States into the war will change the whole situation."

"England will be annihilated," Hitler warned his Yugoslav visitors. "If the British now announce they are a country of long wars and adduce the course of the Napoleonic wars as evidence for this theory, then let me point out that the only reason the British could hold out so long then was because they had the Prussians fighting for them"—a reference to Blücher's opportune arrival at the battle of Waterloo. The Yugoslavs offered one suggestion—that they form a Balkan bloc with Bulgaria and Turkey—but this would have made impossible any attack designed to oust the British from Greece; Hitler dismissed it privately as "a British insinuation." When the Yugoslavs left the Berghof they said they would report to the prince regent in Belgrade and let Hitler know. On the outcome would depend "Marita," and Hitler had reason to be nervous.

The first wave of divisions was now moving toward the frontier with Russia—only a slow procession as yet; not until mid-March would the second wave begin. As Lossberg had pointed out, the German railway network was so superior to the Russian system that when the real race began, Germany could muster seven divisions a day and the Russians only five; the farther west the "Barbarossa" divisions waited the better— "the bigger will be the Russian surprise when the German troop concentration begins." The whole military jigsaw puzzle would be fitted together, each piece numbered and timetabled by the General Staff, in the last weeks before the attack. Only when the puzzle was unveiled would Stalin find Hitler ready to attack Russia.

When Field Marshal von Bock reported to Hitler on February 1, their conversation drifted through the problems of basing great decisions on the rackety foundations provided by Italy's disasters. The attack on Russia would divert world attention from the African calamity. Britain was proving a tough nut to crack; there was no talk of invasion now. But "the people in Britain aren't fools," said Hitler. "They just *act* like fools! They will realize there is no point in fighting on once Russia too is beaten and eliminated." Bock agreed that *if* the Russians stood their ground and fought, they would be defeated; and he wondered whether they could be forced into an armistice? This might be one consequence of the German capture of the Ukraine, Moscow, and Leningrad, replied

Hitler; otherwise the Wehrmacht must advance toward Yekatarinburg. "Anyway," he concluded, "I am glad that we carried on with arms manufacture so that we are now strong enough to be a match for anybody. We have more than enough material and we already have to begin thinking about converting parts of our industry. Our Wehrmacht manpower position is better than when war broke out. Our economy is absolutely firm." The Führer rejected out of hand any idea of yielding—not that Bock had hinted at it. "I am going to fight," he said; and "I am convinced that our attack will flatten them like a hailstorm."

Two days later Field Marshal von Brauchitsch brought Chief of the General Staff Halder to the Chancellery to outline the army's operational directive on "Barbarossa." Halder put the Russian strength confronting them at about 155 divisions—in short, numerically a little more than the German strength but vastly inferior in quality. Although army Intelligence believed the Russians might have as many as 10,000 tanks, compared with their own 3,500, the Russian armored vehicles were a motley collection of obsolete design. "Even so, surprises cannot be ruled out altogether," warned Halder—with some perspicacity, for by June 1941 the Red Army had 967 ultramodern T-34 tanks on the front, and the Germans did not have an antitank gun powerful enough to use against that model. As for the Russian soldier, Halder believed the Germans were superior in experience, training, equipment, organization, command, national character, and ideology. Hitler naturally agreed, but he challenged the army's estimate of Russia's huge manpower reserves and arms potential. He was convinced, however, that the Soviet dictatorship was so hated, particularly by the young Russians, that it would crumble under the first victorious German onslaught. As for Soviet armament, he was something of an expert on arms production, he said; and from his "memory" he unlocked a ten-minute statistical lecture on Russian tank production since 1928, proving in the process just how thinly armored each type was.

Hitler approved the army's directive but once again emphasized the capture of the Baltic coast and of Leningrad. The latter was particularly important if the Russians were falling back elsewhere, as this northern stronghold would provide the best possible supply base for the second phase of the campaign. Finland would assist in the northern theater, dividing her forces for operations against the Murmansk railway in the far north and against Leningrad on the Baltic. Hitler knew that Halder had just had a first round of talks with his Finnish counterpart, General E.

Heinrichs, in Berlin. Hitler was convinced the Finns would make ideal allies, although Finland's political strategy would be problematical as she wished to avoid a complete rupture with the United States and Britain. Hitler had said to his staff, "They are a plucky people, and at least I will have a good flank defense there. Quite apart from which, it is always good to have comrades-in-arms who are thirsting for revenge. . . ."

The army's timetable produced some interesting side-effects which had obviously not occurred to Hitler up to now. Once the second wave of divisions started eastward from western Europe in mid-March, "Attila" (the emergency occupation of Vichy France) would become virtually impossible. With the third wave in mid-April the maximum-capacity transport plan began, and the troop concentrations could no longer be concealed except as a vast decoy operation "to distract from an invasion of Britain"; but when the fourth and final wave of panzer divisions that had been reequipping and resting in central Germany started rolling eastward from April 25 onward, an invasion of Britain would become an obviously impossible cover story. Hitler admiringly agreed with all that Halder had said. "When 'Barbarossa' gets going, the whole world will hold its breath—it won't move a muscle!"

The army directive was forthwith issued. The next day, Admiral Raeder set out the navy's somewhat smaller role (the navy's main enemy was still Britain). Afterward, Raeder told the admiralty that the navy's principal task in "Barbarossa" would be to establish a supply line to Leningrad.

Probably no major campaign has ever been launched upon less Intelligence. The services had furnished Hitler—to say nothing of their lower commands—with only the most inadequate information on the Russians. They were certain of only one thing: the German fighting man's inborn superiority. All else was the product of rumor, speculation, and fragile calculations. Admiral Canaris told Keitel the Abwehr had drawn a blank in Russia. Conditions for espionage were impossible. Maps were nonexistent. The range of the army's radio-monitoring stations was strictly limited. Foreign Armies East appealed to the Luftwaffe to intensify photographic reconnaissance missions, as it would take eight weeks to print the maps and issue them to the troops. The Russian aircraft industry was an unknown quantity on which the veil was only gradually being lifted. Recent indications were that it was being expanded at a disconcerting speed. Göring, apprehensive that the Russian air force might prove more formidable than the army Intelligence figures indicated, arranged for a team of his air ministry engineers to inspect the Soviet air industry, but not until early March did permission for their trip arrive.

This lack of proper Intelligence was the root cause of the ultimate disaster. For while Halder had confidently advised the Führer on February 3 that they would oppose only a small Red Army superiority in numbers, 155 divisions, by early April that figure had been raised (as the Finns and Japanese had always recommended) to 247 divisions; and four months later, when it was too late to retreat, the army admitted it had now identified *360* Soviet divisions in combat with them.

The whole of Hitler's strategy was based on the assumption that Russia would be laid low in a Blitzkrieg of only a few months. Germany's oil and rubber stocks would not hold out much longer. Repeatedly during the latter months Keitel had warned the services to economize on oil consumption so that a stockpile could be built up for "Barbarossa." Now, on February 8, Keitel learned from his staff that while the Luftwaffe and navy would have enough fuel to last until the coming autumn, gasoline and diesel fuel for the army's tanks and motor transport would not hold out beyond mid-August if supplies from Romania dried up—unless of course the oil fields of the Caucasus could be reached in time. Keitel ordered further economies. The rubber situation allowed for even less leeway. Much of Germany's rubber supplies had reached her from the Far East along the Trans-Siberian railroad. War with Russia would cut that link, leaving only an uncertain trickle supplied by blockade-running ships. Later in February the OKW submitted to Hitler and Göring a full survey of the economic side-effects of "Barbarossa." Göring was forced to agree with the OKW's view that possession of the Ukraine would not be enough: Germany would need the oil fields of the Caucasus as well, whatever the cost. Keitel's economics expert General Thomas noted after meeting Göring on February 26: "He shares the Führer's opinion that when German troops march into Russia the entire Bolshevik state will collapse, and that for this reason we need not fear the destruction of the stores and railway system on a large scale, as I do. The main thing is to get rid of the Bolshevik leaders rapidly first of all." Göring's anxiety was the weakness of the German supply lines. "He recalled that supply failures had proved Napoleon's undoing. For this reason he has kept urging the Führer to concentrate more on the supply organization and less on activating fresh divisions, some of which would not come under fire." But far from pulling in his horns, Hitler was already thinking beyond the end of "Barbarossa." On the seventeenth,

Jodl instructed his staff that the Führer wished them to study the problems of assembling troops in Afghanistan for an assault on India.

On Sunday February 16, Hitler's chief Wehrmacht adjutant, Rudolf Schmundt, who had flown to North Africa with Rommel the week before, reported back to the Berghof with photographs of Rommel's arrival and a first analysis of the position.

Hitler saw a possible crisis zone in Libya, for if the Italians were driven out altogether, the British could transfer forces to Syria with complex side-effects on "Marita" and "Barbarossa." Not surprisingly, he awaited Rommel's operations "feverishly," as Schmundt wrote a few days later. Colonel Schmundt described the enthusiasm with which Rommel had thrown himself into his task. Hitler sanctioned all his requests—for antitank guns, mines, and Luftwaffe reconnaissance and close-support aircraft. Rommel's first troops had disembarked at Tripoli in one night and then covered the 350 miles to the Italian front west of El Agheila in twenty-six hours—an accomplishment not without effect on the demoralized Italian troops. Rommel organized a military parade of his troops, whose new tropical helmets and gear gleamed in the African sun. Before he left Tripoli he set up the rapid manufacture of scores of dummy tanks mounted on Volkswagen chassis to dupe the British into thinking he had a powerful armored force. By the twenty-first, the first 35 dummy tanks had arrived at his headquarters—another 170 were being built. His troops had already withstood their first howling *ghibli* (sandstorm) and were advancing on El Agheila. The British were withdrawing from their position there, and the Italians were already acquiring new heart—though their fighter pilots still lacked verve. The letters Rommel sent to Schmundt (which the colonel undoubtedly showed to Hitler) exuded optimism from every line. Hitler decided to send out the 15th Panzer Division as soon as he could.

How eerily different was this new battlefield for Rommel's soldiers—city dwellers or farmers for the most part. The Cyrenaican desert was an almost treeless, shadowless lunar landscape baked by a fierce sun; however, as soon as darkness fell, the temperature plummeted toward zero. There were few valleys, and the monotonous expanse of white or reddish-yellow sand was broken only by occasional herds of sheep and camels tended by migrant Arab tribes. At the end of February Rommel had lost only one man—killed in the dark by his own troops. In mid-March he reported to Hitler in person and then returned to Africa. He detected the weakness of the British forces opposing him—a weakness resulting from the dispatch of over sixty thousand British troops to Greece; without waiting for the new armored division to arrive, and against the explicit instructions of both the German war department and the Italian Supreme Commander, Italo Gariboldi, he launched a bold assault in early April; he did not halt until he had reached the Egyptian frontier and taken three thousand British prisoners, including five generals.

By March the last major crisis before "Barbarossa" had been overcome—or so Hitler believed. At 7 A.M. on February 28, since Greece still proudly refused to offer peace terms to Italy, the German Wehrmacht began throwing three mighty army bridges across the mile-wide, fast-flowing Danube from Romania into Bulgaria.

After several false starts, Hitler dictated to Fräulein Wolf an important letter assuring Turkey's President Ismet Inönü that he saw "no reason, either now or in the future, why Germany and Turkey should ever be enemies." He assured Inönü that the Wehrmacht would stand many miles off the Turkish frontier—unless of course Turkish measures forced him to revise this attitude. (The General Staff and OKW had both worked out contingency plans for a tank campaign against European Turkey in alliance with Bulgaria.) Inönü replied calmly that Turkey's sole desire was to safeguard her integrity, and he warmly recalled her comradeship with Germany in World War I. Hitler was well pleased.

On March 1 we find him in Vienna, where the German-speaking King Boris signed Bulgaria's formal entry into the Tripartite Pact. Who could then have foreseen that this document would prove the death warrant of the king, poisoned by an unknown hand in 1943; or that Fräulein Wolf's shorthand pad with the letter to Inönü would be found by American soldiers raking through the ruins of the Berghof in 1945? So far, however, all Hitler's calculations were again proving correct; within one week, by March 7, 1941, the first German soldiers would be standing on the Greek frontier, facing British and Greek troops as they had in 1918. This time would surely be different: neither Turkey nor Russia would move a muscle. Nothing could save Greece.

Behind the Door

One incident of the climactic summer of 1941 must be examined here lest it become submerged in the noisier events of Hitler's attack on Russia. It serves to illustrate the atmosphere in which that year's more controversial decisions were taken.

A few days after Hitler's combined armies invaded Russia, Sweden as the protecting power gave Germany discreet permission for the Soviet embassy buildings in Paris to be searched. The embassy staff refused to let the police unit in, so the building was forcibly entered by a major general of the German police and a squad of forensic experts of Heydrich's security service. If the reports shown to Hitler—admittedly of Nazi origin and hence possibly tainted—are to be believed, horrifying evidence of the activities of the GPU, the Soviet secret police, was found. Heydrich's summary report to Ribbentrop related: "There were twenty-six Soviet Russians in the building. Five of them (four men and a woman) had locked themselves into strong rooms specially shielded by heavy armorplate steel doors; they were busy destroying documents and other materials in four furnaces specially constructed and installed in there. They could not be prevented from doing this, as even using special technical gear it would still have taken hours to force the rooms open. After the materials had been incinerated, the rooms were then opened from within by their occupants." Heydrich's officers were less impressed by the undiplomatic haul of radio gear, time fuses, detonators, and explosives than by the outside laboratory-type furnaces found in the special wing of the building used by the GPU. Investigation indicated that they had been used for cremating bodies.

Ribbentrop brought this report to Hitler, but Hitler had already heard the details firsthand from Admiral Canaris, one of whose department heads had himself inspected the Paris building. He had recorded: "The inspection yielded an exceedingly interesting insight into the GPU's activities. The completely isolated wing of the embassy in which the GPU's offices and execution chambers were located can only be described as a criminals' and murderers' workshop of the most outstanding technical perfection: soundproof walls, heavy, electrically operated steel doors, hidden spyholes and slots for guns to be fired from one room into another, an electrical furnace, and a bathtub in which the corpses were cut up, completed the macabre inventory of these rooms, in addition to housebreaking implements, poison capsules, and the like. Thus there is every probability that General Miller, and perhaps General Kutiepoff as well, together with many an awkward White Russian emigré or opponent of the Soviets in France, vanished in this way—they literally 'went up in smoke.' "

Hitler ordered the Soviet embassy buildings in Berlin unsealed and searched at once. At first the Swedes refused to allow the safes to be blown open, but eventually they agreed to look the other way. In the Soviet trade mission headquarters at 11 Lietsenburgerstrasse the same armored strongrooms with the same furnaces were found, and again there were stocks of guns and ammunition.

Hitler was a realist. There was no reason why these finds should have shocked him, and there is no evidence that he regarded them as of anything more than propaganda value (not that he could exploit them, for diplomatic reasons). He expected the war in the Soviet Union to be merciless and to obey no conventional rules. For twenty years he had been fighting bolshevism, and its face had changed but little in those two decades. Bolshevik methods were familiar to him, and they had also impressed themselves on those European nations which had however briefly tasted the fruits of bolshevism.[1] The horrors of the Cheka were part of history, but the brutality of the Bolsheviks in the Spanish civil war, in Stalin's half of Poland, and most recently in the hapless Baltic states—occupied by the Soviets in the spring of 1940 under the Ribbentrop-Molotov pact—indicated that this was a permanent trait. In the French campaign, German troops had found ten of their infantry comrades bound hand and foot with their eyes torn out, and an antiaircraft

[1] In a cynical entry in his unpublished diary of August 1941, Goebbels wrote: "A search of the Soviet embassies in Paris and Berlin has brought surprising terror weapons to light. These Soviet embassies are in fact the refuges of criminals. This is inevitable. If a criminal gang comes to power, then they will use criminal means to conduct their policies. It is a good thing that bolshevism is being got rid of once and for all in our eastern campaign. There was after all no room for the two of us in Europe, in the long run."

gunner with his feet sawn off; the culprits turned out to be Spanish Red Guards (all were executed). In the Baltic countries Stalin had appointed commissars who had supervised the deportation and liquidation of the entire intelligentsia within a matter of weeks (as had been done in Poland already); these commissars—said to have been Jewish—had then been replaced by Russians who had disposed of their predecessors.

In the western campaigns Hitler had instructed the Wehrmacht to fight with discipline. In the armistice that followed he had explicitly ordered all troops and civilian personnel in the occupied territories to perform their duties "flawlessly" and with proper reserve toward the former enemy populations; any drunkenness or violence was to be severely punished—if necessary by "death and dishonor." In the interests of the armistice, he had not insisted on the extradition of enemy "war criminals" for trial by German courts. In March 1941, Hitler took no action when his ambassador in Paris recommended executing former Prime Minister Reynaud and Minister of the Interior Georges Mandel on the charge of having organized bands of ununiformed franc-tireurs to gun down German parachutists during "Yellow."

In the eastern campaign, however, no holds would be barred on either side. A member of Jodl's staff later wrote: "For Hitler the Russian enemy has two faces, and one of them is bolshevism, his ideological deadly enemy, which Hitler as Europe's champion intends to put to the sword and 'eradicate with ruthless, remorseless lack of mercy'—you have to hear it from his own mouth, rasping and rolling every 'r.' For Hitler, bolshevism is not an enemy with whom one chivalrously crosses swords. In his view we must expect all manner of knavery and cruelty. So Hitler proposes to meet him with the same fighting methods from the start. He states that 'Them or Us' is to be the pitiless motto of this clash." To some extent the Bolshevik leaders had themselves paved the way for this development by formally renouncing czarist treaties, including the various conventions governing warfare, and by having refused to sign the Geneva Convention of 1929 on the treatment of prisoners of war.[2] They could do what they liked with German prisoners in their hands, but they could expect no quarter from Hitler either.

Göring's previous hint to General Thomas concerning the advisability of rapidly getting rid of the Bolshevik leaders was now—on Hitler's direct orders to Jodl—to be entrenched as a principle in the special guidelines issued to the Wehrmacht for "Barbarossa":

[2] On August 8, the Soviet government offered through Sweden to observe The Hague Convention of 1907 on land warfare, and the Geneva Conventions of 1925 and 1929 on poison-gas warfare and prisoners of war, respectively. By that time the Russians had lost a million soldiers as prisoners to the German army.

The coming campaign is more than just a clash of arms. It will result in a conflict of two ideologies. Given the vastness of the country, it will not be enough to defeat the enemy armed forces if the war is to be ended. The entire area must be split up into states with their own governments, with each of whom we can sign peace agreements. . . . Every revolution of any size creates facts which cannot just be wiped away. Wishful thinking alone will not rid modern Russia of the socialist idea; so this alone can act as the domestic political basis for the creation of these new states and governments. The Jewish-Bolshevik intelligentsia as the present "subjugators" of the people must be got rid of. The former bourgeois aristocracy, in so far as it survives abroad, is also useless—they are rejected by the Russian people and are anti-German in any case. . . . In addition we must do everything to avoid allowing a nationalist Russia to supplant the Bolshevik one, as history shows it will always be anti-German. Our job is to set up as soon as possible, with a minimum of military effort, socialist ministates dependent on us. These tasks will be so difficult that they cannot be entrusted to the army.

The war aims Hitler thus revealed to Jodl were very different from the colonization of the east which was alone his driving inspiration. In July 1943 he was to make this clear. "I consider it a cardinal and catastrophic error, something with the gravest consequences, to take the slightest step that might cause a man to say to himself: 'We are getting out of here anyway; we are not going to remain; there are going to be national states founded here, so we will have to get out.'" A soldier needs "positive war aims" to fight body and soul for his country. What war aim can equal a crusade of imperialist conquest? Hitler's outspoken philosophy in July 1943 was this: "In the end man lives from the soil, and the soil is a goblet passing from lip to lip, which Providence allows to linger longest with the nation that fights for it."

Jodl's staff redrafted the special guidelines for "Barbarossa" during March 1941, as Hitler had asked. The army's actual zone of operations was to be a belt as shallow as practicable, while in the rear Himmler's SS and various "Reich commissioners" would see to the founding of the new state governments. The OKW records speak obscurely of the need to put "all Bolshevik headmen and commissars" out of the way, and they quote Hitler as having stipulated that the political administrations were to start functioning as soon as possible "so that the struggle between the ideologies can be waged simultaneously with the clash of arms." Himmler had been ordered by Hitler to carry out on his own responsibility "certain special duties" of a kind to be expected in a fight between two diametrically opposed political systems. The army's records portray Hitler's purpose more bluntly. Halder recorded the Führer as telling him: "We have to set up de-Stalinized republics. The intelligentsia appointed by Stalin must be destroyed. The Russian empire's command machinery must be smashed. In the whole of Russia it will be necessary to employ the most naked brute force. The ideological ties are not yet strong enough to hold the Russian people together. Once the officials are disposed of, the nation will burst apart." Again there is no evidence that the General Staff contested this broad view.

Halder's quartermaster general (traditionally responsible for army occupation policy) attended that conference; after discussing police matters with Heydrich, a few days later he drafted an army order giving the SS "task forces" a free hand to execute certain grim assignments within the army's zone of operations. In a lengthy speech to his army and Luftwaffe generals at the end of the month—to which we shall return in another context[3]—Hitler also prepared them for the different character of the coming fight in Russia. Communist ideology was compared to legalized criminality. "We must put the arguments of soldierly comradeship right out of our minds," he told his generals. "The Communist is no comrade and never will be." He again explicitly referred to the "annihilation of the Bolshevik commissars and the Communist intelligentsia," and he emphasized that "commissars and GPU officials are criminals and must be treated as such." In conclusion, Hitler noted: "I do not expect my generals to understand my orders to this effect. But I demand that they obey them."

Early in March 1941 the British navy executed a lightning raid on the Lofoten Isles in Norway, shelling the town of Svolvaer, sinking several ships in the harbor, and taking about two hundred German merchant seamen prisoners. Militarily the raid was insignificant, but Hitler treated it as a monstrous blow to German prestige, and it roused in him wholly disproportionate fears for Norway's security. Norway was to be the key to German naval supremacy in future decades—he had commissioned Albert Speer to construct at Trondheim a major new city and naval dockyard, and Todt's labor battalions were already engineering superhighways to the far north, the like of which Norway had never seen before.

While snow settled suddenly around the Berghof, blotting out prema-

[3] See page 241.

ture signs of spring, Hitler issued orders for the immediate investigation of the Lofoten raid and the execution of all Norwegians who had aided the enemy. The army was to install 160 gun batteries along the Norwegian coast forthwith, and Admiral Hermann Boehm, the admiral commanding Norway, was summoned to the Berghof. At this conference Hitler decided it would no longer be possible to release 40 percent of the (very considerable) military strength in Norway for "Barbarossa"; indeed, he actually ordered the Narvik and Kirkenes regions reinforced. For the next three years the fear that the British would mount an invasion of Norway never left him.

As the ice thawed in Central Europe, the Wehrmacht's timetable began to unfold. One of Hitler's secretaries, Christa Schroeder, wrote at the Berghof on March 7: "I feel so cut off from everybody here, so shut in, that it is as though I were deaf. It will soon be time to return to Berlin; we have been down here long enough. We will probably be back in Berlin in the middle of the month. . . . We have to be injected again against cholera and typhus—and that happened before all our big journeys!"

Göring had now returned from his extended leave, and on March 6 he secured a long interview with Hitler in which he repaired the fences that had been broken—particularly by his hated rival Admiral Raeder—in his absence. Raeder had especially regretted the continuing reduction of naval air power that had begun early in 1940, and he had lost no opportunity of criticizing the Luftwaffe commander and exposing the hollowness of his claims to Hitler. From the moment Göring had gone on leave in November, the admiral had argued with the Führer that the surest means of defeating Britain was the blockade of her imports by air and submarine forces operating under a unified—meaning his own—command; his submarine officers at least had a right to adequate aerial reconnaissance over the Atlantic. Hitler had initially regarded the continual in-fighting between Raeder and Göring as proof of the need for a much more powerful OKW. (Another bone of contention between the two commanders was whether torpedo-bomber attacks on enemy shipping were better controlled by the air force or the navy. Hitler irritably declared this was "completely unimportant," all that mattered was that the weapon be effectively employed.) At this time Göring's prestige was low following his defeat in the Battle of Britain. He was also embarrassed by the exaggerated claims of his pilots when "destroyed" enemy aircraft, battleships, and aircraft carriers turned up intact. It is significant that although Göring referred to himself in February 1941 as "the second man in the state," Hitler was privately explaining to Keitel and Jodl that one reason why a powerful OKW would become necessary in the future was that "a man might later step into his shoes who might well be the best statesman but might not have as much military knowledge and ability at his fingertips as he did." This could hardly refer to Göring.

Raeder had become bolder in his attacks on the absent Reichsmarschall, producing air photographs of Portsmouth, Plymouth, and Cardiff to show the ineffectiveness of the Luftwaffe attacks and pointing out that the crescendo of RAF attacks on Germany was proof that the enemy air force was anything but defeated. Only in bombing the sea lanes could the Luftwaffe be used to best advantage. These arguments were accepted by Hitler in his directive for economic warfare against Britain on February 6. He identified the loss of British merchant shipping as the most potent factor in the destruction of the war economy; the effect of Luftwaffe attacks on the British arms industry was noted as "more problematic." In a direct reference to Göring's present tactical directives, Hitler emphasized: "No decisive effect is to be expected from systematic terror raids on residential areas or attacks on coastal fortifications." Hitler ordered the Luftwaffe to transfer control of No. 40 Bomber Wing, equipped with the long-range Focke-Wulf 200, to Admiral Dönitz, the submarine fleet commander, for reconnaissance purposes. Furious, Göring summoned Dönitz on February 7 and bitingly informed him that the navy was laboring under a delusion if it imagined that in this way it was going to scrape together a naval air force; only over his dead body would any of his precious Focke-Wulf 200s be supplied to Dönitz for such unspectacular purposes as aerial reconnaissance. Now that Göring had returned from leave, Hitler wearily yielded to his tantrums.

Hitler nevertheless remained unimpressed by the Luftwaffe attacks on Britain. A French diplomat who had left Britain in December reported to the German authorities that although the night bombing of London and Coventry had affected public morale to some extent, Newcastle, where he had been stationed, had hardly suffered. Hitler personally underlined with blue pencil the man's remarks that "massive attacks on Newcastle had not taken place up to his departure. He was puzzled by this as at present the Vickers Armstrong shipyards at Newcastle were building an aircraft carrier (due to be finished in about six months), two battle cruisers (finished in five or six months), a light cruiser, six or seven destroyers, and three or four submarines." Hitler ordered this

oversight brought to the Luftwaffe's attention, but still he refused to injure Göring's pride—as he himself put it—by giving the navy direct control of the air force units that it needed. Indeed, now that Göring's leave
was over, Hitler laid down a final reorganization of Luftwaffe reconnaissance duties, splitting them up into naval (North Sea) and Luftwaffe (Atlantic) zones, a compromise that positively invited disaster.

In Albania, the minor offensive Mussolini had so pompously launched
on March 9 folded up within five days. Hitler was secretly pleased that
the Duce had again burned his fingers. Now the Greek general commanding the northern army secretly let the Germans know that they
would agree to an immediate armistice in Albania if the Italian troops
there were replaced by Germans; they would also talk about territorial
claims, provided that there were no Italians at the conference table; unless these provisos were met, the Greeks would fight to the finish. Hitler
wanted the British thrown out of Greece and the Peloponnesus, but he
told both Brauchitsch and Raeder that even if Greece would now agree
to do so, Germany would still have to occupy the whole country so that
the Luftwaffe could command the eastern Mediterranean. He nonetheless viewed the coming war with Greece with undiluted distaste. He admired the Greeks as a nation and had still not broken off diplomatic
relations with Athens; as a result, there was a continuous flow of information on the mood there—and the mood of the people was that the
"holy war with Italy" must be fought to final victory.

By March 24, when Hitler departed for Vienna, the British were
believed to have disembarked up to forty thousand troops in Greece.
The OKW instructed the German military attaché in Washington to see
to it that the size of the British force in Greece was given maximum
publicity. "The bigger the British talk, the better will be the propaganda
effect of their defeat." In Vienna, the documents attaching Yugoslavia
to the Tripartite Pact were at last to be signed, and Hitler was in high
spirits as his train pulled into the station. He caught sight of Ribbentrop's corpulent young liaison officer, Ambassador Hewel—easily the
most eligible bachelor on his staff—and teasingly suggested that this was
his thirty-seventh birthday and high time to be married. "I hope in my
old age you will allow me to say, Send all the little Hewels to come and
see me. . . ."

Hitler and his entourage stayed at the Imperial Hotel, redolent with
memories of March 1938. When the day was over, Hewel entered in his
diary: "Ceremonial signing of Yugoslavia's entry to the Tripartite Pact

at the Belvedere. Afterward conferences with [Dragisha] Cvetković"—the Yugoslav prime minister—"and Ciano. Afterward dinner with Schirach, very pleasant. Maria Holst, Fräulein Caspar, etc., were there. Führer spoke the whole time about my getting married." Indeed, among Hewel's possessions is the menu of that dinner—simple enough, but signed by everybody present: Hitler's personal photographer Heinrich Hoffmann, Dr. Karl Brandt, his adjutants, Bormann, and the young Viennese beauties Schirach had selected to grace the table. Hitler scribbled at the top, "To the peacock, from a well-wisher.—Adolf Hitler."

Before Hitler returned to Berlin, his adjutants allowed a "Frau Wolf" in to see him—his younger sister, Paula, working incognito as a secretary for doctors in a military hospital. For a while they chatted about family affairs. Paula said, "Sometimes when I am in the mountains and I see a little chapel I go in and pray for you." Hitler was deeply stirred, and after a time replied, "Do you know it is my absolute conviction that the Lord is holding his protecting hand above me?" Paula had been eleven when their mother died, and Adolf eighteen. He had not seen her for thirteen years after that, but he had let her have his share of their orphans' pension, while he had worked as a laborer in Vienna. In the years of his rise to power, he had annually sent her a ticket to the impressive Nuremberg rally, but she remained of the opinion that it was a pity he had not become an architect as he had always wanted. This was the last time he saw Paula.

It had taken all of March to persuade the ambiguous Yugoslavs to sign the pact, but the psychological blow to Britain was well worth the time invested; in addition, Hitler's armies fighting in Greece would depend on a line of communications extending for some 250 miles along, and only 12 miles away from, the Yugoslav border, so even hostility short of war would be most undesirable. The regent, Prince Paul, had visited him unofficially at the Berghof and explained how touchy public opinion in his country was. It was not until Germany agreed to Paul's terms—Yugoslavian territory would not be crossed by Axis troops, and though Yugoslavia was to make no military contribution herself, she was to receive Salonika as a reward—that the Yugoslav privy council agreed to the signature; however, anti-Italian feeling was running so high in Belgrade that several ministers resigned over the issue. Once the pact was signed, Hitler sent for Keitel and expressed his pleasure that there would be no further unpleasant surprises for them in the Balkans, but when he made the same remark to Ciano he qualified it thus:

"Yugoslavia's domestic affairs could still take a complicated turn despite everything." This was not an example of his famous intuition; the Abwehr report on Yugoslavia had that day noted: "The mood of large circles is black toward Germany. Incidents and provocations are multiplying, particularly in the provinces and villages. The state of affairs is enough to give rise to fears that the government will lose control of the situation. . . ." At 10:20 P.M., Hitler's train left Vienna for Berlin, where he was to meet the Japanese foreign minister on the afternoon of the twenty-seventh.

Seldom was a pact shorter-lived than this one with Yugoslavia. Early on March 27, Hewel brought Hitler the stunning news from Belgrade that there had been a coup d'etat; the prince regent had been overthrown, and with him the Cvetković government. Hitler's first reaction was that this was a bad joke, but the putsch was real enough: crowds were demonstrating outside the German legation, the German tourist office had been destroyed, the Swedish envoy had been mistaken for a German and beaten unconscious, and British flags—distributed by the British legation—were appearing everywhere. There were some American flags as well. Crowds were singing "The Red Flag" in the streets. Serbia was in an uproar; Croatia was still calm. The coup had been engineered by Yugoslavia's air force commander, General Dušan Simović; a Serb known to be hostile to Germany, he was an exponent of Pan-Slavism and perhaps even a Russian agent. His revolutionary Cabinet did not ratify the entry into the Tripartite Pact, but made continuing protestations of loyalty toward Germany. Hitler set little store by them—he had mouthed enough of his own in the past. He stormed that this revolution was as though somebody had smacked his fist into a basinful of water.

The traumatic effect of the Belgrade putsch on Hitler became apparent only later. He saw it as a timely warning never to trust the Slavs. A month later he privately noted:

To go through something like that teaches caution. Nations today are governed less by logic and reason than by hatred and perhaps by money interests as well, and this is how it has happened that one nation after another has been precipitated into misfortune by British promises and lies—Poland, to whom I offered the most favorable terms,[4] France, who did not want a war at all, Holland and Belgium, Norway, and now Greece and Yugoslavia. You may say, the people

---

[4] He was referring to the sixteen-point proposals "offered" to the Poles in August 1939. At the time he had described them privately as terms on which the Poles should "choke."

themselves cannot help it, but I have to deal not with the people but their governments.

On first receiving the news, he had sent for Keitel and Jodl, met them in their conference room, and showed them the Belgrade telegram. His initial anger had yielded almost immediately to delight at the new strategic openings. As a result of his Austrian upbringing, he had always been uneasy about the chauvinistic Serbs in Belgrade. This uneasiness had been reinforced by Intelligence reports that Churchill's agents were plotting the overthrow of Prince Paul. Now he had been forced to abdicate and an officer camarilla had dumped seventeen-year-old King Peter on the throne. Hitler could hardly credit his good fortune that all this had happened now. In mid-May, "Barbarossa" was scheduled to begin; had the overthrow of Prince Paul occurred only then, it would have enormously complicated Hitler's plans. "Luckily the enemy unmasked themselves now, while our hands are still free!" he crowed. Now he would wipe Yugoslavia off the map. Hewel wrote in his diary: "—Göring, Brauchitsch, and Ribbentrop are sent for immediately. Decisions are rapidly taken. The mood is exhilarating. The Hungarian and Bulgarian envoys are summoned forthwith." At 1 P.M. Generals Halder and Brauchitsch arrived. Hitler, sparkling with excitement, took them and Ribbentrop to the map table, where he announced, "I have decided to destroy Yugoslavia. How much military force do you need? How much time?"

Almost at once, Hitler was informed that the Hungarian envoy, Döme Sztójay, had arrived. The war conference was adjourned. The generals had their orders anyway. Ribbentrop had not spoken. Hitler told the Hungarian envoy that now that the Italians had been made a laughingstock by Greece, the whole world thought the Axis powers were finished. His message to the regent of Hungary, Horthy, was this: the hour had struck for Hungary's revenge; the Führer would support her territorial claims to the hilt. "March back into the Banat!" he advised her, and he offered Hungary an Adriatic outlet which Admiral Horthy— the last commander of the Austro-Hungarian navy in 1918—must surely desire: the port of Fiume. After hearing these words, Sztójay was flown to Budapest. Shortly afterward Hitler received the Bulgarian envoy, Draganoff, and offered him what would have been Yugoslavia's share of Greece—Macedonia. "The eternal uncertainty down there is over," he rejoiced. "The tornado is going to burst upon Yugoslavia with breathtaking suddenness."

The next evening the Hungarian, Sztójay, arrived back with a secret letter from Horthy: the regent would be pleased to help, but turned down the offer of territory. Hitler was delighted that Germany and Hungary would now confront the Slav menace shoulder to shoulder, and mused to the envoy, "Now that I reflect on all this, I cannot help believing in a Higher Justice. I am awestruck at the powers of Providence."

In the brief war conference with Halder, Brauchitsch, and Ribbentrop, Hitler had settled the broad plan of attack in the Balkans. "Politically it is vital for the blow to fall on Yugoslavia without mercy; militarily, she must be defeated in one lightning swoop." Göring undertook to withdraw the necessary bomber and fighter squadrons from the west immediately. The Luftwaffe would open the campaign with wave after wave of bombers to destroy Belgrade. By the small hours of the morning following the war conference, the OKW's formal directive was in Hitler's hands: "Yugoslavia is to be regarded as an enemy and is therefore to be destroyed as rapidly as possible, whatever protestations of loyalty she may utter for the time being." General von Rintelen was sent to Mussolini with details for the Italian armed forces.

The attack on Russia must now be postponed for up to four weeks, as the directive made clear. It was a decision Hitler had not taken lightly, for he was well aware of the implications of allowing "Barbarossa" to drag on into the Russian winter. In the event, however, even here fate was on his side: the spring of 1941 had brought unusually heavy rains to Central Europe, and the ground would have been too marshy for the panzer divisions which were the backbone of "Barbarossa" to operate earlier than they did; the rivers and dikes were flooded throughout western Russia. The divisions Hitler now committed to the Balkans would have remained idle until June anyway.

Punctually at 4 P.M. on March 27, outwardly unruffled by the breathtaking events of the past few hours, Hitler received the Japanese foreign minister, Yosuke Matsuoka, at the Chancellery. Some 150,000 Berlin citizens marshaled outside in the Wilhelmplatz thundered a welcome for an ally Germany had always held in higher esteem than Italy.

Hitler saw in Japan's territorial aspirations in the Far East a further powerful means of bringing about Britain's submission. The purpose of his present foreign policy was to urge the Japanese to join the fray now, while the British were still at a disadvantage. In September 1940, Japan had occupied bases in northern Indochina with Vichy approval, but she feared to embark on fresh military exploits while Russia menaced her in the rear. Interestingly enough, given his foreign policy goal, during the first five months of 1941 Hitler refrained from telling the Japanese outright of "Barbarossa" and went no further than oblique hints. We are entitled to ask why, for he himself had emphasized that the Japanese could always be trusted to keep a secret. (The Forschungsamt had long given up as a fruitless exercise the tapping of Japanese embassy telephones, and to German code-experts the Japanese cyphers seemed impregnable.)

It was Admiral Raeder who had first brought Hitler's attention to Singapore, the key to British supremacy in the Far East. Late in December, Raeder had shown him a letter from his naval attaché in Tokyo, reporting that certain Japanese naval circles were seriously in favor of capturing Singapore as soon as possible; Raeder suggested to Hitler that this need not necessarily drag the United States into the war and that it would be very much in Germany's interest if Japan became embroiled with Britain, however lengthy and profitless her campaign. Hitler approved the Japanese proposal, but disappointingly little more was heard from Tokyo. He hinted obscurely to the departing Japanese ambassador, Saburo Kurusu, in early February that "mutual friends could one day become our mutual enemies"—meaning Germany and Russia—but this message left no visible impression on Tokyo. In the middle of the month Foreign Minister Matsuoka had however announced his intention of visiting Berlin. Japanese policy had two broad aims—to keep the United States out of the current war, and to prepare a preventive attack on Singapore *if* this attempt should fail. Japan also wanted to improve her relations with the Soviet Union. To Hitler, these policy aims were inadequate, and he instructed the OKW to draft a plan for wide-ranging joint consultation between Germany and Japan. He rebuked Raeder for expecting everything of Tokyo and offering nothing in return. The Wehrmacht and German industry must give their ally generous insight into all their most up-to-date secret weapons and designs, in the tacit hope that Japan would "take active steps in the Far East as soon as possible," thus simultaneously bringing about the defeat of Britain and keeping America out of the war. In an OKW directive issued early in March, it was pointed out that the attack on Russia would provide Japan with an ideal opportunity to launch her own campaigns, but that "no hint whatsoever is to be given to the Japanese about "Operation Barbarossa."

Matsuoka's personal visit to the Chancellery at the end of March 1941 had been preceded by conversations a month before in which

Hitler and Ribbentrop had urged the new Japanese ambassador, General Hiroshi Oshima, to recommend an attack on Singapore. (Ribbentrop had merely indicated to the ambassador that Germany was keeping calm where Russia was concerned, but that if the Reich should be forced to fight in the east, the outcome would be a total eclipse of the Soviet Union.) The German foreign minister wanted "a lightning strike, if possible without a declaration of war," but Oshima said that Japan now felt it must prepare for war not only with Britain but with the United States and that this would take time; the preparations for attacking Singapore would be concluded by the end of May. On February 27, Ribbentrop therefore cabled his ambassador in Tokyo: "Please use every means at your disposal to get Japan to take Singapore as soon as possible." But the naval attaché in Tokyo reported that the Japanese navy had decided against attacking Singapore alone. Hitler still refused to play his trump card—revealing to the Japanese his firm plan to attack Russia; in response to General Halder's urging on March 17 he merely agreed to drop a hint as to the possibility when Matsuoka saw him; Raeder made the same proposal next day privately, but Hitler again refused.

Hitler and Ribbentrop both chose their words with extreme care throughout Matsuoka's visit. The Reich foreign minister only hinted that a Russo-German war was entirely within the realm of possibility. Hitler observed how cagey Matsuoka was about Singapore—the visitor stressed in painful detail how little weight his voice carried on this issue in Tokyo—and made his own most direct reference to "Barbarossa" in an aside to General Oshima at the luncheon given for Matsuoka on the twenty-eighth. After indicating that the Soviet Union had been behind the Belgrade putsch the day before, he noted: "If the Soviet Union were to attack Japan, then Germany would not hesitate to launch an armed attack on the Soviet Union." This, echoed Ribbentrop, was an "absolute guarantee." When a few days later Matsuoka passed through Berlin again on his way back to Tokyo from Rome, Hitler offered him a similar guarantee in the event that Japan should—through attacking Singapore—find herself at war with the United States. On April 10, Ribbentrop was to be even more explicit, stating that even if the Soviet Union did *not* attack Japan, "Germany might still start a war against the Soviet Union before the year is out; it depends on how she behaves." From intercepted documents, both the German foreign minister and Hitler were by now well aware of Churchill's attempts to panic the Russians into drawing closer to the British camp.[5] But the Japanese response was

---

[5] This being so, there seems no logical explanation for Göring's revealing to his Swedish intermediary, Dahlerus—who would no doubt rapidly transmit it to London—between March 24 and 27,

disappointing—indeed, while passing through Moscow on his return to Tokyo, Matsuoka signed an agreement of neutrality between Japan and Moscow.

Once more, on March 30, 1941, Hitler's generals and admirals were summoned from all over Nazi-occupied Europe to hear a secret speech in Berlin. The Führer chose the New Chancellery's Cabinet Room for his setting as its wood paneling provided the best acoustics. Scores of gilded chairs were fetched from the nearby propaganda ministry—the speech was to last three hours. Despite the imminence of "Marita," and now the attack on Yugoslavia too, Hitler's speech covered the whole European war theater, with most emphasis on the eastern front, and he only touched briefly on the tactical problems in the Balkans during the discussion that followed the simple luncheon.

He explained at some historical length his decision to attack Russia, starting significantly with Britain's refusal to make peace in June 1940. He spoke scathingly of Italy's misfortunes, charitably distinguishing between the plucky but poorly led Italian soldiers and their bumbling, devious political and military commanders. "Why has Britain fought on?" he asked. He identified two primary reasons—the influence of the Jews and of Britain's international financial involvements, and the dominant influence of the Churchill clique. Britain had floated off the sandbanks of despondency by means of purely psychological bubbles: although she had demonstrably lost four hundred thousand tons of shipping at Dunkirk, she had camouflaged the rout as a victorious retreat; the RAF's night bombing of Germany boosted home morale far more than it damaged German industry; British cockiness had been restored by the failure of the dreaded Wehrmacht invasion to materialize, and by Mussolini's defeats in the Mediterranean.

Now Britain was hitching her fortunes to the United States and Russia, declared Hitler. Of the United States he was not afraid—it could never match Germany's soaring aircraft, tank, and submarine production; not for four years would American arms output be going at full blast, and then there was the problem of transporting the arms and troops to the European theater. But Russia must be defeated now. "Now we have the chance to smash Russia while our own back is free. That chance will not return so soon. I would be betraying the future of the German people if I did not seize it now!" Once this land-forces

---

1941, that Hitler was preparing to attack Russia; moreover, in the second week of June 1941 Göring again summoned Dahlerus to Berlin and informed him of the precise date of the attack. There is no indication that Hitler was aware of this.

problem had been settled, in about two years, Germany could set about mastering her other duties in the skies and oceans of the world. He urged his generals to have no moral compunctions about violating their treaty with Russia. It was quite clear why Stalin had cynically signed it; but he also urged them not to underestimate the Russian tanks or air force, or to rely too heavily on Germany's allies in this fight. "The fate of major German formations must not be trusted to the steadfastness of Romanian divisions"—a warning he was himself to ignore at Stalingrad.

Hitler also drilled into his generals that this would be a war between great ideologies, and as such very different from the war in the west. "In the east cruelty now will be kindness for the future." The Russian commissars and GPU officials were criminals and were to be treated as such. "It is not our job to see that these criminals survive."

In a masterpiece of rapid General Staff work, the entire Balkan campaign plan was dismantled and remounted within nine days to include the improvised invasion of Yugoslavia by German forces, with Hungarian and Italian troops in walk-on roles. It was a feat of planning Hitler recognized, but only tacitly.

Hitler meanwhile decided how the carcass of Yugoslavia was to be carved up—the rich and fertile Banat region would be returned to Hungary, the Dalmatian coast and Montenegro assigned to Italy, and Serbia placed under German military rule. Of the former Austrian territory Germany would require only the return of Carinthia and Styria to the Reich. Croatia was to become an autonomous state and choose its own ruler; Greek Macedonia was to be annexed by Bulgaria. It all seemed a very satisfactory end to the Balkan nightmare. Russia's Balkan stance remained uncertain, and in the last few days before launching the invasion of Greece and Yugoslavia, Hitler was in the same agony of apprehension that had gripped him before "Yellow" and the invasion of Norway. Rumors multiplied. Was Stalin offering Yugoslavia's new regime a nonaggression pact? Had he secretly offered the Yugoslavs arms and supplies, as an intercepted message between Belgrade and Moscow had implied? The Russians hotly denied the suggestion—Hungary would never allow Russian arms to cross her territory; but Hitler knew there were other routes to Belgrade, through the Aegean ports of Greece, for example. He warned Antonescu to increase the guard on Romania's frontiers as tension between the Axis and Belgrade rose. On April 5 the Romanian General Staff—regarded by Foreign Armies East as the best source of Intelligence after Finland—reported that the Russians were stepping up photographic reconnaissance sorties over Romania, that sixty or more Russian aircraft had suddenly arrived at Leofa, and that a new paratroop school had just opened at Kiev.

All these warnings sinisterly shaded the Belgrade regime's obvious attempts to gain time. Hitler instructed Ribbentrop to ignore any fresh protestations of loyalty from Belgrade. When Count Ciano telephoned after dinner on March 31 with the news that the deputy premier of Yugoslavia was asking to see Mussolini, Hitler advised, "Yes, but keep him away for the next few days." On April 5 the political clouds suddenly began to clear: Hewel brought him a disturbing Forschungsamt intercept proving that Stalin was on the point of signing a pact with the new anti-German regime in Belgrade (it was signed within the next twenty-four hours). It was, therefore, now or never. All through the fifth, Hitler was on tenterhooks, and he sat up with Hewel and his personal staff talking until five in the morning. Twenty minutes later, his armored and infantry divisions began storming the frontiers of Greece and Yugoslavia; his heavily escorted bomber squadrons were already in the air heading for Belgrade.

A Bitter Victory

To the rest of the world Hitler's lightning campaign against Greece and Yugoslavia proved once more the invincibility of the German Wehrmacht. Within the inner sanctum of his own headquarters, however, it demonstrated the grating lack of harmony within the Axis: the Axis always had been more myth than reality, but never more so than now. Hitler had fully taken into account the susceptibilities of his new allies; in a directive issued at the beginning of April 1941, he stated that while he would himself assign the necessary campaign objectives for the Italian and Hungarian forces he would endeavor to do so in such a way that Mussolini and Horthy might yet appear to their people and armed forces as "sovereign military commanders." Horthy was no problem, but the Duce—his *amour-propre* injured by a succession of defeats—obliged Hitler to adopt public postures and contortions on Italy's behalf that for once united the OKW, the foreign ministry, the army, and the navy in a seething, uncomprehending anger at their Führer's indulgence of his inept ally. But Hitler had a higher aim; he wanted to strengthen the slackened Axis bonds in time for the supreme ordeal yet to come: "Barbarossa," the assault on Russia.

Within twelve days Yugoslavia, her thirty-four divisions rent by the national rift between Serb and Croat, was defeated. The Greek armies capitulated following a heroic struggle shortly after, leaving the British Expeditionary Force fighting a hopeless rearguard action against the German armored and mountain corps which had comfortably sidestepped the formidable Metaxas line to pour into Yugoslavia and Greece. The British had committed their first blunder in purchasing the coup d'etat in Belgrade; the second error was in overestimating the resisting power of the Yugoslav army. When Hitler's Second Army, operating out of Austria, offered the Yugoslav general negotiating the armistice the use of a German plane to consult his government, the worthy officer had to struggle visibly with his qualms about entering such a newfangled device. "I am an old man and have never flown before—but I will do it for my Fatherland!" Besides, Yugoslavia's forces were equipped with German weapons firing German ammunition; how could she possibly have fought a long war?

Hitler had ordered the attack to begin with the saturation bombing of Belgrade—with an eye to the deterrent effect on other powers, notably Turkey and the Soviet Union. Nearly five hundred bomber and dive-bomber sorties had devastated the Yugoslav capital within hours after the campaign opened. Water, gas, and power supplies failed, as many as 17,000 civilians were killed, and the government was forced to flee to the suburbs without having made any provision for this eventuality; robbed of their nerve center, the Yugoslav armies caved in. Over 340,000 Yugoslav soldiers were taken prisoner; the Germans lost only 151 dead. Throughout the campaign, the Italians and the Hungarians— who since Hungary had signed a treaty of friendship with Yugoslavia tactfully waited until Croatia had declared her independence before marching in—displayed a marked reluctance to attack until the enemy had first been soundly beaten and demoralized by the German troops. Hitler fully sympathized with Admiral Horthy's predicament: the latter's prime minister had shown his disapproval of the attack on Yugoslavia by committing suicide on April 3. Horthy expressed to the German liaison officer in Budapest the pious hope that in the coming fighting the Hungarian armies would not lose too much blood or be "led too far astray from Hungary"; at that time he had no knowledge of Hitler's plans for a coalition war against Russia within three months.

On the afternoon of April 9, German radio broadcast the first string of six special bulletins on the victories in the southeast. The Greek army defending Salonika had capitulated. Hewel noted the "magnificent mood" at Hitler's Chancellery. The mood was dimmed briefly that night when fifty British bombers arrived over Berlin, cascading high-explosive and fire bombs over the acres between the Victory Monument and Alexanderplatz. Hitler took refuge in his air raid shelter and, after the raid was over, sent Hewel to tour the blitzed area with a police general. Bellevue Castle, the crown prince's palace, the State library, and the university had been badly damaged; in the State Opera House Unter den Linden the fires were out of control, and when dawn came, this fine building in which the Führer had delivered some of his most significant speeches was a smoldering shell. The raid had killed eleven people. In revenge, a week later Hitler sent the Luftwaffe to raid London continuously for ten hours with a thousand tons of bombs.

Late on April 10 his train left Berlin for Munich; and late on the eleventh he continued through Vienna toward Graz. Here a tunnel took the single-track railway through the Alps. The OKW command train, *Atlas*, halted on the far side of the ice-cold, three thousand-yard-long tunnel; Hitler's *Amerika* stopped before entering it, near the little station of Mönichkirchen. Each train could be shunted into the tunnel in case of air attack. This heavily guarded area was to be his headquarters for the next two weeks. His only contacts with the outside world were the OKW's communications system, the twice weekly showing of rough-cut newsreels at the nearby Mönichkirchener Hof Hotel—projected without sound-track, while an adjutant read aloud the accompanying script—and the visits of his generals and ministers. It was here that a young Luftwaffe lieutenant, Franz von Werra, reported to him. Shot down over Britain, he had escaped from a prison train in Canada. He was a mine of information gleaned in captivity—for example, from German submarine crews, who told him their boats had been detected by some British device called "Asdic."

On April 12, the Nazi banner was already flying over the ruins of Belgrade. On the fourteenth the Greeks began evacuating Albania. On the fifteenth the OKW learned that the British Expeditionary Force was in full flight toward its ports of embarkation. Broadcasting to the Yugoslav nation, Churchill offered deceptive comfort: the British knew what it was like and were still standing right behind them, an awkwardly ambiguous statement which Goebbels instructed his press media to exploit to the full.

Hitler ordered his army and Luftwaffe to use all available means to prevent the escape of the British troops in Greece. Late on the seventeenth, Radio Athens was monitored announcing the inevitability of defeat and appealing to the people to remain calm. Hitler's instructions to the OKW were that if Greece surrendered, all Greek prisoners were to be released—as a mark of his admiration for the valor with which they had defended their frontiers. Prime Minister Alexander Koryzis committed suicide, and on April 20, as Hitler's birthday was being ceremonially observed in his command train at Mönichkirchen, he learned that what was left of the Greek army had surrendered to the SS Leibstandarte, or Life Guards.

In an OKW order of April 19, Hitler had laid down the principle that surrender offers were always to be accepted by German commanders, however small the enemy unit involved. Field Marshal List had therefore formally accepted the army's surrender on April 21 even though the Greek commander, General Tsolakoglu, made it plain that he was *not* surrendering to the Italians, whom his forces had soundly defeated (and indeed not seen for some days). Hitler endorsed List's action, hoping no doubt to present the Duce with a *fait accompli*. Victory over Greece was a bittersweet accomplishment, and in a gush of sentiment, on April 19 he told a Hungarian diplomat that he had not had his heart in fighting the Greeks. "I am fighting a war against Britain, not against these little countries." He claimed that had Greece not allowed the British forces in, he would never have attacked her; now he was bound to disarm her, but he did so without relish and he would take no Greek prisoners.

After this high point Hitler's moral stance toward Greece rapidly deteriorated. Mussolini was speechless with rage that the Greeks had not offered their surrender to the Italians, and bluntly refused to stop the fighting unless the Greeks appealed to *him* for an armistice. Italy, blustered the Duce, had been fighting with 500,000 men and lost 63,000 dead in her six months of war with Greece. Then suddenly the SS Life Guards had advanced so far that they held a bridge which actively blocked the Italian pursuit of the Greeks! Hitler reluctantly backtracked and told Jodl that List was wrong to have accepted the surrender and that the fight must go on until the Greeks surrendered to the Italians too.

The army was furious at this public rebuff. So was Ribbentrop, who visited Hitler that very afternoon, April 21. Hewel noted: "The Chief with the Führer. Reports that the Italians are making the most brazen demands. Surrender talks are in progress with the Greek army. Obstacle: the Italians. Everybody is furious, even the Führer. He is always torn between soldier and politician. Keitel against Ribbentrop." Mussolini's haughty demands brought a comic problem to the Greek tragedy: not only had the Greek army surrendered to the Germans and laid down its arms, but the greater part of it was already in captivity; how were the Greeks now to continue fighting for Italy's benefit? Hitler sent word to the Duce's headquarters that perhaps the Italians would like to send a representative to assist Jodl in settling the surrender terms with the Greeks the next morning, April 22. But Mussolini's forces had opened a bedraggled offensive on the Epirus front as soon as word of the Greek surrender to List reached him; the Greeks were not only still fighting there, they were inflicting heavy casualties on the Italians.

The OKW rushed a draft of the surrender terms to Rome, but Mussolini still churlishly refused to play any part unless the Greeks first offered to capitulate to the Italian commander. He sulkingly announced that he could have finished off the Greeks without Hitler's help—if the five hundred thousand Italian troops had not sufficed, then he would have sent a million. When he read in the draft that the Führer wanted to allow the Greek officers to retain their swords and daggers, he protested in exasperation that these were an enemy who had inflicted nameless indignities on the Italians; but here the Germans were adamant—the whole world had marveled at the Greek army's prolonged resistance, and Hitler considered it proper to recognize their bravery. Apart from this Hitler blindly accepted the Italian demands. To the fury of Admiral Raeder he announced that the Yugoslav and Greek navies were to be handed over to the Italians when they arrived to replace the German troops; to the fury of both the OKW and army, Hitler also bowed to Mussolini's demand that the Axis troops stage a ceremonial entry into Athens, with Italians and Germans side by side. (He himself considered this an unnecessary and objectionable humiliation of a brave enemy.) The nearest Italians were still a week's march away from Athens, which did not make things easier.

When the surrender conference began at Salonika late on April 22, the Italian general present announced that he was not empowered to sign. Inquiries in Rome revealed that Mussolini had personally ordered this; the general would be authorized to sign only if the Greeks offered to surrender on the Epirus front first. For a time Hitler toyed with the idea of leaving the Greeks and Italians to fight it out, west of a certain line to be blocked by German troops. But during the night the Greeks bowed to the inevitable and offered surrender to Mussolini's generals too. At Salonika the surrender document was signed by all three parties on the afternoon of April 23, after Mussolini had played his final trick on Hitler. The Führer had forbidden premature release of the surrender news, but at 10 A.M. the Italians had already suddenly broadcast it to the world. "The enemy armies of Epirus and Macedonia have laid down their arms. The surrender was tendered by a Greek military delegation yesterday at 9:04 P.M. to the commander of the Italian Eleventh Army on the Epirus front. The details of the surrender will now be worked out in complete agreement with our German allies." Discreet inquiries in Rome revealed that Mussolini had personally ordered the early announcement. Hewel summed it up in his diary: "The Italians are acting like crazy idiots."

In Croatia—the northern region of Yugoslavia bordering on Italy and Austria—a breakaway movement had been fomented by Canaris's underground forces. General Sladko Kvaternik, an officer of the old Austro-Hungarian army, had seized power in Zagreb, aided by the Abwehr's "Jupiter" organization, and with Hitler's blessing he had set up an independent state with Dr. Ante Pavelić, the leader of the Ustashi movement who had spent long years exiled in Italy, as its *Poglavnik,* or chief. Major General Edmund von Glaise-Horstenau was appointed German liaison officer responsible directly to Keitel and the OKW. His task would eventually be to build up a Croatian police army of about six divisions. A diplomat of SA general's rank—an increasingly familiar animal in Ribbentrop's ministry—would be Germany's envoy to Croatia.

Hitler's decision to transfer the Dalmatian coastal region of Croatia to Italy caused intense resentment in Zagreb, and Glaise-Horstenau protested vehemently to Hitler at this amputation. However, the Führer closed his eyes to the hatred Germany would reap from the Croats by this action. Meanwhile the Serbs, despised as conspirators and traitors who had sold Yugoslavia to the British and the Bolsheviks, need expect short shrift from Germany. The Luftwaffe's General Helmut Förster was appointed military governor in Serbia, with orders to rule with an iron hand.[1]

In Dalmatia, the Italians needed no prompting to act likewise. On April 24, Canaris's lieutenant, Colonel Lahousen, interviewed General Kvaternik, the new Croat war minister in Zagreb (referred to as "Marshal Kvaternik" by his overenthusiastic followers). Lahousen found that this ancient, upright nationalist's admiration for Germany and her Führer was boundless, but so was his hatred of the Italians, who were now wreaking their revenge on Dalmatia. (The Italians had already posted warnings that they were introducing corporal punishment there.) "The Croats are a people of honor, with a long military tradition," complained Kvaternik, "and it is bitter beyond words to be trodden down and humiliated now by an army that has not been able to pin one victory to its colors." He told Lahousen that when Pavelić had initially returned from his Italian exile, his first private question to him was,

[1] Ribbentrop's specialists had searched the Yugoslav foreign ministry and war department buildings in Belgrade for, *inter alia,* files relating to Serbian secret organizations. Among the documents found was a proposal for the Yugoslav General Staff to poison awkward personalities.

"Ante, have you made any kind of deal with the Italians on Croatia?" Only when his old comrade had categorically denied this did the general offer him his hand. Nonetheless, Lahousen reported to the OKW that the new Croatian leaders would swallow Italy's annexation of Dalmatia —if only because they were sure Mussolini could not hang on to this, the eastern coast of the Adriatic, for long. A few days later Canaris himself met Kvaternik in Zagreb. The general had fresh reports of Italian outrages—soldiers urinating on the Croatian national flag, tearing down the Reich insignia, actively inciting Serbian elements against the Croats, and looting foodstuffs and goods; Kvaternik feared—prophetically, as events turned out—that this "completely irrational political attitude of the Italians" would sow the seeds of serious future danger.

On April 24, 1941, the Hungarian regent, Admiral Horthy, visited Hitler's train—their first meeting since 1938. In the interval, Hitler had received from the admiral many letters, written in a quaint, archaic German style. The most recent had come in mid-April; only Horthy's handwritten draft survives, in Budapest archives. In it, Horthy once more suggested a German attack on Russia and hinted that Hungary would participate if the whole of Transylvania—at present partly under Romanian rule—were promised to him. "Nobody else knows I have written this letter, and I will *never* mention it, even in any memoirs I may write." Horthy warned that an invasion of Britain was fraught with a thousand dangers. "But if Russia's inexhaustible riches are once in German hands, you can hold out for all eternity." On April 19, Hitler acknowledged to the Hungarian envoy Sztójay that Horthy obviously felt deeply—as this letter showed—about the Russian menace; he nevertheless inwardly rejected making any commitment to Hungary at Romania's expense. So now, on the twenty-fourth, he charmed and flattered Horthy, and the regent fawned on him—according to Hewel's diary the Hungarian "talked and talked" during the luncheon, and even argued, using one of Hitler's favorite phrases, that Greece had been defeated because she was a democracy, where "the votes of two idiots count for more than that of one wise man."

Keitel lunched silently with them, listening to Horthy's endless tales from his civilian life as horse breeder, farmer, and racehorse owner. Then Keitel lured him into hunting anecdotes, knowing that Hitler abominated huntsmen as a "green freemasonry" bent only on the cowardly murder of nature's most beautiful creatures—usually, as the Duke of Windsor had once pointed out at the Berghof—from a safe distance and with telescopic sights. Those who knew Hitler well were familiar with his loathing of horses too. (When three years later, SS General Hermann Fegelein, Himmler's new liaison officer, clanked in wearing riding spurs, Hitler sardonically invited him to "gallop next door" to fetch a certain document; purpling with rage, Fegelein vowed never to wear spurs again.)

But nothing could now darken Hitler's mood. The British were in full flight to their ships, albeit destroying every bridge to impede the Wehrmacht's pursuit. When the British evacuation ended five days later, Hitler had killed or captured another twenty-two thousand elite troops. Of the fifty thousand others who escaped, some sailed to Egypt. The rest were on the isle of Crete, and on Jeschonnek's suggestion Hitler ordered an airborne assault on Crete prepared as well. Inexplicably for Hitler, Churchill also survived this second Dunkirk-type fiasco. Through Lisbon, Hitler received word that Churchill was very popular in Britain, and Anthony Eden was being publicly identified with the humiliation in the Balkans.

Hitler's own mind was made up on the Russian campaign, but he still wanted to convince Ribbentrop. He knew he would not win over the foreign ministry as such. He considered its ways conservative, its procedures ponderous, and its attitude to the Party reactionary. Since its failure to give him advance warning of the Belgrade putsch, the ministry's stock had sunk even lower in his estimation. Hitler's tendency to direct foreign policy himself, using Ribbentrop only as a secretary, was strongly exposed again in "Barbarossa." He had decided to appoint not the foreign ministry, but the Party's chief thinker, the Baltic-born Alfred Rosenberg, to manage the new eastern domain—impressed, apparently, by Rosenberg's early writings on the Bolshevik menace. Small wonder that Hewel's diary shows Ribbentrop "off sick" for most of April 1941 —malingering, furious at this fresh erosion of his powers.

On about April 25, Hitler telephoned Ribbentrop in Vienna, summoned him to his special-train headquarters, and told him he had decided finally to attack Russia. Ribbentrop later recalled:

He said that all the military Intelligence reaching him confirmed that the Soviet Union was preparing in a big way along the entire front from the Baltic to the Black Sea. He was not willing to be taken by surprise once he had recognized a danger. Moscow's pact with the Serbian putschist government was a downright provocation to Germany and a clear departure from the German-Russian treaty of friendship. In this conversation I recommended that he listen first to our [Moscow] ambassador, Count [Werner von der] Schulenburg, . . . I wanted to try a diplomatic settlement with Moscow first. But Hitler refused any such attempt and forbade me to discuss the matter with anybody; no amount of diplomacy could change the Russian attitude, as he now recognized it, but it might cheat him of the important tactical element of surprise when he attacked. He requested me to put on a show of complete support for his view, and explained that one day the West would understand why he had rejected the Soviet demands and attacked the East.

Thus, Hitler regarded "Barbarossa" as that most controversial of campaigns—a preventive war.

"What can a war historian tell us about the problems of fighting preventive wars?" he asked Wilhelm Scheidt at this time. Scheidt, a young, well-groomed cavalry captain, had just been introduced as adjutant to Colonel Walter Scherff, Hitler's personal historian. Scheidt knew about "Barbarossa," and replied, "Only somebody with the deepest sense of responsibility can take such a decision, and then only after looking at it from every possible angle. Because he will be risking immense dangers in starting such a war." He would have to accept the odium of being the aggressor, in return for the tactical advantages of surprise. But Hitler mused out loud, "Britain will just have to climb down, once we have defeated her last ally on the continent. If she does not, we shall destroy her, with all the means that we shall have when all Europe as far as the Urals is at our feet."

On April 26, Hitler's train left Mönichkirchen for the former Yugoslav frontier. He motored to Maribor—newly renamed Marburg—and toured the German-speaking provinces his Second Army had regained for the Reich. Everywhere there was a huge and fervent welcome, especially at Marburg's town hall. "Then by train back to Graz," recorded Hewel. "An enormous reception there. . . . The Führer is very happy —a fanatical welcome. Wonderful singing. The museum. Lunch at Hotel Wiesler, then left for Klagenfürt in the evening. On the way Rintelen and Ambassador Benzler joined the train. A conference on setting up a Greek opposition government.[2] Coffee at the castle, with infinitely ugly maidens provided from the Gau's leadership school. But they could sing very nicely." Here in Klagenfürt, Hitler the next day met his old history

[2] On April 22, 1941, General Tsolakoglu, now a captive, had offered to establish a new government in Athens. Keitel instructed the army to release him so that the new government could be set up as soon as Mussolini formally assented.

Benzler was the former German envoy in Belgrade, who now became Ribbentrop's plenipotentiary to the German military governor of Serbia.

teacher, Professor Leopold Poetsch. Of this man he had written in *Mein Kampf* that it had perhaps altered the whole course of his life that fate gave him such a history teacher—able to bring the subject alive.

By April 28, with the swastika over the Acropolis, German paratroops astride the Isthmus of Corinth, and the SS Life Guards Brigade in the Peloponnesus, Adolf Hitler was back in his Chancellery in Berlin.

At five-fifteen that evening, Ribbentrop's ambassador in Moscow was ushered in to him. Count Schulenburg had not been officially informed of "Barbarossa" (Hans Krebs, his military attaché, had been forbidden to tell him). But Schulenburg was no simpleton. The rumors sweeping Central Europe, the evasive responses from Berlin, Hitler's failure to reply to the Soviet proposals of November 25, 1940—these told him all he needed. At Ribbentrop's behest the ambassador had prepared a memorandum begging Hitler to accept the Russian proposals; but in Berlin this document had been toned down by Ribbentrop's own advisers, who pointed out that otherwise Hitler would toss it aside unread. Hitler granted Schulenburg just thirty minutes of his time. To the ambassador it seemed that the Führer had drawn all his preconceived ideas from Vidkun Quisling, who had for many years been Norway's military attaché in Moscow and had first whispered to Hitler that Stalin's empire was already falling apart—that after the very first military defeats the unpopular Bolshevik regime would collapse, and that the Ukraine and other states were struggling to secede from the USSR.

"The Führer receives Schulenburg," noted Hewel. "A superficial conversation about Russia." Hitler asked him, according to Schulenburg's own record, what devil had possessed the Russians that they had signed that pact with the anti-German putschist regime in Belgrade—was it an attempt to frighten Germany? The ambassador's opinion was that the Russians were just openly staking their claim on the Balkans; they were very uneasy about the rumors of a coming German attack as well. Hitler retorted that it was the Russians who had begun the mobilization race, but the ambassador suggested it was characteristic Russian overreaction to German moves. If Stalin had not allied himself with France and Britain when both were still strong and intact, he would hardly opt for them now. (To Hitler this was a facile argument: in 1939 Stalin had *wanted* to encourage war between Germany and the West; how could he have foreseen that Hitler would emerge victorious so soon?) When Schulenburg referred to all the indications that Stalin was desperate to reinforce the friendly ties between Germany and Russia, and was even hinting that he could supply five million tons of grain in 1942, Hitler turned away and ended the interview. His secretary, writing a private letter in the secretaries' room beneath the Chancellery stairs, ended it abruptly with the words: "Oh dear, I must stop now as the table is just being laid. The Chief comes every afternoon to have coffee with us in our 'stair cupboard.' "

The next day Hitler spoke to nine thousand officer candidates in the Berlin Sportpalast. "If you ask me, 'Führer, how long will the war last?' I can only say as long as it takes to emerge victorious! Whatever may come! As a National Socialist during the struggle for power I never knew the word 'capitulation.' And there is one word I will never know as leader of the German people and your Supreme Commander, and again it is 'capitulation'—that is, to submit to the will of another. Never, never! And you too have to think like that." He also hinted that he might yet have to make decisions that some of them might not comprehend, but he justified himself thus: "Where would we be now if we had waited just one week more in the south?"—meaning the Balkans.

His divisions were already pulling out of the Balkans and regrouping for "Barbarossa." He decided now that "Barbarossa" would begin on June 22, a Sunday, with the onset of the final top-capacity transport program one month earlier. On the Russian front the Wehrmacht would have the upper hand only in the central section, while in consequence of the Balkan campaign—which had left the Twelfth Army in southeastern Europe—and the considerable Russian reinforcements pouring into Bessarabia and Bukovina, the German armies in the south would be numerically inferior to the enemy. This was the real strategic cost of "Marita": Army Group South could not mount the pincer movement originally planned to destroy the Russian forces south of the Pripyet Marshes but had to attempt an almost impossible encirclement action with its northern wing while the southern wing was restricted to a tactical defense role. Nonetheless, Brauchitsch was still confident that after four weeks of stiff fighting on the frontier the initial Russian resistance would melt away.

During May the OKW was to begin staff talks with Finland and—less hopefully—with Hungary. The final month in which the real assembly for "Barbarossa" could no longer be concealed was to be camouflaged as a colossal diversion from Hitler's supposedly real intention—to invade Britain.

By this time the most persistent rumors of "Barbarossa" were sweeping Moscow once again. The first wave of reports that Germany was planning to attack Russia had reached Moscow in August 1940—perhaps significantly—but it had ebbed during the autumn only to come thundering back in March. Most of these reports could be traced back to the British embassy, but travelers in Germany were bringing back enough hair-raising and evidently significant tidbits of Intelligence to alarm even the most complacent Kremlin dweller. The most substantial evidence had reached Moscow from Romania and indirectly from Belgrade. Hitler had been most frank in his overtures to General Antonescu—indeed, the Romanian leader had positively canvassed "Barbarossa"; and when Göring had seen him in Vienna on March 5 about increasing Romania's oil output he had explained unambiguously that "one day the other oil supplier might drop out." Göring had asked how many Romanians now lived on Russian territory, and he had made a scooping gesture with his hand by way of explanation. Almost at once Moscow came into possession of photocopies of a document establishing that Hitler had promised that Romania should recover Bessarabia after Russia had been defeated; Hitler learned of this leak by mid-April. At the same time he learned of another, more intriguing leak from Belgrade.

Evidently Hitler had told Yugoslavia's prince regent privately about "Barbarossa" at the Berghof on March 4. In any case, British Foreign Secretary Eden had just told Sir Stafford Cripps as much; Eden had identified his source as King George of Greece, the prince regent's brother. The excellent Hungarian Intelligence service learned of this in Moscow and passed the information back to Admiral Canaris on April 11. In short the rumor was all over Europe. A few days later the unsuspecting German naval attaché in Moscow was cabling that Cripps was now predicting that Hitler would attack Russia on June 22, a canard so "obviously absurd" that he would do all he could to kill it.[3] The OKW evenly dismissed all these rumors as a British attempt "to poison the wells" and instructed its attachés abroad to spread counterrumors that in the first half of May there would be major shifts of Wehrmacht strength to the west.

Stalin's reaction to the warnings was illuminating. At Cripps's suggestion the Yugoslav envoy in Moscow had at the beginning of April warned Stalin about "Barbarossa." Stalin had hedged a guess at the probable date and cockily replied, "Let them come. We will be ready for them!" Hitler's rapid victory in the Balkans literally wiped the smile off Stalin's face. An extraordinary period ensued in which the Soviet

---

[3] At this time, April 24, Hitler himself had not fixed the date of June 22 for certain. But in the first week in April he seems to have discussed June 22 or 23 with Brauchitsch as possible dates. Lossberg meanwhile advised Jodl that since the troop movements would not be completed until the twenty-third, the operation should begin two days after that. Cripps's rumor seems therefore to have been based on a lucky guess.

government tried desperately to appease Hitler: whereas the Soviet-German trade pact of January 1941 had been followed by a noticeable slowing down of Russian deliveries to Germany, now grain, petroleum, manganese, and other materials began flooding westward, and the Soviet government even laid on a special goods train to rush rubber to Germany along the Trans-Siberian railway. But no words spoke more eloquently than the sensational scene at Moscow's railroad station on the day the Japanese foreign minister departed for Tokyo. Stalin did what he had not even done for Ribbentrop—he made a stunning personal appearance on the platform, embraced the Japanese officials, and then searched out Ambassador Schulenburg and loudly pronounced in front of the assembled diplomatic corps, "We must remain friends, you must do all you can for that!" He put his arms around the German envoy's shoulders—perhaps he was drunk, for his left eye was half closed, he groped for the right words, and he looked much older.

As if that were not enough, Stalin swung around toward Colonel Krebs, the acting military attaché, satisfied himself that Krebs was German, and promised loudly, "We will always remain friends with you—whatever may happen!" Hitler had studied all the reports, including one submitted by the Forschungsamt, on this puzzling Moscow scene, and he wondered what to make of it. Equally remarkable was the studied politeness of the Soviet remonstrance over eighty German violations of Soviet air space in the first half of April (one aircraft had landed and been found to contain cameras, exposed films, and a topographical map of Soviet territory); the Soviet protest was mild compared with Jodl's cynical list of "deliberate provocations" by Russian aircraft—eight on April 17 alone—and his warning about the "momentous frontier incidents" that might soon occur if the Russians did not mend their ways. In fact the OKW was worried about this very Soviet reasonableness. After a secret conference with Keitel on Abwehr subversive and sabotage operations planned inside Russia, Admiral Canaris noted: "After my discussion with the chief of the OKW, General Jodl disclosed to me in a conference that they are greatly worried about the Russians' soft and indulgent attitude toward us, and he added half in jest, in a reference to our No. 800 'Special Duties' Training Regiment Brandenburg,[4] 'If these chaps'—meaning the Soviet Russians—'keep on being so accommodating and take offense at nothing, then *you* will have to stage an incident to start the war.' "

---

[4] The German commando regiment.

Finding a suitable incident was traditionally the difficulty of launching a premeditated preventive war, which is what Hitler's eastern crusade had now become. Neither Hitler nor his military advisers were any longer in doubt as to Stalin's long-term intentions. Halder was to state that if the Russian deployments were shown to an impartial military expert he would have to concede that they were offensive in design. Throughout March, Russian troop movements close to the frontier had been so intense, with a heavy flow of reinforcements from Moscow toward Smolensk and Minsk, that eventually Halder felt anxiety about the threat of a Russian preventive action. The danger would be acute at least until April 20, for until then the Russians would have great superiority in strength. "The disposition of Russian forces gives food for thought," Halder wrote on April 7. "If we discount the catchword that the Russians want peace and won't attack anybody themselves, then it has to be admitted that the Russian dispositions could allow them to convert very rapidly from defense into attack—and this could prove highly embarrassing for us." He had Jodl ask Hitler whether the top-capacity "Barbarossa" transport plan should be thrown into action now, six weeks early, but Hitler was against it.

The Führer himself was in no doubt. Stalin's pact with Belgrade, coupled with a communiqué of March 24,[5] provided further justification for "Barbarossa." At the end of it all he was to say, "I didn't take the decision to attack Moscow lightly, but because I knew from certain information that an alliance was being prepared between Britain and Russia. The big question was, Should we strike out first or wait until we were overwhelmed some time in the future?" According to his army adjutant, Hitler's decision was reinforced by Intelligence reports on feverish airfield and arms dump construction by the Russians throughout the spring; there were also reports from Polish agents of Russian troop movements from as far away as the Far East, and of the creation and deployment of new armies for what could only be offensive purposes. The Russians were also instructing their commissars, for example in Leningrad, to get ready for a long and grueling war with Germany.

German Intelligence collected concrete evidence of long-range Soviet

[5] Russia had reaffirmed her nonaggression pact with Turkey to encourage her to adopt a more aggressive role against Germany in the Balkans. The Soviet Union had steadily overcome her traditional distrust of Turkey. On February 18, the Forschungsamt had intercepted a description by the Turkish ambassador in Berlin of his conversation with the Russian ambassador, Vladimir Dekanozov, who had hinted that Turkey and the Soviet Union should exchange ideas on the Balkans. The Germans had then also intercepted the Turkish secret cables from Moscow, in which the ambassador there reported that on March 9 Molotov's deputy Andrei Vyshinsky had first proposed such a communiqué, and explicitly stated that the Soviet Union would "understand" any operation Turkey was forced to launch against "the threat of an attack"; Turkey's acceptance and reciprocation of this assurance on March 14 was also intercepted.

planning. The naval attaché reported from Moscow that the Soviet naval construction program was in the process of building three battle-ships, eleven cruisers, *sixty-one* destroyers, and nearly *three hundred* submarines; most of this fleet would be concentrated in the Baltic. On April 4 the German naval code-breakers noticed that the Russians had suddenly adopted completely new radio- and code-systems for two days —evidently a test of war procedures. After April 7, the German embassy in Moscow observed a steady call-up of reservists and raw recruits. On the eighth, the families of the Russian trade mission began leaving Berlin. Trainloads of the paraphernalia of war were observed moving westward from Kiev to the Polish border. On the ninth, the military attaché in Bucharest reported that Marshal Semën Timoshenko, believed to be the only capable Soviet commander, had just held a council of war at Kiev and ordered an alert for all units on the western front. Rumors swept the Generalgouvernement that Russia would exploit her present brief superiority of arms to strike into Germany, destroying the "Barbarossa" assembly and capturing the huge arms dumps Hitler was moving into the front line. On April 13, Hitler was shown a Forschungsamt summary on the multiplying rumors of war with Russia. On the twenty-third there were fresh reports from Bucharest of immense Soviet reinforcements in Bukovina and Bessarabia, some of the reinforcements arriving from as far away as the Caucasus and Finland; the next day the German military attaché in Bucharest reported that the Russians were evacuating the civilian population along their side of the Prut River front and that shiploads of Red Army troops were arriving at Odessa and being transported by rail to the Bug and Dniestr. On the twenty-fifth the naval decoders intercepted the British military attaché's report to London from Moscow. A thousand people a day were now being called up in Moscow alone, he said, many of them being sent to the Baltic states. "Our military attaché in Budapest, who was traveling to Moscow a few days ago, saw at Lemberg [Lvov] at least one tank brigade . . . on the railway line between Lemberg and Kiev heading westward; he passed seven troop trains of which four were conveying tanks and mechanized equipment and three troops." The German attachés undertaking similar journeys also saw many military transports heading west between Minsk and Baranovichi. By May 5, Antonescu was able to tip off the Germans that Soviet troops were massing between Kiev and Odessa and that reinforcements were still pouring westward from Siberia. "The thing worth noting is that factories around Moscow have been ordered to transfer their equipment into the country's interior."

According to Hitler's Luftwaffe adjutant, the Intelligence brought back by a team of Göring's engineers from a tour of Soviet aircraft factories late in April convinced the Führer there was no time to be lost. These air ministry experts had been allowed to tour eight or nine of the biggest Russian factories producing ball bearings, alloys, aircraft, and aeroengines, and to see the advances made by Soviet research. It was clear that the Soviet air force was a far greater menace than Hitler had bargained for—both in size and aircraft performance. The aircraft factories themselves were the biggest and most modern in Europe—and more were under construction. When the German experts attended a dinner party, the leading Soviet aircraft designer, Mikoyan (who later designed the MIG fighters), stated explicitly, "Now you have seen the mighty technology of the Soviet fatherland. We shall valiantly ward off any attack, whatever quarter it comes from!" Years later Hitler was to describe this commission's report on the Soviet air force as having finally convinced him of the need to attack Russia now.

The voice of Ambassador Schulenburg was a lone voice in the wilderness. In vain he interpreted Stalin's sudden appointment to a government post—Chairman of the Council of People's Commissars—on May 6 as a public rebuke to Molotov for having allowed German-Soviet relations to cool. Undoubtedly it was a historic event in Soviet history, but it could also be interpreted in a more sinister light, as could Stalin's urgent recall of his Berlin ambassador, who a few days earlier had returned to Moscow for consultations. In his May Day speech Stalin had proclaimed: "The Red Army is ready, in the interests of the socialist state, to ward off every blow struck by the imperialists. The international situation is full of unexpected events. In such a situation the Red Army must step up its defensive readiness." Since early May the German military attaché had noted the call-up of the youngest age-group some six months early; and now on Red Army orders foreign diplomats were prevented from traveling freely. On May 13 a German consul in the heart of China, with access to Soviet secret diplomatic circulars, reported that six days before, Moscow had instructed all missions to ascertain the probable attitude of other countries in the event of a German-Soviet conflict. On the sixteenth the Russian envoy in Stockholm was reported to have stated that at no time in Russian history had more powerful troop contingents been massed in the west (which confirmed the estimate of the Swedish air attaché in Moscow that by mid-March alone 60 percent of the Red Army had been massed in western Russia, particularly confronting Romania). And Antonescu's Intelligence service learned that Stalin was saying that "the Soviet government must accept grave sacrifices in order to win time," because the coming war could be postponed, but not prevented; to postpone it, the supply of raw materials to Germany must continue.

The trainloads of rubber, ores, oil, and grain kept rolling westward to Hitler's Germany even as June 22, the date for "Barbarossa," approached; but the date on which Stalin proposed to resume the Soviet program of expansion, now temporarily halted by Hitler's obduracy, also came closer. A year later, the proof of this was in German hands; it will be dealt with in its proper sequence, except for one episode which can for the purpose of this narrative best be related here. On May 5, two secret speeches were delivered at a Kremlin banquet by Stalin to a thousand officers graduating from Moscow's staff colleges. Among the officials who passed through the Kremlin's Trinity Gate that evening were Molotov, Mikoyan, Voroshilov, Kalinin, and Lavrenti Beria; there were also two generals and one major who later fell into German hands and independently described the speeches to German interrogators with a high degree of unanimity.[6] Had Schulenburg—who heard merely that Stalin had delivered a forty-minute speech—been there, perhaps even his optimism about the Soviet Union's designs would have been dispelled.

Marshal Timoshenko had opened the proceedings with a speech and a toast to "our great and wise Stalin." After a formal report by the director of staff studies, Stalin launched into a sober account of the need to modernize the Red Army's weaponry and prepare for the coming war with Germany. He set out these preparations in detail and pointed to certain shortcomings in infantry equipment and tactics. He promised that in two months Russia would have some of the best and fastest aircraft in the world.

New tank models, the Mark 1 and 3, are on their way; these are excellent tanks, whose armor can withstand 76-millimeter shells. In the near future there will also be a new tank graced with my own name. This tank will be a veritable fortress. Today we have up to a hundred armored and mechanized divisions which still need to be organized into an entity. Our war plan is ready, we have built the airfields and landing grounds, and the frontline aircraft are already there. Everything has been done by way of clearing out the rear areas: all the foreign elements have been removed. It follows that over the next two months we can begin the fight with Germany. Perhaps it surprises you that I tell you of our war plans. But we have to take our revenge for Bulgaria and Finland.

[6] Ribbentrop claimed in 1943 that agents supplied details of the speeches to Hitler almost at once. There is no trace of this in surviving German files. Göring made a similar claim after the war.

As for the pact with Germany, that was just camouflage, said Stalin. He explained to his perhaps uneasy listeners that France had only collapsed because her army was without the solid grass-roots support of the French people—it was an army without authority. "Girls even hesitated to marry a French soldier." Hitler on the other hand had enjoyed the unalloyed support of his people so long as he was fighting the obvious injustice of Versailles. But the moment Hitler crossed into Russia he would forfeit the German people's support. The partisan movement painstakingly built up throughout Europe by the Comintern since the war began would assume a vast scale and paralyze the German army's supplies. By the end of the first year Germany would have exhausted her limited stockpiles of scarce raw materials, but Russia was a land of plenty. Above all Germany did not have Russia's limitless reserves of manpower. "Germany may be able to build aircraft and tanks, but she will lack the warriors themselves." Stalin emphasized: "There is no such thing as an invincible army, whatever the country of its allegiance."

A lavish banquet followed in the George Hall of the Kremlin, with drinking far into the night. Perhaps Stalin was drunk by the time he made his second speech—the sources are in conflict on this point. One of the generals, the director of the famous Frunze military academy, was toasting Stalin's genius for "preserving the peace" of Europe when Stalin irritably waved for him to stop, tottered to his feet, and delivered a speech of his own.

> The slogan of peaceful policies is now obsolete—it has been overtaken by events. During the years of the capitalist encirclement of the Soviet Union we were able to make good use of the slogan while we expanded the Soviet Union's frontiers to the north and west. But now we must discard this slogan for the reactionary and narrow-minded slogan that it is, as it will not serve to win us one more square inch of territory. It is time to stop chewing that particular cud, Comrade Chosin: stop being a simpleton! The era of forcible expansion has begun for the Soviet Union. The people must be schooled to accept that a war of aggression is inevitable; they must be in permanent mobilization.

In *this* connection Germany was not explicitly mentioned as the target, but all three of the men interrogated by the Germans said they had no doubt that that was what Stalin meant. (One of them also noted that at the Soviet General Staff college problems of strategic attack alone were analyzed throughout the winter of 1940–1941.) When the director of the chemical warfare academy proposed a toast to their continued friendship with Germany, Stalin angrily interrupted that the German army's victories had only been obtained against small nations up to now. "Many of our officers wrongly overestimate the German army's success. Let's see how good the German army is when it meets an enemy of equal stature!" Raising his glass, Stalin announced a new toast: "Drink to the new era of development and territorial expansion that has begun! Long live the active policy of aggression of the Soviet nation!"

As the storm of applause subsided, Stalin's friend and companion Nikita Khrushchev sprang up and emotionally declaimed: "Never did I dream that in my old age I would live to be given a command in the army of the proletarian world revolution. And now the day is not far off when we who sit here will take the helm and steer our 'ship of history,' not on the slow and stately course we followed hitherto, but . . ." Khrushchev was interrupted by an even more inebriated Marshal Timoshenko. Great—if not always sober or coherent—was the rejoicing within the Kremlin walls that night.

Hess and Bormann

"As a German and as a soldier I consider it beneath me ever to belittle a brave enemy," exclaimed Hitler to his assembled Reichstag deputies on May 4, 1941. "But it seems necessary to me to do something to protect the Truth from the boastful lies of a man who is as miserable a politician as soldier, and is as wretched a soldier as politician." Hitler was declaiming on the Wehrmacht's fresh Balkan triumph.

> Just as he did after Norway and Dunkirk, Mr. Churchill—he also began this campaign—is trying to say something that he might yet be able to twist and distort into a British victory. I don't think that very honest, but in the case of this man it is at least comprehensible. If ever any other politician had met such defeats, or a soldier had encountered such catastrophes, he would not have kept his job six months—unless he was possessed of the same talent that alone distinguishes Mr. Churchill, the ability to lie with devout mien and distort the truth so that in the end the most frightful defeats turn into the most glorious victories. Mr. Churchill may be able to put down a smokescreen before his fellow-countrymen, but he cannot eliminate the results of his disasters.

Hitler went on to say that the British prime minister's appeal three days before to the German people to desert their Führer was explicable only as the fevered outburst of a paralytic or the delirious shout of a chronic drunkard; the same brain had spawned the ill-conceived Balkan expedition as a vain attempt to set southeastern Europe ablaze. Now the brave Greek people had paid for their pro-British monarch's folly. "I regretted it from the start. For me as a German born and bred to revere and respect the art and culture of this country whence the first rays of mortal beauty and dignity emerged, it was a hard and bitter experience to see this happening and be able to do nothing to prevent it." From the

French and British documents found in France he had realized how far the Greek government had drifted into Britain's arms. He heaped praise on Ribbentrop's "unique patience and genius for perseverance" in finally bringing Yugoslavia into the Tripartite Pact; he lavished more praise on the General Staff for their brilliant campaign planning. "One sentence will suffice to distinguish this campaign: to the German soldier nothing is impossible!"

Rudolf Hess, constitutionally "Deputy Führer" of the Party since April 1933 and second in line of succession after Göring, had sat between Hitler and Ribbentrop during the lengthy speech. Ribbentrop was to say a week later that Hess's eyes had looked completely abnormal all evening and that he had seemed mentally disturbed. Hitler did not notice. Hess was an eccentric, a beloved member of the Party's Old Guard, a believer in the supernatural and in herbal remedies; but he also had a brain of surprising shrewdness and a personal courage to match. He had been born in Egypt and was unabashedly pro-British. An enthusiastic pilot whose wings had been officially clipped by Hitler since 1933, he nevertheless found opportunities to fly the latest planes through his personal friendship with the director of air armament, Ernst Udet, and the aircraft designer Willy Messerschmitt. Since the outbreak of war he had taken a keen interest in strategy. Hitler's Luftwaffe and naval adjutants have both stressed Hess's active support for blockading the British Isles as a relatively antiseptic way of imposing Germany's will on Britain, and it was Hess who had persuaded Hitler to force Göring to take the aerial torpedo seriously. Long before the war he had submitted lengthy studies to Hitler on the mass employment of mines in British waters; Hitler had ordered the admiralty to take the matter up, and heard no more until it reemerged as an admiralty proposal.

At the end of Hitler's Reichstag speech, Hess spoke with Hitler privately for about half an hour; no record survives. Hitler disclosed a few days later that on this occasion Hess persistently inquired whether he, the Führer, still stood by the program he had set forth in *Mein Kampf*— of marching side by side with Britain; and that he had confirmed he did. We also have Hess's statement, ten days later, when he was already in enemy hands, that "as recently as May 4, after his Reichstag speech, Hitler declared to me that he had no oppressive demands to make on England."

At eight-fifteen that evening Hitler left by special train with his private staff for the naval dockyard at Gotenhafen, on the Baltic, to inspect Raeder's mighty new capital ships, the *Bismarck* and the *Tirpitz*. The last time he had seen the latter was at her launching at Wilhelmshaven two years before; he still recalled the keen, honest features of the shipyard workers—"A real aristocracy of the working class." But now the battleship was fitting out here in the dismal port of Gotenhafen, beyond the reach of the British bombers, and the *Bismarck* was already straining to sail on her first Atlantic sortie. Gotenhafen itself—the former Polish port of Gdynia—was an economic white elephant built by the Poles in an attempt to ruin Danzig's trade between the wars. It was one of the ugliest cities in western Europe, a sprawling collection of endless suburbs and soulless slums, a sorry contrast to the neat Hanseatic appearance of Danzig. The two huge new battleships dominated the dockyard.

Hitler arrived on May 5 without Admiral Raeder, who wished his fleet commander to see the Führer alone. The navy's plan was to transfer the *Bismarck* and the new heavy cruiser *Prinz Eugen* from the Baltic to the Atlantic coast. Hitler was ferried across to the battleship—a breathtaking spectacle of armor and machinery—in a naval tender. The crew lined up for Hitler's inspection, and he was shown around. There was a moment of levity when Hitler's physician, the portly Professor Morell, became briefly wedged in the slim entrance to one of the 380-millimeter main gun turrets. The *Bismarck,* with her twenty-eight thousand miles of electrical circuits and her radar-controlled guns, was the most advanced warship afloat. Indeed, she was considered unsinkable, and Admiral Günther Lütjens, the gaunt-faced fleet commander, emphasized this to Hitler in his cabin.

He reported on the brilliant marauding operation he had commanded with the pocket battleships *Scharnhorst* and *Gneisenau* during the first three months of the year, raiding Atlantic convoys bringing war supplies to Britain from the United States; and he explained the purpose of the new operation he would command with the *Bismarck* and the *Prinz Eugen*. Hitler was inclined to leave the navy to operate as it saw fit; though it retained its imperial traditions and its antipathy toward all political doctrines, it was fired by a common purpose and fighting spirit of which the National Socialists could approve. (Unlike the services garrisoned in the Reich, the navy was unaffected by prevailing trends of anti-Hitler rebellion, and only three of its officers were to be implicated in the 1944 plot.)

When Hitler did voice his qualms at Lütjens's proposal to risk the capital ships alone against the Atlantic convoys, the admiral put his mind at rest. "Mein Führer, there is virtually nothing that can go wrong for me, with a ship like this. The only danger that I can see is torpedo-aircraft coming at us from aircraft carriers."

Hitler returned to Berlin and then continued south to Berchtesgaden, where he was to meet Admiral Darlan on May 11.

The Führer had belatedly decided to back the Arab "liberation movement" that had broken out in Iraq, and this could best be done with Vichy support from Syria. It is characteristic of Hitler's *ad hoc* strategy that he had hitherto paid no attention to Iraq, a desert country with oil fields in the north and occupied by only small British forces under a ten-year-old treaty. But on April 2 a coup d'etat had brought the anti-British general Rashid Ali el Gailani to power, and when the British thereupon landed in strength at the port of Basra on the Persian Gulf, Rashid Ali's small army encircled the big British air base at Habbaniya some twenty-five miles west of Baghdad and fighting broke out. The Iraqis appealed to Germany for aid. Hitler ordered Vichy arms cached in Syria to be released to them, and German military experts were flown out, followed by a diminutive force of Messerschmitt and Heinkel aircraft, which Darlan allowed to land on the airfields in Syria. The prospects of a Franco-German entente thus seemed auspicious— were it not that a stunning blow now befell Adolf Hitler.

That evening a bulky packet from Rudolf Hess was delivered to the Berghof. Assuming it to contain more of the minister's interminable memoranda, Hitler pushed the packet aside. Toward noon next day, Sunday May 11, he was standing with General Karl Bodenschatz— Göring's representative—in the Berghof's Great Hall when there was a commotion and one of Hess's adjutants burst in, ignoring the protests of the guards. He handed Hitler a slim envelope. Hitler turned it over to Bodenschatz to slit open. There were two pages inside, which the general handed back to him unread. Hitler put on his eyeglasses and began to glance over it indifferently. Suddenly he slumped into a chair and bellowed in a voice that could be heard all over the house: "Oh my God, my God! He has flown to Britain!" A crowd of the curious appeared at the doors, but they were ushered out. Hess's adjutant stated unashamedly that his chief had taken off at Augsburg airfield at 5:40 P.M. the previous evening; when Hitler furiously asked why he had not told anybody until now, the adjutant gave his loyalty to Hess as the reason. Hitler swung around on Bodenschatz. "How is it, Herr General, that the Luftwaffe let Hess fly although I forbade it? Get Göring here!"

But the Reichsmarschall was relaxing at his family castle north of Nuremberg.

It was found that the bulky packet from Hess contained about fourteen pages—a long-winded account of his motives for flying and his proposed peace plan. Apparently written in October 1940, it dealt with technical aspects of a peace settlement—for example, reparations to be paid to Germany. In the shorter letter—which Bodenschatz had just opened—Hess explained that he was flying to Glasgow to meet the Duke of Hamilton, a true friend of Germany whom he had met in 1936; he wanted to try for peace between Germany and Britain before the Russian campaign began. He promised not to betray "Barbarossa" to the British. According to this letter, since November Hess had made three other attempts to reach Scotland; each time an aircraft malfunction had forced him back.

How Hitler's head must have reeled to read all this! Bodenschatz was now on the telephone to Göring. The Reichsmarschall was petulantly asking *why* he was required at the Berghof. Hitler snatched the telephone, shouted, "Göring—you are to come at once!" and slammed the instrument down. Ambassador Hewel telephoned for Ribbentrop: the foreign minister was in conference with Admiral Darlan. That too was abruptly curtailed. Hess's adjutant, the unfortunate bearer of the ill-tidings, was arrested and led away.

A wave of hysterical speculation gripped the Berghof. Could Hess have been a British agent? Might he in fact have gone to Russia? "*Every possible* construction," wrote Schmundt's wife in her diary.

Hitler refused to believe Hess would be disloyal, but pacing nervously up and down his study he confided to Julius Schaub what he feared. "Never mind what he says. If Hess really gets there just imagine: Churchill has Hess in his grasp! What lunacy on Hess's part. . . . They will give Hess some drug or other to make him stand before a microphone and broadcast whatever Churchill wants. I cannot challenge it, because it's Hess's voice and everybody knows it."

Bodenschatz began immediate technical inquiries. He found out that Willy Messerschmitt had himself supplied the advanced Messerschmitt fighter Hess had used, and that Hess had availed himself of the Y-beams navigation system used by the bomber squadrons. Ernst Udet was ordered to come to the Berghof at once: perhaps Hess might have crashed en route, or run into foul weather? But further investigation revealed that ever since August Hess had been supplied with regular weather reports on Britain; giving some innocent excuse, he had also arranged with two radio stations to make a certain broadcast at a specific time so that he could fix his position.

Admiral Darlan—Pétain's deputy premier, foreign minister, navy minister, and minister of the interior—arrived after lunch with Ribbentrop. German-French relations had remained in a limbo of indecision since Montoire; now that Hitler had decided on "Barbarossa," his interest in the Mediterranean had waned, and his inborn mistrust of the French and his anxieties about de Gaulle were not easily overcome. In the Yugoslav files captured in Belgrade, a document had been found strongly indicating that General Weygand was preparing to transfer his allegiance to de Gaulle and that the American ambassador to Vichy had stated that the United States would supply him with equipment and ammunition in that event. The Italians certainly shared Hitler's mistrust. Count Ciano wisecracked to Ribbentrop's interpreter: "The people of Paris say that the British are winning the war. The people of Vichy say that *those pigs* the British will win. *Voilà la différence!*"

Canaris was to note after a meeting with Keitel at this time:

. . . When I turned to our Abwehr subversive operations in Syria and Iraq, the field marshal explained that the Führer is inclined to be skeptical about the French attitude over this issue, as he is indeed about their whole attitude toward collaborating with Germany. He, the chief of the OKW, would in fact term himself a super-skeptic, while Herr von Ribbentrop's views on this were somewhere about the middle. The chief of the OKW mentioned in passing a discussion between the Führer and Herr Ribbentrop on the subject of de Gaulle in the course of which the Führer interrupted Ribbentrop—who had uttered a derogatory remark about de Gaulle—with the words: "Now, now, my dear Ribbentrop, if you found yourself in the same situation you would be the first to become a Gaullist!"

Ribbentrop had seriously flirted with the notion of collaboration with France since February, perhaps in the hope of presenting Hitler with a credible alternative to "Barbarossa" for the defeat of Britain. Late that month he had shown Hitler his ambassador's reply to a secret questionnaire in which he had asked whether a future French government might be cajoled into "declaring war on Britain, placing the French fleet at the disposal of the fight against Britain, and conceding bases to us in French Africa"; Ambassador Otto Abetz had replied that an outright declaration of war would be unlikely, but that a state of war might practically be brought about under certain conditions in which Weygand might even unconditionally follow Pétain. Hitler, however, remained skeptical and cool toward Darlan. A break for tea was taken at five-thirty, but Hewel noticed that the Führer's mind was elsewhere, and the conversation among the dozen people present was stilted and uncomfortable. (Only Ribbentrop continued, in a talk with Darlan next day, to press France to declare war on Britain.) Hitler's mind was on Hess.

The Reichsmarschall arrived at 9 P.M. and threw a quizzical look at Bodenschatz, but the latter had been sworn to secrecy. Now Hitler's resentment was turned on his Luftwaffe commander. (Hewel recorded that night: "According to Bodenschatz's version [Göring] was just as agitated. A long discussion with the Führer downstairs in the Hall: the Führer, foreign minister, Göring, Bormann. Very irritable. Much speculation.") The British had not yet announced anything; throughout this day and the next the argument raged back and forth at the Berghof as to whether Hess had arrived in Britain or was long dead. "A very upset day," wrote Hewel on the twelfth. "Investigations into Hess's flight. . . . Göring and Udet believe Hess could not have managed the difficult flight to Glasgow, as this would call for the utmost flying ability using the most modern equipment. But the Führer thinks Hess *could* have done it."

It was Ribbentrop who sagely pointed out that if they waited any longer, the British might announce the news at any moment to the world —indeed, they could claim that Hess had brought an official offer for a separate peace between Germany and Britain. It might just split the whole Axis wide open.[1] Hitler was aghast. He ordered Ribbentrop to telephone Ciano, and he at once began to dictate the text of a communiqué to the German people. Investigations had meanwhile established that Hess had suffered from a bile complaint for some time and had fallen under the sway of nature healers and astrologers. This facilitated the announcement that while Hess had evidently acted from idealistic motives he was in fact quite mad. "The Führer decides to go ahead with the announcement," wrote Hewel. "He insists on including the passage about it being the action of a madman." By late afternoon the tenth redraft of the communiqué was complete and passed by Hitler. In an agony of fear that the British might still launch their propaganda campaign first, assuming Hess *had* safely arrived, Hitler switched on the radio. At 8 P.M. the German communiqué was broadcast: the Party

---

[1] In September 1943 Hitler was to tell Goebbels: "The British muffed their biggest political opportunity of the war on this occasion."

officially announced that "in a hallucinated state" Hess had taken off from Augsburg in an aircraft and not been seen since. "It is to be feared that Party-member Hess has crashed or met with an accident somewhere." Hitler, noted Hewel, was now "somewhat less tense and more lively." Hours passed and then the BBC finally stirred: Rudolf Hess had landed by parachute in Scotland two nights before. The tension at the Berghof relaxed; indeed a mood of laughter took its place. "Führer wants to wait until the morrow," Hewel ended that day's momentous entries. "The chief is staying at the Berghof."

The Party's anguished investigation into the Deputy Führer's defection continued. For advice on the English mentality, Hess had relied on Albrecht Haushofer, a Berlin professor of geopolitics and son of Munich's eminent Professor Karl Haushofer. The younger Haushofer had been befriended by Hess much earlier and shielded from outrages he might have been subjected to on account of his part-Jewish wife; he had attracted Party hostility by outspoken commentaries on Anglo-German relations in his father's monthly *Zeitschrift für Geopolitik,* with prognoses diametrically opposed to those of the National Socialists. (He had since mid-1938 warned of the growing Anglo-American military alliance and of the futility of Germany's efforts to achieve economic self-sufficiency.) Albrecht Haushofer was summoned to the Obersalzberg on May 12 and ordered to explain his behavior. He admitted that he had made many attempts to correspond with the Duke of Hamilton through Lisbon and Switzerland but said he had received no reply.[2] Haushofer was allowed to return home, but his telephone was tapped by the Forschungsamt and his house was watched.

On May 13 the Party recovered its composure and circulated a second communiqué: papers left behind by Hess—who was more familiar with the Führer's genuine peace proposals than any other person—suggested that he suffered from the hallucination that if he took a personal step with Englishmen known to him from earlier times, he might yet manage to bring about an entente between Germany and Britain. Hitler debated with his advisers about what to do should the British send Hess back. Ribbentrop gained the impression that Hess would be shot. Hans Frank—whom Bormann summoned posthaste to the Berghof along with all the other Party leaders and Gauleiters—later quoted Hitler

---

[2] There is a curious echo of this in British government files on Hess. The Duke of Hamilton first learned of Haushofer's letters from Hess and complained to the government that these peace feelers had never reached him. The secret service requested him to take the matter no further in the national interest.

as telling him: "This man is dead as far as I am concerned: whenever and wherever we find him we will hang him." Frank, who had been through many crises with Hitler as his personal lawyer, found him more upset than he had ever seen him "since the death of his niece Geli Raubal." (Geli had infatuated him and then committed suicide under mysterious circumstances in 1931.)

In time, Hitler's anger softened, though the feud was carried forward by Martin Bormann. Schaub later wrote: "In the years that followed, Hitler seldom mentioned Hess, but when he did it was always to emphasize how highly he had esteemed him—he had always been an upright and honest man until he was led astray." Bormann, of course, was like a dog with two tails to wag—especially since this affair had happened while the Führer was at the Berghof and thus within Bormann's domain. There were many who believed Bormann was morally to blame for Hess's flight, that he had undermined Hess's position so much that the minister had felt compelled to undertake this drastic act to restore his faded status with Hitler. Hitler was certainly not blind to Bormann's pathological ambition, yet in this hour of crisis he wavered. When Göring now asked him whether he proposed to appoint Bormann as Hess's successor, the Führer shook his head and said that he had earmarked Bormann to succeed the Party treasurer Franz Xaver Schwarz; the Reichsmarschall replied succinctly that Hitler was wrong "by a long shot" if he thought that would slake Bormann's ambition. "I care nothing about his ambition," retorted Hitler. Bormann would continue as head of the Party Chancellery; Göring was to look for a suitably youthful candidate to be "Party minister." When Robert Ley also bluntly warned Hitler against appointing Bormann as Hess's successor, he got a similar answer. Small wonder that Bormann's subsequent meteoric rise was to astound them all.

Propaganda Minister Goebbels had by this time also arrived from Berlin. As Goebbels saw it, Hess's act was a momentary aberration, the act of a man who had lost his nerve. After consulting with Hitler, he instructed the propaganda media to pass over the affair as briefly as possible. "We will ignore it for the time being. In any case there is shortly to be a military event which will enable us to distract attention from the subject of Hess to other things." (This must have been a reference to the imminent parachute assault on Crete.) At 3 P.M. Ribbentrop left for Rome to put Mussolini's mind at rest.

By this time the Berghof was packed with the Party leaders and Gauleiters Bormann had summoned. From four until six-thirty, Bormann and Hitler spoke to them about the Hess affair: it was now known that Hess had been "manipulated" by various astrologers, mindreaders, and nature healers who had influenced him to fly to Britain; in doing so he had put the Reich in an impossible predicament with her allies, particularly Italy and Japan. Hewel later described the scene in his diary. As Göring stands behind him with earnest mien "Bormann reads out the letters left by Hess. A dramatic assembly, heavy with emotion. The Führer comes, speaks very humanly, analyzes Hess's act for what it is, and proves he was deranged from his lack of logic: the idea of landing near a castle he has never seen and whose owner, Hamilton, is not even there, etc.; and Hoare is in Madrid.[3] Then from foreign affairs standpoint, and finally the domestic repercussions. A deeply moving demonstration. Sympathy [from the Gauleiters]: 'Nothing is spared our Führer.' Afterward, lengthy discussions." Hewel concluded that Hitler was pleased he no longer had a formal deputy.

After he had finished speaking, Hitler leaned back on the big marble table in front of the Great Hall's picture window, while the sixty or seventy Gauleiters and others pressed around him in a silent semicircle. He caught sight of Gauleiter Ernst Bohle, the Bradford-born Gauleiter of all Germans abroad, and asked him pointedly, "Tell me what you knew of the affair." Bohle guiltily replied that in October Rudolf Hess had asked him to call one evening at his home in Wilhelmstrasse, sworn him to secrecy, and asked him to translate into English a letter he was writing to the Duke of Hamilton; on no account was he to tell Ribbentrop about it. Over the next three months Bohle had several times been called to Hess's office to continue work on the letter, and it was finished by January 7. At this point Hitler took Bohle aside, showed him the letters Hess had left, and asked him to point out paragraph by paragraph which passages had been in the letter Hess carried to the Duke of Hamilton. Hitler was furious that the Gauleiter had aided and abetted

---

[3] Sir Samuel Hoare was the British ambassador in Madrid.—Hitler could not have known that Hess had in fact succeeded in navigating in pitch darkness to within twelve miles of his target, had then parachuted safely (no mean feat for a man of forty-seven on his first attempt), and was actually in conversation with the Duke of Hamilton within a matter of hours. Under interrogation, Hess, speaking good English, explained that this was his fourth attempt to fly to Britain. He had got the idea when he was with the Führer during "Yellow," in June 1940. He had deliberately refrained from attempting the flight while Britain was scoring successes in Libya in case his proposals were interpreted as a sign of German weakness. With the Nazi victories in North Africa and the Balkans the sitation had, however, changed. His knowledge of the Luftwaffe's expansion plans and the submarine construction program made him confident in Germany's ultimate victory. But Hitler had no desire to inflict slaughter and defeat on Britain: From a long and intimate knowledge of the Führer which had begun eighteen years before in the fortress of Landsberg he could give his word of honor that (unlike the Americans) the Führer had never entertained any designs against the British Empire. Nor had he ever aspired to world domination. Mr. Churchill would not, however, be an acceptable negotiating partner. Hess stated that he had come unarmed and of his own free will, and he asked for his release on parole. Churchill ordered his incarceration for the rest of the war.

Hess, but Bohle cleverly cited the *Führerprinzip* in his defense: he had assumed that Hess was acting on the Führer's authority. He escaped unscathed.

Not so the rest. Haushofer joined Hess's two adjutants in a concentration camp. Hitler intervened on behalf of Frau Ilse Hess, but Bormann even had his children, Rudolf and Ilse, rechristened, and ordered his former superior's name to be expunged from the history books. Himmler, his new-found intimate, toadied to Bormann—sending him the letters Hess was writing from British captivity. Even Göring curried favor with Bormann now. Himmler took to greeting Bormann with an exaggerated affection, while the other took both Himmler's hands in his own. They were frequently on the telephone to each other. Woe betide those who fell afoul of Hess's dynamic successor, or strayed from the Party line. Precisely one year later, on May 13, 1942, Party headquarters in Munich telephoned Bormann that the obstreperous Gauleiter Carl Röver of Oldenburg was going the way Hess had gone. Following bouts of paralysis, visits by faith healers, and hallucinations, Röver had that day announced his intention of flying to see Churchill—after first calling at the Führer's headquarters—"as the whole world is mad." By that afternoon Bormann's agents were already on their way to him, armed with *"top level"* instructions. Two days later Röver had died a timely death, Hitler could order a state funeral, and Goebbels could sigh in his diary: "There goes one more member of the Old Guard." Euthanasia had its uses.

On May 12, Hitler had formally replaced Hess's old "Office of the Deputy Führer" with a Party chancellery headed by Bormann; two weeks later he conferred on him the rights of a Reich minister. Bormann now gathered powers the like of which Hess had never had, but Hitler grudged this hard-working, unobtrusive, ruthless manager none of them. A secretary overheard him command Bormann: "Just keep the Gauleiters off my back!" And the forty-year-old Bormann—who in 1930 founded the Party's financial fortunes by an insurance scheme under which millions of SA members paid thirty pfennigs monthly and stuck stamps onto a yellow card which in case of injury in the street fighting proved that they were paid up—did just that. He took the load off Hitler's mind. In alliance with the crafty constitutional expert Lammers, Bormann established a civilian bottleneck through which all state affairs had to pass on their way to Hitler; Bormann had the knack of presenting them to Hitler in a rapid, deliberate way that required only a Yes or No as answer. Hitler's whim, no sooner spoken, became a Führer Command, noted down by Bormann, elaborated by the expert lawyers he had drafted to his staff, duplicated and circulated by Party channels and teleprinters almost instantly. From eight each morning until far into the night Bormann was at Hitler's disposal; he ran the Reich while Hitler directed his war.

Bormann achieved that most dangerous of attributes—indispensability. Hitler ignored the man's sinister side and boorishness: Bormann's one and only public speech, at a Gauleiter conference, was a fiasco. Behind a steering wheel he was reckless in the extreme. Privately Hitler could never forgive Bormann for what he and the Party had done to his Obersalzberg; a future pilgrim's mecca of the worst possible taste, the Berghof was ringed by more and more buildings. The Führer even mentioned to Schaub that he was thinking of moving his permanent residence to Linz or Mohn or Bayreuth because of this. Hitler also disagreed with Bormann's approach to problems dealing with the Church and Jews. Yet Bormann survived until the end, dreaming of the day when he might step into the Führer's shoes. "Bormann clung to him like ivy around the oak," Robert Ley was to say, "using him to get to the light, and to the very summit."

Late on May 14, Ribbentrop returned from his emergency visit to Mussolini. Hewel fetched him from the airport and noted that night: "He reported this evening to the Führer up the mountain: positive." On the sixteenth and seventeenth Hitler was shown the Forschungsamt intercepts on the Italian ambassador's comments on the Hess case. Heydrich meanwhile personally interrogated Gauleiter Bohle.

For Hitler the case was already closed; his eyes again reverted east. The Second Air Force had already begun uprooting its ground organization in the west; by the end of May only a large radio-spoofing organization would remain to deceive the enemy into thinking that Kesselring was still there. On May 10 and 13 the Luftwaffe made its last mass attacks on London, causing immense damage. After that only a skeleton force of aircraft would remain to harass the British defenses and simulate invasion preparations. "Barbarossa" was to be disguised as a master deception plan: "The closer the date of the attack approaches," directed the OKW, "the cruder will be the means of deception we can employ (in the Intelligence channels as well)." The very airborne invasion of Crete was to be referred to openly as "a dress rehearsal for the invasion of Britain," and several ministries were instructed to start planning for the occupation of Britain immediately.

It was also time to start putting out cautious feelers to Russia's other bruised western neighbors. Hungary could not be approached until the last days of May, and Romania even later; but there were military reasons why Finland must be approached now. A grotesque formula had to be adopted by the OKW: despite the friendly contractual relations between Germany and Russia, there was a completely unmotivated Russian buildup on the frontier. The OKW formula explained: "This obliges Germany to concentrate forces there too. In the immediate future a political settlement is intended. If this proves impossible, it will almost certainly be necessary to apply a military settlement, if the choice of date is not to be left to Russia." The staff talks proposed with Finland would establish the basis of their cooperation should war thus break out this summer. In view of Finland's casualties in her recent war with the Soviet Union no heavy burden would be foisted onto her; it would be left to her to decide how to meet the German requests. "The course of this putative war will definitely be as follows: after Russia has lost a certain area on account of the participation of many small nations (a crusade against bolshevism) and in particular on account of the German Wehrmacht's superiority, she will be unable to fight on. The collapse in the north will come fastest and the Baltic will rapidly come into our hands. After the onset of the Russian catastrophe Germany will be the leading and impregnable power in Europe; she can cut back her army to step up Luftwaffe and naval construction programs and defeat Britain, which still rests her hopes on Russia."

Jodl proposed to the foreign ministry that Dr. Julius Schnurre, Ribbentrop's trade expert, who was on friendly terms with the Finnish prime minister and foreign minister, should go to Finland and invite her to send staff officers to Germany at once. Hewel's diary[4] of May 15 notes:

> After lunch the Chief [Ribbentrop] comes with Schnurre up the mountain. Schnurre is given instructions on discussing Russian problem in Finland, and negotiating with [Rysto] Ryti [the Finnish president]. He wants to return via Stockholm, but the Führer is very hostile toward Sweden. Says their ruling class is basically pro-British. If they did show any interest [in "Barbarossa"] then it would only be so they could immediately report what they heard to Britain. He does not want Schnurre to drop any hints at all there except that he had had talks in Finland on the Russian problem. (But even this the Reich foreign minister afterward prohibits.) Schnurre is more optimistic. The Führer reads out a memo by Paul (press department)

---

[4] These extracts are quoted at length, as the diary of the diplomat Walther Hewel has not previously been available to historians.

Schmidt, says it is much too optimistic: it also notes that it would be extremely useful if the whole of Scandinavia joined the Tripartite Pact. The Führer considers this impossible, says even the Reichsmarschall [Göring] has been cured of his infatuation for Sweden. Sweden would willingly sacrifice Finland if Germany lost the war. She is afraid of losing her dominant position in Scandinavia, of encirclement by Finland, Germany, and Norway. Russian ambitions.

Hitler instructed Schnurre to tell Ryti that he had rejected the Soviet demands on Finland during Molotov's November visit to Berlin.

On the eighteenth, French haggling for alleviation of the armistice terms in return for Vichy support in the Middle East again clouded the Berghof atmosphere. "The Führer is still nervous," an entry in Hewel's diary noted. "The French problem is acute. The Führer bitterly reproaches the foreign ministry and especially Ambassador Abetz for tossing concessions to the French; this refers particularly to the release of prisoners. A furious scene. At 7 P.M. Ribbentrop and Abetz in conference with the Führer. Führer somewhat more affable, but is still reluctant to go wholeheartedly into the French affair. Does not want to commit himself too much to France.[5] He always asks himself whether Darlan can hang on at all."

The next day Hitler was more lively and relaxed, and even found words of approval for Italy. "It is quite clear that the Duce is one of the greatest men in modern history. He has extracted from the Italian people every ounce of what there was to be extracted—and what he has extracted from the Italian people is quite marvelous. If he did not get any further, it was simply because he had reached the extreme limit of their capabilities. After him there will not be another with his energy and talents for a long time, so events in Italy will definitely run downhill later." On the following morning, May 20, as Göring's paratroops began their costly assault on the isle of Crete, Hitler drove down to Munich for two days in the quiet seclusion of his apartment there.

Anxieties gnawed within him as he pored over the great charts of Europe, trying to divine what nasty surprises the British might yet spring on him. Earlier in May he had feared the British might invade Portugal or Spain: he briefly received the Spanish ambassador and

---

[5] The fly in the ointment was always Italy, as an entry by Hewel on April 25, 1941, indicates. "Great exasperation at the Italians. Rommel in serious difficulties in Libya"—because of the Italians' failure to transport supplies to him. "Führer uses violent language. In the evening I sat in on a long discussion with the Führer. The invitation to Darlan. Führer: 'France on the one hand, Italy and Spain on the other.' "

warned him of the British activities in Morocco and told him of Abwehr reports on British plans to invade the Iberian peninsula. He took the risk seriously enough—why else should enemy propaganda be harping on alleged German designs down there?—to issue an OKW directive for a contingency plan to expel any British expeditionary force. Spain would present no problem to the Wehrmacht. But Hitler privately admitted to an adjutant, "We must remember that Franco is not a leader like Mussolini or myself—he has a much more omnipotent dictator over him than the Duce or I do, namely the Pope and the Church." Later in May, his anxieties concerned "Barbarossa": was the eastern front not suspiciously quiet now? The OKW circulated to the operations staffs a succinct warning: "The Führer again reminds you that over the coming weeks Russian preventive measures are possible and that steps must be taken in defense against these."

Grand Admiral Raeder came to see him on May 22, and the feeling of coming disaster seems to have grown even more strong within Hitler; when Raeder almost casually mentioned in a discussion of the Battle of the Atlantic that the *Bismarck* and the *Prinz Eugen* had just sailed from Gotenhafen for their first sweep in the North Atlantic, Hitler remembered all the premonitions only half-voiced in his private talk with Admiral Lütjens aboard the battleship at Gotenhafen. He complained uneasily that it seemed a great risk to run for so small a potential profit, and he mentioned Lütjens's own reservations about enemy torpedo-aircraft. He now asked Raeder outright, "Herr Grossadmiral, can't we fetch the ships back?" Raeder however advised him that the warships had already passed into the open North Sea, that enormous preparations had been made—five tankers and two auxiliary ships had been sent out in advance with submarines to rendezvous positions in the North Sea and the Atlantic. To recall the warships now would have a catastrophic effect on naval morale.[6] Hitler bowed to the admiral's experience and raised no further objections.

According to Hitler's naval adjutant, another factor in his anxiety was the wish to avoid provoking the United States by sending the most powerful battleship in the world to cruise on the threshold of its announced sphere of interest. All German policy was geared to depriving Roosevelt of any justification for war—at any rate, as yet. "War with the United States will come sooner or later," he had told his adjutants late in March. "Roosevelt, and behind him the big Jewish financiers, want war

---

[6] Raeder, who knew Hitler could not sleep when his capital ships were at sea, evidently refrained from telling him that at 6:20 A.M. the previous day a British aircraft control station was monitored reporting that RAF aircraft had just been dispatched with orders to search for "two battleships and three destroyers."

—they have no choice, because a German victory in Europe would cause the American Jews enormous capital losses in Europe. I only regret we still have no aircraft able to bomb American towns. I would dearly like to teach the Jews of America what it's like." Exasperating though Lend-Lease was, he said, it had one advantage: the Americans had given him the justification he needed for war. Hitler's policy of nonaggravation meantime did bear fruit: late in April his chargé d'affaires in Washington reported that in contrast to 1917 the American people were not demanding war, as they did not feel the Germans were provoking them. The German admiralty grudgingly conceded that the Führer's policy thus seemed justified, but the restrictions he continued to impose on the hard-pressed U-boat crews in the North and South Atlantic irked nonetheless. They were not to attack American warships or merchant ships, not to board those suspected of carrying war goods to the enemy, not to use their armament even if the Americans were flagrantly violating their neutrality—reporting German movements to the enemy, for example—unless the Americans fired the first shot. Roosevelt, whom Hitler seriously believed to be ill and perhaps even mentally unsound in consequence of his polio,[7] hinted that the American navy would start *convoying* its shipments of war supplies to Britain, which was certain to lead to open hostilities. Hitler approved Raeder's idea that the German press immediately publish an "interview" in which the admiral warned the American people of what Roosevelt's convoy idea must entail.

Hewel's diary of May 22 illustrates Hitler's dilemma over the United States.

. . . Drove up the mountain. Conference with the Chief [Ribbentrop], Raeder, and Keitel on naval strategy, convoy issue, the Raeder "interview," and on Dakar, the Canaries and *the Azores!*[8] Very interesting. The Führer still vacillates in his attitude toward America, as "you cannot peer into Roosevelt's mind." If he wants a war, he will always find the means, even if legally we are in the right. *Japan* holds the key.

This was because Japan was bound by the Tripartite Pact to declare war only if the United States was clearly the aggressor.[9]

[7] According to Julius Schaub, Hitler often discussed this possibility with his physician, Dr. Theo Morell.
[8] Hitler had more than once raised the possibility of occupying the Azores as a staging point for long-range bombers to operate against the United States, perhaps this very autumn of 1941. The navy admitted that the Azores could probably be captured, but they could not be held in the face of British and possibly even American attack.
[9] In a cable of May 23 the German military attaché in Tokyo reported that the Japanese confirmed they would declare war if the United States attacked Germany, but that they could not commence hostilities immediately as they must conclude the conflict with China first.

Even though he has still not made his mind up it is better to keep the
U.S.A. out of the war than perhaps to sink a few hundred thousand
more tons of shipping. Without the U.S.A. the war will be over this
year; with the U.S.A. it will go on for long years to come. A "warning" is agreed on.

Negative comments on Italy's warfare at sea. Mosley is on the Isle
of Man!

Six P.M. the Italians come, under [Ambassador Dino] Alfieri.
Speech on the occasion of second anniversary of the Axis pact. Tea.
Got a date for Cudahy.

John Cudahy, Roosevelt's former ambassador in Brussels and now a
Life magazine correspondent, was brought up to the Berghof next afternoon to interview Hitler for the American press. Cudahy was a rather
naïve, open-faced outsider to the world of power politics, and Hitler's
responses were short-tempered and impatient. Right at the start he
rasped, "Convoys will mean war!" and tried to put out of his visitor's
mind the "ludicrous" notion that the Nazis might ever invade the
Americas. This was just a wicked lie invented to convert American public opinion, said Hitler; indeed, he laughed out loud, dismissed it as a
childish suggestion, and exclaimed, "That is on a level with claiming
that America plans to conquer the moon!" Mindful of the propaganda
meant to distract from "Barbarossa," Hitler added that his OKW was
not planning expeditions to the moon but was busy with projects of
rather shorter range—like Crete, at a range of sixty miles, or Britain at a
range of only twenty. Hewel wrote afterward: "Three P.M., Cudahy, the
U.S. envoy in Belgium, a friend of Lindbergh's. Questions from another
world, childish, as in the years of struggle twenty years ago. But positive. Cudahy deeply impressed."

Hitler's message seems to have been understood by Roosevelt, for
overnight a change was observed in the president's belligerent stand.
Whereas on May 27 in a speech broadcast to the world Roosevelt appeared to utter a solemn commitment to enter the war, at a press conference the very next day he airily dismissed any suggestion of using his
navy to convoy shipments to Britain or of asking Congress for a change
in the Neutrality Law. Nevertheless, in his speech he had said outright,
"From the point of view of strict naval and military necessity, we shall
give every possible assistance to Britain and to all who, with Britain, are
resisting Hitlerism or its equivalent with force of arms. Our patrols are
helping now to insure delivery of the needed supplies to Britain. All additional measures necessary to deliver the goods will be taken." He had

ended the speech with a proclamation of Unlimited National Emergency.

It was a provocative speech but, as Hewel's diary shows, Ribbentrop begged Hitler not to rise to the bait. "Roosevelt speech—weak but a propaganda danger. The man must be stopped from continually getting away with it. The Chief [Ribbentrop] comes to see Führer: a long discussion on this topic. The Führer would dearly like to make a speech, if only because he gets a kick out of it. The Reich foreign minister fears it will degenerate into a mutual abuse match and that the Führer's speech won't get a hearing in the U.S.A. Backward and forward.—In the afternoon we strolled in brilliant weather to the teahouse."

Since Raeder's visit Hitler had been distracted by a domestic incident from closely following the *Bismarck*'s steady progress toward the Americas. A drunken remark made by one of the Reich's senior press officials, Professor Karl Bömer, at a Bulgarian legation reception in mid-May threatened to betray the "Barbarossa" operation. "In four weeks the Russians'll be finished. Rosenberg's going to be Governor General of Russia. I'm going to be my old boss's undersecretary." From the intercepts that resulted, Hitler found out about the incident, summoned Heydrich to the Berghof, and ordered an investigation. Bömer was arrested, but Goebbels sprang to his defense and Heydrich found no evidence of deliberate or accidental treason. Hitler was not satisfied: he wanted Bömer's blood and ordered him tried by the People's Court. "From now on I will take ruthless action against everybody who can't hold his tongue!" Bömer ended up in a punishment battalion on the eastern front.

In Crete the bloody struggle for the island, launched on May 22, was approaching its climax. At Iráklion (Candia) some Greek companies had even joined the German paratroops in fighting the British: war was full of surprises. Late on May 24, Raeder telephoned from Berlin. On leaving the Denmark Straits south of Iceland, the *Bismarck* had stumbled on two British battleships sent to intercept her. She had dispatched the *Hood*—Churchill's most powerful battleship—in less than five minutes. The other British battleship, the *Prince of Wales,* had suffered heavy damage and turned away. But the elation at the Berghof was diminished as further signals came from the admiralty. The *Bismarck* herself had been hit twice, though without casualties, and she was bleeding oil; her speed was reduced, and the British warships seemed to be operating some kind of radar, a possibility not previously admitted. Admiral Lütjens proposed to put into the French port of Saint-Nazaire, leaving the *Prinz Eugen* to continue by herself into the Atlantic, but he could not shake off the pursuing enemy warships. He suggested that Dönitz marshal all available submarines in one area through which he would try to lure the enemy, but next day he announced that his oil was so low that he must steer directly for Saint-Nazaire.

By now the German admiralty knew that every enemy warship from Scapa Flow had sailed against the crippled *Bismarck*. Late on the twenty-fourth Lütjens had reported the first air strikes, so the British aircraft carrier *Victorious* was clearly within range. At the Berghof, Hewel noted: "Frightening hours on the *Bismarck*'s account." Further torpedo attacks were delivered by the aircraft during the midnight hours, but Lütjens dismissed them as "unimportant." By noon of the twenty-fifth, he had at last managed to shake off his pursuers. But for how long? From radio monitoring it was clear the British were throwing all they had into pinning the *Bismarck* down. Göring ordered his commanders to push out air cover as far as possible toward the limping battleship, but the range of his aircraft was insufficient. Hitler grimly radioed Lütjens greetings on his birthday. The mood at the Berghof was further soured by the presence of Heydrich and Goebbels, who were wrangling over the Bömer affair.

When Hitler rose on the twenty-sixth the news awaiting him was that the *Bismarck* had been found by the enemy; shadowed by an enemy aircraft, she still had six hundred miles to go to Brest. Soon after 9 P.M. Lütjens radioed that the aircraft had scored torpedo hits amidships and astern, and at 9:50 came the dread news that the battleship's steering was out of action: the unsinkable *Bismarck* was afloat and her guns were primed, but at best she could only steer a slow and stately circle while the British battle fleet closed in. From radio monitoring, the German admiralty identified at least four battleships and two aircraft carriers closing for the kill; the stormy seas prevented Raeder's destroyers from putting to sea, and Dönitz's submarines were too far off to engage the enemy in time. Shortly before midnight, Lütjens radioed: "Ship unmaneuverable. We are fighting to the last shell. Long live the Führer!" And to Hitler himself, he signaled: "We shall fight to the end trusting in you, mein Führer, and with our faith in Germany's victory undestroyed." Hitler instructed the admiralty to reply, "All Germany is with you. What can be done will be done. The way you do your duty will strengthen our nation in its fight for survival. Adolf Hitler."

During the early hours of May 27 the Luftwaffe scoured the area and ventured ineffectual attacks on British cruisers and destroyers. Ocean-going tugs put to sea. The Spanish government was asked to send out rescue ships. Lütjens's last radio message had come at 6:25 A.M.: "Position unchanged. Windstrength 8 to 9." From then onward there was silence. A funereal gloom descended over the Berghof. An adjutant's wife whispered that mourning clothes might seem in order. At noon Hitler learned that the British government had announced the sinking of the *Bismarck* an hour before.

Disabled and her last ammunition spent, the *Bismarck* had proved unsinkable to the end. She had scuttled herself under the guns of the British navy and sank with her colors honorably flying and the loss of some twenty-three hundred lives. Hitler's sorrow turned to anger. The OKW received instructions that no battleship or cruiser was to put to sea without his previous consent. The gallant Admiral Lütjens had himself warned in one of his last signals that the enemy use of naval radar would force a revision of the German navy's Atlantic cruiser warfare strategy. Hewel wrote on May 27:

> *Bismarck* sunk. Mood very dejected. Führer melancholy beyond words. Uncontrollable fury at the naval staff:
> 1. The ship should never have been sent out raiding;
> 2. After finishing off the *Hood* she should have dealt with the *Prince of Wales* too, and not run away;
> 3. She should have returned straight to Norway and not run straight into the lions' den.
> Red tape and wooden-headedness in the navy. Won't tolerate any man with a mind of his own.
> Reich foreign minister comes in the afternoon. Führer speaks his mind to him, swears and curses and then calms down. A walk to the teahouse. The Führer picks up again, talks about new types of ships and the airborne torpedo as a weapon.

Raeder answered Hitler's criticisms soberly when he next came to the Berghof; he particularly emphasized that for the *Bismarck* to have returned through the northern passages to Norway would have been more risky than continuing into the Atlantic. Hitler asked the admiralty to adopt a policy of conservation of strength until the effect of "Barbarossa" on Britain was known. "Should Britain's collapse threaten to become imminent, some very important duties might present themselves to our surface warships." Though Hitler did not admit it, the *Bismarck*'s loss had certainly not been in vain. She had drawn off no fewer than eight battleships, two aircraft carriers, eleven cruisers, and twenty-one destroyers, creating a diversion which more than ensured the successful conclusion of the invasion of Crete; and the capture of Crete in turn reduced Britain's naval influence in the Mediterranean and paved the way for Rommel's future triumphs in North Africa.

Hitler meanwhile had issued a belated OKW directive ordering support for the Arab "liberation movement" against Britain. Jodl's chief assistant, General Warlimont, had been sent to Paris for a week to resume the military talks broken off in December, and a protocol had been signed granting the French concessions in return for assistance in Syria and Iraq, as well as the future use of the Tunisian port of Bizerte to supply Rommel's troops in North Africa; more reluctantly, the French agreed on principle to let Hitler operate their port at Dakar as a submarine and Luftwaffe base on the west coast of Africa. They also secretly agreed to remove General Weygand from his command, though this was not specifically mentioned in the protocol. It was signed in Paris on the twenty-eighth, and the next day Warlimont flew to the Berghof to report.

Events in Iraq were overtaking Hitler, however. The British were already advancing on Baghdad, and the end could not be far off. In private Hitler cursed the "banqueting diplomats" who had misinformed him. "Unfortunately the Arabs are unreliable and venal. The British and French have grasped that fact. But we cannot give a helping hand everywhere. The Middle East by itself would have been no problem if our other plans"—meaning "Barbarossa"—"were not irrevocable. When they succeed, we can open a door into the Middle East from there." Mussolini was opposed to abandoning the Iraqi rebels and sent word to Hitler thus: "I, Mussolini, am in favor of active support, as this is an opportunity to raise the entire population of the Middle East against Britain. But if Iraq collapses, they will all lose heart again. If the German High Command also decides on active support, then it seems to me necessary to occupy Cyprus as well—after the reduction of Crete and Rhodes—since it lies off the Syrian coastline and holds the key to the entire Middle East." With Crete and Cyprus in Axis hands, the British fleet could scarcely stay safely in Alexandria; the Duce felt the capture of Cyprus would be easier than that of Crete as it was less mountainous and not so heavily fortified. Hitler's first reaction was an outburst: "Mussolini thinks Cyprus should be taken now as well!" And Hewel recorded: "The Führer proposes to agree, and to tell him to do it himself." Nonetheless, Hitler did ask Göring and Jeschonnek whether

Cyprus would be possible. The Reichsmarschall winced, reported on the blood the Luftwaffe had lost over Crete—150 Junkers 52 transports alone—and advised against invading Cyprus. "Since war broke out the Luftwaffe has known no rest. From Crete we shall now be fighting a pitched battle against the British fleet and Tobruk."

Hewel made a lengthy record of Hitler's worried conference with Ribbentrop and the OKW generals on May 29:

> The point under debate is how far to bring in France or to get her involved in a war with Britain. The Führer's view is that the French will only fight, and Weygand will only stay loyal, if they know that they can thereby retain the French empire and are persuaded that the soil on which they fight will by that fight remain French. If Syria could be isolated from the rest, this could be done; but it cannot be isolated, it has to be regarded in its larger context: Syria, Tunisia, Algeria, Morocco, and Dakar. The French are making Bizerte available to us in Tunisia. But now the Italians also want a port there "on principle." Obviously they want to get their foot in the door there, and this is why the French will never give way. . . .
>
> The Führer curses the Italians. He hates the Spanish. Of Italy he says that you can't keep making concessions to somebody who is always running around with his bottom black and blue from beatings, nor will the German people stand for it. And on top of that they are an arrogant bunch. . . . The Führer's view is that when "Barbarossa" is over, he won't need to pay any more attention to Italy! We will then automatically be able to come together with the French. They are counting on kicking the Italians out of Tunisia after the war. He wants to have a talk with Mussolini shortly.

Later that day the foreign ministry's Dr. Julius Schnurre expounded at length but with precision on Finland and Sweden. The Finns had sent generals to negotiate with the OKW and the General Staff in Germany; they had been asked to prepare two divisions to support the operations of Hitler's army in Norway against northern Russia. " 'Barbarossa' is a gamble like everything else," said Hitler after Schnurre left. "If it fails, then it will all be over anyway. If it succeeds, it will have created a situation that will probably force Britain to make peace. What will the United States have to say when all at once Finland is on our side! When the first shot is fired, the world will hold its breath."

Pricking the Bubble

The dazzling heat of high summer had come to the Berghof. It was now early June 1941: with a suddenness that caused an almost perceptible lurch the last echelon of assault troops had set out from Germany for the eastern front—the twelve panzer divisions and twelve mechanized divisions whose location by an enemy must surely unmask Hitler's true intentions beyond all doubt. In less than three weeks "Barbarossa" would begin. It was time to start dropping hints to his prospective allies.

Hitler's last major anxieties had been overcome. Crete was in German and Italian hands. Only Iraq remained a "blemish," though through no fault of Germany's. Rashid Ali had fled to Iran, and the victorious British were evidently regrouping for an invasion of Syria. Yet Hitler was not downhearted. "If we tote up the results of two years of war," he told Göring, "it has to be said: 'There's got to be a limit somewhere.' Iraq was a blemish—so what? I cannot help it. After all, I am not an Arab and the Arabs are no Germans. All in all the Arabs did right"— meaning in their rebellion against the British, now shown to have been premature. "If they had waited any longer, more and more British would have poured in and a coup d'etat would have been quite impossible."

His nagging suspicions about Japan had also been removed. A few weeks before, he had been unsettled by rumors that Washington was offering Japan a nonaggression pact; he had examined this risk from every angle with Ribbentrop here at the Berghof, for both realized that such a pact would be an open invitation to Roosevelt to intervene in the European war. Admiral Kichisaburo Nomura had privately warned Hitler through Raeder that Japan's naval construction program would not allow her to tackle her Far Eastern problem until 1946, as only then would she be strong enough to take on Britain and the United States. To

Hitler Japan's Foreign Minister Matsuoka was dangerously inscrutable. "He combines the hypocrisy of an American Bible missionary with all the wiles of a Japanese oriental," he told Mussolini. But at the end of May he breathed again when Matsuoka loudly proclaimed his unswerving allegiance to the Tripartite Pact.

The first hint was dropped to Mussolini, but the dictator seems not to have grasped its meaning and Hitler did not repeat it. He had asked the Duce to join him at the Brenner Pass on June 2. Hewel accompanied Hitler's party. "Journeyed in wonderful weather to the Brenner. Arrival at 10:15 A.M., followed by talks and lunch at 2:30." Hitler talked alone with Mussolini for two hours before the two dictators were joined by their foreign ministers. When at four o'clock the train set out again for Berchtesgaden, Hewel sat with the Führer. "He is contented; says Mussolini is very confident and sure of victory. Has dropped a hint on Russia 'if the shipping losses alone do not suffice,'" meaning suffice to knock Britain out of the war. No whisper of his latent inclinations to do a deal postwar with France at Italy's expense came through, but he did talk to Mussolini of the possibility that David Lloyd George might succeed a defeated Churchill. "Then we must see what possibility there is of settling our differences."

To the Japanese ambassador, General Oshima, whom he urgently summoned to the Berghof the next day, Hitler put on the appropriate "anti-British" act. Oshima correctly interpreted Hitler's hint at "Barbarossa" and after being lectured by Ribbentrop as well, he personally cabled Matsuoka in strictest confidence. "Both gentlemen gave me to understand that a German-Soviet war probably cannot be avoided." Hitler had bluntly stated on the third that he would always be the first to draw his sword if he detected any hostility in an opponent, and although he did not expressly say so, his remarks to Oshima implied that while the Tripartite Pact was *expressis verbis* not intended as an instrument against the Soviet Union, such was the obligation on Japan—and he would expect the Japanese to honor it. Ribbentrop assured Oshima that the campaign would be over in two or three months—he could not say when it would begin, but "if Japan should find it necessary to prepare for this eventuality, then he would advise her to do so in as short a time as possible." On June 4, Hitler received King Boris of Bulgaria for two hours. Hewel took notes on the encounter, but they appear to have been lost, and since the Bulgarian records fell into Soviet hands in the course of the events Hitler was about to unleash, we are unlikely ever to learn what they discussed.

Now the Soviet Union began to reap the harvest of the hatred she had sown. The Finns confirmed to German officers sent to Helsinki that they were aware of the "historic hour" that was dawning and they would provide Finnish troops, territory, and airfields to assist in "Barbarossa." Antonescu came to Munich and again offered to support the attack with all the military and other resources at Romania's disposal. Even the Turks, Britain's last formal ally, were softening under Papen's pressure, and a treaty with Germany, the victor of the Balkans, was in the cards. Perhaps the activities of the British sabotage agencies influenced them. Not many weeks before, the Turks had intercepted a British launch laden with sabotage materials and explosives heading for their coast; in addition, Turkish police had uncovered a British sabotage ring in Istanbul. In Crete the Germans had uncovered a veritable arsenal of explosives in the house of the British vice-consul at Iráklion, a Major Pendlebury. Pendlebury—real name Kustos—was head of the British secret service in central Crete. His private diary revealed that British secret service headquarters in London had instructed its agents to ignore the prevailing laws and conventions of war.

As for himself, operating on the principle that no questions are asked of the victor, Hitler authorized orders to his Wehrmacht—even in advance of "Barbarossa"—which were so shocking that Keitel later had all copies of them destroyed. Hitler's staff, however, accepted the idea that such orders were necessary. His naval adjutant had himself seen how mercilessly the Reds fought in the Baltic states in 1919. Jodl—convinced that Hitler was of impeccable morality and pursuing only one lofty ideal, a German victory—also decided that his orders were to be obeyed whatever their character.

The decision to liquidate the political commissars attached to Red Army units was to Hitler a logical extension of the fight against the tentacles of Soviet authority—the eradication of the ruling classes. The commissars could be identified as such by the red star embroidered with a golden hammer and sickle on their sleeves. Evidently at Hitler's dictation, Jodl drafted an explanation of the decision to liquidate the commissars (though not all of them). The Bolsheviks could not be counted on to fight "humanely." The commissars in particular would subject German prisoners to spiteful, cruel, and inhuman treatment, for they were the "originators of these barbaric Asiatic fighting methods."

Hitler ordered: "If they are caught fighting or offering resistance, they are to be shot out of hand without exception and immediately." They were francs-tireurs and as such not entitled to be recognized as soldiers. The less active commissars, defined as "political commissars guilty or suspected of committing no hostile acts," were to be spared: Rosenberg had pointed out that initially he would be needing many of the top Russian officials to help him administer the eastern territories. General Warlimont sent out this document, although it was evidently never signed by Hitler, directing the army and Luftwaffe that the orders it contained were to be passed on only by word of mouth below a certain command level.

The role played by Halder and the army General Staff, not to mention the German military lawyers, in drafting these orders was less than glorious. After Hitler had undoubtedly given the initial impetus in his blunt secret speech of March 30,[1] Brauchitsch's staff had drafted two separate orders in weeks of tedious bureaucratic paperwork and discussed them with the OKW. The first was this commissar order, and the second an order restricting the jurisdiction of courts-martial on Russian soil (basically to enable the SS task forces to operate at will). The army wanted Russian civilians to be subject to military law, while the OKW lawyers and General Jeschonnek recalled that Hitler had always been irked by the ponderous procedures of the army courts, believing that only speedy conviction and execution was a true deterrent. It was Halder, however, who proposed the clause reading: "Immediate collective punishments will be enforced against towns and villages from which ambushes or treacherous attacks on the Wehrmacht are made, on the orders of an officer of not less than battalion commander's rank, if circumstances do not permit the rapid arrest of the individual perpetrators." Apart from this, the army's arguments were ignored. In the formal order issued by Keitel on Hitler's behalf in May, the Wehrmacht was instructed that offenses against Russian civilians would *not* be punishable by courts-martial; that francs-tireurs were to be wiped out in battle or "trying to escape." This aroused intense feeling among the army commands. In May, Brauchitsch partially qualified the order by issuing a supplementary order on the maintenance of army discipline, but many of his frontline generals were sick at heart when these two "Barbarossa" orders reached them.

To Hitler, however, the Red Army was not an enemy to be handled with kid gloves. In a Berghof conference on June 5 he again warned his staff of the extensive use the Russians would make of tactics not sanc-

[1] See page 231 above.

tioned by international convention, and he ordered printed instructions to be prepared for the troops—though not distributed as yet, so as not to put ideas into the enemy's head. Hitler anticipated that the Russians might, for example, contaminate long stretches of their roads of retreat with poison gases, or use poisonous additives to spike the food stocks and fresh-water supplies or kill livestock in the areas overrun by the Wehrmacht.

Hitler prepared to leave the Berghof, resolved perhaps not to return until Russia had been defeated. He had recently taken to gathering his friends, his adjutants, and their wives about him in the evenings and rambling on endlessly about Christianity and the Roman Empire. On June 8, Hewel entered in his Berghof diary:

> Raining. The British are marching into Syria. A long conversation alone with the Führer about Russia. Says it will be a "tough proposition" but he trusts in the Wehrmacht. [Russian] air force: numerical superiority in fighters and bombers. He is a bit frightened of air raids on Berlin and Vienna. "The area we are to occupy will not be much bigger than from Denmark to Bordeaux in size. Russians have massed their entire strength on their western frontier, the biggest concentration in history. If "Barbarossa" goes wrong now, we are all lost anyway. As soon as that is all over, Iraq and Syria will take care of themselves. Then I will have a free hand, and I will be able to thrust on down through Turkey as well.
>
> If the French lose Syria—and I am convinced that Syria *is* lost—then there is only the one danger left, that they will lose Algeria as well. If that happens, I will thrust straight down through Spain at once and barricade the Mediterranean against the British. It is just this wretched waiting that makes one so nervous!

A few days later the OKW asked the supreme commanders for their views on a draft directive for the period after "Barbarossa": basically, after sixty divisions and one Luftflotte had been left astride the territories won in the east, the remaining military units would be used to feed manpower back into the naval and Luftwaffe construction industries and to coerce France, Spain, Turkey, and Iran into joining the fight against Britain. A contested invasion of Britain itself was not contemplated in this document. On the eleventh, Hitler sent Schmundt to check if the headquarters being built for him near Rastenburg in East Prussia was ready.

Luftwaffe reconnaissance photographs showed some four thousand

Russian aircraft packing the airfields just across the frontier; radio reconnaissance suggested over a thousand more were waiting farther back. On the diplomatic front something akin to hysteria was overtaking Moscow as the realization of Hitler's mobilization dawned: the Russian shipments to Germany were stepped up; false rumors of German political demands on the Soviet Union multiplied; troop movements and the widespread call-up of Russian reservists were noticed. On June 9 the German embassy in Moscow smuggled a naval officer into a Communist party indoctrination session at which a functionary delivered a violently anti-German talk warning his audience to be on guard over the next few weeks. The speaker said that nobody in Moscow had expected Hitler to conquer the Balkans so rapidly, but once the war became a war of raw materials like petroleum and ore, Germany would be at a disadvantage; for bolshevism, the advantage was that any war of attrition must lead to the annihilation of the middle classes. The Soviet Union's interests would best be served by a period of national peace—while the rest of Europe bled white in war.

Hitler arrived back in Berlin early on June 13 obsessed with the coming campaign. Again he told Hewel his belief that "Barbarossa" must mean the end of Britain's resistance. In his diary Hewel judged the prospects more soberly: "I cannot share this belief, as the British will regard it as a weakening of Germany for a long time to come." In Berlin Dr. Goebbels reported to Hitler on the pre-"Barbarossa" propaganda campaign. Goebbels himself had told his staff that the planned eastern campaign was canceled, and that since the invasion of Britain was imminent, they must now prepare for that eventuality. Through Party channels a wave of rumors had been sent swirling around Germany—that Stalin was to visit Germany, or that he had agreed to lease the Ukraine to Germany for ninety-nine years. On the morning of Hitler's arrival in Berlin the police raided every newspaper outlet in the capital and seized the latest *Völkischer Beobachter;* but enough copies escaped seizure for the impression to be conveyed that in Goebbels's leading article, "Crete as an Example," he had unwittingly betrayed that within two months Britain would be invaded and "Mr. Churchill would be laughing on the other side of his face." But Goebbels was not in disgrace for this lapse—he was seen next day in Hitler's residence, cackling out loud over the success of his rumor-mongering, and the Führer was laughing uproariously and slapping his thigh at each fresh detail of his canny propaganda minister's devices.

It was Saturday the fourteenth. The Reich Chancellery was packed with the Wehrmacht commanders summoned for an all-day series of briefing conferences on the coming campaign. Secrecy was essential, so (paradoxically) uniforms were to be worn. Everybody was assigned different street-entrances by which to arrive at the sprawling Reich Chancellery complex, so that passersby might not sense the urgency of the conferences proceeding behind the tall granite walls that Albert Speer had built three years before. Brauchitsch would arrive through the garden gate in Hermann-Göringstrasse, Göring would enter through Wilhelmstrasse, and the army group commanders through the New Chancellery in Vossstrasse; the first would arrive shortly before 11 A.M., the last just before lunch.

At two o'clock Hitler broke for lunch, which he took sitting at a long oval-shaped table with twenty-eight of his top generals. An hour later he called for silence and spoke of his military reasons for attacking Russia. An unpublished note taken by a Luftwaffe general survives:

Hitler's after-luncheon speech. The main enemy is still Britain. Britain will fight on as long as the fight has any purpose; this is typical of the British, as we have seen from their individual soldier's conduct in Flanders, and it was demonstrated again by Dunkirk, by Greece, and by Crete. But Britain's fight only makes sense as long as they can hope that American aid will take effect and that they may find support on the continent. This explains why they have high hopes that the Russians will intervene and tie down the Germans, wearing down our war economy while the balance of power is tilted by American aid. At present this is very meager; it will not become effective until the summer of 1942, assuming they have enough shipping tonnage to bring it over here; and the shipping losses are increasing.

The proof of [Britain's] advances to Russia is the complete uniformity in their press treatment of Cripps's journey.[2] Russia's attitude is perpetually obscure; she exploited every moment of political or military preoccupation elsewhere to raise immediate political demands. We can see this happening in Russia's intervention in the Polish campaign, and again against the Baltic states and Finland, and now in the Balkans (Bessarabia, and the treaty of friendship with Yugoslavia).

Our attempt to "clarify the position" met with the following objections from Molotov. First question, What does our guarantee to Romania mean and would we object to a Russian military mission? Second question concerning the Dardanelles, and the third about Finland. In other words continual efforts to push in somewhere. Since these efforts coincided chronologically with various temporary weaknesses in the German position, we would have to expect them to use every chance they can in the future to act against Germany's in-

---

[2] The British ambassador, Sir Stafford Cripps, had left Moscow a week before to consult with the foreign office in London.

terests. The Russian armed forces are strong enough to prevent us from demobilizing soldiers and feeding them into the arms and consumer-goods industries so long as this latent Russian threat persists. Even if we made peace with Britain this would still be so. We want this conflict to come early, however; indeed it is absolutely vital if we are not to forfeit the favorable conditions that prevail. The bulk of the Russian forces are standing on the frontier, so we have a good chance of defeating them right there.

Hitler rounded off his speech with a warning that the Russian forces outnumbered the German, but that German command leadership, equipment, and experience were superior. Even so, he warned them against underestimating the Red Army.

It was probably on this occasion that when Göring loudly proclaimed to a cluster of other generals that this would be a victory on the same scale as those that Hitler had already won, the Führer took him by the arm and soberly corrected him. "Göring, it will be our toughest struggle yet—by far the toughest!" Göring asked him why, and Hitler replied, "Because for the first time we shall be fighting an *ideological* enemy, and an ideological enemy of fanatical persistence at that." Three years later Hitler ruefully reminded his generals of these words.

The old familiar bouts of insomnia began to attack him as the last days before "Barbarossa" dragged by. By night he lay awake and asked himself what loopholes in his grand design the British might yet exploit. He believed he had plugged them all: he had sent Göring's deputy, Milch, on an extended tour of Germany's air raid defenses; he had ordered an urgent reinforcement of Holland's coastal defenses; and suspecting that his successful paratroop operation against Crete might stimulate the British to similar ventures against the Norwegian coast or the two Channel Isles as soon as his hands were tied in Russia, he had ordered the island garrisons increased and extensively reinforced with tanks and artillery—the more so as he intended to keep Guernsey and Jersey in German hands after the final peace treaty with Britain. Yet Hitler could still only get to sleep with sedatives, even after staying up until three or four each morning discussing Turkey, Russia, war, and warfare with dutiful but weary henchmen like Himmler, Ley, Hewel, Ribbentrop, and Seyss-Inquart.

On June 18, with the newspapers of every country but Germany openly asking when Hitler's attack on the Soviet Union would begin, the Russians unwittingly caused him his most anxious hours ever when the

Soviet ambassador in Berlin, Dekanozov, asked for an interview with Ribbentrop's state secretary, Baron von Weizsäcker. Hewel, at Hitler's Chancellery, wrote an agitated note in his diary: "Big problem: Dekanozov has announced he is to see the state secretary. What is he bringing? Is Stalin going to bring off a major coup even now? A big offer to us, etc. etc.? [Führer has] a long discussion with foreign minister; Engel [Hitler's army adjutant] and myself going over every possible angle. The Führer and foreign minister will have to vanish—so they can't be reached. Much plotting: Sonnenburg, Karinhall, or Berghof; the train; Wildpark.³ Then one day lying low in the Reich Chancellery." Hewel concluded the entry as follows: "These last days before an action are the most nerve-racking: something unexpected can still occur." The next evening, however, as Hitler was in the middle of dictating his "Barbarossa" proclamation—"To the Troops of the Eastern Front!"—Ribbentrop telephoned that Dekanozov had called on his state secretary at 6 P.M., had discussed purely routine affairs, and had left after cracking a few jokes.

The proclamation was printed and issued secretly to the services on the twentieth. This time its language must have been far above the average soldier's head—it was a *tour d'horizon* of Germany's foreign policy since the war began in 1939; but in its four closely printed pages there were some lines worthy of attention. Here Hitler even claimed that the German people had never wished ill to the inhabitants of Russia. "But for two decades the Jewish-Bolshevik rulers of Moscow have endeavored to set not only Germany but all Europe alight." Hitler said he had never tried to export the Nazi ideology to Russia the way the Kremlin had tried to convert the rest of Europe to communism by means of subversion. In a cynical oversimplification, Hitler reminded his troops: "You, my soldiers, know for yourselves that until a very few weeks ago there was not one German panzer or mechanized division on our eastern frontier." The historic proclamation ended:

At this moment, soldiers of the eastern front, an assembly of strength the like of which in size and scale the world has never seen is now complete. In league with Finnish divisions, our comrades are standing with the Victor of Narvik [Dietl] on the shores of the Arctic in the north. German soldiers under the command of the Conquerer of Norway [Falkenhorst], and the Finnish heroes of freedom under their own Marshal [Mannerheim] are protecting Finland. On the eastern front stand you. In Romania, on the banks of the Prut, and along the

---

³ Sonnenburg was Ribbentrop's country home; Karinhall was Göring's; Wildpark was the site of Luftwaffe headquarters, outside Potsdam.

Danube right down to the beaches of the Black Sea are German and Romanian troops united under Antonescu, the head of state. When this, the biggest front line in history, now begins its advance it does so not just to provide the means of ending for all time this great war, or to defend those countries currently concerned, but for the salvation of our entire European civilization and culture.

German soldiers! You are thus entering upon a harsh and demanding fight—because the fate of Europe, the future of the German Reich, the existence of our nation now rest on your hands alone.

May the Lord God help us all in this struggle.

At the same time he ordered Jodl to advise the Wehrmacht by the prearranged code word that the attack would begin, as planned, early on June 22. Hewel wrote: "A long conversation with the Führer. Expects a lot of the Russian campaign. Wishes he was ten weeks on from hence. After all there must always be a big element of risk. We are standing outside a locked door. [Will we run into] secret weapons? The tenacity of the fanatic? He now has to take sleeping pills to fall asleep. He is still dictating. He told me that this morning [June 20] he again pored over every minute detail, but found no possibility for the enemy to get the better of Germany. He thinks Britain will have to give in—and he hopes it will be before the year is over."

The coming occupation of fresh territories in the east suggested to Hitler an alternative solution of the "Jewish problem." Since the summer of 1940 experts in the foreign ministry had studied the possibility of settling Europe's uprooted Jews on the island of Madagascar. On June 2, 1941, Hitler told Mussolini that after the war every Jew must get out of Europe. "Perhaps we can settle them in Madagascar. Considering our own population density, the island could find room for fifteen million people." (Madagascar is over twice as big as Britain or West Germany; its prewar population was four million.) Hitler did not want the Jews to remain in their present settlement region around Lublin, as the standards of hygiene resulting from the living conditions now imposed on them raised the danger of epidemics. But for the duration of the war the Madagascar plan was out. Hans Frank's Generalgouvernement of Poland would have to accommodate Europe's displaced Jews for the time being. On October 2, 1940, Hitler had discussed this with Frank and Baldur von Schirach, Gauleiter of Vienna. Schirach pointed out that his fifty thousand Viennese Jews were the first due for deportation. Frank reported that Warsaw and other Polish cities had concentrated their

Jews in restricted areas—"ghettos"—and complained that he had no accommodation available for a fresh influx of Jews. But Hitler had dreamed of ridding Europe of the "Jewish plague" since 1921, if not earlier, and he had strong popular support for this program in the Reich. The German army commander of Vienna wrote to the war department in February 1941 welcoming the deportations, as he considered the Jews the principal rumor-mongers; he asked only that an exception should be made for former Jewish officers wounded in World War I. Hitler agreed.

Thus Hitler overrode Hans Frank's practical objections to using the Generalgouvernement as a dumping ground. The problem with the Madagascar plan in wartime was, he told Martin Bormann, how to transport the Jews that far. "I would dearly like to devote my entire fleet of *Kraft durch Freude* (strength through joy) ocean liners[4] to it, but in wartime that's not so easy. I don't want my German crews being sunk by enemy torpedoes." In private—to Keitel, Bormann, and Speer—Hitler described it as his eventual ambition to eliminate all Jewish influence throughout the Axis domains. It would solve many of the infuriating legalistic problems still bogged down in the ministries of Justice and the Interior, about the rights of Jews in the law courts, the status of half-Jews, etc. On June 7, 1941, Dr. Hans Lammers wrote to Martin Bormann: "The main reason why the Führer has not approved the ruling proposed by the Ministry of the Interior is that in his opinion there won't be any Jews left in Germany after the war anyway."

As "Operation Barbarossa" approached, it occurred to Hitler that the new eastern empire would enable him to humor Hans Frank's loud objections to the dumping of Jews on his Generalgouvernement territory and Himmler's growing influence there. Three days before the Wehrmacht attacked Russia, Hitler announced this explicitly to Frank; and the latter accordingly briefed his staff that no fresh ghettos were to be established, "since the Führer expressly stated to me on June 19 that in due course the Jews will be removed from the Generalgouvernement—and that the Generalgouvernement is to be, so to speak, only a transit camp." Seven months later, the Madagascar plan died a natural death. A foreign ministry official would then write: "The war against the Soviet Union has meanwhile made it possible to provide other territories for the final solution. Accordingly, the Führer has decided that the Jews are not to be deported to Madagascar but to the east."

What exactly did Hitler mean by "east" of the Generalgouvernement? On the twentieth, Rosenberg had revealed to Canaris, Heydrich, and a

---

[4] Pleasure liners built by and for the mass German labor union, DAF.

host of other Party and Wehrmacht leaders that White Ruthenia—the area around Minsk—was to be set aside for "undesirables" and antisocial elements from Germany's dominions. Was this to be the new Israel, or did Hitler now use "east" just as a vague generic term, whose more precise definition would be: perdition, oblivion, extermination? The documents at our disposal do not help us.

Two days remained, and Russia was still an enigma behind a sealed door. During a coffee break snatched with his female secretaries in their "stair cupboard" in the Chancellery, Hitler noted that there was something sinister about Russia—something that reminded him of the ghost ship in *The Flying Dutchman*. And when Fräulein Schroeder, a clever, critical, and often dangerously outspoken thirty-three-year-old stenographer who had loyally served Martin Bormann before attracting Hitler's attention in 1933, asked why the Führer kept emphasizing how the "Barbarossa" decision had been the toughest he had ever taken, Hitler frankly replied, "Because we know absolutely nothing about Russia. It might be one big soap-bubble, but it might just as well turn out to be very different."

At 9 P.M. on June 20, Colonel Schmundt, his Wehrmacht adjutant, brought news from the admiralty that showed how fragile was the thread restraining the whole world from war. A German submarine had proudly reported attempting to attack the U.S. battleship *Texas,* since it was encountered ten miles within the North Atlantic blockade zone proclaimed by Germany. Hitler cannot have been pleased, for as recently as June 6 he had patiently explained to Admiral Raeder why he wanted to do everything possible to avoid incidents with the United States. On top of this, a U-boat sank the American freighter *Robin Moore* outside the Atlantic blockade zone, claiming it was carrying contraband goods for the enemy. The U.S. government protested less loudly than the U.S. press—Raeder attributed this to his forthright warnings in May—but again Hitler directed that "for political reasons incidents with the United States are to be avoided completely for the time being."

On the *Texas* incident, Raeder stated the U-boat had acted quite correctly, though he now proposed forbidding attacks on American warships up to twenty miles inside the blockade zone, to rule out navigational errors. Hitler at first agreed, but during the night he had second thoughts and telephoned the admiralty that no attacks whatever were to be made on American warships anywhere in the blockade zone. The following afternoon Raeder came in person to argue against this. The two incidents were a warning to Roosevelt that Germany meant business. Hitler would not budge; there must be no incidents with the United States until the outcome of "Barbarossa" was clear. The same order was issued to the Luftwaffe.

Less than twelve hours remained of the last, tense day before the attack. The foreign ministry telephoned with the unsettling news that the Soviet ambassador was again urgently demanding to see Ribbentrop. The foreign minister became unavailable: Dekanozov was fobbed off with word that he was away from Berlin until evening and that an appointment would be made on his return. In fact Ribbentrop was in the Chancellery and paid several visits to Hitler. Hitler was dictating a proclamation for home consumption and letters to Mussolini, Horthy, and Finland's President Rysto Ryti.

During the afternoon the German naval attaché, who had left Moscow late on the nineteenth (his recall was in response to the fact that the Russians had suddenly recalled their naval attaché from Berlin) arrived by train in the Reich capital and rendered a vivid description of the panic that had broken out in Moscow diplomatic circles; nevertheless, on returning by rail through Poland he had seen less military activity than at any time over the last four months, and certainly far less than he had observed in the Baltic countries recently. Both he and his assistant, who arrived back in Berlin the next day, encountered closed prison trains escorted by blue-uniformed GPU troops—evacuating Polish "undesirables" from eastern Poland. Ambassador Schulenburg meanwhile remained in Moscow. Ribbentrop cabled him to destroy the embassy's code books and radio equipment and to arrange an immediate interview with Molotov at which he was to read out a long rigamarole ending with the words ". . . the Führer has therefore ordered the German Wehrmacht to stand up to this menace with all the means of force at its disposal."

At nine-thirty, Dekanozov was allowed to see Ribbentrop's state secretary. To everybody's relief he was only delivering a formal Soviet complaint about repeated violations of its air space. The parallel complaint delivered simultaneously by Molotov to Schulenburg sounded so wistful that it brought the house down in Hitler's Chancellery when the telegram was read out upon its arrival there in the small hours of the morning. "A series of symptoms gives us the impression that the German government is dissatisfied with the Soviet government . . ." grumbled Molotov. One hour later, along a frontier extending from the Arctic Ocean to the Black Sea, over three million German troops, supported by three thousand tanks and nearly two thousand aircraft, attacked the USSR. Surprise was complete.

His thoughts far from the Chancellery, Hitler sat up with his private staff far into the night. Then he briefly retired to bed, remarking to his adjutants, "Before three months have passed, we shall witness a collapse in Russia the like of which world history has never seen!"

What Hewel described as a "tranquil, self-possessed mood" descended on the Chancellery during the morning of these tumultuous events. It was almost like any other Sunday, except that Hitler and Ribbentrop fell fast asleep after lunch. The foreign minister had summoned the Soviet ambassador at three-thirty that morning to break the grim news to him, and then in rapid succession he summoned the representatives of Germany's allies—Italy, Japan, Hungary, Finland, and Romania. At five-thirty Dr. Goebbels had spoken, and at six Ribbentrop had addressed the press, surrounded by his assembled staff. Many of Hitler's adjutants, wilting under the Central European sun, went swimming.

By the time Hitler awoke late that afternoon, his armies were already many miles inside the Russian frontier, and the first reactions of the world were being monitored. Italy had honored her obligations with notable speed: at 3 P.M. Rome had cabled that Italy regarded herself as at war with Russia since five-thirty that morning. Romanian troops had crossed the Prut and were fighting in the provinces invaded by Russia twelve months before. Madrid telephoned that a Spanish volunteer legion was being recruited to join the crusade. An ecstatic Admiral Horthy exulted at the "magnificent" news and told the German ambassador that this was a day of which he had dreamed for twenty-two years —mankind would thank Hitler for this deed for centuries to come. Hungary dutifully broke off diplomatic relations with Moscow before Hitler retired to bed, but this was as far as it would as yet go. At 6 P.M. a disappointed General Jodl telephoned his liaison officer in Budapest to remind the Hungarians of the historic importance of the hour; but Horthy had gone off to play polo, his Chief of Army Staff was "unavailable," and the defense minister had gone fishing. Just as Hitler expected, the Hungarians, canny as ever, wanted to see the first results of "Barbarossa" before committing themselves.

Again he sat up late with his staff listening to the military reports. The Luftwaffe had bombed Kiev, Kovno (Kaunas), Sevastopol, Murmansk, Odessa, and Zhitomir. The bulk of the Russians' forward air force had been smashed on the ground—over twelve hundred Soviet aircraft had been destroyed. Thousands of prisoners had already been taken. From North Africa came heartening news from Rommel. Of this day Hewel wrote: "11:30 A.M., [Alessandro] Pavolini [the Italian education minister] to see the Führer. I accompany the Führer; he is in a brilliant mood on account of the huge successes in Russia (Luftwaffe) and Sollum (tanks)."

As so often before, Hitler and his staff drove through the sun-drenched streets of Berlin to his special train at the Anhalt station. At half-past noon he left for East Prussia—the twin locomotives hauling him throughout the afternoon and evening across Pomerania, those fields and cities so recently "liberated" from the Poles. Over tea he reminisced with Hewel and the others. "Russia," he said at one point, "is still a big question mark." Long after midnight he was being driven in a column of cars past cordons of sentries guarding a wood about ten miles outside the dreary East Prussian township of Rastenburg. Deep inside this wood was his new headquarters—during the train journey he had decided to call it the Wolf's Lair *(Wolfsschanze)*. When a secretary inquired, "Why Wolf again—just like the other headquarters?" Hitler replied, "That was my code name in the Years of Struggle." It was 1:30 A.M. when he first set foot inside the forbidding compound. From here he planned to command the defeat of the Soviet Union.

PART 3

CRUSADE INTO RUSSIA

The Country Poacher

Thus Adolf Hitler at fifty-two set out to conquer Russia.

In a terrible, unceasing onslaught his gray legions of Wehrmacht and Waffen SS troops fought forward across the drab and windswept plains, the glowing yellow fields of Ukrainian sunflower crops, the swamps around Lake Ilmen, the barren steppe, and the rocky deserts and inhospitable tundra of the north, humming with myriads of unseen mosquitoes, until the spent Nazi tide finally lapped the Caucasus Mountains.

Within a few days Field Marshal Leeb's armored spearheads had reached Dvinsk (Daugavpils); Field Marshal Bock's tanks were encircling a long oval-shaped pocket from Bialystok to Minsk in which eventually 350,000 Russian prisoners would be taken. Within a month Smolensk itself would be in German hands and Rundstedt would be at the gates of Kiev. As the Germans advanced, they found Russian trains still laden with grain and raw materials destined for Germany. Ironically, Hitler's tanks were running on the oil he had procured from Russia.

Yet there were disturbing auguries. Stalin had proclaimed a "patriotic war," and this was a slogan of dangerous magnetism. Moreover, his tanks and aircraft were significantly more modern and plentiful than Hitler had been told; the German General Staff's red-bound manual on the Soviet forces soon became known as the "Red Donkey." Most ominous of all was the frightening tenacity of the Soviet soldier. He was willing to die; he was brave and dogged. Frederick the Great once said, "You've got to shoot every Russian dead twice, and still turn him over to make sure." More than one German officer inspecting a bloody battlefield paid with his life for ignoring this warning. Chief of Staff Halder wrote privately on July 16, 1941: "The Russians drive their men forward into counterattacks without the least artillery support, as many as twelve waves one after another; often they are raw recruits, who just link arms and—their muskets on their backs—charge our machine guns, driven by their terror of the commissars and their superiors. Sheer weight of numbers has always been Russia's *forte,* and now the Russian command is forcing us to slay them, because stand aside they won't." But the Russian soldier was poorly led, his armored units were wrongly employed, and analogous errors were made with the Soviet artillery.

A more fundamental obstacle to the invasion was the nature of the Russian terrain, of which the "Red Donkey" had made no mention at all. Hitler had been undaunted by the sheer distances involved, since unlike Napoleon in 1812 he had the internal combustion engine and the airplane—indeed, he had tempted providence by launching "Barbarossa" on the very anniversary of Napoleon's invasion. But in the months to come Hitler was to learn that horses did have certain advantages over mechanical transport. The Russian roads dissolved into bottomless morasses when the rains came; railroads were few and far between, and only tracked vehicles remained mobile when it rained, so the gasoline for the tanks had to be hauled the immense distances from the railheads by relays of farm carts and tractors.

We shall not analyze the Russian campaign in great detail, except to point out where it bore the stamp of Hitler's own personality or of his ability to inspire faith in his subordinates. It was a gamble: he had held forty-eight divisions in reserve during "Yellow," but he was attacking Russia with only ten or fifteen in reserve. However, the extent of the gamble was concealed from all but his closest intimates. When Ribbentrop came on June 27, Hitler laughingly exclaimed that he felt like the legendary horseman who having unwittingly ridden across the frozen Lake Constance died of horror when he learned what he had done: "If I had had the slightest inkling of this gigantic Red Army assemblage I would never have taken the decision to attack."

Perhaps it was an unconscious foreboding that caused him two days later, even as the German radio was blaring out the first seven special communiqués on "Barbarossa" victories, to think again of his own death and sign a secret constitutional instrument appointing Hermann Göring his successor.

Today Rastenburg is part of Poland, and all that remains of the Wolf's Lair are the ruins of bunkers built to defend Hitler from enemy bombing or parachute attacks that never came. Massive concrete slabs tilt at awkward angles among the trees.

"Security Zone One" was in 1941 a cluster of wooden barracks and single-story concrete blockhouses which were divided into smaller compartments. "Cold and clammy bunkers," wrote one civil servant, "in which we freeze to death at night, can't sleep for the constant rattle of the electric ventilation system and its frightful draft, and wake up every morning with a headache." The whole compound was invisible from the air, concealed by camouflage netting suspended from the treetops. A few hundred yards away, on the other side of the road leading from Rastenburg to Angerburg (General Staff HQ), Jodl's operations staff occupied a similar encampment, "Security Zone Two." When Hitler had predicted that "this whole headquarters will one day become a historic monument, because here is where we founded a New World Order," Jodl had drily replied that it would be better suited as a garrison detention center for Rastenburg. It had in fact been built in one of the marshiest places in Masuria. "No doubt some government department found the land was cheapest here," sighed Hitler. Jodl's staff diarist complained in a private letter dated June 27: "We are being plagued by the most awful mosquitoes. It would be hard to pick on a more senseless site than this—deciduous forest with marshy pools, sandy ground, and stagnant lakes, ideal for these loathsome creatures."

One of Hitler's two private secretaries wrote a closely observed account of her impressions of the Wolf's Lair on June 28. This worm's-eye view of one of the most powerful men on earth deserves quoting at length if only for the scene it sets:

> This time we girls . . . are accommodated as well as the men are. The blockhouses are scattered in the woods, grouped according to the work we do. Each department is kept to itself. Our sleeping bunker, as big as a railway compartment, is very comfortable-looking, paneled with a beautiful light-colored wood; it has a concealed wash basin and a mirror, a small Siemens radio on which we can pick up clear broadcasts of very many stations, and we even have electric heaters (which are admittedly not on) and a good bright light in attractive wall lamps; there is a narrow, hard mattress filled with hay. It is a tight fit but not so tight as to be uncomfortable, and now that I have put a few pictures on the bunker wall it all makes an agreeable impression. There are communal shower rooms, but we have yet to use them as at first there was no warm water and now we like to sleep, as usual, until the very last moment. As the air-conditioning noise bothered us and the draft went right past our heads . . . we have it switched off at night with the result that . . . we walk around with leaden limbs all next day.
>
> Despite all this it is wonderful except for an appalling plague of mosquitoes. My legs have been stung to bits and are covered with

lumps. The antimosquito stuff they give us only works for a short time, unfortunately. The men are better protected by their long leather boots and thick uniforms; their only vulnerable point is the neck. Some of them go around all day with mosquito nets on. I tried it all one afternoon, but found it too much of a nuisance. Indoors it is not so bad with these little monsters. Wherever a mosquito turns up, it is hunted down. In the first few days this led to immediate problems of jurisdiction, as the Chief [Hitler] says it should be the Luftwaffe's job only. Meantime flyswatters of wire mesh have arrived and anybody not doing anything else is sent mosquito-hunting. They say the small mosquitoes are replaced by a far more unpleasant sort at the end of June, and their bites will be far more powerful. God help us!

The temperature here is a pleasant surprise. It is almost too cool indoors. . . . The forest keeps out the heat: you don't notice how much until you go out onto the street, where the heat clamps down on you.

Shortly after 10 A.M. we two go to the mess bunker, No. 1 Dining Room—a long whitewashed room sunk half-underground so that the small gauze-covered windows are very high up. On its walls are wood engravings, one of baskets, another of Henry I, etc. A table for twenty people takes up the entire length of the room; here the Chief takes his lunch and supper with his generals, his General Staff officers, adjutants, and doctors. At breakfast and afternoon coffee we two girls are also there. The Chief sits facing the maps of Russia hanging on the opposite wall, and this naturally prompts him to make repeated remarks about Soviet Russia and the dangers of bolshevism. . . . He must have suffered heavily of late, since the so-called friendship treaty was signed with Russia. Now he makes a clean breast of his apprehensions, again and again emphasizing the enormous danger bolshevism is for Europe and saying that if he had waited just one more year it would probably have been too late. . . .

We wait in this No. 1 Dining Room each morning until the Chief arrives for breakfast from the map room, where meantime he has been briefed on the war situation. Breakfast for him, I might add, is just a glass of milk and a mashed apple: somewhat modest and unpretentious. We girls for our part can't get enough to eat, and after we have eaten our own share (with its small butter portion) we switch place settings while nobody's looking so that we get two or three shares each. Meanwhile we get the Chief to tell us first what the latest war situation is.

Afterward we go at 1 P.M. to the general situation conference in the map room, where either Colonel Schmundt or Major Engel [Hitler's army adjutant] does the briefing. These briefing sessions are extremely interesting. The statistics on enemy aircraft and tanks destroyed are announced—the Russians seem to have enormous numbers, as we have already annihilated over 3,500 aircraft and over 1,000 tanks including some heavy ones, forty-tonners—and our troops' advance is shown on the maps, etc. Now we can see how strenuously the Russians are fighting, and that it would have been fought on even terms if the Russians had any logical leadership, which thank God they have not.

After all we have seen so far, you can say it is a war against wild animals. If we are amazed to have taken so few prisoners, the answer is that the Russians have been whipped up by their commissars into believing the atrocity stories they tell them about our "inhumanity," about what would happen to them if they fell into German captivity. They have been told to fight to the end and to shoot themselves if need be. And they do; for example, at Kovno this happened: our troops sent a Russian prisoner into a Russian bunker to tell the Russians there to surrender, but he seems to have been shot himself by the commissar in there for having agreed to act as intermediary at all. Then the entire bunker was blown up by its own occupants. In other words, perish rather than surrender. There is a GPU commissar attached to each unit, and the commanding officer has to bow to him. Away from their leadership, the troops are just a rabble; they are absolutely primitive, but they fight doggedly on—which is of course a danger of its own and will lead to many a hard struggle yet. The French, Belgians, and so on were intelligent and gave up the fight when they saw it was pointless, but the Russians fight on like lunatics, shivering with fear that something will happen to their families if they surrender—that's what Moscow threatens them with anyway. What is the use of having so many aircraft if they don't have any brains? In the Russian squadrons it has happened, for example, that the squadron commander flew ahead and the others followed him without knowing what the target was, they just flew behind him. If he was shot down, they couldn't even find their own way home as most of them did not even know how to read a compass. . . .

Well, back to the daily routine: after the situation conference it is time for lunch, which is in No. 2 Dining Room for us. As this is very often just a hot pot we mostly pass it up. Anyway, that's what we do when it's peas and beans. If there is nothing important to be done, we sleep a few hours after lunch so we are bright and breezy for the rest of the day, which usually drags on till the cows come home. Then, around 5 P.M., we are summoned to the Chief and plied with cakes by him. The one who grabs the most cakes gets his commendation! This coffee break most often goes on to 7 P.M., frequently even longer. Then we walk back to No. 2 Dining Room for supper. Finally we lie low in the vicinity until the Chief summons us to his study where there is a small get-together with coffee and cakes again in his more intimate circle. . . . I often feel so feckless and superfluous here. If I consider what I actually do all day, the shattering answer is: absolutely nothing. We sleep, eat, drink, and let people talk to us, if we are too lazy to talk ourselves. . . .

This morning the Chief said that if ever the German soldier deserved a laurel wreath it was for this campaign. Everything is going far far better than he hoped. There have been many strokes of good fortune, for example, that the Russians met us on the frontier and did not first lure us far into their hinterland with all the enormous transport and supply problems that would certainly have involved. And again, that they did not manage to destroy their two bridges at Dvinsk. It would have been a big waste of time if we had first had to rebuild those bridges. I believe that once we have occupied Minsk our advance will surge forward. If there are any isolated Communists left among our own ranks, they will definitely be converted when they see the "blessings" of life on the other side. . . .

By June 30 the encirclement of Minsk was completed. Army Group Center destroyed 20 Soviet divisions here, capturing 290,000 prisoners, 25,000 tanks, and 1,400 guns. A captured Russian corps commander confirmed that there were no Red Army forces of any importance east of the Dvina and Dnieper rivers. Halder reflected the optimism at General Staff headquarters when he boasted in his diary on July 3: "It's probably not overstating the case if I maintain that the campaign in Russia has been won in two weeks. Of course that doesn't mean it's *over*." In a letter on June 29, Jodl's war diarist Helmuth Greiner showed that the OKW agreed the campaign was going far better than expected. "With the capture of Dvinsk and Minsk we have covered in one week one third of the way to Leningrad and Moscow; at this rate we would be in both cities in another fourteen days—but we can assume it'll be even sooner."

Hitler shared this view. Staring at the wall map in his dining room, he proclaimed within his secretaries' earshot, "In a few weeks we'll be in Moscow. Then I'll raze it to the ground and build a reservoir there. The name Moscow must be expunged." Ribbentrop addressed his senior diplomats in similar terms a few days later. "In six or eight weeks the Russian campaign will be over. The war against Britain may go on for another six months or for ten years." At about the same time Hitler assured Ambassador von der Schulenburg, who had been repatriated from Moscow: "By August 15 we shall be in Moscow. By October 1 the Russian war will be over."

Hitler had every reason to scent victory throughout July 1941. On

July 2 he was shown a decoded Turkish report quoting both Stalin and Marshal Timoshenko as privately conceding to foreign diplomats that they had already written off Leningrad, Minsk, Kiev, and even Moscow, but that they had taken this into account in their calculations. A decoded morale report from the American embassy in Moscow described air raid precautions there and anxiously noted the food situation and rumors that the Russians were already evacuating their gold reserves to safety. Over lunch with Ribbentrop on July 4, Hitler was already enlarging on his plans for colonizing Russia, as Hewel's diary shows, and contrasting the pure nihilism of the Bolshevik revolution with the basic orderliness of the Fascist revolution. "Where there is no compulsion man will always revert to a rabbitlike existence," he explained. "The Russian peasant doesn't work willingly. This is why the Communist slogans failed, and they had to resort to the collective system—with commissars instead of landowners. It's all the same thing. Slavs can't organize, they can only *be* organized. They need to be in bondage."

The next day, July 5, 1941, with the Russian campaign seemingly drawing to an end, Hitler explained to the same select lunchtime audience why he had attacked Russia without a formal declaration of war or even the pretext of an "incident." "Nobody is ever asked about his motives at the bar of history. Why did Alexander invade India? Why did the Romans fight their Punic wars, or Frederick II his second Silesian campaign? In history it is success alone that counts." He, Hitler, was answerable only to his people. "To sacrifice hundreds of thousands [of troops] just because of the theoretical responsibility-issue [for starting the war] would be criminal. I will go down in history as the destroyer of bolshevism, regardless of whether there was a frontier incident or not. Only the result is judged. If I lose, I will not be able to talk my way out with questions of form. Look at Norway—we would never have succeeded if I had announced my intention first, yet it was vital for the fate of Germany. And vice versa: if Churchill and Reynaud had kept a still tongue in their heads I would probably not have tackled Norway."

Hitler calculated that he would capture Smolensk in mid-July but that it would take until August to assemble his infantry for an attack on Moscow, so meanwhile his tank formations could "mop up" in the north. He was noticeably uncertain about how high to rank Moscow itself on his list of objectives; to him it was just a place-name, he said, while Leningrad was the very citadel of bolshevism, the city from which that evil creed had first sprung in 1917. Strategically he was right to emphasize that victory would hinge not on the capture of Moscow but on the destruction of Soviet military strength; but the General Staff disagreed with him noisily, and this problem, of how best to employ his tanks after the Dnieper and Dvina rivers had been crossed, continued to beset him throughout July. "I constantly try to put myself in the enemy's shoes," he told his generals on July 4. "They have virtually lost the war already. It is good that we wiped out the Russian tank and air forces right at the start. The Russians cannot replace them now." But should he retain his own tank forces for the assault on Moscow or divert them to help Field Marshal Leeb's drive toward Leningrad? "It will be the toughest decision of the whole campaign," Hitler admitted to his staff.

By this time the coalition was complete: Slovakia had declared war on June 23; Hungary and Finland had decorously waited a few more days, until Russian aircraft attacked them, then they too declared war. The Vichy government broke off diplomatic relations with the USSR, and thousands of Frenchmen responded to the call for volunteers to fight bolshevism: 150 airmen volunteered, among them 20 of France's foremost bomber pilots. From Denmark, Norway, Spain, France, Belgium, and Croatia came word of legions being formed to fight in Russia. Hitler directed that those from "Germanic" countries were to be organized by the SS, while the Wehrmacht would attend to the rest. All must swear allegiance to him. Sweden and Switzerland remained the exceptions—"Nations on Furlough," as Hitler contemptuously called them. As he had predicted, the battle against bolshevism was proving a rallying point for all Europe. On July 10, Hewel observed of Hitler: "He predicted it. 'I was forced into this fight step by step, but Germany will emerge from it as the greatest national Power on earth.' He believes that Churchill will topple all at once, quite suddenly. Then in Britain an immense anti-Americanism will arise, and Britain will be the first country to join the ranks of Europe in the fight against America." And Hewel added jubilantly: "He is infinitely confident of victory. The tasks confronting him today are as nothing, he says, compared with those in the years of struggle; particularly since ours is the biggest and finest army in the world."

The Vatican also let it be known that it "welcomed the war" with Russia. That Churchill had broadcast his immediate offer of aid to Russia on the first day of "Barbarossa" did not surprise Hitler. (In private he mocked the strange spectacle of "Churchill, Stalin, and Roosevelt as fighters for freedom!") But that the exiled Dutch queen should broadcast over the BBC her deepest sympathy for the Russian people conveniently revolted him, and he instructed that the Dutch royal family's remaining wealth in Holland was to be confiscated forthwith. Meanwhile, a Dutch East Company was founded in Holland to organize the provision of food for the Netherlands from the Ukraine and to negotiate contracts for Dutch specialists and workers to emigrate to the east. Japan alone shunned what Hitler regarded as her obligations to the Axis: Hitler believed that with "Barbarossa" proving such a crushing success, Axis interests would now best be served by Japan attacking the Soviet Union. He preferred land contact between the Japanese and German armies along the Trans-Siberian railway to an attack on Singapore. The Japanese were forcefully reminded that their foreign minister had himself declaimed in Berlin that no Japanese statesman could uphold Japanese neutrality if Germany became involved in war with Russia. But Japan viewed Hitler's immediate prospects soberly. On July 2, Weizsäcker commented, in his diary: "The Japanese are still playing us along. All we know is that they don't want to attack Singapore as yet. If and when they will help against Russia remains to be seen."

When early victory had seemed certain, Hitler's mind turned to future campaigns. On July 8, 1941, he instructed Brauchitsch not to send any new tanks to the eastern front; the panzer divisions there were to be reduced in number, and idle tank crews were to be sent back to Germany to train fresh tank divisions. On the thirteenth, he confirmed this in an OKW order: in addition to the twenty existing panzer divisions, the army was to establish sixteen more by May 1, 1942—twelve for the east and twenty-four—a whole panzer army—for other tasks. The next day Hitler ruled that after the Soviet Union's defeat, the army would be cut back (apart from these panzer divisions) and naval construction would be limited to requirements for the war with Britain and the United States. The Luftwaffe, however, was to be expanded on a colossal scale, and its factories were to be working at full blast by the spring of 1942. Of his real future aims at this time we are only meagerly informed. Hitler seems to have envisaged a future war—perhaps not in his lifetime —between the New World and the Old. Later in July, gossiping one night about the Englishman's innate sense of authority, he remarked, "I'm sure the end of this war's going to mark the start of a lasting friendship with Britain. But if we're to live in peace with her, we shall have to give her a knockout blow first—the British expect that from anybody, if they are to respect him properly."

Yet there were disturbing facets to that summer of 1941. Stalin had obviously laid immense plans for an offensive into Europe. The Red

Army was far stronger than Hitler's experts had believed. Its air force had some eight thousand aircraft, and Soviet industry was turning out tanks at a rate which Hitler would have dismissed as impossible—had his Intelligence agencies so advised him. On July 15, Jeschonnek's deputy, touring the conquered territories, wrote in his diary: "The Red Army's equipment staggers us again and again. . . . They had laid out enormous fortifications, mostly still incomplete, to guard their Lemberg [Lvov] salient. In this region, sixty-three huge airfields alone, each with two runways and all still incomplete, bear witness to the Russian attack preparations." The next day Stalin's son Jacob, a lieutenant in a Soviet tank division, was captured near Vitebsk. Among "other proof that the Russians were just waiting to get at the Germans" was, according to the Luftwaffe's General von Richthofen, the huge booty of artillery and tanks taken at Dobromysl. "In part they come from the young Stalin's tank division. He has admitted that they were standing by for the big offensive and were smashed to pieces by my squadrons' surprise attack." Hitler learned that on Jacob Stalin there had been found a letter from a friend mentioning that before their "outing to Berlin" he was going to see his Anushka one more time. Interrogation of Stalin junior and the dictator's captured former secretary revealed that Stalin planned to exploit the German intelligentsia to improve the Russian population's caliber; Europe and Asia would then become the invincible bastions of bolshevism, and the victory of the Communist world revolution would be assured.

As a self-professed weapons expert, Hitler was particularly awed by the new Soviet armored fighting vehicles that crawled out of the forests like primeval monsters of whose existence his experts had breathed no word to him: here was a tank of fifty-two tons, its armorplate so thick that only the Luftwaffe's 88-millimeter antiaircraft guns made any impression on it; and here, south of Dubno, were tanks weighing a hundred tons. On July 4, OKW war diarist Greiner—who again stated that in fourteen days they would be in Leningrad and Moscow—confidently asserted: "The Russians have lost so many aircraft and four thousand six hundred tanks that there can't be many left." But by mid-July Hitler's weary gunners had knocked out eight thousand Russian tanks and still they came. At the end of July *twelve thousand* tanks had been captured or destroyed.[1] Visiting Army Group Center on August 4, Hitler wanly admitted to his panzer commander General Guderian:

---

[1] General von Waldau, Jeschonnek's deputy, noted that by July 30 the Germans had taken:
    Army Group South: 162,680 prisoners 4,574 tanks 2,894 guns
    Army Group Center: 580,910 prisoners 5,571 tanks 4,300 guns
    Army Group North: 56,320 prisoners 1,880 tanks 1,200 guns

"Had I known they had as many tanks as that, I'd have thought twice before invading."

The complete failure of his Intelligence agencies rattled Hitler. An Abwehr colonel apprehensively recorded on July 20: "C[anaris] has just returned from the Führer's headquarters and describes the mood there as very jittery, as it is increasingly evident that the Russian campaign is not 'going by the book.' The signs are multiplying that this war will not bring about the expected internal collapse, so much as the invigoration of bolshevism.—C. warns in particular that attempts are being made to brand the Abwehr as the culprits, for not properly informing people about the true strength and fighting power of the Russian army. For example the Führer is said to have remarked that had he known of the existence of the super-heavy Russian tanks he would not have waged this war." Greiner speculated the next day: "What matters is how much material and manpower they can salvage from these debacles. . . . Nobody discussed this at lunch with the Führer yesterday. At first he was very taciturn, and just brooded away, so I took the opportunity to stuff my belly with the best of everything. Then he came to life and delivered a monologue of an hour or more on our brave and gallant Italian allies and the worries they are causing him. . . . You can't help being astonished at his brilliant judgment and clear insights. He looks in the best of health and seems well although he seldom gets to bed before 5 or 6 A.M."

For the ordinary German soldier, the eastern front already had something of a nightmare quality. To this nightmare, Stalin also added the specter of long-prepared partisan warfare.

On July 3, Hitler had been brought the radio monitoring service's transcript of Stalin's first public broadcast since "Barbarossa" began. Effective and cunning—though Stalin had never been much of a rhetorician—it echoed the May 5 secret speech to the generals of which Hitler was to learn shortly. Stalin asked his radio audience: "Are the German Fascist troops really invincible, as their loud-mouthed Fascist propaganda chiefs trumpet to the world? Of course they are not!" He referred to Hitler and Ribbentrop as monsters and cannibals, and claimed that Hitler's ambition was to restore the landowners to power, to bring back the czars, and to destroy the national cultures of the independent constituent republics of the Soviet Union. "He will Germanize them and turn them into the slaves of German princes and barons." He appealed to patriotic Russians everywhere to destroy everything of value in the path of the advancing Wehrmacht—railway rolling stock, crops, fuel, and raw materials. They were to form partisan units behind German lines, to blow up roads and bridges, burn down forests, destroy arms dumps and convoys, and remorselessly hunt down and wipe out the enemy and his accomplices. "This war with Fascist Germany must not be regarded as an ordinary war."

Hitler piously noted: "Thanks to Stalin's slogan that everything is to be destroyed, millions must now starve." The partisan war provided the SS task forces with a fresh rationale for their mass-extermination drives, in which Russian Jews increasingly came to be regarded as "partisan material" and hence ripe for prophylactic massacre. The identification of Jews with partisans was so fixed in Hitler's pathological mind that on July 10 we find him telephoning Brauchitsch about the pointlessness of committing panzer divisions to the assault on Kiev: 35 percent of the city's population were Jews, so the bridges across the Dnieper would not be found intact. Another factor now also weighed with Hitler: should the Red workers rise in response to Stalin's appeal, the vast, sprawling conurbations of Leningrad and Moscow would become deathtraps if Hitler's precious tanks entered them.

Thus he eventually decided that Moscow and Leningrad were to be destroyed, but not necessarily occupied. This destruction he would achieve with the bomber aircraft and by mass starvation. Two days after Stalin's radio speech Hitler told his private staff that Moscow would "disappear from the earth's surface" as soon as its riches were safely in German hands. Unlike his General Staff, who regarded the capital as a strategic target, Hitler saw it only as the seat of bolshevism; on July 8 he told Brauchitsch and Halder that its devastation was necessary to drive out its population, whom they would otherwise have to feed in the coming winter. He ordered the Luftwaffe to disrupt Moscow with a terror raid—ostensibly in reprisal for the attacks on Finnish and Romanian cities—hoping for the kind of national catastrophe that the overcentralization of government in Moscow seemed to invite. "If an earthquake destroyed Moscow today," he explained to the Japanese ambassador, "the whole of Russia would perish." On July 21 and 22 the Luftwaffe raided Moscow, against Jeschonnek's better instincts; but the intercepted dispatches from the city showed that the results were far short of Hitler's expectations.

Emotionally Hitler was far more attracted to the destruction of Leningrad. On July 16, Bormann noted: "The Leningrad area is being claimed by the Finns. The Führer wants to raze Leningrad to the ground—then he'll give it to the Finns." Its capture had been confidently expected by mid-July, but even as the evacuation of the last awkward terrain of marsh and forest west of the city was in progress, a new Russian general took command and ordered the troops not to retreat one more step. Henceforth the Russians clung grimly on with a success that was not without effect on Hitler. It was now that Hitler began seriously to consider detaching General Hermann Hoth's tanks from the army group advancing on Moscow to help Leeb's Army Group North encircle Leningrad; he would then also divert Guderian's panzer group from the Moscow front to Army Group South. This would leave only infantry armies for the final assault on Moscow. On July 21, he visited Leeb's headquarters. The army group's war diary records: "The Führer emphasized that he expects a bitter enemy defense south of Leningrad, as Russia's leaders fully realize that Leningrad has been held up to the nation as a showpiece of the revolution these last twenty-four years, and that given the Slav mentality, which has already suffered from the fighting so far, the loss of Leningrad might result in a complete collapse." As to the fact that this concentration on Leningrad would leave only infantry armies for the assault on Moscow: "The Führer is not concerned by this, since to him Moscow is only a geographical objective."

It was a difficult decision, and flatly condemned by the General Staff. Halder—plagued like Hitler by the mosquitoes and torrid climate—had already noted in his diary on July 14: "The Führer's constant interference is becoming a regular nuisance." Now the general wrote an irritable private letter on July 28. "He's playing warlord again and bothering us with such absurd ideas that he's risking everything our wonderful operations so far have won. Unlike the French, the Russians won't just run away when they've been tactically defeated; they have to be slain one at a time in a terrain that's half forest and marsh; all this takes time and his nerves won't stand it. Every other day now I have to go over to him. Hours of gibberish and the outcome is there's only one man who understands how to wage wars. . . . If I didn't have my faith in God and my own inner buoyancy, I'd go under like Brauchitsch, who's at the end of his tether and hides behind an iron mask of manliness so as not to betray his complete helplessness."

Out of the "preventive war" an old-style war of colonial conquest had emerged. Raw materials such as oil, chrome, and manganese would soon be his in the measure that the Russians were deprived of them. He would construct an oil pipeline from the Caucasus oil fields to Germany. On July 14, Hitler told one visitor to the Wolf's Lair: "We shall not lose our heads as we press onward; we will not advance beyond what we can really hold on to." But there seemed no limit to his territorial ambitions. Germany's domains would extend to the Urals and two hundred miles beyond. The Crimea would become the Riviera of the Reich, settled exclusively by Germans and linked to the fatherland by a broad autobahn. He was overheard to remark: "I entered this war a nationalist, but I shall come out of it an imperialist." It was a role he thoroughly enjoyed. In the relaxed company of his private secretary, walking in the pitch darkness one night among the blockhouses he made a bantering remark that again illustrated this. She had left her flashlight on his desk and kept stumbling in the darkness. An orderly sent to fetch the flashlight reported it missing. In mock-righteous tones that mimicked a Swabian businessman's thick accent Hitler assured her: "Look, I poach other people's countries—I don't pinch their flashlights!" And he added with the loud belly-laugh of which he was still capable in spite of the death and destruction he had loosed: "And that's just as well, because it is the small fry that get strung up. The big fish get away with it."

At a five-hour conference with his chief minions—Rosenberg, Lammers, Keitel, Göring, and Bormann—on July 16, Hitler hammered home the point that Germany alone was entitled to benefit from defeating the Soviet Union. As for their secret aims, while they must be concealed from the world at large the German leaders must themselves be in no doubt: just as she had in Norway, Denmark, Holland, and Belgium—where Germany had already staked her territorial claims in secret, whatever she might publicly profess for tactical reasons—so too in Russia must Germany adopt the pose of a protector. "But let there be no doubt in *our* minds that we shall never depart from these territories." The Crimea and Galicia in particular must be annexed. As for the rest, this "giant cake" must be so cut that Germany could dominate it, rule it, and exploit it properly. "Never again must there be any military power west of the Urals, even if we have to fight a hundred years' war to prevent it." Germans alone must be permitted to bear arms—this was why Hitler would not allow the Slavs, or Czechs, or Cossacks, or Ukrainians to join in his crusade. Since the Ukraine would be most vital as Germany's granary for the next three years, Hitler wanted Gauleiter Erich Koch appointed Reich Commissar—a tough, cruel viceroy who had shown his mettle in the economic management of East Prussia. Gauleiter Heinrich Lohse would rule the Baltic countries, with Siegfried Kasche in Moscow, Alfred Frauenfeld in the Crimea, Josef Terboven in the Kola peninsula, and Schickedanz in the Caucasus.

In Russia—the "future German empire" as he was to describe it some days later—he would encourage neither schools nor religion, a position on which he met the opposition of Alfred Rosenberg and the strongly Catholic Franz von Papen. Papen had sent him a long study urging that now was the right moment to reintroduce Christianity into Russia; Hitler would not hear of it. Wisecracking in his usual way in private, he noted that he might eventually consider letting *all* the Christian sects in "so they can beat each other's brains out with their crucifixes." In this new German empire, soldiers with twelve years of service would automatically inherit a farmstead fully equipped with cattle and machinery. During the last two years of their military service these peasant-soldiers would be trained on similar farmsteads. He asked only that some of this new peasant breed should marry girls from the countryside. They were to retain their weapons, including machine guns, so that they could answer any fresh call to arms against the Asiatic hordes. The NCOs—particularly those of the Luftwaffe and mechanized divisions—were to manage the gasoline stations along the big autobahns. Given a future standing army of 1,500,000 men, about 30,000 would be discharged each year. This soldier-peasant would above all make a far better teacher than the university-trained elementary school teacher, who would always be dissatisfied: not that Hitler planned to educate the Russian masses. "It is in our interest that the people know just enough to recognize the signs on the road," he said.

On July 17, Hitler signed the formal decrees putting these plans into effect. Parallel to Ribbentrop's jealous foreign ministry he set up an East Ministry under Alfred Rosenberg to handle the occupied territories; to complete the parallel he allowed Rosenberg to appoint a liaison officer, Dr. Werner Koeppen, to the Führer's headquarters as a counterpart to Walther Hewel. Heinrich Himmler and Hermann Göring were given sweeping powers to police and exploit these new domains. On July 31, Göring—as head of the Four-Year Plan set up in 1936 to make Germany self-sufficient—signed a document empowering Reinhard Heydrich as chief of the security police to "make all necessary preparations as regards organization and actual concrete preparations for an overall unraveling of the Jewish problem within Germany's sphere of influence in Europe." This amplified his January 1939 order to Heydrich to enforce Jewish emigration from Germany itself.

In some regions, particularly the Baltic countries, the "Jewish problem" had already solved itself since 1939. According to German reports, two days after the Soviet invasion of Lithuania in 1940 all the local businessmen had been ordered into the streets at 7 A.M. "to clean them"; the Russians had then mown them down with machine guns while commissars reported to be Jewish had taken over their businesses for the state. It was this story which at the onset of "Barbarossa" touched off such primitive and bloody pogroms in Latvia and Lithuania that Himmler's task forces complained that only a few hundred Jews remained for them to deal with when they arrived. Leeb's army group brought these massacres by Lithuanian "irregulars" to the attention of Hitler's headquarters on July 5; Colonel Schmundt replied that German soldiers were not to interfere with "these political questions"; it was part of "a necessary mopping-up operation" (*Flurbereinigung*).

The spirit inspiring Hitler in his war against the European Jews is clear from the entry in Hewel's diary on July 10:

> . . . Stayed up until 3 A.M. with the Führer in his bunker. Very hot and very exhausting, interesting though the conversation was.
>
> He says, "I feel like the Robert Koch of politics. It was he who discovered the bacillus, thereby opening up new paths for medical science to explore. And it is I who have discovered the Jews as the bacillus and ferment that causes all decay in society. And what I have proved is this—that nations can survive without Jews; that the economy, culture, art, and so on can exist without Jews and in fact better. That is the cruelest blow I have dealt the Jews."

He reverted to this imagery of the Jewish bacillus a few days later when explaining to the Croatian defense minister why every single Jew must be evicted from European soil. "Because if just one country, whatever the reason, tolerates one Jewish family in its midst, then this will become the seat of a fresh bacillus infection. Once there are no more Jews in Europe the unity of the European nations can no longer be disrupted. It is unimportant where the Jews are sent—whether to Siberia or to Madagascar." He planned, he said, to approach each country with this demand. The last country in which the Jews would hold out would inevitably be Hungary; the remaining European nations must then send her a joint inter-European summons, calling on her to bend to the "iron will" of Europe. At this stage Hitler spoke of habitual criminals who were to be liquidated since "if upright, valuable human beings are risking their lives at the front, it is a crime to preserve these villains," but he did not yet specifically mention Jews in this category. When he next employed this argument, early in 1943, Jews and incorrigible criminal elements were lumped into a single category.

Hitler's part in the unfolding Jewish tragedy cannot be usefully analyzed *in vacuo*. Jews and Bolshevik leadership were pathologically identified in his mind. Given this obsession it was an easy progression to draw the same conclusion about leadership in the United States. In 1939 Hitler had once confided to a bemused General Friedrich von Boetticher, the German military attaché in Washington, that he possessed documents proving Roosevelt's Jewish ancestry and that one day he would release them to an astounded world. In August 1941 in conversation with a Spanish diplomat he reverted to this theme. "The arch culprit for this war is Roosevelt, with his freemasons, Jews, and general Jewish-bolshevism." Three months later he told the Finnish foreign minister, "Be clear about one point: the whole of World Jewry is on the side of the Bolsheviks."

It was to these unidentified Jewish-Bolshevik influences that Hitler ascribed Roosevelt's attempts to provoke a shooting war with Germany in a way that would justify his declaration of war before a reluctant Congress. American troops relieved British forces that had preemptively occupied Iceland in May 1940, thus bringing the United States into the German war zone for the first time. Hans Thomsen, the German chargé d'affaires, telegraphed from Washington that Roosevelt, in conversation with Wendell Willkie, had four times reiterated his firm determination to get into the war as soon as possible. But Hitler was equally determined to avoid war with the United States at this time. On July 13 the diplomat Etzdorf quoted Hitler as saying, "So long as our eastern operations are still running, we won't let ourselves be provoked. Later the Americans can have their war, if they absolutely must." Admiral Raeder begged him to regard the Iceland occupation as sufficient cause, as a *de facto* declaration of war on Germany. Again the diplomat quoted Hitler as refusing; he would do his utmost to prevent Roosevelt from entering the war for one or two more months because the Luftwaffe was still committed to the Russian campaign. Besides, as Raeder informed the naval staff: "The Führer still presumes that a victorious Russian campaign will affect the posture of the United States." Keitel, Raeder, the admirals, and even the army generals writhed under the rigid prohibitions Hitler now imposed. He forbade even the mining of Icelandic harbors. Field Marshal von Bock snorted in his diary on July 25: "Keitel says it isn't easy to take the American occupation of Iceland lying down, and that we've had to restrict our U-boats to attacking only ships definitely identified as enemy so as not to hand the Americans the *casus belli* they are seeking. . . . We did the same thing in World War I, and I fear that—just as happened then—the Americans will find another cause."

Evidence supporting Raeder's point of view kept coming in. It was reported that the American navy had been ordered to fire without warning or provocation on *any* German warship; if the Germans survived long enough to relate this illegal act, the American commander concerned was instructed to deny responsibility and to suggest that a British unit was involved. Thus Roosevelt hoped to provoke countermeasures. The "neutral" United States had meanwhile furnished the British admiralty with sets of her secret codes. All these facts Hitler learned from intercepted U.S. naval code signals. In a speech to his staff on July 17, Ribbentrop said, "If the United States continue to provoke us after Russia's defeat, later they can have their war. We are not fearful of a common front between Britain and the United States."

Three days later Canaris reported: "A certain disenchantment is to be discerned in the Reich foreign minister von R[ibbentrop]. Thus he himself now accepts America's entry into the war as imminent, and for the first time he spoke disparagingly of the 'journalistic' reporting of Thomsen and Boetticher." Ribbentrop's stock with Hitler was currently at its lowest. "The Führer again curses the foreign ministry: 'sluts,' etc.," wrote Hewel. And a few weeks later Hewel quoted Hitler as telling him, "I could not stick working three weeks under your boss!" Hitler, whose lanky SS adjutant Hansgeorg Schulze had just been killed on the Russian front, had recruited his brother, Richard, to replace him; Richard Schulze had formerly been adjutant to Ribbentrop and he and Hewel had often been encouraged by Hitler to make fun of their boss, the foreign minister. "In the evening Schulze and I told funny stories about *kepala orang*,"[2] Hewel wrote circumspectly in his diary. "The Führer laughed a lot, then was lost in thought."

It was no joke to Ribbentrop, however. Ever jealous of his rights, on June 9 Ribbentrop had asked Hitler to transfer the Party's foreign organization (AO, Auslands-Organisation) to his ministry, but Hitler had refused. In July, the question as to whether Rosenberg or Ribbentrop should conduct propaganda in Russia—for example, over the capture of Stalin's son Jacob and on Russian atrocities—caused a further row; Hitler characteristically decided to allow *both* ministers a free hand. Rosenberg's new ministry, set up in mid-July to handle all of Russia and the Baltic countries, was to the foreign minister like a red rag to a bull.

On the twenty-eighth Ribbentrop picked a violent quarrel with Hitler, challenging his very decision to attack Russia. It was a stiflingly hot summer day. Hitler was so enraged that he feigned a stroke, collapsed into a chair, and gasped at the petrified Ribbentrop that he must never

---

[2] Malayan: "head man." Hewel had spent twelve years of his youth in the Dutch East Indies and entered his more private thoughts in his diary in this tongue.

challenge his decisions again. Ribbentrop gave his word. He appears to have suffered the more permanent damage himself, for from that date developed the splitting hemicranial headaches and occasional functional paralysis of the right arm and leg that plagued him until his execution five years later. At this point, Ribbentrop came as near as he ever did to being replaced as minister. By whom? Perhaps by Goebbels, who had schemed patiently for the day when he could supplant him. But Hitler charged Lammers to inform the foreign minister that in time of war the diplomatic service must stand aside, until the guns had finished speaking. Perhaps it was a wider dissatisfaction with the trend of events —he even suspected that the Japanese had made a secret deal with Roosevelt giving him a free hand in Europe—that motivated Hitler's aversion to the foreign ministry.

Adolf Hitler's own health was poor, for the first time in five years. The influence of this on military events in the summer of 1941 cannot be ignored.

After the conclusion of the French campaign a year earlier, he had complained of breathing difficulties and he had been X-rayed in Munich; Dr. Morell had feared pleurisy. The stress of the Russian campaign, coupled with the hot, malarial climate in which the Wolf's Lair had been sited, told severely on the dictator. Worse, the brackish waters of Masuria had infected him with dysentery, and for fourteen days until mid-August he was afflicted by diarrhea, stomach pains, nausea, aching limbs, shivery feelings, and high temperatures. As the crucial strategic controversy developed in these weeks between Hitler and his generals, his ability to overrule them was impaired by his own physical weakness; his own grand strategy, which was to set up a vast encircling movement by Army Groups North and South, enveloping Moscow from the rear, was opposed and circumvented by Brauchitsch and his staff, who favored a direct assault on Moscow by Field Marshal von Bock's Army Group Center. Brauchitsch stayed in Berlin and ignored Hitler's orders; Hitler was confined by circumstances to his field headquarters. When the army Commander in Chief did pay a rare visit to the Wolf's Lair, Hitler vainly warned that the way things were going the fronts would inevitably become static, as they had in World War I. Halder certainly recognized that Hitler was too ill to oppose the army. "Despite his medical indisposition," the general wrote on August 8, "the Führer has given the Commander in Chief the closest instructions on how he wants the air force squadrons used. . . ."

Hitler was still very weak when Goebbels visited him on August 18. "Unhappily, he looks somewhat strained and sickly," the propaganda minister wrote. "This is probably a result of his dysentery, and perhaps also of the drain on his strength of these last few weeks." Only later was Hitler's military plan recognized to have offered the better prospects, for Bock's armies were still outside Moscow when winter set in. "Today I still believe," Göring was to tell his captors, "that had Hitler's original plan of genius not been diluted like that, the eastern campaign would have been decided by early 1942 at the latest."

The illness in mid-1941 cost Hitler more than Moscow, however. On August 14, Dr. Morell performed an electrocardiogram study of Hitler's heart. The graphs were sent to a leading authority on heart conditions, Professor Karl Weber, director of the heart institute at Bad Nauheim; Weber was instructed only that the traces were of a "very busy diplomat." From them Weber diagnosed beyond a doubt that "Patient A." was suffering from a virtually incurable heart disease: rapidly progressive coronary sclerosis. In a man of Hitler's age it was not abnormal, but from now on there would always be the danger of angina pectoris—a violent paroxysm of pain behind the chest bone—or of an embolism—the sudden plugging of a blood vessel, with possibly fatal consequences. There is no evidence that Hitler was told of this heart diagnosis, but his subsequent references to having only two or three more years to live may have been an allusion to this. More likely Morell kept the truth from him, for in the Führer's presence he later insisted that Hitler's heart and other organs were working well. In private, however, Morell began to study textbooks on the heart, and additional medicines were added to Hitler's overflowing cabinet. For repeated periods of two to three weeks Morell took to injecting 0.02 milligrams of a heart tonic, Strophantin, into Hitler's veins; and this he alternated with Prostrophanta, which contained the same ingredients but also glucose and vitamin B complex (nicotinic acid). To overcome the insufficiency of Hitler's circulatory system, Morell was also occasionally administering Cardiazol and Coramin internally to Hitler during the rest of 1941. In the following spring, Morell added to this growing list yet another medicine: Sympathol. A solution about one-hundredth as effective as adrenalin, it was meant to regulate Hitler's heart activity and overcome his heart-vessel insufficiency.

Throughout the coming winter Morell was a daily visitor to the Wolf's Lair. Hitler passively accepted his portly physician's explanations for the growing volume of medication being injected into his veins. "Morell told me my energy consumption is as high as in the tropics, because of my uninterrupted intensive work," Hitler repeated to another doctor. And, "Morell is still researching and his works are still expanding." Yet Morell's "Patient A." was not a medical ignoramus; he was better informed than most laymen. "He knew the connection between blood coagulation and thrombosis, the effect of nicotine on the heart muscles, and the possible relationship between the teeth and an inflammation of the maxillary sinus," commented a doctor who had long conversations with Hitler.

"Long conversations" is perhaps a misnomer. Hitler's conversations were monologues, delivered in a rich Austrian dialect to a handful of cronies assembled in his bunker, or over lunch or dinner at the long oblong table with Jodl at his left, an outside guest like Speer or Goebbels at his right, and his headquarters staff—the liaison officers, the younger adjutants, and secretaries—at their allotted places. Hitler would talk about the Party and Christianity. "We must not try to combat religion, but let it wither away!"

One of Hitler's devoted secretaries wrote in mid-July 1941:

In our evening discussions with the Chief the Church plays a big part. . . . It is all so convincing, what the Chief says, when for example he explains how Christianity by its mendacity and hypocrisy has set back mankind in its development, culturally speaking, by two thousand years. I really must start writing down what the Chief says. It's just that these sessions go on for ages and afterward you are just too limp and lifeless to write anything. The night before last, when we left the Chief's bunker, it was already light. We did not turn in even then, as ordinary people would have, but made for the kitchen, ate a few cakes, and then strolled for two hours toward the rising sun, past farmyards and paddocks, past hillocks glowing with red and white clover in the morning sun, a fairyland on which you just could not feast your eyes enough; and then back to bed. We are incapable of getting up before 2 or 3 P.M. A crazy life . . . A strange calling like ours will probably never be seen again: we eat, we drink, we sleep, now and then we type a bit, and meantime keep him company for hours on end. Recently we did make ourselves a bit useful—we picked some flowers, so that his bunker does not look too bare.

Kiev

In his New Year proclamation Hitler had promised the German people the war would be over by the end of 1941. By mid-August he knew this promise would not be fulfilled. Indeed, by the end of the year none of even his interim objectives—Leningrad, Moscow, or Rostov—had been captured because the invading armies—caught between the doctrines of the General Staff and the intuition of the Führer—were halted by the onset of winter.

The General Staff argued that the enemy's military strength must always be destroyed first; in August 1941 this was the Red Army mass assembled by Marshal Timoshenko in front of Moscow. Field Marshal von Bock's Army Group Center must therefore advance on Moscow; the other two army group operations in the north and the south were seen as strictly subsidiary. Bock, a tall, bony, upright Prussian professional, agreed. But when Hitler visited him on the fourth, as the battle for Smolensk was drawing to its end and another three hundred thousand Russian captives were already being marched westward, it was clear that the Führer had not yet made up his mind on how to fight the next phase of the campaign. For one thing, Hitler was still intoxicated by Bock's "historic triumphs," and his mind was on the New Order he planned for the east. "Now we will put things in order here for a thousand years," he had exclaimed on leaving his headquarters early that morning. For another, what precisely *was* Russia's "military strength"? Halder himself would wanly admit that everybody had underestimated the Soviet colossus. "When we attacked, we assumed there were 200 enemy divisions. To date we have already counted 360. . . . And if we destroy a dozen of these, the Russians throw another dozen in."

Clearly the enemy's military strength was not the finite quantity it had been in "White" and "Yellow." Russia's manpower reserves were virtually limitless. Halder felt that the answer was to attack Soviet industrial conurbations like Moscow. To Hitler the more immediate and final solution lay farther afield—in Russia's raw material centers, the sources of her food, her iron ore, coal, and oil, and particularly the Donets region beyond Kharkov: "That is the entire base of the Soviet economy." To a visiting diplomat he explained, "Soon we will occupy the richest Russian economic regions, bearing 61 percent of their iron and 35 percent of their molybdenum; and when we cut off their oil supplies from the south the fate of bolshevism will be sealed."

By August 6, visiting Rundstedt and General Antonescu at Army Group South headquarters in the dreary Ukrainian town of Berdichev,[1] Hitler's mind was all but made up. He would make his main push southeastward toward the oil fields, while the northern advance on Leningrad from the Luga bridgeheads began. Moscow would be left for last. Meteorologists had assured him the dry weather would remain longer in the center than the south anyway. Yet even so no firm directive was issued.

At the Wolf's Lair Hitler began holding war conferences each morning and evening. These were to become nightmares for their regular participants—theatrical performances dominated by the insistent monologues of the Führer, rambling discourses on generalities intermingled with sudden snap decisions intervening in even the lowest echelons of the army's command. The conferences lasted for hours on end, sapping the energy of his generals, who were grimly aware that they had more urgent business elsewhere. It was not a pleasant atmosphere. Individual generals hesitated to speak their minds in front of such a large and compliant audience. Of Hitler's regular staff only his army adjutant, Major Engel, had a ready wit and biting tongue; the other adjutants were more diplomatic in their approach. As for his commanders, they found out that in private Hitler could be frankly spoken to; but there were few—among them Rundstedt, Reichenau, Guderian, Manstein, and later Milch, Zeitzler, and Ferdinand Schörner—who had the requisite courage.

Life within Security Zone One revolved around Hitler; when he was away visiting the frontline headquarters, it was as though the dynamo had been wrenched bodily out of the powerhouse. Favored indeed were those with special passes to the compound. To these officers and Party officials it seemed an almost unforgivable act on Hitler's part to have

---

[1] Rundstedt's headquarters was in a former Soviet military school. Hewel noted that day: "We strolled through Berdichev. Ruined monastery church. Opened coffins, execution, ghastly town. Many Jews, ancient cottages, fertile soil. Very hot. Three hours' flight back."

brought his female staff with him to this sacred half-acre; Hitler, however, guarded his ladies with an almost comic jealousy, snapping at the young Walther Hewel for getting Gerda Daranowski, Hitler's attractive secretary, to do some typing for him instead of employing a clerk of his own. One of the secretaries wrote:

It's a thorn in some people's side that even in wartime the Chief has his personal staff around him, and particularly of course that we two females are included. An orderly told me of late-night comments in No. 1 Dining Room; I am furious about them, because we aren't here on an outing but because the Chief wants us and maintains he can't work without us. More than once he has stressed in these gentlemen's presence that without us . . . he would be in a hopeless mess. . . . It cannot have been a very pleasant situation when a few days after these utterances the Chief asked his Wehrmacht adjutant [Schmundt] whether a tent has been laid on for his ladies at the next headquarters. The reply was in the negative, so the Führer angrily ordered that accommodation was to be provided for us. "Oh, they had imagined they were only going to stay there in a tent encampment a few days, so we would not be needed!" All these excuses show how much they want to get rid of us. But the Chief has no intention whatever of being talked into it. An omnibus had to be laid on at once for us to sleep and work in. This episode quickly rid me of the illusion that the officers concerned could ever have friendly feelings for us women, whatever the late-night hours spent together in the dining room might suggest: that was just an alcoholic mirage. . . . The men have only one thought—to show themselves in the best light possible. The most ludicrous picture I think is when the Chief is standing with a cluster of his men, and the photographer begins to focus his Leica. At that moment, moving like lightning, they all crowd as close to the Chief as possible—like moths around a flame—so they too can get into the picture. I find this conduct quite absurd.

Three weeks later the same secretary was again complaining of the monotony. "We have now been here nine weeks, and the rumor is we shall stay here until the end of October. . . . I am so sick of inactivity that I recently tried to convince the Chief he needs only *one* secretary . . . but he changed the subject straight away so that I could not even touch on my request to be of some use somewhere else for the duration of the war, either in a hospital or an arms factory." Yet indirectly this secretary was serving a purpose for history, for her writings unmistakably reflect Hitler's inner thoughts. Thus on August 20 we find her recording:

A few days ago we saw here a British newsreel that reached us from

America, showing the horrifying devastation of entire streets in London: all the big department stores, Parliament, and so on are in ruins. The camera showed the huge fires raging, as it panned across whole sections of the city, with warehouse after warehouse forming one sea of fire. The commentary says that the British are sticking it out in the knowledge that Berlin looks just the same. Oh, if the poor British could only guess that the damage they are causing to Berlin is a mere shadow of this in London I am sure they would never go on fighting. Captured British officers themselves say their government is acting wholly irresponsibly. And that is really saying something, if the British admit this, and officers at that. . . .

I long for nothing more fervently than that the British should come forward with peace proposals once we have dealt with Russia. This war with Britain can only result in us smashing each other's cities to smithereens. And Mr. Roosevelt chuckles in gleeful anticipation of the day he will inherit Britain's legacy. I really cannot understand why the British won't listen to the voice of reason. Now that we are expanding to the east, we have no need for their colonies. I find it all so much more practical that everything will be right on our doorstep: the Ukraine and Crimea are so fertile we can plant everything we need there, and the rest (coffee, tea, cocoa, etc.) we can obtain by barter from South America. It is all so simple and obvious. God grant that the British soon come to their senses.

Hitler's was not an isolated view. From Lisbon came word that the Duke of Windsor had privately written to his former host there confirming that he believed Britain had virtually lost the war already and that the United States would do better to promote peace rather than war. Those in authority were, however, bent on Hitler's extinction. In the second week of August, Churchill and Roosevelt had met aboard their warships off Newfoundland, and proclaimed the eight-point Atlantic Charter, affirming that they sought no territorial aggrandizement, that they frowned on all territorial changes that did not accord with the freely expressed wishes of the people concerned, and that all nations should enjoy equal access to the raw materials of the earth and to its oceans. (Russia, which had lost the European territories it had annexed in 1940, subscribed to the Charter in 1942 along with some twenty nations that were then at war with Germany.) On August 25, Britain and Russia invaded Iran, on the pretext of warding off a similar Axis plan. (In fact Hitler had been aware since early July, through an indirect tip from King Farouk, that the British chiefs of staff had decided to occupy the Iranian oil fields.)

More serious than the propaganda dimensions of the Charter were the secret covenants that accompanied it. The United States now took over the naval watch of the Denmark Straits (south of Iceland) and undertook escort duties on North Atlantic convoys. Clearly the distinction between neutrality and belligerency was being increasingly blurred. Goebbels favored publishing the eight points in full, but Hitler was against it. He did, however, approve Goebbels's mischievous idea of immediately following Clement Attlee's broadcast on the Atlantic talks (as Churchill's deputy) with two OKW special communiqués, announcing that the Black Sea ports of Odessa and Nikolaev were now under siege and that the Soviet iron-ore fields were in German hands. In private,[2] Goebbels—not without reason—scoffed at the Charter's meager content. "There is to be no territorial aggrandizement. *Very* impressive, coming from two powers who own half the earth's surface. They wish to see self-government restored to those who have been forcibly deprived of it. This is also thoroughly understandable, as this self-government is to perpetuate the atomization of Europe which is so much in British and American interests. They'll give all countries equal access to the world's raw materials—note that: 'to the raw materials,' and not 'to the *sources* of the raw materials' . . . And disarmament is essential—only of the aggressor-nations, of course, while the peace-loving countries are to remain in possession of their weapons."

Hitler had asked Propaganda Minister Goebbels to come and see him on August 18, 1941. Apparently he was prompted by the growing Catholic clamor against the Nazi euthanasia program.

Early in July the Bishop of Munster, Count von Galen, had blown the lid off the scandal in a pastoral letter, and on the twenty-seventh he had instituted private criminal proceedings against persons unknown, explaining from his pulpit on August 3 that under German law he was obliged to report any knowledge of a crime being committed. For the Nazi party and government alike it was acutely embarrassing: Hitler's arbitrary 1939 law authorizing euthanasia had never been published. Bormann was eager to bring the Party's fight against the Church right out into the open and submitted to Hitler a memorandum on the desirability of executing the bishop. But short of treason by the bishop there was no way. Goebbels supported Bormann, arguing that Galen had spiced his sermon with wholly unfounded charges—that permanently disabled Wehrmacht battle casualties were being murdered, for example. But Hitler sagely disregarded Goebbels's advice, and instead on August

[2] An unpublished segment of his diary.

24 he ordered the entire secret euthanasia operation shut down immediately.

It was characteristic of his slackening grip on domestic affairs in Germany that the euthanasia operation continued nonetheless.[3] Immersed in "Barbarossa," Hitler was even unaware that Martin Bormann was already waging open war on the Church. Hitler's movie cameraman Walter Frentz heard Hitler say *in jest* to Bormann over lunch in 1941, "If you had your way, Herr Bormann, all the monasteries would be shut down!"—which was precisely what Bormann was doing. On another occasion Hitler said, "If my mother were still alive, she'd definitely be a churchgoer and I wouldn't want to hinder her. On the contrary, you've got to respect the simple faith of the people." Goebbels uncomfortably noted this in his diary. But according to Hitler's doctor, Hasselbach, the spectacle of the worthies of the Church of England now praying for the victory of bolshevism satisfied the Führer that all clergy *were* hypocrites. (He seemed to have forgotten that he himself had temporarily allied himself with bolshevism.) He assured Goebbels and Rosenberg that he would not easily forgive the German church leaders their behavior during this emergency period. But first the war must be won, and until then the Party must proceed slowly against the Church. On July 30, 1941, Bormann personally circularized all the Gauleiters on Hitler's orders, instructing them to refrain from any persecution of the religious communities, since this would only divide the nation Hitler had so arduously united.

Goebbels brought with him to Hitler's headquarters on August 18 radical proposals for intensifying the surveillance and persecution of the remaining Jews in Germany. "In the eastern campaign," his memorandum read, "the German soldier has seen the Jew in all his cruelty and repulsiveness." Jews had allegedly mutilated German soldiers or shot them down from the rear. "Clearly when the soldier comes home from the wars, he must not find any Jews here waiting for him." Ever since the summer of 1940 Goebbels had impatiently prepared for the rapid deportation of Berlin's seventy thousand Jews to the east—to Poland; but the war needs for transport overrode his ambitions, and he told the Berlin police that they could not begin the big roundup until the war was over. Now, in August 1941, Goebbels and Heydrich jointly proposed harsh measures to hound and intimidate the Jews—banning them from certain districts, from all public entertainment and eating places, and from non-Jewish shops. On August 17, Heydrich recommended to Bormann that all Jews should be forced to wear a distinctive emblem, to

---

[3] It continued until February 1945, evidently on the local initiative of Gauleiters and doctors.

make their surveillance as potential enemies of the state easier. Goebbels supported him. "One only needs to imagine what the Jews would do if they had us in their power, to know what we must do now that we are on top."

Afterward Goebbels wrote: "I manage to get my way completely with the Führer on the Jewish matter. He agrees we can introduce a large, visible badge for all the Jews in the Reich, to be worn by all Jews in public, so as to obviate the danger that the Jews will act as grumblers and defeatists without being detected. And in future we will allocate to Jews who don't work smaller food rations than to Germans; this is only right and proper—those who don't work won't eat. After all, of Berlin's 76,000 Jews, for example, only 26,000 work; the rest are sustained not only by the toils but also by the food rations of the Berlin public! Incidentally, the Führer agrees that as soon as the first transport possibilities arise, the Berlin Jews will be deported from Berlin to the east. There they will be taken in hand under a somewhat harsher climate."

Goebbels noted that Hitler also reminded him of his January 1939 Reichstag speech.

> The Führer is convinced that the prophecy he uttered then in the Reichstag—that if the Jews once more succeeded in provoking a world war, it would end with the destruction of the Jews—is coming true. It is coming true these weeks and months with a dread certainty that is almost uncanny. In the east the Jews will have to square accounts; they have already footed part of the bill in Germany and they will have to pay still more in the future. Their last refuge will be North America, and there too they will one day, sooner or later, end up footing the bill. Judaism is a foreign body among the cultured nations, and its works these last three decades have been so devastating that the popular reaction to it is absolutely comprehensible, necessary, indeed one might almost say self-evident. At any rate in the coming world the Jews will have little cause for mirth. . . .

Heydrich ordered that in the future Jews would have to wear yellow-and-white armbands to distinguish them; early in September, when the law was published, it was amended to a yellow star. As soon as "Barbarossa" was over, Hitler had agreed, the deportation of Berlin Jews could commence.

August 18 was a beautiful summer day at the Führer's headquarters, and Hitler's dysentery had passed, so he spent the four hours of his talk with Goebbels strolling in the woods—the first time he had done so in five weeks. Goebbels detected the strain in Hitler's features, but for a man of fifty-two the Führer's vitality and application were remarkable. He asked Goebbels about the mood in Berlin, which had recently undergone small-scale British and Russian air attacks. He had no worries about the morale of his people as a whole, though he strongly distrusted the intellectuals, and he promised Goebbels he would speak to the nation in the autumn.

The Wehrmacht's big push southward would shortly begin. "The Führer is not concerned with occupying particular regions or cities," wrote Goebbels. "He wants to avoid casualties if at all possible. Therefore, he does not intend to take Leningrad [Goebbels wrote "Petersburg"] or Kiev by force of arms, but to starve them into submission; once Leningrad has been cut off, his plan is to destroy the city's lifelines with his Luftwaffe and artillery. Probably not much will be left of this city. This is presumably justified by expediency. No doubt," gloated Goebbels, "there will be a degree of chaos among its millions of inhabitants. But the Bolsheviks would not have it otherwise. Our first Luftwaffe attacks will hit the water, power, and gas stations." Even as they were talking, a message was handed to Hitler that, true to the letter of Stalin's orders, a Russian town had burned its entire food stocks shortly before its capture. Hitler ordered the town left to starve so that other towns might have second thoughts about relying on the Wehrmacht's benevolence.

The exhausted German panzer divisions would shortly recuperate, continued Hitler to Goebbels. He hoped to be beyond Moscow by the time winter set in—presumably in mid-October. He put Stalin's losses at three million dead already. Perhaps, he mused wistfully, Stalin might even now sue for peace. "He has of course little in common with the plutocrats in London; nor will he let Britain dupe him as it did the potentates of those minor countries who allowed London to lead them to the slaughter. He is a hard-bitten realist, and the moment he sees that the Bolshevik system itself is on the verge of collapse and can only be salvaged by surrender, then he will certainly be willing to do so." When Goebbels asked what then, Hitler disclosed that he would agree to a peace request provided he was given considerable territorial safeguards and the Red Army was dismantled to the last rifle. "Bolshevism without the Red Army is no danger to us." Peace, thought Hitler, might come upon them quite unexpectedly—after all, nobody had expected at the beginning of January 1933 that thirty days later Hitler would be in power.

"The Führer is convinced that Moscow and London were in the same line of business long before June," wrote Goebbels. Their aim had been identical, the destruction of the Reich. He was overwhelmed at the very thought of what it would have meant if the Bolshevik hordes had swarmed into highly civilized central and western Europe. "Perhaps we still do not fully know the precarious position we were in this June. Autumn would definitely have brought the showdown." He admitted that German Intelligence had been grossly misled on Russian tank and aircraft strengths, and this had led to errors of judgment. "For example the Führer had estimated there were five thousand Soviet tanks, whereas in reality they had something like twenty thousand. We thought they had around ten thousand aircraft; in fact they possessed over twenty thousand, albeit largely unsuitable for battle." Hitler consoled himself with the idea that had he known the truth he might never have ordered "Barbarossa," but he could not conceal from his shrewd propaganda minister his inner annoyance at having been fooled by the earlier reports from the Soviet Union. "He has worried a lot over this," observed Goebbels. And—indignantly—"The Bolsheviks deliberately set out to deceive us."

The advancing German armies had certainly found concrete indications of Stalin's true disposition toward western Europe. Captured Russian generals admitted they had been hampered in their enforced retreats by a total lack of maps of their own country; on the other hand, they had been furnished with entire truckloads of maps of Germany. While some German division commanders began "Barbarossa" with nothing more detailed than maps torn from automobile club handbooks, they found the enemy had better large-scale maps of Germany, Austria, and Silesia than they did themselves. Air reconnaissance now revealed that Stalin had established a huge complex of arms factories beyond the Urals. The Russians had also built several completely unpublicized highways along which they advanced, while the Wehrmacht adhered to the only roads they were aware of—the lanes that turned to swamps as soon as the rains fell. It also appeared that the German war department had been furnished by Communist agents with maps depicting completely fictitious roads and obstacles. In Red Army barracks were found dummy German soldiers that had been manufactured for target practice long before June 1941. From the absence of any Soviet written orders for actual operations in western Europe, it seems unlikely that anything *was* planned as early as the autumn, but most of Hitler's commanders—including Bock, Kluge, Richard Ruoff—agreed that the Führer had selected the proper time to strike.

Hitler properly realized that fast-flowing transport of supplies to his armies was the key to victory. Aided by thousands of prisoners, army engineers labored around the clock to repair the demolished Russian railway lines and re-lay them on the different German gauge. By mid-August a twin track extended as far as Smolensk. As Hitler repeatedly remarked, he was not going to make the mistakes "a certain other famous man"—meaning Napoleon—had made.

On the seventeenth, he had educated his staff on the dangers of overoptimism. "Always credit the enemy with doing just what you least want," he told Hewel. For example, he tried to envisage what Stalin would do if the Pripyet Marshes did not exist. On August 19, Martin Bormann quoted Hitler as remarking, "It'd be a good thing if the German people had a war every fifteen or twenty years. An army whose only job is keeping the peace ends up playing soldiers—look at Sweden and Switzerland!" And, "If it is held against me that my warmaking has cost one hundred thousand or two hundred thousand lives my answer is this: through my activities so far the German nation has already gained over two-and-a-half *million* people. Even if I ask ten percent of this as a sacrifice, I have still given ninety percent."

On August 18, the day of Goebbels's visit, Brauchitsch submitted to Hitler a written argument for the immediate resumption of the attack on Moscow, as the city's capture would take at least two months and Guderian's and Hoth's tanks first needed overhauling. The OKW operations staff agreed—though Colonel von Lossberg, Jodl's army aide, seemed pessimistic. Hewel noted: "A wager with Lossberg. I say the war will be shorter than World War I; he says it'll be longer."

Hitler rejected Brauchitsch's memorandum outright. It was most urgent, in his view, to deprive Stalin of his raw materials and arms industry. Besides, a rapid advance southward would encourage Iran to resist the Anglo-Russian invasion which he already knew was in the cards; in any case, he wanted the Crimea in German hands: it was from Crimean airfields that Russian bombers had recently attacked Romania. Hitler was plagued at night by a recurring nightmare—the petroleum fields of Ploesti, ablaze from end to end. His panzer generals Hoth and Guderian lamented that their tanks were largely in need of overhaul. Hitler did not believe them, as he had heard the same story before Dunkirk. After meeting with them at Borisov on August 4—where Guderian had claimed that he alone needed three hundred new tank-engines—Hitler told Keitel in exasperation that the two generals were obviously just

claiming that their tanks needed overhauling to conceal their own arrogant disapproval of his grand strategy.

Well, he was Führer, and now he was in better health too. On August
21 he dictated a brusque letter to Brauchitsch beginning with the words
"The army's proposal for continuing the operations in the east, dated
August 18, does not accord with my intentions. I order the following"—
and he restated the objectives he had been demanding since December
1940. In the north, the isolation of Leningrad; and in the south, the
capture of the Crimea, the Donets industrial and coal regions, and the
Caucasus oil fields. Field Marshal von Bock's Army Group Center, facing Moscow, was to remain on the defensive.

This rude rebuff caused uproar in the army. Halder literally wept
over Hitler's "pamphleteering," as he believed that Hitler was throwing
away the year's main chance. Brauchitsch suffered his first mild heart
attack. For many nights his adjutant heard him arguing with Hitler in
his sleep. He lacked the courage to resign as yet. Halder, made of
sterner stuff, wrote to his wife on August 23: "Tortured days lie behind
me. Again I offered my resignation to stave off an act of folly. The outcome was completely unsatisfactory. . . . The objective I set myself—
namely to finish off the Russians once for all before the year is out—will
not be achieved. . . . History will level at us the gravest accusation that
can be made of a High Command, namely that for fear of undue risk we
did not exploit the attacking impetus of our troops. It was the same in
the western campaign. But there the enemy's internal collapse cast a
merciful veil over our errors."

Bock's diary bespoke an equally anguished heart. "I don't want to
'capture Moscow'! I want to destroy the enemy's army, and the bulk of
that army is *in front* of me!" He telephoned Colonel Schmundt asking
that the Führer at least give a hearing to Guderian, who was warning
that his tanks urgently needed rest and rehabilitation. Guderian's controversial midnight conference with Hitler on August 23, without
Halder, can be reconstructed from his private letters and the diary of his
Chief of Staff. After hearing Hitler's case for the main thrust to continue
now toward the south, Guderian recognized that the Führer was right
and pocketed his own doubts; but he made one condition—that his
Panzer-Gruppe should be committed in its entirety to this thrust and not
to two divergent campaigns. Hitler agreed. "I returned," wrote Guderian afterward, "on the twenty-fourth, well satisfied and with high
hopes." Hitler had been "as always very nice and clear-thinking, and
unambiguously insistent on the direction I am now taking."

Bock's wrath and Halder's indignation, when they learned of Guderian's "defection," were immense and deviously expressed: Guderian commenced his southward thrust on August 25—but Halder confiscated his most powerful corps, the Forty-Sixth Panzer, and assigned it to the Fourth Army on the Moscow front. With only two corps, Guderian's offensive limped and stumbled, although his troops fought well. "Since the twenty-seventh I've been fighting for reinforcements, but they are granted me only in driblets and too late," he wrote in one letter. His Chief of Staff observed in his diary that Guderian "has the impression that [Bock and Halder] are still hanging on to their old plan—the advance on Moscow." By early September it was clear, as bad weather arrived, that the Red Army north of the Desna River had eluded him. Not until September 19 did Kiev fall to Reichenau's Sixth Army. A week later the huge encirclement action to the east of Kiev was over, with four Soviet armies wiped out and 665,000 prisoners taken; it was a famous victory, but the war was far from won.

At the end of August 1941, Hitler again found time for his allies. Italy had dispatched an expeditionary corps to the Ukraine, presenting the German army transport officials with the unenviable choice of transporting either the unloved Italians or the supplies essential to the Wehrmacht offensive. Goebbels had recently told Hitler that the Italians planned a North Africa propaganda film in which the part played by Rommel's forces would be ignored. Mussolini might need such a film for domestic consumption, but it would have fateful consequences in Germany. Hitler instructed Goebbels to refuse the Italian request for assistance. At the German première of another Italian film, there were hoots of laughter when the Italian troops were praised as "speedy"; Hitler ordered the offending sound-track obliterated before the film's release. "Otherwise, particularly in Austria, the entire Axis relationship would be damaged." His cynicism was manifest when in August Mussolini's son Bruno was for a time reported missing in action. "It's a pity that Mussolini's son was not killed in action after all. Fascism could have done with that at present."

The Duce arrived at the Wolf's Lair on August 25. Hewel noted: "War conference, then a communal meal in the dining bunker and a talk with my Chief [Ribbentrop]. In the evening a cold buffet in the garden. Vittorio Mussolini is particularly unattractive and dumb. . . ." The next day Hitler showed Mussolini over the battlefield at Brest-Litovsk, where the two-ton projectiles of his 620-millimeter mortars had reduced the citadel to ruins. He admitted that his military Intelligence had grossly misinformed him about the Soviet powers of resistance, but he predicted that final victory would be his by the spring of 1942. He was already manufacturing the extra naval and Luftwaffe equipment needed to invade Britain—or so he told Mussolini.

That evening both dictators left for the Führer's southern headquarters site in Galicia. Their two trains were shunted into specially modified tunnels for the night, and Mussolini joined Hitler for a confidential talk—pouring his heart out for the first time about the very real difficulties his Fascist revolution was in.[4] In 1943 Hitler reminisced: "We were speaking that night about the Russian commissar system, how you could not have two masters, and so on. He began to brood, and I went and dined in his train. Then he suddenly said to me, 'What you were saying, Führer, about not having two masters in one army, is quite right; but tell me, what can you do if you have got officers with reservations about the regime and about its ideologies . . . who say—the moment you talk of your ideology or of raison d'état—'We are monarchists: we owe our allegiance to the King!' " This admission of impotence in face of the Italian monarchy was a shock to Hitler, and he never forgot Mussolini's words.

The next day, August 28, both dictators flew across the fertile Ukrainian countryside for hours until they reached Rundstedt's command post at Uman. Keitel was to write: "The impression left by the sheer expanse of black soil and the—by German standards—immense harvest-lands of the Ukraine was overwhelming. For miles on end one often saw in the gently undulating open and treeless landscape nothing but the shocks of one enormous, endless wheatfield. One could sense the virginity of the soil." Three months later, in talking to a foreign diplomat Hitler described his own vivid impressions—how he had found himself surveying areas where the milk and honey flowed, where the soil was more fertile than anywhere else in Europe, "and yet the people were pitiful and impoverished beyond comprehension. I must have seen thousands of women there, but not one of them was wearing even the cheapest ornaments. In their wretched hovels there was neither cutlery nor other household goods. And this misery prevailed in a region whose soil was capable of the biggest harvest imaginable. Today there still lives there this terrified, scared mass of people, trembling with constant fear

---

[4] On August 30, 1941, Canaris returned to Berlin from talks with his Italian counterpart, Colonel Cesare Amé. He told his Abwehr staff: "A. describes the situation in Italy as very grave and hinted particularly at serious ill-feeling in army circles toward the Duce and the Fascist regime. A. believes that when the three hundred thousand Italian prisoners of war return they will want the System to give a very clear explanation of why this war was fought. The surprise caused by the eastern campaign has had an extremely unpleasant effect on the Italian people, and A. has great apprehensions about the coming winter of war."

of their commissars. Only when these pitiable creatures saw with their own eyes the commissars being shot did they gradually turn back into human beings again."

And Joachim Ribbentrop on his return from the Ukraine to Hitler's headquarters wrote his own private—and premature—panegyric on the Wehrmacht's achievement in conquering the east. "The Führer is exceptionally pleased with the way things are going. I firmly believe we will reach our target by winter—we shall have finally annihilated the fighting remnants of the Red Army and captured the main centers of population, raw materials, and industry so that even if the Soviet Union does not collapse completely it will be virtually incapable of regeneration in the coming winter, *i.e.,* they will in effect cease to be of value as an ally to Britain. And perhaps then after all the moment will come when the west adopts a different tone of voice, and we can achieve (albeit after a considerable detour) what we had in mind these last few years"—meaning concord with Britain. But he added: "Admittedly the interests of our allies now have to be taken fully into account." Hitler had evidently told Ribbentrop nothing of his secret talks with Mussolini; the foreign minister had to glean what information he could from the Forschungsamt's intercepts of the Italian ambassador's subsequent reports to Rome on *his* conversations with the Duce.

The summer would soon be over. At the end of August, Christa Schroeder wrote:

Our stay here at the headquarters gets longer and longer. First we thought we would be back in Berlin by the end of July, then they talked of mid-October; and now they are already saying we will not get away before the end of October, if even then. It is already quite cool here, like autumn, and if it occurs to the Chief to spend the winter here we shall all be frozen. This protracted bunker existence can't be doing us any good. The Chief does not look too well either, he gets too little fresh air and now he is oversensitive to sun and wind the moment he goes out in his car for a few hours. I would have loved to stay in Galicia—we were all in favor of it—but security there is not good enough. They say there are incidents there every day, and as they can't cordon off the area there as at our present headquarters the danger would be too great. But the countryside down there has a surprising charm, with woodland on one side and gentle slopes on the other and the cattle silhouetted against the blue sky while the farmers plod behind their plows. How romantic the peasant cottages look, all battered and windblown, with thatched roofs and scarcely a window in them, a wishing-well in front of them with a bucket on a rusty chain and a few sunflowers; the women are suntanned and barefoot with large dark cloths wrapped around their heads and reaching down to their waists—they stand there beside their cow, a little mournful, a little mysterious, but absolutely part of the landscape. It reminds me somehow of home.

The whole countryside there is freer. Here in the forest it all crowds in on you after a while. Besides, there you didn't have the feeling that you were locked in: you saw the peasants working in the fields and it made you feel free, while here we keep stumbling on sentries and are forever showing our identity cards. Well, I suppose that wherever we are we're always cut off from the world—in Berlin, at the Berghof, or on our travels. It is always the same sharply defined circle, always the same circuit inside the fence.

Just what Hitler's New Order would be in Europe was a secret he closely kept. That Slavs and Bolsheviks—particularly if they were Jewish —would not prosper under it was obvious; but the positions of countries like Italy, France, Hungary, and even Russia were still undefined. Hungary's astute military experts were not optimistic about "Barbarossa," and public opinion in Hungary frowned on Horthy's associations with the Nazis. The pro-German army Chief of Staff, General Henrik Werth, had been replaced by the isolationist General Ferenc Szombathelyi, and when Horthy visited Hitler on September 8 it was to ask for his divisions to be withdrawn from the battlefield. They visited Marienburg (now Malbork) in East Prussia together, and Horthy was deeply impressed at the genuine popular acclaim for the Führer. "We don't have your Jewish problem," Hitler pointedly explained. To his private staff he observed as the regent left, "Hungarians will always be Hungarians."

Oddly enough, it was Mussolini who had raised the New Order issue, although Italy by the extravagance of her claims on France was doing most to hinder it. Hitler's naval adjutant, Puttkamer, wrote revealingly on August 11, 1941:

At lunch yesterday the Führer spoke about our relationship with France. This elicited for the first time the reason why he doesn't take up any of the proposals made about it. He said he thought that a man like Darlan is being perfectly honest and that it was quite possible to achieve a bearable relationship with France by progressing from armistice to a preliminary peace. This was absolutely possible, in his view, even if we made stiff demands: France expected them, would uphold them, and would join the war at our side. So—*if* we were alone—everything could be attained. The decisive obstacle was however Italy's claims—Tunis and Corsica. No French government could uphold these. But he couldn't persuade the Italians to drop them; he had to associate himself with these claims too. He couldn't barter our ally Italy against France, he said. So that's the real reason, which was news to both me and Jodl, whom I discussed it with.

On September 8—the day of Horthy's arrival—Hitler told Hewel: "These are all just alliances of expediency. For example, the German people know that our alliance with Italy is only an alliance between Mussolini and myself. We Germans have sympathies only with Finland; we could find some sympathy for Sweden, and of course with Britain." Here he must have sighed, for he added: "A German-British alliance would be an alliance from people to people! The British would only have to keep their hands off the Continent. They could keep their empire—and the world if they wanted!"

However, Churchill was still in power, and any New Order must take account of that. Hitler's conquest of the Ukraine would mean that he no longer needed the raw-material regions of France. As he explained to his ambassador in France, Otto Abetz, on September 16, the Soviet iron-ore fields at Krivoi Rog alone would yield a million tons of ore a month. Hitler would insist only on Alsace and Lorraine, and the Channel coast facing England—he had thought a lot about the latter, but felt he could not relinquish it now, as he might have to reconquer it in years to come. Nor could he overlook the need for France to participate in the defeat of Britain. Given what he saw as modest claims, Hitler assured Abetz that France would certainly have a share of the pickings from the New Order. Turkey's position was more ambivalent. Britain had tried to restore her own standing after Ankara signed its ten-year treaty with Germany on the eve of "Barbarossa", but the Turkish foreign minister secretly assured Hitler's shrewd ambassador, Franz von Papen, that every true Turk longed in his heart for a German victory.

In his diary of September 15, 1941, Weizsäcker described Hitler's foreign policy in these words: "The quasi-depression of four weeks ago has been cured, probably the physical malaise too. An autobahn is being planned to the Crimean peninsula. There is speculation as to the probable manner of Stalin's departure. If he withdraws into Asia, he might even be granted a peace treaty. . . . He's unlikely to be replaced, let alone eliminated by a general." The next day, Papen also raised Stalin's future with Hitler, and the Führer repeated what he had told Goebbels a month before—that once the Wehrmacht had occupied a certain forward line in Russia, it might be possible to find common ground with the Red dictator, who was after all a man of enormous achievements. As another diplomat—Hasso von Etzdorf—noted on September 22: "[Hitler] sees two possibilities as to Stalin's fate: either he gets bumped off by his own people, or he tries to make peace with us. Because, he says, Stalin as the greatest living statesman must realize that at sixty-six you can't begin your life's work all over again if it will take a lifetime to complete it; so he'll try to salvage what he can, with our acquiescence. And in this we should meet him halfway. If Stalin could only decide to seek expansion for Russia toward the south, the Persian Gulf, as he [Hitler] recommended to him once [November 1940], then peaceful coexistence between Russia and Germany would be imaginable."

Papen for his part impressed on Hitler the need to promote a "constructive peace plan" after Russia's overthrow, a plan capable of inspiring all Europeans. From what Ribbentrop learned, Hitler agreed with Papen and planned a series of bilateral agreements with each European country, rather than one overall conference—except perhaps for the final grand act of ratification.

"The Führer then turned to his plans for the east," relates the only existing record of Hitler's conversation with Abetz on September 16:

Petersburg [Leningrad], the "poisonous nest" from which for so long Asiatic venom has "spewed forth" into the Baltic, must vanish from the earth's surface. The city is already cut off. It only remains for our artillery and Luftwaffe to bombard it to pieces, destroying the water mains, the power stations, and everything the population needs to survive. The Asiatics and the Bolsheviks must be hounded out of Europe, this "episode of two hundred fifty years of Asiatic pestilence" is at an end. The Urals will be the frontier beyond which Stalin and his like can do as they please. But he [Hitler], by launching occasional expeditions across the Urals, will also ensure that Stalin gets no respite there either.

After the expulsion of the Asiatics, Europe will never again be dependent on an outside power, nor need we "care two hoots" about America. Europe will meet its own raw material needs, and it will have its own export market in the Russian territories so we will no longer need the rest of the world's trade. The new Russia this side of the Urals will be "our India," but far more handily located than that of Britain. The new Greater German Empire will embrace 135 million people, and it will rule 150 million more.

The backbone of the new empire would be the Wehrmacht and above all the SS—the capable new elite, alone in Hitler's view entitled to rule the Slavs and the inferior races of the east.

Himmler and Heydrich were frequent guests at the Wolf's Lair. On one occasion in September Hitler found himself lunching with Himmler and six SS generals (albeit some of only honorary rank: Bormann, Dietrich, Schaub, and Karl-Hermann Frank). In public Hitler talked with Himmler only of innocuous matters—architecture, the salon of Frau Bruckmann, or the relative nutritive values of the potato and the soya bean. In private they elaborated ways of fighting the growing Hydra-headed partisan movements throughout the Nazi-occupied territories. Hitler linked these movements with Stalin's July broadcast, and he condemned as far too mild the treatment so far meted out to captured offenders. On September 7—as Himmler was at the Wolf's Lair—he ordered that if the murderer of a German NCO in Paris was not found immediately, fifty hostages were to be shot; and in future the ratio was to be a hundred "Communists" for each German life taken. (The German military commander admittedly protested, and Hitler left the final scale of reprisals to his discretion.) The partisan threat was particularly severe in the Balkans, and on the sixteenth Hitler signed an order giving his local army commanders special powers; but the enemy purpose was being achieved, for more and more divisions would have to be diverted to this counterinsurgency campaign, and the differences between an initially passive population and their German occupiers hardened into an implacable hatred.

The siege of Leningrad symbolized the brutalization of this war. Four million people now packed the city's streets. By mid-September Leeb had taken the last high ground to the south. Already his tank crews could see the glittering gold spires of the admiralty building. The Russians had evacuated the main munitions factories in July, and a chaotic attempt at getting the women and children to safety had begun. But with the German capture of Petrokrepost the city was now cut off; in a formal directive, Number 35, issued on September 6, Hitler ordered Leningrad to be so thoroughly isolated by his ground forces that by mid-September at the latest he could recover his tanks and Richthofen's air squadrons for the main assault on Moscow after all. On September 9 the Luftwaffe began around-the-clock bombing operations. Jeschonnek's deputy wrote in his diary: "We hope to have achieved a tight encirclement of Leningrad within a week. Food already appears to be short there." On the tenth, Rosenberg's liaison officer reported to him from Hitler's headquarters:

For three days now our 240-millimeter guns have been firing into the city. Richthofen's bombing has destroyed the big waterworks. The

Russians have only evacuated the Stakhanovite and other top-grade workers needed to expand their industry beyond the Urals; apart from that the entire population has remained and actually been swollen by the evacuation of the surrounding suburbs. Already it's almost impossible to get bread, sugar, and meat in Leningrad. The Führer wants to avoid house-to-house fighting, which would cost our troops heavy casualties. The city is to be just shut in, shot to pieces by artillery and starved out. A few days or weeks here or there make no difference, as the besieging army won't have to be very big. The Finns have suggested diverting Lake Ladoga into the Gulf of Finland—which lies several meters lower—to wash away the city of Leningrad.

On September 12, General Halder emphasized to Leeb's army group that his tanks would shortly be needed for the attack on Moscow. This provoked angry protests from the tank commanders. General Hans Reinhardt protested at the shattering effect this order to halt was having on his men. "The city is spread out before them, and nobody is stopping them going right on in!" But Hitler agreed that the tanks should not be committed; Leningrad should be destroyed by bombardment instead. Admiral Raeder asked him to spare at least the dockyards for the German navy; this too Hitler refused, but as regards the tanks Keitel telephoned Leeb to postpone their withdrawal by forty-eight hours. On the twelfth the Luftwaffe commander, Richthofen, entered in his diary: "Colonel Schmundt came this afternoon to lecture the higher echelons of the army on how the Führer sees things. Very necessary, unfortunately, as Halder and Brauchitsch either told them nothing at all or got it all wrong. [Schmundt] talked about the problem of Finland and Leningrad. Over L. the 'plow shall pass!'" On September 16 the tanks were finally halted, and their withdrawal to the Moscow front began. As for Leningrad, on September 27 the naval staff learned that "any surrender offer is to be rejected."

Kiev at least was in German hands. The news broke at Hitler's headquarters late on September 19. For days afterward he spoke at lunch and dinner of his plans for Europe. Dr. Fritz Todt came, and so did Gauleiter Koch, whose mission would be to tame the Ukraine for western Europe's needs. Dr. Werner Koeppen, Rosenberg's liaison officer, recorded these historic conversations:

Lunchtime, September 19
    Dr. Todt related his impressions of his latest journey to Oslo and Trondheim, and of the first ground broken for the major traffic link between Germany and Denmark. The Führer talked about his plan to rebuild Trondheim afresh in terrace-form, so that every house will be

in the sun all day long; this presents no traffic problems, as Trond-heim's main traffic will always rely on its waterways. The Führer then spoke of the need to build one autobahn to Trondheim, and another down to the Crimea. After the war the German citizen shall have the chance of taking his Volkswagen and looking over the captured terri-tories in person, so that if need should arise he will also be willing to fight for them. We must never repeat the prewar error of having the colonial idea the property of only a few capitalists or corporations. In the future the road or autobahn will play an incomparably larger part in public transport than the railway, which will take care of goods transportation. Only road travel enables you to get to know a coun-try. The railway traverses distances, but the road opens them up.

He planned the New Order as a deliberately European *Raumpolitik*. Earlier, as he told Seyss-Inquart on the twenty-sixth, it was downright absurd that though a vast, only sparsely populated empire lay in the east with almost inexhaustible resources and raw materials, western Europe struggled to meet its needs by imports from colonies far overseas. In time of war those sea lanes could always be endangered. "This is why it is unimportant how long we have to go on fighting in the east. Once we have securely occupied the vitally important European regions of the Soviet Union, the war east of the Urals can go on a hundred years, for all we care." Meanwhile the 130 million people living in Europe's new eastern empire would be a captive market for virtually every industrial product Europe manufactured, from a simple water-glass to the largest artifact. The east would supply raw materials. Hitler had just learned, for example, that rubber was being grown near Kharkov—he had himself already seen excellent samples of it. "The giant farms Stalin has intro-duced will probably be the best way to use the land in the future too, as they are probably the only way of cultivating the land intensively . . ." He felt that most Russians had become quite accustomed to being treated like animals.

The Ukrainians, he had said at lunch a few days earlier, were lazy, amorphous, nihilistic, and Asiatic in their ways; they would never under-stand such concepts as duty or the ethos of work; they responded only to the whip. "This is why Stalin is one of the greatest living men, be-cause he succeeded in forging this Slav rabbit family into a nation, albeit only by the cruelest coercion." Both Hitler and Koch rejected any no-tion of a "Free Ukraine" for this reason. Chaos came naturally to the Ukrainians, it was their natural ambience. Half an education would make them dissatisfied and anarchistic; hence Rosenberg's ambition to found a university at Kiev must be rejected. If the occupying authorities controlled the alcohol and tobacco supplies, they would have the population eating out of their hands. In private conference with Hitler and Keitel, Koch emphasized the need to be brutal right from the start if the errors of 1917–18, stemming from vacillating occupation policies, were to be avoided. Hitler agreed. He suggested that the British rule over India must be the model for their own administration of the east. Koch departed from the Wolf's Lair amid the congratulations of Hitler's staff: Koch was undoubtedly the "second Stalin" the Ukraine needed.

"The frontier between Europe and Asia," reflected Hitler over dinner on the twenty-third, "is not the Ural Mountains but there where the settlements of Germanically inclined people end and unadulterated Slav settlements begin. It is our task to push this frontier as far east as possible, and if need be far beyond the Urals. It is the eternal law of nature that gives Germany as the stronger power the right before history to subjugate these peoples of inferior race, to dominate them and to coerce them into performing useful labors. I admit this has nothing to do with Christian ethics, but the very fact that it is according to the more ancient and well-tried laws of nature makes it the more likely to last a long while."

In the "Protectorate" of Bohemia-Moravia, draconian measures succeeded. By 1941 Hitler had incarcerated twenty-five hundred Czech "opponents," but in October 1940 he had stipulated that "the trials are to be postponed until the war's over, when they will be drowned by the noise of victory celebrations." For insurgents and rebels Hitler preferred to use the firing squad—formal trials just produced folk heroes like Andreas Hofer and Leo Schlageter (Germans executed by the French occupation forces in the Twenties). But since "Barbarossa" a wave of opposition had appeared in the Protectorate. Crops had been sabotaged, there were slowdowns and stoppages and terror incidents. Rumor reached Hitler that a full-scale uprising was being plotted. "Only now do they realize that there is no escape. As long as the great Russia, mother of all Slavs, was there they could still hope." Obviously the ailing and respectable Baron Konstantin von Neurath was too inefficient as Reich Protector to crush the mutiny at birth. Koeppen quoted Hitler's remarks at lunch a few days later: "He keeps repeating that he knows the Czechs of old. To them Neurath was just a friendly old duffer whose blandness and good humor they rapidly mistook for weakness and stupidity. . . . The Czechs are a nation of 'cyclists'—they bow from the waist upward, but the legs still kick!"

On Bormann's advice Hitler sent Neurath on extended sick-leave and appointed the feared SS General Reinhard Heydrich—head of the SS main security office—Acting Protector. ("It was at my suggestion that Heydrich was appointed!" Bormann later crowed in his diary.) When Bormann, SS Reichsführer Himmler, Heydrich, and Karl Frank (Neurath's state secretary) came to the Wolf's Lair on September 24, Hitler told Heydrich his job would be "a fighting mission," of only limited duration. He gave Heydrich carte blanche, signed in his own hand, to do as he saw fit, and he pointed out: "You observe that wherever I believe the unity of the Reich to be at risk I appoint an SS commander to safeguard it." Heydrich proudly flew to Prague on September 27 and arrested the rebellious ringleaders—among them General Alois Eliaš, the prime minister. The next day Heydrich phoned Himmler that Eliaš had confessed to being in contact with the exiled Beneš government in London. Eliaš was tried in public and condemned to death. But Hitler decided he was of more value as a hostage for the Czechs' good behavior, and he survived until May 1942.

Hitler briefed Heydrich fully on the position of his Protectorate in the New Order. Heydrich reported this secretly to his local German governors in Prague on October 2: Germany was to remain permanently in occupation of certain European countries. Norway, Holland, Flanders, Denmark, Sweden, and—because of the fifth- and sixth-century Germanic invasions—Britain too were nations of Germanic origin; they would be led humanely and justly into a closer alliance with the Reich. Heydrich also closely followed Hitler's "thoughts on the final solution" of the vexing Slav problem. One day the Protectorate would be permanently settled by Germans. "This does not mean," said Heydrich, "that we now have to try to Germanize all Czech rabble. . . . For those of good race and good intentions the matter is simple; they will be Germanized. For the rest, those of inferior racial origin or with hostile intentions, I shall get rid of them—there is plenty of room in the east for them." Inferior but well-meaning Czechs would probably be sent to work in the Reich. The more difficult category—those of good racial characteristics but hostile intentions—would have to be liquidated, if all attempts at Germanizing them failed; it would be potentially too dangerous to turn them loose in the east.[5]

[5] Hitler had used the same language to Neurath, State Secretary Karl-Hermann Frank, and the minister of justice in September 1940: "Czechs turned down on racial grounds or anti-Reich in attitude were not to be assimilated. This category was to be eliminated *(sei auszumerzen)*." In conversation over lunch on October 6, 1941, Hitler announced that the Jews in the Protectorate were all to be deported eastward. "If the Czechs still don't behave themselves then, the Führer will amend their protectorate status: Moravia will be completely detached from Bohemia and large

Hitler advised Heydrich to introduce the Czech workers to both the carrot and the stick. In any factory where sabotage occurred, ten hostages were to be shot; but in factories with a good output and a sabotage-free record the workers were to get extra rations. Heydrich went much further, introducing the Czechs for the first time to the full Bismarckian social security program. This social experiment lasted until May 1942, when Heydrich was assassinated in Prague by Free Czechs agents parachuted into the country.

"The Czech workers have accepted the liquidation of the conspirators quite calmly," Koeppen had written when Heydrich first reported back from Prague, over dinner on October 2. "The most important thing to them is to have enough food and work. . . . One worker has even written to Heydrich, stating his full name, saying that Czech history has always been like this: each generation has to learn its lesson and then there is peace for a time. He added that nobody would object if another two thousand of them were shot, either." The Nazis rose to the occasion.

For Hitler the last act of "Barbarossa," as he thought, had now begun. At five-thirty on the morning of October 2, 1941, Field Marshal von Bock's army group—nearly two thousand tanks commanded by Guderian, Erich Hoepner, and Hoth, and the armies of Maximilian von Weichs, Günther-Hans von Kluge, and Adolf Strauss—opened the first phase of "Operation Typhoon," the attack on Moscow. Hitler calculated that four weeks of fighting weather still remained.

At 11:30 P.M., after his supper with Heydrich, he took his special train to Berlin, where he was to speak to the German people.

---

parts handed over to the Lower Danube Gau. Gauleiter Dr. [Hugo] Jury has been waiting long enough for his missing capital city Brünn [Brno]. After this war the Führer proposes to transplant all the racially valueless elements from Bohemia to the east."

Cold Harvest

Only the weather could now thwart him. On October 2, 1941, as "Typhoon" began, lunch started fifty minutes late at his headquarters as he listened to the first reports on this last battle, designed to destroy Marshal Timoshenko's armies. When the meal began, he was at first unusually silent, brooding on the great events unfolding five hundred miles to the east. He broke the silence only to ask about the weather prospects for the next few days, and then again, in a forced attempt to put his mind elsewhere, to reminisce about the Berghof—where even now Martin Bormann's construction crews were carrying out still further architectural "improvements" to the mountainside.

Yet Russia's weather was in no way unpredictable: the first daytime frost always comes on the eighteenth of October (while frost at night might come as early as the end of September). Peter the Great knew this, for he had forbidden ships to leave the Baltic ports after October 18 for fear of the winter storms. The Russian winter reaches its peak every eighteenth of January—with the notorious "Jordan's frost"—with Fahrenheit temperatures of zero in Leningrad and minus five in Moscow itself. No snow would actually stick until late November, however; and once, in 1913, there had been no snow until February.

As soon as Hitler had believed Leningrad encircled and Rundstedt's operations at Kiev far enough advanced, he had ordered the army to prepare this attack on Timoshenko's forces west of Moscow, using the armored divisions and Luftwaffe units no longer needed by Leeb or Rundstedt; he would have liked "Typhoon" to begin in mid-September, but the army had explained why the attack could not be launched before the end of the month. The Luftwaffe command showed the earliest apprehensions about "Typhoon's" prospects. Indeed, as early as August 14, Jeschonnek's deputy, Hoffmann von Waldau, had privately written at Luftwaffe headquarters: "It is all getting very late: at the end of October the war will die out in the snow." And on September 9, three days after Hitler issued the directive for "Typhoon," Waldau gloomily predicted: "We are heading for a winter campaign. The real trial of this war has begun. My belief in final victory remains." West of the Russian capital, meanwhile, Timoshenko had prepared line after line of defensive positions, while an apparently inexhaustible flow of new divisions poured into the front, making a mockery of the German army theoreticians' dreams of eliminating the enemy's military strength.

In an exultant proclamation to his three million soldiers on the eve of "Typhoon," Hitler appealed to them to give "the last mighty heave necessary to smash the enemy before winter breaks upon us." He opened their eyes to the scale of the effort already made since June—two thousand road bridges built for the troops, over four hundred railway bridges constructed, eighteen thousand miles of railway track restored to working order, including ten thousand miles already relaid to the standard European gauge. Now he was to speak to the ordinary Berliners. "Quite apart from the transport problem," mocked Hitler over lunch on October 1, "Russia won't be helped much with one week's British tank output allocated to her, as she is losing more tanks in a day than Britain can turn out in a week. The only palpable relief for Russia would be if Britain could force us to withdraw tanks and aircraft from the eastern front, and this she can only do by invading the Continent. Churchill has warded off this Stalin demand by arguing that the invasion danger increases with the approach of dull and foggy weather again, and that he needs his forty-five divisions to defend the British Isles." Hitler made fun of the British suggestion that he had not spoken in recent months as he had nothing cheerful to tell the German people. "Over this period Churchill has admittedly made almost a dozen speeches, but if you compare actions and achievements, then I am quite content to stand before history as I am." His table companions laughed heartily; two days later they recognized that Hitler had just tried out his next big speech on them.

At 1:30 P.M. on October 3, 1941, his train arrived in Berlin. He lunched with his staff, then drove through streets of cheering crowds to the Sportpalast, where he now delivered one of the most stirring speeches of his life—wholly *ex tempore* and hence "enormously devout," as Hewel afterward reported. Hitler was exhilarated by the welcome the capital gave him. "It was the same atmosphere as at the most wonderful of our meetings during the years of struggle. The reason was that no special tickets had been distributed—the audience really was a cross section of the people. The enthusiasm and acclaim of the Berliners lining the streets to the stadium were also bigger and more genuine than for a long time. The ordinary people really do make the most appreciative audience, they are the people who deep down inside know they support me. They are marked by that kind of stability that can stand the heaviest burdens—while our intellectuals just flutter here and there."

In his tumultuous speech he outlined his unifying role in Europe—how Italy, Hungary, the Nordic countries, and then Japan had come closer to Germany. "Unhappily, however, not the nation I have courted all my life: the British. Not that the British people as a whole alone bear the responsibility for this, no, but there are some people who in their pigheaded hatred and lunacy have sabotaged every such attempt at an understanding between us, with the support of that international enemy known to us all, international Jewry. . . . As in all the years I strove to achieve understanding whatever the cost, there was Mr. Churchill who kept on shouting, 'I want a war!' Now he has it.'' Hitler scorned the Churchill clique who were claiming that in these last three months he had met defeat after defeat in Russia; the truth was that the Wehrmacht's divisions had advanced from one victory to the next, tirelessly and courageously, the infantry marching two thousand miles and more since the spring. "If people now talk of lightning [*Blitz*] wars, then it is these soldiers who are responsible for it; their achievements are like lightning, because never in history have there been advances like these. . . . Of course there were also a few historic lightning retreats too," he scoffed, talking about the British regiments, "and these certainly beat our operations for speed; but then there were not such great distances involved, as they always kept that much closer to the coast!"

Within an hour Hitler's train was bearing him back to headquarters. Victory in Russia seemed certain. Guderian was approaching Orel. Like two fishermen's nets flung out over the sea, Bock's armies were hauling in their catches at Vyazma and Bryansk. Another 673,000 prisoners would be found inside. On the Sea of Azov, Rundstedt destroyed the Soviet Eighteenth Army and took another 100,000 prisoners. In front of Moscow Timoshenko seemed unaware of what was happening to his own armies—some were attacking, others retreating, while all the time Bock's nets pulled tighter.

A grim jocularity overcame Hitler—he began talking freely at mealtimes again, gossiping about the different kinds of caviar and oysters and the mysterious bacteria that had massacred the crabs some decades before. Russia? "We are planning big things for our share of the territory, 'our India'—canals and railroads, the latter with a new gauge of ten feet. The population . . . must vegetate. For Stalin's rump-empire [beyond the Urals] bolshevism will be a good thing—our guarantee of their permanent ignorance." Thus wrote Weizsäcker of Hitler's ambitions. They were an open secret. In his mind's eye, Hitler transported himself fifty years onward, to when there would be five million German farmers settled there to tend the crops. "He does not attach the slightest importance to overseas colonies," wrote Koeppen. "On this score he would most rapidly reach agreement with Britain. Germany only needs a little colonial soil to cultivate tea and coffee—everything else he would produce on the Continent itself. Germany's colonial needs would be satisfied by the Belgian Congo. Our Mississippi must be the Volga—not the Niger."

Outside the dining bunker at midday on October 5, Hitler espied a large table, groaning under a display of agricultural products from East Prussia, for this was Harvest Thanksgiving day. He jested that this vegetarian display with its many hues and colors was far more attractive than if, for example, a pile of "butchered animal carcasses" had been put there—a comment that enjoyed only a mixed reception since there were the most luscious pork chops for lunch that day. At dinner the next day, Hitler was again in an expansive mood. Major Engel, his ebullient army adjutant, had been bitten by a dog, so Hitler uncorked a stream of witticisms about the fearful consequences if rabies should take hold at his headquarters. Dinner was short, so that the latest uncensored newsreel films could be shown. Hitler saw for himself his troops battling forward under General von Manstein, now commanding the Eleventh Army in the assault on the Crimea; he also saw the northern armies frustrating the frantic Russian attempts to relieve Leningrad.

By October 7, the Bryansk pocket was completely sealed, and the armored divisions were about to close the other huge ring around Vyazma. Jodl stated that the Red Army was about to lose seventy-two divisions in the two pockets, and that so far radio reconnaissance had only located one solitary division outside them. Gripped by this military drama, Hitler did not eat that day—although Himmler was guest of honor, it being his forty-first birthday. Hewel marveled in his diary: "Vyazma has been captured. The net tightens around Timoshenko's army. Jodl says, 'The most crucial day of the whole Russian war,' and compares it with Königgrätz."

Intercepted code-messages from diplomats in Moscow suggested that the end there was not far off. The Turkish ambassador told of tens of thousands of casualties and an indescribable turmoil and confusion; parts of the city's population were already fleeing for the Ural Mountains. Immense German plans were hatched in this flush of victory—the General Staff looking beyond Moscow, Hitler looking to the south. For a time, elated by his SS Life Guards' capture of Mariupol (Zhdanov) on the Sea of Azov, Hitler considered throwing them a hundred miles forward to Rostov on the Don—the very gateway to the Caucasus and the oil fields there. ("The fact that in the not too distant future we'll have used up every last drop of gasoline makes this a matter of the utmost urgency," Keitel told Canaris later in October.) General Eduard Wagner, the army's quartermaster general, wrote privately late on October 5: "Now the operation is rolling toward Moscow. Our impression is that the final great collapse is immediately ahead, and that tonight the Kremlin is packing its bags. What matters now is that the panzer armies reach their objectives. Strategic objectives are being defined that would have stood our hair on end at one time. East of Moscow!! Then I think the war'll be over and perhaps we'll see the collapse of their system too, which would see us a fair bit further on in the fight against Britain. I keep having to marvel at the Führer's military judgment. This time he is intervening—and one can say, decisively—in the operations, and so far he has been right every time. The major victory in the south is *his* work alone."

On October 8, Jodl repeated his triumphant verdict: "We have finally and without any exaggeration won this war!" At dinner Hitler exultantly scoffed at the distortions being put about by London's "Press Jews"— claims so foolish that a schoolboy with an atlas could refute them. In France Admiral Darlan had now spoken out in favor of a German-French entente. "Success," commented Hitler, "is always the best basis for bargaining."

On the eastern front it had now begun to rain.

In Kiev—and later in Odessa—there was an urban variation on the scorched earth theme: the Russians had booby-trapped entire buildings, to blow them up by remote control after the Germans moved in. According to the Soviet radio, Leningrad had been similarly prepared. Moscow would be no different. On October 7, Hitler signed an OKW order forbidding Bock to accept Moscow's surrender, if offered; no German troops were to set foot there or in Leningrad—these cities were to be encircled and wiped out by fire and bombardment. Small gaps might be left on the far side of the Moscow ring, to allow the citizenry to flee eastward into the Soviet lines and increase the chaos there. A few days later, Heydrich asked Himmler to make it clear to the Führer that responsibility for the effective destruction of Leningrad and Moscow rested solely with the Wehrmacht commanders. He said the SS agents who had penetrated into Leningrad reported that the damage so far was quite negligible, and that if they had learned anything from Warsaw it was that artillery alone was not enough—massive use had to be made of fire bombs and high explosives.

The coming victory over Russia promised to relieve Hitler of immense strategic burdens. Japan would then be free to wade into the United States, which would then hardly be in a position to come to Britain's aid in her final fight with Germany. Roosevelt for his part increased his efforts to swing American public opinion around to supporting war with Hitler now, and he sent Averell Harriman to assist Britain's Lord Beaverbrook at a Moscow conference on ways of rushing military support to Stalin. On October 6, Hitler was handed the decoded text of Roosevelt's letter introducing Harriman to Stalin:

> Harry Hopkins has told me in great detail of his encouraging and satisfactory visits with you. I can't tell you how thrilled all of us are because of the gallant defense of the Soviet armies. I am confident that ways will be found to provide the material and supplies necessary to fight Hitler on all fronts, including your own. I want particularly to take this occasion to express my great confidence that your armies will ultimately prevail over Hitler and to assure you of our great determination to be of every possible material assistance.

Hitler had the text of this letter released throughout the Americas, without revealing how he had obtained it; he also, to the intense irritation of Roosevelt, amended the president's salutation ("My Dear Mr. Stalin") to "My Dear Friend Stalin"; and where Roosevelt had prudently concluded with "Yours very sincerely," the German propaganda text ended with an oily "In cordial friendship."

Roosevelt had long gone beyond strict neutrality. Early in September a U-boat had given him the welcome chance by attempting to torpedo the American destroyer *Greer* (which had reportedly been cooperating with a British plane chasing the submarine); as a result of this attack, on the eleventh Roosevelt ordered the navy to "shoot on sight" any warships of the Axis powers encountered in seas, "the protection of which is necessary for American defense." Hitler no longer believed the isolationists could keep the United States out of the war, in spite of efforts such as those by Charles Lindbergh, who used the American radio networks to denounce "warmongers," among whom he included not only Roosevelt and the British but the Jews as well. Admiral Raeder implored the Führer to permit German warships to meet force with force, since Roosevelt's announcement was tantamount to a localized declaration of war under international law; but after discussing this from every angle with Raeder and U-boat commander Admiral Dönitz—as well as with Ribbentrop—Hitler remained unconvinced that the military advantages would outweigh the political risks involved in firing back on any U.S. naval attackers, and his restrictions on the warships remained in force. He was not frightened of Roosevelt or the United States. Handed an American magazine which quoted annual statistics on tank and aircraft production in the United States, Hitler scoffed that the figures were ludicrously low—less than one month's output of the German munitions industry. As for quality, he rocked with laughter when he saw the first newsreels of the United States' two mechanized divisions on maneuvers (the film reached him through South America).

Hitler could not conceal his disappointment at the current aimlessness of Japanese foreign policy, which he had closely followed through the telegrams intercepted by the Forschungsamt and foreign ministry decoders. The Japanese had refused to show the Germans the texts of their secret exchanges with the Roosevelt administration, but in September Hitler explained to his staff that he was loath to put pressure on Tokyo to enter the war in case this was construed as proof of German weakness. By October 1941 Hitler no longer feared this construction; he even somewhat prematurely directed his press chief, Dr. Otto Dietrich, to announce to the world—and Tokyo in particular—that the Russian campaign had been won. But Tokyo's secret talks with Washington still continued; her economy was suffering from the overlong interruption of the Trans-Siberian railway by "Barbarossa"—far longer than the "two months" Hitler had promised—and on October 16 the Japanese Cabinet resigned. To Hitler's annoyance the new prime minister was General Hideki Tojo, and his foreign minister was Shigenori Togo, the former Japanese ambassador to Berlin; Hitler intensely mistrusted the latter, despite his German wife. He saw in all this just Japanese playacting designed to assuage domestic public opinion, while the Japanese continued to wriggle out of their commitments for a few more months. The truth was, as he revealed by an aside to Ciano on October 25, that Hitler was completely in the dark as to Japanese war plans. "We cannot expect Japan to pursue anything but a purely Japanese foreign policy," he had also said in September. "We must just contrive to wait until they themselves consider the time ripe for intervention." As for North America,

Hitler learned that Pope Pius XII had instructed Roosevelt's special emissary Myron C. Taylor that any extension of the war by the United States would be frowned on. Indeed, the Vatican had flatly refused to pronounce the war of the democracies against National Socialism a "just war"; Hitler learned this on October 7.

That same day Field Marshal von Bock was ordered to proceed with his drive on Moscow and the first snow drifted out of the sky onto Hitler's headquarters. On the sixteenth a fighter pilot arriving at the Führer's headquarters to receive the Knight's Cross announced that six inches of snow was covering the whole countryside. On the seventeenth the temperature at Leningrad fell to 32°F.; in the far north it was 5°. The next day for the first time the weather was so bad as to prevent any noticeable change in the front lines. Bock's army group was paralyzed by the snow, slush, and slime. Nothing could move except on foot or in the lightest of handcarts, for the roads were few and far between and it was on these that the Russians now concentrated their defense. The only good highway—from Smolensk to Vyazma—had been booby-trapped with high-explosive shells, whose remote-controlled detonation caused sudden craters thirty feet wide and eight feet deep. Each night the temperatures fell and froze the snow and mud; each morning the thaw set in, and the roads were again impassable.

"The Russian roads beggar description," wrote one of Canaris's aides touring the eastern front. "They are frequently up to one hundred yards wide and people use them as they choose. Their surface is a thick, cloying layer of slime of varying depth: if you drive slowly, it bogs your truck down, and if you drive faster, you start sliding and skidding; despite the width of the roads it is enormously difficult to take evasive action, for all the traffic in both directions tries to keep to the same beaten tracks; as these ruts are very difficult to get out of, collisions occur." As the German troops struggled to advance through this filth and slush they encountered mournful columns of Russians trudging westward into captivity. There were hundreds of thousands of them, and they presented the German military authorities with problems of feeding, transportation, and accommodation they had never clearly envisaged. "The columns of Russian prisoners moving on the roads look like half-witted herds of animals," Canaris's aide noted. Barely guarded and kept in order by the fist and whip, these wretched prisoners marched until they were exhausted by hunger or disease; they were then carried by their comrades or left at the roadside. "The Sixth Army [Reichenau's] has ordered that all prisoners that break down are to be shot. Regrettably this is done at the roadside, even in the villages, so that the local population are eyewitnesses of these incidents." In the prison camps the food was so meager that cannibalism broke out. "The population," the report continued, "greet the German soldiers as liberators from the yoke of bolshevism. But there is a danger that this extremely useful mood, which is displayed by their great hospitality and many gifts, will turn into the opposite if dealt with wrongly."

The first big anti-Jewish SS action occurred at Kiev at the end of September. The report to Canaris by the previously mentioned aide noted: "Orders are that the Jews are to be 'resettled.' This takes place as follows: the Jews are ordered at short notice to report to specific collecting points with their best clothes and their jewelry on the following night. No distinctions are made as to class, sex, or age. They are then taken to a preselected and prepared site outside the town concerned, where they have to deposit their jewelry and clothes under the pretext of having to complete certain formalities. They are led away from the road and liquidated. The situations that arise in the process are so horrifying that they can not be described. The effects on the German squads are inevitable—the executions can usually only be carried out under the influence of alcohol. An SD officer ordered to act as an observer related how he had nightmares of the most terrible kind for days afterward. The native population react to this liquidation program, of which they are fully aware, calmly and sometimes with satisfaction, and the Ukrainian militia actually take part." There were even protests that some Jews were escaping the net cast by the SS task forces.[1]

The actual origins of the Kiev pogrom are obscure. The report of the security police suggests that the massacre was a reprisal impatiently demanded by the Ukrainians themselves, since it was the Russian Jews who were reported to have acted as NKVD agents and set fire to the city after the Germans moved in. Whatever the origin, on the last two days of September 33,771 Russian Jews were executed at Kiev. One month later the figure had risen to 75,000.

There are compelling indications that all this was planned long before "Barbarossa" began: at a course for SS task force commanders at Düben in June, Heydrich had instructed them—according to Walter Blume, one such commander—that these *Ostjuden* were the intellectual reservoir of bolshevism and "in the Führer's view" were to be liqui-

[1] Thus a renegade Russian major named Chumak wrote in a report in December 1942 (forwarded by Colonel Gehlen, the new head of Foreign Armies East, to his superiors): "Take the Ukraine: for twenty-three years this nation had to bear the Jewish yoke without protest and in far greater degree than any other nation in Russia. . . . Yet even though all the Jews were shot between September 28 and October 1 [1941], Kiev is now swarming with them again, and all of them have been issued Russian papers."

dated. Himmler, the SS Reichsführer, had orally briefed them in the same sense in May, and late in September he toured the task force head-quarters and announced to them—for example to Otto Ohlendorf, com-manding Task Force D, in a speech at Nikolaev—that he alone "in asso-ciation with Hitler" was responsible.

Himmler's formulation was perhaps purposefully vague. There are documents which strongly suggest that Hitler's responsibility—as distinct from Himmler's—was limited to the decision to deport all European Jews to the east, and that responsibility for what happened to Russian Jews and to European Jews after their arrival in "the east" rested with Himmler, Heydrich, and the local authorities there—who took full ad-vantage of the atmosphere of hatred and contempt for human life created by their Führer. On September 18, 1941, Himmler wrote to Arthur Greiser, the brutal Gauleiter of the Wartheland—that is, the Pol-ish territories annexed in the German invasion two years earlier:

> The Führer wishes the old Reich territory and the Protectorate [of Bohemia-Moravia] to be cleansed and rid of Jews, from west to east, as soon as possible. As a first step I am therefore endeavoring to transport—this year as far as possible—all the Jews of the old Reich and Protectorate into the eastern territories annexed by the Reich in 1939 first of all; next spring they will then be deported still further eastward [into Russia].

The first sixty thousand, Himmler advised, would be sent to the Lodz ghetto soon to spend the winter there. Heydrich would be in charge of this "migration of the Jews." Evidently the second phase, dumping them into Russia itself, could not be begun until the Russian campaign was finished and the military pressure on the railroads was relaxed.

Hitler's own attitude is illuminated by an incident at this time. On September 20, he learned that the Bolsheviks were maltreating the large colony of ethnic Germans on the Volga: thousands were being liqui-dated, and the rest deported to Siberia, according to his sources. The foreign ministry recommended "reprisals against Jews in the occupied eastern territories," or even against those in the Reich. But Baron Adolf von Steengracht, Ribbentrop's representative, noted that "the Führer has not yet decided," and the next day Koeppen recorded that Hitler had decided to reserve reprisals against the Jews "for the eventuality of an American declaration of war." When Goebbels saw him two days later, he wrote in an unpublished section of his diary, only: "The Führer's opinion is that bit by bit the Jews must be got out of Germany altogether"—so even to Goebbels, his most trusted and anti-Semitic minister, Hitler made no specific mention of any extermination of either the German or the Russian Jews.

The Russian Jews had few champions. There was almost no German army opposition to their liquidation—it was regarded even by Manstein as a salutary preventive measure, wiping out the reservoirs of partisan activity before they became active. Reichenau, commanding the Sixth Army, justified it as part of the German mission to rid Europe permanently of the "Asiatic Jewish danger." In a message to his troops he proclaimed:

> In the east each soldier is not only a warrior abiding by the usual rules of war, but also the uncompromising bearer of a pure German ideal and the avenger of the bestialities committed against Germans and related races.
>
> This is why the soldier must understand why we have to exact a harsh but just retribution from the Jewish subhumans. This serves the added purpose of stifling at birth uprisings in the rear of the Wehrmacht, since experience shows that these are always conceived by Jews. . . .

Hitler considered the proclamation "excellent," and Quartermaster General Eduard Wagner circulated it to other commands as an example.

Yet no direct report by Himmler or Heydrich to Hitler on the barbarous massacres of Russian Jews they themselves had witnessed has ever come to light. At supper on October 5, for example, Himmler, who had just returned from his extended tour of the Ukraine on which he had visited Kiev, Nikolaev, and Kherson, related to Hitler his impressions of Kiev. Werner Koeppen, who was a guest at Hitler's table that evening, recorded Himmler's comments: "In Kiev . . . the number of inhabitants is still very great. The people look poor and proletarian, so that we could 'easily dispense with 80 or 90 percent of them!' The Reichsführer proposes (and the Führer immediately agrees) that the oldest Russian monastery at Kiev should be confiscated to prevent its becoming the focus of orthodoxy and nationalism. The monastery is at present being guarded by German troops because of its priceless religious treasures."

Hitler's surviving adjutants, secretaries, and staff stenographers have *all* uniformly testified that never once was the extermination of either the Russian or European Jews mentioned—even confidentially—at Hitler's headquarters. Even SS General Karl Wolff, Himmler's Chief of Staff and liaison officer to Hitler, was at this time ignorant of the program that now got under way.[2] Colonel Rudolf Schmundt, a regular visi-

[2] He began to suspect in August 1942. See page 429.

tor to the Russian front, appears to have suspected what was going on there; for when Hitler's movie cameraman Walter Frentz willingly accompanied Himmler to Minsk on an outing with stage designer Benno von Arent, he found himself the horrified witness of a mass open-air execution; Schmundt advised him to destroy the one color photograph he took, and "not to poke his nose into matters that did not concern him."

By mid-October 1941, despite the foul weather, the Russian front was cracking in every joint. Hitler was still fired with optimism. On the thirteenth he and Ribbentrop first began laying the foundations for a Nazi version of a united Europe. Hewel wrote: "Reich foreign minister visits the Führer: first thoughts on a European manifesto. Probably in the economic sphere first of all, and probably at the beginning of the winter. Führer is in very best and relaxed mood." Over dinner he revealed that he had been thinking of calling together the economic experts of Denmark, Norway, Holland, Belgium, Sweden, and Finland to bring it home to them that Russia was an outlet for all their surplus population and a source of all the raw materials they might require. "I think it not impossible they would then come over into our own camp with flags flying." He unfolded his economic ideas—based on European self-sufficiency—to his own minister of economics, Walther Funk, the same day; Funk was enthusiastic. Hitler had a vision in which the Danube, which is linked by the Black Sea to the Dnieper and Don, would now be joined by canals to the Main and Oder. "All those who have a feeling for Europe can join in this work," meaning the colonization of the east. And: "Everybody will be able to participate, in one form or another, in this European economy." (A month later he was to say, "With our new economic organization, the political center of Europe is shifting. England will be nothing but a vast Holland. The Continent is coming back to life.")

His feelings toward the British people remained unchanged. One evening, an English magazine was passed around the little group chatting in his bunker. One photograph showed seven or eight RAF airmen clustered in front of their bomber aircraft; all were young and keen-looking. Hitler tapped the picture and sighed, "I wonder how many crews like these Göring could show me!" But there was an underlying bitterness against the "uncomprehending" British government which had followed its invasion of Iran with a demand that the Iranians surrender to them the German colony there of 220, and hand over 21 to the Russians. Hitler, who had agreed in secret negotiations to repatriate 1,140 sick

British prisoners, partly from the hospitals of Dunkirk, in exchange for 44 German prisoners in a similar condition, stopped the exchange when the British interned and flatly refused to release the German colony in Iran.

When Todt and Fritz Sauckel—Hitler's manpower commissioner—dined with Hitler on October 17, they were brimming with everything they had just seen in the east. Again Hitler dreamed aloud of the vast construction projects whereby he would open up the east in a manner similar to the way the Americans had colonized the west. "Above all we must lay roads," Koeppen wrote that night.

He told Dr. Todt he must expand his original projects considerably. For this purpose he will be able to make use of the three million prisoners for the next twenty years. The major roads—the Führer spoke today not only of the highway to the Crimea but also of one to the Caucasus and of two or three through the more northern territories—must be laid across the areas of greatest scenic beauty. Where the big rivers are crossed, German cities must arise, as centers of the Wehrmacht, police, administration, and Party authorities. Along these roads will lie the German farmsteads, and soon the monotonous steppe, with its Asiatic appearance, will look very different indeed. In ten years four million Germans will have settled there, and in twenty years at least ten million. They will come not only from the Reich but above all from America, and from Scandinavia, Holland, and Flanders too. And the rest of Europe shall play its part in this opening up of the Russian wastes as well. No Germans will set foot in the Russian towns, insofar as they survive this war (which Leningrad and Moscow certainly will not); let them continue to rot away in their filthy vegetable existence far from the great highways! The Führer then reverted to the theme that "contrary to what some people think" no education or welfare is to be laid on for the native population. Knowledge of the road signs will suffice, there will be no call for German schoolmasters there. By "freedom" the Ukrainians understood that instead of twice they now had to wash only once a month—the Germans with their scrubbing brushes would soon make themselves unpopular there. He as Führer would set up his new administration there after ice-cool calculations: what the Slavs might think about it would not put him out one bit. Nobody who ate German bread today got worked up about the fact that in the twelfth century the granaries east of the Elbe were regained by the sword. Here in the east we were repeating a process for a second time not unlike the conquest of America. For climatic reasons alone we could not venture further south than the Crimea—he did not mention the Caucasus at this point —even now hundreds of our mountain troops on Crete had malaria! The Führer kept repeating that he wished he was ten or fifteen years younger so he could live through the rest of this process.

The remorseless advance of the German armies to the east and southeast continued. The Ninth Army took Rzhev, the Romanians took Odessa, German tanks rolled into Taganrog, mountain troops captured Stalino, Reichenau captured Kharkov and Belgorod, and Manstein's Eleventh Army at last broke through into the Crimean peninsula.

At the same time, the next phase of the deportation of Europe's Jews began. The evidence is that Hitler's intention was twofold—to establish a Jewish labor force for his grandiose plans in the east, and to hold them hostage. (The "Jewish hostage" motif appears again late in 1943.[3]) There was no word of massacring them. On October 6, 1941, Hitler again pronounced at lunch, as Koeppen noted: "All the Jews must be removed from the Protectorate—and not just to the Generalgouvernement but right on to the east. It is only our heavy need for war transport that stops us doing this right now. At the same time as the Jews from the Protectorate, all the Jews are to disappear from Berlin and Vienna too. The Jews are everywhere the grapevine along which enemy news reports filter into every nook and cranny of our nation with the speed of the winds." Hitherto Adolf Eichmann, one of Himmler's leading experts on Jewish affairs, had continued holding regular conferences with his regional officials on the various problems associated with the "Madagascar plan"—for example, the reeducation of professional Jews into the laborers, farmers, and artisans that would be needed in the new island-state. But on October 18, Himmler scribbled on his telephone pad the message he had just dictated to Heydrich: "No emigration by Jews to overseas."[4] Instead, on October 15, 1941, the big exodus from Europe to the east began—the Jews being herded initially into camps in Poland and the Lodz ghetto. "In daily transports of a thousand people, 20,000 Jews and 5,000 gypsies are being sent to the Lodz ghetto between October 15 and November 8," Heydrich informed Himmler on October 19. For the time being Himmler reluctantly kept the ablebodied Jews alive for the work they could perform; but farther east the Gauleiters had no intention of preserving the unemployable Jews: a letter dated October 25 in SS files states that Adolf Eichmann had now

---

[3] When Hitler forbade the liquidation of Rome's Jews: see page 628.
[4] On February 10, 1942, a foreign ministry official noted that since "Barbarossa" had acquired other territories suitable for a solution of the Jewish problem, "the Führer has accordingly decided that the Jews are to be deported not to Madagascar but to the east."

approved Gauleiter Lohse's proposal that those arriving at Riga should be killed by mobile gas-trucks. This initially *ad hoc* operation gathered momentum. Soon the Jews from the Lodz ghetto and Greiser's territories were being deported farther east—to the extermination camp at Chelmno. There were 152,000 Jews involved in all, and Chelmno began liquidating them on December 8.

At this stage of the Jewish massacre it is possible to be more specific about the instigators, because on May 1, 1942, Greiser himself mentioned in a letter to Himmler that the current "special treatment" program of the hundred thousand Jews in his own Gau had been authorized by Himmler "with the agreement of" Heydrich. Hitler was not mentioned. Meanwhile, from mid-November 1941 onward, the Reichsbahn trainloads of Jews—rounded up in Vienna, Brünn (Brno), Bremen, and Berlin—headed direct to Minsk, while others went to Warsaw, Kovno, and Riga. At Kovno and Riga the Jews were invariably shot soon after. At Minsk the Jews did not survive much longer: Richard Kube, Rosenberg's general commissioner of White Ruthenia, recorded on July 31, 1942, that 10,000 had been liquidated since the twenty-eighth, "of which 6,500 were Russian Jews, old folk, women and children, with the rest unemployable Jews largely sent to Minsk from Vienna, Brünn, Bremen, and Berlin in November last year on the Führer's orders." It is not without evidentiary value that Himmler's handwritten telephone notes include one on a call to Heydrich on November 17, 1941, on the "situation in the Generalgouvernement" and "getting rid of the Jews"; two days later Heydrich circulated invitations to an interministerial conference on the Final Solution of the Jewish Problem—delayed until January 1942, it became notorious as the Wannsee Conference.

No documentary evidence exists that Hitler was aware that the Jews were being massacred upon their arrival. His remarks, noted by Bormann's adjutant Heinrich Heim late on October 25, 1941, indicate that he did not favor it: "From the rostrum of the Reichstag I prophesied to Jewry that if war could not be avoided, the Jews would disappear from Europe. That race of criminals already had on its conscience the two million dead of the Great War, and now it has hundreds of thousands more. Let nobody tell me that despite that we cannot park them in the marshy parts of Russia! Our troops are there as well, and who worries about them! By the way—it's not a bad thing that public rumor attributes to us a plan to exterminate the Jews. Terror is a salutary thing." Hitler added that, just as he was sidestepping an open clash with the Vatican by postponing the final reckoning with Bishop von Galen until later, "with the Jews too I have found myself remaining inactive.

There's no point adding to one's difficulties at a time like this."[5] Hans Lammers testified later that this was undoubtedly Hitler's policy, for when he tackled Hitler on a statement by Himmler that the Führer had charged him with deporting the Jews from Germany, Hitler confirmed this but added, "I don't want to be bothered with the Jewish problem again until the war is over."

This does not gainsay the fact that Hitler felt a deep revulsion for Jews. On November 5, for example, Koeppen noted after dinner: "The Führer denies that Jews have any talent for anything. They surpass the other races in only one respect—the art of the lie and its unscrupulous application. . . . Shut them up together with only their own kind, in other words where their lying loses its effectiveness, and their 'talents' desert them and the Jew descends into squalor and poverty. While the Aryan races are improved the more they are allowed to coexist with their racial equals, the Jews suffer by it and degenerate into animals. With their lie that they are a *religious* community, and by calling their money markets temples, they pulled the wool over the eyes of tolerant bygone generations right up to the present day. In reality no Jew has ever delved into the metaphysical—their whole religion is based on the laws of race."

In most circumstances Hitler was a pragmatist. It would have been unlike him to sanction the use of scarce transport space to move millions of Jews east for no other purpose than liquidating them there; nor would he willingly destroy manpower, for which his industry was crying out. Heinrich Heim recalls one exasperated comment by Hitler when Allied radio broadcast an announcement that the Jews were being exterminated: "Really, the Jews should be *grateful* to me for wanting nothing more than a bit of hard work from them." It was Heydrich and the fanatical Gauleiters in the east who were interpreting with brutal thoroughness Hitler's decree that the Jews must "finally disappear" from Europe; Himmler's personal role is ambivalent. On November 30, 1941, he was summoned to the Wolf's Lair for a secret conference with Hitler, at which the fate of Berlin's Jews was clearly raised. At 1:30 P.M. Himmler was obliged to telephone from Hitler's bunker to Heydrich the explicit order that Jews were *not to be liquidated;* and the next day Himmler telephoned SS General Oswald Pohl, overall chief of the

---

[5] In March 1942 a memo was inserted in a Reich justice ministry file of correspondence with Lammers's Reich Chancellery to the effect that Hitler intended to postpone solution of the "Jewish problem" until after the war. The memo was catalogued as Item No. 4 on a "Staff Evidence Analysis Sheet" (Nuremberg document 4025-PS) when the file was first examined by Allied investigators at the Ministerial Collection Center in West Berlin in June 1946. It is now missing. Dr. Robert Kempner, the Nuremberg prosecutor who certified copies of those items produced as trial exhibits (US-923) in August 1946, evidently did not find this document.

concentration camp system, with the order: "Jews are to stay where they are."[6]

Yet the blood purge continued. The extermination program had gained a momentum of its own. Hans Frank, announcing to his Lublin cabinet on December 16, 1941, that Heydrich was calling a big conference in January on the expulsion of Europe's Jews to the east, irritably exclaimed, "Do you imagine they're going to be housed in neat estates in the Baltic provinces! In Berlin"—and with Hitler in East Prussia this can only be taken as a reference to Heydrich's agencies—"they tell us: why the caviling? We've got no use for them either. . . . Liquidate them yourselves!"

During October 1941 the Russians stubbornly prevented Hitler from encircling Leningrad completely when the Finnish and German armies advancing on either shore of Lake Ladoga were unable to meet. Partly for political reasons, Mannerheim—the Finnish commander—ignored Hitler's appeals to penetrate more steadfastly onto Russian territory; Field Marshal von Leeb was unable to advance the whole way to meet him. To encourage Mannerheim to resume the offensive, Hitler ordered Leeb to strike with his Sixteenth Army toward the city of Tikhvin—which would cut the sole railway line between Leningrad and Moscow.

By this time, mid-October, Moscow's fate seemed sealed. The Communist party headquarters, the government, and the diplomatic corps had been evacuated. On the night of October 16 the files of the Frunse military academy—to which Stalin had delivered his anti-German speeches in May were burned. Nobody knew who had started the panic or ordered the evacuations. Then the rains came and "Operation Typhoon" slithered to a halt. Bock's army group foundered in an unprecedented autumn morass of mud, rain, and slush. His generals had never seen anything like it. Trucks sank up to their axles and had to be winched out. Many were literally torn apart in the attempt. Of half a million vehicles, suddenly the German army lost 150,000. The enemy was fighting only a few miles from his arms factories and arsenals, and could use an intact network of railways around Moscow. But as they had withdrawn, they had methodically ripped up every railway track and tie to deny this weatherproof form of transport to the Germans. The Luftwaffe's deputy chief of staff General Hoffmann von Waldau, who had confidently predicted on October 10: "As long as the weather does

---

[6] Himmler's original note on his telephone conversations of November 30, 1941, appears as a facsimile illustration, page 550.

not continue to deteriorate (and at present it is fine, 28° to 22°) the enemy will not be able to prevent us from encircling Moscow," followed this with a frustrated diary entry six days later: "Our wildest dreams have been washed out by rain and snow. . . . Everything is bogged down in a bottomless quagmire. The temperature drops to 11°, a foot of snow falls, and then it rains on top of the snow." Leeb's tanks attacking Tikhvin had to be left behind; on October 24, Hitler decided to abandon the operation, but two days later Leeb came in person to Rastenburg and persuaded him—against Hitler's better instincts as the army group's war diary records—to allow it to proceed. In the Ukraine low clouds, icing, and snow were grounding the Luftwaffe. In the attack on Rostov, General von Kleist's tanks were running out of gasoline.

Thus Hitler's bold hopes for the *rapid* overthrow of Stalin's regime were thwarted by the weather. Now all the other strategic issues which he had optimistically adjourned—the Battle of the Atlantic, North Africa, the partisan war, the British second front, and the enemy's bombing offensive, not to mention the possibility of open war with the United States in 1942—had to be squarely met. In the northern theater, an unusually early winter had begun. Over lunch on October 26, Hitler asked the army's quartermaster general, the ebullient Eduard Wagner, to what extent he had provisioned the eastern armies with winter gear. Both the Luftwaffe and the SS had prepared for their winter campaign in Russia in February or March 1941, and during the summer Hitler had continually reminded Wagner to see to army winter needs. However, Wagner's private letters indicate that he had only addressed himself to the problem on October 19; but now he assured Hitler that by October 30 both Leeb and Rundstedt would have received half their winter equipment, while the numerically far bigger Army Group Center would have received only one-third. (He mentioned that the Russians' destruction of the one railway along the Sea of Azov would delay supplies to the south.) "The Führer was extremely nice and friendly to me," wrote Wagner.

In fact, Wagner and the General Staff were more optimistic than Hitler. On October 29, Wagner noted that an enemy pipeline had been captured, still spewing forth gasoline, and this would enable the tanks to press on into Rostov. "Everything else is also moving again, and we're convinced we'll shortly finish off Moscow." The Crimea was captured, and Manstein's advance troops were already outside Sevastopol—the ancient fortress at its southern point. But winter was unmistakably closing in: on October 30, Admiral Canaris flew in to Rastenburg, his plane almost colliding with another in the fog. Hitler ran into him on the way to the map room, and asked what weather Canaris had seen at the front. Canaris told him "Bad!" and Hitler gestured with annoyance. (A member of the admiral's staff wrote: "They're all getting on each other's nerves—a bad case of the camp jitters.") The next day snow settled on the Wolf's Lair too. On November 1, Hitler spent an hour at General Staff headquarters, inspecting for himself the winter equipment Wagner had organized. He made no comment, but Wagner noted: "He looked at and listened closely to everything; he appeared fresh and lively and was in a good mood."

But a mood of restlessness, of uneasiness and annoyance, beset him. The war might now go on for two more years, he realized; and what would be left of Germany and the flower of her manhood when it was over? Already a hundred and fifty thousand men had died since "Barbarossa" began; a war like this was bound to disrupt the national metabolism, if the good blood was being constantly drained away while the evil and pernicious elements were leading their "charmed" existence in the concentration camps, and all because the Russians had proved tougher than he had bargained for, and because that "drunken poltroon" Churchill refused to admit the mess he was getting his empire into. Thus Adolf Hitler argued with himself in the months to come. From reliable sources he knew Stalin had warned Roosevelt that his munitions would be exhausted by early December, but he also knew—from radio intercepts—that Churchill was moving heaven and earth to start shipments of arms to Archangel. Hitler ardently hoped that one day the opposition to Churchill's war policies would cause his undoing. "It's significant that Britain has already had to lock up over nine thousand people in concentration camps for this reason," he remarked on October 22. "Unfortunately the leading pro-Germans like Rothermere and Lord Londonderry are too deeply in the Jewish thrall to be able to put up any real opposition."

Even at this late date he still longed for the great Anglo-German concord which would restore immediate peace. However, from a remark made by Lord Halifax in Lisbon it was clear that Churchill was just waiting for some such hint of an offer—presumably after Russia's seemingly inevitable defeat—to give him a chance of publicly rebuking the Führer and restoring Roosevelt's faith in Britain. Hitler did not expect Roosevelt to start massive arms deliveries to Russia at this point, and even if Stalin did manage to discharge his present military bankruptcy, what was there the United States could offer? At best an obsolete tank model, for American artillery was useless, and the much vaunted Flying Fortress bombers were—Göring had assured him—of such poor quality, thanks to mass-production methods, that they would be easy prey for any German fighter. In short, neither Britain nor the United States could save Russia. Thus he deceived himself.

Hitler's continued wooing of Britain was both illogical and detrimental to his own war effort. It was the reason he gave Colonel Wilhelm Speidel for rejecting the French offers of collaboration—that it would stand in the way of the later concord with Britain. And when Raeder's Chief of Staff, Admiral Fricke, argued with compelling logic that Britain's military defeat was necessary for any New Order in Europe, and that this defeat could only be achieved by concentrating on the submarine war in the Atlantic, Hitler explained that he was even now ready to make peace with Britain, as the territory Germany had already won in Europe was adequate for the German people's future needs. The admiral gathered that to Hitler a colonial empire in central Africa was of only secondary interest. "Evidently," the admiral reported, "the Führer would be glad for Britain, once the eastern campaign is over, to show signs of sense (*not* that the Führer expects it of Churchill) even if it meant that Germany could not win further ground than she already occupies." Hitler was not bothered about any "formalized, legalized" termination of the war, the admiral concluded.

Hitler's attitude toward Britain was a disappointment to his naval staff. In a nutshell, Hitler's strategy was governed by the need to avoid defeat by Britain, rather than by the necessity of defeating her outright now. Britain's bombing offensive against the northwest coast (and, of course, Italy) was becoming a serious nuisance to morale; Hitler ordered Göring to increase aircraft and antiaircraft production. Britain would not risk invading the French mainland yet, but she might attempt to seize back one of her Channel Isles. Hitler therefore sent Colonel Schmundt to inspect those islands' defenses; afterward, he ordered the army to appoint particularly active garrison commanders to each island and to multiply their infantry and artillery defenses. Britain might invade northern Norway and cut off Germany's iron-ore and nickel supplies; here too Hitler ordered the reluctant navy to take precautions, although Raeder thought it unlikely Britain would risk such an invasion in winter. Most promising for the enemy would seem to be an invasion somewhere in the Mediterranean, perhaps on Sardinia or Pantelleria.

The Mediterranean had quietly become one of the most vulnerable areas of Axis operations, particularly now that Mussolini's very position was threatened by domestic unrest. The British, with sea and air superiority in the Mediterranean, were slowly but surely throttling the seaborne supplies to North Africa, of which Rommel and the Italian troops needed some five thousand tons a day. Hitler sadly reflected that if he could capture Gibraltar it would solve the whole problem with one blow, but without Spain's consent this was impossible. As Rommel's supply predicament worsened, Hitler angrily complained that the Wehrmacht commanders had not kept him informed of the situation; but this was not true, for Raeder had predicted this since early July and had demanded that Göring divert Luftwaffe units to safeguard the supply line to Tripoli. In September, Hitler had ordered the Tenth Air Corps to do so, but Jeschonnek had got him to change his mind by arguing that the Luftwaffe was barely capable of fulfilling its "Barbarossa" tasks as it was. In vain Raeder cabled Hitler that victory in Russia would hardly depend on whether or not thirty or forty aircraft were switched to the Mediterranean. Not until mid-October did Hitler tell Mussolini in a letter that Göring would furnish Luftwaffe support, but by then the rot had set in.

At the end of the month he ordered the navy virtually to abandon the Battle of the Atlantic and switch its submarine force to the Mediterranean too. Italy's tottering regime must be militarily buttressed at all costs. The food shortage and British bombing raids had badly impaired Italian morale. Hitler told Admiral Fricke on the twenty-seventh that the Italian royal family, the anti-Fascist elements, the freemasons, and the Vatican were all deeply opposed to the war. "Let there be no mistake—the Fascist regime is not as secure as the German government. Any change of government in Italy would spell the end of the Fascist regime, and Italy would unquestionably cross into the enemy camp." Large sections of the Italian public were pro-British. The defection of Italy would moreover lead to the loss of France to the enemy as well, and hence the defection of Spain. The "safeguarding of our Continental territory is now our first strategic commandment for the time being," Hitler ordered. Because of this, the active war against Britain must be abandoned: the *Schwerpunkt* (focus) of U-boat operations must be moved from the Atlantic to the Mediterranean; he wanted twenty-four submarines stationed there as soon as possible. In vain Fricke argued that now—with Russia on the verge of collapse—was no time to remove the noose from Britain's neck, and that Italy must do more to escort the supply convoys to Tripoli herself—either by sealing off the Straits of Sicily with minefields or by eliminating Malta.

In Hitler's view the risk to Italy, to the soft underbelly of Europe, was too real to let the rot in the Mediterranean go on.

A Test of Endurance

In Stalin, Hitler unquestionably now knew, he had met his match. As the Soviet resistance hardened despite each fresh catastrophe inflicted on its armies, Hitler's admiration for his Bolshevik adversary grew. "This Stalin is obviously also a great man," he kept telling his baffled generals. "To claim anything else would not make sense. Historians of the future will have to set out from the fact that today's events are governed by the collision or collusion of great, towering personalities whose paths cross like this only once in many centuries."

The Wehrmacht had captured over three million Russian prisoners. No estimate could be put on the Red Army's casualties. The Soviet Union had lost most of its aluminum, manganese, pig iron, and coal resources. As soon as Hitler's armies could penetrate beyond Rostov into the Caucasus, Stalin would lose 90 percent of his oil as well. This was why Hitler could only smile confidently when he read in Intelligence reports that Stalin was rebuilding his armies beyond the Urals. Hitler learned that Averell Harriman said in confidence early in November 1941 that the Russian leader took three days to agree to the western condition that the Soviet Union must not make a separate peace with Hitler, and even then he made his agreement conditional on receiving adequate war supplies from the West. In Moscow, meanwhile, tens of thousands of people were being evacuated. Some of those who had to stay in the capital tried to obtain swastika flags and German dictionaries in anticipation of the city's capture.

For the first two weeks of November the German armies were held immobile by the mud and mire. The Russians were able to build line after line of defensive positions. There were those generals—Erich Hoepner among them—who bitterly criticized their army superiors for not giving the panzer *Gruppen* their head in the October offensive but rather tying them rigidly to the infantry armies; this overcautiousness, bordering on defeatism, had deprived Hoepner of the chance of destroying all the Russian reserve forces as well. Now these reserves, augmented by workers from the Moscow factories and freshly arrived Siberian divisions—magnificently equipped with winter gear—were pouring into the capital's defenses and bracing for the frost, which would give the Germans firm ground on which to resume the attack.

Germany had still suffered no military reverses, and this was a position of strength from which Hitler was willing to envisage offering peace terms to the enemy. There are several indications of this. The most curious is the manner in which he and Ribbentrop allowed the unsuspecting former ambassador to Rome, Ulrich von Hassell, to pursue his clandestine peace feelers with American officials from September on; Heydrich submitted a full report on Hassell's activities to Ribbentrop early in November and inquired whether the ambassador was "acting with the consent or instructions" of the government. Since the secretary of the principal American involved was one of Heydrich's agents, and she and Hassell conversed freely on the telephone, it is not surprising that this conspiracy was known to the authorities. The American had asked Hassell to meet him in Lisbon; Hassell proposed Switzerland instead and sent the American a memorandum—which also fell into the hands of the German authorities—to the effect that many intelligent Germans, even if they did not fear losing the war, dreaded the devastation that even victory would entail. Since "that man down south"—meaning Mussolini—was also said to think the same way, perhaps the memorandum to the United States ambassador to Rome, William Phillipps, should suggest putting out feelers to the Duce too. "At present not clear as to the How of peace—but great haste called for as otherwise danger that the various parties will go too far out onto their respective limbs to be able to go back." Hassell urged the Americans not to insist at this stage on "top authority"—meaning Hitler's written sanction for the dialogue.

By early November, Ribbentrop's diplomatic seismographs detected other signs that the Führer wanted peace. Etzdorf, Ribbentrop's liaison officer to the General Staff, listed them thus: "Ambassador von Bergen is to be replaced at the Vatican by a more active personality, one better able to monitor the peace possibilities coming through there. Everything relating to peace in the [foreign] press is to be carefully collected and immediately submitted. The same procedure is to be followed with regard to Russia's domestic situation." As for Japan: "The Führer is not particularly interested in Japan entering the war; it would only make peace more difficult." Weizsäcker, Ribbentrop's state secretary, held out no hope of peace to the army, however. He told Halder that there was no evidence that Britain was inclined toward a cessation of hostilities; he felt that any moves initiated by Germany would be rebuffed.

By the end of the month Hitler knew Weizsäcker was right. British foreign office instructions to ridicule any "peace offensive" by Hitler reached German hands. Churchill had emphasized in a Mansion House speech that to talk of Europe's future was not the sole prerogative of "those who are causing the cold blood of execution yard and scaffold to flow between the German race and other European countries." An economically self-contained Europe was, he warned, equally impracticable. "The present peace offensive," the foreign office instruction continued, "comes not, as it was intended to do, at a moment of victory over Russia, but when Germany is further away from victory than at any previous time. Hitler doubtless intended to proclaim the New Europe from the Kremlin. He is now an ersatz victor making an ersatz peace offer from an ersatz Kremlin." Hitler reminded one minister arriving in Berlin for the fifth anniversary of the Anti-Comintern Pact that Lord Halifax had bragged of being "a strong enough man" to ignore the countless letters from all over England demanding peace in 1940; this was proof, said Hitler, that the "Jewish-Bolshevik" suicidal forces still had the upper hand in London. Wistfully he added that what irritated him most was that "that cretin Churchill" was interrupting him in his mighty task of cultural reconstruction.

For Hitler, the thrills of warmaking had long palled; but not for the generals. Halder's private letters home proudly reveled in the advances "his" army had achieved. Although his own Intelligence staff warned that the Russians were moving reinforcements west of Moscow, Halder turned a blind eye on these unpalatable signs and commanded Bock's army group to delay its Moscow offensive until the logistics buildup would support a far more ambitious offensive. The Ninth Army would lunge far beyond Moscow toward Kalinin, the Volga reservoir, and Selizharovo; the Third and Fourth Panzer Gruppen would make for Vologda, and Guderian's Second Panzer Army was even assigned Gorki as its final objective for the winter. Hitler pocketed his doubts and approved the plans. On November 11 Jodl signed a directive to the army groups setting out these far-flung ambitions to be achieved before the heavy snowfalls began: "The goals would justify an extreme exertion to sever the two supply lines used by Anglo-American war materials, and to improve and safeguard our restricted petroleum supplies, by advancing on Stalingrad and a rapid capture of Maykop in the south, and the capture of Vologda in the north." Halder stoutly defended these aims at a staff conference in Orsha on November 13—optimistically counting on six weeks' campaigning before winter really closed in—but neither Bock nor Rundstedt would hear of them; thus a limited advance on Moscow only was finally approved. Had Halder's grand strategy been adopted, Hitler would undoubtedly have lost his entire eastern army in the catastrophe that shortly unfolded.

In fact Hitler was on the horns of a dilemma. Even if the nearest Russian oil fields at Maykop *could* now be seized, he lacked the tankers to bring the oil to the Mediterranean theater, where it was most needed by Italy. He had postponed his assault on the main Caucasus oil fields until 1942, but since these were likely to be so thoroughly destroyed that it would hardly be possible to produce any oil until 1943, Keitel's petroleum experts questioned whether there was any real point in invading the Caucasus at all. To Hitler, there was; he wanted to rob Stalin of his oil resources, and he had heard of British plans to establish a front in the Caucasus as well.

In another sense, Hitler showed a curious optimism. Halder wrote: "All in all he gave an impression of anticipating that when both warring parties realize that they are incapable of destroying each other there will result a negotiated peace." It was the vision of a second Verdun that kept recurring to Hitler; and the condescendingly chivalrous notion that since Stalin had fought well and fearlessly, he should be spared the fate he no doubt otherwise deserved.

With the return of the long nights, the British bombing had resumed. On November 7 no fewer than four hundred RAF bombers attacked Berlin, Mannheim, and half a dozen other targets. When Hitler arrived in Munich the next afternoon to speak at the annual beer-cellar gathering of his Old Guard, the city's population had all but fled in fear of the almost inevitable nightly air raid.

That same night a most severe blow befell the supply lines to Rommel's force in North Africa. Although Italian warships had provided strong cover, an entire Italian supply convoy of seven ships was sunk by a small British force comprised of two light cruisers and two destroyers. Admittedly there was compensation in the fact that one of Raeder's U-boats sank the aircraft carrier *Ark Royal* a few days later and another sank the battleship *Barham* before November was over, but when the British counteroffensive opened in North Africa on the eighteenth the German and Italian divisions besieging Tobruk were weak, low in fuel, and short of men and materials. Supply shipping losses were now running at sixty thousand tons a month. Rommel managed to inflict heavy losses on the enemy, but he then took the hard decision to abandon Cyrenaica. In December, however, the tide turned again in his favor: Field Marshal Kesselring arrived in Rome as Hitler's newly appointed "Commander in Chief South," and with him he brought the air power needed to regain air supremacy in the Mediterranean. On the nineteenth, bold Italian midget submariners disabled Admiral Sir Andrew Cunningham's last two battleships at Alexandria, the *Queen Elizabeth* and the *Valiant,* and he lost more big warships the next day in a minefield off Malta. Soon the British possessed only three cruisers and a handful of destroyers and submarines in the area between Gibraltar and Alexandria. New blood began to flow into Rommel's Afrika Korps.

The unexpected prolongation of the war faced Hitler with fundamental decisions on armaments policy—for soon he expected to be confronting three world empires. The wasteful use of scarce resources might have been tolerable in the Blitzkrieg economy of 1940, but it would be no longer. His munitions minister, Fritz Todt, returned from a tour of the Russian front and in a private talk with Hitler on November 29, 1941, summed up his prognosis thus: "Given the arms and industrial supremacy of the Anglo-Saxon powers, we can no longer militarily win this war!" Hitler calmly inquired, "How am I supposed to end it, then? I can't see much possibility of ending it *politically*."

Even before "Barbarossa," Hitler had realized that German arms production was inefficient. The aircraft industry was beset by primadonna personalities and producing a plethora of outdated aircraft. The Luftwaffe had no long-range aircraft for reconnaissance or bombing far into the Atlantic or beyond the Urals. The new generation of fighters which Göring had promised was still unfit for squadron service. General Ernst Udet, the director of air armament, recognized his share of the blame and shot himself in November. To succeed Udet, Hitler appointed Field Marshal Erhard Milch, Göring's bustling deputy who had founded Lufthansa and built the secret prewar Luftwaffe. But it would be 1943 before Milch's appointment could have any real effect. In the last week of his life Hitler ruefully admitted that he had erred in so blindly accepting Göring's advice about Luftwaffe matters all along.

Tank design was different. Here Hitler considered himself an expert, and he was indeed far ahead of the professionals. By November 1941 he feared that the tank's useful offensive life would soon be over as the Allies had clearly got wind that summer of the German army's secret antitank shells with tungsten cores. Hitler's still-embargoed other secret weapon, the Redhead "hollow-charge" shell, would soon have to be given its debut as well. All this meant that the German panzer divisions would have to complete Hitler's program of territorial conquests quickly, and this meant building tanks stronger and in greater quantity than the British or Russians could. The huge Russian tank output, and the appearance of the Soviet T-34, had shaken him badly; when Todt now told him of two more new Russian types he had examined at Orel, Hitler exclaimed in exasperation, "How can such a primitive people manage such technical achievements in such a short time!"

Nine months had passed since Hitler had called his own first tank-design symposium at the Berghof on February 18, 1941. Then he had demanded the modification of the Mark III and Mark IV tanks to mount much heavier caliber long-barreled guns—50 and 75 millimeters, respectively—despite the design objections raised by the experts. When Keitel demurred at releasing twenty thousand skilled workers from the army for tank production, Hitler snapped that it was better than losing perhaps ten times as many soldiers because of the lack of a powerful tank force. The modified tanks were demonstrated to him at the Chancellery six weeks later. Hitler climbed all over them and asked for the turret to be rotated. The gunner explained that he first had to duck his head inside—at which Hitler angrily stopped the demonstration. "Obviously the gunner must be able to keep his eye to the eyepiece at all times!" A further symposium followed on May 26 at the Berghof: Hitler demanded an even heavier gun in future tanks and instructed both the Henschel tank works and Professor Ferdinand Porsche to produce prototypes mounting the 88-millimeter heavy gun. The designers were aghast, but Hitler announced that in future campaigns his tanks would travel to the battlefields "in the outer reaches of Europe" by train, so the load-bearing ability of roadbridges would no longer impose a limit on his tanks. He pictured to them the "morale and physical effect" of a direct hit by such a shell on a cast-steel tank turret—it would burst asunder. In Greece his SS Life Guards had destroyed enemy tanks at ranges of up to seven thousand yards with this fearful weapon.

Much had happened since that February symposium. The enemy's T-34 was vastly superior to the newest German Mark IV. At an arms conference on November 29, Hitler again warned Todt and Brauchitsch that the age of the tank would soon be over; he asked them to concentrate on three basic tank designs—a light tank for reconnaissance, like the present Mark III; a medium tank, the Mark IV; and a heavy tank (the later Panther) to outclass the Russian T-34. A superheavy tank was also to be blueprinted by Porsche for the future.

In mid-November 1941 Field Marshal von Bock's drive toward Moscow was resumed. He was confident of success, and General Halder swallowed his own misgivings and gave Bock free rein. Bock's northern wing began to move on the fifteenth, followed by the southern wing two days later. All Hitler's commanders had assured him that the Red Army lacked depth; but the enemy's resistance before Moscow was ominously vehement, and he began to suspect that he had again been wrongly advised. He saw victory at Moscow slipping through his fingers; he bluntly told the ailing Field Marshal von Brauchitsch—who had suffered a fresh heart attack a week before—that it was a question of the army's *will* to victory.

Meanwhile, General von Kleist's First Panzer Army had managed to seize Rostov on the Don, only to be thrown back again on November 28. Temperatures of 14°F. gripped the front. Fuel and equipment shortages dogged every move. The troops lacked ice axes, glycol antifreeze had to be flown in, the tank engines refused to start. (The army's quartermaster general had not informed lower levels of a simple "cold-start" procedure first demonstrated by the Luftwaffe in 1939.) Hitler's generals were gripped by apathy. Reichenau's Sixth Army had found comfortable winter quarters which they were very loath to leave; this enabled the enemy before them to regroup against the desperately harassed Kleist.

The temperature was still falling all along the front. Ribbentrop came on the twenty-second, no doubt to discuss the big demonstration of European solidarity he was about to stage in Berlin. But on the twenty-fourth Hewel noted: "Führer is dissatisfied with Ribbentrop's draft speech, lots of corrections, etc. His mind is on Africa." And one of Hitler's adjutants, Major Engel, wrote the next day: "In the evening a further lengthy debate on future operations. The Führer explains his great anxiety about the Russian winter and weather conditions, says we started one month too late. The ideal solution would have been the surrender of Leningrad, the capture of the south, and then if need be a pincer around Moscow from south and north, following through in the center . . . but time is his greatest nightmare now."

Hitler listened to Ribbentrop's Berlin speech on the radio. It was an important address to the ambassadors and foreign ministers of Germany's allies and friendly neutrals; "Europe's struggle for freedom" was its theme. Had the Soviet Union been on the brink of defeat it would have been timely and well-chosen; but Ribbentrop made the British government the butt of his leaden witticisms, goaded by the constant and effective British propaganda charge that he as Hitler's foreign minister was to blame for this war. Ribbentrop lauded Hitler's unexampled and benign patience toward Britain in these words: "If any sane person examines the advantages offered by the Führer's foreign policy to Britain, then he must clutch his head at the thought of the blindness with which the British statesmen were stricken, because the Führer not only offered a comprehensive territorial and maritime guarantee to the British Isles but even offered to supply German forces to help safeguard the British Empire." Ribbentrop referred to his own endeavors to bring the two countries together: "I will be happy to leave it to History to judge whether the sapient British propagandists are right in claiming that I advised the Führer that Britain would never fight, and that I was ignorant of the British and their national character."

Soon after Ribbentrop's radio broadcast was over, he himself was on the phone asking if Hitler had liked his speech. The Führer had not, and he was still fulminating against Ribbentrop, the foreign ministry, and the speech when his train left headquarters to take him to Berlin at 7 P.M. that evening.

In Berlin a round of receptions for the new signatories of the Anti-Comintern Pact began. They made a curious bunch. The Hungarians had to be kept apart from the Romanians. Serrano Suñer had to be received jointly with Ciano. Ciano was accorded the same frozen politeness as had been his lot on his recent visit to the Wolf's Lair. The Turks, who had also been invited to join the pact, had refused point-blank; from decoded British admiralty telegrams Hitler knew that Turkey was again playing a double role and negotiating with the British for destroyers and submarines; and her Chief of Staff had even taken to referring to the Germans as *les boches* in conversation with British officers. Vichy France, despite Pétain's jostling for German favors, was not invited to join the pact, as Hitler still evidently hoped to treat with Britain some day at France's expense. A French volunteer legion was now fighting under Bock's command, and from decoded American cables the Germans knew that Pétain had commended Germany for adhering to the armistice conditions. Hitler had kept his promises, and Pétain accordingly supported his plans for a New Order, from which he felt that France could only profit. But Hitler's latent resentment had its psychological roots too deep in recent history to be easily overcome, as his surly reply to a letter from the French marshal showed: Hitler reminded Pétain that France had declared war on Germany, not vice versa, and he said that Germany's recent execution of French "Communists" in reprisal for the assassination of German officers doing their "lawful duty" was fully justified. The Führer drew a passionate comparison between what he presented as Germany's restrained presence now in France and the French troops' unruly behavior in the Rhineland between the wars, when they had driven German citizens from the sidewalks with their riding crops, and the rape of more than sixteen thousand German women had gone unpunished.

A major source of discontent in France was that Germany—like France after World War I—was still detaining over a million French prisoners of war. Hitler could not dispense with this labor force, for the German agricultural and armament economy relied heavily on prisoners. Hitler had recently put Göring in charge of employing three million Russian prisoners, remarking that such stubborn fighters must make good workers too. But the army had paid scant attention to their welfare and accommodations; hunger, exhaustion, lack of medical care, and fierce typhus epidemics took their toll. Albert Speer, Hitler's chief architect, had asked him on November 21 to provide forced labor for his work in rebuilding Berlin. (Now that Hitler was in the capital again, Speer lunched with him and then showed him the latest scale-models of Berlin's new buildings, set up in the Model Room at the Chancellery—finely detailed miniatures of the vast Great Hall, the Office of the Reichsmarschall, and the new stadium.) Hitler granted Speer's request for thirty thousand Russian prisoners to help in the construction work. The Führer assured Speer that he proposed to start work on this huge reconstruction of Berlin before the war was over—no war was going to keep him from putting these plans into effect.

While he was in Berlin, on November 27, Hitler learned that the protracted talks between Japan and the United States had broken down. He had a private meeting with the Japanese ambassador, General Oshima, who tried unsuccessfully to warn him of what was coming; two weeks later Hitler admitted to his military staff that he should have paid closer attention to the cautious hints that Oshima dropped. Unlike Ribbentrop, who wanted the Japanese to strike northward into Russia, Hitler preferred that they should thrust southward to embarrass the British. He felt that attacking Vladivostok would not help now, as he considered

"Barbarossa" all but over. Indeed, at the end of October Hitler had been against any Japanese involvement, as this would have made the peace settlement more complicated. Militarily, Japan was an unknown quantity. Her population was bigger than Germany's, so she could raise perhaps 120 divisions; but the world knew nothing of any Japanese tank, aircraft, or warship capabilities.

The United States was also evidently having second thoughts about fighting a war in Europe. Several American destroyers and merchant vessels had recently been sunk by U-boats, but Roosevelt had shown little firm reaction. The German foreign ministry answered General Halder's inquiry about whether Roosevelt was likely to declare war with a decisive negative. As late as December 6, Hitler would be shown dispatches from Hans Thomsen, his chargé d'affaires in Washington, listing the reasons why the United States would not declare war yet. This firm suggestion that Roosevelt—alarmed at the Soviet Union's imminent collapse—now wanted to avoid armed conflict until his rearmament was ready, persuaded Hitler that war between the United States and Japan might serve his purposes after all: it would tie this powerful enemy down in the Pacific at least throughout 1942, which would give him time to realize his own ambitions in Russia. Admiral Raeder and the hard-pressed U-boat commanders in the Atlantic would certainly welcome such a showdown.

As Hitler's policy toward the United States swung around during November 1941, so did that of Japan as hopes dwindled in Tokyo that Roosevelt would relax the oil and economic sanctions imposed on Japan. The German attachés in Tokyo both warned Berlin that Japan would enter the war before the year was out. Indeed, the naval attaché cabled on November 5 that a senior Japanese naval officer had advised him that "the government has as good as made up its mind to fight America. The southern campaign will most probably begin this year." In due course Tokyo would approach Germany for a pact binding each country not to make a separate peace with the United States so long as the other was still fighting. Sure enough, such a request was received by Ribbentrop on the eighteenth; he agreed "in principle," fearing that otherwise Japan might reach a compromise with the United States. For the next week the reports reaching Hitler were conflicting.

Then on November 28 he received one from Hans Thomsen in Washington reporting that Cordell Hull had handed to the Japanese what amounted to an ultimatum which "is bound to result in the immediate breakdown of the talks." The Americans demanded a nonaggression treaty, the evacuation of Indochina, and Japan's withdrawal from the

Axis. Hitler discussed the implications of this with his political and military advisers at the Chancellery late that day, then sent Ribbentrop to inform the startled General Oshima—startled, for the ambassador himself was unaware the Japanese-American talks had collapsed—that if Japan did reach a decision to fight "Britain and the United States," they must not hesitate, as it would be in the Axis interests. Oshima inquired in puzzlement whether he was to infer that Germany and the United States would soon be at war, and Ribbentrop replied, "Roosevelt's a fanatic. There's no telling what he'll do." Ribbentrop then gave the Japanese the assurance they had wanted:

> If Japan becomes engaged in a war against the United States, Germany will of course join the war immediately. There is no possibility whatever of Germany entering into a separate peace with the United States under such circumstances. The Führer is adamant on that point.

Even so, Ribbentrop does seem to have had doubts. On the train carrying them both back to East Prussia the next day, November 29, he asked Hitler what Germany's posture would be if Japan actually *attacked* the United States; the Tripartite Pact only obliged Germany to assist if Japan was the victim of an attack. Hitler cast these diplomatic niceties aside; if Germany welshed on Japan in the event of Japan's attacking the United States, it would be the end of the Tripartite Pact. "The Americans are already shooting at us—so we are already at war with them."

Some days passed before Hitler's attention was again called to Japan, for he was virtually incommunicado—touring his army headquarters on the tottering eastern front. Only then was he shown the latest telegram from Tokyo, reporting Roosevelt's ultimatum to Japan; the Japanese had assured the German ambassador they would honor Germany's interests, and they again asked for Germany and Italy to stand at her side under the Tripartite Pact. In fact the secret instructions to Ambassador Oshima in Berlin were couched in even plainer terms: he was to inform Hitler and Ribbentrop confidentially that war between Japan and the Anglo-Saxon powers might be ignited "quicker than anybody dreams"; and he was to propose an agreement binding Germany and Italy to join in too.

Oshima saw Ribbentrop forthwith, on December 2, and again the next day; but the Nazi foreign minister had to prevaricate because he still could not reach the Führer. By scrambler-telephone he evidently managed this late on December 4. That night Rome was asked to approve the German counterproposal for an agreement, and at 4 A.M. Ribbentrop handed Oshima the agreed text of a German-Italian-Japanese treaty. This more than met Japan's requirements. It did not even ask for Japanese intervention against Russia as the price. "Our view," Ribbentrop cabled his man in Tokyo, "is that the Axis powers and Japan regard themselves as locked in one historic struggle."

Neither he nor Hitler realized that Japanese aircraft carriers had already sailed with war orders ten days before.

Hitler's eyes were of course elsewhere. As winter closed in, barbarous fighting erupted everywhere on the Russian front, where the army's all-out assault on Moscow was beginning. The fighting was of unexampled savagery. On both sides, prisoners were frequently shot out of hand—the Spanish "Blue Division" took the fewest prisoners. Villages were starved to feed the Germans and razed to the ground to deprive the Russians of cover; and warm clothing was stripped off captives. A captured Russian battalion commander related what happened to three Waffen SS soldiers in his area: "When the regiment's commissar, Zhukenin, of the 508th Infantry Regiment, asked an officer what he was fighting for, he replied, 'For Hitler!' So the commissar kicked him in the groin and shot him." The other two shared his fate. A captured Russian order stated that only three prisoners were to be taken in an infantry division's coming attack; the rest were to be slain. Meanwhile autopsy reports revealed that Russian troops defending the beleaguered Leningrad had resorted to nature's most primitive crime—cannibalism. German corpses found behind the Russian lines lacked parts of their bodies, although the uniforms nearby were undamaged.

The cruel Russian winter fell equally on the opposing armies, but it was unequally felt. Stalin's troops were well-clad, skilled in winter warfare, with skis and equipment adapted to sub-zero temperatures; they were also fighting close to their industrial base. Not so Hitler's armies. While the Luftwaffe and SS were more adequately provided, the German army's meager winter supplies were still bottled up by the chaotic railroad system at Minsk and Smolensk far to the rear. Different and feuding railroad authorities operated the networks in Germany, Poland, and occupied Russia. German locomotives were not only the wrong gauge, but their external "gossamer" of plumbing and pipework made them easy prey for the sub-zero winters. The retreating Russians had methodically wrecked the water towers, bridges, and railroad installations as well as the rolling stock. In consequence, the supply of food, equipment, and ammunition to the entire eastern front suddenly choked to a halt. Instead of seventeen supply trains a day, each army on the Leningrad front was lucky to get one; instead of eighteen, Guderian's Second Panzer Army was getting only three. It became apparent that the German railroads had unloaded their most infuriatingly feckless and inept staff members onto the Polish and Russian networks.

When at last winter clothing did reach the fighting troops, it was useless against the Russian winter. Many weeks earlier Brauchitsch had paraded before Hitler a dozen soldiers outfitted with the army's special new winter gear. Only now did Hitler learn that those dozen outfits were all the army had. The blame for this fraud lay squarely on the General Staff. Meanwhile Hitler's armies were trapped in blizzards and snowdrifts outside Moscow—and were slowly freezing to death.

The reverse suffered by the First Panzer Army on the Don at Rostov was a bitter pill for Hitler to swallow, because now an Intelligence report confirmed that his own original strategy—of conquering Russia's southern petroleum oil fields first—was what the Soviets had feared most. Marshal Timoshenko had just delivered a secret speech to the supreme defense council in Moscow:

> If Germany succeeds in taking Moscow, that is obviously a grave disappointment for us, but it by no means disrupts our grand strategy. . . . Germany would gain accommodation, but that alone will not win the war. The only thing that matters is oil. As we remember, Germany kept harping on her own urgent oil problems in her economic bargaining with us from 1939 to 1941.
> So we have to do all we can (a) to make Germany increase her oil consumption, and (b) to keep the German armies out of the Caucasus until the oil shortage in Germany begins to hurt.

So far, Timoshenko continued, Marshal Semën Budënny had had to wage a scorched-earth campaign and ignore his own colossal military casualties. "This first phase of the war has been decisively won by *us*, however much a glance at the map may give the public a different impression." The Red Army's task now was to throw the Germans back just far enough to destroy the caches of tanks and ammunition it had built up for the Caucasus offensive. This would win a few precious months for new Soviet armies to be raised, for Britain's General Archibald Wavell to establish his Caucasus front in Iraq and Iran, for the evacuated Soviet factories to resume production, and for the American supplies to start to flow.

How Hitler must have cursed the General Staff for having foisted its Moscow campaign on to him. With winter upon him, he had no option but to see it through, although the armies' reserves were at an end and the physical conditions were brutal in the extreme. How far the army faithfully called his attention to these adverse conditions is controversial even now. The two army group commanders, Bock and Rundstedt, believed that Hitler was not being told the blunt facts; so did Kleist's Chief of Staff Zeitzler. Guderian—commanding the Second Panzer Army south of Moscow—blamed his immediate superiors too. "We must face the melancholy fact," he wrote privately, "that our superior command has overreached itself; it didn't want to believe our reports on the dwindling combat strength of our troops, it made one fresh demand after another, it made no provision for the harsh winter, and now it's been taken by surprise by the Russian temperatures of −30°F. . . . While the Luftwaffe is methodically commanded, we in the army have to put up with horrifying bungling and aimlessness."

This lack of *Zivilcourage* was first brought home to Hitler by the immediate sequel to the loss of Rostov. First, the city proved far larger than shown on the General Staff's maps. Second, Kleist's frantic warnings about his panzer army's long exposed left flank and the severe icing conditions were withheld from Hitler. When Kleist was forced to withdraw his spearhead—intending to fall back on the Mius, which had been adequately prepared for a long defense—Hitler had on November 30 vetoed this: Rundstedt, the army group commander, was to order Kleist to defend a line five miles forward of the Mius. In the course of the evening, Brauchitsch received Rundstedt's uncompromising reply refusing to carry out what he evidently believed to be only Brauchitsch's order. "If my superiors have no faith in my leadership, I must ask to be replaced as Commander in Chief." Hitler sacked Rundstedt that same night, replacing him with Reichenau; the newcomer was ordered categorically to halt the panzer army's retreat.

Hitler backed this order with a personal visit to Kleist's battle headquarters at Mariupol (Zhdanov), on the Sea of Azov. He took no General Staff officers with him—just his adjutants. He had intended sacking both Kleist and Zeitzler, but SS General Sepp Dietrich, whose SS Life Guards Division had been in the thick of the fighting, pluckily defended his superiors; and Schmundt told Hitler that Zeitzler had now shown him copies of the panzer army's frantic signals before the Rostov operation. These messages had accurately predicted this very outcome. Hitler was astonished that they had been withheld from him. He exclaimed, "So the panzer army saw it all coming and reported to that effect. It bears none of the blame, then." He telephoned Jodl's staff in this vein on December 3: Kleist's panzer army bore none of the blame for the Rostov crisis. "It reported to the army group as early as November 21 and 22 about its great anxiety over the threat to its eastern flank and the complete lack of any reserves. Army Group South has moreover claimed that it forwarded details of this menacing situation to the war ministry." Clearly the messages had been suppressed by the General Staff. Thus Hitler's confidence in Rundstedt was restored—though characteristically of Hitler the dismissal remained in force.

The Rostov setback paled into insignificance against what now occurred at Moscow. General Kluge's powerful Fourth Army had begun its big push on December 1 through the forests and swamps west of the capital; Hoepner's Fourth Panzer Army and Guderian's Second Panzer Army began an enveloping action to the north and the south, respectively. On December 2, through snowstorms and blizzards, a reconnaissance battalion of the 258th Infantry Division reached Khimki, on the very outskirts of Moscow; but it was driven back by armed Russian workers. Thus German troops came within twelve miles of the city center before exhaustion overcame them.

This was the German army's trauma. Moscow was being evacuated; its streets and public buildings were being mined for demolition. Yet by December 4, with temperatures of −6°F., both Hoepner's tanks and Kluge's infantry were at a standstill. Guderian, visiting the battlefield, found his tank crews still optimistic, while their corps and division commanders were not. But Field Marshal von Bock warned the OKW by telephone that his troops would soon be able to proceed no farther. "If the attack is not called off until then," he warned Jodl, "it will be almost impossible to go over to the defensive." On the fifth, Guderian—up at the forefront of his army with the 296th Infantry Division—realized that his own attack was hopeless too. His Chief of Staff recorded in his diary: "Twenty-five degrees below zero this morning. Tank turrets frozen solid, frostbite taking heavy toll, artillery fire has become irregular as gunpowder evidently burns differently." As the hours passed, the temperature sagged to *thirty-five degrees* below zero. "Our troops no longer had the strength to carry the attack victoriously through to Moscow," Guderian described privately on the eighth. "And so with a heavy heart I had to decide late on December 5 to call off the now pointless attack and fall back on a relatively short line I had already chosen earlier, which I can just about hope to hold with my remaining forces. . . . Fortunately we have been able to hang on to our fine tanks—at least insofar as they are still running."

On December 5, as Hitler's offensive slued to a halt, four Soviet armies opened their counterattack north of Moscow. Next day ten more armies—one hundred divisions—fell upon Bock's exhausted and frozen troops on a two-hundred-mile front on either side of Moscow. Thus the real emergency began. The Luftwaffe was grounded. Gasoline fires had to be lit in pits under their tanks for four hours to thaw out the engines. The telescopic gunsights were useless, and every caliber of gun and cannon jammed. The oil congealed in the tank tracks. The Russians used special winter oils and lubrication techniques, and now their formidable T-34 tank appeared en masse, with its armor impregnable to the standard German 37-millimeter antitank shell. "From the depths of Russia, undreamed-of masses of humanity were hurled against us," recalled an OKW staff officer. "I can still see the situation maps of the next days and weeks: where until now the blue of our own forces had dominated the picture, with the enemy's red only sparsely sketched in, now from Leningrad right down to the Sea of Azov thick red arrows had sprung up on every sector of the front, pointing at the heart of Germany. Only thin blue lines wound their tortuous way around this broad-arrowed onslaught."

Meanwhile the paraphernalia of modern war accumulated by the Wehrmacht in its seven years of preparation for this moment congealed into frozen impotence, paralyzed by the icy grip of a sub-Napoleonic winter. If battle casualties were not dragged under cover, they were dead within half an hour from exposure. Guderian lost twelve hundred men to frostbite in one division in one day. On the ninth, one corps reported fifteen hundred cases; three hundred fifty men had to have limbs amputated. Eleven hundred army horses perished every day.

"In wave after wave of densely packed soldiers, the enemy offensive rolled across the snowscape toward us. Our machine guns hammered away at them without letup, you could not hear yourself speak. Like a dark and somber carpet a layer of dead and dying stretched across the snow in front of us, but still the masses of humanity came on at us, closer and closer, seemingly inexhaustible. Only when they came within hand-grenade range of us did the last of these attacking Russians fall to our machine guns. And then, as our gunners began to breathe again, there was a fresh stir in the distance, a broad dark line on the horizon, and it all began again." Thus a German officer described the rearguard actions north of Moscow.

Even a healthy commander would have quailed inwardly before such an onslaught. But Field Marshal von Brauchitsch was already a sick man: he had suffered heart attacks in November, and the tongue lashing to which Hitler had recently subjected him had not aided his convalescence. On December 6, as the great Russian offensive began, he tendered his resignation to Hitler. He must have known that he would otherwise be made the scapegoat. Hitler stalked up and down the room for ten minutes without answering; then he replied that he could not agree to any change at this moment. Brauchitsch left the room without a word.

From the Russian front came the ominous sounds of an impending avalanche. But even Hitler now saw that Brauchitsch was a sick and exhausted man. Who could replace him? The names of Manstein and Kesselring were whispered to him. Colonel Rudolf Schmundt persuasively urged Hitler to become his *own* army Commander in Chief, issuing orders directly through Halder to the army. Hitler said he would think it over. In fact he had already begun to act the role—or rehearse it: by early December 7 it was obvious that the corps holding the embattled salient at Tikhvin despite blizzards and catastrophic losses was in danger of being encircled. Hitler decided to abandon the city, which was largely gutted and ruined anyway, and confirmed this in a direct telephone conversation with Leeb, commander of Army Group North, at 7:04 P.M. He did not consult Brauchitsch at all. Halder sorrowfully wrote in his diary: "Today's events are again stunning and shameful. The Commander in Chief [Brauchitsch] is barely even used as postman now. The Führer deals over his head with the army group commanders direct. The terrible thing is, however, that the High Command does not grasp the condition our troops are in, and is relying on patchwork operations where only bold decisions can be of use."

Yet the High Command—and that meant Hitler—was all too aware of Germany's precarious position now that her offensives had been halted. The uneasiness of the German people was as nothing compared with Hitler's own private nightmare, for only in him were all the threads of foreign Intelligence and strategic decisions combined. As the usual faces gathered in his bunker after dinner that Sunday evening, December

7—the women secretaries, Bormann's adjutant Heim, a doctor, and Walther Hewel—Hitler reflected that the emergency collection of warm winter clothing now beginning throughout Germany on behalf of the troops on the eastern front was an admission of bad planning intelligible to even his most loyal followers.

Toward midnight the buzz of conversation was stilled as Heinz Lorenz, a press officer, burst in. An American radio station had just announced a surprise Japanese air attack on the U.S. fleet in Pearl Harbor, Hawaii. Japan was at war with Britain and the United States.

It was so unexpected—Hitler's immediate reaction was to slap his thighs in delight and joyously proclaim, "The turning point!" Then he bounced out of the bunker and ran through the icy darkness to show the news bulletin to Keitel and Jodl. To Hewel, Hitler rejoiced: "Now it is impossible for us to lose the war: we now have an ally who has never been vanquished in three thousand years, and another ally"—he added, paraphrasing a remark Napoleon had also made about the Italians, a remark which he had read in Talleyrand and which had been drifting around his magpie memory ever since—"who has constantly been vanquished but has always ended up on the right side."[1]

In Berlin, the Japanese ambassador was calling on Ribbentrop. Ribbentrop assured him that Germany and Italy would immediately declare war on the United States too. In fact, Hitler took two days over this decision (the records give no indication of a reason). Meantime the news of Japan's triumph hardened. In a carbon copy of the Japanese attack on the Russians at Port Arthur in 1904,[2] torpedo planes had sunk five battleships and badly damaged three more at Pearl Harbor; air bases in the Philippines had been bombed, and the northeastern corner of Malaya had been invaded at Kota Bharu. The British battleships *Prince of Wales* and *Repulse* were sent to combat the invasion and sunk two days later by Japanese aircraft.

Hitler issued to the admiralty orders that German submarines and warships might forthwith open fire on American ships as and where they met them; and before he left for Berlin on the evening of the eighth, he discussed at length with his staff how best to declare war on the United States so as to make a good impression on his own people. That he would declare war was a foregone conclusion; not even Göring, Hitler's

[1] Napoleon had said, "The Italians have never yet ended a war on the same side as they started it —except when they changed sides twice."
[2] Liddell Hart effectively quoted the 1904 *Times* on the Port Arthur attack: "The Russian squadron was open to, and invited attack. The invitation has been accepted with a promptness and punctuality that do high honor to the navy of our gallant allies," *i.e.*, the Japanese. (*History of the Second World War*, London, 1970.)

second man, was consulted on that point. In Washington the mood was reported to be grave; public opinion was consoled with the bromide that the United States had not yet lost a war, but late on the eighth, the west coast of the United States was panicked by a false air raid warning, followed the next noon by an alert on the Atlantic seaboard, with warnings broadcast on the radio that German bomber squadrons were approaching! Hitler scoffed some weeks later, "Roosevelt declares war"—presumably meaning the covert shoot-on-sight phase existing since September—"and thereupon not only allows himself to be thrown out of East Asia wholly unprepared, but lets his merchant shipping ply peacefully back and forth along the American coast for us to pick off like sitting ducks. He drives pell-mell out of Washington because of air raid dangers, onto his estate, then back to Washington. . . . He makes his whole country hysterical, the way he goes on."

Hitler arrived in Berlin with Keitel, Jodl, Schmundt, and other members of his staff at 11 A.M. on December 9. The German chargé in Washington had now confirmed that Roosevelt was unlikely to demand war with Germany and Italy under the circumstances, unless he felt it necessary to beat Hitler and Mussolini to such a declaration for reasons of personal prestige; Roosevelt would do all he could to avoid open war in the Atlantic, a war on two fronts. To Hitler, however, this was the delicious moment when he could deliver to that "lout" Roosevelt the public smack in the eye he deserved. Late on the ninth the Washington embassy was instructed to burn its secret files and code books. Hitler began to prepare a speech for the Reichstag; the foreign ministry furnished him with a list of all Roosevelt's violations of neutrality.

Shortly after 2 P.M. on the eleventh Ribbentrop read out Germany's declaration of war to the American chargé in Berlin: now President Roosevelt had the war he had been asking for, Ribbentrop concluded.

There was little to distinguish Hitler's Reichstag speech that afternoon: he referred to the Chicago *Tribune,* which had recently published "war plans" revealing Roosevelt's intention of invading Europe in 1943, and he read out the text of the agreement just signed with Japan. Yet deep within, instinct was warning the Führer that he ought *not* to be welcoming the events that must now unfold. Major von Below, his Luftwaffe adjutant, who had met him at the railroad station in Berlin, found him uneasy about the long-term effects of Pearl Harbor. Ribbentrop also professed (later) to have been distraught at the manner in which the Tripartite Pact, made to keep the United States *out* of the war, had now brought her into direct confrontation with the Reich. But neither he nor Hitler raised any obstacles to the military convenant drafted by the Japanese and dividing the world into operational zones: west of the meridian of 70 degrees east, Germany and Italy would operate; all the world east of that line, including British India, would fall to Japan. Only this, the German leaders reasoned, would bring Japan into a sharp and prolonged conflict with Britain and exclude any possibility of a separate peace.

Despite the strategic benefits—Japan's advance on Singapore and Australia would force Britain to withdraw Indian and Anzac forces, particularly from the Mediterranean, and the United States would have to cut back her arms supplies to Britain and the Soviet Union—Hitler was heard to mutter, "I never wanted things to turn out like this. Now they"—meaning the British—"will lose Singapore!"[3] It was after he had returned to the Wolf's Lair, with the "Barbarossa" campaign on the brink of its first winter crisis, that he made to Walther Hewel the remark that has already been reported: "How strange that with Japan's aid we are destroying the positions of the white race in the Far East—and that Britain is fighting against Europe with those swine the Bolsheviks!" His foreign minister soberly warned him: "We have just one year to cut off Russia from her American supplies arriving via Murmansk and the Persian Gulf; Japan must take care of Vladivostok. If we don't succeed and the munitions potential of the United States joins up with the manpower potential of the Russians, the war will enter a phase in which we shall only be able to win it with difficulty." To this Hitler made no reply.

[3] And see Hitler's revealing remark on the fall of Singapore, page 407 below.

Hitler Takes Command

In the dark months of that winter Hitler showed his iron determination and hypnotic powers of leadership. We shall see how these qualities and the German soldier's legendary capacity for enduring hardship spared the eastern army from cruel defeat that winter. Where his generals saw an ignominious withdrawal as their only salvation, Hitler told them to stand firm until the spring thaw arrived to halt the enemy offensive. When they demurred, argued, and disobeyed, Hitler dismissed and disgraced them, and himself took command of the German army, until a new spirit gradually prevailed along the eastern front.

Hitler's powers to influence were remarkable. A division was reported to be retreating. Hitler telephoned its commander. The general's dejected voice reached him—barely a whisper, from a frozen, inhospitable wilderness hundreds of miles away. Hitler rebuked him: "You know perfectly well that it's just as cold thirty miles further back! The eyes of the German people are on *you*." His few words implanted a new sense of purpose in the general, and the division stood its ground. Soon hardened commanders were swearing they had seen Hitler in the thick of battle—"We thought it was all over, but then the Führer toured our sector calling for one last ounce of effort from us, and we pulled through!" But many more months would pass before he risked leaving his headquarters.

> I had to act ruthlessly. I had to send even my closest generals packing, two army generals, for example, whose strength was gone and who were at the end of their tether. . . . In winter one of them came and announced, "Mein Führer, we can't hold on any longer, we've got to retreat." I asked him, "Sirrrr, where in God's name are you thinking of retreating to? How far?" "Well," he answered, "I don't really know!"—"Do you plan to drop back thirty miles? Do you think

it isn't all that cold there, then? And do you imagine your transport and supply problems will be any better there? And if you retreat, do you intend to take your heavy weapons with you, can you take them?" This man answered, "No, it can't be done."—"So you're planning to leave them to the Russians. And how do you think you're going to fight further back if you haven't got any heavy weapons?" He responded, "Mein Führer, save at least the army, whatever happens to its guns." So I inquired, "Are you planning just a retreat to the Reich frontier, or what? Where do you plan to call a halt?" "Well, mein Führer," he rejoined, "we probably won't get any choice." I could only tell these gentlemen, "Get yourself back to Germany as rapidly as you can—but leave the army in my charge. And the army is staying at the front."

After declaring war on the United States, Hitler remained briefly in Berlin. The public mood was grim. The churches were full—a disturbing sign, but Hitler admitted to his secretaries that there was nothing he could do against the churches until the war was over. As in the case of the "Jewish problem," Hitler felt he already had enough on his plate.[1]

In the east military disaster was looming. The Soviet counteroffensive had torn open a thirty-mile-wide gap between Kluge's and Guderian's armies. Bock's Army Group Center had no more reserves. On December 9 Guderian had warned him: "Something like a crisis of confidence has broken out among the troops." More and more Russian troops and tanks poured through the breach. The most effective antitank weapon, the Redhead shell with a hollow-charge warhead—which Hitler had first seen demonstrated on November 25—had immediately been embargoed by him to keep it secret from the enemy. Whenever Russian tanks appeared, the German infantry were taking to their heels. The fear of Russian captivity, and the lack of weapons, fuel, fodder for the horses, and reserves, produced a crushing sense of inferiority.

Hitler sent the army's ailing Commander in Chief von Brauchitsch to the Moscow front to see the situation for himself. Guderian met him on December 14 at Roslavl; he wrote afterward: "It took a twenty-two hours' drive through the blizzard to reach him. I think he got the most urgent points I made." Brauchitsch ordered Guderian to hold the line forward of Kursk and Orel, but like Bock and Kluge the tank commander knew only one solution: retreat while the going was still good! Hitler turned a deaf ear on them all. "I can't send everybody home just

---

[1] After discussing a proposed Sportpalast speech with Hitler on December 14, 1941, Rosenberg noted: "I said I took the view that I shouldn't mention the stamping out of Judaism. The Führer took my point and commented that as they had thrust this war onto us and brought about all this destruction, it was no wonder if they were the first to feel the consequences."

because Army Group Center is beginning to leak," he argued; and he was encouraged by anguished appeals from the other sector commanders not to let a general rout begin.

Army Group Center's most urgent need was for reserves. Late on December 14 Hitler ordered Jodl to find out how much could be scraped together in the Reich; General Friedrich Fromm explained that his Replacement Army had a number of divisions under training, convalescing, or temporarily released to industry. Half an hour after midnight Hitler ordered Fromm to come to the Chancellery. The general undertook to raise four and a half divisions at once from all over Germany, equipped with winter clothing and skis. At 1 P.M. the next day Hitler telephoned Field Marshal Leeb, who was now asking permission to pull back his army group (North) to the Volkhov River; Hitler pointed out that this would open up the railroad link to Tikhvin for the Russians and enable them to pour more troops and supplies into Leningrad. Again he could not trust Brauchitsch or Halder to make this plain enough. He ordered Leeb to bring General Ernst Busch—commander of the Sixteenth Army besieging Leningrad—to the Wolf's Lair in person the next day.

As his special train left Berlin that evening, Hitler drafted his first Halt Order to the eastern front. "Any large-scale retreat by major sections of the army in midwinter, given only limited mobility, insufficient winter equipment, and no prepared positions in the rear, must inevitably have the gravest consequences." The Fourth Army was ordered not to fall back one foot. This controversial order was hotly debated during the night. Its critics argued that what mattered now was not clinging to frozen territory but preserving the army's fighting power for 1942; others, among them Jodl, replied that only such a holding order made sense. A colonel argued that it was time for strategic command of the war to be delegated to an acknowledged expert like General von Manstein; Jodl— emerging from Hitler's conference car—pointed out that the Führer could not stand that general too near him. "Besides, the Führer has already decided on a different way of resolving the command problem."

It was 11 A.M., December 16, when Hitler arrived back at the Wolf's Lair. His Halt Order was dictated to Bock over the telephone by Halder at 12:10 P.M. Hitler made it obvious that he was going to ignore Brauchitsch and deal directly with the army groups in the future. But the damage had already been done. When Leeb now came, Hitler had to agree to Army Group North's proposed withdrawal. "If you had been

given the Third Panzer Group as I wanted, at the time the enemy
south of Lake Ladoga was still weak, you would have encircled Leningrad immediately and made land contact with the Finns." This plan the
General Staff had prevented.

Indeed, Hitler no longer trusted Brauchitsch's judgment. On December 16 he had his chief adjutant, Rudolf Schmundt, flown to the Moscow front; and that afternoon Schmundt returned with an accurate account of Guderian's litany of worries, told him in an hour-long
conference on Orel airfield. At last the truth was reaching Hitler. Waiting for the Führer to telephone him about reinforcements that evening,
Guderian—racked by sciatica—wrote to his wife: "I only hope it's not
too late. The consequences don't bear thinking about. We've been put in
a hideous position by our total underestimation of the enemy and the
haphazard preparation for a winter campaign in Russia. Heaven knows
how we're going to extricate ourselves. . . . I'm just glad that the
Führer at least knows what's happening, and I hope he'll come to grips
with his customary verve with the bureaucratic wheels of the war department, railroad, and other machinery. . . . I lie awake at night racking my brains about how I can help my poor men, who have no protection against this fierce winter weather."

Toward midnight Bock telephoned Schmundt with the text of his
three-day-old report to Brauchitsch, openly warning that a momentous
decision would shortly confront them. It read: "The Führer must decide
for himself whether my army group must stand and fight, thereby risking its total destruction, or retreat, entailing precisely the same risk. If
he decides on retreat, then he must realize that it is unlikely that enough
troops will ever get back to the new line to hold it, and that it will be
unprepared for them and not all that much shorter." Brauchitsch had
suppressed this report rather than show it to Hitler. Over the phone
Bock now added that his 267th Infantry Division had that very day
been forced to abandon its entire artillery in the retreat. Hitler telephoned him in person. "In this situation there is only one answer, and
that is not to yield one inch—to plug the gaps and hold on!" Bock grimly
replied that his front might cave in any moment. Hitler responded
clearly, "That is a risk I must just take."

"There is only one thing that ails our front," he explained to Brauchitsch and Halder a few moments later. "The enemy just has more soldiers than us." This was why they must rush the simplest reinforcements
—riflemen, each provisioned with eight or ten days' canned food, alcohol, and chocolate—by train to the Russian front. A thousand trucks
must be supplied to Bock as well, and two thousand SS troops must be

flown east from Cracow. At 3 A.M. he telephoned Guderian with details of the reinforcements that he was airlifting to the front.

Later that day, December 17, General von Richthofen came to the Wolf's Lair with Göring. The Luftwaffe corps commander wrote in his diary:

> Jeschonnek and I went in to see the Führer. He's a bundle of nerves, but clearheaded and confident. . . . I kept emphasizing that what matters now is keeping our troops alive and fighting where they are. What the front lacks is riflemen, winter gear, and food, but above all the will to stand fast. . . . I emphasized the need for him to appeal to each soldier in person, then it will be all right. . . . The Führer listened with enormous interest and concentration. He's planning a major proclamation. Reichsmarschall [Göring] and I were very persuasive. Führer swears loudly about the army commanders responsible for much of the foul-up. Is grappling with big reshuffle. Brauchitsch already out, Halder, Keitel, etc. are to follow him. He asks my opinion on various army commanders: not a pleasant job, but I spoke my mind bluntly while stressing my own bias.

Hitler himself signed the famous order that now went out to the eastern front. After minor frontline corrections, Army Group North was to stand fast to the last man. Army Group South was also to stand fast. The same went for Bock's Army Group Center.

> Major withdrawal movements cannot be made. They will result in the complete loss of heavy weapons and equipment. Under the personal leadership of commanders and officers alike, the troops are to be forced to put up a fanatical resistance in their lines, regardless of any enemy breakthrough in their flanks and rear. Only this kind of fighting will win the time we need to move up the reinforcements I have ordered from the home country and the west.

Richthofen was to receive one long-range fighter and four bomber squadrons from the west. The chief of air training was to release five transport squadrons to the front, and the aircraft pools of every ministry and headquarters unit were to be ruthlessly stripped of all but the most essential transport planes as well. "The most important thing is to *furnish riflemen* (in simple replacement battalions) to the weakest of the divisions. There is less urgency for the transport of tanks."

This was no time to respect personal feelings, either. If Bock was unwell, then a tougher commander must replace him: Hitler ordered Field Marshal von Kluge to take over Army Group Center. Hitler attached no blame to Bock and asked Schmundt to make this plain to the field marshal.

Less cordial was his parting now with Field Marshal von Brauchitsch, the army's Commander in Chief. Hitler clearly held him responsible for withholding from him, whatever the motives, urgent and serious messages from frontline commanders. The impression he had gained on his visit to Rundstedt's army group two weeks earlier was confirmed by the inexplicable suppression of Bock's alarming message of the thirteenth. Later in December, Hitler issued a Basic Order to all Wehrmacht commands, reminding them of the need to respect such reports as an indispensable instrument of leadership—"It is the duty of every soldier to report unfulfilled orders and his own errors truthfully"—and to report without exaggeration or dangerous embellishment.

More serious were the recent indications of Brauchitsch's inability or reluctance to execute Hitler's orders. According to Major von Below, Hitler's Luftwaffe adjutant, the incident that was the last straw had occurred in Berlin, in that midnight conference between Hitler and General Fromm. "Here Hitler found out that the orders that had reached the Replacement Army were different from those he had issued. After this nocturnal conference Hitler decided that Brauchitsch would have to resign his command of the army." Several days had followed in which Hitler thought of appointing another general in his place. By December 19, however, his mind was made up: he would follow Schmundt's advice and take command of the army himself. He knew of no general capable of instilling the National Socialist spirit into the army, he explained to Brauchitsch in a loud voice that day, and he added almost inaudibly, "We will remain friends."

He repeated to Halder his motives for taking command himself. He explained that Halder would have to carry on as before, while Keitel assumed the ministerial functions of the war ministry. It surprised many that Halder had not shared the fate of Brauchitsch; but Hitler needed the Chief of General Staff for his ability and experience, and the ambitious general learned to swallow his aversion as a professional to the "upstart" dictator. Meanwhile, Hitler and Schmundt composed an Order of the Day to the soldiers of the army and the Waffen SS: "Our country's struggle for freedom is approaching its climax. We are faced by world-shaking decisions. The prime bearer of the struggle is the army. As of today I have therefore taken command of the army myself. As a soldier in many battles of World War I, I share deeply with you the determination to win through." A second document he signed that day was a letter to the commanders of the Luftwaffe and the navy in which he formalized his action:

> As of today I have decided to take command of the army myself.
> The Chief of the Army General Staff will be subordinated directly to myself.
> The Chief of the Wehrmacht High Command, Field Marshal Keitel, will exercise on my behalf the remaining powers of the army Commander in Chief as the supreme commanding and administrative authority of the army . . .
>
> *Adolf Hitler.*

General Guderian was the next to go. It had slowly dawned on his superiors that he was ignoring Hitler's Halt Order and preparing his Second Panzer Army's retreat; this was clear to Halder from the way the tanks were being regrouped around Orel and the army being echeloned in depth. Kluge, who had succeeded Bock, was no friend of Guderian, and when the panzer general arrived at Hitler's headquarters on December 20 Kluge angrily telephoned Halder and Schmundt to warn them that Guderian had obviously lost his nerve.

Guderian dramatically set out to the Führer the condition of the Second Panzer Army: his troops were exhausted and outnumbered; it was impossible to dig in, as the ground was frozen solid. Hitler retorted, "Then use your heavy artillery or mortars to blast out craters and install trench heaters in them." At one stage he caustically inquired of Guderian: "Do you believe that Frederick the Great's grenadiers enjoyed dying for their country either?" Guderian for his part hinted that it was high time for Hitler to rid himself of chairbound experts like Keitel, Jodl, and Halder, who had never seen the front line. (He had just written in a private letter: "They simply signal impossible orders to us and turn down all our requests and demands. What gets on my nerves is the feeling that I'm not getting through to them—that I'm powerless to prevent my being sacrificed to these conditions.") He flew back to Orel the next day and briefed his commanders on Hitler's renewed Halt Order. But his tanks' stealthy withdrawal still continued. Finally, on December 25, Kluge refused to work with Guderian any longer: one or the other of them must go. Shortly before midnight Hitler telephoned Kluge back: Guderian was being relieved of his command forthwith.

Something of the loneliness of absolute power must have gripped him in these weeks. Could he be certain that his single-handed decisions were right—or would the ultimate blame for military disaster now attach to him? There was nobody to whom he could unburden himself. With Eva Braun he could not discuss the war, and anyway she was far away in Bavaria. The women on his staff occasionally glimpsed the inner man. A few days earlier a record player had been installed in the Führer's Bunker—the concrete blockhouse in which he lived, in case of an enemy bombing raid or paratroop assault—and every evening he listened to Richard Strauss and Hugo Wolf *Lieder*—and of course to Wagner. How the girls loved to listen to Strauss's "Heimliche Aufforderung" as Heinrich Schlusnuss sang it, or to the gentle tenor voice of Peter Anders. "How beautiful these *Lieder* are," wrote one of the secretaries. "They envelop you in warmth and love, and even the Chief seems touched by them, because yesterday evening he told us two girls, 'Children, you must use every hour that's given you!' "

But with the command of the German army, an avalanche of work descended on him. He had ordered Halder to attend his war conferences each day in person with his staff, but Halder was no glutton for responsibility, and it was this that weighed so heavily. For weeks on end Hitler knew no regular routine. His midday meal used to start at 2 P.M.; now it was taken hours later—once as late as 6 P.M. This in turn dislocated the supper times, and the tea-party routine which previously had begun regularly in his bunker at 10 P.M. now never started before midnight. Once that winter it started after 2 A.M., which meant that his weary partners were unable to retire to bed before four or five. There was no exercise for anybody: the bunkers were warm, but outside it was cold and the roads were blocked by snow or treacherous with ice. While his secretaries preferred the warm, cozily furnished offices, Hitler slept in his bunker, with the ventilation system humming all night and the draft blowing on his head.

At the conference Guderian had attended on December 20, Hitler had issued a string of further draconian orders to steady the ragged eastern front. He told Halder: "The will to hold out must be brought home to every unit!" He recognized the troops' natural tendency to cling to the sheltering villages, but he demanded that heated dugouts be improvised between them too: the men must learn to dig in and "put up with" enemy breakthroughs. Any Russians who did penetrate must be mopped up by hunting parties in the rear. Indeed, the rear area must become one vast defense zone in which the enemy would be forced again and again to stand and fight—every field bakery must learn to defend itself, as must the Luftwaffe's ground organization. The attacking Russians must find no shelter, no stone standing atop another. This was the ruthless policy Stalin had employed in his retreat that summer; how much more effective it would be in winter. Every village the Germans had to abandon must be burned down regardless of its inhabitants. Their warm clothes were to be taken from them. Any villages or woodlands falling into Russian hands were to be methodically destroyed by the Luftwaffe. The enemy must live from hand to mouth. Above all the morale of the troops had to be restored, and their fear of the Russian enemy and winter dispelled.

He embodied these principles in a new order to the three army groups in the east. Every officer and man must realize one thing: a retreating army must expect a far crueler winter than the army that held out where it was—however ramshackle its positions. "The Russians will follow hard on the heels of any withdrawing army, allowing it no respite, attacking and assailing it again and again; nor will such an army come to any halt, as it lacks any kind of prepared positions in the rear. The phrase 'Napoleonic Retreat' is threatening to come true." Hitler held out one hope to his commanders: the Russians would slowly bleed to death in their own offensive. They were already throwing their very last reserves into the fight, and these were no match for the German soldier.

Hitler's message was distributed to every officer on the eastern front. If his armies could only hold out long enough, he would transport to them fresh riflemen and ammunition, and they would win time to salvage precious equipment disabled near the Russian lines.

Christmas at Hitler's headquarters was always a cheerless affair, very different from that celebrated at the Berlin ministries, for example. Hitler received his staff in turn, handed them an envelope containing a small sum in Reichsmarks, and sometimes sent them a packet of coffee with a typed note of good wishes. Hewel wrote in his diary on the twenty-fourth: "A dejected Christmas. Führer's thoughts are elsewhere. No candles lit." Two days before, Hitler had learned from Kluge that the General Staff were sending hundreds of half-frozen troops by air to Smolensk without weapons or winter gear. He had shouted into the telephone: "Another *Schweinerei!* I was told that everybody going to the eastern front was being equipped with machine guns and rifles." Kluge warned him: "I have a feeling we shall be facing a major decision tomorrow." Hitler confidentially gave him the authority to withdraw sectors of his army group if need be—a measure of his trust in this field marshal. More important, Hitler also lifted the embargo on the Redhead hollow-charge antitank shells.

A fragment of another famous diary, that of Canaris, graphically portrays the atmosphere:

December 24, 1941.

A grave crisis is looming up on the eastern front, particularly for Army Group Center. If the Russians keep up their pressure it may end in catastrophe. Fateful consequences are now arising from the fundamental errors made in planning the operations of October 15 (no single main point of effort) and in allocating our forces (no tactical reserves anywhere, let alone strategic), and above all from our downright criminal underestimation of the enemy. General Schmundt is drawing comparisons with 1812 and talks of the "moment of truth" for National Socialism. The equipment losses are horrifying: trucks, guns, and aircraft have to be destroyed or abandoned because we lack the fuel to bring them back.

All this has a grim effect on our soldiers' fighting morale, as they suddenly realize that they are being badly led. The Führer's actions (retiring von B[rauchitsch] and a number of commanders) are quite right and have befallen those who are by no means blameless, whatever people may say about them. . . .

Our own treatment of Russian prisoners is having awful consequences. In the retreat from Moscow we had to abandon German field hospitals as well. The Russians dragged out the sick and injured, hanged them upside down, poured gasoline over them, and set them on fire.[2] Some uninjured German soldiers had to watch this torture; they were then kicked in the groin and sent back to the German lines with instructions to describe how the Bolsheviks were reacting to news of the mass executions and barbaric treatment meted out to their comrades in German captivity. On another occasion German prisoners were beheaded and their heads laid out to form the SS symbol.

The Russian army communiqué never reports numbers of prisoners taken, but just registers laconically that "fifty officers and two thousand enlisted men were liquidated"—meaning the modes of execution described above.

Hitler also received ample evidence from the Forschungsamt intercepts that the Red Army was shooting German prisoners of war. When the International Red Cross now proposed that both sides return to the

[2] Jodl's naval staff officer, Commander Wolf Junge, described similar reports, adding: "When a major German field hospital had to be abandoned to the enemy at Kaluga in December 1941, our troops laid a pistol on each invalid's bed; we left them the choice of whether or not to fall alive into Russian hands" (unpublished memoirs of Junge).

accepted conventions, Hitler refused, telling Keitel and Jodl that he did not want his troops to get the idea that the Russians would treat them decently in captivity; besides, if he had to furnish lists to the enemy, the Russians would soon observe that many of their prisoners in German hands were no longer alive (a consequence of the heartless neglect and epidemics to which they had been exposed).

The year's end had come. They had attained none of their strategic objectives. Almost hourly Hitler was to be seen clinging to the long-distance telephone linking him with Kluge and the eastern front. The dam might break at any moment. Kluge was again asking for minor withdrawals, and Hitler was grimly observing that they might just as well fall back on the Dnieper or even the Polish frontier. The Russians were not even first softening up the Germans with artillery bombardment. Hitler related to the field marshal how as a simple infantryman in Flanders he and his comrades had withstood ten days of ceaseless bombardment and nevertheless had held the line. Kluge rejoined that Hitler had not been fighting at twenty-five degrees below zero. "My corps commander has told me that if the 15th Infantry Division is ordered to stand fast, the troops are so exhausted they will not obey." Hitler angrily said, "If that is so, then it is the end of the German army," and he ended the conversation.

None of Hitler's staff would forget the New Year's Eve that followed. In the far south, Manstein's first assault on the fortress Sevastopol had failed—indeed, General Hans von Sponeck had surrendered Kerch to the enemy. Throughout the day Kluge had been on the phone to General Halder, begging for permission to withdraw the Fourth Army, the right wing of Hoepner's Fourth Panzergruppe, and the Ninth Army into a new line. Hitler flatly refused. Any strategic retreat was bound to touch off a general collapse; he demanded a fight to the finish in order to win time until the reinforcements arrived. Kluge phoned Halder soon afterward: if General Strauss's Ninth Army stood fast, it would be wiped out in the next two or three days. Then they would have no alternative but to witness the honorable collapse of the entire army group within a week.

Supper was again served late. Hitler dozed off afterward, exhausted, while the last minutes of the old year ticked away. His staff gathered expectantly in the mess and waited for him. But at eleven-thirty Kluge phoned urgently from the front, and for the next *three hours*—the time is graven in the diaries of Bormann, Hewel, and the army group itself—

Hitler wrangled with the field marshal, arguing and cajoling—stopping only for a half-hour debate with Halder—on the need to stand fast. Kluge argued for a compromise—something between the extremes represented by Guderian's stealthy retreat and the Führer's adamant orders, as he put it. He asked Hitler to trust him. Halder, however, supported Hitler completely. Hitler refused outright to grant Kluge freedom to withdraw what amounted to a ninety-mile section of the front over twenty miles. Again Kluge was ordered to hold the front. Not until 2:30 A.M. did Hitler arrive for tea with his intimate staff. "I am glad I know how to overcome even the greatest difficulties," he said. "Let's hope 1942 brings me as much good fortune as 1941. The worries can stay. So far the pattern has always been this: the hardest times come first, as a kind of preparation for the really great events." Turning to Hewel, who had shared his captivity in Landsberg prison, he added, "You have been through times like this yourself!" In the corner the phonograph was playing Bruckner's Seventh, but nobody was in a mood to appreciate it.[3]

It was on this occasion that Ribbentrop first broached with Hitler the possibility of an armistice with Russia. But Hitler merely replied that only a clear victory or defeat was now possible in the east. Over the next weeks and months there were to be many attempts at mediation, but Hitler ignored them all. On January 1, 1942, he was shown an intercepted Italian dispatch from Tokyo indicating that Japan wanted to mediate. The problem remained Britain: she had sworn never to negotiate a peace with Hitler, and only the severest military setbacks would make her reverse this decision; Ribbentrop's officials also argued that Germany must show she was a fit partner to negotiate with, and this meant an end to the "barbarism" in Europe. If Britain would now concede, Germany would leave the British Empire—minus the conquests by Japan—intact; however, in the future Britain must keep her nose out of Europe. As for France, Hitler quoted Bismarck's sentiments after the French capitulation at Sédan: the individual Frenchman might nurture some friendly feelings for the Germans; the French as a nation would al-

---

[3] One of Hitler's secretaries wrote two weeks later: "On New Year's Eve we were all in a cheerful enough mood at supper in the No.2 mess. After that we were ordered over to the regular tea session, where we found a very weary Chief, who nodded off after a while. So we accordingly kept very quiet, which completely stifled what high spirits we had been able to summon up. After that the Chief was away for three hours in conference, while the menfolk who had been mustered to offer New Year greetings hung around with doom-laden faces not daring to allow a smile to pass their lips. I just can't describe it—at any rate it was so ghastly that I broke down in tears in my bunker, and when I went back over to the mess I ran into a couple of the lads of the Escort Command, who of course saw at once that I had been crying—which set me off all over again, whereupon they tried to comfort me with words and alcohol, successfully. And then we all sang a sea chantey at the tops of our voices—'At Anchor off Madagascar, and We've Got the Plague Aboard!' "

ways hate them. He proposed therefore to leave France outside the New Europe, outside the three great walls he was now thinking of—an East Wall from Leningrad to Rostov, a North Wall along the Norwegian coast, and a West Wall along the new frontier with France.

Hitler's ruthless leadership stabilized the front for just long enough. In mid-January 1942 he could authorize Kluge to withdraw the more exposed sections of his army group. But by now a new defensive line had been prepared, reserves were arriving, warm clothing had been contributed by the German public, and most of the heavy equipment could be salvaged in time.

The winter crisis had been mastered. But the cost in officers was high —ousted by Hitler *pour encourager les autres*. General Otto Förster, the engineer-general who had already incurred Hitler's displeasure once in a 1938 dispute over fortifications, was dismissed for withdrawing his corps; General von Sponeck, who had abandoned Kerch, was sentenced to be shot (though Hitler later commuted this sentence). General Hoepner, who prematurely withdrew his panzergruppe to the winter line on January 8, was dismissed from the army in disgrace. (He and Sponeck were both executed three years later in another context.) Field Marshal von Leeb was retired from Army Group North. General Strauss was sacked from the Ninth Army. Many lesser commanders shared their fate. The Luftwaffe, and particularly Richthofen, kept Hitler zealously briefed on the army generals' shortcomings. Field Marshal von Reichenau was killed by a stroke; Bock, his health miraculously recovered, was appointed to replace him at Army Group South.

One new face drew Hitler's attention. In January the First Panzer Army's Chief of Staff lunched with him one day and reported on the imaginative emergency measures he had taken to protect the army's southern flank, suddenly exposed when the Sea of Azov froze hard enough for the enemy to cross: he had improvised squads of soldiers convalescing along the coast, fitted them out with guns and ammunition and even ice yachts for patrolling the sea. "The panzer army has really done everything it could!" said Hitler in congratulation. Eight months later it was this general—Kurt Zeitzler—whom he selected to replace Halder as the Chief of General Staff.

Over the next weeks, Hitler rejected every effort made to lighten his burden by relaxing his direct control. On January 16 he refused to sign two decrees drafted by Lammers to that effect. Indeed, he shouldered still more authority. General Hoepner, outraged at the loss of his "well-earned pension rights," instituted a lawsuit against the Reich in the Leipzig courts and won. Hitler, enraged by the blindness of the legal profession to the disciplines of war, declared himself above the law and summoned the Reichstag on April 26 to endorse a decree to that effect.[4] The decree gave him powers over every person in the Reich "regardless of their so-called well-earned rights." It puzzled many Germans that an absolute dictator should need to arrogate seemingly superfluous powers to himself, but as Goebbels learned, Hitler's aim was to legalize in advance the radical steps he planned against "reactionaries, civil servants, lawyers, and certain sections of the officer corps."

The tactical withdrawal he had ordered in mid-January in Russia was followed a month later by an immensely more dramatic withdrawal in the west, as the navy's battleships at Brest were forced to abandon the Atlantic theater on Hitler's orders.

Here his motive was primarily one of preventive strategy. Throughout December and January, Intelligence reports had trickled into his headquarters indicating an Anglo-American plan to invade northern Norway in the spring. The sources were ominously similar to those proven accurate in the anxious spring of 1940: on December 25, Berlin learned from a decoded dispatch that the Finnish envoy in Washington had quoted his colleagues there about Allied preparations to invade northern Norway. A British raid on the Lofoten Isles soon after was regarded by Hitler not only as a personal insult but as a forerunner of a later invasion. It also reminded him of his reliance on Swedish iron and Finnish nickel supplies from Petsamo (Penchenga). He suspected that the enemy had secretly promised Narvik to Sweden; while Sweden's king and army were said to be pro-Hitler, her financial institutions and Social Democrats were not and might well cut off all the iron ore if Britain ever did occupy Narvik.

With this in mind Hitler ordered the reinforcement of Norway, particularly by his navy. The time for sweeping forays into the Atlantic was over anyway. The battleships *Scharnhorst* and *Gneisenau,* still denied access to French North African and Spanish ports, had been bottled up at Brest on France's Atlantic coast since the spring and had been regularly crippled by bomb damage ever since. Hitler was impatient at their enforced idleness. On December 26 his naval adjutant put to him the admiralty's request for extra air support for their next exercises. This was the last straw. "I was always a champion of big ships before,"

4 See page 416 below.

Hitler announced. "My heart was in them. But they've had their day. The danger of air attack is too great." He sent for Raeder to discuss withdrawing the battleships—to Norway, where, out of RAF bomber range, they would have a new lease on life. On December 29 he told Raeder to bring them back from Brest. Since routing them around the British Isles would invite certain disaster, Hitler suggested taking the British channel defenses by surprise—sailing the warships back through the English Channel. The navy was aghast; but Hitler bluntly gave them the alternative of that or decommissioning the warships where they lay and employing their armament and crews elsewhere.

Hitler explained to his naval adjutant on January 4 that surprise was of the essence. "Therefore any steps which might somehow alert the British must be avoided," the adjutant noted. "If the withdrawal comes off, he would like to see every ship possible transferred to Norway. This is the only step likely to have a deterrent effect on the British. Since Churchill has stated that the British still have the bloodiest sacrifices to bear, he considers an invasion of Norway quite likely. Naturally Churchill may have meant something else, but he, the Führer, will not rest in this respect until our fleet is there." The navy outlined its plan to him a week later, while Colonel Adolf Galland, the famous fighter ace and commander, explained how he proposed to give the warships air cover during their Channel dash. Hitler was taken aback by Vice Admiral Otto Ciliax's insistence on reaching the seventeen-mile-wide Dover Straits at high noon, but this was inevitable if the warships were to slip out of Brest under cover of dusk. Raeder was unhappy about the whole venture, but the alternative did not bear thinking about. The attempt would be made in one month's time.

It was probably not until early February 1942 that Hitler could form any realistic picture of the Moloch of defeat from which he had snatched his army. By January 10 the army had registered 30,000 frost casualties, with 2,200 soldiers suffering amputation, but this proved only an interim figure; by February 20 the army had counted 112,627 frost victims, of which no fewer than 14,357 were amputees. "Barbarossa" had now cost the German forces close on 1,000,000 casualties, including 200,000 dead. The bitterness within the army's ranks was directed not at Hitler but at his generals.

One vivid narrative by an ordinary soldier filtered up through SS channels to Martin Bormann and probably reached Hitler too. It recounted how his battalion had marched about aimlessly for some three hundred miles before being hurled into action on the Donets, where the Russians had already overwhelmed the defenses.

Too late and without any heavy guns, without even a single antitank gun our battalion was thrown into the breach as a so-called stopgap force. The Russians came at us, of course, with heavy tanks and enormous masses of infantry and pushed us back. Our machine guns wouldn't fire because of the bitter cold, and our ammunition ran out. For one whole day our battalion was encircled in a village where we had dug in. We tried a breakout by night as a last hope, an act of madness, but it came off. Meantime the entire front was beginning to cave in, about sixty miles across. Everywhere troops were flooding back in disorder, losing their heads. In vain officers confronted them at pistol point trying to restore order in this chaos; panic had broken out everywhere. . . . You saw scenes we had never witnessed even with the Russians, and only rarely with the French in France: columns of troops streaming back, often several side by side on one road; steel helmets, guns, gas masks, and equipment littered the whole area. Hundreds of trucks set on fire by our own troops because they could not move them for lack of gasoline or because of the frost and snowdrifts; blazing ammunition dumps, clothing stores, food depots. The roads of retreat strewn with dead horses and broken-down vehicles. Upon this scene of chaos there pounced *German* dive-bombers, adding the final touches of perfection to the destruction. . . . The injured lay where they fell. Shapeless huddles of misery, swathed in blankets, their legs wrapped in rags and bandages, hobbled along the roads looking like something from scenes of Napoleon's retreat. For four days our battalion fought on, screening this hideous retreat. By the fifth day the Russian tanks had overtaken us, shot us to pieces, and wiped out the rest of our battalion. I myself escaped the tanks—which took a fiendish pleasure in hounding down each of our men until he was flattened beneath the tank tracks—by running into a deep pit where the snowdrifts barred the tanks' pursuit. . . .

With his own eyes this man had seen the three divisions in his sector wiped out. "We, the survivors of this catastrophe, have only one wish: that the Führer wreak a terrible judgment on the guilty ones."

Long before the passing of the old year, Hitler's thoughts had been with the coming spring offensive. He hoped to begin advancing Army Group South into the Caucasus as soon as the weather cleared—perhaps late in April 1942. As he explained to the Japanese, from whom he concealed none of his true ambitions, a southern thrust rather than the capture of Moscow offered many advantages: it would cure the oil problem, it would keep Turkey neutral, and if all went well the autumn of 1942 might see the Wehrmacht advancing on Baghdad. He disclosed his strategic plan to Field Marshal von Bock on January 18, before Bock flew to take command of his Army Group South at Poltava, seven hundred miles away. But Hitler already realized that the war would continue into 1943: on February 9, Göring conferred with him on "responsibility for the prompt provision of locomotives for the winter of 1942–43"; the equipment was to be of a kind capable of surviving the Russian winter.

Hitler's allies were initially unenthusiastic about a spring offensive. Finland feared war with the western powers. Mannerheim virtually declined to advance on the vital Murmansk railroad; he demobilized 180,000 of his troops that spring and went over to the defensive. But Field Marshal Keitel in an undoubted feat of diplomacy persuaded both Romania and Hungary to increase their contingents on the eastern front. Romania agreed to restore her expeditionary force to its previous strength, and Hungary, not to be outdone—and fearing that Hitler would favor the Romanians in the inevitable postwar struggle for the Transylvania region—followed suit, offering a complete Hungarian army of two hundred thousand men. Italy also agreed to send more divisions east. Hitler for his part tactfully respected everybody's feelings: the allied armies would not come under German command; and the Hungarians and Romanians would nowhere find themselves adjacent, so they could not get at each other's throats. Bulgaria, with its strong pro-Russian currents of sympathy, remained nonaligned. Her king, although an admiring follower of Hitler's, was pleased that the Führer expected nothing more of Bulgaria's army than that it dissuade Turkey from foolish undertakings. Turkey's feelings were evidently warming toward Hitler anyway, even as the spring thaws melted northward across Russia; the Turkish president privately assured Franz von Papen that he was as convinced as ever of Germany's ultimate victory and was resolved to withstand British pressure on Turkey to abandon her neutrality. Learning from Forschungsamt intercepts that a disgruntled Britain was discontinuing her arms supplies to Turkey, in April Hitler agreed that Germany would supply the Turks with tanks, guns, submarines, and aircraft.

Neutral nations and Germany's allies were not the only ones demanding the products of the German arms industry. The catastrophic material losses of the German army that winter had to be made good. Anticipating a swift defeat of Russia, in mid-1941 Hitler had ordered production effort switched to the navy and Luftwaffe, and now the army's needs, particularly in ammunition, could barely be covered. In November 1941 the economics ministry had declared its virtual bankruptcy: General Hermann von Hanneken saw no way of increasing arms production on the present raw materials basis. Hitler himself had to devise the ways and means of rationalizing arms production and surmounting red tape. Seated in his private plane on December 3, while flying to the eastern front, he had dictated to Munitions Minister Fritz Todt a three-page decree ordering the simplification and expansion of arms production. Basically, future arms manufacture was to be concentrated in the most efficient factories, turning out standardized and unsophisticated weapons by mass-production means. Todt initiated a radical reform of the arms industry's structure. On January 10 Hitler ordered the industry to revert to its earlier preferential treatment of the army's needs at the expense of the Luftwaffe and navy (although "the long-term objectives remain unaltered," *i.e.*, the focus of the fighting effort of the latter two services was to be directed against the western Allies). At the end of January, Todt outlined to Hitler his detailed proposals—basically the arms combines would supervise their own projects and a "fixed contract price" system would be introduced to dispose of the current iniquitous "cost-plus-profit" system, with its inherent deterrent to any factory to cut weapons production costs. As a result of Todt's reforms, between February and July 1942 German arms production was to increase by 55 percent. On February 7, Todt reported to Hitler and dined with him at the Wolf's Lair; by 9:45 A.M. the next morning he was dead, his charred remains lying in the wreckage of his Heinkel which had crashed on takeoff at Rastenburg airfield.

Hitler was desolate at the loss of this old friend. He ordered the air ministry to design a cockpit-recorder, to install in future planes, to register the cause of any accidents. His Luftwaffe adjutant witnessed Hitler's receipt of the news from the airfield. "He showed the barest flicker of emotion. The only thing he said was, after a few minutes, that only Albert Speer could be considered a suitable successor. As that day wore on, and more frequently with the passing years, he talked of Dr. Todt and how grievous a blow his death was for him." Speer had just arrived the previous evening from a hazardous tour of the construction gangs he had late in December supplied to the eastern front to speed up the relaying of railroad track and reconstruction of transport installations. Hitler called him into his office and informed him of his selection as Todt's successor.

For the second time in two weeks Hitler returned to Berlin, this time to bury his loyal friend, Munitions Minister Fritz Todt.

These were momentous hours. As his train pulled into the Reich capital, his battleships were in the English Channel. At noon they would be passing through the Straits of Dover, and still the British seemed totally unaware of them. In the Far East, the final Japanese assault on Singapore, bastion of the British Empire there, had just begun. It looked like the end of India, too. In North Africa, General Rommel's corps, nourished with fresh tanks and men, had gone over to the counteroffensive and thrown the British back three hundred miles and out of Cyrenaica. From decoded British foreign office instructions to missions abroad Hitler could savor the harsh mood of realism now again pervading London in view of the German army's unbroken powers of resistance and his imminent spring offensive. Yet his feelings on the coming British disgrace were mixed. To the Japanese he seemed to relish every moment. "If Britain loses India, their world will cave in on them. India is the heart of the British Empire. It is from India that Britain has won her entire wealth." But to his staff he showed a different face. To Goebbels on January 29 he had lamented the sad losses being inflicted on the White Man in the Far East. In speaking to Antonescu on February 11 he referred to the latest dispatch from Singapore as "perhaps a somewhat melancholy piece of news." It was rumored that he privately went so far as to admit he would dearly like to send the British twenty divisions to help them throw the Yellow invaders out.

Yet the clock could not be turned back. Hitler mentioned to Goebbels that every Englishman he had met before the war had agreed that Churchill was a nincompoop—"even" Chamberlain took that view. The propaganda minister did not share Hitler's and Ribbentrop's evident belief that these February disgraces would lead to Churchill's final downfall, though both would have liked to see Sir Stafford Cripps take his place.[5] Hitler believed Cripps even more inept than Churchill ("It's not enough to be called Cripps, you've got to have *Grips* [brains] as well," he wisecracked). Goebbels agreed that in any normal country a Churchill would long ago have got his just deserts; but the British were an odd folk, and probably too inert to take action.

By the early hours of February 13, the German fleet's strategic with-

[5] The German admiralty also believed Churchill impregnable. Etzdorf recorded: "In Ambassador [Karl] Ritter's view, the political leadership has certain hopes that the loss of Singapore might have far-reaching effects on the British public as far as the dropping of Churchill and a willingness for peace are concerned. The naval staff thinks otherwise. There is no hope *whatever* of the British suddenly giving way to make peace." The admiralty felt that even if Australia and India were lost, Churchill, in view of his ties to the United States, would probably reform the Empire as a British Commonwealth of Nations with Canada as its centerpiece.

drawal from the Atlantic to northern waters had been successfully completed. The *Scharnhorst* had reached Wilhelmshaven, despite minor damage from two mines. The *Gneisenau* had reached Kiel, also dented by a mine. The *Prinz Eugen* had got through completely unscathed. In the belated air battles the British had lost twenty bombers, sixteen fighters, and six torpedo planes; Galland had lost only seven fighters. The London *Times* commented hotly: "Vice Admiral Ciliax has succeeded where the Duke of Medina Sidonia failed. . . . Nothing more mortifying to the pride of sea power has happened in home waters since the seventeenth century." Hitler, who had remained in hourly contact with the admiralty, and who had "trembled for the safety of our ships," as Goebbels witnessed, now breathed again.

Next day he spoke to ten thousand newly commissioned lieutenants assembled in Berlin's Sportpalast. The photographs show him—looking stern and flanked by Keitel, Milch, and Himmler—gripping the speaker's lectern. He made every officer present believe that in this hour of crisis he alone could turn the tide. Normally such speeches ended in silence, but as he left the platform a thunderous cheering broke out, and out of the clamor swelled ten thousand voices united in the national anthem. Despite the reverses in Russia, his prestige was at its height. The next evening, February 15, his train bore him back toward his headquarters in East Prussia. Toward midnight, Joachim Ribbentrop came along the swaying corridor with news that Churchill had just broadcast the fall of Singapore: Lieutenant General A. E. Percival had capitulated that evening with his seventy thousand men to General Tomoyuki Yamashita, commander of the Japanese Twenty-fifth Army. To Fräulein Schroeder, Hitler's secretary, the foreign minister dictated a gloating draft communiqué for the Axis press to publish next morning. Hitler read it with an expression of distaste. Then shaking his head he advised Ribbentrop: "We have to think in terms of centuries. Who knows, in the future the Yellow Peril may well be the biggest one for us."[6] He tore the document in half.

[6] Yet a few weeks later the same Hitler privately scoffed at the foreign journalists who accused him of betraying his own race and conjuring up a "Yellow Peril" through his alliance with Japan. "It was the British who appealed to the Japanese in World War I to give us the *coup de grâce* . . . the essential thing is to win, and to that end we are quite ready to make an alliance with the Devil himself."

Hitler's Word Is Law

The first half of 1942 was again to bring the Soviet Union to the brink of defeat. From the intercepted messages passing between east and west, Hitler could follow Stalin's exasperated demands for an Allied Second Front and his veiled threats to conclude a separate peace with the Nazis. But now that he had survived the winter, Hitler no longer wanted to settle his differences by negotiation. As soon as the ground dried out and he had restocked his depleted divisions in the far south, he would go over to the offensive. The German soldier's self-confidence had been restored: with the Führer's prodding they had mastered the terrors of the Russian winter, where even a Napoleon had failed. At the end of February the foreign diplomats in Berlin were informed that the Führer had now decided to fight to the bitter end. All further attempts at mediation, of which the latest were quietly proposed by Turkey, were discouraged.

Initially, as Hitler's secretary vividly described, the mood at his head-quarters upon his return from Berlin was bleak. "After two days of warmer weather the temperature suddenly dropped again," she wrote on February 27, 1942. "Although by day it is only about zero, the biting east wind makes the cold far far worse. . . . The Chief is always dog-tired, but he won't go to bed, and this is often a torment for the rest of us. We used to play records most evenings, and then you could fall back on your own thoughts; but since Todt's unfortunate end the music evenings have been few and far between, and as his tea circle always consists of the same faces, there is no stimulus from outside and nobody has any personal experiences to relate, so the conversation is often tedious and indifferent to say the least. In fact, the conversations run around and around in the same circles. Thank goodness we have a cat that often sits up with us. Its playful antics . . . are a welcome relief and help to bridge the awkward silences. I like him most of all, because if he jumps on to my lap I can warm my freezing hands under his soft fur— it's bliss! There is also a Scotch terrier, but he is not all that popular as he is obstinate and capricious (besides which the Chief says he looks like a scrub brush and he'd never let himself be photographed with it). . . ." Goebbels found the terrier still being given the run of Hitler's bunker at the end of March. "At present there is no creature closer to him," observed the propaganda minister.

Hitler's health had suffered from the winter, but he allowed himself no respite. In December he had jibed to Halder: "You fine generals only play ball so long as everything's going well. The moment things get sticky you report sick or tender your resignation!" If Germany was to survive, *he* could not resign; the worry, the extremes of temperature, and the general strain on his sclerotic arteries began to tell on him. Dr. Morell added an ever-increasing variety of medicines to the Führer's medicine chest: the heart tonics "Strophantin" and "Prostrophanta" first, then the stimulants "Cardiazol" and "Coramin" to overcome the insufficiency in Hitler's circulatory system. In 1942 Morell began administering "Sympathol." Hitler passively accepted Morell's increasing doses. "Morell tells me that my intense rate of work uses up so much energy that he has to give me so many injections—just as if I were in the tropics," he would explain. Or again: "Morell is still researching. He is still pushing out the frontiers of our knowledge." His faith in Morell's "Vitamultin" vitamin tablets was so great that he ordered billions of them dispensed regularly to the armed forces despite expert opinion that they were valueless. And when the winter of 1941 brought a plague of lice to the eastern front, it was Morell's invention, "Russla" powder (a foul-smelling concoction), that was prescribed to the reluctant troops. Morell's royalty profit was commensurate.

For all Morell's endeavors, visitors to Rastenburg that spring found Hitler gray, drawn, and ailing. He confided to Goebbels that he suffered attacks of giddiness; and as he described the winter crisis he seemed to age visibly. "The Führer describes to me," wrote Goebbels of a conversation on March 19, "how close we were these past few months to a Napoleonic winter. Had we weakened for just one instant, the front would have caved in and a catastrophe ensued that would have put Napoleon's far into the shade. Millions of fine soldiers would have been exposed to death by starvation and cold, and our workers—not to mention the intelligentsia—probably forced into bondage. Most of the blame for this is Brauchitsch's. The Führer has only words of contempt for him: a vain, cowardly wretch, unable even to grasp what was happening, much

less master it. By his constant interference and disobedience he completely wrecked the entire plan of campaign in the east, which had been
devised in crystal clarity by the Führer. The Führer had a plan which
was bound to lead to victory. Had Brauchitsch done what was asked of
him and what he should in fact have done, then things in the east would
look very different than they do today. The Führer had no intention
whatever of aiming for Moscow; he wanted to cut off the Caucasus
[from the rest of Russia], thus hitting the Soviet system at its most
vulnerable point. But Brauchitsch and his General Staff knew better:
Brauchitsch kept hammering on about Moscow. He wanted prestige victories instead of real ones."

In retrospect, the issues all seemed much clearer to Hitler than at the
time.

For the coming German offensive in the east, Hitler had again established a clear list of priorities. This time General Halder accepted
them. As Hitler set them out in a conference on March 28, 1942, a
carefully phased series of campaigns would begin in the far south as
soon as the ground dried out: in the Crimea, Manstein would destroy
the Russian forces in the Kerch peninsula; he would then storm Sevastopol, using the techniques of World War I—sheer weight of artillery
bombardment. Then Bock's army group would attack the Izyum salient
east of Kharkov. The main summer offensive, "Blue," would open with
the capture of Voronezh on the Don; then the armies would roll
southeastward down the Don toward Stalingrad, digging in along the
river for winter quarters. Hitler assured Goebbels that by October his
armies would be able to go into these winter quarters. By early September he hoped they would have reached the Caucasus Mountains. De-
pending on the summer victories, he would decide later what operations
to undertake in the center and against Leningrad. The directive for
"Blue" was issued on April 5. After the defeat of Stalin's main armies,
Hitler planned to construct an immense East Wall beyond which there
might well rage a Hundred Years' War against the scattered remnants of
the Bolshevik forces. "Russia will then be to us what India is to the
British," he told Goebbels.

More than one voice doubted the prospects of this great offensive.
Keitel mentioned—but only to his subordinates—as early as December
1941 the possibility that it might fail; his staff experts correctly suspected that damage to the Caucasus oil fields might be so extensive as to
render their capture pointless. General Fromm, commander of the Re-

placement Army, doubted there would be enough manpower or munitions to execute "Blue" over such vast distances. Göring also doubted whether the Russians would be defeated that summer. However, Hitler had no real option but to strike out toward the Caucasus oil fields. He needed the oil; and so did Stalin—so the Red Army would surely stand and fight rather than withdraw beyond the Don. Already the Soviet Union had lost the iron ore of Krivoi Rog and the manganese of Nikopol; the armorplate of their latest tanks was consequently of poor quality. But if "Blue" succeeded, Stalin would have no coking coal, or oil either. Now even General Halder saw the point, and when the admiralty persisted in arguing for the capture by Rommel of the Suez Canal the general impatiently replied that Rommel's army would be too weak to withstand the enemy's counterattack from the Middle East and Red Sea *unless* the German armies were also astride the Caucasus. Besides, Halder pointed out: "The Caucasus operation is still absolutely vital for our oil supply position." He held that only victory in the Caucasus would ensure the Reich's ultimate survival in the war.[1]

The oil shortage was certainly a compelling argument to use with the admiralty. The German and Italian navies were virtually immobilized; production of aviation fuel was just enough to cover monthly requirements, but so low as to make expansion of aircraft production pointless; and in May 1942 Keitel also had to find 60,000 tons of fuel for agricultural purposes in the Ukraine and for Atlantic defensive projects. The 1942 output of gasoline for motor transport would be 77,000 tons a month less than the average monthly consumption (219,000) in 1941. Hitler signed a government decree restricting the use of motor cars to official use only—and even then a bona fide justification was needed.

Unaware that Rommel's army stood astride undreamed-of oil fields in Libya, Hitler still relied on Romania's resources. Hungary showed little inclination to part with her supplies, and Hitler had evidence that both she and Romania were secretly stockpiling oil for the private war they were planning to wage on each other in the future. But he was unwilling to put pressure on Marshal Antonescu to increase oil deliveries. Antonescu claimed that 80 percent of Romania's output was already earmarked for the Axis, and Hitler, fearful that something might happen to this loyal friend, instructed Keitel that the Romanians were to be given "kid glove treatment" and there was to be no question of imposing a military "petroleum dictator" on Antonescu. With blithe lack of vision,

[1] Halder's words are quoted as above by his naval liaison officer in German admiralty archives. After the war, he and departmental heads like General Adolf Heusinger claimed to have been unanimous in opposing the Caucasus campaign.

Antonescu's government insisted that Germany pay for all her oil with gold, and in advance; had Romania foreseen into which neighbor's coffers that gold would eventually vanish, she might have acted otherwise.

Hitler had always been a champion of the radical act. In every SS barracks hung one of his favorite Nietzsche texts: *Praised be that which toughens.* Much of his admiration of Stalin was inspired by the dictator's successful brutality. He, Hitler, would try to emulate him, but often did not succeed: he had not determined to bomb London until too late. To the Japanese ambassador, General Oshima, he mentioned that he intended to kill all survivors of torpedoed Allied merchant ships out of cruel "necessity"; but when he put this idea to the admiralty as a means of intensifying the tonnage war, Raeder would not hear of it.

The fear of reprisal did not dissuade the British from opening up in March 1942 a massive area-bombing offensive against German and German-occupied cities. On the night of March 3, RAF planes dropped over 450 tons of bombs on a Paris arms factory, killing 800 French civilians. Hitler ordered the Luftwaffe to execute an immediate reprisal on a British target. "The main thing is to achieve the maximum shock and terror effect." But a few days later he canceled the order, explaining to Jeschonnek that he wanted to avoid provoking air raids on German cities; besides, the British were not coming to Germany in any strength, he argued, and the Luftwaffe was incapable of meting out appropriate annihilation raids on English cities. A week later, a force of 200 RAF bombers laden primarily with incendiaries all but destroyed the medieval Baltic town of Lübeck, leaving 320 dead and hundreds of injured in the ruins. It was a Saturday night, and Hitler's temper was not improved when it was found impossible to reach anybody at Berlin's civilian ministries or military headquarters: all of them were closed—apparently from lunchtime on Saturday until 9 A.M. on Monday! Nobody knew where the ministers themselves could be reached.[2] The raid was a clear attempt to provoke Hitler into withdrawing Luftwaffe strength from the Russian front for reprisals; in this it was unsuccessful, for Jeschonnek firmly believed the Russian threat must be liquidated before all else. But Hitler did order reprisal attacks on English towns, to be chosen for their

[2] This was typical of the comfortable life led by most of the Nazi ministers. Only a week earlier, on March 21, Hitler had issued a secret decree insisting that these ministers and generals set an example to the public and warning that he would act ruthlessly and without regard for rank against any of them dealing, for example, in the black market. Somehow Göring escaped censure, though he was the worst offender.

defenselessness and cultural value—the same criteria as Churchill had applied. Exeter was the first town to suffer; London was explicitly embargoed from attack. After a series of Allied fire-raids on the Baltic port of Rostock, Hitler told Goebbels that terror could only be answered with terror. "The British belong to that class of human beings whom you can only talk with after you have smashed their teeth in."

It was an unedifying sight—the two opposing leaders, well-bunkered in their respective capitals, trading blows at each other's innocent citizenry. How Stalin, who had long learned to "think in terms of centuries," must have relished it![3] During the spring, it became obvious that the British regarded their new area-bombing offensive as the second front that Moscow was clamoring for.

The British had no alternative as yet. To invade Norway or North Africa would require a shipping fleet they would soon no longer possess, thanks to the U-boats. From Stockholm, Hitler learned that Churchill had promised the exiled Norwegian government not to invade Norway—not in 1942, anyway; and the king of Sweden privately assured Hitler that he would oppose any Allied designs in northern Scandinavia. As for the Continent, the British would be foolish to count on an internal uprising in Europe, Hitler told Mussolini. (There was no more opposition in Germany—in Berlin he had fewer than two thousand critics, or so he believed. The cheering Berlin crowds after his Reichstag speech on April 26 were seen as proof of that.) However, his intuitive sense of strategy warned him late in March that the Cherbourg and Brest peninsulas might be the target of an Allied invasion. On March 27 he ordered all available reserves "immediately" moved into the region west of Caen and Saint-Nazaire, and he gave instructions that the U-boat base at Saint-Nazaire itself was to be closely reinforced. The very next morning the British launched a commando raid on the base.

The aging destroyer *Campbelltown,* accompanied by a swarm of torpedo boats and motor launches laden with commandos, had entered the base before dawn on March 28, rammed the lock gates of the huge drydock, and been abandoned. The warships had flown the German ensign and employed secret German signal codes, but this should not have surprised the defenses to the extent it did. The commandos were wiped out by the port's defenders, and only four of the eighteen torpedo boats and

[3] The Soviet ambassador in London allegedly remarked to Sir Alexander Cadogan at the end of 1940 that his country was content to see the two sides exhaust themselves. He was in the daily habit, he said, of totting up the aircraft losses in the Battle of Britain together, in one column; whereas Churchill and Hitler were more myopically setting them down against each other.

launches employed escaped destruction. French dockyard workers and sightseers were still clustered curiously around the abandoned *Campbelltown* at 11:45 A.M., when its hidden cargo of time-fused explosives blew up, killing sixty of them—though not before the ship's secret papers had been salvaged by the Germans, including what was apparently the latest chart of Allied minefields. The naval staff was well pleased, but Hitler was not. He sent for Raeder and expressed his displeasure at the fact that the raiding force had sailed so far up the Loire; and more importantly he ordered the Atlantic defenses still further strengthened to make such raids impossible in the future.

Over 140 British prisoners had been taken at Saint-Nazaire. Hitler sent his interpreter Paul Schmidt to interrogate them. The interrogation reports submitted to Hitler showed them to be the cream of Churchill's forces—well-informed, proud, and patriotic. Schmidt found most of them bitter that they should be fighting Germany, a brother country. They no longer believed Britain could win, he reported, but felt that the war would "just fizzle out." Goebbels's English-language propaganda was said by these prisoners to have a big listening public but to be using the wrong approach. Most riveting were the remarks of a territorial army major, a London industrialist and friend of Anthony Eden, who said that his war-weary countrymen would make peace the next day if they could be convinced their country's very existence was not threatened. According to this major, the British hated the Japanese but nevertheless felt that Britain ought to be in the same camp as the Germans, not fighting them. "We all like the Germans. . . . It's just that we are certain that Hitler is planning to conquer the world." Told that Hitler had no designs on Britain at all, the major is said to have exclaimed, "Then why not tell our government and people that! I would be willing to go to the British government and tell them what your peace terms are, and I give my word of honor to return to captivity here. But for God's sake do it now, before the hundreds of thousands who will die on both sides in this summer's fighting are sacrificed!"

This offer was not taken up, but many of Hitler's coming decisions—for example his rejection of the joint "India Declaration" approved by Italy and Japan and designed to encourage mutiny in that endangered dominion—were guided by a desire to preserve the prevailing undercurrents of peace perceptible to him in Britain. The British authorities continued, however, to represent Hitler's war aims to the British people very differently, for example there was a pronouncement soon afterward by Lord Vansittart, diplomatic adviser to the Cabinet, that Germany intended to exterminate twenty million Britons or transport them as slaves to Africa. So the British fought gamely on.

Hitler was now fifty-three. On his birthday there were letters from Eva Braun and her mother, and from his sisters Angela and Paula. He wrote back thanking them and sending them ham he had just received from a Spanish admirer—with a warning to them to cook it thoroughly before eating. Raeder, Göring, Milch, Ribbentrop, and a host of lesser dignitaries attended the birthday luncheon held in a dining room decked out with tablecloths and flowers. The headquarters officers and staff were given a glass of Piesporter Goldtröpfchen and cups of real coffee. All the children of the neighborhood were marshaled outside by SS adjutant Schulze and photographed plucking at the Führer's uniform and thrusting flowers into his hands. After lunch the first two Tiger tanks were demonstrated to him. From Berlin Goebbels had sent a newfangled device, a tape recorder with tapes of many symphonies and orchestras. Hitler could hear for himself how much better the Berlin Philharmonic was than its Vienna counterpart, which had an aged string section; and now he discovered Hans Hotter as the up-and-coming baritone who would be ideal for Bayreuth.

In the east the roads and fields were drying out; the snow had vanished almost everywhere. In the Crimea spring was already in full bloom. Never in his life had Hitler yearned so painfully for the onset of that season. He never wanted to see snow again. It had cost him six months of his precious last years—the vital years. After a certain age, he reflected, man's creative genius gradually abandons him. The strenuous bunker life in East Prussia had sapped his strength. The first white hairs were appearing on his head.

Hitler's doctors prescribed the solitude of the Berghof, and he himself was only too eager to put the horrors of the Russian front out of his mind. (Only a few days earlier a Russian deserter had brought over nauseating details of the one million dead in Leningrad and of the cannibalism widespread among the beleaguered Russian army units and population there.) He therefore asked Ribbentrop to arrange an early meeting with Mussolini, and to make plain that he would prefer Salzburg to some Italian venue. Mussolini meekly agreed, and Hitler's train left the Wolf's Lair late on April 24 on the first leg of the long journey to Bavaria; it was followed by Ribbentrop's equally impressive train. "A wonder that the foreign minister allows anybody to take precedence over him!" joked Hitler, long aware of Ribbentrop's tiresome vanity.

In Berlin he was to address the Reichstag, asking for powers that would neutralize the meddling lawyers of the ministry of justice for all time. He himself drafted the necessary decree and showed it to Hans Lammers four hours before the speech began on April 26. Lammers he could trust—he knew how to manufacture the quasi-legal tools needed to buttress the affairs of an authoritarian state. "He doesn't get legalistic theorizing confused with the realities of life," Hitler said some days later. Lammers suggested that it would suffice for the Reichstag to pass the law by acclamation; Göring would follow Hitler's speech with a formal approval of the law as President of the Reichstag. The little charade was performed at the end of the afternoon's speeches. The Reichstag records show Hitler thundering:

> . . . I do however expect one thing: that the nation give me the right to take immediate action in any way I see fit, wherever I do not find the obedience unconditionally called for by service of the greater cause. This is a matter of life and death to us. (*Loud applause.*) At the front and at home, in transport, civil service, and the judiciary there must be obedience to only one idea, namely the fight for victory. (*Stormy applause.*) Let nobody now preach about his well-earned rights.[4] Let each man clearly understand, from now on there are only duties.

Göring appealed to the deputies to empower the Führer to do "everything in the cause of, or contributing to, the fight for victory." Regardless of rank or position, Hitler could punish any German as he saw fit, dismissing him from any office or command without the need for regular procedures. As one man the Reichstag deputies rose from their seats and signified their assent with shouts of Heil and a singing of the national anthem. At 4:24 P.M., when the session ended—the last time the Reichstag would ever meet—Adolf Hitler was himself the Law.

That evening Hitler continued his journey to Bavaria. The days in Munich and at the Berghof passed all too rapidly. Unfortunately, the Obersalzberg was carpeted with fresh fallen snow as he arrived—snow seemed to dog him everywhere. But the snapshots Eva Braun pasted into her album show a misty-eyed Führer affectionately playing with Herta Schneider's children and fondling Bella, the new Alsatian bitch he had just bought from a minor postal official in Ingolstadt to keep Blondi, his

---

[4] A reference to General Hoepner's lawsuit. See page 401.

other Alsatian, company. The advantage of taking Bella for walks was that she would not start talking politics or war with him.

The two days of talks with Mussolini yielded nothing new. The atmosphere was more cordial than on their previous meeting in August 1941. In the first meeting at Klessheim, near Salzburg, Hitler painted the German position in Russia in optimistic terms. Mussolini responded by quoting the New York *Herald Tribune*'s assessment that Russia had "a dying army." When the Duce mentioned the growing grain shortage in Italy, Hitler promised that in 1943 the Ukrainian harvest would yield at least seven million tons. Both agreed that a watchful eye was needed on France; but at the other end of the Mediterranean, Turkey was slowly but surely edging around to the Axis camp, if only in consequence of her hatred of the Russians. There was ample proof of this. Turkey had recently imposed a crippling fine on the British envoy to Bulgaria, whose luggage had mysteriously blown up in a Constantinople hotel! She had vigorously prosecuted the Soviet agents behind a recent bungled attempt at assassinating Franz von Papen in Ankara. And she was currently negotiating with Germany for the purchase of German submarines, tanks, and guns.[5]

The second meeting between the dictators was at the Berghof. Generals and field marshals took the place of the foreign ministers who had attended the first meeting (but no admirals, as the German naval staff later lamented). The Italians pressed their case for an early capture of Malta, "Operation Hercules." Hitler conceded that if successful, "Hercules" and the subsequent destruction of the British stranglehold on the Middle East would be a turning point for the Axis, but he viewed the operation with scarcely concealed distaste—not only because it was to be a primarily Italian operation (and hence in his eyes predestined to ignominious failure), but because despite all the arguments of Raeder, Kesselring, and the Italians to the contrary, he still argued that the war could only be won in the east. The Mediterranean theater was a sideshow of value only for tying down enemy forces. In deference to the alliance, Hitler paid lip service to the needs of "Hercules": since April 2, German and Italian bomber forces had been mercilessly softening-up Malta for invasion, attacking airfields, dockyards, and warships with

---

[5] Hitler wanted to make the sale of U-boats conditional on Turkey's allowing a similar number of German submarines to slip clandestinely through the Dardanelles into the Black Sea. This the Turks rejected. Hitler withdrew a similar proposal about torpedo boats, to be disguised as merchant ships, when he was reminded that plans were far advanced to transport these down the autobahn to Linz and from there along the Danube directly into the Black Sea.

savage side-effects testified to by the appeals reaching Hitler via neutral channels to allow British hospital ships through to the island. In mid-April, he had also agreed to supply German parachute troops for the eventual invasion, provided the British did not in the meanwhile spring surprises on him in Norway or France. This was the basic offer he repeated to Mussolini at the Berghof, but his heart was not in it. He knew from the aerial photographs spread out before them that the island was heavily fortified and unsuitable for glider landings. Rommel's offensive in North Africa must begin before the British could start theirs, and given the limited Axis air strength in the Mediterranean, "Hercules" would have to be postponed at least until after that. Early in May, therefore, the OKW laid down that Rommel should launch "Theseus," as his offensive was called, at the end of the month, with "Hercules" postponed until mid-July or mid-August. The actual objectives of Rommel's offensive were themselves a matter of disagreement: the Italians wanted him to halt on a line between Sollum and the Halfaya Pass, but Hitler wanted Egypt. A Finnish report had claimed that 90 percent of the Egyptian population was anti-British, so it must be "ripe for revolution" in Hitler's view.

At the beginning of May, Hitler returned to the Wolf's Lair in East Prussia. Bella went with him, sleeping in his train compartment and lying at the foot of the camp bed in his bunker. Perhaps Hitler saw in the massive Alsatian something of a watchdog, for over the last few days reports had trickled in of a plot to assassinate him; there were indications that Russian assassins were being sent to do the job.

Bella did have her disadvantages, though. She woke regularly as clockwork at 9 A.M. in the pitch-dark bunker bedroom, bounded onto Hitler's bed, and began to paw him affectionately. Since he seldom went to bed before three or four, this was a nuisance; besides, he liked to lie in bed for an hour or two each morning, catching up on his reading. His intake of information was staggering, a necessity if the Führer principle was to be maintained. The breakfast trolley outside his bedroom door groaned with fresh files each morning. Ambassador Hewel logged over eleven hundred different diplomatic papers passing through his hands to Hitler in 1941; by early April 1942 he had already submitted over eight hundred more. Now as Commander in Chief of the army he assumed a workload that would have crushed many men. He boasted: "Although the Russian front is three times as big as the front was in France, there is not one regiment or battalion there whose situation is not followed three times a day here at Führer Headquarters."

We shall never know all the Intelligence data on which Hitler based his decisions. The Forschungsamt archives were later destroyed, and the remarkable output of the post office went from his hands straight to the document-shredder machine. (A few weeks earlier the Post Office had begun unscrambling the enemy's sole radio-telephone link between London and Washington, and a regular flow of transcripts had reached Hitler through Himmler ever since March 1942; the transcripts included even the top-secret conversations between Roosevelt and Churchill.) Missing too are the secret cables decoded by Ribbentrop's cryptanalysts —Swiss, Turkish, British, Italian, American, French, and a host of other codes. Decoded confidential Turkish and Yugoslav dispatches from the Soviet capital enabled Hitler to follow Stalin's guesswork over Germany's coming offensive—Hitler's aim was to feign transport and other preparations for a renewed offensive against Moscow, to distract attention from his real objectives: Voronezh and the south. He also learned of the crippling Russian famine, of the arrival of American tanks and aircraft, and details of Russian aircraft production. The decoded American telegrams from Cairo to Washington were even better: in February, the Italians deciphered one in which Washington inquired about the possibility of invading northwest Africa. At the end of April, Cairo was heard advising Washington of the crucial position in Malta: antiaircraft ammunition was running out, and there was no gasoline for the motor transport. Other American messages betrayed the strength and dispositions of the forces opposing Rommel. The Abwehr units in the east were also functioning; late in April they were able to quote a member of the Soviet party leadership, Nossenko, on a resolution of the latest session of the Central Committee's presidium—"to snatch the operational initiative out of German hands before their offensive begins." The Red Army would go over to the offensive on the symbolically significant first of May (in fact, the offensive began soon after).

Hitler also learned much from orthodox diplomatic sources. Early in April he heard from Buenos Aires that Britain was mass-producing one-kilo bombs with long time-fuses. He at once ordered the Luftwaffe to begin its own mass production of such weapons. From diplomatic sources too he heard the first rumors that Vice-Admiral Sir Louis Mountbatten was preparing an amphibious invasion of France. Probably one of the more damaging items was the confirmation blurted out by Churchill—who evidently forgot the wartime slogan "walls have ears"— that the mounting shipping losses were bringing Britain to "the brink of her most critical moment since war broke out." This quotation reached Hitler through Spain and encouraged him to step up his U-boat and Luftwaffe offensive on the Atlantic and Arctic convoys. In the last week of May, convoy PQ. 16 to North Russia was attacked; 7 ships were sunk, with 32,400 tons of war supplies including 147 tanks, 77 aircraft, and 770 motor vehicles. Every Allied vessel sunk reduced the threat of a Second Front. From the intercepted enemy cables Hitler also knew precisely the terms of the Anglo-Soviet pact being hammered out in London: Stalin was demanding the restitution of his pre-1941 frontiers (which included the Baltic states and parts of Finland and Romania) and much of southeast Europe; Anthony Eden, Churchill's foreign minister, was inclined to agree, but the Americans as yet were not.

During May 1942 Hitler's armies regained the military initiative in the east. Only the growing partisan menace in the rear of Kluge's Army Group Center gave cause for concern. Persuaded that Moscow was the objective of Hitler's summer offensive, the Russians had infiltrated and parachuted tens of thousands of partisans into this area (though Hitler forbade his staff to refer to them as "partisans," just as in an internal edict he denied the bombers of Rostock and Lübeck the right to the title "Royal Air Force").

The partisans were blowing up railways and bridges, burning down factories and food stores, and intimidating the relatives of Russians working for the Axis. In the eyes of many Germans a great opportunity had been lost—that of winning at least the traditionally anti-Soviet Ukrainians to their cause. This had been Reichenau's last message to Hitler before he died in January 1942. It was the advice of Goebbels, and particularly of Rosenberg as well. The latter, officially Hitler's minister for the eastern territories, watched in despair as one plenipotentiary after another muscled in on his regional governments—each with Hitler's special warrant, like Albert Speer's for the construction of roads and railways, or Fritz Sauckel's for the procurement of workers for the Reich. Rosenberg bitterly told Hitler on May 8 that with greater tact those workers could have been procured voluntarily; by rounding them up like slaves, Sauckel—as Hitler's manpower dictator—was merely driving hordes of Russians before him into the forests, thus supplying new recruits for the partisan armies. Gauleiter Erich Koch, his own Reich Commissar of the Ukraine, was even worse than Sauckel and quite out of Rosenberg's control. "I know that we always used to say the Slav liked a good whipping," said Rosenberg, who went on to complain that some Germans in the Ukraine were taking this literally and strutting around with whip in hand; this was a bitter blow to the Ukrainians' self-esteem. Hitler approved an order Rosenberg had drafted curbing Koch's excesses, but in private he believed Koch's doctrine was the proper one. Göring also supported the tough line, telling his generals in April after a conference with Hitler: "The Russians are an enemy with barbaric methods. We are not going to introduce such methods ourselves, but it will be necessary for us to express ourselves more harshly."

Large-scale antipartisan sweeps with code names like "Hanover" and "Brunswick" began in May. The Hungarian contingent counted 117 prisoners and 4,300 dead in one such operation alone. Hitler welcomed the idea of using Russian prisoners themselves to help fight the partisans, but nobody, certainly not Rosenberg, could persuade him to appoint at least "puppet" Russian governments in the conquered regions. And so the increasingly barbaric struggle behind the German lines went on, with more and more of the local population being won around to harbor and encourage the partisan fight against the Germans.

The General Staff suggested that Hitler allow the use of poison gas to combat the partisans—thereby countering illegal warfare with illegal weapons. Hitler would not hear of it—even though he was to say when the analogous problem of fighting Tito's guerrillas in Serbia was discussed that the situation there was just like that in Russia: it would be impossible to be too tough with them. "We can only get our way by acting brutally and casting off all our European inhibitions." Similarly, he flatly forbade the General Staff to study the problems of bacterial attack, except in a purely defensive light. What may have been a hangover from his own gassing experience in World War I kept him adamant to the end. Although the British employed phosphorus in their bombs, Hitler forbade its use in the Luftwaffe's, as it caused skin injuries and its fumes were poisonous. Since German scientists had developed nerve-gases (Sarin and Tabun) and bacterial weapons to a degree of sophistication unknown to the enemy, Hitler's otherwise inexplicable inhibitions were not without effect on the war effort.

For the coming summer offensive, Hitler's armies would rely heavily on their own "partisan" operations, though they were not on the massive scale employed by Stalin. In mid-April he summoned Colonel Lahousen, Canaris's chief of Abwehr subversive and sabotage operations, to discuss these with Jodl and himself at his headquarters. The final plans, as described by Lahousen to army representatives in May, relied heavily on "what we may term reeducated prisoners of war" in addition to the regular commando regiment, the "Brandenburg" Regiment, which in earlier campaigns had performed classic holding operations at the bridges of Gennep, the Dvina River, and the Vardar bridge at Aziupolis. The Russian prisoners who had volunteered proved surprisingly effective, filtering in their own uniforms or plain clothes through Russian lines to execute clandestine missions against their former comrades; furnished with the necessary passwords, they were able to return through the German lines unscathed. Army Group South, and particularly the Seventeenth Army, had high praise for them.

During April, single pairs of Abwehr agents had already parachuted into Voronezh, Stalingrad, Krasnodar, and other areas to sabotage key railway lines, power stations, and pipeline installations. Special task forces had also been trained—one to defend the Maykop oil fields, another to cut the railway line from Moscow through Rostov to Baku, and a third to organize an uprising in Georgia. In each force one-third were German specialists, the rest, native emigrants or prisoners of that region. The biggest force had been organized for the Caucasus offensive that coming summer—the "Bergmann" Battalion, 200 German language experts and 550 "reeducated" Russian prisoners from the North Caucasus and Caucasia (Georgia, Azerbaijan, and Armenia). When the hour struck, their task would be to infiltrate into the Caucasus Mountains to clear and hold key passes and to arm the anti-Soviet sections of the population. These were operations in which neither Germans nor Russians could expect any mercy if captured.

Casualties were high. On May 22 the first major operation began—"Graukopf," devised by Army Group Center: 350 Russians wearing their original uniforms infiltrated the Soviet lines, disarmed 500 troops, destroyed communications, liquidated political commissars, and spread panic and suspicion; only 100 survivors returned to the German lines. And more than one Abwehr raiding party left the German lines in a painstakingly rebuilt Russian aircraft, only to be shot down in flames within minutes by alert German antiaircraft gunners.

With overwhelming air superiority, the German spring offensives were opened by General von Manstein's Eleventh Army in the Crimea on May 8, 1942. Within four days he had all but won the battle for the Kerch peninsula. By May 15, some 170,000 Russians were his prisoners. The remaining Soviet forces in the area were dead or hiding out for a fanatical last stand in caves and quarries, or had committed themselves on rafts to the Black Sea.

The second offensive, "Fridericus," was scheduled to begin on the eighteenth, with Kleist's *Armeegruppe* and the Sixth Army pinching off the Izyum salient east of Kharkov. But the Russians launched a spoiling attack first, throwing an unprecedented weight of tanks into the salient on the twelfth, in a drive for Kharkov. This sent tremors around the entire southern front and threatened to unhinge the whole summer campaign. By evening the Soviet tanks were less than fifteen miles from Kharkov. Field Marshal von Bock, the army group commander, telephoned Halder that evening that "Fridericus" would have to be abandoned in favor of a frontal defense of Kharkov. But the Chief of General Staff replied that Hitler thought differently. No troops were to be redeployed for the repair of "minor blemishes." Bock retorted, "This is no 'blemish'—it's a matter of life and death!" He saw their only salvation in withdrawing three or four of the infantry and armored divisions allocated to Kleist for "Fridericus" and giving them to General Paulus's Sixth Army to stall the Russian onslaught on its right wing, south of Kharkov. He telephoned this suggestion to General Halder urgently on May 14—the most crucial day of the battle. Hitler would not hear of it.[6] With the main Crimea fighting over, he could release the Luftwaffe squadrons at once to aid Bock. He ordered that "Fridericus" was to commence as planned in the south—indeed, one day early, on the seventeenth. He telephoned Bock himself, explaining to the harassed field marshal that at a time like this a counterattack was the very best solution possible, as it would inevitably take the weight off the Sixth Army. To ensure that there was no "misunderstanding," Hitler ordered Halder to confirm the instructions to Bock's army group in writing.

For two days there was crisis after Kleist's offensive began. Hitler insisted that his generals keep their nerve. Sooner or later the Russians would realize they were about to be encircled. The resulting battle, heavy with carnage, was later seen as one of the boldest and most interesting operations of the war. By the twenty-second, Kleist had linked up with the Sixth Army and encircled the enemy. Within the next week 239,000 prisoners and over 1,240 captured or destroyed tanks were counted on the bloody battlefield, and Hitler had regained the Donets River.

---

[6] Afterward everybody claimed paternity of this bold decision. Halder even added a footnote to his published diaries, where he had originally entered only that Bock's "proposal is turned down," to the effect that this was on his, Halder's, advice to Hitler. But the war diaries of the OKW historical section and of Bock himself show beyond the shadow of a doubt that the decision, and hence the credit for the victory, was Hitler's, and that Halder had argued *against* it.

Hitler's ebullient mood emerges from the diary of Richthofen, who lunched with him on May 21. "Führer very nice to me, calls me his specialist, etc. At lunch he held forth to our immense amusement with an endless flood of easy arguments as to the 'Special Privileges of Smokers' —for example, the right to drive off mosquitoes from all nonsmokers; and on the idiocy of winter sports, on the protests of mountaineers at the building of mountain roads and railways, on hunting and the raising of deer in order to shoot them, on deer themselves as foodstuffs (after they've eaten five times their own weight in foodstuffs first), and on trophy-hunting: 'Why don't soldiers mount the jawbones of dead Russians in their rooms, then?' And so on."

Victor of the battle of Kharkov, Hitler returned briefly to Berlin. He told Goebbels on the twenty-ninth that the grand objective of "Blue's" first operations would be the Caucasus. "Then we'll strangle the Soviet system at its Adam's apple, so to speak." The Russians were starving and lacked tanks. Halder persistently assured him that Stalin's reserves were drying up. Rumors that Stalin was mobilizing a reserve of over one hundred divisions beyond the Urals for the coming winter—not to be tapped even if Moscow itself was endangered—were discounted.

A record of Hitler's secret speech to the new officer generation on May 30 survives. It was a summary of Social Darwinism, the survival of the fittest—a eulogy of toughness and brutality. Just as Charlemagne had used harsh measures to build his empire, the little nation of Prussia unifying all the Germans in Europe by using force to impose its will on the reluctant, so the new Wehrmacht must employ brute force in the east if it was to win the new *Lebensraum* that the Reich needed to survive. Perhaps Hitler's experiences in World War I had made him callous of human life. Wilhelm Scheidt, the assistant of Hitler's court historian, once heard him say, "I want to raise a younger generation that will put fear into the hearts of the world—in its eyes I want to see the fires of a savage beast!" More than once in private he commended Stalin's harsh leadership, for this alone had saved the Red Army from extinction. "If we cannot emulate their toughness and ruthlessness," he began saying, "we might as well give up the fight." Yet he was also fiercely proud of the ordinary German soldier: he drew comparisons between a beleaguered garrison which had just withstood a Russian siege of four months, and the American troops who surrendered the fortress of Corregidor in the Philippines with hardly a casualty, even though they still had food for another two months. Thought-provoking though the captured Russian newsreels of the nightmare battle for Moscow were, with the abandoned German tanks, guns, and trucks heaped black against the snow and the thousands of ill-clad, hungry German prisoners being herded away to an uncertain fate, it was the faces of these unknown, unsung soldiers that gave Hitler hope, for he was convinced that they betrayed no trace of fear or *personal* surrender.

The cloak-and-dagger war of agents and assassins was by no means confined to the east. As early as January 1942, Canaris had warned of the arrival of the first Allied agents in Denmark; two had parachuted from an aircraft south of Copenhagen on December 28, and since one parachute had failed to open, the *corpus delicti* was there for the Danish police to find the next morning—complete with ten pistols, a wireless transmitter, and a device whereby a pistol strapped to the man's ribs could be fired by raising his hands, ostensibly in surrender. By May, Allied secret service activity in Norway was also evident: aircraft were being blown up by altitude-activated sabotage devices; German officials were being assassinated. Josef Terboven, Reich Commissar for Norway, was summoned to confer with Hitler, and Himmler reported the results to Heydrich soon after. On the twenty-seventh, Heydrich's own turn came—he was mortally wounded as he drove into Prague in his open Mercedes.

In this ugly underground war the Allied aim—later admitted—was to "set Europe on fire" by provoking savage Nazi countermeasures against the indigenous population. Such cold-blooded tactics had Hitler's approval. In revenge for Heydrich's death the Germans liquidated Lidice, the village found to have harbored the Czech born assassins, and Heydrich's short-lived attempt to woo the Czechs with socialist experiments ended. But Hitler's own aim was clearly to present a minimal profile to the Czechs. In an urgent circular to the Gauleiters, which was prompted by the growing public demand for the deportation of the Czechs from Bohemia and Moravia to follow that of the Jews, Bormann admonished: "On the Führer's instructions I am to make it clear that there is to be no open discussion of the Czech problem in Party meetings, let alone in public."[7]

The second British provocation was an air raid, and clearly designed to impress the Russian allies. At this very moment, as Hitler knew from his Forschungsamt decoders, Molotov was conferring secretly with Churchill in London. As Hitler's train bore him back to East Prussia,

---

[7] Bormann's circular was dated June 8, 1942. Four days later Himmler approved an outline *"Generalplan* East" providing for the eventual resettlement of eastern Europe's inhabitants (the Poles, Czechs, Ukrainians, and Ruthenians) in Siberia.

after speaking to the officer candidates in Berlin, alarming reports reached him of a colossal British air raid on Cologne. The local Gauleiter reported that the damage was vast. Göring, however, comfortably holidaying at his castle outside Nuremberg, claimed that since his air defenses had destroyed nearly forty of the bombers and "only seventy or eighty" had actually attacked, the occasion had been an overwhelming Luftwaffe victory. Hitler believed the Gauleiter in preference to Göring —the more so when Churchill announced that a thousand bombers had taken part in the bombing; even Churchill could hardly get away with exaggerating by a multiple of ten, reasoned Hitler. He was prepared to accept that the RAF had sent over perhaps three hundred, no doubt as a gesture to the Kremlin. When General Jeschonnek insisted on the Luftwaffe's less credible version, Hitler abruptly replied, "I have never yet capitulated before an unpalatable truth. But I must see straight, if I am to draw the right conclusions." The obvious conclusion after Cologne was that the enemy had decided to make their interim Second Front a determined attempt to attack the civilian population, killing as many as possible until the Nazi regime surrendered. Some five hundred died in Cologne, and another forty-five thousand were made homeless. Frustratingly, Göring made no secret to Hitler of the Luftwaffe's inability to exact revenge.[8] Hitler now regretted his own "reticence" with the Luftwaffe's bomber force in earlier campaigns. Warsaw had first been given a "fair" chance to surrender; he had not bombed Brussels or Paris at all, let alone Copenhagen or Oslo. "It would have been a scandal if these cities' priceless treasures had suffered from air bombardment," he told a neutral diplomat. But now the boot was on the other foot: quite without their wanting it, the peoples of Europe were breathing a new climate of brutality.

Germany's contribution to this new climate, the elimination of the Jews from central Europe, was now gathering momentum. Hitler's radical followers saw the eleven million Jews as "Europe's misfortune"—as an eastern plague threatening friend and foe alike. Hitler felt that in time all Europe would understand his hatred. "Somehow we must get rid of them, if they are not to get rid of us," reasoned Josef Goebbels. It seemed no coincidence that the Jews were at the bottom of the spreading partisan movement everywhere.

The precise mode of "elimination" met with varying interpretations.

[8] In mid-August 1942, Hitler was advised that from now on no real effect could be expected from the Luftwaffe's attacks on Britain.

Hitler's was unquestionably the authority behind the *expulsion* operations; on whose initiative the grim procedures at the terminal stations of this miserable exodus were adopted, is arguable. In January 1942, Reinhard Heydrich, chief of the Gestapo, had briefed the leading government officials in Berlin thus: the Führer had sanctioned the evacuation of all Jews to the eastern territories, substituting this for the overseas deportation originally planned. In the east they would build roads, until they dropped. At a further Heydrich conference early in March the awkward problem posed by half- and quarter-Jews was examined. One solution would be to sterilize them, but it would take ten days' hospital treatment to sterilize each of the seventy thousand people involved, so this procedure would have to wait until the war was over; a "top level" opinion—*i.e.,* Hitler's—was quoted to the effect that a sharp distinction must be made between Jews and non-Jews, as it would not be acceptable for a mini-race of semi-Jews to be perpetuated in law. In a paper circulated early in March 1942, Heydrich's office advised the ministries that Europe's eleven million Jews were to be concentrated "in the east" for the time being; after the war they might be allocated a remote territory like Madagascar as a national home. Thus the official version.

The actual operation proceeded differently. Starting in March and April the European Jews were rounded up in occupied France, Holland and Belgium, and in the eager Nazi satellite Slovakia; for political reasons Hungary—which had nearly a million Jews—and Romania were not approached yet but were told that their Jewish "problems" would be left unresolved until the war was over. From Hans Frank's Generalgouvernement of Poland too—beginning with the ghettos of Lublin—the Jews set out eastward under the direction of one of the cruelest SS leaders, Brigadier Odilo Globocnik, the Trieste-born former Gauleiter of Vienna. Upon arrival at Auschwitz and Treblinka, four in every ten were pronounced fit for work; the rest were exterminated with a maximum of concealment. Two documents shed some oblique rays of light on the level of responsibility for this. At a cabinet meeting in Cracow on April 9, Hans Frank disclaimed responsibility for the disruption in the work process caused by the order to turn over all Jews for liquidation. "The directive for the liquidation of the Jews comes from higher up."[9] In a letter of June 26 it became clear that Himmler was anxious to conceal the massacre, for Globocnik was quoted as being eager to get it over with as quickly as possible in case one day *force majeure* should

---

[9] The semantics are significant. Frank said ". . . from higher up" (*von höherer Stelle*). Were the allusion to Hitler, Nazi usage invariably preferred *"von höchster Stelle,"* i.e., the *"top level,"* which actually occurs in the previous paragraph, or even *"von allerhöchster Stelle."*

prevent them completing it: "You yourself, Reichsführer, once mentioned that you felt the job should be done as quickly as possible if only for reasons of concealment." The concealment was almost perfect, and Himmler's own papers reveal how he pulled the wool over Hitler's eyes. On September 17, while the murder machinery was operating at peak capacity, the Reichsführer still calmly jotted down in his notes for that day's Führer conference: "Jewish emigration—how should we proceed?" And in March 1943 he was to order a too-explicit statistical report rewritten to remove a stray reference to the massacre of Europe's Jews before it was submitted to the Führer![10]

The ghastly secrets of Auschwitz and Treblinka were well kept. Goebbels wrote a frank summary of them in his diary on March 27, 1942, but evidently held his tongue when he met Hitler two days later, for he quotes only Hitler's remark: "The Jews must get out of Europe. If need be, we must resort to the most brutal methods." Hitler repeated the gist of this to Goebbels on April 26, adding that he had put Himmler in charge of resettling Germany's Jews in the eastern ghettos. Goebbels did not enlighten him. Over lunch on May 15, Hitler again merely spoke of transporting the Jews eastward and indignantly referred to the misplaced sympathies of the bourgeoisie. How well the Jews were faring, compared with the German emigrants of the nineteenth century— many of whom had even *died* en route! Over lunch on the twenty-ninth (as Goebbels's unpublished diary records) Hitler again dwelt on the best postwar homeland for the Jews. Siberia was out—that would merely produce an even tougher baccilus strain of Jews; Palestine was out too— the Arabs did not want them; perhaps central Africa? At all events, he summed up, western Europe must be liberated of its Jews—there could be no homeland for them here. As late as July 24, Hitler was still referring at table to his plan to transport the Jews to Madagascar—by now already in British hands—or some other Jewish national home after the war was over.

In reality, Himmler was simultaneously throwing the murder machinery into top gear, while he was careful not to place responsibility for the massacre itself on Hitler in writing. (Thus on July 28 he wrote to SS General Gottlob Berger: "The occupied eastern territories"—meaning Poland—"are to be liberated of Jews. The Führer has entrusted me with the execution of this arduous order. Nobody can deprive me of this responsibility.") On July 19, three days after seeing Hitler, Himmler ordered the "resettlement" of the entire Jewish population of the General-gouvernement to be completed by the last day of 1942. Each day after

[10] See page 549 below.

July 22 a trainload of five thousand Jews left Warsaw for the extermination center at Treblinka; each week two trains left Przemysl for the center at Belsec. Moreover, in August the first informal approach was made to the Hungarians to begin deporting their one million Jews to the east immediately. Count Döme Sztójay, the Hungarian envoy in Berlin, warned Budapest on August 15 that this was a "radical departure" from Hitler's previous ruling that Hungary's "problem" could be left until after the war. "The Germans are determined to rid Europe of the Jewish elements without further delay, and intend—regardless of the nationality of these Jews and provided that transport facilities exist—to deport them to the occupied territories in the east, where they will be settled in ghettos or labor camps and put to work. . . . According to absolutely reliable information, Reichsführer Himmler has informed a meeting of SS leaders that the German government desires to complete these deportations within a year."

What had inspired Himmler with this urgency? Undoubtedly—according to the retrospective view of his Chief of Staff, General Karl Wolff—it was the assassination of Reinhard Heydrich in Prague. Initially the Nazis blamed it on Jewish agents and believed it. Eyewitnesses have described the traumatic effect on Himmler: he appeared for dinner that day with Hitler ashen-faced and barely able to speak. Since a Jewish congress meeting in Moscow had according to Goebbels's diary just broadcast directives to world Jewry to launch a war of assassination, the Nazis assumed Heydrich was the first victim. Goebbels ordered the arrest of five hundred Jews in Berlin as hostages and persuaded Hitler on May 29 that every remaining Jew should be evicted from the city forthwith. Hitler instructed Speer to replace the Jews in the arms industry by foreign workers. As a worried Goebbels put it, there were still forty thousand Jews with "nothing more to lose" at large in Berlin, and the prospect of some *Ostjude* pumping bullets into him was not an appealing one.

By August 1942 the massacre machinery was gathering momentum—of such refinement and devilish ingenuity that from Himmler down to the ex-lawyers who ran the extermination camps perhaps only seventy men were aware of the truth. It is conceivable that Hitler was unaware that his November 1941 order forbidding the liquidation of the Jews[11] was being violated on such a scale. Early in August, Himmler made to

[11] See page 357.

Wolff the melancholy confession that for the sake of the German nation and its Führer he had shouldered a burden of which nobody could ever learn, in order that the "Messiah of the coming two millennia" might remain personally uncontaminated. At the time, Wolff was unable to elicit from Himmler precisely what that burden was.

"Blue"

In mid-1942 Hitler launched his rebuilt armies into "Operation Blue"—
the summer campaign that he hoped would leave him master of all
Europe as far as Astrakhan, Stalingrad, and Baku. This was the big
push that would indeed bring him to the Volga by September—and to
the Caucasus Mountains, beyond which lay the Caspian Sea and the
Middle East. Yet great though the advances the Wehrmacht now made
were, strategically the Soviet command remained the victor as autumn
approached, for after Kharkov, which Hitler considered one of Stalin's
most costly errors, the Red Army was never again to allow the Germans
to encircle them. Each successive phase of "Blue" netted a smaller haul
of prisoners and booty than the last. The Russian commander Marshal
Timoshenko no longer committed his forces to fixed pitched battles but
instead withdrew and regrouped to the far side of the lengthening German left flank as the Sixth Army advanced on Stalingrad.

We shall see how through the stubbornness of his army generals like
Bock and Hoth, and the persisting inadequacy of the army's supply arrangements, Hitler was cheated of the ultimate autumn victory; his armies were never quite fast enough to catch up with, and scythe down,
the withdrawing enemy. And when the Red Army did stand and fight, it
was on its own terms: with winter drawing on and at the extreme limit
of the German lines of supply.

Yet the summer operations started promisingly enough. Emboldened by
the victory at Kharkov, Hitler's attention was attracted to the two Russian armies orphaned by the disaster—the one east of Izyum and the
other, far larger, northeast of Kharkov. He decided on a short postponement of "Blue," the main summer campaign, while two preliminary

battles ("Fridericus II" and "Wilhelm," respectively) were fought to wipe out these tempting enemy concentrations. He flew to Field Marshal von Bock's headquarters at Poltava on June 1 and won his generals' support, explaining that this was an opportunity they would be foolish not to seize while they could. "What we defeat now can't interfere with our later 'Blue' offensive," he said. "Wilhelm" began nine days afterward, followed by "Fridericus II" on the twenty-second. Meanwhile General von Manstein had begun the long-drawn-out final bombardment and assault on the Crimean fortress of Sevastopol.

"Blue" itself—originally scheduled for mid-June—was provisionally set down for the twenty-second. In the interval Hitler ministered to his coalition.

On June 4, 1942, he made one of his very rare flights outside the Reich frontiers, to honor Finland's Marshal Mannerheim on his seventy-fifth birthday. In the dining car of Mannerheim's special train, its broad windows overlooking the unique Finnish landscape and sunlit Lake Saimaa, Hitler was tempted by the polished and fertile speech of President Ryti to rise in reply himself. While the local German envoy looked on disapprovingly, he delivered *ex tempore* a tactful speech on his difficult position during Finland's 1940 winter war with Russia. One witness, General Waldemar Erfurth, was so taken with the Führer's charm that he said that "there can be no doubt that on June 4, 1942, Hitler was in complete possession of his mental faculties." After Hitler's four-engined Focke-Wulf took off again, a flattered Mannerheim commented, "He is phenomenal!" and his Chief of Staff agreed.

Two days later Hitler received Miklos von Kállay, the new Hungarian prime minister. Kállay had brought a secret written undertaking from Horthy to bury the hatchet with Romania—but only until the war was over. Thereafter the Hungarians desired "both the Lord God and the Führer"—as Hitler laughingly put it the next day—to turn a blind eye on their fight with Romania. It would be, Kállay ingeniously suggested, a struggle between Europe and Asia, since the Hungarian frontier was where the Orthodox ceased to hold sway.

Flying back from Finland, Hitler heard that Heydrich had died of his wounds.

In private he bitterly regretted the foolhardy bravado—riding in an open car—which had cost the life of such an irreplaceable man. He ordered Heydrich's name graven on the Party roll of honor; an SS regiment on the eastern front was named after him. The state funeral was held in Berlin on June 9 in the Chancellery. Czech president Emil Hácha and his government attended. Six hundred of Germany's leading men gathered behind Hitler to pay homage to the Gestapo chief most of them had inwardly feared. Hitler used to call him "the man with iron nerves"; according to his historical officer, Scheidt, Hitler was even grooming Heydrich to become his successor and had appointed him Acting Protector of Bohemia and Moravia in Baron von Neurath's place in September 1941 as a first step in this direction. In Prague, Heydrich had modeled himself on Hitler, eliminating the noisy intellectual opposition and winning the workers over. He had introduced the first social security system they had ever known, and by the time of his assassination the first twenty workers' convalescent homes had already been built. On the day he died, fifty thousand Czech workers demonstrated against the British-inspired act in Prague. As Siegfried's "Funeral March" died away, Himmler spoke, recalling the day Heydrich had taken up the reins in Bohemia and Moravia: "There were many in Germany, and many more among the Czechs, who thought the dreaded Heydrich was going to rule by blood and terror." But he had not, Himmler explained. He had merely acted radically against the "unruly dissidents," restoring respect for German rule and beginning his internal social reforms soon after. Himmler—who had had cause enough to fear him in the past—spoke with evident emotion now that Heydrich was safely dead. Hitler laid his wreath, and then Heydrich's remains were borne in stately procession to east Berlin, to be buried at the Invalidenfriedhof cemetery along with those of Ernst Udet, Fritz Todt, and many of Hitler's other friends. All their tombs and monuments have vanished now.

Before President Hácha left Berlin, Hitler advised him to keep the Czechs in rein. If there was any repetition of the anti-German outbreaks that had caused him to appoint Heydrich in September, he would seriously consider deporting all the Czechs from Bohemia and Moravia. Hácha asked permission to warn his people of this grim prospect. Hitler recommended that he do so. At 11:10 P.M. the Führer left for Bavaria.

The records show him fulfilling few engagements. At the Osteria restaurant in Munich the next day he lunched with the architect Frau Gerdi Troost and Winifred Wagner's family. In Eva Braun's album a couple of photographs dated June 14 show the Führer and her walking their respective dogs on the Berghof terraces. But the war conferences continued.

On the fifteenth, Admiral Raeder came up to the Berghof for one of his rare meetings with the Führer; he was anxious to press the case for the attack on Malta and to obtain permission for the battle fleet in Norway to launch its most ambitious operation against the Arctic convoys yet—code-named "The Knight's Move." Hitler's enthusiasm for capturing Malta had long since waned, even though the parachute general Kurt Student spoke highly of the German and Italian paratroops he was training in southern Italy, and the Chief of Air Staff, General Jeschonnek, also strongly supported it. German air raids on Malta had long dwindled, and the island's air defenses were being reinforced with fresh aircraft, crews, and fuel. In May, Student had briefed Hitler on British fortifications and defenses in Malta; to Hitler it seemed that more was known of the probable British tactics than the Italian. Jodl's naval staff officer had told the admiralty: "The Führer has little confidence in the operation's success, as the Italians' assault strength is wholly inadequate and the Italians don't have the least idea of secrecy. It seems to be a particularly difficult task, far tougher than Crete, which was difficult enough as it was." Hitler offered a string of specious arguments against invading Malta: even if they succeeded, the Italians could not keep the island garrison supplied (to which the admiralty acidly pointed out that at present the far more difficult supply line to Rommel's army in North Africa was still open). Even more farfetched was Hitler's claim that Malta served their strategy better in British hands, as its supply convoys then offered sitting targets in the antishipping war. Admiral Raeder was at loggerheads with Hitler over other matters and unable to put his case —that the capture of Malta was the *prerequisite* for any advance on the Suez Canal—more strongly. Hitler had allowed the "theoretical planning" for Malta to continue during May, but now, on June 15, he offered the admiral little hope. On no account could the Axis run the risk of failure through Italian shortcomings again. One suspects, however, that a different factor operated too—that Malta was *British,* and Hitler's "soft" line toward Britain still prevailed; nothing must prejudice the chance of an Anglo-German settlement in the autumn, after "Blue" had brought Russia to her knees.

Over 200 submarines were now in or entering German service—a fruit of the prudent policy of conservation Hitler had enforced in 1940. On May 1 there were 85 prowling the Atlantic alone, with 19 in the Mediterranean, 20 in northern waters, and over 100 fitting out in the Baltic. The submarine admiral, Dönitz, had made a fine impression on Hitler at their last meeting in East Prussia in mid-May. Hitler regretted not having devoted more shipyard capacity to submarine construction rather than to big warships—costly white elephants, rendered obsolete by the aircraft carrier and the airborne torpedo. Capital ships, in Hitler's eyes, served only a deterrent purpose, tying down enemy warships far from where the enemy would like to commit them. For this reason he had at first been averse to the admiralty's plan for "The Knight's Move," in which the entire German battle fleet in Norway—the *Tirpitz,* the *Hipper,* the *Lützow,* the *Scheer,* and a dozen destroyers—were to seek to wipe out the next Allied convoy, PQ. 17, bearing supplies to North Russia. On no account must the *Tirpitz* go the way of the *Bismarck.* But Raeder's liaison officer assured him early in June that no risk would be involved at all, provided that the Reichsmarschall was ordered to give them Luftwaffe support and—above all—adequate aerial reconnaissance. Given the right circumstances, the operation might annihilate the convoy down to its very last ship. When Admiral Raeder left the Berghof on June 15, he had Hitler's cautious permission to proceed—provided that Allied aircraft carriers in the vicinity had first been precisely located and bombed to a standstill.

On the Russian front, operation "Wilhelm" was over. The enemy was tensely awaiting Hitler's next move. Intelligence agents reported that Stalin had held a two-day council of war in Moscow beginning on June 10 and that he had opted for a purely defensive strategy, regrouping along the Don and Volga and keeping the Germans out of the Caucasus. It seemed clear that the Russians were no longer deceived by Kluge's noisy preparations west of Moscow—indeed, on June 16 an Allied press agency in Moscow quoted German strategic designs for the summer at such length that it was obvious there was a leak in German security somewhere. Hitler was perplexed and furious; Halder's General Staff must be the culprit, he suspected. Either somebody had been talking too much on the telephone, or—just as had happened before the invasion of Poland, Norway, and the Low Countries—it was deliberate treason.[1] History seemed to be repeating itself with a vengeance: Hitler was infuriated to learn that the senior General Staff officer of a panzer division had crash-landed in no-man's-land with the complete secret plans for the first stage of "Blue"—the tank thrust to the Don at Voronezh—just as had happened in the notorious Mechelen affair in 1940. His generals had apparently learned nothing from that incident. He decided to make an example of them: the staff officer involved this time was beyond punishment, having been killed by the Russians; but Hitler sacked all the

[1] Some months later an extensive espionage network centering on a Luftwaffe staff officer was uncovered. See page 466.

officer's superiors, including the corps commander. Nor was Field Marshal von Bock spared a tongue-lashing when Hitler saw him the day after his return to the Wolf's Lair.

Hitler himself signed a new order expanding the security rules he had laid down after the Mechelen incident. "Security during the preparation of major operations is of particular importance because of the prime risk that operational orders falling into enemy hands might be exploited in time; this would jeopardize the entire success of the operation, or at the very least the negligence or disobedience of individual officers would be paid for in the blood of German soldiers." Not even the scrambler telephone was safe for discussing strategic plans, he warned. Couriers were to be armed and provided with means for igniting secret documents. No secret documents were to be carried by plane to headquarters forward of army level. As it was, he hoped the Russians could not react fast enough, since "Blue" was due to begin before June was over; he coolly ordered the strategic plan to be left unchanged.

Toward midnight on June 21, Hitler's train left Munich for Berlin. Bock's operation "Fridericus II" (east of Izyum) was to begin at 2:15 A.M. Hitler's thoughts must have gone back to that night twelve months earlier, when he had spent agonizing hours waiting for the onset of "Barbarossa." If it had not been for his stubborn army generals last summer, Russia would have long been defeated!

During the night, his train pulled into a station for twenty minutes. The telephones were linked up—and there was joyous and totally unexpected news from North Africa: the fortified port of Tobruk, which had withstood Rommel's siege for eight months in 1941, had fallen in as many hours. Thirty-three thousand British prisoners surrendered to the German and Italian troops, together with five generals and a vast quantity of tanks, guns, gasoline, and supplies.

Now Rommel must strike while the iron was still hot. In Berlin there was a letter from Mussolini clearly stating the Italian view that Rommel must pause while "Hercules," the assault on Malta, was launched. But already Rommel was preparing to sweep eastward into Egypt. He still had fifty tanks, and two hundred more were being repaired after the month's battles. Hitler cabled Rommel immediately, promoting him to field marshal. He trusted him implicitly. When Goebbels now referred at lunch to Rommel's irrepressible popularity—along with Dietl, Rommel was the very personification of the ideal German soldier-type—Hitler enthusiastically agreed: Rommel's ability was above question. For example, back in May Rommel had predicted every detail of this last offensive—even that the British would fall right into his trap by withdrawing into what might seem to them an ideal triangle of territory but which was actually one in which German 88s could shoot them to pieces. Hitler told his staff that he would, if need be, telephone Mussolini to give Rommel a free hand by postponing "Hercules" until the end of August. The message he then telegraphed to Rome was high-flown and urgently persuasive; without even mentioning Malta, he described the victory wrought by the German and Italian divisions in Libya as a turning point in history. Churchill's Eighth Army was practically in shreds. Since the British themselves had obligingly built a railroad from Tobruk almost as far as Egypt, a relentless pursuit must now follow. He closed thus: "The battle's Goddess of Fortune draws nigh upon the commanders only once; he who does not grasp her at that moment will seldom come to grips with her again." Mussolini allowed himself to be persuaded. "Hercules" was postponed until early September. Late on June 23, Rommel's *Panzerarmee Afrika* crossed into Egypt on a broad front. Within a week he hoped to be in Cairo.

The Italian command and Field Marshal Kesselring, Hitler's Commander in Chief South, watched Rommel's eastward progress into Egypt with mounting apprehension. Each mile lengthened his supply lines and shortened the enemy's; each mile brought the enemy airfields in the Nile Delta closer. Hitler remained optimistic. Although Rommel had received barely three thousand tons of supplies for the entire army during June, Hitler saw Egypt already in his hands. "Rommel must be given all the supplies he needs," he announced at supper on June 28, when the news arrived that four enemy divisions were now encircled in the fortress of Marsa Matrûh. He agreed with Keitel's prediction that "when the Germans captured Alexandria the *entire* British public would be thrown into a far greater rage than at the surrender of Singapore." It would stir them up against Churchill. "Let's hope that the American legation in Cairo continues to keep us so excellently informed of British military plans with its badly enciphered cables." To Hitler and his ministers it must have seemed that the British public's morale was cracking; otherwise thirty-three thousand men could not have surrendered Tobruk with barely a fight. After "Blue" was over in the autumn, an Anglo-German settlement seemed certain.

The British fleet evacuated the harbor at Alexandria and escaped to the Red Sea. But the British army was preparing to hold out some sixty miles west of Alexandria, at El Alamein, and Field Marshal Rommel now had only seventy tanks and armored cars at his disposal.

"Operation Blue," Hitler's great summer offensive in Russia, had begun
early on June 28, 1942. German and Hungarian divisions commanded
by General von Weichs punched through the Russian front and swept
eastward toward the Don city of Voronezh. Two days later General
Paulus's Sixth Army began an advance that was eventually to take it
southward along the Don. Hitler—encouraged by the evidence presented
to him by Halder—believed the Russian reserves were all but exhausted;
so sure was he of a swift collapse that he began thinking of taking two
armored divisions from "Blue" for a later assault on Moscow. Yet the
auguries of impending disaster were there: the army's quartermaster
general warned that their fuel would last them only until mid-September. And the outcome of both "Wilhelm" and "Fridericus II" in
terms of prisoners and booty was disappointing—a sign that the Russians
had learned their lesson at Kharkov and a similar disaster on the Volkhov River far to the north; they were no longer rash enough to let themselves be encircled. Hitler had anticipated an elastic strategy from Marshal Timoshenko, his Russian adversary in the south, but he hoped to
thwart this by moving his tanks down the Don fast enough to prevent
the enemy's withdrawal beyond it.

Once again his generals thwarted this bold plan, though this time his
own tongue-tied inability to speak forcefully to his top commanders—
and especially those of the aristocracy—was to blame. The General Staff
had proposed gaining time by launching Phase II of "Blue" with infantry divisions alone, but Hitler and Bock maintained that only tanks
could move south fast enough to prevent the enemy's escape. This did
not prevent Bock from acquiescing in General Hoth's armored drive toward Voronezh. Remembering Dunkirk in 1940 and Leningrad in 1941,
Hitler feared that Voronezh would swallow up his precious armor for
days on end, and he expressed growing impatience as the days passed.
Keitel recognized all the familiar omens of trouble and begged him to fly
out to Poltava in person and order Bock to leave the city alone. At this
stage the capture of the city was unimportant, provided the railways and
aircraft factories could be destroyed.

Tactically this was right. Hitler made the three-hour flight to Poltava,
arriving at 7 A.M. on July 3; but confronted by the granite-faced field
marshal, he lost his tongue. He became affable and friendly, joked about
the way Churchill sacked every general who had a run of bad luck, explained why he did not fear an Allied Second Front, hedged about the
risk that the Russians—who knew the German overall plan—might yet
elude his armies, and assured Bock that the Red Army had sapped its

last reserves. Far from flatly forbidding Bock to take the city of Voronezh, he wrapped up his directives in a double negative so vague that as the Führer was leaving Bock queried, "Am I right in understanding you as follows: I am to capture Voronezh if it can be done easily or without bloodshed. But I am not to get involved in heavy fighting for the city?" Hitler confirmed this with a silent nod.

Back at the Wolf's Lair his courage returned to him. As the days passed, it became more evident that neither Weichs nor Bock appreciated the urgency of making ground to the south. He watched impatiently; the city was captured easily enough on July 6, but the two armored divisions there were immediately subjected to a fierce Russian counterattack. As the unwanted battle for the city developed, precious time was being wasted. He ordered the two divisions out and to the south, but now they had to await the arrival of supporting infantry; not until the eighth could they disengage themselves from Voronezh, and after one day's southward progress their fuel ran out. The army's quartermaster general, Eduard Wagner, should have provided for this unexpectedly rapid offensive in his logistics, but he had not; at the Wolf's Lair he unjustly laid the blame on Bock. Two full days had been wasted by Voronezh. Boiling with anger, Hitler could see the Russian forces slipping away. Was this not the same Bock who had thwarted his grand designs in 1941? And had not Bock—against his own staff's advice, as they had just told Schmundt at Poltava—argued for the purely defensive treatment of Kharkov in May? Bock was having a run of bad luck; Hitler discussed him with Keitel and Halder on July 13—and then sacked him. He told Schmundt he still admired the man, but in the present crisis he could work only with generals who followed his directives to the letter.

The damage was already done, however. Keitel later told Bock: "For months afterward the Führer kept harping on 'those forty-eight hours lost at Voronezh' as time wasted to catastrophic effect." When the first phase ended on July 8, Weichs had rounded up only 28,000 prisoners and 1,000 tanks; and the Sixth Army had accounted for only 45,000 prisoners and 200 tanks. A week later, the second phase, an attempted encirclement of the enemy north of the Donets River, ended with the capture of Millerovo; this time there were only 14,000 prisoners. In retrospect, it should have been clear at once that the majority of the Red Army had escaped. But Hitler, ill-advised by his General Staff, evidently considered these low hauls further proof that the Red Army was on its last legs: how else can we interpret his decisions during July 1942 to transport five divisions of the Eleventh Army from the Crimea to the far north, and to withdraw some of his finest units to the western front as well?

Since the second half of June 1942 Hitler had felt insecure in the west. On the twenty-first, the Third Air Force had brought back photographic reconnaissance Intelligence from southern England revealing nearly three thousand small craft assembled between Portsmouth and Portland, and numbers of unfamiliar craft drawn ashore at Southampton and Poole. In occupied France the sabotage of railroads and cables was increasing. Hitler had visions of massive paratroop and glider landings—cutting the vital rail and road links to prevent him moving up reserves when the main seaborne invasion started. Halder suggested sending an armored division to the west; Hitler agreed, and ordered that three others already in reserve there should remain, together with the SS division "Das Reich" and the Seventh Air Division of paratroops. On June 26 he decided that "if the Russian resistance during the coming operations should be less than expected," the two SS divisions "Adolf Hitler Life Guards" and "Death's Head" would also be transferred to the west. Three days later he conferred with Rundstedt's new Chief of Staff in the west, the bustling General Zeitzler, with Speer, and with the general in charge of engineering and fortifications, Alfred Jacob, on their western defenses. He explained that in view of the enemy's political obligations, a major Anglo-American invasion attempt was quite possible. Having thrown the British out of the Continent once, he did not fear them; he told foreign diplomats he was relishing the chance of teaching the Americans a lesson too—his Waffen SS elite were just itching to get their hands on American troops.

With remarkable prescience, Hitler predicted in a directive of July 9 that the Allies would most probably invade either somewhere between Dieppe and Le Havre or in Normandy, as these coastal areas were within Allied fighter range and suitable for small-craft crossings. "In the event of an Allied invasion I will proceed to the west and take command myself." Whether Hitler expected a full-scale Second Front *soon* is uncertain. He believed that Churchill's recent visit to Washington had been to advise against such an invasion until 1943 and that Stalin was consequently being advised to stave off defeat until then.[2] There might still be

---

[2] This may have been deduced from the intercepted radiotelephone traffic between London and Washington (see page 446). Hitler mentioned "Churchill himself as proof." His belief was confirmed by General Franco, who had it from a reliable agent that Churchill's main purpose in Washington that June had been to convert Roosevelt to a position opposing Stalin's demand for

a diversionary maneuver in the west, but it was unlikely. On the other hand, desperate leaders might be driven to desperate remedies. True, Rommel's Egyptian offensive had been halted at El Alamein, but else-where the outlook was black for Britain. On July 1, Manstein took Sevastopol and was promoted to field marshal. In the Arctic German submarines and bombers sank twenty-four of the thirty-six Allied mer-chant ships bound for North Russia in convoy PQ. 17; the *Tirpitz* and the battle fleet had not even had to go into action. In the west, there-fore, Churchill might find his hand forced over a Second Front—any-thing was possible.

At the daily war conferences, Hitler's advisers were confident of victory in the east. General Halder studiously curried Hitler's favor. An adju-tant noted one day that July: "The Chief of Staff is visibly at pains to sweeten the atmosphere. Luckily for him the situation is obviously well under control. Von Gyldenfeldt [a staff officer] and I are furious at the way he misses no opportunity of denigrating the former Commander in Chief [Brauchitsch] in his absence—and sometimes quite cleverly too—and tries to put the blame for all the previous decisions and ideas that were contrary to Hitler's. Today [Halder] said, 'Mein Führer, had the field marshal listened to you and me a bit more often, we would have been standing there or there by now.'"

In Hitler's eyes the east was already a German empire. On July 9 he discussed with Himmler the final plans for settling the South Tyroleans from Italy in the Crimea once the war was over. On the sixteenth he told Himmler he had no intention of overtly annexing Transcaucasia to the German empire; it would suffice to put a guard on the oil fields and frontiers and leave a Resident-General to protect German interests in the "Free Caucasian Protectorates," as they would be known. On the twenty-third he instructed Bormann to issue to Reichsleiter Rosenberg broad guidelines for population control in the east: the native popula-tion was to be kept down by encouraging abortion and contraceptive techniques; German standards of sanitation and public health would not be enforced (*i.e.,* the natives were not to be immunized or vaccinated). When Hitler learned that his troops had fathered over a million offspring with Russian women, he instructed Himmler to identify all the children concerned, select those that were racially promising, and "re-cover" them for Germany; if the mothers were also sound and racially

---

a Second Front in 1942. Churchill had, reported Franco, warned that on no account must such an invasion fail—it might be the beginning of the end.

acceptable, they could come too, otherwise they would not see their children again. Still uneasy at the prospect that in later generations even the rejected offspring might "improve" the Russian bloodstock, Hitler ordered the widest distribution of contraceptives to his troops in the east forthwith. As for education, Himmler told his police officials: "I can only repeat what the Führer has asked. It is enough if, firstly, the children are taught the traffic signs at school so that they won't run under our cars; secondly, they learn to count to twenty-five; and thirdly, they can write their names as well. No more is necessary."

With mounting public unrest over food rationing in Germany, Hitler also ordered a more ruthless exploitation of the occupied countries. Göring told the Gauleiters assembled in Berlin: "Why should we hunger! Let the people in the countries we occupy eat Cossack saddles!" To Gauleiter Koch, his viceroy in the Ukraine, Hitler confirmed all Himmler had said. People everywhere in Europe ate better than those in Germany, he felt. It was setting back arms production; and if the bread ration was not increased, he foresaw political problems too. Koch was made responsible for extracting at least three million tons of grain from the Ukraine forthwith; the Ukrainian people were racially "inferior"—they would find some other way to survive soon enough.

For the final heave on the eastern front Hitler transferred to a forward headquarters in the Ukraine, code-named "Werewolf," at Vinnitsa. At 8:15 A.M. on July 16 his entire staff flew in sixteen planes to the new site. A secretary wrote soon after: "The airfield was an imposing sight—with the great aircraft lined up ready to take off, their engines turning over, and the air filled with the deep roar of vibrating wings and wires until one after another they rolled down the runway and lifted into the air." Three hours later they touched down at Vinnitsa. Krupp and Mercedes automobiles carried them along rustic lanes to the three-cornered copse concealing Werewolf—a summer camp of log cabins and wooden huts. Here Hitler's commandant feared only a Soviet paratroop attack, perhaps disguised in German uniforms, so the Führer found none of the concrete bunkers characterizing the Wolf's Lair at Rastenburg. But the cabins were damp, the climate was humid, and the site swarmed with deadly anopheles mosquitoes.

Each evening everybody had to swallow Atabrine, a bitter anti-malaria concoction against which the tongue rebelled. The windows were screened with gauze, but still the mosquitoes got in. At night it was icy cold. By day Vinnitsa sweltered in the Ukrainian high summer.

Hitler detested the camp. He suffered splitting headaches and could not think straight. The newly creosoted wood gave off an acrid stench in the baking sun. He easily found fault with everybody. OKW diarist Greiner noted privately: "The climate and heat here get the Führer down. He longs for his old bunker [at Rastenburg], which is a sure sign of where we'll be quartered this winter. . . . By then our operations in the Caucasus will be virtually completed anyway."

Throughout July 1942 Hitler based his command decisions on the assumption that the Red Army was on its last legs. It was a fatally incorrect assumption, but there is no evidence whatever that General Halder advised him differently until August, and by then it was too late to undo the damage already done. Soon, he felt, Rommel would be astride the Suez Canal; the old strategic vision of crossing the Caucasus Mountains and advancing southward through Georgia recurred to Hitler. These would be the two arms of a pincer whereby he would conquer the Middle East. He informed Albert Speer that in future the army's supporting industry—manufacturing tanks and guns—would have equal priority with the Luftwaffe's. With Transcaucasia a German dominion, his oil nightmare would be banished. Once he said, "If I cannot capture at least Maykop, I cannot fight on." If he could get the oil fields at both Maykop and Grozny, producing five million tons a year, and even more if his armies captured the Baku oil fields south of the Caucasus, then Stalin would have to concede defeat. This was the reward at stake in August and September 1942.

There seemed sound evidence that the Russians were collapsing. In front of Paulus's Sixth Army the enemy was in full flight toward Stalingrad. Mass Soviet desertions were reported by Kleist's First Panzer Army. The Russian command seemed to be losing control. In a string of directives issued late in July, Hitler confidently asserted that the three-week campaign had thus far attained virtually all the targets he had set for the southern front. The operations against Marshal Timoshenko had gone "far better and faster" than expected. Hitler claimed: "Only puny elements of Timoshenko's armies have managed to escape encirclement and get south of the Don." Already he had divided Army Group South into two new army groups, A and B; to the former he had reluctantly appointed Field Marshal List, and to the latter, General Baron von Weichs. These two groups would now *diverge* across the Don —List's group, by far the weightier, to encircle the escaping Russians south of Rostov and then conquer the Caucasus and the Black Sea coast; and Weichs striking southeastward toward Stalingrad and the Volga. If Stalingrad itself could not be overrun at once, it was important to reach the Volga south of that city, as Hitler was convinced that the river was Stalin's main waterway from the oil fields to central Russia. After Stalingrad, the armored divisions would roll down the Volga to Astrakhan on the Caspian Sea.

These directives—inspired by the belief that Timoshenko was finished —were already a momentous departure from his April 1942 directive for a *phased* campaign in the south, and Hitler went even further, ordering Field Marshal von Küchler's Army Group North to prepare a fresh assault on Leningrad in September, followed by an attempt at cutting the Murmansk railroad at Kandalaksha in the autumn. Then Stalin would be deprived of both the Caucasian and the northern routes of Allied supplies.

Over the last week of July 1942, however, Hitler's attention was drawn back to Stalingrad, to the capture of which he had assigned only one of the four German armies in the south, Paulus's Sixth Army. All the signs were that the enemy was preparing a last stand there, rather than on the Don. The General Staff learned on July 15—and presumably told Hitler—of a high-level Moscow council of war two days before called by Molotov, Voroshilov, and General Boris Shaposhnikov, the Soviet Chief of Staff, with Allied representatives. Shaposhnikov announced a strategic retreat to the Volga, to force the Germans to winter there. "Counterattacks are to be attempted at two places, the first north of Orel and the second north of Voronezh. Air force and armored troops will take part. A diversionary thrust will be made at Kalinin. Stalingrad, Novorossisk [a Black Sea port], and the Caucasus are to be held."

Nobody had foreseen that Stalin would voluntarily yield so much ground for a dubious strategic advantage, but the Intelligence certainly seemed confirmed by reconnaissance and other sources. Rostov, far to the west, was captured after fierce fighting on July 23, but the enemy escaped, blowing up the bridges behind him. Two days later the entire west bank of the Don was in German hands as far as Voronezh. Hitler's spearheads were about one hundred miles from Stalingrad. In a directive on July 23, Hitler predicted that Timoshenko would reinforce his armies at Stalingrad from the Caucasus region and defend the city with great tenacity. But again the German army's supply organization broke down. For days on end the Sixth Army's tanks were stranded without gasoline; violent rainstorms were blamed for delaying the German supply columns (without, mysteriously, delaying the simultaneous Russian retreat). Worse still, on July 25, Quartermaster General Wagner switched all logistics effort away from the Sixth Army to the Caucasus operation. For the first (and only) time Hitler heard the voice of General von Weichs on the telephone, pleading for the decision to be reversed; Hitler overruled Wagner, but for ten days the Sixth Army was emasculated by this lack of fuel and ammunition, while the gloating Russian commanders had time to build a line of defense far to the west of Stalingrad.

In the stifling atmosphere of Hitler's Ukrainian headquarters violent arguments broke out in the thin-walled wooden conference hut—Halder raging in private at this layman's "grotesque" ignorance of strategy, and the Führer retorting that Halder had repeatedly ignored his orders to transfer a panzer corps from the Rostov group to support the Sixth Army. Uglier still was the enmity smoldering between Jodl's staff—Hitler's military "think-tank"—and Halder's General Staff. "The General Staff is the last of the Masonic Lodges," Hitler lamented. "Unfortunately I forgot to dissolve it."

His troops fought on. On July 26, List's army group swept across the Don for the attack on the Caucasus; it was supported by Richthofen's Fourth Air Force. Three days later the last railroad linking the Caucasus with central Russia was blown up by German tanks.

Now Hitler considered the Caucasus his for the taking, and he refocused his attention on the fighting west of Stalingrad. Halder wrote the next day, July 30: "At the Führer's conference General Jodl took the floor and bombastically pronounced that the fate of the Caucasus will be decided at Stalingrad." This was what Halder had been arguing for a week himself. It was decided to transfer the Fourth Panzer Army from List to Weichs at once. In vain List protested when Halder phoned him that evening that the transfer would leave his left flank exposed; he pointed out that now his group too was suffering fuel delays, and he underlined the gamble they were taking by driving southward into the Caucasus with such a weak force, unprotected on its flank. When he asked that at least the "Gross Deutschland" Division should not be transferred to France, Halder was equally adamant. (Hitler had rhetorically asked him only a few days before: "What is the use of victories in Russia if I lose western Europe?") In a directive signed by Halder the next day, the Fourth Panzer Army was ordered to the Stalingrad front. Halder said that while the enemy could no longer move significant reinforcements up against List from the Russian interior, they must assume that "the enemy will concentrate all available strength on Stalingrad to keep the vital Volga artery open."

Thus two German armies, each with less dependable allied forces in train, were assigned to each of Hitler's southern strategic targets—

Stalingrad and the Caucasus. If the enemy's reserves *were* finished, this was an adequate disposition; if they were not, it was not.

From the documents available it is clear that Hitler did not fear any serious risk of "losing western Europe" until 1943, but there were persistent rumors that something more immediate was in the air. An Abwehr agent in British embassy circles in Madrid reported that Britain was assembling twenty-four hundred launches—calling them in from as far afield as Gibraltar, the Mediterranean, and West Africa—for a determined "invasion attempt" on the Channel or French Atlantic coast toward the end of August. On July 18 a week of talks between Churchill and Roosevelt's confidant, Harry Hopkins, began in London. Two days later a batch of intercepted transatlantic telephone conversations was sent to Himmler—and no doubt Hitler—with an SS general's comments: "Although only code words are employed in these intercepted telephone conversations, I deduce the following: today and tomorrow there must be a highly important meeting between the British and Americans. This conference will probably determine where the Second Front is to be established and when. The main people speaking are General Staff officers, ambassadors, and ministers."[3] On August 13 a highly trusted Abwehr agent in southern England reported that the invasion target would be the Channel port of Dieppe.

Hitler was confident he could thwart any immediate British adventures; of those that might be launched in 1943 he was less certain. By mid-August he had 29 divisions in the west under Rundstedt's command, including the "Hermann Göring," 2 parachute, 2 SS, and 4 panzer divisions; the crack infantry division "Gross Deutschland" was also transferring from the eastern front. He had no fears for Norway so long as the nights were short; what might happen outside Europe did not concern him either. But the more he studied the bulky military atlases his experts had compiled on the Channel and Atlantic coasts of France, Belgium, and Holland, the more apprehensive he became: the maps and overlays spoke glibly of "field-type defenses" and used vague military jargon that he suspected concealed a multitude of weaknesses. He sent out Walter Frentz, his staff movie cameraman, to tour the

[3] On July 24, 1942, the London conference approved Britain's proposal for an invasion of Northwest Africa, "Gymnast"—shortly rechristened "Torch"—rather than the American plan to invade Cherbourg or Brest—"Sledgehammer."

The archives are silent on just what the intercepted conversations revealed. Others, less revealing, between Churchill and a Mr. Butcher in Washington on July 22, and between General Mark Clark, General Snyder, etc., were returned by Hitler to Himmler and are in his files.

coastline and photograph what he could find. The color photographs revealed that the whole coastline would be wide open to a determined Allied assault; what had already been built was useless—the very first wave of enemy bombers would pulverize the structures. Mile after mile of coastline was bare of any fortification whatever. He resolved to build an impregnable fortress line along the entire Atlantic coastline facing Britain.

Albert Speer and the military experts were summoned to the Werewolf headquarters on August 13 and informed of this decision. Hitler lectured them in detail on his requirements for this "Atlantic Wall": it must be such that with an armed force of half a million troops the entire coastline could be defended; assuming 150,000 troops in reserve, the rest would man 15,000 bunkers. A girdle of bunkers spaced at fifty-yard intervals would protect each of the ten most vital war bases; the rest would be spaced at hundred-yard intervals along the entire coast. Cost was no obstacle. "Our most costly substance is the German man. The blood these fortifications will spare is worth the billions!" Decoy sites, minefields, barbed-wire entanglements, and tank traps would complete the defense of western Europe. The Wall was to be completed by the end of April 1943. The submarine bases and naval gunsites were to get special treatment—walls and ceilings of twelve-foot-thick concrete capable of withstanding the heaviest bombs or naval gunfire. Hitler wanted his troops able to sleep or perform their bodily functions undisturbed by the heaviest bombardment. Heavy machine-guns, tanks, and antitank guns must all come under cover, for Hitler predicted that any invasion would begin with the saturation bombardment of the entire area. "It is wisest to consider our own Luftwaffe so weak in the west as to be non-existent," Hitler warned. The individual bunker design must take everything into account. The Russians were not expected to initiate poison-gas war, but Hitler felt that the Americans probably would, and he suspected that they had developed a brand of gas capable of penetrating existing German gasmasks. He therefore ordered that all bunkers must be gastight and have oxygen supplies on hand. The Allies might use napalm bombs, so the bunkers must have steps and ledges to check the flow of blazing oil. Each bigger bunker must have flame-throwing gear. The whole Atlantic Wall must be so formidable that the enemy would think twice about even testing it; and when an invasion did begin, it would have to be in such strength that it would be no problem for Hitler to distinguish the real *Schwerpunkt* from any diversionary feints.

The Atlantic Wall's purpose must be to prevent the enemy from even securing a foothold in western Europe. It would take Hitler two or three days to rush reserves to the main landing zone, by which time the enemy could have landed up to three hundred thousand troops—once that foothold was granted them. He predicted to his generals now, in August 1942, that the invasion proper would be preceded during the night by waves of parachute and glider sabotage troops with orders to disrupt the transport and signals systems and to disable headquarters units; next would come wave after wave of heavy bombers, saturation-bombing the invasion defenses. The invasion would follow at dawn, with three or four thousand landing craft and total enemy air superiority. But by 1943 the Atlantic Wall he had envisaged would be a match for all that. Of course, as he told a Balkan diplomat on August 14, those mad British might venture something *before* then. "If only soldiers had the say in Britain, this operation they are peddling around as their 'Second Front' would not take place. But as lunatics like that drunkard Churchill, and Maccabeans and numskulls like that brilliantined dandy Eden, are at the tiller, we have to be prepared for just about anything!"

What occurred just five days later was indeed a baffling *coup de théâtre* by the British: two brigades of Canadian troops were landed with thirty tanks and British commando detachments on either side of Dieppe. Within less than nine hours the raid had ended in a complete debacle. The Germans, alerted by the chance meeting of a coastal convoy with the raiding force, wiped out the entire force. The British lost a destroyer, 33 landing craft, over 100 planes, and 4,000 troops, of whom 1,179 lay dead on the beaches or the few yards they had penetrated along the promenade. As the minute-by-minute reports from the Luftwaffe and army flooded into Hitler's headquarters in the Ukraine he was unperturbed; Rundstedt's radio message at 6:15 P.M. that no armed Englishman was left ashore provoked the barest flicker of a smile. Hitler sent his chief interpreter, Paul Schmidt, to question the prisoners. Schmidt wrote a few days later: "Militarily speaking, Dieppe was a total fiasco for the British. They ran slap into an ambush on the beaches and nothing worked out for them. The troops probably fought as well as ever, but their top commanders must be frightful. One prisoner bluntly told me: "The men who ordered this raid and those who organized it are criminals and deserve to be shot for mass murder!" Yet all the prisoners thought highly of Churchill, despite his blunders; he was the only leader capable of pulling Britain through the war, they felt.

Politically, Churchill's Dieppe decision was inept. Apparently—as the captured maps and 121-page British operation orders revealed—all this bloodshed and military effort had been squandered only in order to destroy Dieppe harbor and some guns and radar sites; Stalin's chagrin at the failure was obvious. Hitler was nonplussed that Churchill had even dispensed with paratroops: had these landed in the rear and fought off the reserves, Dieppe might have ended very differently. He was encouraged by the appalling quality of the new British "Sten" gun and of the Churchill tanks and equipment the enemy had obligingly ferried across and left on permanent display on the beaches and promenade of Dieppe. But he knew the real invasion would be different. For political reasons he ordered the OKW to proclaim that Dieppe *was* the Second Front; but in September, secretly addressing his western commanders, he predicted that in the real invasion the enemy would rely far more on air power. "We must realize that we are not alone in learning a lesson from Dieppe. The British have also learned. We must reckon with a totally different mode of attack—and at quite a different place." The Atlantic Wall would now play a vital role. "If nothing happens in the west next year, we have won the war."[4]

He considered his personal impressions of the western enemy as largely confirmed. British morale was evidently as brittle as the low-grade steel of the tanks stranded on the beaches. The sophistication of the Canadian assault troops was minimal. One had never heard of Roosevelt; another, asked if he knew of any Germans, replied, "Yes, General Rommel and Lili Marlene." Few even of the officers believed in a British victory now, Schmidt reported.

True, the Allies had no cause for complacency. In mid-August a Mediterranean relief convoy bound for Malta had met with a disaster even more crippling than PQ. 17. Only five of the heavily escorted tankers and merchantmen reached harbor: in three days the Germans had sunk the aricraft carrier *Eagle,* badly damaged the carrier *Indomitable,* and sunk the cruiser *Manchester;* and the Italians had sunk the cruiser *Cairo* and torpedoed the cruisers *Nigeria* and *Kenya* as well.

In the Far East, British and American possessions were falling into Japanese hands. Singapore, Hong Kong, the Philippines, Java, and Sumatra; after the monsoon season, late in September, the Japanese might attack Ceylon and India too. Yet the basic weakness of the Axis was becoming clear: not only could Hitler and Ribbentrop not agree on their policy toward Japan, but the Japanese showed no inclination to pursue a joint military strategy. Ribbentrop wanted Japan to strike northward into Russia and counseled Ambassador Oshima to that effect. But Hitler rebuked his foreign minister and pointed out that this was just what

---

[4] This unpublished speech of September 29, 1942, is referred to at greater length below, page 469. Captain S. W. Roskill, the British official historian, suggests in *The War at Sea,* Vol. II, page 251, that the Germans drew the wrong conclusions from Dieppe. This was certainly not true of Hitler.

Churchill wanted, as it would take Japanese pressure off Australia and India. Halder and the naval staff both shared this view: Japan must shift her naval effort to the western Indian Ocean, at the expense of her ambitions in the Pacific.

The Japanese kept their own counsel, while Hitler, on the other hand, apprised Tokyo of even those most secret plans he dared not impart to the talkative Italians, and he also entrusted all Germany's military inventions and techniques to Japan; he received nothing in return. Late in July 1942 the General Staff noted with resignation that nothing was known even to the Führer of Japan's actual intentions; and when joint staff talks between General Jodl and a Japanese mission were held on August 5, the latter flatly rejected all the German advice. "You must not demand too much of Japan," the Japanese said.

The Black Spot for Halder

Once before, in July 1918, German troops had invaded the Caucasus. The Turks had caved in the Russian front and marched into Transcaucasia, and the Germans had followed from across the Black Sea; then too the Ukraine had been in German hands. The analogy between then and now, the late summer of 1942, was close indeed! But if in 1918 the Germans had needed the oil only for their military machine, in 1942 they needed it for the Ukraine too. Hundreds of thousands of useless tractors littered the collective farms, unable to sow or harvest until once more the oil of Baku began to reach them. The projected eight million tons of Ukranian grain for Europe would remain a dream unless Hitler could get to Baku.

Between his armies and Baku stood the Caucasus—seven hundred miles of untamed, jagged mountains capped by an eighteen-thousand-foot extinct volcano, Elborus. Flanked at one end by the Black Sea and at the other by the Caspian Sea, these mountains had throughout history proved a sure barrier to military ambitions. The Alps had repeatedly been crossed, from the time of Hannibal down through that of the medieval German emperors. Not so the Caucasus: the Mongol invaders, Timur, the Seldshuks and Osmans, had all skirted around its eastern end; Islam had to take to the Caspian in its northward crusade; so did Peter the Great when he invaded northern Persia. The Caucasus itself was impregnable. The German occupation forces had held its passes with a solitary company of riflemen in 1918.

Hitler had long ago decided to set a historic precedent. Field Marshal von List's army group had been directed to cross the mountains to the Black Sea coast so that the Russian navy there would be finally eliminated. The Führer was unimpressed by the obstacles. At one war conference Göring leaned over the maps, tapped the mountain range with his sausage fingers laden with glittering rings, and coolly announced, "There is not all that much difference between the Caucasus and Berlin's Grunewald!"

From now on, however, the campaign in Russia suffered from the faulty planning and Intelligence of the summer. Hitler's armored divisions outpaced their supply lines and came to a halt; they relied on one solitary low-capacity railroad running eastward from the Donets Basin, but this ended far short of the battlefields and there was not enough truck transport to bridge the gaps. Oil and gasoline were available, but they were at the wrong places. In the center and northern front, guerrilla warfare behind the German lines increased, and Hitler had to sign a special directive on uniform countermeasures. Ill-advised by Halder and army Intelligence throughout the summer on Stalin's remaining reserves, Hitler had committed his armies to too many campaigns on too many fronts, leaving the uncertain divisions of his allies to guard the flanks. But these allies—Romanian, Hungarian, and Italian—were low in morale and inadequately equipped, and out of thin air the enemy was producing fresh divisions all along the front. Hitler had no reserves to meet this unexpected situation. A tug-of-war developed over every German division temporarily withdrawn from the battlefields. Meanwhile the Russian generals captured in the fighting just smiled faintly when interrogated about the forces still at Stalin's disposal: "You are in for the surprise of your lives!"

Hitler was determined not to be surprised. The Russians would unquestionably first strike at the Hungarian and Italian armies on the Don; several times during August he asked Halder to back up the Hungarians with German artillery and antitank defenses, and on the sixteenth he shrewdly prophesied that Stalin might repeat the 1920 ploy used against the White Russian army—attacking across the Don at Serafimovich and striking toward Rostov. The Italian Eighth Army would probably collapse, and the entire southern front would then be threatened. Repeatedly throughout August Hitler ordered Halder to shift the 22nd Panzer Division from the Stalingrad fighting to an area behind the Italian army. Halder paid no heed; there is no reference to Hitler's order in Halder's diary or in the records of the army group concerned. History was to show that Hitler's fears were well founded.

Russia's strength was anything but exhausted. On August 2, Halder's chief of eastern Intelligence, Colonel Gehlen, had indicated that in July alone Stalin had produced 54 new infantry divisions and 56 new armored divisions. Halder sent all Gehlen's figures to Hitler the next day, frankly admitting that earlier Intelligence figures had been underestimations; but he added that the enemy had achieved this feat only by employing far more female labor than had Germany, and he suggested that since Stalin could now fall back only on eighteen-year-olds for recruits they need expect only 30 more divisions to be raised at most. In addition, once Stalin had raised these divisions he would still have to solve the problem of equipping and arming them. In July the Red Army had lost 3,900 tanks, and since they were importing only 400 and manufacturing less than 1,000 a month, sooner or later their tank supply would be exhausted. But even Halder's forced optimism evaporated two weeks later. Gehlen's new figures now gave Stalin the equivalent of 593 divisions, of which an awe-inspiring number was being held in reserve. Hitler pathetically clung to his earlier information—his entire strategy in Russia had been based on it. As the truth finally dawned on him, his anger at Halder and the army's generals increased. He nevertheless insisted that Gehlen must have been duped by the Russians. According to Halder, Hitler foamed: "I, the head of the greatest industrial nation— I, assisted by the greatest genius of all time," referring to Albert Speer, "I, whose drive makes the whole world tremble, I sweat and toil to produce just six hundred tanks a month. And you are telling me that Stalin makes a thousand!" But it was too late to turn back now. Hitler's only hope lay in depriving the Russians of the economic basis for continued defense.

That basis lay in the Caucasus.

On August 9, General Ruoff's command had captured Krasnodar, and Kleist's tanks rolled through Maykop; but the oil fields were in ruins. Hitler called on Field Marshal List to strike through the mountains to the ports of Tuapse and Sukhumi as rapidly as possible, thus depriving the Russian fleet of its last sanctuaries and enabling the German army to ferry supplies to the Caucasus by sea. But only one road crossed the mountains, that from Armavir through Maykop to Tuapse. The Fourth Air Force were optimistic still. But on August 11 the OKW Intelligence chief, Canaris, visiting Hitler's headquarters, wrote in his diary: "Keitel more candid than usual this time, does not share Richthofen's optimism. He does not doubt that the Russians will try to hold the western Caucasus and in particular block the road from Armavir to Tuapse." Six days later Kleist's armor reached the eastern end of the mountain ridge, where it was stalled by stiffening enemy resistance and air attacks. The Russians had marshaled over three thousand planes in this theater, including trainers and Lend-Lease aircraft. Time was running out for Hitler. Seized by uncertainty, he sent one after another of Jodl's officers to investigate on the spot and spur the army generals on. He suspected them of frittering away their strength in the Caucasian Highlands instead of building up their main thrusts to Tuapse and Sukhumi. Speer has testified to Hitler's cold fury on August 21 when List's mountaineers proudly announced that they had scaled the Elborus and raised the swastika from its peak. Army cameramen had filmed the dramatic scene. Hitler raged that his army's ambition should be to defeat the Russians, rather than conquer mountains. Jodl—a Bavarian and mountaineer like List himself—defended the field marshal and for the first time Hitler rounded on Jodl too. He fumed at List in particular and at the army's leaders in general, storming at their "arrogance, incorrigibility, and sheer inability to grasp fundamentals." By the end of August, List's offensive had petered out—defeated by impassable roads, wrecked suspension bridges, dense fog, and driving rain and snow.

To the northeast, Weichs's Stalingrad offensive was faring better, despite the oppressive heat of high summer in the arid steppes. General Hoth's Fourth Panzer Army, plagued by fuel and ammunition shortages and nonexistent roads, halted just south of the city. But on August 23, Paulus's Sixth Army covered forty miles, and at 4 P.M. one of his corps commanders reached the Volga at a point just north of the city. With 88-millimeter guns the first Soviet ships were sent to the bottom of the Volga before night fell, but here too the Red Army's resistance was stiffening.

Hitler had no reserves left. Since early August fierce Russian attacks had gnawed at the marrow of Field Marshal von Kluge's Army Group Center. Hitler had ordered him to erase a Russian salient at Sukhinichi —one hundred fifty miles southwest of Moscow—left over from the winter crisis; this attack, "Whirlwind," would create the platform for a possible later attack on Moscow itself. Russian spoiling attacks on General Walther Model's Ninth Army at Rzhev and Subtsoff left Hitler unconcerned. Perhaps he hoped to repeat his Kharkov victory.[1] When Kluge appealed for permission to cancel "Whirlwind" and use the five hundred tanks to save the Ninth Army instead, Hitler would not hear of it. Provided the armored divisions held their thrust tightly together, like a rapier lunging toward Sukhinichi, "Whirlwind" was bound to succeed.

---

[1] There was an essential difference. "Fridericus" at Kharkov (page 423) was a pincer attack; for lack of reserves Hitler could mount "Whirlwind" only with the southern arm of the pincer, the Second Panzer Army.

Kluge stomped out of Werewolf saying, "Then you, mein Führer, must take the responsibility!"

The attack began on August 11, in difficult terrain—heavily fortified, marshy forests alternating with treacherous minefields. Kluge allowed the divisions to splay out; their casualties were horrifying. Halder remained optimistic of success; General Adolf Heusinger—chief of his operations staff—roundly disagreed. The attack failed.

Again summoned to Werewolf on August 22, Kluge was rebuked by a disappointed Hitler and instructed to recast "Whirlwind" as a purely holding operation. This first major setback of 1942 vexed Hitler deeply. Four months later he complained, "Our worst mistake this year was that attack on Sukhinichi. It was a copybook example of how *not* to stage an attack. They attacked in just about every direction that they could, instead of holding it tightly and narrowly together and thrusting rapidly through with the five armored divisions. We had some five hundred tanks committed to the attack on Sukhinichi. And what did they do?—Splattered them all over the place: that was a 'famous victory'!"

Model's Ninth Army at Rzhev began bleeding to death. Hitler injected the "Gross Deutschland" Division into its rump, but at a stormy war conference at noon on August 24, Halder demanded permission for Model to retreat, as his army's casualties could not be sustained. One regiment had lost eight commanders in a week. The army was in danger of burning itself out.

Hitler's hatred of the General Staff boiled over. Perhaps it was the insufferable heat; perhaps it was Halder's dry, monotonous voice, or his perpetual sneer, or the Mafia-like cluster of staff officers around him. More likely it was the parallel with the winter Moscow crisis that suddenly reminded Hitler that Halder was a reactionary relic of the Brauchitsch era. "You always seem to make the same suggestion—retreat!" he rebuked the general. This idea had to be stamped out in the army, once and for all, he stormed. If Model complained that the reinforcements being sent him were useless, then he must be made to realize that the Russian reinforcements were even more so. Hitler ended his furious tirade by saying, "I must demand the same toughness from my commanders as from my troops." For the first time, Halder lost his temper. "I *am* still tough, mein Führer. But out there our fine riflemen and lieutenants are dying by the thousand just because their commanders are denied the only possible decision—their hands are tied." To everybody's embarrassment Hitler interrupted him with a calculated injury: "What, Herr Halder—you who were as chairbound in the Great War as in this—what do you think you can teach me about the troops!

You, who haven't even got a wound stripe on your uniform!"—and he pounded the black stripe on his own chest.

Halder visited Hitler in private afterward and tried to reason with him: it was a crime against German blood to set tasks to sons of German mothers that were downright impossible. Hitler accused him of turning soft and of losing his nerve now that the troops were beginning to suffer casualties again.

Field Marshal von Manstein, the conqueror of Sevastopol, had been among the hushed and embarrassed witnesses of Hitler's outburst against Halder. Manstein had arrived from the Crimea, en route to the north where his Eleventh Army was slated to launch the final assault on Leningrad in September.

Beleaguered since September 1941, Leningrad was the key to the fighting both in the Baltic and in Finland. Until it was destroyed, Hitler could not release his divisions there to strengthen General Dietl's army in Lapland, where the enemy might at any time seize the only nickel mines under German control; neither Jodl nor Dietl thought either side could secure strategic victories in such formidable terrain, but Hitler disagreed. Were he Stalin or Churchill, he would risk anything to knock out those nickel mines: within a few months no more German tanks or shells could be produced. In late July he had directed the army to storm Leningrad early in September. For this operation, "Northern Lights," he promised Field Marshal Georg von Küchler, the commander of Army Group North, a veritable orchestra of artillery unparalleled since Verdun—nearly a thousand guns marshaled around the city's flat outskirts to pave the way for the infantry assault by "sheer brute force." Among the siege artillery was the 800-millimeter "Dora," a colossal weapon with only forty-six rounds of ammunition left over from Sevastopol; there were two 600-millimeter, two 420-millimeter, and six 400-millimeter howitzers as well. On August 8, Küchler had told Hitler that he hoped to finish off Leningrad by the end of October, but Jodl interjected that this was too long; "Northern Lights," he noted, was not an end in itself so much as a preparation for the campaign in Lapland. At Jodl's suggestion, Hitler brought in Manstein to direct the assault on Leningrad, since Küchler appeared to lack the necessary impetus.

The trainloads of artillery arriving from the Crimea had not passed undetected by the enemy. By late August the outlying population was flocking into Leningrad, until perhaps a million refugees were there. Stern measures of defense had been prepared, including the preparation of demolition charges around the biggest buildings. The German navy eagerly awaited the day when it could take over the huge shipyards, and it begged Hitler to avoid damaging them.

Hitler feared that the Russians would spoil the attack by striking first at the narrow German salient west of Lake Ladoga—a vulnerable bottleneck of German troops which sealed off Leningrad by land; the Russians only kept the city alive by hazardous shipments across the lake itself. Throughout August, Hitler had anxiously ordered Halder to ensure that the Eighteenth Army had enough tanks and artillery to defend the bottleneck without draining away the strength Manstein's Eleventh Army would need for "Northern Lights." Halder, apparently bent on documenting his disapproval of Hitler's leadership by petty obstructionism, at first refused the demands then bluntly disobeyed them.

On August 23, Hitler told Küchler he was putting Manstein in charge. Together they pored over the air photographs of the city. Hitler was apprehensive about house-to-house fighting breaking out in this endless maze of streets and buildings. As Küchler pointed out, when the assault began, hundreds of thousands of workers would down tools, reach for their rifles, and stream into the trench fortifications. Only days of terror-bombardment, directed against the factories, munitions works, Party buildings, and control posts would prevent this. (Manstein later told Küchler he did not believe, from his experiences with Sevastopol, that the Russians could be terrorized by bombardment.) Hitler feared a more fundamental danger—that Stalin would attack the bottleneck first. He knew that the first nine Tiger tanks were on their way from Germany. "I would set up the first Tigers behind the front line there," he told Küchler. "Then nothing can go wrong. They are unassailable. They can smash any enemy tank onslaught." Hitler decided that Manstein should launch "Northern Lights" on September 14, after Richthofen had spent three days softening up the city with his bomber squadrons. With Richthofen at Stalingrad, Hitler told Jeschonnek, that battle was already 100 percent won; with Richthofen at Leningrad, the odds on victory would rise to 150 percent.

Manstein was less hopeful, and on August 24 he told Hitler as much —particularly if the Finns would not attack Leningrad simultaneously from the north. On August 27 the Russians struck just where Hitler had feared, at the vulnerable bottleneck. Deep wounds were riven in General Georg Lindemann's Eighteenth Army here, and the Eleventh Army had to divert its strength to his support. The attack on Leningrad receded ever further into the future. The much vaunted Tiger tanks were a disappointment.

And all the time the thermometer at Hitler's headquarters camp continued to rise as the Ukrainian sun beat down. The ground was rock-hard, the grass had turned brown and dry, the trees and shrubs were grimy with dust, and clouds of dust hung in choking layers over every road. "Much though we long for rain and cool weather," wrote the OKW diarist Greiner from Werewolf on August 31, "we dread them too because then it rains in torrents and every lane will become a quagmire within minutes and the humid heat here is said to be particularly grim. In the forest camp we can just about bear the heat, but we mustn't try to leave the forest shade." As he ended the letter the first rain began to beat down on the wooden roof, and steam rose from the undergrowth.

In Egypt weeks of enforced inactivity had blunted the edge of Rommel's offensive. Ahead of his German and Italian divisions lay Montgomery's Alamein line—a forty-mile-long swath of minefields powerfully defended by tanks and aircraft.

With the revival of Malta, after a British convoy had reached the island in June, the supplies getting to Rommel had dwindled to a trickle. Hitler's instinctive dropping of the "Hercules" plan to invade the island now cost the Germans dear. As the water drought had tormented the British defenders at Hacheim in June, now in July and August the lack of gasoline tortured Rommel. In June and July his aircraft had flown twelve thousand sorties. But by early August he was down to his last few hundred tons of gasoline. Under cover of increasing air supremacy, the British attacks began. The first signs of panic were seen in the Italian divisions. The Germans had to regroup to plug the gaps, and every mile of desert cost Rommel more precious gasoline. The enemy's fighter bombers roamed the desert almost unimpeded. Jodl's deputy, Warlimont, flew out to North Africa at the end of July to see for himself; he reported vividly to Hitler on the plight of Rommel, who was confronting an enemy growing stronger each day on the ground and in the air. Hitler impatiently swung around on Göring: "D'you hear that, Göring! Saturation bombing raids in mid-desert!"

It was not even as though Hitler intended to *stay* in the Mediterranean. This was Italy's *Lebensraum* in his view; Germany had no title to it—indeed, not only was its climate wrong for the Germanic races, but the south had always been a source of mischief in German history. He was already thinking of turning Crete over to Mussolini. The Italians were not slow to stake a formal claim to the island on the pretext that Rommel's coming offensive in Egypt would make a strong Italian contingent unavoidable. Admiral Raeder demurred, since the naval staff wanted Crete retained to strengthen Germany's postwar hand in the south. Jodl's staff proposed to filibuster against the Italian claim; but Hitler adhered to his doctrinaire attitude, favoring Mussolini. Anti-Italian feeling ran high among the Germans, particularly since the Italian *comando supremo* favored its own contingent in North Africa with three times the volume of supplies that was provided to the Germans, although there were nearly a hundred thousand German troops there compared with only forty-eight thousand Italians! When Rommel launched his long-prepared assault at El Alamein on August 30, the enemy outnumbered him so heavily, and his oil reserves were so low, that by September 3 his Panzer Army Africa was back where it had started.

Raeder and the naval staff warned insistently that this was a turning point in the war. The army refused to agree. Halder believed that Rommel would demonstrate his superior leadership and seize the initiative as soon as the British launched their own offensive, "presumably next spring"; Jodl also persuaded Hitler that the Egyptian offensive had not failed, as the enemy would scarcely succeed in penetrating Rommel's Alamein position. Therefore no steps were taken to restore Germany's lost air supremacy in Africa. Hitler was convinced that no harm could come to the Axis there—and certainly not in 1942.

It was autumn. In the fine oak forests around Hitler's headquarters the scent was unmistakable. The fields had been harvested, the sunflowers had been laid out to dry on the roofs, and bulging watermelons—used here only as cattle fodder—lay everywhere; the poppies were blackening, the ears of corn yellowing, and summer was truly over. Hitler did not know it, but ahead of him lay only an unbroken succession of defeats, withdrawals, and disappointments.

He was already preparing for a long war. He had postponed the capture of Baku until 1943. He harried his subordinates into speeding up construction of the Atlantic Wall. He turned a baleful eye on partisan activity in Holland and Denmark. He ordered Kluge to speed the construction of a rear line of defense along the central eastern front. When General von Weichs arrived at Werewolf in mid-September, Hitler also ordered him to build a defensive line north of Stalingrad as soon as it had been captured and the armies were pressing on to Astrakhan.

Tantalizing and provocative, Stalingrad seemed to Hitler and his field commanders as good as theirs—there lay the rub. Hitler told Halder he wanted the virulently Communist city's entire male population "disposed of" and the women transported away. Paulus's troops were already fighting in the outskirts, from house to house and street to street. Each day, Richthofen's bombers were pouring a thousand tons of bombs into the Russian positions; Richthofen himself—tough and dynamic—was personally supervising the operations from a fighter airfield ten miles west of Stalingrad. But ground conditions were truly appalling. A two-mile-high pall of choking dust lay over the battlefields. Progress was slow. Richthofen voiced biting criticism of the field commanders Paulus and Hoth, claiming that with more spirit they could have taken Stalingrad in two days. He himself had found difficulty in spotting any enemy at all, while from his plane he had seen German troops bathing in the river instead of fighting.

In the Caucasus, Field Marshal Wilhelm List fared little better. His mountain divisions were at a virtual standstill in the narrow passes—still twenty miles and more from the Black Sea coast. Hitler's army adjutant, Major Gerhard Engel, returned with a vivid description of the mountain terrain. There were only four mule paths across the mountains, and the modern and highly mechanized German divisions could scarcely make use of them in their attempt to reach the sea. Hitler was impatient at List's slow progress. Jodl courageously defended the army group's achievements and pointed out that it was a consequence of the Führer's own orders for "Barbarossa" that the mountain divisions had neglected their specialized equipment and were thus now little more than glorified infantry divisions; Hitler claimed he had ordered their proper fitting out as mountain divisions before "Blue" began, in July, but Jodl replied that Hitler's memory was at fault. It was symptomatic of the deteriorating situation that even these two men were falling out with each other. Previously, the OKW's outstanding chief of operations had schooled himself to accept Hitler's orders implicitly; once Jodl had explained to Halder that he always remembered what his grandmother had told his mother on her wedding day: "In matrimony the husband is always right! And if he says, 'The water's running uphill today' my answer is, 'Yuh, Yuh, it's up there already!'"

At the end of August, Hitler had summoned List to headquarters. Faced with the conservative, powerfully religious field marshal, Hitler's tongue again clove to the roof of his mouth. He swallowed all his private dislikes—his complaint that List had prevented the SS tanks from breaking into Rostov, his anger at the Elborus flag-planting incident, his impatience over the lengthy delay in ferrying the Romanians across from the Crimea, and List's general insubordination. He engaged List in affable conversation, lunched privately with him, then sent him back to the Caucasus. Once the field marshal had left, Hitler criticized the way he had arrived armed only with a 1:1,000,000 map of southern Russia without any of his forces shown on it—although standing orders prohibited taking strategic maps on plane journeys. To Hitler, List seemed hopelessly "at sea." List for his part did not elaborate on the formidable mountain terrain barring his advance to the coast. Meanwhile, two of Jodl's officers sent to investigate the delays in the crossing of the Strait of Kerch had scored some success in getting things moving; two days later the crossing was successfully accomplished, and a slow advance along the coast road itself began. Hitler failed to see why the crossing could not have been made a month before, as he had directed in July; did none of his commanders appreciate the urgency of their campaigns? From Hitler's mood his adjutants guessed that a storm was about to break.

His antipathy toward General Halder, the Chief of General Staff, still smoldered. He complained in private of Halder's animosity and negative attitude. "With Jodl I know where I am. He says what he thinks. But Halder just stands there like somebody with a guilty conscience." He could not abide specialists; his verdict on the Halder type was summed up in a *bon mot* coined in happier times—"A specialist is a man who explains to me precisely why something can *not* be done!" Halder had done nothing to wed the army to National Socialism. To Hitler's staff it was plain that the general had been passed the Black Spot; thus Halder was now treated as though he had an infectious disease. In his absence, there were debates at the war conferences on who ought to succeed him. Hitler observed that he really needed an old-fashioned "quartermaster," a man of drive and imagination, and he recalled that Kleist's panzer army had had such a Chief of Staff in Kurt Zeitzler. Göring's imminent arrival was announced, and his liaison officer General Karl Bodenschatz slipped out to meet him. When the Reichsmarschall entered the hut he announced portentously, "Mein Führer, I have been racking my brains all night on a successor for Halder. What about General Zeitzler?" This was characteristic of the way the Göring-Bodenschatz team worked. Jodl spoke out on Halder's behalf in the days that followed. Together with General Scherff, Hitler's court historian, he drafted a memorandum proving that Halder's staff had only been following Hitler's own orders in the weeks before the impasse in the Caucasus. But Hitler—tormented by the heat, the rows, and the realization that victory in Russia was finally slipping from his grasp—was already beyond reason.

The storm broke on September 7. Jodl himself had flown out to Stalino to confer with List and his mountain corps commander General Konrad, a close friend of Jodl's since they had been cadets together in Bavaria. He returned to Vinnitsa that evening and reported to Hitler in private, giving a horrendous picture of the conditions in the Caucasus. The Fourth Mountain Division was being asked to advance on the Georgian coastal towns of Gudauta and Sukhumi along a mountain path over sixty miles long. All its supplies would have to be carried by mule, of which nearly two thousand were still needed. The Russians would only have to demolish all the bridges. The simultaneous advance on Tuapse, the port farther west, would be incomplete before winter set in. The generals felt there was no alternative to withdrawing from these Caucasus passes and concentrating on the "road" to Tuapse.

Jodl courageously quoted these views to Hitler. It provoked a furious scene. Hitler ranted that Jodl had been sent down there to get the offensive moving again; instead, he had allowed his insubordinate Bavarian comrades to hoodwink him. ("All generals lie," was Hitler's favorite watchword.) The Führer said that not since the notorious Hentsch affair in World War I had an army been so betrayed.[2] He ended the conference and stalked out, refusing for the first time to shake hands with Keitel and Jodl as he went—a snub he persisted in until the end of January 1943. And whereas at midday he had entertained his staff and guests—Milch, Speer, and Koch—at luncheon, as he had done regularly since May 1940, he announced that he proposed to dine alone in his own quarters from now on. He left them in no doubt of his mistrust of them.

The real cause of Hitler's anger remains a matter for conjecture. His subsequent actions give some clues. After supper he sent for Julius Schaub, his personal majordomo; the crippled minion hobbled in, and Hitler asked him to arrange for a "Wehrmacht hut" to be erected nearby. Then he sent for Bormann and asked him to provide teams of stenographers to record every word spoken at the war conferences; the stenographers were to be housed in the Wehrmacht hut. Never again would Jodl or anybody else be able to put words into his mouth. Evidently Jodl had tactlessly suggested that it was Hitler's own directives, faithfully complied with, that had caused the Caucasus stalemate, for Hitler now also demanded to see every scrap of paper referring to the

[2] The German army's High Command had sent Lieutenant Colonel Hentsch, a General Staff officer, out to inspect the armies on the Marne. He was then blamed for the resulting retreat of those armies.

command of List's army group. Jodl could have kicked himself for such an elementary *faux pas*. His own rule had always been that the dictator's reputation for infallibility must remain immaculate; the blame must always be laid upon insubordinates, for they were many—never placed on Hitler, for he was only one.

The clean sweep began at once. Over the next days Hitler contemplated replacing Keitel with Kesselring; he told Jodl he could not work with him any longer either and proposed replacing him with Paulus as soon as the general had taken Stalingrad. On September 9, the day the first Reichstag stenographers flew in from Berlin, he repeated his intention of ridding himself of Halder, as the general's nerves were evidently not equal to the strain. That afternoon he sent Keitel to drop the necessary hint to Halder. Keitel was also to tell Halder that Field Marshal List's resignation was required. For the time being he, Hitler, would command Army Group A in the Caucasus—the ultimate in anomalies, for he was after all Commander in Chief of the Army and Supreme Commander of the Wehrmacht as well. Keitel took the news to List in person.

List resigned that same evening, but Halder seems to have believed the ax would not fall on him as well. After all, Jodl continued in office and so did Keitel. But with Jodl the situation was different: Hitler still warmed toward him; his balding pate was a familiar sight across the map table, and above all he was loyal—apart, of course, from the one lapse about the blame for the Caucasus stalemate. Jodl commented to his own deputy, "The Führer will have to cast around a long time to find a better army general than me, and a more convinced National Socialist!" So he stayed on, while Hitler treated him with silent contempt for many weeks. Meanwhile the war conferences no longer took place in Jodl's map room but in his own quarters. They were conducted in monosyllabic brevity by an angry Führer while relays of stenographers recorded every word and interjection.

Under Martin Bormann's supervision the first three stenographers were sworn in on September 12 and a second batch two days later. The verbatim record of proceedings in the Wehrmacht hut came to some five hundred pages a day, every page checked and doublechecked by Hitler's adjutants and then locked away. "When we win a battle, my field marshals take the credit," Hitler explained. "When there's a failure, they point at *me*." He could trust nobody—but the SS. After the stenographers had been sworn in, he turned to SS aide Richard Schulze, promoted him to Personal Adjutant, and ordered him to sit in on every military meeting, no matter how confidential. The towering SS captain became a familiar sight.

Two years later Hitler, in conversation with a medical specialist, revealed a further motive for introducing the stenographers. The doctor mentioned that Kaiser Wilhelm II had suffered an ear complaint similar to Hitler's and inquired whether the Führer had ever read J. D. Chamier's biography of the Kaiser; Hitler had, and admitted that English though the author was the Kaiser had emerged well—perhaps better than he deserved. The doctor's note of this conversation continues:

> Hitler then said that a foreigner probably finds it easier to pass judgment on a statesman, provided that he is familiar with the country, its people, language, and archives. "Presumably Chamier didn't know the Kaiser personally, as he was still relatively young," I said. "However, his book not only shows a precise knowledge of the archives and papers, but relies on what are after all many personal items like the Kaiser's letters and written memoranda of conversations with friends and enemies. Of course in the Kaiser's time ideas were communicated far more frequently in writing than nowadays when we have the telephone, telegraph, aircraft, and car." Hitler then said that for some time now he has gone over to having all important discussions and military conferences recorded for posterity by shorthand writers. And perhaps one day after he is dead and buried an objective Englishman will come and give him the same kind of objective treatment. The present generation neither can nor will.

By mid-September 1942 the General Staff had reverted to the comforting theme that the Russians were finished—their lack of strategic reserves demonstrated by their urgent transfer of divisions from along the front to the Leningrad and Stalingrad crisis areas. Hitler optimistically spoke to Weichs and Paulus of future campaigns and of the capture of Astrakhan on the Caspian Sea. On September 13 the systematic assault on Stalingrad began. The next day even Richthofen believed the Russians were flagging. In his private diary Weizsäcker quoted his friend General Halder thus: "He says that above all he's leaving his post without worries for the army. The Russians are too far weakened to be the danger to us they were last winter. The weak spot is Africa." (Halder hated Rommel.)

But now the Russians began a heroic struggle for Stalingrad, contesting every street, every ruined building, and every yard of the battered city. Throughout late September Hitler's anxiety about the Don front, defended only by his poorly armed and unenthusiastic allies, mounted. Halder still had not executed Hitler's order for the 22nd Panzer Division to be placed in reserve behind the vulnerable Italian Eighth Army on the Don. On September 16, Hitler again ordered the transfer. Was it inertia or pigheadedness on Halder's part? Hitler, seething over the gradual stagnation of the summer offensive, suspected the former. It was time for Halder—who had identified himself so closely with Hitler's military ambitions and cast of thought in the first months after Brauchitsch's dismissal—to be ejected from the war machine like a spent cartridge case. On September 17, Hitler finally resolved to appoint the bustling General Zeitzler in his place; he turned down Keitel's suggestion that either Manstein or Paulus would be better, and he sent Schmundt, his chief adjutant, to Paris the next day accompanied by General Günther Blumentritt, who was to replace Zeitzler as Rundstedt's Chief of Staff.

It was late on September 23 before Schmundt arrived back at Hitler's Ukrainian headquarters, bringing a puzzled—and still unenlightened—Zeitzler with him. An hour after midnight Hitler had him fetched from the guest house, and launched into an impassioned monologue on List and Halder—the latter was "more of a professor than a soldier." When the red-faced Zeitzler tried uncomfortably to defend his chief, Hitler cut him short, rose to his feet, and announced that Zeitzler was to replace Halder forthwith. "I hereby promote you to full general." Thus at forty-seven Zeitzler was one of the army's youngest three-star generals and suddenly catapulted into the highest post of the army's General Staff. A rotund, florid, jovial soldier—known throughout the army as "Thunderball" because of his dynamic years as Chief of Staff to General von Kleist—he provided a change from Halder that could hardly have been more dramatic.

Halder attended his last frosty war conference the next midday. Afterward Hitler took leave of him, while Keitel and the stenographers stood by; he rebuked the general for losing his nerve and for lacking the kind of fanatical idealism that Moltke had displayed on behalf of the monarchy. When Major Engel, the army adjutant, collected Halder outside the door the general was still weeping—as another general put it, Halder had been kicked out like a dog caught piddling on the carpet. A victory mood reigned among the OKW officials, who rejoiced at the disgrace Hitler had inflicted on the General Staff. Schmundt proclaimed that the last barrier had fallen; the "spirit of Zossen" would now be stamped out, and the German army steeped through and through in the true spirit of National Socialism.

The new Chief of Staff was certainly more closely aligned with the Party than Halder, but he was by no means complaisant. Keitel accordingly warned him: "Never contradict the Führer. Never remind him that once he may have thought differently about something. Never tell him that subsequent events have proved you right and him wrong. Never report on casualties to him—you have to spare the nerves of this man." But Zeitzler retorted, "If a man starts a war he must have the nerve to hear the consequences." Court historian Scherff shared Keitel's view. Once he told an army general that there had been errors, but it would be harmful to draw the Führer's attention to them as he might then lose faith in his "instinctive touch"; it was the overall picture that mattered.

Hitler tolerated Zeitzler's robustness willingly at first. He hoped Zeitzler would succeed in remolding the General Staff, and he even drafted two orders for Zeitzler to deal with first: the one dispensing with the older army commanders—some of them were over sixty—and the other scrapping the traditional red-striped trousers and insignia of the General Staff. Zeitzler refused to inaugurate his office with such radical decrees. The traditions of the General Staff could not be disposed of at a stroke, even by an absolute dictator. Yet there was sound reasoning behind the desire for younger commanders—as the successes of Rommel, Model, Paulus, and Dietl, all in their early fifties, showed. In a third decree, Hitler subjected the personnel decisions of the General Staff to the Army Personnel Branch instead of to the Chief of Staff, and he also made his own chief adjutant, General Schmundt, head of that branch—thus for the first time acquiring absolute control over all senior army appointments. The brazen "freemasonry" of General Staff officers must lose its monopoly within the army. Hitler ordered:

a) There is only one officer corps. The best officers are to be given additional training to equip them for early entry to high front-line commands;
b) There is to be no limit on the number selected for training. . . .

In this way a tidal wave of youthful, active frontline commanders, equipped with the skills of the General Staff, promoted in leaps and bounds while still at the peak of their mental and physical abilities, would flood new life into the weary outer reaches of the German army. Halder's replacement by a general eleven years his junior was therefore just the forerunner of a much more fundamental revolution.

Hitler's aversion to the professional staff officer found further justification late in September: the Gestapo pounced on a Communist espionage ring extending across western Europe, one of whose principals was a staff officer attached to the air ministry. They had transmitted to their Russian paymasters details of Hitler's headquarters, his planned offensive in the Caucasus, and exaggerated statistics on German aircraft production and much else. The shortwave radios were distributed by the Soviet embassy in Berlin just before "Barbarossa" began, and they were serviced by a young Communist, Hans Coppi, aided by the Countess Brockdorff-Rantzau. The leading figure was Dr. Arvid Harnack, a civil servant in the economics ministry. The spy ring was a polyglot mixture of nobility and plebs, although Hitler scornfully observed that not one German worker had chosen to identify himself with them—the 117 members finally rounded up were either "warped intellectuals" like Lieutenant Harro Schulze-Boysen of the air Intelligence staff, who fancied himself as the defense minister in a Red Germany, or small fry trapped into betraying their country for sexual or monetary favors.

The first trials began some months later. The American-born Frau Mildred Harnack, was sentenced to six years' jail, the countess to ten years'; the rest were to be hanged—a mode of execution stipulated by Hitler as befitting this offense; he also demanded a retrial of the two women, and they were eventually hanged.

The summer of 1942 was over; as Hitler flew back to Berlin on September 27, the first autumn thunderstorms were drenching the capital. A mood of melancholy gripped the people—tired of waiting for the word that Stalingrad had fallen. The Reich press chief had already ordered the printing of special editions, but the event itself was thereby brought no closer. In bloody house-to-house fighting Paulus's troops stormed factory after factory, captured the waterworks, the South Station, and almost all the Volga River bank; the swastika had been hoisted above Communist party headquarters. Hitler was optimistic but failed to inspire even his most dedicated followers with the same hope.

Domestic morale was sagging: the British night-bombing raids on city centers were proving more than the fighter and antiaircraft defenses could handle. He ordered the Luftwaffe to build flak towers in Munich, Vienna, Linz, and Nuremberg—the fear that these cities might be laid waste was a "constant nightmare," he told his staff. During September heavy raids were made on Bremen, Duisburg, Düsseldorf, and Munich. On other nights isolated aircraft sent millions of city dwellers and factory workers to shelters and basements for hours on end. The Luftwaffe, itself in a period of technical innovation, had neither long-range strategic bombers nor high-speed fighter-bombers comparable with those of the enemy; the four-engined Heinkel 177 was a failure, plagued by engine failures and still totally unfit for squadron service, and the much-vaunted Messerschmitt 210 fighter-bomber had had to be scrapped outright earlier in 1942. Its outstanding successor, the Messerschmitt 410, had only just made its first flight. Hitler understood nothing about aircraft and had confidently left the Luftwaffe's future in Göring's hands. He began to suspect that his confidence had been misplaced. Increasingly he turned to the Chief of Air Staff, the youthful General Jeschonnek, for advice, excluding the pained and pompous Reichsmarschall Göring; or he discussed Luftwaffe policies with the eminently more capable Number Two, Field Marshal Milch, and the Reich's economic affairs with the munitions minister, Albert Speer, or with Goebbels.

To Goebbels he admitted that he was glad Munich had been bombed —he even found perverse relief in the damage to his own apartment there. The bombing would do the dour Bavarians good. The citizens had turned their backs on the war to such degree that he was pleased the British had drawn their attention to it again. Standing with Goebbels in the Chancellery galleries, where prewar Berlin had seen such spectacular gatherings, Hitler spoke of his longing for peace, which would enable him to return to these elegant surroundings with an easy conscience. Goebbels found him lively and good-tempered; the Führer had just addressed twelve thousand young officers and been fortified in spirit and resolution by the experience. Hitler confided that despite the winter, once Stalingrad had fallen he expected to fight on southward through the Caucasus, as the climate there would permit the campaign to continue. By early 1943 he hoped the huge power station at Zaporozh'ye would be working again, and then the mines and quarries of the Donets would begin producing for Germany.

In one respect Hitler still seemed too indulgent to Goebbels; the propaganda minister pointed out that in every offensive they lacked that final 10 percent of effort that decided between failure and outright success. The German public was awaiting a command for the total mobilization of its resources. Germany was confronted by a totalitarian state wholly committed to the war, while she herself was permitting useless expenditure of effort on, for example, gilding the trappings of Hans Frank's palaces in Poland. Hitler, inexplicably, still hesitated to proclaim a Total War, and thus the precious months were squandered.

Anxiety about the western defenses never left him. For example, Germany's possession of the Finnish nickel mines at Petsamo (Pechenga) was vital to her war effort. Thus he ordered every available warship to remain in northern waters now that the nights were lengthening again. In Holland, Hitler knew that the British secret service was parachuting

tons of sabotage material to its agents. Himmler's Gestapo had long penetrated the spy net and ambushed each successive shipment of agents and equipment—a self-perpetuating "England Game" on which the Führer was kept constantly informed.

Even placid little Denmark, the crucial link with Scandinavia, was growing restive. On King Christian's birthday, September 25, Hitler had sent the customary greetings; he received a reply that could only be regarded as deliberately brusque. As Goebbels put it, Europe's monarchs needed socking on the jaw now and then to stuff some sense into them. So Hitler recalled his envoy and military commander from Copenhagen, sent the Danish diplomats in Berlin packing, rejected the apologies belatedly offered by the crown prince, and—after keeping the luckless Danes in agitated suspense for four weeks—delegated the former Gestapo official Dr. Werner Best to act as his strongman in Copenhagen. He instructed Best to ignore the Danish monarchy completely and ensure that Danish Nazis were introduced into a new government—which was to be "legal and complaisant," though "with no support among the Danish people." If the aged king should die, the Wehrmacht was forbidden to join the official mourning.

What Hitler most feared, however, was an enemy invasion of France. The Dieppe raid had shown that this was not impossible. "As you all know," he reminded Göring, Speer, Rundstedt, and a handful of selected generals in the Chancellery's Cabinet Room on September 29, "I have never capitulated. But let us be quite plain about one point: a major enemy landing in the west could precipitate a real crisis." The enemy would have absolute air supremacy. The invasion defenses would be pummelled by bombers and ships' artillery. Only the strongest concrete bunkers and antitank defenses along the entire coastline could ward off an invasion.

The army's transcript of his three-hour secret speech noted:

Finally the Führer repeated that he saw only one remaining danger for the outcome of the war and that was the emergence of a Second Front in the west, as the fighting in the east and the home base would be directly endangered by this. The enemy could launch their Second Front anywhere else they liked, as long as it was as far as possible from Europe. At present he saw his main job as being to spare his country from being turned into a battlefield, which would be the immediate result of an invasion in the west. If we can prevent that until the spring [by which time the Atlantic Wall's fifteen thousand bunkers would be built] nothing can happen to us any longer.

We have got over the worst foodstuffs shortage. By increased pro-

duction of antiaircraft guns and ammunition the home base will be protected against air raids. In the spring we shall march with our finest divisions down into Mesopotamia, and then one day we shall force our enemies to make peace where and as we want it. Once before the German Reich suffered from its own excessive modesty. The new German Reich will not make the same mistake in its war aims.

The next day he spoke to the German people—for the first time for many months, he apologized, as he had less time for speechmaking than a prime minister who could cruise for weeks around the world in a white silk blouse and floppy sombrero or some other ludicrous garb.

It is of course impossible to talk with these people about Beliefs. If somebody believes that Namsos was a victory, or Andalsnes—if somebody describes even Dunkirk as the biggest victory in history or sees in some nine-hour expedition [Dieppe] a flabbergasting sign of national triumph—obviously we cannot even begin to compare our own modest successes with them! . . . If in these last few months, and in this country there are only a few months available for campaigning, we advance to the Don, finally reach the Volga, overrun Stalingrad and capture it—and of that they can be certain—in their eyes this is nothing! If we advance to the Caucasus, that is as unimportant as that we occupy the Ukraine, have the Donets coal in our domain, have 65 or 70 percent of Russia's iron ore, open up the biggest grain region in the world for the German people and thus for Europe, and also take over the Caucasian oil wells. All that is nothing! But if Canadian troops, wagged by a tiny English tail, come over to Dieppe and just manage to hang on there for nine hours before they are wiped out, then that is an "encouraging, astounding proof of the inexhaustible, triumphant energy typical of the British Empire!" What are our Luftwatte, our infantry, our tanks against these? What is the effort of our engineers, our railway construction teams—what are our gigantic transport systems, built by us to open up and rebuild half a continent in a matter of months, compared with these? . . . If Mr. Churchill now says, "We want to leave the Germans to fret and ponder on where and when we will open the Second Front," then I can only say, "Mr. Churchill, you never gave me cause to worry yet! But that we must *ponder*—you've got a point there, because if my enemy was a man of stature I could deduce fairly accurately where he would strike; but if one is confronted by military nincompoops, obviously one hasn't the faintest idea, for it might be the most lunatic undertaking imaginable. And that is the only unattractive feature—that with paralytics and drunkards you can never tell what they'll be up to next."

Africa and Stalingrad

Hitler believed he had good reason to face the coming winter with optimism. The railway transport crisis had been overcome. The harvest throughout occupied Europe was better than expected. Albert Speer was harnessing Germany's latent industrial might to mass-produce tanks and guns. Under Field Marshal Milch the Luftwaffe's production lines were being reorganized. The Atlantic coast was being fortified. The navy was in Norway; the submarines were blocking the Allied convoy routes in the Arctic. The Reich's domains extended farther than ever before in history.

On October 1, 1942, Field Marshal Rommel—amiable and reserved—visited Hitler at the Berlin Chancellery. He explained why he had had to abandon his offensive against the British El Alamein position, attributing it solely to the shortcomings of the Italian officers and British air supremacy. But when Rommel reported that British planes were knocking out his tanks with 40-millimeter shells Göring scoffed, "Out of the question—the Americans only know how to make razor blades!" Rommel retorted, "Herr Reichsmarschall, I wish we had blades like that." Hitler showed him the prototypes of new self-propelled assault guns Albert Speer had collected at the Chancellery that morning—formidable low-chassis armored vehicles mounting the well-proven 105-millimeter guns and presenting a remarkably small target profile to the enemy. He told Rommel of the new Tiger tanks and promised to send forty of them and all the gasoline Rommel needed across to Africa by means of countless Siebel ferries—small flat-bottomed ferries with powerful antiaircraft defenses. The promises remained unfulfilled. Rommel later wrote that Hitler had been misled by his armaments production experts, but even Speer had only promised Hitler a dozen of the assault guns by the end of October. Hitler was an optimist, however; he told Rommel of a weapon of such appalling power it would blast a man off his horse two miles away. Evidently his imagination had run riot on Speer's sober account of Germany's modest atomic research effort some months before. He liked Rommel, too—he was planning to make him Commander in Chief of the army when the time came.

Hitler returned to the Ukraine on October 4. Halder was finally gone. Zeitzler's verve infected every war conference, evoking from Hitler Napoleon's maxim *"activité, activité, vitesse!"* Zeitzler took control of the eastern front, while Jodl and the OKW controlled the other theaters—a division of responsibility reflected in the war conferences at headquarters, where Zeitzler first briefed Hitler on the Russian front, not infrequently in strict privacy, followed by Jodl on the "OKW theaters." Hitler encouraged the innovation, seeing in Zeitzler the tactical experience needed for Russia and in Jodl the broad strategic vision Zeitzler lacked for the other theaters. Zeitzler toured the southern front at once, returned to Vinnitsa, and issued over Hitler's name a string of realistic orders designed to increase the army's fighting strength—from the proper use of modern weapons, ammunition, and minefields down to the introduction of special rations for combat troops.

Nor were either of these military advisers sycophants. On one occasion the stenographers caught their breath as General Jodl, propped on an elbow on the map table, glanced briefly at Hitler and replied, "Mein Führer, that is an order I will *not* comply with." On another occasion Zeitzler warned that unless a certain salient was withdrawn, the troops would lose confidence in their leadership. Hitler, his awe of the newcomer now diminished, thundered at him, "You're just a staff officer. What do you know about the troops!" Zeitzler sharply reminded the Führer that in August 1914 he had gone to war as an infantry ensign—his knapsack on his back and his rifle on his shoulder—to fight in Belgium. "For bravery in the face of the enemy I was promoted to lieutenant. For three years I commanded a company and for one year I was regimental adjutant. I was wounded twice. I think my combat experience is as good as yours." Hitler paled, instructed the general to proceed with the conference, and avoided attacking him personally after that.

Thus Zeitzler's position became entrenched. Keitel, by way of contrast, had long forfeited Hitler's esteem. Hitler took to making "good-humored" fun of his absent commanders. "My field marshals are great tacticians," he guffawed once. "By tactics, of course, they mean retreating!" Enjoying the dutiful laughter he added, "My field marshals' horizon is the size of a lavatory lid!" Field Marshal Keitel did not move a muscle as the others laughed. The next day an adjutant informed Hitler that Zeitzler wanted a brief private word with him; the meeting took place at midnight. He cordially shook the general's hand. "What can I do for you?" "Mein Führer," replied Zeitzler, "I must speak my mind. As an army general I take exception to the language you used about our field marshals. May I ask you not to use expressions like that in my presence again?" Hitler was dumbfounded, then gave him his hand. "I thank you." As Zeitzler later put it, the Führer was unpredictable. When Antonescu visited him three months later, Hitler introduced Zeitzler to him with the words "This is my new Chief of General Staff. A man of iron nerves and great war experience."

The war had taken on many new dimensions since 1939. In the east and southeast armies of partisans and bandits were fighting a new kind of campaign. In the west too the Allies were emulating—and far surpassing —the tactics of the Abwehr in commando warfare. These peripheral successes struck a raw nerve in Hitler, whether the target was a secret radar site in France or a German oil dump in North Africa. He showed little inclination to mercy when the commandos were caught: in August, six Britons captured in North Africa behind the lines had caused great damage and many German casualties; two of them were wearing items of German uniforms. Hitler ordered their execution. As he warned his western commanders in October, unless they closed their hearts and acted ruthlessly against the Allied commandos, they would find themselves enmeshed in a partisan struggle no less gruesome than that in the east. Never before had "illegals" played such a part in war—disrupting transport, intimidating the pro-Germans, and sabotaging vital installations. One saboteur could paralyze a power plant and thus deprive the Luftwaffe of thousands of tons of aluminum. The British commandos concealed their uniforms under civilian clothing, so they could escape or surrender as they chose—"The worst possible abuse of the Geneva Convention," said Hitler, conveniently forgetting the tactics he had devised for the invasion of Holland.

A commando-training manual fell into his hands, with diagrams on how to slit human throats and how to truss prisoners so that a noose around their neck would strangle them if they moved. Some corpses trussed like this had been found. Similar instructions captured in North Africa had been commendably disowned by the British government. In September he was told that the British had machine-gunned the survivors of a sinking German minelayer. "It is essential that we give the British as good as we get—an eye for an eye and a tooth for a tooth," fulminated Hitler. "We must declare at once that henceforth parachuting airmen will be fired on, that our submarines will shell the survivors from torpedoed ships, regardless of whether they are soldiers or civilians, women or children! . . . The British are realists, devoid of any scruple and as cold as ice; but as soon as we show our teeth, they become propitiary and almost friendly!" He ordered the navy to commence reprisals, but Raeder demurred. German career officers were too steeped in the traditions of "old-fashioned" wars—the kind fought before the strategic bomber and the atomic weapon—to accept Hitler's radical ideas.

On his return to Vinnitsa on October 4 news reached him of a British commando raid on the tiny Channel island of Sark the night before. The island was guarded only by a rifle company. The commandos had seized five army engineers sleeping in a hotel, manacled them, and then shot and stabbed them to death before withdrawing. Hitler immediately ordered all the prisoners taken at Dieppe manacled as a reprisal until the British government undertook not to repeat such methods; the British proclaimed they would retaliate against the same number of Axis prisoners in their own camps. Hitler had meanwhile drafted a text for the daily OKW communiqué broadcast on the seventh: "The terror and sabotage squads of the British and their accomplices act more like bandits than soldiers. In the future they will be treated as such by the German troops and ruthlessly put down in battle, wheresoever they may appear."

General Jodl urged Hitler to leave it at that—the warning words would alone deter, no need actually to put them into practice. Hitler disagreed. He grumbled about his generals' timidity and their unwillingness to carry out even his order for the liquidation of the Soviet army commissars. "The war ministry is to blame; they always wanted the soldier's profession to be on a par with the parson's!" Keitel and Jodl refused to draft the new order, so Hitler dictated it to one of his own secretaries. He justified it by referring to the commandos' methods as being outside the Geneva Conventions. "Captured papers show that they are ordered not only to manacle their prisoners, but to kill their defenseless prisoners out of hand the moment they feel such prisoners might become a burden or hindrance to them in the prosecution of their purposes." Jodl, unhappily distributing Hitler's order to the commanders on October 19, urgently warned them not to let it fall into enemy hands.

Thus the reported tactics of the British commandos had tragic consequences for many others who fell into German hands. A thirst for revenge also played its part. For example, the record of Hitler's war conference on October 23 began: "In reprisal for the fresh British air raid on a casualty clearing station in Africa the Führer has ordered the immediate execution of the Briton captured during the sabotage attack on the power station at Glomfjord." A week later an attempt by six British sailors to destroy the battleship *Tirpitz*—wintering in a Norwegian fjord —came to grief when their two-man torpedoes were lost in foul weather. Himmler reported to Hitler that all were in plain clothes and that their ship had flown the Norwegian flag. Norwegian frontier guards had captured them, but the six had opened fire with concealed weapons, and five had escaped into Sweden; technically, they were clearly illegals. Hitler ordered the sixth, a twenty-year-old seaman who had been shot through the legs by his Norwegian captors, to be executed. Three weeks later the same fate met the fourteen British survivors of a commando-style attack launched on a hydroelectric power station in Norway: the first glider had crashed into the sea, killing all aboard; the second had crashed with its towing aircraft into a hillside. The Norwegian police rounded up the survivors. The Germans found extensive sabotage equipment in the wreckage. In accordance with the new Commando Order, all fourteen were shot before darkness fell.[1] Some of them *had* been in uniform, and this may have given Hitler misgivings, for when Britain formally protested months later, Hitler dictated to Jodl a note of reply: Insofar as they were in uniform and executing an obvious military mission, enemy soldiers would be treated according to the Convention; but soldiers "dropped behind our lines for clandestine sabotage operations" in unorthodox or civilian clothing, or equipped with "treacherously concealed firearms," would be put to death.

In the Balkans a partisan war of unexampled ferocity was raging, thanks to the devious policies of the Italians and the ineptness of the puppet governments Hitler had established. In April 1941, Yugoslavia had been dismembered into Croatia, governed by a "Poglavnik," Ante Pavelic, and Serbia, which came under German military rule. The Italians had occupied Montenegro and part of Croatia, and they were annexing large stretches of the Croatian coastline. By May 1941 partisan warfare had broken out throughout what was formerly Yugoslavia. In Serbia it was ruthlessly quelled by the Germans; but in Croatia rival armies of guerrillas and bandits roamed the land, terrorizing the pro-Germans,

[1] The target, the Vemork power plant at Rjukan, had been selected because of its importance for the German atomic research program.

robbing and plundering and murdering, paralyzing the new Croatian state's machinery from the outset. The Četniks, led by Draža Mihajlovič, were fighting for the restoration of the monarchy in Yugoslavia; the partisans, led by Tito, were fighting for Communist ideals; the Ustasha, the Croatian government troops, were fighting an ineffective campaign against them all, hampered by a lack of even the simplest weapons, since the Italians were failing to supply them. Mussolini complained that the Croats were persecuting the Serbian minority and had killed two hundred thousand men, women, and children. His own Second Army, commanded by the controversial General Mario Roatta, sided not with the Ustasha but the Četniks—even to the extent of arming them against Tito's partisans. The Italians were weaving a tangled web indeed.

It was not only that all this laid bare the growing divergence of German and Italian aims. Croatia was of great strategic importance: across the country passed the German supply lines to Salonika and North Africa; and it exported oil and two hundred thousand tons of bauxite to Germany annually. Order and control were imperative to the Nazis. But the Italians were suppressing the Croat population and actively shielding the Jews—the very subversive elements against whom the Poglavnik was struggling to apply repressive laws similar to those enforced in Germany. Hitler thrashed out this explosive situation with the Poglavnik and the German military commanders late in September. He had two divisions in Croatia, and a Croat battalion was already fighting before Stalingrad; more were being trained—an entire foreign legion—by the Waffen SS, but now the Poglavnik would need them to restore order in Croatia. All this was the result of Roatta's strange dealings, but Hitler was loath to embarrass Mussolini, and the papers sent down to Rome were stripped of any references that might offend Italian susceptibilities. As Ribbentrop wrote in mid-October: "The German-Italian alliance is and always has been the basis of our foreign policy."

In private Hitler regretted the Italians' kid-glove treatment of the Serbs. Only brute force bereft of inhibitions would work—just as only brute force would work in the war against the partisans in Russia. "On principle, when combatting illegals, anything that works is right—and I want that hammered into everybody," he laid down. "This gives everybody the freedom of action they need. . . . If the illegals use women and children as shields, then our officer or NCO must be able to open fire on them without hesitation. What matters is that he gets through and wipes out the illegals." Hitler wanted no "pedantic" disciplinary action against the officer afterward. Himmler took the hint. In August, September, October, and November his security forces counted 1,337 dead Russian partisans and executed a further 8,564 taken prisoner. His report to Hitler for the same period listed 16,553 "partisan accomplices and suspects" captured, of which 14,257 were executed; an additional 363,211 Russian Jews were claimed to have been executed under the same heading.

Hitler could look east without qualms. General Ruoff's Seventeenth Army was still struggling through the mountains toward Tuapse and the Black Sea. Yard by yard Stalingrad was being overrun. Soon his armies could have their well-earned winter respite. On October 14 he issued orders for winter positions to be built along the current front line—making rigorous use of prisoners, civilians, and women to aid in their construction. The next day Field Marshal von Richthofen, one of Hitler's favorite Luftwaffe commanders, called. Richthofen's diary reports: "The Führer was in good humor because of Stalingrad and of having got rid of Halder. Particularly affectionate to me . . . . The Führer curses with vehemence (and justification) the name of List. My operational plans [in the Caucasus] are approved. I tell him something of our infantry weakness, our tactics, and above all our difficult terrain. Zeitzler is stout and cheerful. . . ."

A few days later, Ruoff's campaign finally ground to a halt. In the last week of October the spirit of Paulus's troops in Stalingrad also flagged. Richthofen wrote: "The main reasons lie in the weariness of the combat troops and commanders, and in the army's pedantic tolerance of a ration strength of twelve thousand men per division, of whom only a thousand are actually in the front line. . . . I tell Paulus of this, but he naturally doesn't agree." Zeitzler still spoke highly of Paulus to Hitler. But on October 26 he admitted at Hitler's war conference: "In the Sixth Army's view the enemy's resistance at Stalingrad is so stiff that the fighting will not result in the city's capture until November 10."

The capture of the Caucasian oil fields was impossible before winter, so on October 7, Hitler had ordered the Luftwaffe to destroy the Soviet oil fields around Saratov and Grozny. Two weeks later he added Astrakhan and Baku to the target lists. Maykop had been in German hands since August, but it was a shambles—the oil wells either blown up or cemented over. The army's petroleum brigade reported that a year's reconstruction effort would be needed. Now Hitler was told that much more convenient oil fields were available in the Taman peninsula. For three months the petroleum brigade had done virtually nothing at Maykop on the blithe assumption that Baku and Grozny would shortly be in German hands. After Hitler's orders for the bombing and sabotage of those oil fields, the severity of the oil crisis became apparent to everybody. The Italian navy shrieked for more oil without satisfactorily explaining what it had done with the thousands of tons Germany had already supplied. The German admiralty pointed out that the transfer of the *Scharnhorst, Nürnberg, Prinz Eugen,* and *Lützow* to Norway would alone cost nine thousand tons of fuel oil, leaving only one thousand tons for actual operations in November and two thousand tons in December.

German manpower was an equally scarce war commodity. Industry relied on the 6,000,000 foreign workers procured by Hitler's labor dictator, Fritz Sauckel—but while Sauckel insisted they must be properly fed, the local Gauleiters often thought differently. Speer promised to raise three divisions from German munitions workers, but he shortly reduced his offer to only a quarter of the 50,000 men he originally spoke of; the divisions never actually materialized. The army itself was 1,000,000 men under strength. Not so the Luftwaffe: Hitler had always believed its strength was only 1,600,000 men—now he learned that it was bloated to 1,980,000 men in anticipation of the doubling of its squadron strength, something long since abandoned by Hitler as impracticable. Hitler ordered both the navy and the Luftwaffe to transfer manpower to the anemic army, but Göring decided instead to create twenty Luftwaffe "field divisions" rather than see his airmen forced into the army's reactionary field-gray ranks. Thus to satisfy Göring's stubborn vanity 220,000 of his troops were to find themselves fighting—often at the most crucial sectors—inadequately trained and with no combat experience.

Coupled with these manpower and materials shortages was the complete bankruptcy of Hitler's Intelligence services by the autumn of 1942. Colonel Reinhard Gehlen's army Intelligence consistently predicted until early November that the Russian offensive would open not in the south but against Smolensk or even Velikiye Luki, on the northern front. Admiral Wilhelm Canaris's Abwehr produced equally convincing evidence that the Allies were planning a Second Front not, for example, in North Africa, but against the Cherbourg peninsula. As General Fromm—responsible for raising the new divisions—commented, "If the attacks on Cherbourg and Velikiye Luki coincide, they may cost us the war." Moreover, Hitler was still misled as to Stalin's coming strength. (On October 21, Keitel said, "The Führer is convinced the Russians are collapsing. He says that twenty million will have to starve.") The first three Luftwaffe field divisions were sent to Velikiye Luki, as were sections of the Eleventh Army—which meant finally abandoning the assault on Leningrad. But a Russian attack on Smolensk would be even more likely, in Hitler's view, so he transferred the Seventh Air Division paratroops and the 20th Panzer Division there as well. These were fatal errors.

Yet Hitler did not accept Gehlen's judgment willingly. By October 26 he was clearly rattled by concrete evidence of Russian plans to cross the Don just where the Axis front was weakest—held only by the reluctant Italians and Romanians. The army group interpreted the dense night traffic toward Serafimovich as unimportant replenishments, but when the enemy started constructing heavy bridges across the Don, Hitler knew differently; he had built bridges across rivers himself and knew what it presaged. He ordered more Luftwaffe field divisions moved into the endangered Italian and Romanian sectors. He was convinced Stalin planned to strike westward toward Rostov—and strike before 1942 was over! The General Staff disagreed. On November 6, Gehlen insisted there were no signs of any Soviet offensive in the south in the near future; far more likely was a drive against Smolensk, followed by a thrust to the Baltic to cut off the whole of Army Group North. Thus the Russians would wipe out the threat to Moscow and win a prestige victory relatively easily, while in the south the logistical and transport difficulties would surely dissuade them. Nor, stated Gehlen, would the Russian offensive begin before the ground froze over. He was to prove wrong on all counts.

Hitler also saw no cause to suspect that the Mediterranean theater would soon be in an uproar. In mid-October indications had multiplied that the Allies might invade West Africa; however, the OKW considered this unlikely before spring. But the Führer's agents in Spain could see the Allied shipping build up at Gibraltar, and this indicated some operation *within* the Mediterranean. Respect for Mussolini's feelings figured among his reasons for not reinforcing the Vichy French forces in French North Africa. The Italians were less sanguine and actively prepared to invade Tunisia (a French domain) the moment the enemy should arrive.

Rommel was in Germany on sick leave. He had told Hitler that the El Alamein position was virtually impregnable. But late on October 23, General Montgomery launched a massive and unheralded attack with 150,000 men supported by over 1,000 tanks and 800 planes. The Axis was outnumbered nearly 2 to 1. Rommel's stand-in was killed by a heart attack and by the next day one panzer division had only 31 of its 119 tanks left. The enemy's American Sherman tank seemed invincible. Rommel, who hurried back to Africa, found his army's fuel and ammunition almost at an end. Despite the Luftwaffe's around-the-clock bombing of Malta, the Axis supply convoys to North Africa had been cut to pieces. The Italian sectors of Rommel's front dissolved overnight; tens of thousands surrendered to the British. His supplies dried up. The Luftwaffe commander in the Mediterranean wrote in his diary: "The blackest day was October 26: a big tanker and a smaller merchantman were sunk just short of Tobruk after we had escorted them successfully for two days. Thus a crisis of undreamed-of proportions has emerged for the panzer army. The failure of the Italian fighter escort is to blame —it just did not show up. . . . Kesselring came, worried out of his mind. Lunch was like in a mortuary. . . . Everybody's hopes were pinned on the second tanker, which sailed on October 28. In the night it was reported sunk." On the thirty-first he wrote: "The situation at the front is slightly better. The British have taken some heavy blows and have to regroup. They will begin again in one or two days. A weak relief is the docking of the *Brioni* on the thirtieth, bringing some ammunition and fuel." Indeed, both Rommel and Kesselring—and the Italian High Command—were confident that the crisis had been overcome. Hitler willingly believed them.

In what now followed, the human element weighs as heavily as the military. Hitler was preoccupied by the eastern front; besides, his headquarters was in the midst of returning from the Ukraine to East Prussia —forty-nine trainloads of officers and men, machinery and paraphernalia. On November 2 all hell broke loose in North Africa again, as General Montgomery hurled his tanks and artillery against Rommel's well-fortified minefields at El Alamein. The line was breached, and enemy armor began to pour through. In his interim report, received by the OKW that evening, Rommel suddenly sounded despondent and anxious:

> Despite today's defensive success, the army's strength is exhausted after ten days' tough fighting against British ground and air forces many times its superior. Therefore the army will no longer be capable of impeding the strong enemy tank formations expected to repeat their breakthrough attempt tonight or tomorrow. For want of motor transport it will not be possible for the six Italian and two German nonmotorized divisions to withdraw in good order. A large part of these units will probably fall into the hands of the enemy's mechanized formations. But even our mobile troops are embroiled in such heavy fighting that only part will be able to disengage themselves

from the enemy. Such ammunition stocks as there are lie close to the front lines, while in the rear there are no stocks worth talking of. Our meager fuel supplies will not permit any withdrawals over long distances. It is certain that the army will be attacked day and night by the British air force on the one road available to it.

In this situation the gradual destruction of the army must therefore be assumed as inevitable, despite the heroic resistance and exemplary spirit of the troops.

sgd. ROMMEL, *Field Marshal*

At 11 P.M. Hitler telephoned Jodl's staff officer, Colonel Christian, to ask if there was any more news from Rommel, and to check with Rome to find out. There was no news. In North Africa, however, Rommel had succumbed to a black despair. Still a sick man and cowed by the ceaseless British bombardment, he had already ordered his army to abandon El Alamein—without notifying anybody to that effect. The retreat began at 10 P.M. To cover himself, Rommel later dispatched to his superiors a lengthy but seemingly routine daily report, near the end of which he surreptitiously buried the announcement that he had bowed before the enemy's strength and would withdraw from El Alamein the next day, November 3: "The infantry divisions will already be withdrawn during the coming night, November 2–3." To announce a strategic decision in such a furtive way was, as Jodl's deputy, Warlimont, later pointed out, against all accepted military usage. The result was that Rommel's illicit retreat was already twelve hours old when Hitler first learned of it.

At midnight, Rome advised Colonel Christian that the routine report from Rommel was just being decoded, and it arrived by teletype at the Führer's headquarters at 3 A.M. But Jodl's night duty officer, an elderly major of the reserve, overlooked the vital sentence announcing the retreat and left the report unforwarded until morning. It was belatedly rushed over to Hitler at 9 A.M.: thus he was awakened with the news that Rommel was retreating. In the angry scene that followed, he blamed Keitel in particular for the OKW's lackadaisical attitude. For a time he suspected that the OKW had deliberately sat on Rommel's report in order to confront him with a *fait accompli* in Africa. "At this critical moment Rommel turned to me and the Fatherland!" he exclaimed. "We should have been stiffening his resolve. If I'd been awakened I would have taken full responsibility and ordered him to stand fast. But our Mr. Warlimont is snug asleep while Rommel is appealing to me!"

Hitler believed he could still give Rommel—a sensitive, almost childlike personality—the inspiration he seemed to be begging for. While the chief of the Italian *comando supremo* signaled Rommel to hold the El Alamein position "whatever the cost," at 1 P.M. on November 3 Hitler radioed to Rommel the following message, finely attuned to the susceptibilities of the field marshal:

> With me the entire German people is watching your heroic defensive battle in Egypt, with rightful confidence in your leadership qualities and the courage of your German and Italian troops. In your situation there can be no thought but of persevering, of yielding not one yard, and of hurling every gun and every fighting man available into the battle. Considerable air force reinforcements are being transferred over the coming days to Commander in Chief South [Kesselring]. The Duce and the *comando supremo* will also do their utmost to furnish you with the means to keep up the fight.
>
> Despite his superiority the enemy must also be at the end of his strength. It would not be the first time in history that the stronger will has triumphed over the stronger battalions of an enemy. To your troops therefore you can offer no other path than that leading to Victory or Death.
>
> *sgd.* ADOLF HITLER

The night duty officer was fetched. Hitler questioned him in person, warning, "If you don't tell me the absolute truth, I'll have you dead inside ten minutes!" Rommel also was interrogated by radio, asked to state the precise time that the infantry retreat had begun. He radioed back: "In the latter part of the night"—so it seemed that, but for the report's inexcusable delay, Hitler could still have stepped in to forbid the retreat. Punishment was swift: the major was reduced to the ranks and sent to the front; his superior, Warlimont, was evicted from the OKW and the Führer's headquarters that same day. But Rommel's reply was, of course, a lie: his retreat had begun at 10 P.M., before his report had been dispatched. On Schmundt's insistence, Warlimont was reinstated, and even the major's lapse was not held against him long.

Another field marshal would have paid dearly for this deceit. Guderian had been sacked, Hoepner discharged from the army, and Sponeck condemned to death for just such actions as this. But by adroit public relations Rommel had developed a charisma which made even a popular dictator hesitate to take disciplinary action.

Rommel wavered throughout the day. He rescinded his order to retreat, but already it was too late. Half his troops and 40 percent of his artillery were lost. As November 3 ended, he had only twenty-four tanks left. The next day he and Kesselring reported separately that the battlefront no longer existed, and formally asked permission to revert to "mobile warfare," defending every foot of ground until the new line at Fûka was reached. Hitler sourly replied that evening, "In view of the way things have gone, I approve your decision." He had no choice, though privately he doubted Rommel could hold the Fûka or any other line. He felt Rommel's nerve had failed him.[2] Two years later he brooded: "He should have stood his ground up front [at El Alamein], that was his only chance of saving anything. He didn't compensate for the enemy's superiority of numbers by heading for the wide-open spaces—that was where their superiority really began to take effect. At that bottleneck, just forty miles across, you could just about survive an attack. But the moment you were forced out and lost the cover of the [Qattara] depression to your left, all the lessons of desert warfare showed you were liable to be leapfrogged again and again by the enemy. . . ." Too late, Hitler ordered reinforcements rushed to North Africa—the deadly Tiger tanks, guns, ammunition, fuel, two fighter squadrons from Russia, and a bomber squadron from Norway. These steps "would have brought far more realistic relief if only one-quarter fulfilled two weeks ago, than at this present juncture of the battle," a local Luftwaffe commander observed. In Africa a rout that was to end dismally in Tunis six months later had begun.

Hitler's attention was still captured by events in the east, where he feared his armies were about to lose the initiative. As the rumored Russian offensive against Velikiye Luki in the far north failed to materialize, he began to plan his own attack, now that he had been duped into moving his reserves up there.

While at the southern end of the front the First Panzer Army's advance on Ordzhonikidze was going well, in Stalingrad the infantry was losing heart. Perhaps Paulus himself was to blame. Field Marshal von Richthofen was to note in his diary in mid-November:

> . . . Telephoned Zeitzler about the need for really energetic leadership in the battle for Stalingrad, or for the attack to be called off otherwise. If the mopping-up is not done now, with the Volga icing over and the Russians in Stalingrad in dire distress, we will never pull it off. Besides, the days are getting shorter and the weather worse. Zeitzler promised to tell the Führer; he shares my view. During the night a Führer Order came to the Sixth Army in line with my tele-

2 See Hitler's remark in December 1942, page 502. Throughout November, Rommel's private letters betrayed an increasing despondency. On December 11 he actually wrote his wife: ". . . I would be grateful if you would send me by secret courier a small English-German dictionary. I think I'm going to need it."

phone suggestion. But I still don't think it will work. I stressed to Zeitzler that the commanders and combat troops in Stalingrad are so apathetic that only the injection of a new spirit will get us anywhere. I suggested the commanders—who are otherwise trustworthy enough—should be sent on leave for a while to let very different types take their place. But "up top" there isn't the toughness for that.

As with Rostov the year before, the sheer size of Stalingrad had taken Hitler by surprise; it sprawled over an area about the distance from Berlin to Brandenburg. But he accepted Paulus's assurances that the battle was all but won.

Hitler was still hypnotized by the obvious Russian preparations north of Stalingrad. The OKW historian recorded: "War conference with Führer on November 2: . . . The Russian attack feared across the Don toward Rostov is again discussed. More and more Russian bridges are being built there. The Luftwaffe is to submit reconnaissance mosaics. The Führer orders very heavy air attacks on the bridge sites and troop assembly areas suspected in the forests on the other river bank." On the fifth the historian noted: "According to Chief of General Staff [Zeitzler], a council of war was attended by all supreme commanders in Moscow on November 4: the Big Push is apparently planned for the Don or central fronts before this year is out." Soon after, two thousand enemy vehicles were glimpsed massing north of Kletskaya, and the headquarters of a new Russian army group, the "Southwest Front," was detected at nearby Serafimovich. But even now Gehlen's estimate was that the Russians just planned to cut the one railroad supplying Paulus's army in Stalingrad from the west.

Hitler feared that Stalin was capable of more.

Before this fear materialized, momentous events occurred in the Mediterranean, shaking the Axis partnership to its very foundations.

Throughout October the Abwehr and SS Intelligence agencies had been swamped with "enemy invasion plans." Some spoke of Norway, others of the Channel coast or the Mediterranean. Hitler intuitively believed only the latter: as the Italian divisions marched into enemy captivity in Egypt, Mussolini's prestige was already crumbling. Air raids on Italian towns had sapped morale. A further military setback in the Mediterranean might force Italy out of the war—indeed, diplomatic sources in Rome detected the first neutralist undercurrents in government circles there. The whiff of treason was already in the air. Hitler's military liaison reported on November 6 that Mussolini thought the time now ripe to make amends to Stalin. Small wonder that Hitler believed he could postpone his next meeting with the tired and ailing Fascist dictator no longer, urgently though he himself was needed at his East Prussian headquarters.

Besides, he had gradually become aware that an immense fleet of ships was assembling at Gibraltar, a fleet far bigger than the harbor at Malta could accommodate; so this was no mere supply convoy. Hitler had recently suspected that the enemy would invade Sardinia or Corsica prior to striking at the Italian mainland itself. Much of the Luftwaffe's strength had been withdrawn eastward from Sicily, but Hitler had ordered all available German submarines to the western Mediterranean. As late as November 4 the navy would have none of this, insisting that the enemy was just preparing to fight a big supply convoy through to Malta. If this was an invasion fleet, where were the troop transports? On the sixth they changed their tune. The armada had sailed, and Italian Intelligence now reported what the German Abwehr had not—that the vessels had trucks and invasion tackle on their decks and they were joining convoys of ships streaming eastward through the Strait of Gibraltar. The navy judged that the enemy planned to invade Libya, in Rommel's rear; less likely targets would be Sicily, Sardinia, or the Italian mainland; French North Africa was considered least likely of all, as the enemy would hardly drive France into Hitler's arms. Though both Mussolini and the Luftwaffe believed an enemy invasion of Algeria far more likely—beyond the range of Axis air power—Hitler had by November 7 bowed to the navy's judgment that the likely targets were Tripoli or Benghazi, and he ordered emergency measures there, including street barricades.

He personally radioed to the handful of submarines and torpedo boats in the Mediterranean: "Army's survival in Africa depends on destruction of British naval forces. I expect determined, victorious attack." But the navy had stationed these ships in the central Mediterranean, far to the east of where the enemy's invasion designs lay. The failure of Hitler's Intelligence service was thus to cost many German lives over the months to come.

Early on the afternoon of November 7, 1942, Hitler's train left Rastenburg for Berlin and Munich—where he was to meet the Italians.

At a 7 P.M. war conference, Jodl briefed him on the latest position of the enemy armada in the Mediterranean: it was still heading due east and would probably pass through the Strait of Sicily. But one of the last

Intelligence reports had mentioned Oran as an invasion target, and Hitler's ears had pricked up at this, for Oran would lie outside Axis aircraft range. Toward the end of the conference, the naval staff telephoned Hitler's train with confirmation: from the armada's 6 P.M. position and the ships' speeds, the Italians deduced that it *must* be an invasion of Algeria—they would hardly risk forcing the Strait of Sicily in broad daylight. Hitler accepted this calculation. It was a bitter pill to swallow, and his disappointment at his Intelligence agencies must have been profound. But he remained outwardly calm and detached.

His train was halted by a signal at a little railroad station deep in the Thuringian forest. Walther Hewel was called to the stationmaster's telephone—the foreign ministry was on the line. British radio stations were announcing that an American invasion force was disembarking at Algiers, Oran, and Casablanca.[3] Before the train moved off, Hitler ordered all the necessary countermeasures put into effect. In a speech some hours later, President Roosevelt was heard justifying the invasion action as being necessary to thwart a threatened invasion by the Axis. Roosevelt appealed to the Vichy French forces not to resist, but the aged Marshal Pétain, deeply shaken by Roosevelt's "perfidy," ordered his troops to defend France's African possessions to the bitter end.

Ribbentrop could not be reached, so at 2:30 P.M. Hitler ordered the train stopped again, and Walther Hewel telephoned to the foreign ministry the text of urgent new instructions that Hitler wanted transmitted immediately to Ambassador Otto Abetz in France:

> Ambassador Abetz is to approach the French government immediately and is to inquire whether they are seriously willing to fight with us against the British and Americans. This would entail that France not only break off diplomatic relations with those two countries, but also declare war on them as if she had been attacked by an enemy. If the French government makes an unambiguous declaration like this, then we would be ready to go through thick and thin with the French government.

At Bamberg railroad station, shortly before Munich, Ribbentrop stepped aboard Hitler's train. He had hastily flown down from Berlin after arranging for Count Ciano to come at once to Munich—Mussolini being indisposed. Hitler wanted to discuss this new opportunity of re-

[3] The various enemy invasion convoys had suddenly headed sharply south, soon after the Italian sighting at 6 P.M. As Hitler sourly pointed out in April 1944: "The few invasions they have carried out so far completely escaped our notice. . . . Take the North African invasion!" And Keitel agreed: "We were saying right up to the last moment that they'd sail on through. Their vanguard was off Sicily, and we said they were going right on through. Then all at once they made a right-about turn and did a beeline for the shore."

versing Germany's policies toward France, but Ribbentrop brimmed
with gloomier topics. From the latest Allied figures on the size of their
invasion fleet, it was obvious the Germans had overestimated their
U-boats' abilities to strangle the western powers. The entire Axis position in the Mediterranean was endangered—unless Hitler could let up on
commitments elsewhere. "Give me permission to put out peace feelers
to Stalin, via his ambassadress in Stockholm, Madame Kollontay," appealed Ribbentrop, "even if we have to sacrifice virtually everything we
have conquered in the east!" Hitler rose angrily to his feet, reddened,
and refused to discuss anything but North Africa. A momentary military
weakness was no time in which to put out peace feelers to an enemy
poised to strike.

At 3:40 P.M. on the eighth, the train pulled into Munich. As always the
actual occurrence of the feared event had lifted the torturing burden of
uncertainty and indecision. At last he knew where the Second Front was
—and it was not the European mainland. Now he must airlift troops to
Tunisia to bar the American advance. Now the Italians must occupy
Corsica. Now Germany must make Crete the mightiest bastion of Axis
power in the Mediterranean. Now France must join the Axis cause.

At six o'clock, in a buoyant mood, he delivered his anniversary
speech to the Party's Old Guard at the Löwenbräukeller. Two passages
of the rambling, defiant rhetoric need quoting here. In the first he reminded them of his 1939 Reichstag prophecy concerning the fate of the
Jews. "Of those who laughed then, countless already laugh no longer
today; and those who still laugh today will probably not laugh much
longer either." The second passage he must later have regretted; too
willingly believing a message from General Georg von Sodenstern, Chief
of Staff of Army Group B, that Stalingrad was virtually theirs, Hitler
boasted: "I wanted to reach the Volga—at a particular spot, at a particular city. By coincidence it is blessed with Stalin's name . . . it is a vitally important city, because there you can cut off thirty million tons of
river transport, including nine million tons of oil, it is there that the
grain of the mighty Ukrainian and Kuban regions flows in for transportation to the north, there the manganese ore is processed—it was a
huge shipment complex. That was what I wanted to capture, and, do
you know, modest as we are—we've got it too! There are only a few
more tiny pockets! Now some may say, 'Then why don't you fight faster?'
—Because I don't want a second Verdun, that's why." Unable to eat his

words just two weeks later, Hitler found himself politically committed to a strategy in Stalingrad which increasingly proved to be untenable.

Hitler's newfound fondness toward the French, inspired by glowing accounts of the fierce fight put up by French warships defending Casablanca and Oran against the American invaders, lasted less than one day. As the hours of November 9 ticked away he began to suspect that the French commanders were trying to make a deal with the enemy, if indeed they had not clandestinely done so long before. On the eighth he had still believed General Henri-Honoré Giraud to be in France; the next day he found out that Giraud had slipped across to Africa aboard an enemy submarine to act for Eisenhower in Algiers. Admiral Darlan, the French Supreme Commander, had "by chance" been in Algiers for some days and appeared to be directing the French resistance, which in the port itself collapsed on the first evening. But Hitler believed that Darlan and General Alphonse Juin were still loyal—perhaps they were in enemy hands and being forced to issue the cease-fire orders to their troops.

Giraud's switch to the Allies was too blatant to ignore, however. Captured in May 1940, he had broken parole two years later and escaped to unoccupied France, where he had resisted Hitler's blandishments to "do the decent thing" and report back to the prison camp. The reprisals that his behavior had inflicted on his fellow officers in German hands failed to make Giraud reconsider. He gave his word to Hitler's emissary that he would never go to North Africa but would remain in unoccupied France. He gave his written undertaking to Marshal Pétain to do nothing against Germany. All these promises Giraud had now broken. Hitler's fury at Giraud's escape to Africa was matched by his contempt for Himmler's secret agents who had constantly shadowed him but failed to prevent it.[4]

By the time Count Ciano was ushered into his study at the Führer Building in Munich late on the ninth, profusely apologizing for Mussolini's inability to leave Rome, Hitler's old hostility toward France had rekindled in full. He barked at the Italian foreign minister that he had decided to occupy the rest of France—the French were incorrigible, they

---

[4] One of the many legends created by the postwar trial at Nuremberg is that Hitler ordered Keitel to arrange for the assassination of Giraud. No documentary evidence whatever has come to light for this. Hitler's contempt for governments that worked by assassination *is* well-documented, curiously enough—though in his own mind he evidently considered it proper to liquidate those he considered guilty of criminal treason, for example, Ernst Röhm or Otto Strasser. It is a fine distinction.

would never learn to love either the Germans or the Italians. An Axis bridgehead must be established in Tunisia forthwith. Whatever France's Premier Laval—due at 10 P.M.—might say, Hitler's mind was already made up. His troops were already massing along the demarcation line in France. "Strike, strike, strike!"—It was the old Prussian remedy when all else failed.

Laval was delayed by fog; his car arrived in the small hours of the night. Hitler postponed seeing him throughout the tenth, as the mists in North Africa were clearing. He was seen deep in conference with Ribbentrop, Himmler, and the generals. Himmler's files bulge with the Intelligence reports the SS put to Hitler that day: his agents at Vichy had intercepted Darlan's message to Pétain during the night demanding the execution of renegade officers. But Darlan seemed to be playing a double game, for the SS agents also learned that French reserve officers were being called up, that Darlan's staff was preparing to leave Vichy, and that all his war ministry files were being burned. General Auguste Noguès, the French resident-general in Morocco, was believed to be making a deal with the Americans. At midday, Darlan's name appeared on an order for all resistance to cease. For twenty-four hours, Hitler continued to hope that Darlan's name was being abused by the enemy. But Pétain broadcast Darlan's dismissal early that afternoon, November 10, which strongly suggested that Darlan *was* a traitor to the Axis cause. The luckless Pierre Laval was received now with barely concealed brusqueness. Hitler told him of his demands for immediate access to Tunis. Laval temporized and was coldly ushered out.[5] At twenty past eight that evening Hitler issued the order for his troops to occupy a Tunis bridgehead and the rest of France the next morning. It stated that as far as the French authorities were concerned "the occupation is being carried out in accord with the wishes of the French government." "Just like 'Otto' in 1938?" the Luftwaffe generals in Paris asked General Jeschonnek in Munich. "Jawohl, just like Austria."

This time there were no cheering crowds. In southern France the occupation was greeted with a mixture of apathy and official correctness. The real French hatred was reserved for the Italians occupying Corsica and the Riviera—with a sluggishness that infuriated Hitler—and arriving in Tunisia in the wake of the Germans. The Italians in southern France had far overstepped the lines agreed on with the French. Hitler learned that Laval had been overheard on the twelfth shouting into a telephone

---

[5] According to Jodl's naval staff officer—though not according to the official record of the meeting—"Laval was willing at Munich to request us to march in, *à la Hácha;* but only if the Italians would not march in too, and that was the end of that idea."

that if Italy did not withdraw her troops in twenty-four hours he would declare war on her! This was a feud Hitler wanted to keep out of, and when Göring asked if German antiaircraft guns could be stationed in the new Italian zone, he would not hear of it: the German and Italian zones must be clearly separated by the Rhone. The Italian antics drove Hitler's last few supporters in France into open hostility and defection. But a member of Jodl's staff reported late on November 14: "The Führer's actions are governed by his consideration for Italy. He believes it absolutely vital to bolster the Duce in every way we can, and this is why he categorically refuses to oppose Italy's claim to leadership in the Mediterranean, including the coast of southern France, or to present the Italians with *faits accomplis.*"

"Operation Brown," the hasty creation of an Axis bridgehead in Tunisia, was going well, but on November 12 the French forces in North Africa capitulated to the enemy. Upon Darlan's recognition by the Allies the next day as French head of state there, his defection could be doubted no longer. Hitler realistically assumed that no Frenchman could be trusted to collaborate with him. For two weeks, however, he simulated trust in the French navy. He had no option, as he had no *military* means of detaining the French fleet of three battleships, an aircraft carrier, and over thirty destroyers at Toulon; he therefore accepted perforce the loyal promises of the navy's senior admirals not to open hostile action against the Axis and to defend Toulon themselves to the best of their ability; in return, Hitler excluded Toulon from occupation by the Italians. For a brief period a regular French infantry division defending the coast between Toulon and Marseilles actually came under German command. But Hitler silently prepared for the worst. A Luftwaffe general noted on November 16: "The Führer fears the French will create an enclave paving the way for an Anglo-American invasion; that must be prevented." Intercepted telephone conversations of French naval officers revealed that the renegade Admiral Darlan was secretly being toasted in Paris as a national hero. The Germans also learned to their chagrin that the apparently senile Pétain could have been communicating secretly with Darlan all the time by underwater cable; so much for his protestations of loyalty broadcast by radio! Hitler ordered the Luftwaffe's bomber and minelaying squadrons to stand by on two hours' notice in case the French fleet suddenly set sail, and on November 18 he decided to make a clean sweep—all Pétain's armed forces were to be disarmed, and the Toulon enclave overrun. A date eight days hence was set for "Operation Lilac." Mussolini was not informed

(Hitler wanted absolute secrecy); but in spite of Raeder's frantic objections, Hitler stipulated that the Italians should nonetheless be given the Toulon dockyard and the French fleet—or whatever remained of it.[6] "Lilac" began before dawn on the twenty-seventh; by noon the French fleet no longer existed, its battleships blazing, stranded hulks, all but a handful of the rest scuttled or blown up by their crews. Hitler gave the Italians the wreckage to pick over. The French people seemed undistressed. They had lost their army, their navy, and their empire; "America will see us through all right," was the average Frenchman's philosophical belief. Throughout occupied France new painted slogans appeared overnight on a thousand walls: *Vive l'Amérique!* and patriotically, *1918!*. Germany's defeat was regarded as a certainty now.

All this was reported to Hitler. By now he had resigned himself to a long stay in south Germany and was living at the Berghof. Snow gripped the mountains as far as the eye could see. He badly needed respite. North Africa was causing ominous rumblings everywhere. Even neutral Sweden was becoming rambunctious, and the partisans in the Balkans were encouraged to redouble their insurgency. In Germany the public stoically steeled itself for eventual defeat. East Prussia would fall to Poland or even Russia; Germany would be maimed and dismembered. The diplomats again hinted that this was their last chance to extend feelers toward Stalin—while the Red Army was still being held at bay. Hitler hesitated. That a huge Russian offensive was coming he knew—but surely it was not coming yet. How else could he interpret the army's Intelligence reports? There was still time!

But there was not. On November 19, 1942, the phone rang at the Berghof and General Zeitzler, the army's Chief of Staff fighting an almost forgotten war from his headquarters in East Prussia, came on the line. A heavy artillery bombardment had begun on the Don front north of Stalingrad; it had become a saturation barrage, and now masses of tanks, black with Russian troops, were swarming forward. The Romanians were in full flight. It was all happening just where Hitler had predicted. The next day another offensive started, this time south of the city. Two days later Stalingrad was encircled, and the fiercest drama of the war began.

[6] Hitler also ordered all stores and ships at Marseilles turned over to Italy, except for oil dumps. Italy's oil demands were a sore point, especially since Raeder had learned that the last five thousand tons he had sacrificed to Italy had been deliberately contaminated with gasoline to render it unfit for the Italian navy's use—though suitable for civilian purposes. After Italy's defection in 1943, the Germans discovered tens of thousands of tons of oil secretly hoarded by the Italians.